NELSON EDUCATION SERIES
IN HUMAN RESOURCES MANAGEMENT

3RD EDITION

INDUSTRIAL
RELATIONS
IN CANADA

3RD EDITION

INDUSTRIAL
RELATIONS
IN CANADA

ROBERT HEBDON
McGILL UNIVERSITY

TRAVOR C. BROWN
MEMORIAL UNIVERSITY

SERIES EDITOR:
MONICA BELCOURT
YORK UNIVERSITY

NELSON
EDUCATION

NELSON EDUCATION

Industrial Relations, Third Edition

by Robert Hebdon and Travor C. Brown

Vice President, Editorial Higher Education:
Anne Williams

Publisher:
Jackie Wood

Executive Marketing Manager:
Amanda Henry

Developmental Editor:
Elke Price

Photo Researcher:
Natalie Barrington

Permissions Coordinator:
Natalie Barrington

Production Project Manager:
Jaime Smith

Production Service:
Cenveo Publisher Services

Copy Editor:
Kelli Howey

Proofreader:
Pushpa

Indexer:
BIM Indexing Services

Design Director:
Ken Phipps

Managing Designer:
Franca Amore

Interior Design:
Sharon Lucas

Cover Design:
Sharon Lucas

Compositor:
Cenveo Publisher Services

Digital Development Editor:
Becky Ranger

**Library and Archives Canada
Cataloguing in Publication**

Hebdon, Robert, 1943–, author

Industrial relations in Canada /
Robert Hebdon, Travor C. Brown.
— Third edition.

Includes bibliographical references
and index.

ISBN 978-0-17-658057-5 (pbk.)

1. Industrial relations—Canada—
Textbooks. I. Brown, Travor,
1968–, author II. Title.

HD8104.H43 2015

331.0971   C2015-901885-4

ISBN-13: 978-0-17-658057-5
ISBN-10: 0-17-658057-3

To my grandchildren in order of appearance: Sarah, Dylan, Celeste, Nathaniel, Violet, Maya, and Zev
—Robert Hebdon

To my wife, Andrea, and our three children, Davin, Alex, and Maddi. On a regular basis you prove to me the power of collective bargaining!
—Travor C. Brown

BRIEF CONTENTS

CONTENTS

ABOUT THE SERIES

The management of human resources has become the most important source of innovation, competitive advantage, and productivity, more so than any other resource. More than ever, human resources management (HRM) professionals need the knowledge and skills to design HRM policies and practices that not only meet legal requirements but also are effective in supporting organizational strategy. Increasingly, these professionals turn to published research and books on best practices for assistance in the development of effective HR strategies. The books in the *Nelson Education Series in Human Resources Management* are the best source in Canada for reliable, valid, and current knowledge about practices in HRM.

The texts in this series include:

- *Managing Performance through Training and Development*
- *Management of Occupational Health and Safety*
- *Recruitment and Selection in Canada*
- *Strategic Compensation in Canada*
- *Strategic Human Resources Planning*
- *Industrial Relations in Canada*
- *Research, Measurement, and Evaluation of Human Resources*
- *International Human Resources: A Canadian Perspective*

The *Nelson Education Series in Human Resources Management* represents a significant development in the field of HRM for many reasons. Each book in the series is the first and now best-selling text in the functional area. Furthermore, HR professionals in Canada must work with Canadian laws, statistics, policies, and values. This series serves their needs. It is the only opportunity that students and practitioners have to access a complete set of HRM books, standardized in presentation, which enables them to access information quickly across many HRM disciplines. Students who are pursuing the CHRP (Certified Human Resource Professional) designation through their provincial HR associations will find the books in this series invaluable in preparing for the knowledge exams. This one-stop resource will prove useful to anyone looking for solutions for the effective management of people.

The publication of this series signals that the HRM field has advanced to the stage where theory and applied research guide practice. The books in the series present the best and most current research in the functional areas of HRM. Research is supplemented with examples of the best practices used by Canadian companies that are leaders in HRM. Each text begins with a general model of the discipline and then describes the implementation of effective strategies. Thus, the books serve as an introduction to the functional area for the new student of HR and as a validation source for the more experienced HRM practitioner. Cases, exercises, and endnotes provide opportunities for further discussion and analysis.

As you read and consult the books in this series, I hope you share my excitement in being involved and knowledgeable about a profession that has such a significant impact on the achievement of organizational goals, and on employees' lives.

Monica Belcourt, Ph.D., CHRP
Series Editor
October 2014

PREFACE

The field of industrial relations is both complex and fascinating. At its heart, it examines the relationship among three actors: labour (employees and their associations), management (employers and their associations), and government and associated agencies. Shifts in the makeup of the Canadian economy, changes in the demographics of the workforce, and ongoing difficulties related to technological and legal frameworks have proven challenging to all three actors.

It is indeed an interesting time to study the field of industrial relations, and the authors are delighted to launch the third edition of *Industrial Relations in Canada* during this period of change. Before completing Ph.D.s at the University of Toronto and joining academia, the authors of this textbook were practitioners in the field and therefore offer a unique perspective. Robert Hebdon worked for several years with the Ontario Public Service Employees Union (OPSEU), while Travor Brown worked in a variety of human resources and labour relations roles with Abitibi-Price and Nortel Networks. Robert also worked as a neutral arbitrator in between union and academic careers. Moreover, their collective experience includes public-, private-, and nonprofit-sector as well as U.S. and Canadian work experience. This combination of practical and "real world" experience is apparent throughout the chapters of this textbook.

Given the authors' combination of practical and academic experience, this text is grounded in leading research and examines true-to-life issues. Each chapter starts with an opening vignette, contains a minimum of two inserts (labelled "IR Today" and "IR Notebook") concerning authentic IR issues, and includes examples, many from real Canadian organizations. In addition, each chapter ends with a case, discussion questions, and Internet exercises. All these elements are designed to bridge the academic content of the text and the real-world issues in the field. Given the vast quantity of material readily available on the popular website YouTube, we have also included numerous YouTube references in this edition. These, too, are indicated with a Weblink icon.

As former students, we appreciate the need for key points and hands-on activities. Therefore, we have included learning objectives at the beginning of every chapter, key terms in bold in the text and in the margins (and at the end of each chapter), and end-of-chapter summaries. We have also included two collective bargaining activities and several arbitration cases. These activities can be assigned by the instructor to give students a taste of the topic at hand from a practitioner's perspective.

We hope that students and instructors will find the third edition of this textbook helpful as they seek to understand this dynamic area. We look forward to their feedback and suggestions for future editions.

NEW TO THE THIRD EDITION

In response to feedback from faculty reviewers and users who have read earlier editions of *Industrial Relations in Canada*, we have made significant changes to this edition as highlighted below. Also, over 35 photos have been added with captions to capture the essence of the topics discussed, and the interior design has been updated and now appears in colour.

CHAPTER 1—INTRODUCTION

- Chapter 1 has been thoroughly updated to include coverage of recent faculty strikes and the temporary foreign worker debate and impact on youth employment (*IR Today 1.2*).
- The coverage of the Dunlop model is presented in a more concise manner while still retaining its key elements.
- Public and private examples have been added to help students better understand how they can apply their IR knowledge.

CHAPTER 2—LABOUR HISTORY

- Stronger emphasis has been placed on Canadian labour history, with less focus on U.S. events, while still covering the importance of how U.S. events have shaped Canada.
- A new section has been added covering the future of industrial relations in Canada and how current and past history may shape its future.
- The end-of-chapter case has been updated to reflect the merger of the CEP and CAW to form Unifor.

CHAPTER 3—ECONOMIC, SOCIAL, AND POLITICAL ENVIRONMENTS

- The new opening vignette discusses Canada's widening income gap between top earners and others in society.
- Statistics and coverage, including boxed features, have been thoroughly updated with discussions of job losses in Canada, unfounded myths of the economic impact of immigrants, Canada's Temporary Foreign Worker program, child poverty, and Canada's changing workforce composition.

CHAPTER 4—THE LEGAL ENVIRONMENT

- The most recent Supreme Court decisions on bargaining rights for the RCMP and the right to strike are included.

CHAPTER 5—THE UNION PERSPECTIVE

- A new opening vignette has been added: Call Centre Workers at Answernet Telepartners Join the Union.
- Union membership data has been updated; new figures illustrate union density by gender, and unionization rate by age and by region.
- A new end-of-chapter case has been added, entitled Democracy and Finances in an OPSEU Local.

CHAPTER 6—THE MANAGEMENT PERSPECTIVE

- Numerous new Canadian examples have been added, as well as a new opening vignette (Canadian Hockey League) and text boxes.
- Historical detail is presented more concisely to enable a stronger focus on current events.
- New coverage of interactional justice and nonstandard work arrangements has been added.
- There is a greater focus on three management strategies and their impacts on unions: high performance HRM, nonunion representation (NER), and nonstandard work arrangements.
- The coverage of TQM and associated areas of LEAN and ISO has been reduced.

CHAPTER 7—NEGOTIATIONS

- A new opening vignette on the Canadian diplomat strike and a new IR Today about the NHL Lockout have been added.

CHAPTER 8—COLLECTIVE AGREEMENT ADMINISTRATION

- The majority of coverage of grievances and arbitration has been placed in Chapters 9 and 10, respectively.
- Examples and collective agreement quotes have been updated throughout the chapter. The current examples come from a wide range of jurisdictions and industries.
- To help students better understand how to interpret clauses, new exercises and examples have been added. For example, exercises to interpret layoff and seniority clauses and salary scales (using the current trend of signing bonuses) have been included, and two new examples showing different cost implications of different clauses/options have been added.
- In order to make the clauses relevant to students, examples from service industries, airlines, and education have been added, including a new IR Today 8.2: Collective Agreement Language Concerning Cell Phones.

CHAPTER 9—CONFLICT RESOLUTION: GRIEVANCES AND STRIKES

- Given their importance, internal conflict resolution procedures are covered in Chapter 9, while third-party conflict resolution, including arbitration, is now covered in Chapter 10.
- Coverage of illegal work stoppages/wildcat strikes (for example, Air Canada) has been enhanced, and new coverage of work to rule (such as the Newfoundland nurses' overtime strike), essential services agreement, mandatory strike vote, replacement workers, and reinstatement rights has been added.

CHAPTER 10—THIRD-PARTY DISPUTE RESOLUTION PROCEDURES

- Third-party conflict resolution procedures, including arbitration and mediation, are now more clearly and fully discussed in their own chapter.

CHAPTER 11—IMPACTS OF UNIONIZATION

- Coverage of profit, innovation, investment, employment, and ROI has been expanded, with a broader focus on "firm measures."
- New examples including high-tech, space, and knowledge industries have been added, along with a new section on innovation.

CHAPTER 12—PUBLIC-SECTOR ISSUES

- A new opening vignette on the Quebec municipal workers' one-day strike to protest pension reform plan has been added.
- To highlight key points that flow from the chapter, a new IR Today box on GO Transit and a new IR Notebook about the B.C. teachers' strike have been added.

As a part of the process needed to earn a professional HR designation, granted by the HR Provincial Associations, applicants must undergo two assessments, one a knowledge-based exam and a second assessment based on experience. Because the competencies required for the knowledge exams may differ by province, we have not provided lists or links in this edition. Those interested in obtaining an HR designation should consult the HR association in their province.

// INSTRUCTOR RESOURCES

The Nelson Education Teaching Advantage (NETA) program delivers research-based instructor resources that promote student engagement and higher-order thinking to enable the success of Canadian students and educators. Be sure to visit Nelson Education's **Inspired Instruction** website at www.nelson.com/inspired to find out more about NETA. Don't miss the testimonials of instructors who have used NETA supplements and watched student engagement increase!

The following instructor resources have been created for *Industrial Relations in Canada, Third Edition.* Access these ultimate tools for customizing lectures and presentations at www.nelson.com/instructor.

NETA TEST BANK

This resource was prepared by Ron Alexandrowich at York University. It includes over 420 multiple-choice questions written according to NETA guidelines for effective construction and development of higher-order questions. Also included are true/false and short-answer questions.

The NETA Test Bank is available in a new, cloud-based platform. **Nelson Testing Powered by Cognero**® is a secure online testing system that allows instructors to author, edit, and manage test bank content from anywhere that Internet access is available. No installations or downloads are needed, and the desktop-inspired interface, with its dropdown menus and familiar, intuitive tools, allows instructors to create and manage tests with ease. Multiple test versions can be created in an instant, and content can be imported or exported into other systems. Tests can be delivered from a learning management system, the classroom, or wherever an instructor chooses. Nelson Testing Powered by Cognero for *Industrial Relations in Canada* can also be accessed through www.nelson .com/instructor.

NETA POWERPOINT

Microsoft® PowerPoint® lecture slides for every chapter have been created by Linda Yates Cameron of Sheridan College. There is an average of 25 slides per chapter, many featuring key figures, tables, and photographs from *Industrial Relations in Canada*. NETA principles of clear design and engaging content have been incorporated throughout, making it simple for instructors to customize the deck for their courses.

NETA INSTRUCTOR'S MANUAL

The Instructor's Manual to accompany *Industrial Relations in Canada*, Third Edition has been prepared by the text's authors, Robert Hebdon and Travor Brown. This manual contains learning objectives, chapter summaries, suggested classroom activities, and suggested answers to all end-of-chapter discussion questions, using the Internet features, exercises, and cases, and teaching notes for the end-of-book simulations to give instructors the support needed to engage students within the classroom.

IMAGE LIBRARY

This resource consists of digital copies of figures, short tables, and photographs used in the book. Instructors may use these images to customize the NETA PowerPoint or to create their own PowerPoint presentations.

DAY ONE

Day One–Prof InClass is a PowerPoint presentation that instructors can customize to orient students to the class and their textbook at the beginning of the course.

MINDTAP

Offering personalized paths of dynamic assignments and applications, **MindTap** is a digital learning solution that turns cookie-cutter into cutting-edge, apathy into engagement,

and memorizers into higher-level thinkers. MindTap enables students to analyze and apply chapter concepts within relevant assignments, and allows instructors to measure skills and promote better outcomes with ease.

A fully online learning solution, MindTap combines all student learning tools—readings, multimedia, activities, and assessments—into a single Learning Path that guides the student through the curriculum. Instructors personalize the experience by customizing the presentation of these learning tools to their students, even seamlessly introducing their own content into the Learning Path.

// STUDENT ANCILLARIES

MindTap: Stay organized and efficient with **MindTap**—a single destination with all the course material and study aids you need to succeed. Built-in apps leverage social media and the latest learning technology. For example:

- ReadSpeaker will read the text to you.
- Flashcards are pre-populated to provide you with a jump start for review—or you can create your own.
- You can highlight text and make notes in your MindTap Reader. Your notes will flow into Evernote, the electronic notebook app that you can access anywhere when it's time to study for the exam.
- Self-quizzing allows you to assess your understanding.

Visit http://www.nelson.com/student to start using MindTap. Enter the Online Access Code from the card included with your text. If a code card is *not* provided, you can purchase instant access at NELSONbrain.com.

ABOUT THE AUTHORS

Robert Hebdon

Professor Bob Hebdon joined McGill University's Faculty of Management in 2000. After graduating from the University of Toronto with an M.A. in economics in 1968, he worked for the Ontario Public Service Employees Union for 24 years. He completed his Ph.D. in industrial relations at the Centre for Industrial Relations at the University of Toronto in 1992. His academic career began at Cornell University, where he taught collective bargaining for seven years at the School of Industrial Relations. In 1999 he taught at the University of Manitoba in the Faculty of Management. Professor Hebdon also has experience as a neutral in labour–management relations acting as an arbitrator in Ontario. He won the 2007 Morley Gunderson Prize in Industrial Relations in recognition of his outstanding professional achievement and his significant service to the Centre for Industrial Relations and Human Resources at the University of Toronto.

His research interests include public-sector labour relations and restructuring, collective bargaining, dispute resolution, and industrial conflict. He has published in a wide variety of major journals, including *American Economic Review*, *Industrial and Labor Relations Review*, *Berkeley Journal of Industrial Relations*, *Journal of Policy Analysis and Management*, *Relations industrielles*, *Journal of Collective Negotiations in the Public Sector*, *Labor Studies Journal*, and *Arbitration Yearbook*.

Travor C. Brown

Dr. Travor C. Brown is the Director of the Masters of Employment Relations (MER) Program and a Professor, Labour Relations & Human Resources Management with Memorial University. Since joining Memorial University, he has received several teaching and research awards. He has also taught at the University of Toronto and University of Ulster (Northern Ireland). He holds a B.A. (Memorial University), a Master of Industrial Relations (University of Toronto), and a Ph.D. in Industrial Relations (University of Toronto).

Prior to taking academic appointments, Dr. Brown worked with Nortel Networks and Abitibi-Price. With these firms, he gained extensive real-world labour relations and human resources experience in Canada and the United States. This industry experience continues today, as Dr. Brown regularly provides consulting services to a number of private, public, and nonprofit organizations.

Dr. Brown's research tends to focus on areas related to diversity/equity, training and development, and performance appraisal. Many of his studies have taken place in unionized workplaces. His work has been published in several journals, including *Personnel Psychology*, *Journal of Management Education*, *Relations industrielles*, *Canadian Journal of Behavioural Science*, *Canadian Journal of Administrative Sciences*, *Human Resources Development Quarterly*, *Applied Psychology: An International Review*, and *Small Group Research*.

ACKNOWLEDGMENTS

As we move to the third edition of this textbook, we want to acknowledge and thank the many people who aided us in the process. While our names may appear on the cover, this text would have never come to life without the assistance of the following people.

First are the reviewers who took the time to read (and provide feedback on) early versions of the chapters and those who assisted in reviewing the earlier editions of this textbook. Their helpful suggestions resulted in a number of improvements to the text, and we thank each of them: Ron Alexandrowich (York University), Stan Arnold (Humber College), Tim Bartkiw (Ryerson University), Lori Buchart (Mount Royal University), Shelagh Campbell (Saint Mary's University), Gordon Cooke (Memorial University), Dennis Fong (Seneca College), Amanda Hudson (York University), Randy Joseph (University of Lethbridge), Ted Mock (Seneca College), Carol Ann Samhaber (Algonquin College), Andrew Stevens (University of Regina), Scott Walsworth (University of Saskatchewan), and Linda Yates Cameron (Sheridan College).

Second, we thank the research assistants who spent many hours online, at the library, or editing chapters: Adrian Beaton and Vipul Khatter. We also thank the research assistants who assisted us with the previous edition: Kimberly Chaulk, Tara-Lynn Hillier, Krista Stringer, David Parsons, Christian Keen, and Elliot Siemiatycki. Your efforts greatly enhanced the manuscript.

Third, we thank our colleagues, students (past and present), as well as our friends currently working in the field for their ideas, their feedback, and their "sympathetic ears" as we went through this process. In particular, we thank Scott Walsworth and Andrew Luchak, who allowed us to incorporate material from them into our bargaining and arbitration exercises.

Fourth, in many cases the examples we used in this textbook came from friends and contacts currently working in the field of industrial relations. Our thanks to you for providing us with ideas we could incorporate into the text as we tried to "make the content real."

Fifth, we cannot thank enough the team at Nelson—Elke Price, Developmental Editor; Jackie Wood, Publisher; Jaime Smith, Production Project Manager; Dave Stratton, Marketing Manager; Natalie Barrington, Permissions Researcher; Monica Belcourt, Series Editor; and Kelli Howey, Copy Editor—for their assistance and support. We are lucky to have had such a dedicated team of supporters guiding us each step of the way.

Finally, we thank our families, for their ongoing support and love.

INTRODUCTION

LEARNING OBJECTIVES

BY THE END OF THIS CHAPTER, YOU WILL BE ABLE TO DISCUSS

- the similarities and differences among such terms as labour relations, human resources, employment relations, and industrial relations;
- a systems framework that can be used to assess and understand industrial relations issues;
- the differing views in the field of industrial relations; and
- how this textbook is structured to follow the industrial relations system framework.

The subway stops, the chime sounds, the doors open, and Andrew Chen and Lauren Major enter the train to look for seats. They have about a 30-minute ride before they reach their stop for U of T, where they are both taking classes. Lauren looks at Andrew and says, "Just saw a tweet from my friend Jack at Mount Allison. He says the faculty strike there is finally over. He's been pretty stressed that the strike will extend the term. He was worried he'd need to pay an extra month of rent and not be able to start his summer job on time."

Andrew nods, "I heard something about that. Let me see what I can find out." Pulling out his phone, he does a quick search. "...the strike lasted about 3 weeks.... Faculty were on strike for pay and workload reasons.... Yes, you're right, students feared an extended term or the potential loss of mid-term break. Wow it even says that the strike cost students $1300 in tuition."

Leaning over to look at his phone, Lauren asks, "What else does it say?" Andrew replies: "Let's see... It says that the government brought in a special mediator from Toronto to try to settle the strike. You should see the comments posted on these stories. Some say profs going on strike hurt students, others stating that, in the long run, the strike will benefit students as it could reduce number of profs quitting to take jobs in other schools. What divided views! What else? UNB profs were on strike as well. Seems there was a strike vote, mediation, conciliation … do you know what all those terms mean?"

Lauren says, "I really wish I better understood the issues concerning industrial relations. I have no idea what a strike vote or conciliation are. Do you know much about industrial relations?" Andrew laughs. "Studying engineering. I can tell you how this train operates, but I have absolutely no idea about any of this stuff."

Sources: "New Brunswick names mediator in bid to end Mount Allison University strike." *CTV News.* (10 February 2014). Retrieved from http://www.ctvnews.ca/canada/new-brunswick -names-mediator-in-bid-to-end-mount-allison-university -strike-1.1679521; "Mount Allison University students demand an end to faculty strike." *Atlantic CTV News.* (12 February 2014). Retrieved from http://atlantic.ctvnews.ca/mount-allison-university -students-demand-an-end-to-faculty-strike-1.1683416; "Mount Allison University says strike over, classes back on." *CBC News.* (16 February 2014). Retrieved from http://www .cbc.ca/news/canada/new-brunswick/mount-allison-university -says-strike-over-classes-back-on-1.2539297; "Mount Allison students excited to be back to class." *CBC News.* (17 February 2014). Retrieved from http://www.cbc.ca/m/ touch/canada/newbrunswick/story/1.2539979; "Mount Allison professors holding strike vote." *CBC News.* (13 January 2014). Retrieved from http://www.cbc.ca/news/canada/new-brunswick/ mount-allison-professors-holding-strike-vote-1.2494424.

strike
an action by workers in which they cease to perform work duties and do not report to work

// WHAT IS INDUSTRIAL RELATIONS?

While you may not realize it yet, issues related to this textbook occur all around you. If you look at any media outlet you will see news coverage of labour disputes and **strikes** such as the Mount Allison strike that opens this chapter. You will also see stories on poor working conditions in developing countries, protests concerning the growing inequality between the rich and the poor in our country, the strength of the economy as it relates to employment, etc. Similar topics are often discussed amongst your friends in conversations concerning the pros and cons of different careers, jobs, and workplaces. Broadly speaking, all these topics relate to employment. The employment relationships between employers and employees can be characterized in a number of ways. In this section of the book, we will review and discuss

Students supporting the faculty strike at Mount Allison.

Scott Doherty/Sackville Tribune-Post

several of the common names (or terms) relevant to this course and provide recent job examples for each term. These include:

- industrial relations
- labour relations
- human resources management (human resources)
- employee relations
- employment relations

INDUSTRIAL RELATIONS

The term *industrial relations* has often been used by academics to examine all employment issues and relationships between employees (and their **union** if they are unionized), employers (and managers who act on their behalf), and governmental agencies (as well as their associated legislation and policies). As a result, the field of industrial relations has been argued to include the study of both union and nonunion employment relationships.

However, more recently, the term **industrial relations** has become synonymous with issues concerning unionized employment relationships. For example, a recent job posting for an Industrial Relations Manager position presents duties related to interpreting the **collective agreement** and preparing for **collective bargaining**—all issues pertaining to a unionized workplace (Industrial Relations Manager, 2015). (Perhaps because of the narrowing view of the term, some academic programs have changed names in recent years. For example, the former Master of Industrial Relations (MIR) degree at the University of Toronto is now the Master of Industrial Relations and Human Resources (MIRHR). In contrast, a similar program offered at Queen's University continues to use the MIR designation. (See IR Today 1.1.)

union
a group of workers recognized by law who collectively bargain terms and conditions of employment with their employer

industrial relations
the study of employment relationships and issues, often in unionized workplaces

collective agreement
a written document outlining the terms and conditions of employment in a unionized workplace

collective bargaining
the process by which management and labour negotiate the terms and conditions of employment in a unionized workplace

---

IR TODAY   1.1

INDUSTRIAL RELATIONS IN UNIVERSITIES

Part of the university experience is self-exploration and determining potential career interests. Since you will be studying the field of industrial relations this term, it's a good time to explore different programs and career options in the field. There are several English and French programs dedicated to the study of employment relationships in North America. We list some below.

English Programs

Cornell University ILR School
http://www.ilr.cornell.edu
Memorial University MER program
http://www.business.mun.ca/programs/masters/mer/

Queen's University MIR program
mir.queensu.ca
University of Toronto MIRHR program
http://www.cirhr.utoronto.ca/programs/mirhr-overview/
University of Toronto undergraduate Employment Relations program
http://www.wdw.utoronto.ca/index.php/programs/employment_relations/overview/
Warwick University IR master's programs
http://www2.warwick.ac.uk/fac/soc/wbs/research/irru/masters_programmes

LABOUR RELATIONS

labour relations
the study of employment relationships and issues between groups of employees (usually in unions) and management; also known as *union-management relations*

The term **labour relations** refers to the examination of the relationship between groups of employees (usually labour unions) and their employers (including management groups). Consequently, the term is often considered interchangeable with *union–management relations* and has often focused on issues concerning collective employment relationships. Not surprisingly, Heathfield, when discussing careers, stated that "labour relations relations staff members deal almost exclusively with unionized workplaces" and focus on issues related to collective agreements, collective bargaining, and conflict resolution (Heathfield, 2014).

HUMAN RESOURCES MANAGEMENT

human resources
the study of the employment relationship between employers and individual employees

Whereas *labour relations* examines collective employment relationships between groups of employees (usually in labour unions) and their employer, **human resources** focuses on the employment relationship between the individual employee and his or her manager or employer. Thus, the area examines topics such as selection, compensation, and training. Jobs in this field are increasingly requiring applicants to have a Certified Human Resources Professional (CHRP) designation (CHRP, 2015), with demonstrated Required Professional Capabilities in areas such as staffing, total compensation, and employee and labour relations (CCHRA, 2014). In fact, this text has been designed with the RPCs in mind. More details about human resources can be found in Chapter 6.

EMPLOYEE RELATIONS

employee relations
the study of the employment relationship between employers and individual employees, usually in nonunion settings

Like human resources, the phrase **employee relations** has also been used to describe the employment relationship between individual employees and their employers, particularly in the United States. In fact, in the labour movement, it has often been considered a strong anti-union term. In Canada, we see the term used in differing contexts, including unionized workplaces. For instance, Alberta's *Public Service Employee Relations Act* relates to unionized, public-sector employees, and there are unions who use the term *employee relations* in some of their staff's titles. Likewise, the Nova Scotia Government and General Employees Union (NSGEU) website uses the term *employee relations* officers for some of its staff's roles (NSGEU, 2014). Given the diversity in perspectives concerning the term *employee relations*, it will not be used in this text.

EMPLOYMENT RELATIONS

Employment relations is perhaps the newest term. It was proposed by Meltz (1997) in essence to represent the comprehensive study of all employment relations (i.e., union and nonunion). In many ways it can be seen as the term designed to encompass the academic term *industrial relations*. The term has started to be used more frequently in the field. For example, U of T's Woodworth College offers an undergraduate employment relations program, and Memorial University a Master of Employment Relations (MER) degree. (See IR Today 1.1.)

In looking at the job market, we can see a considerable range in terms of the duties of jobs in this field. For example, a job posting for a position entitled "Senior Advisor, Employee Relations" at VIA Rail focused very much on unionized employment issues of collective bargaining and collective agreements (VIA Rail, 2014). In contrast, a position called "Senior Employee Relations Consultant" at CIBC (2014) focused on tasks related to "advice, investigation and conflict resolution on workplace issues, Human Resources policies & programs, and human rights and employment legislative requirements"–with no discussion of unionized issues. As these job ads show, the phrase *employment relations* does encompass union and nonunion environments.

> **employment relations**
> the study of employment relationships and issues in union and nonunion workplaces

INDUSTRIAL RELATIONS AND THIS TEXTBOOK

Because there are a variety of terms representing different forms of employment relationships, it is important that we map out the focus of this text. Both authors of this text have been schooled in the field of industrial relations and, more specifically, completed graduate education centred on the broader definition of *industrial relations* as the comprehensive study of all employment relationships (both union and nonunion). As a result, we use industrial relations frameworks to examine issues relevant to this text. In addition, the focus of much of this text will be on issues related to labour relations. For example, you will see chapters examining contract administration, collective bargaining, strikes, etc. To better understand some of the core industrial frameworks used to examine employment relationships, we now turn to a discussion of the industrial relations system framework that grounds this text.

// THE INDUSTRIAL RELATIONS SYSTEM

Unlike other courses you may have taken, the field of industrial relations is relatively new. It is an interdisciplinary field that encompasses knowledge and scholars from a broad range of subject areas (e.g., business, economics, law, history, sociology, psychology, and political science) in an effort to examine employment relationships and issues. For example, business scholars may look at the impact of collective agreements on management flexibility; economic scholars may examine the impact of unions on wages; law scholars may examine the impact of legislation on access to unionization; history scholars may examine the evolving and historical nature of employment relationships; sociology scholars may examine the dynamics and processes involved in workgroups; psychology scholars may look at issues related to employee satisfaction and motivation; and political science scholars may examine issues related to the roles of unions in the political process. Given the broad scope of the topic, attempts to build unifying frameworks and theories are relatively new, dating back only to the 1950s. In this section, we will present the two most commonly used system frameworks in North America, namely, that of American John Dunlop and that of Canadian Alton Craig.

DUNLOP'S INDUSTRIAL RELATIONS SYSTEM MODEL

John Dunlop was one of the first scholars to develop a systematic method to analyze employment relationships in North America. This model consists of actors, a shared ideology, and contexts, as well as a web of rules.

ACTORS

When Dunlop studied employment relationships and issues, he described three distinct actors:

SPECIALIZED GOVERNMENTAL AGENCIES The role of this actor is to develop, implement, and administer legislation and policies pertinent to the employment relationship.

A HIERARCHY OF MANAGERS AND THEIR REPRESENTATIVES This actor represents the business owners and the management staff hired to run the business. The role of this actor is to manage the workers and workplace in question. In North America, we often look at a single management actor when examining an employment relationship (e.g., see the opening vignette in which the employer is Mount Allison). Yet there are also a number of associations that represent groups of employers. A current example would be the Newfoundland and Labrador Employers' Council (NLEC, 2014), whose website presents its role as providing "advocacy, communication and training for its members in matters that affect the employment relationship."

A HIERARCHY OF WORKERS (NONMANAGEMENT) AND ANY SPOKESPERSONS This actor represents the nonmanagement workers in the employment relationship and any relevant associations. In most cases, these associations consist of labour unions representing the workers.

SHARED IDEOLOGY

Dunlop (1958, p. 16) defined shared ideology as "a set of ideas and beliefs commonly held by the actors that helps to bind or integrate the system together as an entity." This shared ideology was seen to define the role and function of each of the actors and required that all three actors respect and value the roles of the other two.

CONTEXTS

Dunlop envisioned that the three actors might be influenced by any of several environmental contexts:

MARKET AND BUDGETARY CONSTRAINTS While Dunlop focused mostly on the product market, he saw two key areas as critical to the employment relationship: product and labour. As we will discuss in Chapter 5, unions seek to influence both the supply and the demand of labour. In so doing, unions can impact the wages employees earn, as well as the final cost of the product/service that is produced by the organization. Thus, the issue of budgetary constraints becomes key, particularly for the actor of management.

TECHNICAL CHARACTERISTICS OF THE WORKPLACE AND WORK COMMUNITY This context focuses on how work is structured and performed, including such factors as the processes used to produce goods and services, the stability of the workforce and operations, the size of the workgroup, job tasks, hours of work, and the technology/machinery used.

DISTRIBUTION OF POWER IN THE LARGER SOCIETY This context examines the power relationship among the actors within a particular employment relationship in the broader society. In particular, Dunlop (1958, p. 11) noted that the distribution of power among the actors reflects "their prestige, position, and access to authority figures within the larger society [that] shapes and constrains an industrial relations system." Power is important because the actor with the most power will have the greatest ability to influence both the dynamics of the employment relationship and the terms and conditions of employment.

WEB OF RULES

Perhaps the most complicated and contested element of Dunlop's system is the web of rules. Dunlop discussed that the employment relationship consisted of a web of rules that outlined the rights and responsibilities of the actors in question. More specifically, he presented three key elements concerning rules.

PROCEDURES FOR ESTABLISHING RULES This element focuses on the processes used for making the rules and who has the authority to make and administer the rules that govern the workplace.

SUBSTANTIVE RULES These rules pertain to outcomes of the employment relationship—for example, for the employee, compensation, job and performance expectations, and worker rights and duties.

PROCEDURAL RULES Dunlop envisioned procedural rules as those rules that could determine and/or apply substantive rules—for example, rules concerning how wages are determined, rules concerning work schedules, and rules concerning how an employee is able to use or earn vacation time.

CRITICISMS OF DUNLOP'S INDUSTRIAL RELATIONS SYSTEM

As outlined by several authors, there has been considerable debate concerning the merits of Dunlop's systems approach over the past 40 years (Craig, 1988; Hyman, 1989;

Kochan, Katz & McKersie, 1986; Meltz & Adams, 1993; Wood, Wagner, Armstrong, Goodman & Davis, 1975). A number of criticisms of Dunlop's systems approach follow.

First, the model is descriptive in nature, as it essentially consists of a classification system. Thus, while it allows us to examine an industrial relations issue, it lacks the ability to predict outcomes and/or relationships.

Second, the model underestimates the importance of power and conflict. For example, the model assumes the concept of shared ideology—that all actors see a legitimate role for each of the three actors. As we will see in greater detail in Chapter 6, many scholars are questioning this concept of shared ideology, particularly as it relates to the importance and role of labour unions.

Third, the model is static in nature. At no point does it examine how events from one employment relationship can impact other employment relationships, or even the same relationship at a later time.

Fourth, the model cannot explain the rapid decrease in unionization, particularly in the United States. Rather, the framework is often assumed to ground itself in the premise of unionized workplaces being the norm.

In summary, Dunlop's model is a classic work in the field of industrial relations that will continue to be studied for years to come. However, as is often the case with the first model in any discipline, it has been, and will continue to be, expanded upon by subsequent work. In the Canadian context, one of the most studied expansions of Dunlop's model is that of Craig (1967, 1988; see also revision in Craig & Solomon, 1996). Readers familiar with the sciences will note that Craig's model is similar to the systems models used in biology. In biology, we see that a plant takes air from the environment and, through a series of internal conversion systems, takes the carbon dioxide it needs and then releases oxygen back into the environment. Similarly, in Craig's model, we see that the industrial relations actors take elements from the external environment and convert these inputs into outputs through a series of conversion mechanisms. These outputs then flow back into the environment through a **feedback loop**. Figure 1.1 shows our adaptation of Craig's model. As this expanded systems framework will form the basis of this textbook, we will now take time to walk through it.

feedback loop
the mechanism by which outputs of the industrial relations system flow back to the external environment

EXTERNAL INPUTS

The left-hand side of the model shows that several external inputs (or environmental subsystems) are important elements of the industrial relations system. These inputs can be legal, economic, ecological, political, or sociocultural in nature.

LEGAL SUBSYSTEM

In Chapter 4, we more fully discuss the importance of the legal subsystem in industrial relations. In brief, three areas of law are key to the study of industrial relations: (1) common law, which is the earliest form of employment law and applies to nonunion employment relationships; (2) statutory law, or laws concerning minimum employment standards and employment discrimination, covering issues such as minimum wage, overtime payment, and employers' discrimination based on factors not linked to job performance (e.g., race, gender, age)—note that these laws apply to union and nonunion employment relationships; and (3) collective bargaining law, or legislation pertaining to unionized employment relationships.

FIGURE 1.1

INDUSTRIAL RELATIONS SYSTEM MODEL[1]

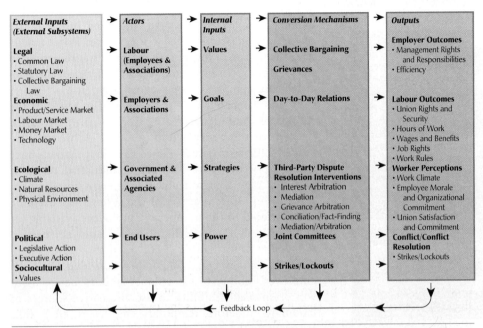

[1] Adapted from: Craig, A. W. J., and Solomon, N. A. (1996). *The System of Industrial Relations in Canada*, 5th edition, pg. 4. Toronto, Ontario: Prentice Hall Canada Inc. Reprinted with permission of estate of Alton J. Craig.

It is also important to note that Canada has a decentralized legal framework, with most provinces having their own provincial laws. In fact, with the exception of industries key to national safety and security (e.g., communication, interprovincial transportation, railways, airlines, banks), most workplaces fall under provincial legislation. The Mount Allison case discussed in the opening vignette is an example, and would be subject to New Brunswick legislation.

ECONOMICS SUBSYSTEM

Since Chapter 3 provides a full overview of the economics subsystem, we now briefly introduce four key elements to this subsystem: product/service markets, labour markets, money markets, and technology.

One can think of product/service markets in terms of the availability of products or services from competitors as well as an organization's relative competitive position in its market (e.g., Does the firm have a large market share? Does it face considerable competition from other service/product suppliers?). A good example is provided by the retail industry. In the recent past, Canadians would have purchased most of their products from their local retailers or outlets of national chains such as Sears, The Bay, Zellers, and K-Mart. However, the movement to Internet-based shopping through websites such as Amazon and eBay means that Canadian retailers now face competition from firms in numerous countries—some of the previously referenced national retailers have even ceased

Government poster highlighting revisions to the temporary foreign worker policy.

operations in recent years. In fact, in the first three months of 2015, national retailers such as Future Shop, Smart Set, Target, and Sony all declared plans to cease Canadian retail operations. These competitive factors in the product/service market can play a large role in industrial relations. For example, employers' collective bargaining proposals are often based on factors related to the product/service market (e.g., the impact of the union's suggested wage increase on the total product/service cost, how wage increases and associated costs compare to competitors' costs, etc.).

Labour markets can be thought of in terms of the supply of, and demand for, workers with the skills needed for the workplace in question. As we will discuss in Chapter 2, issues related to labour markets have been important to the history of industrial relations and can play a significant role in any employment relationship. Often, actors of the system will examine issues related to the number of employees available (or labour supply) and the number of employees needed (or demand for labour). For example, unions will often encourage employment practices that limit the employer's ability to use contact labour; management will often seek flexibility to use alternative sources of labour (contractors, temporary employees, etc.). Take for example the issue of temporary foreign workers outlined in IR Today 1.2. See how the issues related to supply of temporary foreign workers are presented as it relates to demand for Canadian labour.

IR TODAY   1.2

TEMPORARY FOREIGN WORKERS AND EMPLOYMENT IN CANADA

As we discuss in this chapter, the field of industrial relations examines many employment-related topics. A current Canadian debate relates to the impact of temporary foreign workers on the employment of Canadians. For example, an article in the *Vancouver Sun* stated that:

> The federal government should put the brakes on the runaway growth of the Temporary Foreign Worker program, imposing yearly caps until a review determines whether its continued expansion is in the national interest, according to a Carleton University economics professor.
>
> The number of workers admitted under the controversial program has more than doubled nationally

over the last 10 years, increasing to 213,573 in 2012 from 102,932 in 2003, Citizenship and Immigration Canada figures show....

The people who come in under the program range from seasonal agricultural workers to highly skilled IT professionals, but it is the fast-food industry's use of such workers that has been under scrutiny in recent days after Ottawa announced it was investigating a McDonald's franchisee in Victoria for allegedly abusing the program.

The Sun reported Wednesday on a Kelowna-area Dairy Queen employee who said she went

---

from 30-plus hours a week to weeks at a time without a shift after temporary foreign workers arrived from the Philippines. The worker, Alisha Harris, is an 18-year-old Grade 12 student who was working to earn money for university tuition.

Alexandra Fortier, a spokeswoman for Employment Minister Jason Kenney, said Wednesday that the government's assurances of protection for Canadian workers also apply to part-time employees. The risk that temporary foreign workers will take employment opportunities away from young Canadians is not one that should be lightly dismissed, according to Christopher Worswick, an economics professor at Carleton.

"The kinds of jobs that are more and more likely to be filled by TFWs (such as less-skilled fast-food-industry jobs and hotel work) were traditionally first jobs for many young Canadians and/or supported them while they pursued post-secondary education," he wrote in an October 2013 report on the economic implications of changes to the temporary foreign worker program. "If employers are able to bring in TFWs rather than raising wages to induce young Canadians to take these jobs or perhaps move to regions where such jobs exist, this could mean that young Canadians may face even greater difficulties in becoming established in the labour market and accumulating the skills they need to move into higher-skilled occupations."

The reason employers choose to bring in foreigners rather than hire local youth is the "elephant in the room" in the debate around temporary foreign workers, Worswick said, and it has to do with work ethic. There are many low-income workers around the world who would welcome the chance to work in Canada if it meant a better life for their family. Given this motivation, they are likely to work harder and be less likely to complain about working standards than a similarly trained Canadian worker, according to Worswick.

Employers "may see an opportunity to gain extra profit by either advertising jobs at too low a wage (given the job requirements) or perhaps by being overly critical of Canadian applicants, so they could gain permission to hire a TFW who would be more productive." Worswick called this "the greatest challenge regarding the Temporary Foreign Worker Program."

Moreover, the Canadian Labour Congress (CLC) argues that:

Roughly 75% of the new jobs created in Canada in 2010 and 2011 were filled by temporary foreign workers despite the fact that 1.4 million Canadian residents were unemployed," says Ken CLC President Ken Georgetti. The CLC research used numbers from the Statistics Canada's Labour Force Survey and from Citizenship and Immigration Canada.

The federal government was forced in April to make changes to the Temporary Foreign Worker Program (TFWP) after clear evidence that employers were using the program to import vulnerable migrant workers at a time of continuing high unemployment in Canada.

Georgetti provided examples of migrant workers and job creation in Canadian provinces:

- In British Columbia, the influx of temporary foreign workers exceeded the net number of jobs created between 2008 and 2011. B.C. created 52,100 net new jobs in those years, and in 2011 there were nearly 70,000 temporary foreign workers in the province.

- In 2009, Alberta imported 28,547 temporary foreign workers as the provincial economy shed 28,500 net jobs.

- In Saskatchewan, on average between 2008 and 2011, 65% of net new jobs created were held by temporary foreign workers.

- In Manitoba for 2011, approximately 70% of the net new jobs created were held by temporary foreign workers.

- In Ontario, the economy shed over 164,000 jobs in 2009, but 60,000 temporary foreign workers arrived in the province. In 2011, 56% of net new jobs were held by temporary foreign workers.

- In Quebec, 90% of the net new jobs created in 2011 were held by temporary foreign workers.

New Brunswick lost 3,400 jobs in 2010 and 4,100 jobs in 2011, but the number of temporary foreign workers arriving in the province increased to 1,819 in that year.

Nova Scotia created only 300 net new jobs in 2011, but over 2,800 temporary foreign workers arrived in the province.

Prince Edward Island created 1,400 net new jobs in 2011, and 42% of these jobs were held by temporary foreign workers.

Newfoundland and Labrador lost over 6,000 jobs in 2009, yet nearly 1,400 temporary foreign workers arrived in the province that year. In 2011, 22% of net new jobs created were held by temporary foreign workers.

Georgetti adds, "Let me be clear. We welcome migrant workers when there are demonstrated shortages of workers in Canada, but we want to ensure that those migrant workers are protected on the job and welcomed into the community. They should be placed into the permanent immigration stream, not exploited in temporary migration schemes."

Sources: Carman, Tara. (16 April 2014). "Temporary foreign workers drive youth out of labour market, economics professor says. *Vancouver Sun.* Retrieved from http://www.vancouversun.com/Temporary+foreign+workers+drive+youth+labour+market+economics+professor+says/9746008/story.html; and Canadian Labour Congress. (10 May 2013). "Migrant workers account for most new jobs: CLC has crunched numbers between 2008–2011." Retrieved from http://www.canadianlabour.ca/national/news/migrant-workers-account-most-new-jobs-clc-has-crunched-numbers-between-2008-2011. Used with permission.

Money markets also play a key role in the industrial relations system. As outlined by the Bank of Canada (2010; also Côté, 2011), the Canadian economy is impacted by global issues, in particular those of its largest trading partner, the United States. Consequently, issues concerning the money market are very important. If, for example, the Canadian dollar increases in value by 5 percent relative to American currency, a Canadian product then costs 5 percent more in the United States, based only on money market factors. Conversely, if the **exchange rate** drops 5 percent relative to the U.S. dollar, Canadian products are then 5 percent cheaper in the States. It is also important to remember that the Bank of Canada can also adjust **interest rates** on the basis of exchange rates and that interest rates can impact **inflation** (Bank of Canada, 2006, 2010). For these reasons, actors of the industrial relations system, whether or not they are involved in exporting or importing products and services, can be impacted by the money market.

Technology can impact the industrial relations system in a number of ways. It can result in new work methods, job redesign, and, in some cases, layoffs or lower levels of employment as fewer employees may be needed. For example, technology allows work to be performed almost anywhere in the world, particularly in the technology and call-centre industries. In fact, we even see companies in emerging markets such as India marketing their "cost-efficient" services (Outsource2india, 2014). Closer to home, you will see that many stores now have self-checkouts, where customers check themselves out, reducing the number of cashiers needed.

exchange rate
the value of one country's currency relative to another country's currency

interest rate
the rate a bank charges for borrowing money

inflation
the increase in prices over time

ECOLOGICAL SUBSYSTEM

The ecological subsystem includes the physical environment, climate, and natural resources that influence actors and the industrial relations system. For example, the large concentration of petroleum-based companies in Alberta is largely due to the availability of natural resources (i.e., oil) in that province; the physical environment (i.e., access to the Pacific Ocean) explains the importance of shipping employment in British Columbia; and the presence of iron ore explains the prevalence of mining in Labrador. In addition, the climate, in terms of seasons and weather, can influence when unions would likely strike. Not surprisingly, then, Saskatchewan snowplow and salt truck drivers walked off the job in January, a month known for snow (Canwest News, 2007), while their counterparts in Pennsylvania recently threatened to go on strike in the month of February (WTAE, 2014).

POLITICAL SUBSYSTEM

Canada's political subsystem is founded on a form of democracy in which citizens elect politicians to represent them in various forms of government (i.e., municipal, provincial, federal). These governments have the ability to pass legislation. In the industrial relations field, governments use legislative action to create and amend legislation relative to employment issues. Recent examples include the temporary foreign worker program highlighted in IR Today 1.2 as well as legislation ending **mandatory retirement**, where workers were forced to retire at age 65 (Warren & Kelloway, 2010).

Governments can also use executive action (e.g., passing emergency legislation to end a strike). The first usage of such legislation in the federal jurisdiction was in the railway sector in 1950 (Library of Parliament, 2011). However, as we will discuss in Chapter 12, we see its usage in some public-sector disputes.

> **mandatory retirement**
> a requirement that employees retire at age 65

SOCIOCULTURAL

The **values** and beliefs of the society in which the actors operate can also influence the actors, providing a sense of what is perceived as being fair and appropriate in terms of the employment relationship. In fact, we often see public opinion survey results reported in the media during large strikes, particularly when they relate to public services. As noted in the opening vignette we also see that people can post comments on media stories. Information from such sources can be used by both sides to gauge the extent to which the public supports the positions of labour and/or management.

> **values**
> a set of standards or principles

ACTORS

The actors of the industrial relations system are influenced by the previously discussed external inputs. The actors shown in Figure 1.1 mirror those of Dunlop (1958) and include

- labour (employees and their associations);
- employers and their associations; and
- government and associated agencies.

In subsequent chapters, we will provide more details on each of these actors and their roles in the industrial relations system. Note that we have added a fourth actor, the end user of the services/products generated from the employment relationship in question. We have added this fourth actor because scholars now note the importance of the end user in the industrial relations system (Bellemare, 2000).

INTERNAL INPUTS

While the actors of the system are influenced by the external inputs, they, too, provide inputs to the system in terms of their values, goals, strategies, and power. Each actor of the system will have values that guide their actions. Using Barbash's (1987) equity-efficiency theory, we could argue that employers may hold the values of profitability and competitive advantage; in contrast, labour may hold values relative to fair treatment of workers. These differing values would cause employers to develop **goals** that maximize efficiency, while labour would seek to maximize equity.

Strategies would then be developed by both actors to achieve their desired goals. The relative **power** of the actors would help determine which parties' goals were achieved.

CONVERSION MECHANISMS

The processes that the actors use to convert internal and external inputs into outputs of the industrial relations system are known as **conversion mechanisms**. Note that many of these conversion mechanisms are akin to what Dunlop called procedural rules, as they can be methods for determining how workplace outcomes are determined. In Chapters 7 to 10, we will discuss many of the following conversion mechanisms in more detail:

- Collective bargaining, by which the parties negotiate a collective agreement.
- Day-to-day relations. The day-to-day activities in the organization represent conversion mechanisms; for example, prior to launching a formal grievance, a worker may meet directly with his or her manager to resolve an issue.
- Conflict resolution mechanisms, such as grievances procedures. A grievance procedure allows employees (and/or their union) to submit a written complaint that the collective agreement has not been followed.
- Various third-party dispute resolution interventions:
  - Interest arbitration. A third-party process used when parties cannot reach a collective agreement on their own. The decision of the arbitrator(s) becomes a binding collective agreement. This process is most often used by actors who are unable to legally strike (i.e., police, firefighters, etc.).
  - Mediation. A process whereby a third party attempts to facilitate a resolution between labour and management. Note that mediators do not have the power to enforce a resolution.
  - Grievance arbitration. A third-party resolution process used when employers and labour cannot resolve a grievance in a mutually acceptable manner. In such cases, the arbitrator(s) makes a final and binding resolution to the conflict at hand.
  - Conciliation. In many Canadian labour relations laws, a conciliator must assess the proposals of both employers and labour and submit a report to the appropriate federal or provincial minister of labour prior to a strike/lockout taking place.
  - Fact-finding. A process mostly used in British Columbia that is similar to conciliation.
  - Mediation/arbitration. A process that starts off with a third party acting as a mediator. If, however, the parties fail to reach an agreement on their own, the third party becomes an arbitrator and makes a binding decision.

goal
that which a person seeks to obtain or achieve

strategies
processes developed and implemented to achieve goals

power
the ability to make someone agree to your terms

conversion mechanisms
the processes used to convert inputs into outputs of the industrial relations system

Essential service roles such as police officers are often not eligible to strike.

- Joint committees. Many organizations have joint labour-management committees to examine issues of common concern, particularly health and safety joint committees.

- Other workplaces use committees for broader issues, and some jurisdictions, such as Newfoundland and Labrador and British Columbia, even promote their usage and provide assistance in establishing such committees (Labour Relations Agency, 2013; Labour Relations Board British Columbia, 2014).

- Strikes and lockouts. Work stoppages can be both a conversion mechanism and an outcome. When used as a conversion mechanism, strikes and lockouts are used to bring closure to the negotiation process and produce a collective agreement.

IR NOTEBOOK 1.1

RELEVANT JOURNALS

The field of industrial relations is studied in many social science disciplines. Since you may be assigned term papers concerning matters related to employment relationships, or you may wish to further your study of certain topics, the following list of journals may be helpful. Articles from many of these journals were referenced in the creation of this textbook. Journals with a Canadian focus are marked with an asterisk.

- *Academy of Management Journal*
- *Administrative Science Quarterly*
- *American Sociological Review*
- *British Journal of Industrial Relations*
- *Canadian Journal of Administrative Sciences**
- *Canadian Public Policy**

- Employee Relations
- Employee Relations Law Journal
- European Journal of Industrial Relations
- Human Relations
- Human Resource Development Quarterly
- Human Resource Management
- Human Resource Management Journal
- Industrial and Labor Relations Review
- Industrial Relations (Berkeley)
- Industrial Relations Journal
- Journal of Applied Psychology
- Journal of Industrial Relations
- Journal of Management
- Journal of Management Studies
- Journal of Occupational and Organizational Psychology
- Journal of Organizational Behavior
- Journal of Social Psychology
- Journal of Vocational Behavior
- Labor Economics
- Labour History
- Journal of Vocational Behavior
- Labor Law Journal
- Labour/Le Travail*
- Organization Studies
- Organizational Behavior and Human Decision Processes
- Personnel Psychology
- Relations industrielles/Industrial Relations*
- Sociology
- Work & Stress
- Work, Employment, and Society

OUTPUTS

The outputs may be thought of as the results, or outcomes, of the conversion mechanisms. As such, they are similar to what Dunlop called substantive rules. Often, such outputs may be captured in a collective agreement between labour and management (Craig, 1988). The collective agreement (which will be discussed more fully in Chapter 8) outlines key agreements and procedures reflecting the employment relationship in question. Elements that can be considered outputs of the industrial relations system include, but are not limited to, the following (as you read through the textbook, many of these outcomes will be discussed in more detail):

- Employer outcomes. For example, the rights and responsibilities of management in the employment relationship, as well as efficiency elements (productivity, profitability, etc.).
- Labour outcomes. Equity issues or ways to instill fairness in the workplace, including
  - the rights of, and security for, the union;
  - hours of work, including schedules, overtime, etc.;
  - wages and benefits;
  - job rights (e.g., job assignment and selection, layoff provisions, **seniority**); and
  - work rules, or rules that employees and employers are expected to follow.
- Worker perceptions. Workers' reactions in terms of
  - work climate, or workers' sense of the overall work environment in the organization at hand;

seniority
the length of time a person has been a member of the union

- employee morale and organizational commitment, or the extent that employees are satisfied with and committed to their organization and workplace; and
- union satisfaction and commitment, or the extent that employees are satisfied with and committed to their union.
- Conflict. An output of the system can be conflict (e.g., strikes and lockouts).

// VIEWS OF INDUSTRIAL RELATIONS

As one examines the industrial relations system outlined in Figure 1.1, it is clear that industrial relations can be seen as an interdisciplinary field, involving scholars from various social science disciplines. Thus, it should not be surprising that several different viewpoints have been used within the field. For an in-depth, historical look at how these social disciplines have shaped the teaching and research of Canadian industrial relations, see Hébert, Jain, and Meltz (1988). In the present section, we will briefly summarize several of the more prevalent views.

NEOCLASSICAL ECONOMICS VIEW

As outlined by Gunderson (1988, p. 50), the **neoclassical economics view** examines "the application of basic principles of neoclassical economics to ... the market for labour services." In particular, this view emphasizes factors concerning the supply and demand of labour, or workers. The "free market" assumption governing this economics view is that the number of people willing to work at a given wage rate (i.e., labour supply) is equal to the number of workers needed by organizations (i.e., labour demand). As a result, collective bargaining and unions can be seen as an artificial barrier to the free market in that they can artificially influence the supply and demand of labour. As such, researchers with this view often examine issues concerning the impact of unions on wages, productivity, etc.

> **neoclassical economics view**
> a view of industrial relations grounded in economics that sees unions as an artificial barrier to the free market

PLURALIST AND INSTITUTIONAL VIEW

Led by scholars such as John R. Commons (1918) and Selig Perlman (1928), this view largely grew out of what is known as the "Wisconsin School." While the pluralist view began in economic circles, it is in direct contrast to that of neoclassical economics. Rather than considering unions an artificial barrier to the free market, the **pluralist and institutional view** believes that labour unions act as a countervailing force that attempts to balance the interests of employers and employees. As the name implies, this view emphasizes the need for strong institutions as well as multiple (i.e., plural) actors in the employment relationship. Perhaps American scholar Kaufman (2003, p. 25) best summarizes this view when he states,

> **pluralist and institutional view**
> a view of industrial relations stressing the importance of institutions and multiple actors (including labour) in the employment relationship

> the Wisconsin strategy [which founded the institutional view] looks to use institutions such as trade unions, government, and corporations to establish a set of "working rules" that lead to stable, full employment conditions in labor markets, a level playing field in wage determination, and democratic mechanisms for due process and voice in the firm.

As this quote suggests, the systems framework is pluralist in nature. It is worth noting that the systems framework, and the pluralist view in which it is grounded, has traditionally been the predominant view of industrial relations in Canada (Craig, 1988).

HUMAN RESOURCES/STRATEGIC CHOICE

As we will discuss in more detail in Chapter 6, a seminal work by Kochan, Katz, and McKersie (1986) suggested that the American industrial relations climate had shifted significantly in the 1970s and 1980s. In brief, the evidence collected by these scholars suggested that Dunlop's shared ideology no longer existed and that there was a movement away from unionization toward nonunionized employment relationships. Moreover, Kochan, Katz, and McKersie argued that employers were implementing deliberate strategies designed to minimize unionization and the role of collective bargaining. Hence, their model is often referred to as the *strategic choice perspective*.

A key element of this perspective is the importance of human resources strategies and practices linked to the firm's overall business strategy. While human resources strategies and practices are not anti-union per se, they are often designed to foster cooperation between employees and employers. As such, this view has historically been presented as paying very little attention to the role of unions in the employment relationship (Kervin, 1988). In fact, if you look at many HR textbooks you will notice very little coverage of union issues, or at most a single chapter that attempts to present how HR differs in unionized workplaces. Thus, the human resources view may be seen to minimize the inherent conflict between the employer (who seeks to maximize efficiency and owner/shareholder gain) and the employee (who seeks to maximize equity and worker gain). In fact, some scholars have argued that the human resources perspective minimizes the elements of democracy in the workplace (since it does not focus on collective representation) and the inherent conflict between management and worker as they attempt to achieve their competing needs (Godard, 2010; Godard & Delaney, 2000).

POLITICAL ECONOMY

political economy
a view of industrial relations grounded in socialism and Marxism that stresses the role of inherent conflict between labour and management

Unlike many of the industrial relations views discussed previously, **political economy** is heavily grounded in the fields of sociology and political science rather than economics. While the pluralist and human resources perspectives are viewed as minimizing (if not ignoring) the inherent conflict between employers and employees, the political economy perspective does the reverse—it sees inherent conflict between employer and employee. This view has been more prevalent in Europe, where it is often associated with the University of Warwick Industrial Relations Research Unit (Ackers & Wilkinson, 2005) and scholars such as Richard Hyman (1989). The view largely took root in the United Kingdom in the 1970s, following a period of extensive strikes, the breakdown of national-level collective bargaining, and high levels of unemployment. During this time, there was a focus away from the institutional view, with an emphasis on stability and shared ideology, toward a more radical view that focused on "class struggle and workers' self-activity" (Ackers & Wilkinson, 2005, p. 449). This view stresses the need to look more fully at societal and political factors. In fact, Hyman (1994, p. 171) argues that the actions of management, labour, and governments

> *cannot sensibly be studied in isolation from their environing social relations.... Only if we understand how labour power is transformed ... and the social and economics forces that structure this transformation, can we make sense of the rules that apply to the employment relationship....*

In brief, a goal of Marxism was to overthrow management and allow employees to have more control of their workplace.

// OUTLINE OF THE TEXT

As discussed earlier in this chapter, we will largely focus on issues concerning union–management relations, but we will use industrial relations frameworks and a pluralist view to guide us. Accordingly, the industrial relations system shown in Figure 1.1 will provide the foundation of this text and will be used to guide us through the chapters.

First, we will examine the external inputs important to employment relationships. To provide context to the system and the inputs, we first overview labour history in Chapter 2. In particular, the economics subsystem and other environmental inputs will be presented in Chapter 3, while we will pay particular attention to the legal subsystem in Chapter 4.

Second, we move to an examination of the actors, including a discussion of internal inputs (e.g., values, goals, strategies, and power) as well as the history between them. Accordingly, we will focus the actors of labour and management in Chapters 5 and 6, respectively.

Third, we shift to a discussion of the conversion mechanisms. Specifically, we discuss contract negotiations (Chapter 7); collective agreement administration (Chapter 8); conflict resolution procedures, in particular strikes and grievances (Chapter 9); as well as third-party dispute resolution processes (Chapter 10).

Fourth, we discuss the outputs of the system. In particular, Chapter 11 examines the impacts of unionization, with particular focus on the elements of equity and efficiency.

Fifth, we look at the industrial relations system and the role of the feedback loop in terms of the dynamics of employment relationships. Thus, we end our text with a discussion of several special cases and issues in the field of industrial relations. More specifically, we discuss industrial relations issues related to the public sector in Chapter 12.

// SUMMARY

While scholars argue that "industrial relations is one of the oldest and most established ... social science disciplines that feed into business and management studies" (Ackers & Wilkinson, 2005, p. 444), there is considerable debate concerning what is and is not industrial relations. No single theory can be said to ground the field, and several terms can be used to describe various issues germane to it (e.g., industrial relations, employment relations, labour relations, etc.).

Given the diversity of perspectives in the study of employment relationships, several key views related to this text and the field of industrial relations must be kept in mind: neoclassical economics, pluralist/institutional, strategic choice/human resources, and political economy. In particular, it is important to note that the pluralist/institutional view, and specifically the systems approach, will provide the foundation for this textbook. As we move from chapter to chapter, we will focus on several key elements of the systems model presented in Figure 1.1. More specifically, we will (1) start with a review of the external inputs (or environmental subsystems), such as law and economics, (2) move to a discussion of the actors and their associated internal inputs (e.g., values, power, strategies, and goals), (3) present various conversion mechanisms (e.g., collective bargaining and strikes), (4) discuss outputs (e.g., terms and conditions for the employment relationship), and (5) finish with an overview of emerging trends in Canada.

KEY TERMS

collective agreement 3
collective bargaining 3
conversion mechanisms 14
employee relations 4
employment relations 5
exchange rate 12
feedback loop 8
goal 14
human resources 4
industrial relations 3
inflation 12
interest rate 12
labour relations 4
mandatory retirement 13
neoclassical economics view 17
pluralist and institutional view 17
political economy 18
power 14
seniority 16
strategies 14
strike 3
union 3
values 13

DISCUSSION QUESTIONS

1. Many of your peers may argue that the field of industrial relations is dead and that it has no relevance to today's youth. What do you think?

2. The topic of unionization often sparks considerable debate. A recent CLC (2014) Web posting states that: (1) over one-fifth of workers aged 15–29 are unionized, and (2) these unionized youth earn $5.50 per hour more than their nonunion counterparts. Present arguments from the employer and the union concerning the pros and cons of this $5.50 wage difference.

3. IR Today 1.2 examined the issue of foreign temporary workers. In your opinion, do these workers take jobs away from youth? Why or why not?

4. Many students will take this course in a business school. From your perspective, should industrial relations courses be required in business schools?

5. Unions are increasing their focus on youth workers. In your opinion, what should unions do to make them more appealing to youth?

USING THE INTERNET

Although we are early in the textbook, you will quickly see that many of the topics we cover in this course are relevant to you today and as you move throughout your career. Have a look at the following YouTube piece concerning youth, employment, and unionization: http://www.youtube.com/watch?v=8oEMbYj-kk0. Alternatively, go to YouTube and search on the key words of labour, union, and youth.

1. In your opinion are the concerns of youth presented accurate? Are there major concerns of young workers not presented?

2. Figure 1.1 presents numerous outputs of the IR system. Do you feel, based on this video and your own experience, that the desired outcomes for older workers and younger workers differ? Justify your answer with examples.

3. Looking at the IR system presented in Figure 1.1, which of the external inputs do you believe are creating the challenges for youth noted in this video?

4. To what extent are the differing perspectives of industrial relations discussed in this chapter present in the video?

EXERCISES

1. Watch the national or local evening news or go to a media website. Examine the stories that cover issues related to employment relationships and then group them into three themes: (a) collective bargaining/negotiations, (b) strikes, and (c) other areas. Is there a predominant theme? If so, why do you think it exists?

2. Issues related to the fair treatment of workers in developing countries often appear in media. Find a recent story on the topic. Which elements of Figure 1.1 are covered in that story?

3. Get a story concerning a labour dispute or strike from a newspaper or another media outlet. Using the IR system presented in this chapter, please answer the following:

   a. Can you see elements of external inputs in the story?

   b. To what extent are the four actors presented? Who represents these four actors?

   c. What conversion mechanisms, if any, are presented?

4. Most university faculties are unionized. Examining the university you are currently attending,

   a. name and identify the four actors of the industrial relations system;

   b. discuss the relevant internal inputs of these actors; and

   c. identify the external inputs that you feel have the greatest impact on the actors at this time

5. Professors who teach industrial relations come from a broad range of backgrounds, and most schools have websites listing professors' education, teaching experience, and research areas. Take a look at the Web pages of the faculty who teach topics related to industrial relations at your institution. On the basis of the website data provided, which of the industrial relations views do you expect to see emphasized in their courses? Explain.

On January 13, 2014, approximately 550 professors, librarians, and teaching staff walked off the job—effectively cancelling classes at all campuses of the university. The primary areas of dispute appeared to be wages and working conditions.

At the time of the strike the gap between the parties was significant. The Association of University of New Brunswick Teachers (AUNBT) sought a wage increase of approximately 23 percent over four years, to bring the salaries of its members in line with comparable Canadian universities. In contrast, the University had offered an increase of 9.5 percent.

Approximately two weeks into the strike, Jody Carr (New Brunswick's Minister of Post-Secondary Education, Training and Labour) made an important announcement. While the Minister would not comment on whether back-to-work legislation would be used to force an end to the dispute, he did state that the government had ordered the parties back to the bargaining table. Carr also stated that Brian Keller, who was chosen from a list from the union and the university, had been appointed as a special outside mediator. Media reports suggest that both UNB administration and AUNBT were pleased with Mr. Keller's appointment given his extensive experience; notably, Keller had served as vice-chair of both the Canada Labour Relations Board and the Ontario Labour Relations Board. After only two days of talks involving the special mediator, the parties settled. The final settlement consisted of a 2.5 percent increase in the first two years of the settlement; the salary increase in the third year of the agreement would be determined by arbitration.

Student and public reaction to the strike was closely monitored by media. Students protested and sought a refund for lost classes. At the end of strike, reading week was cancelled and there were minor changes to class and exam schedules. All exams ended by April 30. In an unprecedented move, the university passed on any savings from the strike to students. Full-time students received a $200 tuition rebate for lost class time.

Sources: "New Brunswick picks mediator to settle UNB strike." *The Globe and Mail.* (27 January 2014). Retrieved from http://www.theglobeandmail.com/news/national/education/new-brunswick-picks-mediator -to-settle-unb-strike/article16525173/; "UNB and striking faculty reach tentative agreement." *CBC News.* (30 January 2014). Retrieved from http://www.cbc.ca/news/canada/new-brunswick/unb-and-striking-faculty -reach-tentative-agreement-1.2517406; "UNB March Reading Week cancelled, pending senate approval." *CBC News.* (31 January 2014). Retrieved from http://www.cbc.ca/news/canada/new-brunswick/ unb-march-reading-week-cancelled-pending-senate-approval-1.2518263; "UNB and striking faculty ordered back to bargaining table." *CBC News.* (27 January 2014). Retrieved from http://www.cbc.ca/news/ canada/new-brunswick/unb-and-striking-faculty-ordered-back-to-bargaining-table-1.2512666; McCain, K., Campbell, H. E. A., Cogger, J., Goddard, K., & Whitney, B. (7 February 2014). "University to distribute net funds saved from labour disruption to students." UNB Labour Relations. Retrieved from http://www .unblabour.ca/bargaining-updates/2014/2/6/university-to-distribute-net-funds-saved-from-labour-disruption -to-students; Student Representative Board of Governors; McPhee, E. (28 January 2014). "Student dem-onstrations continue / Media blackout on negotiations," *Brunswickan.* Retrieved from http://thebruns.ca/ student-demonstrations-continue-media-blackout-negotiations/.

QUESTIONS

1. Using the industrial relations model presented in this chapter (Figure 1.1),
   a. identify and name the actors in this case;
   b. discuss what external inputs you feel are most relevant in this case; and
   c. name and identify the conversion mechanisms and outputs presented in the case.

// ENDNOTE

1. A preliminary version of this model was presented at the 2007 Annual Meeting of the Canadian Industrial Relations Association of Canada (see Brown, 2007).

// REFERENCES

1. Ackers, P., & Wilkinson, A. (2005). British industrial relations paradigm: A critical outline history and prognosis. *The Journal of Industrial Relations, 47,* pp. 443–456.

2. Bank of Canada. (April 2006). Fact sheets: The exchange rate. *The Bank in Brief.* Retrieved 29 June 2006 from http://www.bankofcanada.ca/en/backgrounders/bg-e1.html

3. Bank of Canada. (December 2010). *Financial system review.* Retrieved 11 January 2011 from http://www.bankofcanada.ca/en/fsr/2010/highlights_1210.pdf

4. Barbash, J. (1987). Like nature, industrial relations abhors a vacuum. *Relations industrielles, 42,* pp. 168–179.

5. Bellemare, G. (2000). End users: Actors in the industrial relations system? *British Journal of Industrial Relations, 38,* pp. 383–405.

6. Brown, T. C. (2007). What happened to the "I" in IR? The role of individual measures in IR theory and research. Paper presented at the annual meeting of the Canadian Association of Industrial Relations, Montreal, 5–7 June.

7. Canwest News. (8 January 2007). Snowplow operators drift toward strike. Retrieved 25 April 2014 from http://www.canada.com/story.html?id=6bda1940-011b-4de1-bb9e-2ab2e782b6ac

8. CCHRA. (February 2014). Specifications for the National Knowledge Examination. Toronto: CCHRA.

9. CHRP. (2015). Become a CHRP. Retrieved 21 April 2015 from http://www.chrp.ca/?page=Become_CHRP

10. CIBC. (2014). Retrieved 5 May 2014 from https://cibc.taleo.net/careersection/1/jobdetail.ftl?job=515942&src=JB-10304

11. CLC. (2014). The union advantage for young workers. Retrieved 5 May 2014 from http://www.canadianlabour.ca/about-clc/union-advantage-young-workers

12. Commons, J. R. (1918). *History of labor in the United States.* (Vols. 1–2). New York: Macmillan.

13. Côté, A. (10 January 2011). Household finances and economic growth. Remarks by Agathe Côté, Deputy Governor of the Bank of Canada to Canadian Club of Kingston. Retrieved 13 January 2011 from http://www.bankofcanada.ca/en/speeches/2011/sp100111.pdf

14. Craig, A. W. J. (1967). A model for the analysis of industrial relations systems. Paper presented to the annual meeting of the Canadian Political Science Association.

15. Craig, A. W. J. (1988). Mainstream industrial relations. In G. Hébert, C. J. Jain & N. M. Meltz (Eds.), *The state of the art in industrial relations* (pp. 9–43). Kingston, ON: Industrial Relations Centre, Queen's University, and Centre for Industrial Relations, University of Toronto.

16. Craig, A. W. J., & Solomon, N. A. (1996). *The system of industrial relations in Canada* (5th edition). Toronto: Prentice Hall Canada Inc.

17. Dunlop, J. T. (1958, 1993). *Industrial relations system.* New York: Henry Holt and Company.

18. Dunlop, J. T. (1993). *Industrial relations system.* (Revised edition). Boston, MA: Harvard Business School Press.

19. Godard, J. (2010). What is best for workers? The implications of workplace and human resource management practices revisited. *Industrial Relations: A Journal of Economy and Society, 49*(3), pp. 466–488.

20. Godard, J., & Delaney, J. (2000). Reflections on the "high performance" paradigm's implications for industrial relations as a field. *Industrial and Labor Relations Review, 53*, pp. 482–502.

21. Gunderson, M. (1988). Labour economics and industrial relations. In G. Hébert, C. J. Jain & N. M. Meltz (Eds.), *The state of the art in industrial relations* (pp. 45–71). Kingston, ON: Industrial Relations Centre, Queen's University, and Centre for Industrial Relations, University of Toronto.

22. Heathfield, S. (2014). What do employees who work in labor relations do? About.com Human Resources. Retrieved 2 May 2014 from http://humanresources.about.com/od/jobdescriptions/f/hr_job_lr.htm

23. Hébert, G., Jain, C. J., & Meltz, N. M. (Eds.). (1988). *The state of the art in industrial relations.* Kingston, ON: Industrial Relations Centre, Queen's University, and Centre for Industrial Relations, University of Toronto.

24. Hyman, R. (1989). *The political economy of industrial relations: Theory and practice in a cold climate.* Basingstoke: Macmillan.

25. Hyman, R. (1994). Theory and industrial relations. *British Journal of Industrial Relations, 32*, pp. 165–180.

26. Industrial Relations Manager. (2015). Retrieved Aug 21 2015 from https://ca.linkedin.com/jobs2/view/44901885?trk=jserp_job_details_text

27. Kaufman, B. E. (2003). John R. Commons and the Wisconsin School on industrial relations strategy and policy. *Industrial and Labor Relations Review, 57,* pp. 3–30.

28. Kervin, J. B. (1988). Sociology, psychology and industrial relations. In G. Hébert, C. J. Jain & N. M. Meltz (Eds.), *The state of the art in industrial relations* (pp. 187–234). Kingston, ON: Industrial Relations Centre, Queen's University, and Centre for Industrial Relations, University of Toronto.

29. Kochan, T., Katz, H., & McKersie, R. (1986). *The transformation of American industrial relations.* New York: Basic Books.

30. Labour Relations Agency. (13 December 2013). *Labour Management Committee.* Retrieved 27 April 2014 from http://www.gov.nl.ca/lra/union/lmc.html

31. Labour Relations Board British Columbia. (27 April 2014). *Joint Consultation Committees (JCC).* Retrieved 27 April 2014 from http://www.lrb.bc.ca/mediation/joint.htm

32. Library of Parliament. (20 November 2009). *Federal back to work legislation 1950 to date.* Retrieved 11 January 2011 from http://www2.parl.gc.ca/Parlinfo/compilations/houseofcommons/legislation/LegislationBackToWork.aspx

33. Meltz, N. M. (1997). Introduction to employment relations. Paper presented to the Conference on Teaching in Human Resources and Industrial Relations, Atlanta, GA.

34. Meltz, N. M., & Adams, R. J. (1993). *Industrial relations theory: Its nature, scope, and pedagogy.* Rutgers University: Scarecrow Press.

35. NLEC. (2014). About. Retrieved 5 May 2014 from http://www.nlec.nf.ca/about/

36. NSGEU. (2014). NSGEU staff. Retrieved 5 May 2014 from http://nsgeu.ca/about/how-nsgeu-works/nsgeu-staff/

37. Outsource2india. (2014). About us. Retrieved 25 April 2014 from http://www.outsource2india.com/AboutUs.asp

38. Perlman, S. (1928). *A theory of the labor movement.* New York: Macmillan.

39. VIA Rail. (2014). Senior advisor, employee relations. Retrieved 4 May 2014 from http://www.jobboom.com/en/job-description/human-resources/senior-advisor-employee-relations/montreal-region/via-rail-canada-inc/2014153

40. Warren, A. M., & Kelloway, E. K. (2010). Retirement decisions in the context of the abolishment of mandatory retirement. *International Journal of Manpower, 31,* pp. 286–305.

41. Wood, S. J., Wagner, A., Armstrong, E. G. A., Goodman, J. F. B., & Davis, J. E. (1975). The "industrial relations system" concept as a basis for theory in industrial relations. *British Journal of Industrial Relations, 13,* pp. 291–308.

42. WTAE. (4 February 2014). Snow plow drivers avoid strike with tentative agreement on new contract. Retrieved 25 April 2014 from http://www.wtae.com/news/local/snow-plow-drivers-may-strike/-/9681086/24268520/-/cscn4sz/-/index.html#ixzz2zuZ4GeuJ

LABOUR HISTORY

LEARNING OBJECTIVES

BY THE END OF THIS CHAPTER, YOU WILL BE ABLE TO DISCUSS

- the preunionization work environment and the movement toward unionized relationships;
- the relationship between the Canadian and American labour movements;
- how exclusive jurisdiction, business unionism, and political nonpartisanship have divided the labour movement over time;
- how significant events from the 1850s to the present day have shaped the history of workplace relations; and
- how current and past history may shape the future of labour in Canada.

On the morning of May 15, 1919, a group of female telephone operators took actions that started one of the more memorable events in Canadian labour history. While they ended their shifts as normal, no one came in to replace them. The operators were holding a sympathy strike in support of the metalworkers. By 7:00 a.m., the phone system was no longer functioning. A few hours later, at 11:00 a.m., Alex Sheppard (a union leader with the metalworkers) placed a One Big Union (OBU) hat on his head and marched to the intersection of Portage and Main. Workers from various establishments followed. The general strike was now in full gear.

Within twenty-four hours, between 20,000 and 35,000 mostly nonunion workers had left their workplaces. Winnipeg, Canada's third-largest city, was at a standstill. Workers from public services (e.g., postal workers, waterworks, police, firefighters), the private sector (e.g., cooks, waiters, retail staff), manufacturing, and building trades were on strike.

Employer and government concern over the strike led to several key events. Employers organized a group called the Citizens Committee of One Thousand, which declared the strike a revolutionary conspiracy. On June 6, the federal government amended the *Immigration Act*. Any non-Canadian-born person deemed to be a revolutionary could now be immediately deported. In addition, the government amended the *Criminal Act*. As a result of these legislative changes, several strike leaders were arrested and jailed on June 17. From 1919 to 1920, the federal government would pay over $196,000 for the prosecution of these labour leaders.

Saturday, June 21 marked a dark day in the strike. Thousands of strikers gathered in front of city hall in defiance of the mayor's ban on parades. The mayor called in the North West Mounted Police, who, along with federal troops, charged the crowd. By the end of the afternoon, downtown Winnipeg was empty, one person was dead, and another thirty were injured. The day became known as Bloody Saturday. Concerned that more violence would occur, the strike leaders declared an end to the strike on June 26.

The two groups key to the start of the strike (metalworkers and phone operators) made no gains. Metalworkers did not receive any wage increases; phone operators were rehired only if they promised to never again go on a sympathy strike.

Sources: D. J. Bercuson. (1990). *Confrontation at Winnipeg: Labour, industrial relations and the general strike.* Montreal and Kingston: McGill-Queen's University Press; Canadian Museum of Civilization, 2002; J. Chaboyer and E. Black. (2006). "Conspiracy in Winnipeg: How the 1919 general strike leaders were railroaded into prison and what we must do now to make amends." Retrieved from http://www.policyalternatives.ca/documents/Mardtoba_Pubs/2006/Conspiracy_in_Winnipeg.pdf; Government of Canada. (2006b); M. Horodyski. (1986). "Women and the Winnipeg General Strike of 1919." *Manitoba History, 11* (Spring). Retrieved from http://www.mhs.mb.ca/docs/mb_history/11/women1919strike.shtml; T. Mitchell. (2004). "Legal gentlemen appointed by the federal government: The Canadian state, the Citizens' Committee of 1000, and Winnipeg's seditious conspiracy trials of 1919–1920." *Labour/Le Travail, 53*, pp. 9–46; Mitchell and Naylor, 1998.

// PREUNIONIZATION

Today as you read this chapter you may be working or may have recently finished a summer job. As an employee today, you have many rights and protections that your grandparents never had. For example, you are entitled to work in a safe work environment, you have access to breaks, you have freedom from discrimination, you are entitled to a minimum wage and to be paid overtime on certain days or after a certain number of hours worked, etc. You even have the right to refuse work that is unsafe. Many of us now take these rights as "givens." We often forget that these rights were the result of victories won by the labour movement over the past hundred years or so. To understand just how far we have come, let's review the type of workplace practices that existed prior to the rise of the labour movement.

MASTER–SERVANT RELATIONSHIP

Prior to unionization, the employment relationship was best described as the **master–servant relationship**. As the name implies, the employer, as the master, made all the rules. The employee, as a servant, was required to follow these rules. As such, employees had limited protection or rights. This was because the basis of the relationship was common law. Under common law, the employment contract required that employees perform the work and employers pay workers' wages (Kahn-Freund, 1967). There was such a power imbalance between workers and employers that employees were often coerced into agreeing to employment terms and conditions (Fox, 1974). It was illegal for workers to quit; for them to bargain collectively or to form a union was deemed a conspiracy; and management controlled virtually all aspects of the employment relationship (Labour Law Casebook Group, 2004). As we note later in the book, **common law** exists today, and is often used to refer to the law regime for nonunion employment. However, employees under common law today have many more rights than they did 100 years ago.

While employees of today can look to unions or governmental agencies for protection from abusive workplace practices, this was not always the case. Unions at that time were illegal, and the laws of the day did little to protect employees. In essence, there were only two actors in the industrial relations system at that time: employers and employees. There were no "associations" (e.g., unions), and the third actor (i.e., government) was largely absent. In fact, as outlined by the Labour Law Casebook Group (2004), the laws and courts did little to protect employees; rather, they provided additional power to the employer. For example, the *Master and Servant Act* stated that workers who refused to report to work or failed to follow lawful orders were guilty of a criminal offence. This act even provided special penalties for workers who attempted to bargain collectively to seek wage increases. Even the rights to choose your employer or leave your employer were restricted. England's *Statute of Artificers* (1563), from which Canada's common law originated, required workers to accept jobs when they were offered and allowed employers to punish people who left a job before the work was completed (Fox, 1985).

As you can see, preunionization workplaces and work practices looked very different from what you would see today. There was little consideration of workers and their rights, and minimal employment protection from courts and legislation. It was this very environment, and the large power imbalance between workers and employers, that led to the rise of a labour movement. In the sections that follow, we will present some of the more significant milestones in that history.

// THE MOVEMENT TO UNIONIZATION

In this section, we will walk through the significant events related to unionization and workplace relationships. (See also Table 2.1.) We will start with pre-1900 Canada and then move chronologically to present-day events.

THE EARLY YEARS (PRE-1900)

The early years in the labour movement were marked by a number of important developments including the introductions of new model unionism, the *Trades Union Act*, the

TABLE 2.1

SOME KEY DATES IN CANADIAN LABOUR HISTORY

Year	Events
1872	Nine-Hour Movement
	Trade Union Act
1886	Trade and Labour Congress (TLC) founded
1902	Berlin Convention results in foundation of National Trades and Labour Congress (NTLC)
1907	*Industrial Disputes Investigation Act* (IDIA)
1919	The Winnipeg General Strike
1944	Wartime Labour Relations Regulation (P.C. 1003)
1945	Rand Formula
1956	Canadian Labour Congress (CLC) formed
1961	New Democratic Party (NDP) formed
1967	Public Service Staff Relations Act (PSSRA)
1975–78	Anti-Inflation Board (AIB)
1985	Canadian United Auto Workers formed
1996	Days of Action
2013	Formation of Unifor

American Federation of Labour, the Trades and Labour Congress of Canada, and the Knights of Labor.

NEW MODEL UNIONISM

In the 1800s, in their study of British unions, sociologists Beatrice and Sidney Webb (1898) described an event they called **new model unionism**. A key element of these new world unions was that they were craft-based—all members performed the same trade or specialty.

Generally composed of specialist employees performing a common trade, new model unions often restricted access to the trade through the use of **apprenticeships**. In so doing, unions minimized wage competition by influencing the supply of labour in terms of the number of craftsmen available to perform the work. As a monopoly supplier of labour, these unions usually sought to negotiate solutions to any workplace issues versus going on strike.

While the Webbs focused on British unions, we will see that Canada had similar issues concerning trade unions in the late 1800s. Arguably, it is new model unionism's focus on trades that may have led to the use of the term **trade union**.

> **new model unionism**
> the movement to trade (or craft) unions
>
> **apprenticeship**
> a process in which trainees learn a trade under the supervision of a senior tradesperson
>
> **trade union**
> unions that organize all workers of a trade regardless of their industry or workplace

THE NINE-HOUR MOVEMENT AND *TRADE UNION ACT* OF 1872

The 1870s were marked by several key events in Canadian labour history. The Nine-Hour Movement of 1872 (see IR Notebook 2.1) was sparked by a group of about 1,500 Hamilton workers who sought a reduction in the length of the workday, defying the legislation of the day (CBC, 2006b; Kealey, 1995). That same year, Toronto printers went on strike against the *Globe* founder, George Brown. While the movement became widespread, it did not result in significant gains. However, the movement is believed to have influenced the prime minister of the day (Sir John A. Macdonald) to create the *Trade Union Act*. Declaring himself "the working man's friend," Macdonald had his government introduce legislation that permitted employees to join unions (Government of Canada, 2006a). That same year, an amendment to the *Criminal Law Amendment Act* (1872) stated that it was no longer a conspiracy or a crime for a person to join a union. That being said, the *Criminal Law Amendment Act* did allow jail penalties for striking. Nevertheless, the passage of these two legislations provided the foundation for the birth of a formalized Canadian labour movement.

IR NOTEBOOK 2.1

THE NINE-HOUR MOVEMENT

The late 1800s were marked by numerous events resulting from employee discontent with the working conditions and practices of the time. Perhaps one of the best known was the Nine-Hour Movement, which occurred in 1872. The following passage from http://www.thecanadianencyclopedia.com provides an excellent summary of those events:

> The nine-hour movement was an international phenomenon, taking place in Canada between January and June 1872. The movement's goal was to standardize shorter working days. Though this particular mandate was unsuccessful, the movement did have an impact, including setting the foundation for the Canadian Labor Union.

Background

> The nine-hour movement was an international workers' attempt to secure shorter working days. In Canada, the movement took place between January and June 1872. Beginning in Hamilton, the demand for the nine-hour day (some workers were expected to labour as long as 12 hours) spread quickly to Toronto and Montréal, gathering support in Ontario towns from Sarnia to Perth. Echoes were heard as far east as Halifax. For the first time, Canadian labour organized what might be considered the beginnings of a unified protest movement.

Movement Leaders

> Among the leading figures in the shorter-hours mobilization were Toronto's J. S. Williams and John Hewitt, a printer and a cooper, respectively; Hamilton's James Ryan, a Great Western Railway engineer; and James Black, employed at Montréal's Grand Trunk Railway works. Railway mechanics like Ryan and Black would figure prominently in the attempt to create a broad, pan-Canadian movement of agitation around the shorter-hours question. Ryan traveled to Montréal, developing a coordinated strategy of specific actions in Hamilton and Toronto that might be supported by Montréal workers. He also encouraged the formation of nine-hour leagues. Unlike anything that had appeared in Canada before, these leagues united union and non-union workers, breaking down barriers between them and building connections across central Canada. By March 1972, with Black as its president, Montréal's Nine Hour League boasted 2,000 members.

Development

At the height of the agitation for shorter hours, the Ontario Workman *newspaper was founded on cooperative principles in Toronto by J. S. Williams and other printers affiliated with the Toronto Typographical Union (TTU) Local 91. With Williams as its editor, this pioneer labour newspaper was a reflection of the complicated mix of forces, old and new, that the mobilization for the nine-hour day drew together.*

On the one hand, Williams challenged employers with labourers' collective strength. As a prominent figure in the shorter-hours movement and a leading member of the TTU Vigilance Committee, he helped organize an April demonstration of 10,000 and led a highly publicized strike against Toronto's master printers. The latter job action culminated in Williams's arrest on conspiracy charges. On the other hand, Williams and a number of other Toronto leaders retained close connections to Conservative Party leader Sir John A. Macdonald. It was Macdonald who later provided funds to keep the Ontario Workman *afloat and in the hands of his Tory workingman friends.*

Between March and April, the controversy around the eventually unsuccessful Toronto printers' strike reminded workers how antagonistic employers were to labourers' new initiatives. Trade unions were declared illegal in Canada, as they were judged to be conspiracies in restraint of trade under a particular reading of older British law. Undaunted, John Hewitt championed the formation of the Canadian Labor Protective and Mutual Improvement Association in Hamilton on 3 May 1872.

Meanwhile, Hamilton leader James Ryan aimed to strategically stagger demonstrations over the course of May and June 1872, culminating in a massive show of force. However, the printers' strike, as well as related attacks launched by the newspaper owner George Brown and other employing printers, forced Ryan to act sooner. On 15 May, Hamilton's "nine-hour pioneers" defied opposition with a procession of 1,500 workers, a virtual general strike of the city's skilled workingmen. At this point in the movement, labour reform seemed attainable.

Impact

Despite the momentum felt in the spring of 1872, the nine-hour movement was largely unsuccessful. Employer hostility and waning post-Confederation prosperity spelled its defeat. Also significant were divisions within the working class. Women and unskilled workers figured peripherally at best, ensuring that the struggle touched certain sectors more fully than others.

However, the nine-hour movement was not an utter failure. Workers declared that their interests, institutions and political stance were reflective of their distinct economic needs. The Canadian Labor Protective and Mutual Improvement Association gave way to the Canadian Labor Union (CLU), formed in April 1873.

The CLU was possible, it could be argued, because working-class activists won major concessions immediately after the demise of the nine-hour movement of 1872, including the limited right to associate in trade unions, the repeal of repressive legislation, the passage of laws strengthening workers' opportunities for action against employers, and franchise extension.

Sir John A. Macdonald, Canada's prime minister at the time, had seen the possibility of class struggle rear its worrisome head in the newly formed country's nine-hour leagues. He feared what he called "the Chartist proclivities" of Canadian workingmen, a reference to the British Chartist movement of the 19th century, which produced demands for universal suffrage and untold battles between employers and labourers. Macdonald thought that in granting the emerging workers' movement concrete, if curtailed, concessions, he would consolidate a relationship with labouring people that would last into the next decades. During the 1880s, however, Canadian workers organized more trade unions, fought more strikes and developed a more wide-reaching movement, centered in the Knights of Labor, than had ever been imaginable in the early 1870s.

The nine-hour movement was a forerunner of these 1880s developments, a transition in the struggle to create institutions and mobilizations of Canadian workers.

The Nine-Hour Movement laid the foundation for many of the elements in current labour and employment standards acts. For example, many laws now require that overtime be paid for an employee working more than eight hours per day. To this day, some of the issues we face (e.g., what is deemed to be a "normal" workday) have been traditional topics on the labour agenda.

Source: Written by Bryan D Palmer. Courtesy of *The Canadian Encyclopedia*, Historica Canada, http://www.thecanadianencyclopedia.ca/en/article/nine-hour-movement/.

AMERICAN FEDERATION OF LABOR AND THE TRADES AND LABOUR CONGRESS OF CANADA

Cigar maker Samuel Gompers was the first president of the American Federation of Labor (AFL). In 1886, he founded the AFL as a federation of trade unions built upon three key principles. As this chapter will show, these three principles both united and divided the labour movement in Canada and the United States for more than half a century. These principles were as follows (AFL, 2006):

EXCLUSIVE JURISDICTION Gompers believed that unions should be craft- or trade-based. This meant that only wage earners could be union members and that each union would be responsible for a single occupation or trade: "one union per craft; one craft per union." Thus, only one union could represent bricklayers, another union could only represent blacksmiths, etc. As we will see later in this chapter, this **exclusive jurisdiction** view conflicted with that of groups like the Knights of Labor, which were open to skilled and unskilled labour.

BUSINESS UNIONISM (OR PURE-AND-SIMPLE UNIONISM) Gompers believed that the primary focus of unions should be the economic well-being of their members rather than political reform. He felt that the best way to ensure workers' rights was to ensure they had economic security. In fact, he is often quoted as saying, "more, more, and more"—referring to more economic gains for workers. Because of this view, North American unionism is often referred to as "bread and butter" unionism or **business (or pure-and-simple) unionism**—its focus being to make certain there was bread and butter on the tables of workers. Accordingly, the AFL did not seek to overthrow capitalism or business owners, as was the case of **socialist unionism**. Rather, Gompers advocated that unions needed to operate in the capitalistic economy with the goal of getting the best deal possible for their members.

POLITICAL NONPARTISANSHIP Gompers believed that labour should practise **political nonpartisanship**—that is, it should not align itself with any one political party or group. Rather, he asserted that labour should create its own priorities, clearly articulate these priorities, seek the endorsement of existing political parties for these priorities, and mobilize members to vote for those politicians or parties that supported labour's priorities. Among IR circles this became known as "rewarding friends (those that supported labour's priorities) and punishing enemies (those that did not support labour's priorities)."

exclusive jurisdiction
what exists when a single union represents all workers of a trade or occupational grouping

business unionism (or pure-and-simple unionism)
unionism that focuses on improving wages and the working conditions of its members

socialist unionism
unionism that challenges capitalism and seeks equity for union and nonunion members

political nonpartisanship
a belief that unions should not be aligned with any political party

As will be shown later in this chapter, the guiding principles that grounded the formation of the AFL, summarized in Table 2.2, have both divided and united the labour movement in Canada.

The same year that the AFL was formed in Ohio, the Trades and Labour Congress (TLC) was formed in Canada. It was largely composed of Canadian affiliates of the AFL; however, it also included groups such as the Knights of Labor, which included unskilled workers.

We should point out that the AFL was not the first trade federation in Canada. Its lineage can be traced to the 1873 Canadian Labour Union (CLU) (Kealey & Palmer, 1995; Palmer, 1983).

The CLU was made up of about thirty-five unions. Its mandate was "to agitate such questions as may be for the benefit of the working classes, in order that we may obtain the enactment of such measures by the Dominion and local legislatures as will be beneficial to us, and the repeal of all oppressive laws which now exist" (Ottawa & District Labour Council, 2005). Accordingly, the CLU's priorities went beyond those of Gompers's AFL and included mandating shorter working hours, ending private employers' use of convict labour, restricting the use of child labour (particularly for children under ten years of age), setting minimum standards for the sanitation and ventilation of factories, creating a government statistics bureau to track information related to wages and working conditions, and instituting resolutions related to public education (Ottawa & District Labour Council, 2005).

An Irish printer named Daniel O'Donoghue, considered by many the "father of the Canadian labour movement," was key to the formation of the CLU (O'Donoghue, 1942–1943). Unfortunately, due to economic downturns of the 1870s, the CLU was short-lived. However, as the economy improved, so did the cause of labour. In the 1880s, O'Donoghue was involved in organizing the initial meeting of the Trades and Labour Congress, which replaced the defunct CLU (Ottawa & District Labour Council, 2005). As you will see in IR Notebook 2.2, O'Donoghue's involvement in politics and the Knights of Labor contradicted the three core values of Gompers's AFL. This early linkage between politics and labour may also explain why, even today, Canadian labour is considered more socialist than their American counterpart.

TABLE 2.2	
GUIDING PRINCIPLES, OR "DIVIDE AND CONQUER"?	
Exclusive jurisdiction	The concept that each union would be responsible for a single trade; often referred to as "one union per craft; one craft per union"
Business unionism (*or* pure-and-simple unionism)	The view that labour unions should seek to improve the economic well-being of its own members rather than to seek to overthrow capitalism or business owners.
Political nonpartisanship	The view that labour should not align itself with any one political party or group, but rather support those politicians who support labour

CHAPTER 2 Labour History

DANIEL O'DONOGHUE: THE FATHER OF THE CANADIAN LABOUR MOVEMENT

Daniel O'Donoghue is considered by many to be the founding father of the Canadian labour movement. Born in Ireland in 1844, he immigrated to Canada at the age of six. At fourteen, he became a printing apprentice. Given the shortage of jobs, he moved to New York, where he was exposed to the printers' union. After returning to Canada to work with the *Ottawa Times*, he, at the age of 21, organized the first printers' union in Ottawa. Union members saw their wages increase to $8 a week in 1869 and $10 in 1873.

Given his success with the printers' union, O'Donoghue was a natural for a leadership role in Ottawa's new trades council, which was formed in 1872. In fact, O'Donoghue held a role as a founding member, secretary, and president of the Ottawa Trades Council. He also participated in the formation of the first national labour federation, the CLU, and became its first vice-president in 1873.

His influence in the labour movement resulted in his being nominated in, and winning, a provincial byelection in Ottawa. He held the position of an independent "working man's representative" from 1874 to 1879. During that time, he focused on a labour agenda by pressing the government of the day to act on trade union issues related to workplace conditions, unemployment, and immigration.

Upon losing his seat in 1879, he returned to his labour movement roots. He moved to Toronto, where he was involved in the revival of the Toronto and District Labour Council. He was a member of this council as a representative of both the Typographical Union and the Knights of Labor. Moreover, O'Donoghue became secretary of the legislative committee in 1883 and was involved in organizing the first meeting of the Trades and Labour Congress in 1886.

During the 1880s and 1890s, O'Donoghue held several positions within the provincial government. Three years after it created a Bureau of Industries (1882), he was named the bureau clerk. In this role, he often wrote on issues important to labour (e.g., poor working conditions, the work of trade unions, etc.). In 1900, O'Donoghue left this position because he was assigned to the federal government's first Department of Labour. There, he worked as a fair wages officer, ensuring people employed under government contracts had fair pay and working conditions.

O'Donoghue died in 1907. During his years in the labour movement, he clearly played a key role in both the transformation and documentation of Canadian labour history.

Sources: O'Donoghue, J. G. (1942–1943). Daniel John O'Donoghue: Father of the Canadian Labour Movement. *CCHA Report, 10.* pp. 87–96. Retrieved from http://www.umanitoba.ca/colleges/st_pauls/ccha/Back%20Issues/CCHA1942-43/Donoghue.html; Ottawa & District Labour Council (2005). Daniel O'Donoghue (1844–1907). Retrieved from http://www.ottawalabour.org/index.php?p=history_daniel.

THE KNIGHTS OF LABOR

The Knights of Labor was first formed in 1869 in Philadelphia. Based in the United States, it was originally a secret society, similar to the Freemasons, but it removed the cloak of secrecy in 1881. It was more radical in nature, and three factors differentiated it from other labour organizations of the day (Knights of Labor, 2009):

1. It believed in the creation of a single large union for skilled and unskilled workers; thus, it did not follow the doctrine of "one union per craft; one craft per union."

2. It was opposed to strikes. The Knights leadership felt that strikes led to hardship for workers. However, while the leadership may have opposed strike action, its membership did not. Members of the Knights were actively involved in many large strikes (Kealey & Palmer, 1995).

3. The Knights sought to establish cooperative businesses, which would be owned and operated by members of the union rather than employers per se. This was in direct contrast to the idea of "bread and butter" or business unionism espoused by Gompers.

Because of the initial secrecy of the Knights of Labor, it is difficult to completely track its history. Kealey and Palmer (1981, 1995) have documented the Knights' history in Canada, in particular in Ontario. It is estimated that the Knights organized a minimum of 21,800 workers nationally, more than 18 percent of whom were employed in the manufacturing sector in 1881 (Kealey & Palmer, 1995).

1900–1920: THE YEARS OF STRUGGLE

The years between 1900 and 1914 marked one of the most accelerated phases of economic development in Canadian history (Palmer, 1992). During the same period (1901–1913), there were fourteen large strikes in which some form of violence occurred; in eleven of these, the militia or military were called in (Canadian Labour Congress, n.d.). This period also marked the beginning of World War I. Thus, this early part of the twentieth century laid a foundation in the Canadian labour movement as well as created a rift between the skilled (i.e., trades) and unskilled workers that would last almost half a century. Some of the important events of this period included the Berlin Convention, the introduction of the *Industrial Disputes Investigation Act* (IDIA), the Winnipeg General Strike, and One Big Union. We will now discuss each in more detail.

THE BERLIN CONVENTION, 1902

Following the lead of the AFL, the Trade and Labour Congress's 1902 convention created a large divide in the Canadian labour movement—one that would remain for fifty years. Held in Berlin (now Kitchener), Ontario, this convention resulted in the TLC becoming composed solely of unions affiliated with the AFL. Unions that did not share the three core philosophies of Gompers's AFL (i.e., exclusive jurisdiction, business unionism, and political nonpartisanship) were ejected from the TLC. These expelled unions were largely industrial-based unions of less-skilled workers (including the Knights of Labor) and split off to form the National Trades and Labour Congress (NTLC) in 1902, which later became the Canadian Federation of Labour (CFL) in 1908 and the All-Canadian Congress of Labour (CCL) in 1927 (Canadian Labour Congress, n.d.; MacDowell, 2006).

INDUSTRIAL DISPUTES INVESTIGATION ACT (IDIA), 1907

Conciliation services had been offered by the federal Department of Labour starting in 1900 with the passage of the *Conciliation Act* (Kealey, 1995). William Lyon Mackenzie King, who would later become a prime minister, had firsthand experience with it, given his role as the chief conciliator of the department. King had attended Harvard and the University of Chicago, where he examined issues relevant to labour relations. In 1907, when he held the position of deputy minister of labour, he created the *Industrial Disputes Investigation Act* (IDIA). The act, which would become a cornerstone of Canadian law, marked an ongoing trend in Canadian legislation, namely the need for third-party intervention prior to a strike (Heron, 1989). Many of the key elements of the IDIA still hold true today, causing some historians arguing that "the IDIA laid the foundation for the particular industrial relations system that exists in Canada" (Kealey, 1995, p. 417).

The act required that all workers and employers in certain industries (i.e., resources, utilities, transportation) submit their disputes to a three-person conciliation board prior to a strike or lockout. Parties would present evidence to the panel, and the panel would issue a report. However, there was a required "cooling-off" period once the board completed its report, during which the parties were not permitted to proceed to work stoppage (Heron, 1989).

THE WINNIPEG GENERAL STRIKE

This chapter's opening vignette presented an overview of the strike itself. Now we need to set the context of that historic event. In the early days of May 1919, the building trades were on strike. The metalworkers joined them, as both sought to have their unions recognized as well as their working conditions and wages improved. They took their cases to the Winnipeg Trades and Labour Council (WTLC). The WTLC held a vote for a general strike of all unions to support the metal and building workers. Support was impressive: over 11,000 voted in favour of the strike as against about 500 who opposed it (Mitchell & Naylor, 1998). Estimates suggest that the votes cast in favour of it cut across occupations, with 149 police staff supporting the strike (11 did not), all 278 waiters and cooks supporting it, and 250 postal workers supporting it (19 did not) (Canadian Museum of Civilization, 2002). The Collections Canada website hosts a silent film of the strike that you might find interesting (Collections Canada, n.d.).

While the vignette suggests that the strikers did not achieve their goals, the strike did result in a number of positive changes in relation to one actor of the IR system—the government (Government of Canada, 2006b). In the 1920 Manitoba election, labour candidates won eleven seats, four of which were won by strike leaders. The next year, James Woodsworth (a Methodist minister who was involved in the strike) was elected as the first independent labour member of Parliament (MP). Woodsworth would later form the Co-operative Commonwealth Federation, the precursor to the present-day New Democratic Party (NDP).

Library and Archives Canada C-037329

C-037329

Postwar labour unrest fuelled the Winnipeg General Strike in 1919.

As suggested by the opening vignette's account of strike leader Alex Sheppard wearing an OBU hat, the OBU is often associated with the Winnipeg General Strike. OBU was radical in nature with a social unionism orientation. One of its key demands was the introduction of a six-hour workday to minimize unemployment. OBU's Canadian roots date back to the March 1919 Western Labour Conference in Calgary (Heron, 1989; Palmer, 1983). During this conference, a referendum was held to separate from the TLC and create a new militant labour organization, OBU (Mitchell & Naylor, 1998).

OBU differed from the TLC in several important ways. It focused on organizing all workers (not just craft/trade workers), identified closely with the revolutions taking place in Germany and Russia (greetings were even sent from the Calgary conference to the Bolsheviks and Spartakists), and had a strong link to the Socialist Party of Canada (SPC), given that several OBU leaders were members of the SPC (Mitchell & Naylor, 1998). OBU is estimated to have had a total membership of 50,000 in 1919 and about 1,800 some eight years later (Palmer, 1983). While relatively short-lived, OBU is considered by some historians to have been the most influential socialist labour organization in Canada (Palmer, 1983).

It is interesting to note that OBU's lineage can be traced to two other labour groups: the Knights of Labor and the Industrial Workers of the World (IWW). As argued by Kealey and Palmer (1995, pp. 239–240), "it was the fires of the Knights of Labor it (OBU) chose to rekindle. ... The Knights were regarded as 'a mass organization grouped into geographic units' that prefigured the industrial unionism of One Big Union."

The IWW, or Wobblies, were socialist in nature. They argued that workers received low wages, toiled hard, and had limited security; however, they, as the producers of goods, had the ability to shut down the economy if they worked in a single, united force (Palmer, 1983). Like the Knights, the Wobblies were open to various ethnic groups as well as unskilled labour. The Wobblies' presence in Canada was largely contained to the 1910s. At their high point, 40 percent of the railway construction workers who built the Canadian National Railway (CNR) and the Grand Trunk Pacific were Wobblies. By the end of 1918, the IWW membership of Canada was, in essence, nonexistent (Palmer, 1983). Nevertheless, the group still exists, continues to advocate the concept of one big union, and is actively seeking to unionize workers by industry versus trade (IWW, 2014).

THE 1930s AND 1940s: DECLINE AND RESURRECTION

The stock market crash of 1929 created a period called the **Great Depression**. During the worst years of the Depression (the mid-1930s), the statistics tell a sad tale of the plight of the working class. In 1933, 32 percent of workers were unemployed; in 1935, about 20 percent of the entire country was receiving some form of social assistance (Palmer, 1983). The economy was in a tailspin. Yet it was during these turbulent times that important changes

> transformed the Canadian industrial relations system from one that combined ad hoc coercion and conciliation in an unpredictable nature to one that endorsed compulsory bargaining ... through an extraordinary complex of administrative boards and a mystifying maze of what soon ... would become "labour law." (Kealey, 1995, pp. 433–434)

Two elements critical to this transition were the *Wagner Act* of the United States and the removal of the Congress of Industrial Organizations from the AFL.

Great Depression
a period of significant economic downturn resulting from the stock market crash of 1929

THE WAGNER ACT

In 1935, Senator Robert Wagner introduced a bill to create the *National Labor Relations Act* (which is often referred to as the ***Wagner Act***). The NRLA set forth several key elements that remain core to current labour relations law in the United States (National Labor Relations Board 60th Anniversary Committee, 1995) and Canada:

1. It created an independent agency (the National Labor Relations Board–NLRB) to enforce the rights of employees to bargain collectively rather than to mediate disputes.

2. It required that employers bargain collectively with certified unions (e.g., when the majority of workers in an appropriate bargaining unit seek collective representation).

3. It defined unfair labour practices on the part of employers (e.g., bargaining directly with employees, disciplining employees for union activity).

4. It gave the NLRB the ability to order remedies for employer violations of the NLRA, including back pay and reinstatement of employees.

5. It adhered to the doctrine of exclusivity. Only one union, the one that the majority of workers selected, would represent the entire bargaining unit.

6. Perhaps most important to both workers and employers of the day, it encouraged collective bargaining.

Clearly this act contrasted with the common law, or master–servant, work relationships of the time—and as is shown in a historical piece on the *Wagner Act*, reaction from employers was not positive. While the *Act* certainly changed the face of employment relations from the 1930s to the present day, not all scholars agree that it was a positive move. For example, Adams (1999, 2002) argues that it created a culture of animosity between the actors of labour and management. Nevertheless, as we will show in our discussion later in the chapter, the NLRA is important to Canadians as it became the blueprint for Canadian labour legislation.

COMMITTEE OF INDUSTRIAL ORGANIZATION, 1935

While many of the early unions were focusing on organizing all the workers of a craft or trade, the economy was in transition. Prior to the 1930s, some unions had organized all workers (regardless of trade) in sectors such as mining, but the 1930s saw a rapid increase in industrial (i.e., factory-based) workplaces and **industrial unions** (Palmer, 1983). While the traditional wisdom of the union movement was to divide the employees of each factory into the appropriate craft unions, the 1935 AFL meeting called this practice into question. In fact, the leader of the United Mine Workers, John Lewis, is said to have punched the leader of the carpenters' union while announcing the need for (and creation of) an industrial-focused organization within the AFL. This group, called the Committee for Industrial Organization (CIO), sought to organize the nonunion workers in industrial settings. The CIO became a large social movement as workers in various industries (e.g., auto, electrical parts, steel) hosted "sit-ins" to improve their workplaces. As in the past, the craft-based values of the TLC proved to be solid. In 1937, the CIO was expelled from the AFL. The committee became an independent congress, namely, the Congress of Industrial Organizations (Heron, 1989).

CANADIAN IMPLICATIONS

A trend of this period was that actions in the United States were often transplanted to Canada. For example, in 1937, Nova Scotia became the first Canadian jurisdiction to pass a Wagner-type law requiring that employers bargain collectively with recognized unions (Kealey, 1995). Similarly in 1939, the TLC followed the AFL's lead and expelled CIO-affiliated unions. These CIO affiliates formed the Canadian Congress of Labour (CCL), together with the All-Canadian Congress of Labour (Palmer, 1983). However, it was the outbreak of World War II and the creation of the *Wartime Labour Relation Regulation*, also known as "P.C. 1003," that were perhaps the most significant events of this period.

P.C. 1003, 1944

After the outbreak of the war, the federal government's use of wartime emergency measures meant that it had jurisdiction over most labour relations issues. The conciliation procedures of the day (the IDIA) were unable to address the labour issues. Thus, the *Wartime Labour Relation Regulation* (P.C. 1003) was tabled by the government of Mackenzie King in February 1944. In essence, it copied the key elements of the *Wagner Act* (i.e., certification procedures, employer duty to bargain in good faith, unfair labour practices, etc.). However, it also put in place requirements in terms of

- mechanisms to handle workplace disputes during the term of the collective agreement (i.e., a grievance procedure); and
- conciliation procedures prior to strike (Kealey, 1995).

THE RAND FORMULA, 1945

With the growing number of industrial unions, the implementation of formal procedures for union certification, and the introduction of compulsory collective bargaining among certified bargaining units, the 1940s saw a large increase in the number of unionized workers. However, unions lacked financial security. In a landmark decision to settle a Ford strike in Windsor, Ontario, Justice Ivan Rand decided that all union dues would be paid directly to the union (i.e., deducted from the workers' pay through a **dues check-off**), regardless of whether or not the person chose to be a union member. Workers in a bargaining unit certified under the *Labour Relations Act* would not be required to join the union but would nevertheless have to pay union dues. This became known as the Rand Formula (Heron, 1989). Ontario's minister of labour declared it a "resounding blow for the advancement of labour's rights … [and] a great milestone in the development of labour-management relations" (Palmer, 1983, p. 242).

> **dues check-off**
> a process whereby union dues are deducted automatically from pay

THE 1950s AND 1960s: RECONCILIATION AND EXPANSION INTO THE PUBLIC SECTOR

While the 1940s marked large increases in the number of industrial unions and the legal entrenchment of labour rights, it had left a labour movement divided largely along skilled (i.e., trade) versus unskilled (i.e., industrial) lines. The 1950s and 1960s provided an environment of reconciliation between these two groups, the formation of a union-backed labour organization, and landmark legislation permitting the unionization of public-sector employees.

CANADIAN LABOUR CONGRESS (CLC), 1956

After a fifty-year divorce, skilled and unskilled workers were reunited. The newly formed AFL-CIO was created in the United States, and shortly thereafter Canadian labour groups also reunited. Specifically, the industrial-based CCL and the trade-based TLC formed the Canadian Labour Congress (CLC) in a convention held in Toronto in April 1956. Almost 60 years later, it remains the largest federation of Canadian labour, representing 3.3 million Canadians. As stated by the former president of the CLC, Ken Georgetti,

> Delegates to the Founding Convention in 1956 called for the establishment of a national health care scheme, a bill of rights, improvements to unemployment insurance, elimination of discrimination against women, equal pay, a national pension scheme, and increases to federal and provincial minimum wages. (CLC, 2006)

The merger required compromise on both sides. You will note that we see elements of social and business unionism in the previous quote. The TLC had traditionally adhered to principles of political nonpartisanship; the CIO had traditionally supported the reform-oriented Co-operative Commonwealth Federation (CCF). The compromise became the creation of a political education department that would be tasked with aiding in the formation of a new political party encompassing unions, farmer organizations, cooperatives, and other progressive organizations. This compromise position is believed to have been brokered as the CCF was largely defunct and "even the 'old guard' within the TLC recognized that Liberal and Conservative parties offered labour no real voice and even worked against labour in moments of crisis" (Palmer, 1983, p. 254). In 1961, the NDP was formed, with the support of labour. Even today, the bond between the NDP and labour remains strong. At the 2013 NDP convention, the President of the CLC spoke to the NDP delegates (Georgetti, 2013).

PUBLIC SERVICE STAFF RELATIONS ACT (PSSRA), 1967

As will be discussed in detail in Chapter 12, employees in the public sector historically had limited rights in terms of appealing, or influencing, their employers' decisions. However, in 1961, the government introduced a new *Civil Service Act* that allowed workers to appeal certain employment decisions (i.e., promotions, transfers, demotions, suspensions, and terminations). Moreover, what was perhaps the second-most-important piece of labour legislation in Canadian history (the first being P.C. 1003) was passed on March 31, 1967. That day, government passed the *Public Service Staff Relations Act* (PSSRA), which enabled federal government employees to bargain collectively with their employer (Felice, 1998).

The PSSRA marked an important turn in Canadian labour relations for two reasons. First, its passage, combined with the passage of similar laws in provincial jurisdictions, resulted in the public sector representing a large percentage of the unionized work force in Canada. As you will see throughout the cases, opening vignettes, etc., of this textbook, the public sector represents a significant player in Canadian labour relations today. Second, it marked an important departure from the United States, where civil servants are largely prohibited from bargaining collectively.

THE 1970s AND 1980s: CHANGING RELATIONSHIPS WITH GOVERNMENTS AND THE UNITED STATES

The 1970s and 1980s marked turbulent times in the Canadian economy. Concerns over the fluctuation of oil prices, skyrocketing inflation, and the movement to freer trade made for challenging years in the labour movement. In the United States, it marked a time of attack on the labour movement in terms of both legislation and employers' actions. As we will discuss in detail in Chapter 6, it was a period of management and governments taking action to move the American workforce toward being union-free and/or reducing the power of unions. However, in Canada, it showed our increasing independence from the American labour movement. In particular, it marked the removal of Canadian auto workers away from the United Auto Workers (UAW) union to form an independent Canadian union. Now let's look at a few of these events in greater detail.

WAGE AND PRICE CONTROLS AND LEGISLATION

This period of history included several pieces of legislation that restricted labour's ability to seek wage increases. In 1973, inflation rose to over 13 percent and showed little sign of slowing down (Bank of Canada, 2006). In an effort to reduce inflation in the economy, in 1975 Prime Minister Pierre Trudeau went against his 1974 election platform and passed legislation designed to restrict wage increases. This was done through the Anti-Inflation Board (AIB), which monitored wage settlements from the private and public sectors for the years 1975–1978. The AIB, and its effectiveness, was subject to great inquiry during this period (Auld, Christofides, Swidinsky & Wilton, 1979; Lipsey, 1981; Reid, 1979). Thirty years later, we continue to see Bank of Canada reviews of the AIB program (Sargent, 2005).

In the early 1980s, we again saw a spike in the inflation rate, as it passed the 12 percent mark (Bank of Canada, 2006). In 1982, the federal government brought in what was known as the "6 and 5" program. In an effort to curb inflation, public-sector increases were frozen at 6 percent in the first year and 5 percent in the second (Sargent, 2005). This trend of freezing and/or restricting wage increases continued into the new millennium as we discuss in more detail in Chapter 12. For example, in April of 2004, four provinces reported that they were going to implement wage freezes, spending cuts, or layoffs in the public sector (Centre for Industrial Relations, 2004); some ten years later, in 2013–14, there were open debates concerning the need for public-sector wage freezes in several provinces including Alberta, Ontario, and Quebec (Bell, 2013; CBC News, 2014a; The Canadian Press, 2014).

FREE TRADE AGREEMENTS

The 1980s also marked the first major trade agreement between Canada and the United States (Haggart, 2001). In the fall of 1987, a free trade agreement was finalized; it became effective January 1, 1989. In the 1990s, Mexico joined the United States and Canada to form the *North American Free Trade Agreement* (NAFTA). Arguments for the agreements included a belief that reducing trade barriers would lower tariffs as well as improve Canadian productivity and standard of living (Haggart, 2001). Labour opposed the deal, fearing that it could lead to reduced wages and/or lower job security.

Some 25 years after, the impact of these trade agreements remains heavily debated (Sergie, 2014). On one hand, Ed Fast, then Federal Minister of Trade, has stated:

> *Twenty-five years on, history has shown that trade is the best way to create jobs, growth and long-term prosperity for hard-working people around the world …The historic agreement reached in 1987 placed Canada and the United States at the forefront of trade liberalization, and, to this day, is the world's greatest free trade success story. (Foreign Affairs, Trade and Development Canada, 2012)*

On the other hand, there is little evidence that Canada's productivity level has caught up with that of the United States, nor is there any evidence that our standard of living has improved (Wise, 2009). While it is difficult to assess the full impact of free trade on employment, some economists state that the free trade agreement was partially responsible for reducing wages and employment in the recession of the 1990s (Haggart, 2001). Additional research suggests that the removal of trade tariffs associated with free trade reduced wages for workers, with the median worker experiencing a real wage decline of 2 percent (Townsend, 2007).

Even today, labour remains particularly vocal against the agreement. According to Jim Stanford (2012), an economist with the CAW, "it's hard to find any concrete economic evidence whatsoever that this historic deal actually helped Canada" given that:

- the percentage of Canada's exports to the U.S. has not changed (stable at 19 percent of Canada's GDP);
- Canada's exports to the U.S. today mainly comprise largely unprocessed primary and resource products, versus the manufactured goods (including automobiles, electronics, and machinery) before free trade;
- Canada now represents only 14 percent of imports into the U.S., a drop of 5 percent since the NFTA;
- Canadian productivity relative to the United States has dropped by almost 20 percent since 1980; and
- the median income of families has not changed.

Perhaps Sergie (2014) best sums up the experience by stating that some

> *(t)wenty years after its implementation, the North American Free Trade Agreement … helped boost intraregional trade between Canada, Mexico, and the United States, but has fallen short of generating the jobs and the deeper regional economic integration its advocates promised decades ago.*

CANADIAN AUTO WORKERS UNION (CAW)

The 1980s furthered the trend toward a less U.S.-dependent labour movement. As will be discussed in more detail in Chapter 6, the 1980s in the United States were marked by concession bargaining as well as less-labour-friendly governments and employers. These changes played very strongly in the U.S. automotive industry. However, as fully outlined by Gindin (1995), the Canadian division of the union saw things differently than its American parent. In the late fall of 1984, Bob White, then director of the CAW, sought increased autonomy for the Canadian branch of the UAW, including allowing the Canadian division to set independent goals, have its own ability to call a strike, and access the strike fund. When these requests were denied, he set into motion a plan that would create an independent Canadian union. In the fall of 1985, the Canadian UAW was formally established. The next year, the union was renamed the Canadian Auto Workers. The CAW has since merged with the Communications, Energy and Paperworkers Union of Canada (CEP) to become Canada's largest private-sector union (Unifor, 2015).

THE 1990s AND BEYOND: INCREASED RESISTANCE

The 1990s and the new century have proven to be challenging environments for labour. As already discussed, the 1990s marked the expansion of the free trade zone to include Mexico in what became known as NAFTA (Haggart, 2001). Some other key events of this period included a restructuring of the Canadian economy (associated with an increased focus on global markets), significant levels of government restructuring, increased use of legislation to replace collective bargaining in the public sector, as well as increased collective protests.

ECONOMIC RESTRUCTURING AND GLOBAL MARKETS

The 1990s marked a turbulent time in Canada's economy. A speech by the governor of the Bank of Canada, Gordon Thiessen (Bank of Canada, 2001) overviews the severity of the situation in the early 1990s. The level of inflation was four times that of 1970; large government deficits were making investors wary of Canadian bonds (causing a "premium" in interest rates); and unemployment rates were above 10 percent. Excerpts from Thiessen's speech best illustrate the severity of the country's economic state at that time:

> By the early 1990s, the realities of the New World economic order were becoming clearer to Canadian companies too. Only, at that time, they were also coping with the fallout from the high-inflation years, especially the sharp drop in the prices of speculative investments and the burden of servicing large debts, as well as with declining world commodity prices.

> Working their way out of these difficulties was disruptive and painful for Canadian businesses. Defaults, restructurings, and downsizings became the order of the day. With all this, unemployment took a long time to recover from the 1990–91 recession and, in many instances, wages and salaries were frozen or reduced.

The economy picked up speed in the late 1990s, and there were positive economic signs and times at the start of the millennium (Thiessen, 2001). However, the first decade of the millennium was marked with two recessions, the first in 2001 largely due to a decline in the technology sector and the second in 2008 due to a crisis in the real estate and financial sectors that resulted in a global economic downturn (Bordo, 2008; Latham & Braun, 2008).

During this timeframe, sectors of the economy that were traditionally union strongholds faced severe job losses. Perhaps no industry has been as hard-hit by either competitive pressure or job loss as the manufacturing sector—one of the traditional strongholds of labour. Reports from numerous sources outline the challenges experienced in that sector. One CLC report highlighted that in a four-year period from August 2002 to October 2006:

- over 250,000 jobs (over 10 percent of positions) had been lost due to layoffs, plant closures, and nonreplacement of retirees;
- job loss in unionized firms had almost doubled that of nonunion jobs (16.4 percent versus 8.7 percent); and
- the rate of job loss differed across industries, with one-third of jobs being lost in the textiles, clothing, and leather-products manufacturing groups.

Several years later, an analysis of Canadian employment by Bernard (2009) reinforced the CLC report. He concluded that over 320,000 jobs (or 14 percent of all jobs) disappeared from the manufacturing sector between the years 2004 and 2008. In particular, the textile and clothes manufacturing sector was decimated, with almost half of the jobs lost in that period. Perhaps more alarming for labour was that many of these lost jobs were unionized. While 32.2 percent of manufacturing job were unionized in 2004, only 26.4 percent were in 2008. Interestingly, for the rest of the economy unionization rates remained largely stable (30.1 percent in 2004, 29.5 percent in 2008). And more recent data from the CLC suggest that in the one-year period between May 2012 to May 2013, over 100,000 manufacturing jobs were lost in Canada (CLC, 2013).

Similarly, the Canadian economy since 1990 has also been marked by strong job loss and competitive pressures in the union strongholds of the resource sector (e.g., fishing and forestry). For example, Human Resources and Development Canada (HRDC, 2004) suggested that job loss in the B.C. salmon fishery was estimated to have been nearly 50 percent during the 1990s. Factors potentially contributing to this job loss included growth in foreign competition in terms of increased supply from other sources and the removal of trade barriers between Canada and the United States. In Newfoundland, a province with a population only slightly higher than 500,000, the collapse of the cod fishery resulted in more than 25,000 people losing their jobs (Sinclair, 2003). In both cases, significant government aid was needed to ease the impact of these losses on the workers affected and to help them transition to new industries.

The forestry industry throughout Canada has been hard-hit since the start of the new millennium. The situation in the first decade of the new millennium was described by the union (the Communications, Energy and Paperworkers) and the employers (e.g., the Forest Products Association of Canada) as a "perfect storm" (CBC, 2006a). Over a five-year period, some 40,000 people have lost jobs in this sector due to economic trends (e.g., the higher Canadian dollar), competition from lower-cost regions (e.g., China, Russia), more efficient European mills, and a decrease in demand because of the movement to computers versus paper (CBC, 2006a). In fact, in British Columbia alone, it is estimated that 20,000 workers lost their jobs between 2007 and 2009 (Hamilton, 2009). Unfortunately, more recent data confirm the challenges in this sector. A report from the Standing Senate Committee on Agriculture and Forestry (2011) concluded that between 2000 and 2008 employment in this sector dropped by 37 percent and over 100,000 jobs.

As these examples from manufacturing and natural resource industries show, many union strongholds in the private sector have seen challenges at least partially attributed to global trade (and trade liberalization). As we look to the future, it is important to note that the Canadian Government has continued to negotiate other trade agreements. At the time of writing the text, two additional trade agreements were in the works. In October 2013, the Comprehensive Economic and Trade Agreement (CETA) between the European Union and Canada was signed (European Commission, 2013).

A few months afterwards, in June 2014, the federal government signed a free trade agreement with South Korea, known as the Canada–South Korea Free Trade Agreement (CKFTA) and expected to come into effect in 2015 (Beltrame, 2014). Given these historic trade agreements, we can expect that the labour movement will continue to see a Canadian economy that is increasingly impacted by global trade.

European Commission President José Manuel Barroso and Canadian Prime Minister Stephen Harper shake hands after signing the free trade agreement between the European Union and Canada.

GOVERNMENT RESTRUCTURING

The previously discussed issues of competition and job loss in the private sector were also at play in the public sector in the 1990s and beyond. The public sector, which is also a union stronghold, faced severe restructuring. As pointed out by a Bank of Canada report by Fenton, Ip, and Wright (2001), the 1990s saw significant changes in the public sector as a result of an increased focus on debt- and deficit-reduction. In fact, this report highlighted an overall loss of about 6 percent of Canadian public-sector jobs between the years 1992 and 1998 (with an 18 percent drop in federal government jobs) in contrast to an overall increase of 11 percent in U.S. public-sector jobs.

In more recent years, there is again focus on job cuts in the broader public sector. In the 2012 budget, the federal government announced that it would cut 19,000 jobs (of which 12,000 would be from retirements and voluntary departures), with most job cuts in 2014–2015 (CBC News, 2012). By April 2014, the government had already cut 20,000 jobs since 2010 and was expected to see another 8,900 cuts within three years (CBC News, 2014b). These same cuts were coupled with cost-cutting reductions in the pensions area.

Similar cuts have been implemented and debated at the provincial level. For example, the 2013 budget of Newfoundland and Labrador included a cut of 1,200 jobs through a combination of retirements, not filling open positions, and layoffs (Bailey, 2013). More recently, in the 2014 Ontario provincial election, the PC party's platform included a plan to eliminate 100,000 jobs in the public sector (Leslie, 2014). This again shows how a traditional union stronghold of public-sector employment is seeing a decline.

The decrease in public-sector jobs in Canada has been attributed to several factors—specifically, an increase in contracting out, **privatization**, and an increased use of contractors and consultants rather than full-time employees (Fenton, Ip & Wright, 2001). As we will discuss in Chapter 6, this trend toward employing contractors and consultants is not unique to the public sector. Nevertheless, the aforementioned Bank of Canada report suggests that of the nearly 40,000 permanent jobs lost in the federal public sector between 1995 and 1998, about 10,000 were due to privatization or devolution. In fact, one federal government report states that between 1985 and 2005, close to thirty federal **Crown corporations**, with a value approaching $12 billion, were privatized through either sales to private firms or sales of shares on the stock market (Padova, 2005). Some of these privatized corporations included Canadair Inc., Canadian National Railways (CNR), and Petro-Canada.

privatization
the transfer or contracting out of services to the private sector

Crown corporations
corporations owned by the government

LEGISLATION REPLACING COLLECTIVE BARGAINING

Given the significant changes taking place in the public sector in the 1990s, one would expect to have seen unions fighting hard to minimize the impacts of such changes on their members. However, public-sector unions faced a great deal of restrictions on their ability to negotiate on behalf of their members. For example, since the 1990s we have seen frequent usage of **back-to-work legislation**, whereby striking workers are legislated to cease their strikes and return to work. However, a trend since the late 1990s has been that wages and benefits issues, which are normally negotiated by unions, have been increasingly included in back-to-work legislation. A few examples of such "expanded" back to work legislation include the 1997 Canada Post strike (Came & DeMont, 1997), the 2004 Newfoundland provincial government strike (CBC, 2004), and the 2005 British Columbia teachers' strike (CBC, 2005). These issues will be discussed in more detail in Chapter 12.

back-to-work legislation
legislation requiring that strike action cease and employees return to work

INCREASED COLLECTIVE PROTEST

Public-sector restructuring led to resistance from labour. For example, when Bob Rae's NDP government was in power in Ontario, it announced what it called a Social Contract. In an effort to save jobs and maintain pay levels in the public sector, Rae's government required that public-sector employees take twelve unpaid days off per year—these became known as "Rae Days" (Hebdon & Warrian, 1999). Labour was strongly opposed to such actions. Similarly, when Mike Harris's Conservative government came into power, there were severe budget cuts. In response, labour leaders called for a massive public strike against the government and a public strike/rally at Queen's Park, the Ontario legislature (CBC, 2004). This resulted in the "Days of Action," a five-day protest against the Conservative government in October of 1996. One estimate suggests that a quarter of a million people took part in the protest on October 26, 1996 (Heron, 1998), making it perhaps the largest strike since the Winnipeg General Strike.

Similar large-scale protests against public-sector cuts have occurred recently in Britain and Wisconsin. In Britain, as many as 1 million public-sector employees walked off the job in 2014 to protest pay freezes, pension changes, and reducing living standards (Taylor & Mason, 2014). In early 2011, tens of thousands of public-sector workers marched into the state capital protesting a budget bill that restricted unions to bargaining only over wages and losing the ability to bargain benefits and pensions (Bruce, 2011).

More recently, we continue to see larger collective protests almost reminiscent of the 1960s. For example, in 2012 there was a significant student protest against the Quebec government's plan to increase tuition. In total over 175,000 students went on strike for a period of several months, holding 170 protests against the government's proposed 75% tuition increase. The strike gathered significant media attention, and labour groups inside and outside of Quebec provided financial support for the cause and encouraged students in other provinces to show support for the students, particularly given the government's decision to pass emergency legislation that restricted protests (The Canadian Press, 2012).

// IMPLICATIONS FOR THE FUTURE OF LABOUR

As this chapter reveals, labour has both influenced and constantly adapted to changes in the external inputs of the IR system. Given where we are today, a natural question is what elements of the past may be reflected in the future. We see three potential trends; namely, a movement toward larger unions, social unionism, and a global labour movement.

LARGER UNIONS

Reflecting on the OBU and larger protests of the 1910s, we are starting to see a movement toward larger protest events and unions. For example, the CAW and CEP recently merged to create the largest public-sector union in Canada, called Unifor (Unifor, 2014a). Interestingly, Unifor's website clearly states that it advocates for all workers (both employed and unemployed), suggesting a departure from "bread and butter" unionism.

SOCIAL UNIONISM

Labour's support of the Quebec student strike, Unifor's positioning of itself as the advocate for employed and unemployed people, and the more social orientation of Canadian labour versus the United States may all be potential indicators that Canada is moving to a more social unionism focus. As one example, look at the broader social issues included in the messaging concerning the formation of the new union Unifor:

> *Nationally the new union will focus on collective bargaining with the aim of providing for its members better wages, pensions and benefits, protecting rights and respect at the workplace, improving health and safety, promoting democracy at work, as well as organizing. The new union will cultivate equality, transparency and democracy of its structures. In a broader society among others the union will commit to the fight for freedom, civil liberties and democratic trade unionism, support an environmentally sustainable future, resist corporate globalization, contribute to global union solidarity and work to end war and contribute to world peace.* (M1 Secretary, 2012)

While this quote does not call for the movement to a radical, social union approach, it clearly shows how Unifor is not positioning itself solely within the confines of business unionism. For a detailed look at the difference between social and business unionism, please see IR Today 2.1.

Members of the newly formed Unifor union march during a Labour Day parade.

BUSINESS VERSUS SOCIAL UNIONISM

As we covered earlier, mainstream labour in Canada has often focused on exclusive jurisdiction, business unionism, and political nonpartisanship. The Industrial Workers of the World (IWW), which is organizing Starbucks, adheres to a very different set of principles as shown at www.iww.org. Let's take a look at a section from the website:

Industrial Unionism—*The IWW organizes industrially rather than by trade. These Industrial Unions are to be grouped together into six Departments. Our goal is to organize all industries into One Big Union. here we explain this concept.*

Solidarity Unionism—*is the term we use for the guiding strategic principles of the IWW as opposed to 'Business Unionism.' We strive to build unions based on the direct strength of workers on the job, without regard to government or employer 'recognition.' It also refers to a strategy that eschews traditional contracts as our end goal. Instead we seek to win gains and build power through direct action tactics, rejecting concessionary bargaining and the prevalent 'no-strike' and 'management rights' clauses most traditional trade unions are all too willing to accept. Here you can find out more about our the IWW's unique* and innovative organizing strategy, Solidarity Unionism.

How the IWW Differs from Business Unions—*The business unions foster a state of affairs which allows one set of workers to be pitted against another set of workers in the same industry, thereby helping defeat one another in wage wars. Moreover, the trade unions aid the employing class to mislead the workers into the belief that the working class have interests in common with their employers. The IWW offers a different vision*

The IWW Stance on Political Parties and Anarchism—*To the end of promoting industrial unity and of securing necessary discipline within the organisation, the IWW refuses all alliances, direct or indirect, with any political parties or anti-political sects, and disclaims responsibility for any individual opinion or act which may be at variance with the purposes herein expressed.*

The IWW's Stance on Ecology—*Between these two classes a struggle must go on until the workers of the world organize as a class, take possession of the means of production, abolish the wage system, and live in harmony with the Earth.*

Source: IWW (2014). About the IWW. Used with permission. Retrieved from http://www.iww.org/content/about-iww.

GLOBAL V. NATIONAL

During the 1980s we saw the movement toward an independent, national labour movement, a departure from the historical ties between Canadian and American labour. Recently, we have seen that labour, like management, is moving toward a global forum. As one example, Unifor has ties with "IndustriALL Global Union, which represents 50 million workers in the mining, energy, automotive and other manufacturing industries in 140 countries" (Raina, 2014). Perhaps this is a resignalling of a return to a less nationally focused labour movement.

// SUMMARY

As we have seen in this chapter, the past century has resulted in significant changes to the employment relationships between Canadian employers and their employees. The beginning of the twentieth century marked a time when employees had few rights. It was illegal for employees to form groups and bargain collectively. As the years progressed, there was a movement to permit the formation of collectives, albeit with restrictions on the actions they could take (e.g., conciliation prior to strike). The early 1900s also saw a focus on trade unions, which are formed by employees of a specific trade (or craft). The 1940s and 1950s marked significant changes in terms of a transition in the economy and the labour movement to industrial workplaces and unions rather than trade unions, as well as legislation that permitted (and even encouraged) collective bargaining. This was followed by landmark legislation of the 1960s that permitted public-sector unionization.

However, the years that followed have been less favourable to labour. The 1980s and beyond represented times of increased government intervention on labour's ability to negotiate wages and benefits, increased competition from international sources, and a stronger employer focus on efficiency. Moreover, the new century has marked a time of significant job loss in many of the traditional strongholds of labour.

Through the years, we have also seen two important trends. First, we saw how the elements of exclusive jurisdiction, business unionism, and political nonpartisanship both united and divided the labour movement. While these guiding principles led to the formation of the AFL, they also led to a huge rift between industrial and trade unions that lasted more than fifty years. Second, we saw how the Canadian labour movement shifted from merely following the lead of the American movement in the early years to setting out on its own path.

As this chapter has clearly shown, the nature of the relationship between employers, employees, and their associations and governments is constantly shifting. If the past one hundred years are any indication, we will continue to see significant developments unfold throughout the twenty-first century.

KEY TERMS

apprenticeship 29
back-to-work legislation 46
business unionism (or pure-and-simple unionism) 32
common law 28
Crown corporations 45
dues check-off 39
exclusive jurisdiction 32
Great Depression 37
industrial unions 38
master–servant relationship 28
new model unionism 29
political nonpartisanship 32
privatization 45
socialist unionism 32
trade union 29
Wagner Act 38

WEB LINKS

Obama and Unifor–Why Join a Union?
http://www.youtube.com/watch?v=NnYDzJkXXVM

Knights of Labor:
http://www.6hourday.org/knightsoflabor.html

Winnipeg General Strike footage:
http://www3.nfb.ca/objectifdocumentaire/index.php?mode=view&language=english&filmId=3

IWW and its campaign to organize Starbucks:
http://www.starbucksunion.org

A YouTube posting concerning the *Wagner Act*:
http://www.youtube.com/watch?v=i2GSnBhYpvc

AFL-CIO:
http://www.afl-cio.org

Canadian Labour Congress:
http://canadianlabour.ca

IndustriALL Global Union:
http://www.industriall-union.org/

DISCUSSION QUESTIONS

1. This chapter shows that collective representation has taken many forms over the past hundred years. For example, the change from trade-based to industrial-based unions. Do you believe that in 2030 we will still have forms of collective representation in Canada? If so, do you think they will be any different than the unions of today?

2. Why do you think North American labour has adopted more of a business unionism than a social unionism perspective?

3. Gompers clearly decided that labour should not have affiliations with any political party. In Canada, we see stronger links between labour and political parties. Do you feel that Gompers was correct in his assertion of political voluntarism? Why or why not?

4. While it is clear that the *Wagner Act* provided the blueprint for the North American industrial relations system, there is debate concerning its effectiveness. From the perspective of labour, what do you see as the advantages and disadvantages of this legislation?

5. The chapter clearly shows that union strongholds are in decline at present. Do you feel that this is signalling the end of the labour movement? Why or why not?

6. The economy is clearly becoming more global. How do you feel that this will impact the future of IR in general and labour more specifically?

USING THE INTERNET

1. North American unions are often perceived as being more "bread and butter" versus socialist in nature. Yet in Canada, we see that several unions and the CLC deal with issues important to both unionized and nonunionized workers (e.g., equality, minimum wage). Have a look at the CLC website and those of two or three large unions (e.g., Unifor, CUPE, provincial government unions). Do you see issues relevant to nonmembers?

2. Labour has played an important role in history. Have a look at the following sites to see how Canadian labour history is presented. Note that in some cases you may need to search using the words *labour history* or *Canadian workers* to find the information:

   http://www.civilization.ca

   http://www.collectionscanada.ca

   http://canadianlabour.ca

   http://www.pc.gc.ca

   http://www.canadianheritage.org

3. You may be surprised to discover just how much labour history material can be found on the Web. For example, YouTube has extensive coverage of issues. Go to that site and search the terms "labour," "union," "Wagner Act," etc.

4. You may be asked to write a labour history paper in this course. The website of the *Journal of Canadian Labour Studies/Revue d'Études Ouvrières Canadiennes* may help you gather information for this paper: **http://www.lltjournal.ca/index.php/llt**

5. As we presented in the chapter, of the national parties, the NDP has always been seen as the most friendly to labour. To more closely examine the relationship between the two, go to

   • the CLC website (**http://www.clc-ctc.ca**) and search for the term "NDP."

   • the NDP website (**http://www.ndp.ca**) and search for the term "CLC."

EXERCISES

1. If you have access to grandparents or other senior citizens, why not conduct your own "labour history" interview? Sample questions might include

   • Tell me about the work practices at your first job (e.g., pay, leaves, hours of work, rights).

   • Were you ever a member of a union? If so, which one? Did you and your peers think that unionization was a good thing? Why or why not?

   • What was the most important change you saw in terms of employment rights in your work life?

2. Have a look at recent union or labour congress websites and publications. Based on what you find, what will historians state were the biggest issues of this year?

3. As this chapter demonstrates, the relationship between unions, governments, and political parties is complex and dynamic. Have a look at recent media (i.e., newspaper, television, Internet) coverage of elections, public policy, or economy issues. To what extent are the roles or the views of labour presented?

4. Many students are employed full- or part-time as they take courses. How do you think the labour movement has impacted the rights you have as an employee today versus if you had been employed in 1900?

5. Throughout history, unions have sought to improve the working conditions and wages of their members. Find recent media (i.e., newspaper, television, Internet) stories of union campaigns. To what extent are issues of working conditions and wages still prevalent in these stories?

CASE FROM UAW TO CAW TO UNIFOR

As shown by the discussion of the 1940s Rand Formula decision, the UAW had a long history in Canada. For much of that period, the Canadian union members simply followed the directions provided by their American leaders. However, the 1980s marked a turbulent time in the auto industry. There were numerous layoffs and increased competition from non–North American manufacturers. The following events show how the CAW was created in this turmoil to become Canada's largest private-sector union.

In 1982 negotiations, the president of General Motors made a public statement that if Canadian workers did not follow the concessions of their American counterparts, there would be plant closures and relocations. GM settled with small gains for workers and without a strike. However, the Chrysler negotiations that followed resulted in a strike. As Gindin (1995) states, after a five-week strike, Chrysler agreed to accept the opening-day proposals of the union—Canadian workers even won a wage increase. In so doing, the Canadians had shown they were a force to be reckoned with.

The next round of bargaining came in 1984. GM settled in the United States with no wage gains for workers. After a thirteen-day strike, Canadian workers earned an annual increase that their American counterparts did not. This again signalled the independence, and strength, of the Canada component of the UAW. In December of that year, Bob White (then Canadian director of the UAW) called for a vote regarding the formation of a new, independent Canadian union. Only four of the 350 delegates voted against the call for the Canadian union.

In September of 1985, after nine months of negotiating the terms of separation, the legal and monetary issues were settled; the Canadian UAW was formed. In 1986, it was renamed to the Canadian Auto Workers (CAW).

In the twenty years that followed, the CAW became the largest public-sector union in Canada. Since its founding, it has merged with more than thirty other unions/locals and now represents workers in many industries outside of the auto sector (e.g., airline, fishery, retail, mining, rail). Given the diversity of its membership, the CAW has taken a leadership role in the areas of equity. In fact, since 1986, it has held an annual human rights conference. As its human rights policy states, Unions emerged to not only collectively protect workers from the arbitrary use of power by employers and governments, but also to create a culture of equality and dignity for all members in their ranks. Achieving higher wages and better working conditions for workers is no more important in the final analysis than achieving solidarity amongst all workers (CAW, 2006b).

The CAW fight for equity among disadvantaged workers even includes workers not represented by it. For example, the CAW website shows policy and discussion papers on issues ranging from employment insurance to protection of workers in the sex trade. It is a union that has clearly made a mark on the country.

In 2013, the CAW and the CEO joined forces to create Unifor. Unifor is Canada's largest private-sector union representing over 300,000 workers in a wide range of industries including communications, manufacturing, national resources, transportation, and service. The union has a broad mandate. It positions itself as representing all workers, both employed and unemployed. The union continues to focus on economic gains for its members and social justice, as shown by "What we stand for" on its webpage (see Unifor, 2014c), where the first paragraph states:

> *Unifor strives to protect the economic rights of our members and every member of the workforce (employed or unemployed). Unifor advocates for and defends the economic rights of working people, safer workplaces, secure employment, wages and benefits that provide a decent standard of living and dignity and respect in the workplace*

That page goes on to present core principles related to union renewal/generational change: democracy, equity, inclusiveness, accountability, solidarity, militancy. The union is also part of a global network of unions called IndustriALL, which represents 50 million employees in 140 countries.

Sources: CAW, 2005, 2006a, 2006b, 2006c; Gindin, 1995; M1 Secretary, 2012; Raina, 2014; Unifor, 2014a, 2014b, 2014c.

QUESTIONS

1. How does the CAW relationship with the UAW in the 1980s contrast with the historical relationship between the American and Canadian labour movements?

2. Discuss how Unifor can be seen to have both a "bread and butter" and a "social justice" orientation.

3. The CAW was considered to be a tough bargainer. Does the case provide evidence to support this claim?

4. As is shown in the chapter, the large labour federations have often had rifts and separations. If Unifor ever left the CLC, do you believe it has sufficient membership diversity to form an organization that would rival the CLC?

5. The case makes reference to the global labour group IndustriALL. Do you feel that such global linkages are needed for the labour movement today?

// REFERENCES

1. Adams, R. J. (1999). Why statutory union recognition is bad labour policy: The North American experience. *Industrial Relations, 30,* pp. 96–101.

2. Adams, R. J. (2002). The *Wagner-Act* model: A toxic system beyond repair. *British Journal of Industrial Relations, 40,* pp. 122–127.

3. American Federation of Labour–Congress of Industrial Organizations. (2006). Samuel Gompers (1850–1924). Retrieved 10 November 2006 from http://www.aflcio.org/aboutus/history/history/gompers.cfm

4. American Federation of Labor–Congress of Industrial Organizations. (2007). George Meany (1894–1980). Retrieved 1 July 2007 from http://www.aflcio.org/aboutus/history/history/meany.cfm

5. Auld, D. A. L., Christofides, L. N., Swidinsky, R., & Wilton, D. A. (1979). The impact of the Anti-Inflation Board on negotiated wage settlements. *Canadian Journal of Economics/Revue Canadienne d'Économique, 12,* pp. 195–213.

6. Bank of Canada. (2001). Canada's economic future: What have we learned from the 1990s? Remarks by Gordon Thiessen, Governor of the Bank of Canada to the Canadian Club of Toronto. 22 January 2001. Retrieved 1 February 2011 from http://www.bank-banque-canada.ca/en/speeches/2001/sp01-1.html

7. Bank of Canada. (2006). Canada's inflation performance, and why it matters. *Why Monetary Policy Matters: A Canadian Perspective.* Retrieved 1 December 2006 from http://www.bankofcanada.ca/en/ragan_paper/inflation.html

8. Bailey, S. (26 March 2013). Newfoundland and Labrador budget cuts jobs, costs as deficits mount. *Huffington Post.* Retrieved 14 July 2014 from http://www.huffingtonpost.ca/2013/03/26/newfoundland-and-labrador-budget-cuts_n_2956760.html

9. Bell. R. (18 February 2013). Alberta nixes wage hikes—three-year freeze on pay expected to save $54M. Retrieved 4 July 2014 from http://www.calgarysun.com/2013/02/19/alberta-nixes-wage-hikes--three-year-freeze-on-pay-expected-to-save-54m

10. Beltrame, J. (11 March, 2014). Harper announces free trade deal with South Korea—Canada's first agreement with an Asian country. *National Post.* Retrieved 11 July 2014 from http://news.nationalpost.com/2014/03/11/stephen-harper-announces-free-trade-agreement-with-south-korea-canadas-first-such-deal-with-an-asian-country/

11. Bernard, A. (2009). Trends in manufacturing employment. *Perspectives on Labour and Income, 21*(1), 27–35. Retrieved 11 February 2011 from CBCA Business (Document ID: 1680692901).

12. Bordo, M. (2008). An historical perspective on the crisis of 2007–2008. (Working Paper 14569). National Bureau of Economic Research. Retrieved 4 July 2014 from http://www.nber.org/papers/w14569

13. Bruce, M. (17 February, 2011). Wisconsin teachers protest Ed budget, union cuts. *ABC News.* Retrieved 14 July 2014 from http://abcnews.go.com/Politics/wisconsin-protests-news-wisconsin-governor-scott-walkers-proposal/story?id=12942012

14. Came, B., & DeMont, J. (15 December 1997). Postal strike ends. *Maclean's.* Retrieved 19 December 2006 from http://www.thecanadianencyclopedia.com/index.cfm?PgNm=TCE&Params=M1ARTM0011454

15. Canadian Auto Workers. (2005). National executive board discussion paper on the sex trade. Retrieved 6 December 2006 from http://www.caw.ca/whatwedo/women/sextrade.asp

16. Canadian Auto Workers. (2006a). CAW mergers. Retrieved 6 December 2006 from http://www.caw.ca/whoweare/mergers/cawmergers.asp

17. Canadian Auto Workers. (2006b). Policy statement on human rights: Workers' rights. Retrieved 6 December 2006 from http://www.caw.ca/whoweare/CAWpoliciesandstatements/policystatements/cawrights_index.asp

18. Canadian Auto Workers. (2006c). Unemployment insurance and labour market deregulation. Retrieved 6 December 2006 from http://www.caw.ca/whoweare/CAWpoliciesandstatements/discussionpapers/unemployment_index.asp

19. Canadian Labour Congress. (2006). 50 years of making a difference. *Canadian Labour Online, 7* (November 1). Retrieved 10 November 2007 from http://canadianlabour.ca/index.php/canadianlabouronline/November_1_2006__Iss

20. Canadian Labour Congress. (n.d.). About the CLC. Retrieved 11 July 2014 from http://www.canadianlabour.ca/about-clc

21. Canadian Museum of Civilization. (2002). Labour's revolt: Winnipeg General Strike. Retrieved 27 November 2006 from http://www.civilization.ca/hist/labour/labh22e.html

22. The Canadian Press. (22 May 2012). Trade unions outside Quebec funding student protests: Ontario Federation of Labour president calls on Ontario students to follow Quebec's lead. CBC News. Retrieved 14 July 2014 from http://www.cbc.ca/news/politics/trade-unions-outside-quebec-funding-student-protests-1.1283329

23. The Canadian Press. (27 March 2014). Public sector employees can't be bullied: Ontario public sector union president. Retrieved 4 July 2014 from http://toronto.ctvnews.ca/public-sector-employees-can-t-be-bullied-ontario-public-sector-union-president-1.1748933#ixzz36VHFKpv2

24. CBC. (2004). Ontario's Conservatives: In transition. 17 September 2004. Retrieved 5 December 2006 from http://www.cbc.ca/news/background/provpolitics

25. CBC. (2005). B.C. teachers end strike. 23 October 2005. Retrieved 19 December 2006 from http://www.cbc.ca/canada/story/2005/10/23/teachers-sunday051023.html

26. CBC. (2006a). Forestry pulp and paper. 13 April 2006. Retrieved 5 December 2006 from http://www.cbc.ca/includes/printablestory.jsp

27. CBC. (2006b). Strikes: A Canadian history. 22 February 2006. Retrieved 10 November 2006 from http://www.cbc.ca/news/background/strike

28. CBC News (29 March 2012). Budget cuts 19,000 public service jobs. Retrieved 4 July 2014 from http://www.cbc.ca/news/politics/budget-cuts-19-000-public-service-jobs-1.1170727

29. CBC News. (2014a). Quebec financial experts recommend public-sector wage freeze: Financial report says balancing Quebec's budget "more difficult than anticipated." 25 April 2014. Retrieved 4 July 2014 from http://www.cbc.ca/news/canada/montreal/quebec-financial-experts-recommend-public-sector-wage-freeze-1.2621757

30. CBC News. (2014b). Thousands more public-sector jobs than planned to be cut, watchdog says. 17 April 2014. Retrieved 4 July 2014 from http://www.cbc .ca/news/canada/ottawa/thousands-more-public-sector-jobs-than-planned-to -be-cut-watchdog-says-1.2613897

31. Centre for Industrial Relations. (2004). Provincial budgets bring job cuts and wage freezes for government employees across Canada. *Weekly Work Report*, April 5. Retrieved 27 November 2006 from http://www.chass.utoronto.ca/cir/ library/wwreport/wwr2004_04_05.html

32. CLC. (2006). *The manufacturing crisis: Impacts on workers and an agenda for government action.* Ottawa: CLC.

33. CLC. (7 June 2013). Georgetti comments on Statistics Canada job numbers: Says government fails to consult labour on job plans. Retrieved 4 July 2014 from http://www.canadianlabour.ca/national/news/georgetti-comments -statistics-canada-job-numbers-says-government-fails-consult-labour-

34. Collections Canada. (n.d.). Winnipeg General Strike, May 15–June 25, 1919 [silent film]. Retrieved 27 November 2006 from http://www.collectionscanada .ca/05/0509/050951/05095176_e.html

35. Cross, A. (3 May 2012). Canada's "Maple Spring"? Dissecting the longest student strike in Quebec's history. *National Post.* Retrieved 14 July 2014 from http://news.nationalpost.com/2012/05/03/quebec-student-strike/

36. European Commission. (18 October 2013). EU and Canada strike free trade deal. Retrieved 11 July 2014 from http://trade.ec.europa.eu/doclib/press/ index.cfm?id=973

37. Felice, M. (1998). A timeline of the public service commission of Canada. Retrieved 1 December 2006 from http://www.psc-cfp.gc.ca/research/timeline/ psc_timeline_e.htm

38. Fenton, P., Ip, I., & Wright, G. (2001). *Employment effects of restructuring in the public sector in North America: Working paper 2001–19.* Ottawa: Bank of Canada.

39. Foreign Affairs, Trade and Development Canada. (3 October 2012). Harper government celebrates 25th anniversary of Canada–U.S. Free Trade Agreement. Retrieved 11 July 2014 from http://www.international.gc.ca/ media_commerce/comm/news-communiques/2012/10/03a.aspx?lang=eng

40. Fox, A. (1974). *Beyond contract: Work, power and trust relations.* London: Faber & Faber.

41. Fox, A. (1985). *History and heritage: The social origins of the British industrial relations system.* London: George Allen and Unwin.

42. Georgetti, K. (12 April 2013). Speaking notes to the federal New Democratic Party convention. Retrieved 4 July 2014 from http://www.canadianlabour.ca/ news-room/speeches/speaking-notes-federal-new-democratic-party-convention

43. Gindin, S. (1995). *The Canadian autoworkers: The birth and transformation of a union.* Toronto: James Lorimer and Company.

44. Government of Canada. (2006a). 1873–The Canadian labour union: The birth of Canadian organized labour. Retrieved 9 November 2006 from http://www .canadianeconomy.gc.ca/english/economy/1873Canadian_Labour_Union. html

45. Government of Canada. (2006b). 1919–The Winnipeg General Strike. Retrieved 26 November 2006 from http://www.canadianeconomy.gc.ca/English/economy/1919Winnipeg_general_strike.html

46. Haggart, B. (2001). *Canada and the United States: Trade, investment, integration and the future.* Ottawa: Government of Canada (Economics Division). Retrieved 27 November 2006 from http://dsp-psd.communication.gc.ca/Collection-R/LoPBdP/BP/prb013-e.htm#4

47. Hamilton, G. (29 April 2009). B.C. forest job losses climb to more than 20,000; Workers forced to move to Alberta for retraining. *Vancouver Sun.* Retrieved 11 February 2010 from http://www2.canada.com/vancouversun/news/business/story.html?id=0d724d33-5f7b-48c2-b811-e9d706cebfdd&k=34782

48. Hebdon, B., & Warrian, P. (1999). Coercive bargaining: Public sector restructuring under the Ontario Social Contract, 1993–1996. *Industrial and Labor Relations Review, 52,* pp. 196–212.

49. Heron, C. (1989). *The Canadian labour movement: A short history.* Toronto: J. Lorimer.

50. Heron, C. (Ed.). (1998). *The workers' revolt in Canada, 1917–1925.* Toronto: University Press.

51. Human Resources and Development Canada. (2004). *Summative evaluation of HRDC's component of the Pacific fisheries adjustment and restructuring program: Final report.* Ottawa: Government of Canada.

52. IWW. (2014). About the IWW. Retrieved 2 July 2014 from http://www.iww.org/content/about-iww

53. IWW Starbucks Workers Union. (2014). About us. Retrieved 2 July 2014 from http://www.starbucksunion.org/about

54. Kahn-Freund, O. (1967). A note on status and contract in British labour law. *Modern Law Review, 30,* p. 635.

55. Kealey, G. S. (1995). The Canadian state's attempt to manage class conflict. In G. S. Kealey (Ed.), *Workers and Canadian History* (pp. 419–440). Montreal and Kingston: McGill–Queen's University Press.

56. Kealey, G. S., & Palmer, B. D. (1981). The bonds of unity: The Knights of Labor in Ontario, 1880–1900. *Social History, 14,* p. 369–411.

57. Kealey, G. S., & Palmer, B. D. (1995). The bonds of unity: The Knights of Labor in Ontario, 1880–1900. In G. S. Kealey (Ed.), *Workers and Canadian History* (pp. 238–288). Montreal and Kingston: McGill–Queen's University Press.

58. Knights of Labor. (2009). The official website of the Knights of Labor. Retrieved 10 February 2011 from http://www.6hourday.org/knightsoflabor.html

59. Labour Law Casebook Group. (2004). *Labour and employment law: Cases, material and commentary* (7th edition). Toronto: Irwin.

60. Latham, S. F., & Braun, M. R. (2008). The performance implications of financial slack during economic recession and recovery: Observations from the software industry (2001–2003). *Journal of Managerial Issues,* pp. 30–50.

61. Leslie, K. (9 May 2014). Tim Hudak's public sector cuts would eliminate 100,000 jobs. Retrieved 4 July 2014 from http://www.huffingtonpost.ca/2014/05/09/tim-hudak-public-sector-job-cuts_n_5295017.html

62. Lipsey, R. G. (1981). The understanding and control of inflation: Is there a crisis in macro-economics? *Canadian Journal of Economics/Revue Canadienne d'Économique, 14*(4), pp. 545–576.

63. Unifor, "New Union in Canada Takes Shape." Used with permission. http://www.uniformediaone.ca/2012/10/new-union-in-canada-takes-shape/

64. MacDowell, L. S. (2006). Industrial unionism. *The Canadian encyclopedia.* Retrieved 24 November 2006 from http://www.thecanadianencyclopedia.com/index.cfm?PgNm=TCE&Params=A1ARTA0003990

65. Mitchell, T., & Naylor, J. (1998). The prairies: In the eye of the storm. In C. Heron (Ed.), *The workers' revolt in Canada 1917–1925* (pp. 176–231). Toronto: University of Toronto Press.

66. National Labor Relations Board 60th Anniversary Committee. (1995). *The first sixty years: The story of the National Labor Relations Board 1935–1995.* Chicago: American Bar Association. Retrieved 28 November 2006 from http://www.nlrb.gov/About_Us/History/thhe_first_60_years.aspx

67. O'Donoghue, J. G. (1942–1943). Daniel John O'Donoghue: Father of the Canadian Labor Movement. *CCHA Report, 10* (pp. 87–96). Retrieved 7 November 2006 from http://www.umanitoba.ca/colleges/st_pauls/ccha/Back%20Issues/CCHA1942-43/Donoghue.html

68. Ottawa & District Labour Council. (2005). Daniel O'Donoghue (1844–1907). Retrieved 7 November 2006 from http://www.ottawalabour.org/index.php?p=history_daniel

69. Padova, A. (2005). *Federal commercialization in Canada.* Ottawa: Government of Canada.

70. Palmer, B. D. (1983). *Working-class experience.* Toronto: Butterworth.

71. Palmer, B. D. (1992). *Working-class experience* (2nd edition). Toronto: McClelland & Stewart.

72. Palmer, B. D. (2006). Nine-Hour Movement. Retrieved 8 November 2006 from http://www.thecanadianencyclopedia.com/index.cfm?PgNm=TCE&Params=A1ARTA0005757

73. Raina, J. (28 February 2014). Support letter for IndustriALL Global Union. Retrieved 14 July 2014 from http://unifortoyota.ca/2014/04/support-letter-from-industriall-global-union/

74. Reid, F. (1979). The effect of controls on the rate of wage change in Canada. *Canadian Journal of Economics/Revue Canadienne d'Économique, 12,* pp. 214–227.

75. Sargent, J. (2005). *The 1975–78 anti-inflation program in retrospect.* Bank of Canada working paper 2005–43. Ottawa: Bank of Canada.

76. Sergie, M. (14 February 2014). NAFTA's Economic Impact. Retrieved 10 July 2014 from http://www.cfr.org/trade/naftas-economic-impact/p15790.

77. Sinclair, P. R. (2003). "A very delicate world": Fishers and plant workers remake their lives on Newfoundland's Bonavista Peninsula after the cod moratorium. *Maritime Studies, 2*(1), pp. 89–109.

78. Stanford, J. (6 October 2012). Did this historic trade deal help Canada? No. *The Globe and Mail*. Used with permission of the author. Retrieved 11 July 2014 from http://www.theglobeandmail.com/globe-debate/ did-this-historic-trade-deal-help-canada-no/article4593360/

79. Standing Senate Committee on Agriculture and Forestry. (2011). *The Canadian forest sector: A future based on innovation*. Final Report of the Hon. Percy Mockler, Chair, Hon. Fernand Robichaud, P.C., Deputy Chair. July, 2011. Retrieved 4 July 2014 from http://www.parl.gc.ca/content/sen/committee/411/agfo/rep/ rep02jul11-e.pdf

80. Taylor, M., & Mason, R. (10 July 2014). Strikes by public sector workers largest in three years: Up to 1 million expected on streets in mass industrial action protesting at pay freeze and pensions as result of austerity cuts. *The Guardian*. Retrieved 14 July 2014 from http://www.theguardian.com/society/2014/ jul/10/strikes-public-sector-industrial-action-pay-pensions

81. Thiessen, G. (22 January 2001). Remarks by Gordon Thiessen Governor of the Bank of Canada to the Canadian Club of Toronto: Toronto, Ontario. 22 January 2001. Retrieved 4 July 2014 from http://www.bankofcanada.ca/ wp-content/uploads/2010/01/sp01-1.pdf

82. Townsend, J. (2007). Do tariff reductions affect the wages of workers in protected industries? Evidence from the Canada–U.S. Free Trade Agreement. *Canadian Journal of Economics, 40*, pp. 69–92.

83. Unifor. (2014a). History & mission. Retrieved 11 July 2014 from http://www .unifor.org/en/about-unifor/history-mission

84. Unifor. (2014b). Sectors. Retrieved 14 July 2014 from http://www.unifor.org/ en/member-services/sectors

85. Unifor. (2014c). What we stand for. Retrieved 15 July 2014 from http://www .unifor.org/en/why-unifor/policies

86. Unifor. (2015). Why join Unifor? Retrieved 21 April 2015 from http://www .unifor.org/en/why-unifor

87. Webb, S., & Webb, B. (1898). *History of trade unionism*. Printed by the authors especially for the Amalgamated Society of Engineers. ASIN: B00085AVQA.

88. Wise, C. (2009). The North American free trade agreement. *New Political Economy, 14*, pp. 133–148.

CHAPTER 3

ECONOMIC, SOCIAL, AND POLITICAL ENVIRONMENTS

LEARNING OBJECTIVES

BY THE END OF THIS CHAPTER, YOU WILL BE ABLE TO DISCUSS

- the supply of and demand for labour;
- the elasticity of supply and demand and its impact on labour power;
- the impact of free trade, deregulation, and privatization on unions;
- the importance of work–leisure decisions;
- the institutional and noncompetitive factors that affect labour supply;
- recent demographic changes in the labour force;
- the social conditions of the labour market;
- public attitude toward unions in North America;
- current trends in income distribution and poverty;
- the impact of compositional shifts in the labour market on labour;
- the importance of achieving a work–life balance;
- the structural elements of the political system that help labour; and
- globalization and politics.

CANADA'S INCOME GAP IS AMONG FASTEST GROWING IN OECD

OTTAWA—Canada is among the worst countries in the developed world in terms of the widening income gap between top earners and others in society, according to the Organization for Economic Co-operation and Development.

The analysis shows income inequality is on the rise in most developed economies, but the trend has particularly taken hold in the United States and Canada.

The OECD report shows the top one per cent of Canadian pre-tax income earners captured 37 per cent of the overall income growth between 1981 and 2012, and now swallow up 12.2 per cent of the country's income pie.

In the U.S., the top one percenters captured 47 per cent of income growth in the country during the period—and now take in one-fifth of the country's pre-tax annual income.

Meanwhile, incomes among the poorest households have not kept pace with overall income growth, the OECD says. In fact, stripping away the top one percenters would leave overall income growth considerably lower in many countries.

This is why the majority of the population can't reconcile their countries' economic growth rate with improvements in their incomes, the report speculates.

...

The OECD, whose 34 member countries are among the world's wealthiest, warns the problem will worse[n] unless steps are taken to ensure top earners pay their fair share of taxes.

"Without concerted policy action, the gap between the rich and poor is likely to grow even wider in the years ahead," predicted OECD Secretary-General Angel Gurria. He notes that in almost all OECD countries, governments have substantially cut top personal tax rates in the past three decades.

As a result, the OECD is calling for a rollback in those tax rate cuts, as well as abolishing or scaling back on a wide range of tax regulations that disproportionately go to top earners, including on stock options, fringe benefits and income from capital and investment.

The OECD report shows Canada is near the top of the heap in terms of both growth in income disparity over the past three decades and in absolute terms. With the one per-centers capturing 12.2 per cent of the income pie in 2012, Canada ranks only behind the United States (20 per cent), Great Britain (12.9 per cent), and Germany (12.7 per cent) in terms of income disparity among the 18 relatively rich countries compared.

Source: Julian Beltrame. (30 April 2014). "*Canada's income gap among fastest growing n the OECD,*" The Canadian Press. Used with permission of The Canadian Press. Retrieved from http://www.ctvnews.ca/business/canada-s-income-gap-among-fastest-growing-in-the-oecd-1.1799525.

Spencer Platt/Getty Images

Growing income inequality sparks North American protests.

CHAPTER 3 Economic, Social, and Political Environments

The environment of industrial relations helps shape the labour–management relationship and such system outcomes as wages, benefits, work rules, and conflict. In this chapter, we examine how the labour market, social conditions, and the political environment affect industrial relations.

// THE ECONOMIC CONTEXT

MACROECONOMIC POLICY

The Canadian economy sank into a deep recession in late 2008. Recovery has been slow and unsteady. How has the Canadian economy performed compared to the other advanced economies? According to the Organisation for Economic Co-operation and Development,

> Canada did not suffer as much during the 2008–2009 global recession as most other countries and its economy has since rebounded sharply....
>
> While unemployment is declining in Canada, the share of the unemployed looking for a job for more than one year was still 12.1% in the first quarter of 2014–4.8 percentage points above its pre-crisis level, although well below the OECD average....
>
> Although Canada has weathered the recent global recession comparatively well, employment prospects for young adults have barely improved. In the second quarter of 2014, the unemployment rate of youth (aged 15 to 24 years) was more than double that of prime-aged workers (aged 25 years and over), 13.4% as compared to 5.9%. The proportion of young Canadians, who were neither employed nor in education and training (NEET), has also risen by 1.4 percentage points since the onset of the crisis to 9%. By comparison, the NEET rate barely increased in the OECD area as a whole. The 2014 Employment Outlook shows that individuals with lower educational attainment and weaker information-processing skills are more likely to be NEET and this association increases with age. (OECD, 2014, pp. 1–2)

Arguably the most important single influence on industrial relations has been the federal government's **macroeconomic policy** with respect to the liberalization of markets. Almost all industries have been affected either directly through **deregulation** or **privatization** (or both) (e.g., trucking, airlines, and communications) or indirectly through policies that promote free trade in goods and services (e.g., the **North American Free Trade Agreement** among Canada, the United States, and Mexico). The net effect of these liberalization policies on workers is in dispute, but there can be little doubt that firms are under greater competitive pressure due to tariff reductions or deregulation policies.

Globalization has resulted in greater mobility of capital and increases in the flow of goods and services. It has also meant increased worldwide competition between firms and between nation states over attracting foreign investment. But global competition is not the only pressure on labour markets, as Gunderson and Verma (1992) point out:

> ... the labor market is subject to the forces of continual technological change, industrial restructuring, just-in-time delivery systems, deregulation, privatization, public sector retrenchment, and the ever-present threat of recession.

Research shows that deregulation policies, at least as they were applied in Australia, may have negative consequences for the economy by increasing inequality in the labour market (Neville & Kriesler, 2008).

---

macroeconomic policy
a policy that applies to economy-wide goals, such as inflation, unemployment, and growth

deregulation
a policy designed to create more competition in an industry by allowing prices to be determined by market forces

privatization
the transfer or contracting out of services to the private sector

North American Free Trade Agreement (NAFTA)
a free trade agreement among Canada, the United States, and Mexico that was signed in 1994 and included a labour side agreement, the North American Agreement on Labor Cooperation

THE LABOUR MARKET[1]

For nonunion firms, labour market forces will largely determine employee compensation and conditions. When the growth of the supply of labour through population growth and immigration is insufficient to meet the future labour demand, lower economic growth will result. For the Ontario version of the problem of low population growth see the report of the Ministry of Finance (2014). The main implication of this is that our current high standard of living will be difficult to maintain unless the demand for labour is matched by supply.

SUPPLY AND DEMAND FRAMEWORK

The purpose of this section is to provide the reader with the tools to analyze the impact of economic conditions on industrial relations (Gunderson & Riddell, 1988). To do this, we need to employ some of the basic supply and demand analysis of economics. In Figure 3.1, we portray a typical labour market equilibrium in which supply (SS) and demand (DD) curves for labour determine the quantity of labour supplied at the competitive wage (Wc) and employment level (Nc). If the demand for labour shifts to D1D1 due to external factors such as the oil sands boom, we can predict some outcomes. The new equilibrium shows higher wages (Wc1) and a higher employment level (Nc1).

FIGURE 3.1

LABOUR MARKET EQUILIBRIUM

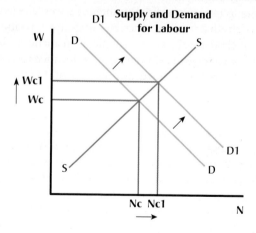

ELASTICITY OF SUPPLY AND DEMAND

The reader will note that the effect of the demand shift will depend on the slope of the supply curve (SS). The steeper the supply curve, the greater is the increase in wages, caused by a shift in demand. A steep supply curve is what economists call an inelastic supply of labour. Conversely, a flat supply curve indicates an elasticity of supply for labour, because a small increase in the wage rate will significantly increase labour supply. Thus, the wage elasticity of supply is measured by the proportionate (or percentage) change in labour supplied, caused by a proportionate (or percentage) change in the wage rate. Proportions or percentages of elasticity are used because wages and labour are measured in different units.

elasticity of supply (demand)
the labour responsiveness of supply (demand) caused by a change in the wage rate; for example, if a small increase in wages causes a large increase in the supply of labour, the supply curve is said to be *elastic*

The same reasoning applies to **elasticity of demand** for labour. The steeper the demand curve, the greater the inelasticity of demand, since a relatively small increase in the quantity demanded will cause a relatively large increase in wages. Conversely, a flat demand curve indicates an elastic demand, because a large increase in the demand for labour will have a relatively small effect on the wage rate.

LABOUR POWER AND MARSHALL'S CONDITIONS

The shape of the demand curve is important, because it influences a union's ability to raise wages without significantly affecting employment levels. This effect is known as the *wage-employment tradeoff*.

What factors determine the shape of the demand curve for labour? How does the shape of the demand curve affect labour power? We know from economic theory that the demand for labour is a "derived" demand, because it is determined solely by supply and demand forces in the market for the firm's product. Marshall (1920) describes four theoretical conditions that determine the wage elasticity of labour as we have defined it (i.e., the employment responsiveness to an increase in wages).

PRODUCT MARKET The more competitive the product market, the greater the employment impact of a wage increase and the elasticity of demand for labour. This is known as the *wage–employment tradeoff* in the sense that when a union increases wages, the higher costs may be reflected in reduced sales. Reduced sales cause reduced demand for labour. Hence, unions will tend to have more power when there is less competition in the firm's product market. Industries where firms have some degree of monopoly power can more easily absorb a wage increase without affecting employment levels. They can do this because their monopoly power gives them room to raise prices without suffering lower sales (and thus employment levels). Thus, to the extent that free trade increases market competition, union power will be reduced. In terms of elasticity, the more inelastic the demand for labour, the lower the employment tradeoff from a wage increase and the greater, therefore, union power.

The case of Sears Canada's planned outsourcing of 1,600 call-centre jobs across Canada illustrates the effect of the wage–employment tradeoff in a highly competitive environment (see IR Today 3.1).

SUBSTITUTION EFFECT The easier it is to substitute capital (machines, new technology, etc.) for labour, the less power labour will have to raise wages. The firm that can easily substitute other factors of production for labour will possess more bargaining power. This substitution effect may be a longer-term phenomenon, since technological change may take years to implement. Certain jobs are more essential to the production process than others and hence harder to substitute. For example, airlines cannot function without pilots, and buildings cannot be constructed without electricians.

LABOUR INTENSITY Labour intensity is the degree to which labour costs account for production costs. Thus, an industry is labour-intensive if labour costs are a high proportion of total costs. The smaller the proportion of total costs labour is, the lower the employment impact of a wage increase will be, thus giving labour more power. In firms that are highly capital-intensive (e.g., high tech, printing, aerospace), labour will have more bargaining power according to this theory, because firms can absorb a wage increase without a serious impact on total costs and employment. On the other hand, many highly labour-intensive public services, such as police and teachers, will have less bargaining power.

SEARS CANADA TO CUT JOBS THROUGH OUTSOURCING

Another round of job cuts is rippling through the operations of Sears Canada Inc. affecting more than 1,600 positions as the company looks for ways to lower expenses.

The retailer says it has eliminated 283 jobs at warehouses across much of the country in a move to simplify logistics. The warehouses affected are in Calgary, Montreal, Belleville and Vaughan, Ont., and a Vancouver suburb. Sears Canada will also outsource the 1,345 associate jobs at its three customer call centres in Toronto, Montreal and Belleville, Ont., over the next nine months.

IBM will become the third-party vendor for customer services, with its English-language phone operations being handled out of the Philippines and French calls going to an office in Europe, said spokesman Vince Power.

The company's call centres handle catalogue orders, gift registry and parts and repair services.

Sears Canada has been scaling back its call centres for several years. The company closed its Hamilton office in 2008, laying off about 140 mainly part-time staff. A year later it shuttered the Regina office, laying off 250 people.

....

Sears Canada is trying to reduce costs and improve its overall business as part of a three-year turnaround plan. The company is dealing with intense competition within the retail sector and a slate of aging stores that it began plans to renovate before the departure of its previous CEO, Calvin McDonald.

Source: David Friend. (15 January 2014). "Sears Canada to cut more than 1,600 jobs, many through outsourcing." The Canadian Press. Used with permission of The Canadian Press. Retrieved from http://www.ctvnews.ca/business/sears-canada-to-cut-more-than-1-600-jobs-many-through-outsourcing-1.1641043#ixzz3Dyf98CmT.

MARKET FOR SUBSTITUTES Finally, the more competitive the market for substitute factors of production is, the greater the bargaining power firms will have. The cheaper and more available these substitutes, the greater the impact on employment, and hence the greater the employer's bargaining power.

A clear implication flowing from the economic theory discussed above is that the more competitive the economy, the greater the bargaining power of employers. Thus, given our earlier discussion of globalization and the shift to freer markets, we can infer a parallel shift to greater bargaining power on the part of management.

To summarize, demand is more inelastic and unions will have more power when

- product markets are less competitive;
- labour costs are a small proportion of total costs;
- the market for substitutes is less competitive; and
- it is harder to substitute labour for capital.

NONECONOMIC SOURCES OF UNION POWER

Unions also derive power from sources other than labour markets. They are more powerful when they build strong links with their local communities. Evidence reveals, for example, that unions have successfully forged alliances with community groups to

- assist in organizing new members;
- strengthen positions in bargaining;
- support political lobbying campaigns;

- oppose plant closures; and
- support strikes and other industrial actions (Craft, 1998).

SUPPLY OF LABOUR

What factors in society determine labour supply? The number of workers is a function of such elements as population growth, immigration, retirement choices, work–family decisions, career patterns, leisure choices, and labour mobility.

POPULATION AND IMMIGRATION

Labour-force growth is fuelled by population growth and immigration. Population growth is determined by births less deaths plus net immigration (immigration less migration). Female fertility rates have an important effect on future labour-force growth. Canada has lower rates than the United States, but about the average of other developed countries.

It seems clear that economic prosperity depends on labour force growth, which in turn must rely on immigration because fertility rates are too low. IR Notebook 3.1 reveals that Canada's immigration is significantly contributing to our economic well-being.

IR NOTEBOOK   3.1

FOR CANADA, IMMIGRATION IS A KEY TO PROSPERITY

Canada has become an attractive pole for immigrants from around the world who are looking for a host country that will give them good opportunities. According to the Organization for Economic Co-operation and Development, Canada's annual immigration flow is now proportionately one of the highest among OECD members, at 0.7 per cent of its population.

In 2011, there were 249,000 new permanent residents, after a record year of 281,000 in 2010. (The official planned admission range is between 240,000 and 265,000 new permanent residents a year.) That is not counting the 190,800 temporary foreign workers that were admitted in 2011 as well as the 98,400 foreign students who came to benefit from our universities and may decide to stay and put their skills to use in Canada's industries.

There are many myths floating around about immigrants, ranging from them being low-skilled workers to them having difficulty integrating into the labour force. A quick read through the OECD's 2013 International Migration Outlook debunks all of those myths – and makes the reader realize just how well Canada is faring on the immigration front.

Time to address unfounded myths about immigrants

The OECD finds that employment for foreign-born Canadian citizens has gone up since 2008, while it has stalled for native-born citizens. The employment rate for Canadian immigrants in 2012 was the third highest in the OECD. This shows that immigrants are quickly integrating into the labour force and putting their skills to work.

For that matter, it is worth noting that more than 50 per cent of Canadian immigrants are highly educated, putting Canada at the top among the OECD countries. As well, a significant number of the almost 100,000 foreign students visiting Canada each year decide to stay after getting a degree from one of our world-class universities (McGill, University of Toronto, UBC, etc.). Many other immigrants are also looking in Canada's direction, attracted by job prospects and the open-arm culture for which Canadians are known.

One reason why foreign immigrants favour Canada as a destination is the labour mobility it offers. According to its latest Global Competitiveness Report published last month, the World Economic Forum ranks Canada as the world's seventh most efficient labour market.

High labour-market efficiency means that workers are more likely to be allocated to their most effective use and provided with an environment where they are encouraged to give their best effort. On a macroeconomic level, this also means that the country's work force is flexible enough to shift workers from one economic activity to another—for example, from factories in Quebec and Ontario to oil sands in Alberta—rapidly and at low cost. It also means that there are strong incentives in place for employees, promoting meritocracy and providing equity in the business environment.

Canada has gone to great lengths to liberalize its labour market, and it is paying off. Canada's labour market now offers a great deal of mobility to its workers; it is quite easy for anyone to move from Montreal to Toronto, Calgary or Vancouver (and vice versa). As a former Quebec minister responsible for economic development and trade, let me tell you that I am proud to have had the opportunity to work with my provincial counterparts on internal trade agreements, fostering Canada's economic ties, and ultimately strengthening the federation.

Positive implication on Canadian economic growth—and real estate

Canada's strong economic performance since 2008 is explained by many factors, including well-capitalized banks, massive public infrastructure spending—and a strong influx of immigrants. Immigration last year explained two-thirds of Canada's population growth of 1.2 per cent, well ahead of the 0.7 per cent and 0.3 per cent seen in the United States and the euro zone, respectively.

Why is this so important? Because without this immigration flow, Canada's population aged between 20 and 44 years old would be declining. That cohort, which constitutes most of the labour force, is the one that creates new households, buys new houses, has children and pays the greater part of taxation revenue. Without immigration, Canada's natural population growth would not be enough to sustain economic growth and welfare. Quebec, given its demographic structure, especially needs immigration to increase its labour force in the short term so as to sustain the costs of its social programs.

We also note that a large percentage of every province's immigrants are in the 20-to-44 age group, meaning that the benefits of household formation are spread all across Canada. This helps explain why the housing market in Canada has been so resilient during the past five years.

I am happy to see that one of Canada's strengths is clearly working in its favour. As Canadians, we need foreign talent to sustain the country's demographic and economic growth, and we have just the labour market to attract it. Canadians need immigration just as much as immigrants need a destination such as Canada. Immigration, as it turns out, is most likely the key to Canada's prosperity.

Source: Clement Gignac and Sebastien McMahon. (7 October 2013). "For Canada, immigration is a key to prosperity." *The Globe and Mail.* Used with permission of the authors. Retrieved from http://www.theglobeandmail.com/report-on-business/economy/economy-lab/for-canada-immigration-is-a-key-to-prosperity/article14711281/.

Clément Gignac is senior vice-president and chief economist at Industrial Alliance Inc., vice-chairman of the World Economic Forum Council on Competitiveness and a former cabinet minister in the Quebec government.

WORK–LEISURE DECISIONS

Economists see a tradeoff choice between leisure and work. In this decision-making framework, leisure is treated as an ordinary commodity. The impact of a wage increase on leisure is analyzed in terms of substitution and income effects. On the one hand, as our incomes rise, we may substitute leisure for work because more goods and services per hour of work can be purchased. But higher incomes make both leisure and work more desirable. That is, we can afford more leisure, but we may also find work more attractive because of the higher pay rate or salary. Thus, in theory, there are two opposing effects on the leisure–work tradeoff when our wages rise.

Economics texts typically discuss the dominance of the income effect over the substitution effect in terms of the long-term decline in hours worked. In Canada, for example, hours declined from an average of 58.6 hours per week in 1901 to 39.2 hours in 1981 (Gunderson & Riddell, 1988). But more recently, from 1979 to 2000, average annual hours worked decreased only 1.7 percent (OECD, 2001). This relative stability in hours in Canada is in contrast to double-digit decreases in hours in France, Germany, Japan, and Norway over the same period. In the United States and Sweden, average hours have actually increased over the period (Hayden, 2003). If we apply the work–leisure framework to the pattern of stability in hours worked in Canada, it indicates that the long-term substitution and income effects are offsetting each other. The slight decrease in average annual hours indicates that the income effect is only slightly greater than the substitution effect.

NONCOMPETITIVE AND INSTITUTIONAL FACTORS

We have analyzed the labour market assuming that markets are competitive, that labour is always mobile (meaning workers can always relocate), and that there are no institutional barriers to competition. In practice, markets are not always competitive, workers are not mobile, and there may be substantial institutional barriers to competition.

> **monopsony**
> occurs when a firm is the sole market buyer of a good, service, or labour

NONCOMPETITIVE FACTORS In economic theory, **monopsony** exists when a firm is not a wage-taker but a wage-setter. This situation is somewhat analogous to monopoly in the product market. The firm is so dominant in the labour market that it has some control over the wages offered. Theory predicts lower wages and employment levels in monopsonistic markets. For example, researchers have found the markets for teachers and nurses to be monopsonistic (Currie, Farsi & Macleod, 2005; Luizer & Thornton, 1986). In the market for nurses in California, private hospitals exercised their monopsonistic power through an increase in workload (patients per nurse) and not wages (Currie, Farsi & Macleod, 2005). Some important research on this topic has revealed significant new evidence of very high levels of monopsony power, particularly in markets for nurses and teachers (Ashenfelter, Farber & Ransom, 2010). Their policy remedies for these market imperfections are unionization or minimum wage laws.

A key economic assumption is that labour is perfectly mobile, but if this is not the case, less than optimal outcomes may result. In a recent analysis of interprovincial movement of labour in Canada, several barriers to mobility were identified (Finnie, 2004). It was found that the probability an individual changed his or her province of residence from one year to the next over the 1982–1995 period was lower if

- the person's home province had a large population;
- language was a factor;
- the person lived in a larger city versus a smaller city, town, or rural area;
- the person was older, married, or had a family;
- the provincial unemployment rate was low or there were low levels of individual unemployment insurance or social assistance; and
- the person was a prime-age male with low income.

Finally, labour mobility as measured by the propensity to move to another province was relatively stable over time. However, there were gender differences, with men's rates declining slightly and women's holding steady or rising a little over the fourteen-year period (Finnie, 2004).

The lack of labour mobility has also been shown to exacerbate wage inequality in international trade agreements (Devillanova, Di Maio & Vertova, 2010).

INSTITUTIONAL BARRIERS TO SUPPLY Other barriers to the supply of labour are institutional in nature. Labour supply may be inhibited by governments through a lack of resources to training or higher education, resulting in a restriction on the supply of graduates to a given occupation or profession. Applying Weber's (1922) theory of social closure, research has shown that various occupations erect barriers to entry to restrict supply and thereby affect earnings (Banerjee & Phan, 2014; Weeden, 2002). Professional associations and craft unions use licensing and certification requirements, association memberships, and educational credentialling to restrict entry into the occupation.

The temporary foreign worker case described in IR Notebook 3.2 is indicative of how labour supply can be affected by government policy. The Notebook presents both the government and opposition views of the controversial program.

IR NOTEBOOK   3.2

NEW REFORMS FOR THE TEMPORARY FOREIGN WORKER PROGRAM

On June 20, 2014, the Honourable Jason Kenney, Minister of Employment and Social Development, and the Honourable Chris Alexander, Minister of Citizenship and Immigration, announced a comprehensive overhaul of the Temporary Foreign Worker Program (TFWP).

Here are the government reform highlights:

The reforms cover three key areas:

- reorganizing the TFWP to offer greater clarity and transparency
- restricting access to the TFWP to ensure Canadians are first in line for available jobs; and
- stronger enforcement and tougher penalties.

Here are some opposing views of the reforms:

A) NDP.

The changes announced today to the Temporary Foreign Worker Program don't go far enough to fix it and show the depth of the Conservatives' incompetence in this file.

"The Conservatives are trying to reverse the damages they've caused by making the program easier to abuse," said Jinny Sims (Newton–North Delta), NDP critic for Employment and Social Development. "But their changes aren't actually making sure employers hire Canadians first or protecting temporary foreign workers from abuse.

The Conservatives' changes to the Program offer nothing new to protect temporary foreign workers from exploitation, nor do they present a pathway to citizenship. The recruitment rules remain the same, rather than requiring employers to advertise for longer or at higher wages. And the Conservative government is not replacing all of the funding it has cut for gathering current Labour Market Information.

"Time and again, we've seen this government introduce half measures and not enforce them," added Sadia Groguhé (Saint-Lambert), NDP Deputy critic for Employment and Social Development. "Why should Canadians trust them now? Why not be fully transparent, and publish positions and wage levels of temporary foreign workers, in addition to the employers?"

B)

The changes to the temporary foreign workers program also received opposition from Maritime labour ministers concerned about how the lobster and seafood industry would be affected. The changes would phase out over three years the use of temporary foreign workers at fish processing plants.

The ministers argue that like agriculture (which is exempt from the program), certain fisheries have a harvest time and their workforce is aging and from rural communities that are becoming increasingly depopulated.

"I haven't found a minister anywhere in Canada who is happy with it," said PEI's Innovation Minister Allen Roach.

Sources: Jane Taber. (2 July 2014). "PEI, Nova Scotia join Alberta in opposing changes to foreign worker program." *The Globe and Mail*. Retrieved from http://www.theglobeandmail.com/news/politics/maritime-labour-ministers-oppose-changes-to-foreign-worker-program/article19407487/; Employment and Social Development Canada. (2015). "Temporary Foreign Workers, Web Highlights." Reproduced with the permission of the Minister of Employment and Social Development Canada, 2015. Retrieved from http://www.esdc.gc.ca/eng/jobs/foreign_workers/reform/highlights.shtml; Tom Mulcair, NDP. (20 June 2014). "Conservative reforms not enough to fix broken Temporary Foreign Worker Program." Used with permission. Retrieved from http://www.ndp.ca/news/conservative-reforms-not-enough-to-fix-broken-temporary-foreign-worker-program.

UNIONS AND LABOUR SUPPLY Research reveals that craft unions' control of labour supply through access to apprentice programs and **hiring halls** has positive and negative effects. On the one hand, European experience shows that without proactive government regulation, minorities and women will tend to be excluded from unionized construction work (Byrne, Clarke & Van Der Meer, 2005). But in the United States, evidence shows that unions have positive effects in terms of higher graduation rates for women involved in joint union–management apprentice programs (Berik & Bilginsoy, 2000). Research also shows that apprenticeship training and hiring halls tend to increase union productivity, while jurisdictional disagreements and restrictive work rules lower it (Allen, 1984). Jurisdictional disputes are found in the construction industry and involve interunion rivalries between craft unions (e.g., labourers and carpenters) over the appropriate trade to perform a particular task. Research on the union impact on training in Germany indicates that by imposing minimum wages and wage compression, unions increase on-the-job training (Dustmann & Shonberg, 2009).

DEMOGRAPHIC FACTORS

Demographic factors are important determinants of labour force patterns. Like most industrialized countries, Canada experienced a postwar baby boom between 1947 and 1966 (Foot & Soffman, 1996). This large baby-boom cohort created challenges for organizations. The traditional hierarchical management structure and conventional career patterns were disrupted by the higher numbers of boomers in the middle ranks. Thus, a substantial mismatch emerged in the 1980s between labour force structure and organizational needs (Foot & Venne, 1990). Organizations found solutions in "flattening organization hierarchies and adopting and rewarding spiral career paths" (Foot & Venne, 1990).

// SOCIAL CONDITIONS

In this section, we examine some of the social conditions that exist in Canada that, to some extent, provide a test of the effects of globalization and are part of the environment of industrial relations. We look at support for unions and worker satisfaction, and then discuss some evidence on trends in income distribution and poverty in a North American context. Finally, employing the concept of a work–life balance, we will look at societal changes that have disturbed this delicate balance.

PUBLIC ATTITUDES TO UNIONS

It has been argued by some that unions have outlived their usefulness as organizations. Union decline, so goes the argument, is an inevitable consequence of several factors:

- globalization and the greater pressures on firms to be competitive;
- more individual protection under employment laws;
- changes in the nature of work, with employees exercising greater control over scheduling (e.g., telework, self-employment); and
- improved human resources practices geared toward individual needs.

If this argument is valid, surely the demand for unionization should be falling over time. The demand for unionization is rarely measured by researchers or opinion seekers. A less direct question about support for unions, however, has been surveyed in the population. Of course, the desire to be a union member and showing general support for unions are distinct things. But the support question is probably correlated with the desire to unionize and thus a useful indicator.

Opinion polls are random samples of the population that provide only snapshots of population preferences. Their reliability as indicators of preferences, therefore, increases as results are repeated over time. We will first look at the longest repeated sample on the question of support for unions provided by the Gallup Organization in the United States.

The Gallup Organization has asked the same question to Americans for almost seventy years: Do you approve of unions? As is shown in Figure 3.2, there is no long-term decline in the support of the American population for unions. (We discuss this topic further in Chapter 5.)

FIGURE 3.2

U.S. UNION APPROVAL: GALLUP POLLS 1936–2014

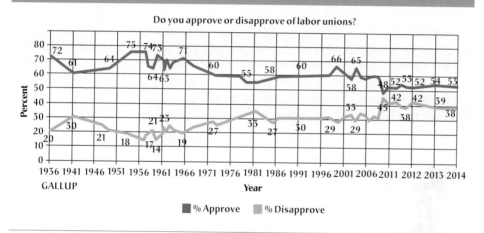

Source: Gallup, Labour Unions, Used with permission. Retrieved from http://www.gallup.com/poll/12751/labor-unions.aspx.

IR NOTEBOOK   **3.3**

POLL RESULTS SHOW MAJORITY OF CANADIANS HOLD FAVOURABLE VIEW OF UNIONS

A majority of Canadians believe that unions and employee associations play a positive role in Canadian society, according to the most recent public opinion poll commissioned by CAUT (Canadian Association of University Teachers).

In a Harris/Decima survey conducted last month, 56 per cent of Canadians had favourable views of unions,

with 70 per cent saying unions are still needed today. By contrast, just 28 per cent of Canadians hold negative views of unions and a similar number said they are no longer needed.

Support for unions is highest in British Columbia where 63 per cent of respondents held positive views of unions.

The survey also found that Canadians are suspicious of politicians who hold anti-union views. A clear majority—53 per cent—of respondents said they are suspicious of government and politicians who try to limit collective bargaining and the political power of unions.

"It's a pleasant surprise that in spite of the anti-union posturing by the federal and some provincial governments, most Canadians continue to hold positive views of unions and employee associations," said CAUT's associate executive director David Robinson.

Robinson added that a strong majority of Canadians are opposed to so-called "right to work" legislation that would allow individuals to opt out of paying dues even though they would continue to receive benefits negotiated by the union.

According to the survey, two-thirds of Canadians think everyone in the workplace should be required to pay union dues if they benefit from the union's work.

However, Robinson noted that Canadians are divided in their views of public sector unions. Forty per cent believe that governments should have the right to impose contracts on public sector workers, while 42 per cent disagree.

Similarly, Canadians were equally split over whether public sector unions should have the right to strike. Forty-four per cent backed taking away the right of public sector unions to strike, while 42 per cent disagree.

The telephone poll of 2,000 adult Canadians, conducted Nov. 7–18, 2013, has a margin of error of ±2.2 per cent, 19 times in 20.

Source: CAUT. (December 2013). "Poll results show majority of Canadians hold favourable view of unions," *CAUT Bulletin*, *Vol. 60*, No. 10. Used with permission. Retrieved from https://www.cautbulletin.ca/en_article.asp?articleid=3754.

In Canada, similar questions have been asked at various times about union support and desire for unionization. The most recent 2013 poll (summarized in IR Notebook 3.3) was conducted by Harris/Decima and showed similar results to the Gallup polls in the United States. A majority (56 percent) of Canadians hold favourable views of unions, and 70 percent believe that unions are still necessary. This support for unions does not provide evidence of a long-term decline in demand for unionization and those who argue this position.

WORK ATTITUDES

Demand for unionization may stem from workers' dissatisfaction with their jobs (Barling, Kelloway & Bremermann, 1991). To examine this question, we have drawn from a joint Canada–U.S. population survey conducted in 1996 (Lipset, Meltz, Gomez & Katchanovski, 2004). Despite the general support for unions indicated above, workers displayed very positive attitudes toward work and conditions (see Table 3.1). Attitudes were very similar between Canadian and American workers, with 86 percent and 85 percent, respectively, indicating satisfaction with their jobs. High proportions of those surveyed also thought they were fairly paid and took pride in their work.

We can only conclude from these apparently contradictory results that the majority of Canadian and American workers want unions for reasons other than economics or job dissatisfaction. Employee demand for a collective and independent voice in the workplace in Canada and the United States appears to be strong despite some profound changes over the past three decades in work organization, labour force composition, and the individualization of human resources.

TRENDS IN INCOME DISTRIBUTION AND POVERTY Critics of globalization and free trade policies argue that a consequence of these trends is a widening income gap between the rich and poor. Restructuring policies, so the argument goes, have disproportionate negative effects on workers who lack the necessary skills and training to compete in the new economy. This is an important factor for those who have concerns about the human condition, for in the United States, high rates of income inequality have been associated with low rates of economic growth (Hsing, 2005). It has also been argued that the replacement of relatively-high-paying unionized manufacturing jobs with lower-paying service-sector jobs will result in a smaller middle class and a widening gap between high- and low-income groups.

We begin by looking at child and family poverty rates in Canada. In 1989, coincidently the same year that Canada signed the Free Trade Agreement with the United States, the Canadian House of Commons unanimously adopted a resolution to achieve the goal of eliminating poverty by the year 2000. Here is what the Conference Board of Canada concluded about child poverty in Canada in 2013:

- Canada scores a "C" grade and ranks 15th out of 17 peer countries.
- More than one in seven Canadian children live in poverty.
- Canada's child poverty rate increased between the mid-1990s and the late 2000s. See IR Notebook 3.4.

IR NOTEBOOK   3.4

PUTTING CHILD POVERTY IN CONTEXT

Children who experience poverty, especially persistently, are at higher risk of suffering health problems, developmental delays, and behaviour disorders. They tend to attain lower levels of education[1] and are more likely to live in poverty as adults.[2]

Moreover, the failure to address poverty may place a heavy burden on a country's economy. As the OECD has concluded, "failure to tackle the poverty and exclusion facing millions of families and their children is not only socially reprehensible, but it will also weigh heavily on countries' capacity to sustain economic growth in years to come."[3]

The Conference Board of Canada uses the OECD's relative measure of child poverty,[4] which calculates the proportion of children living in households where disposable income is less than 50 per cent of the median in each country.

How does Canada compare to its peer countries?

At 15.1 per cent, Canada's child poverty rate is over four percentage points higher than the 17-country average. More than one in seven Canadian children live in poverty. Canada ranks 15th on this indicator and scores a "C" grade.

The Nordic countries—Denmark, Finland, Norway, and Sweden—have the lowest rates of child poverty, with less than 7 per cent of children living in poor households. The relationship between social spending and poverty rates has become more obvious over time, so it is no surprise that the leading countries boast strong traditions of wealth redistribution.

The U.S. still has the highest poverty rate among industrialized countries, earning a "D" grade.

Is the child poverty rate declining in Canada?

Not according to the latest statistics from the Organisation for Economic Co-operation and Development (OECD). In 1989, the Canadian House of Commons unanimously resolved to eliminate child poverty by the year 2000, and there was some initial success; the child poverty rate fell from 15.8 per cent in the mid-1980s to 12.8 in the mid-1990s. Since then, however, the rate has increased—to 15.1 per cent in the late 2000s—reversing earlier progress.

Footnotes:

1. Marc Frenette, Why Are Youth From Lower-Income Families Less Likely to Attend University? (Ottawa: Statistics Canada, 2007).

2. Dominique Fleury, "Low-Income Children," Perspectives on Labour and Income 9, 5 (Ottawa, Statistics Canada, May 2008), 1 (accessed September 9, 2009).

3. OECD, Combating Poverty and Social Exclusion Through Work, Policy Brief (Paris: OECD, 2005).

4. Absolute poverty thresholds consider people to be living in poverty if their income is not enough to cover the costs of a given basket of goods in a particular year, updated annually for inflation. Relative poverty thresholds consider people to be living in poverty if their income cannot afford them the goods and services that are customary in a given society.

Source: The Conference Board of Canada. (January 2013). Child Poverty. Used with permission. Retrieved from http://www.conferenceboard.ca/hcp/details/society/child-poverty.aspx.

Child poverty is part of a larger problem with our current model of globalization. There is mounting evidence that income inequality has also become a major policy question in the world economy. Economic orthodoxy predicts that income and wealth will be evenly distributed among the population under capitalism. This economic assumption has recently been challenged by new evidence showing that both income and wealth are increasingly going to the high-income cohort of industrialized economies (Picketty, 2014; see also the opening vignette). The implications of inequality were identified in a recent report of Oxfam. Here are comments on the report from Professor Joseph Stiglitz, Columbia University, winner of the Nobel Prize for Economics:

> The extreme inequalities in incomes and assets we see in much of the world today harms our economies, our societies, and undermines our politics. Whilst we should all worry about this it is of course the poorest who suffer most, experiencing not just vastly unequal outcomes in their lives, but vastly unequal opportunities too. Oxfam's report is a timely reminder that any real effort to end poverty has to confront the public policy choices that create and sustain inequality. (Oxfam, 2014)

Another study revealed that earning inequality increased for both union and non-union workers in the United States from 1982 to 1990 (Chaykowski & Slotsve, 1996). The inequality found in the latter study, however, was significantly less for unionized workers. Evidence also showed a decline in earnings of the middle-income earners and increased polarization for male workers in the U.S. from 1968 to 1990 (Beach, Chaykowski & Slotsve, 1997). Another study could not rule out deindustrialization as a significant cause of increased earnings inequality (Chevan & Stokes, 2000). More recent data revealed a direct link between union decline and wage inequality in U.S. labour markets (Kim & Sakamoto, 2010).

The Gini coefficients shown in Table 3.2 are measures of income inequality (after tax and transfer) with a 1 value indicating perfect equality and higher values greater inequality. Countries are ranked from the highest inequality to the lowest. Ginis are shown after the effect of taxes and transfer payments. Income after taxes and transfers is often labelled **disposable income**. It captures the impact of such factors as the progressive tax structure and the social safety net. In 2010, we see that Mexico and Turkey representing the developing economies have the highest income inequality with Ginis of .466 and .417, respectively. Surprisingly, the United States has the next highest inequality index of the twenty-four countries in the sample. Canada's Gini of .319 ranked as the tenth worst in the sample. The Scandinavian nations and other European nations had the lowest Ginis, reflecting, in part, their superior safety nets and more progressive taxation policies. The figure also shows Ginis from an earlier period when available. The early period varied but was mostly the mid 1980s, approximating the start of globalization and trade liberalization. What is particularly disturbing about inequality is that it has risen in all of the countries where data were available except Greece and Turkey over this longer term.

> disposable income
> income after taxes
> and benefits from
> social programs
> (e.g., unemployment
> insurance payments)

CHANGING WORKFORCE COMPOSITION In 1965 Canada's workforce was almost 70 percent male, but by 2005 almost half of the workforce (46 percent) was female. The change was due to a doubling of the female labour participation rate (Human Resources and Skills Development Canada [HRSDC], 2004). Here is a Statistics Canada update of changes in the composition of the labour force:

- On July 1, 2014, Canada's population was estimated at 35,540,400, up 386,100 or 1.1% from July 1, 2013.

- This increase was slightly lower than the one observed over the previous year (+1.2% in 2012/2013), but similar to the average annual population increase of the last 30 years (+1.1%).

- Since 1993/1994, net international migration has been the main source of population growth for Canada. In 2013/2014, net international migration was responsible for two-thirds of the country's population growth.

- Over the last year, population growth was negative in Newfoundland and Labrador (−0.2%) and New Brunswick (−0.2%).

- Growth was above the national level (+1.1%) in Nunavut (+3.2%), Alberta (+2.8%), Saskatchewan (+1.7%) and Manitoba (+1.3%).

- On July 1, 2014, 15.7% of Canada's population was aged 65 and older. Thirty years earlier, this proportion was 10.0%.

- The highest proportions of seniors aged 65 and over among the population were in New Brunswick and Nova Scotia (18.3% in both cases) and the lowest in Nunavut (3.7%).

TABLE 3.2

GINI COEFFICIENTS FOR SELECTED OECD COUNTRIES, EARLY PERIOD AND 2004–2011*

YEAR COUNTRY	EARLY PERIOD*	2004	2005	2006	2007	2008	2009	2010	2011
Mexico	0.452	0.474	..	..	..	0.475	..	0.466	..
Turkey	0.434	0.430	..	..	0.409		0.411	0.417	0.412
United States	0.336	0.360	0.380	0.384	0.376	0.378	0.379	0.380	0.389
Portugal	N/A	0.382	0.376	0.369	0.364	0.358	0.340	0.345	0.341
United Kingdom	0.309	0.331	0.335	0.339	0.341	0.342	0.345	0.341	0.344
Japan	0.304	..	..	0.329	..		0.336	..	..
Australia	0.309	0.315	..	..	..	0.336	..	0.334	..
Greece	0.352	0.336	0.346	0.341	0.335	0.331	0.332	0.338	0.335
New Zealand	0.271	..	..	..	..	0.330	0.324	..	0.323
Canada	0.299	0.322	0.317	0.317	0.318	0.321	0.320	0.319	0.316
Italy	0.291	0.331	..	..	..	0.317	0.315	0.321	0.321
Spain	N/A	0.331	0.323	0.315	0.306	0.315	0.329	0.334	0.344
Korea	N/A	..	..	0.306	0.312	0.314	0.314	0.310	0.311
Ireland	N/A	0.323	0.323	0.315	0.303	0.295	0.312	0.313	0.302
France	0.277	0.283	0.288	0.293	0.292	0.293	0.293	0.303	0.309
Germany	0.251	0.285	0.297	0.290	0.295	0.287	0.288	0.286	0.293
Netherlands	0.272	..	0.284	0.280	0.295	0.286	0.283	0.283	..
Finland	0.209	0.267	0.266	0.268	0.270	0.266	0.260	0.265	0.265
Belgium	N/A	0.287	0.279	0.265	0.277	0.265	0.269	0.264	..
Austria	N/A	0.269	0.261	0.268	0.269	0.262	0.269	0.269	0.282
Czech Republic	0.232	0.269	0.261	0.261	0.257	0.260	0.258	0.258	0.256
Sweden	0.198	0.234	..	..	..	0.259	0.269	0.269	0.273
Norway	0.222	0.276	..	..	..	0.250	0.245	0.249	0.250
Denmark	0.221	..	0.232	0.239	0.246	0.242	0.238	0.252	0.253

* The early period varies but generally ginis were available as early as the mid-1980s.

Note: The Gini coefficient is based on the comparison of cumulative proportions of the population against cumulative proportions of income they receive, and it ranges between 0 in the case of perfect equality and 1 in the case of perfect inequality. It is calculated after taxes and transfers.

Source: Based on data from OECD Dataset: Income Distribution and Poverty, Gini Coefficients (2014). Used with permission. Retrieved from http://stats.oecd.org/.

- On July 1, 2014, people under the age of 15 accounted for 16.1% of Canada's total population.

- Population estimates show, for the first time, that there are more persons aged 55 to 64, the age when people typically leave the labour force, than those aged 15 to 24, the age when people typically enter the labour force. (Statistics Canada, 2014b)

In order to prevent labour shortages caused by inadequate labour force growth and low fertility rates, Canada has increasingly relied on immigration. Immigrants tend to have higher levels of education and skills than those of other OECD countries. Canada also appears to be doing a good job of integrating immigrants into the labour force (refer to IR Notebook 3.1 earlier in this chapter).

AN AGING POPULATION

According to HRSDC, the percentage of the population 65 and over will grow from 12.7 percent in 2001, to 14.4 percent in 2011, and to 17.9 percent in 2021 (see Figure 3.3; HRSDC, 2002).

FIGURE 3.3

PROJECTED AGE AND GENDER PROFILE OF THE LABOUR FORCE, 2021

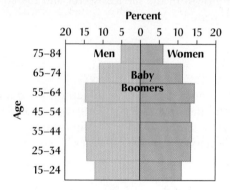

Source: Employment and Social Development Canada. (2015). "Overview of the aging workforce challenges: Diagnostic." Reproduced with the permission of the Minister of Employment and Social Development Canada, 2015. Retrieved from http://www.rhdcc-hrsdc.gc.ca/eng/lp/spila/wlb/ aw/08overview_diagnostic.shtml.

A consequence of the aging population is an increase in poverty for persons above the age of 55. Research indicates that poverty for elderly families is on the increase in Canada (Milligan, 2008); that Canadian social programs for the elderly are woefully inadequate (Audet & Makdissi, 2009; MacDonald, Andrews & Brown, 2010); and that the recession has made matters worse (OECD, 2009).

EMPLOYER CHALLENGES TO WORKFORCE AGING

The Department of Human Resources and Skills Development has produced some tangible recommendations for employers to consider. It is contemplated that policies and/or

Mature workers continue to work after 65 years of age.

collective agreements (if unionized) might permit, enable, and legitimize the following:

- elimination of age discrimination; adoption of proactive measures in the workplace, in human resources practices
- safer workplaces, healthier environments, holistic approach to wellness
- flexible work arrangements, job redesign
- appropriate training opportunities
- flexible retirement options (HRSDC, 2005)

IMPACT OF COMPOSITIONAL CHANGES ON UNIONS

MORE WOMEN

There was a substantial shift in the proportion of women in unions from just 12 percent in 1977 to 48 percent in 2004 (Statistics Canada, 2004). By 2012 slightly more female than male employees belonged to a union or were covered by a collective agreement, at 32.8 percent for women and 30.3 percent for men (ESDC, 2015). This shift reflected, in part, the significant growth of the services sector and the corresponding decline in manufacturing over the period.

OCCUPATIONAL SHIFTS

Over the past ten years, unions have made significant gains among women, youth, and workers in public administration and in the fast-growing childcare and home-support sectors. On the other hand, unions lost members in manufacturing and technical health fields (medical, dental, veterinary, and therapeutic).

CONTINGENT WORKERS

What is contingent work? Armstrong-Stassen (1998) defines five types of alternative work arrangements: part-time work, temporary or contingent work, flextime, compressed work weeks, and teleworking.

1. *Part-time.* According to Statistics Canada (1995), a person is considered to be employed part-time when the number of hours worked at the main job is usually less than thirty hours per week.
2. *Contingent.* There is no accepted definition of contingent work. It falls into two broad categories of workers: (1) those who have traditionally worked on a temporary or casual basis and (2) a smaller but growing group of professional and technical contingent workers who desire the freedom and flexibility provided by contingent work (see Koen, Mitchell & Crow, 2010).
3. *Flextime.* Flextime, as the name indicates, permits employees to start earlier or later as long as the required number of hours are worked per week

(Christensen, 1990). The advantage for employees is that they can travel outside of morning and/or afternoon rush hours and may be better able to juggle family commitments (e.g., day care, school, etc.) (see Zeytinoglu, Cooke & Mann, 2009).

4. *Compressed work weeks.* The compressed work week involves reallocating the work time by condensing the total hours in the traditional work week into fewer days (Duxbury & Haines, 1991). A typical example is the four-day, forty-hour work week (4/40), in which employees work four ten-hour days. While the longer work day can create more pressure, some employees prefer this schedule because of the increased number of days off.

5. *Teleworking.* Teleworking may involve working at home, a satellite work centre, or other nontraditional workplace, either full-time or part-time, and using telecommunications and the electronic processing of information (Gray, Hodson & Gordon, 1993; Long, 1987; Morganson, Major, Oburn, Verive & Heelan, 2010).

Unions have had less success organizing contingent workers. In 2013, for example, 24.5 percent of part-time employees were in unions, compared to 32.3 percent full-time (Statistics Canada, 2014a).

Work in Canada is undergoing significant structural change. Part-time employment (less than thirty hours per week) represented only 4 percent of the workforce in the 1950s. It has been estimated that contingent workers have grown over the past twenty years to 30 percent of the labour force. It is predicted that the "nonstandard" job of today will become the standard job of the future (Armstrong-Stassen, 1998). In the next section, we examine and define various emerging forms of work.

LABOUR AND EMPLOYMENT RELATIONS CHALLENGES

One result of these new forms of work is that the typical firm today has a significant part of its workforce made up of part-time and contingent employees. This new structure poses major challenges for labour and employment relations. Collective bargaining was designed for workers in a stable year-round employment relationship. The new work forms represent a significant change in the balance of power between labour and management in favour of management. Even if unions were able to organize the new groups, it is not clear that labour boards would find that a sufficient community of interests exists to warrant a single bargaining unit. Another difficulty, at least for the affected employees, is the inapplicability of existing law to many of the categories of employees outside of the core workforce. Most employment laws were designed to cover the core workforce and therefore may have minimum (hourly, weekly, or yearly) thresholds to qualify for benefits.

WORK–LIFE BALANCE

The economic and social changes discussed above have put substantial pressure on individuals in the workplace. Work–life balance (WLB), defined as the desire on the part of both employees and employers to achieve a balance between workplace obligations and personal responsibilities, offers a useful framework for analyzing the effects of environmental changes.

Work–Life Conflict (WLC) occurs when the cumulative demands of work and non-work roles are incompatible in some respect so that participation in one role is made more difficult by participation in the other. Sometimes described as having too much to do and too little time to do it, role overload is a term that is sometimes used as a means of examining the conditions that give rise to WLC. WLC has three components . . .

1. *role overload;*

2. *work to family interference (i.e., long work hours limit an employee's ability to participate in family roles); and*

3. *family interferes with work (i.e., family demands prevent attendance at work). (HRSDC, 2004; see also Lero, Richardson & Korabik, 2009 and Winefield, Boyd & Winefield, 2014).*

Having introduced the concept of work–life balance, we want to provide an analysis of how the changing environment of industrial relations has placed pressures on workers and managers. To do this, we construct a systems framework with three categories of the environment: economic, social, and demographic (see Figure 3.4). To some extent, this framework provides a summary of the environmental changes described above.

FIGURE 3.4

A FRAMEWORK FOR ANALYSIS OF WORK–LIFE BALANCE

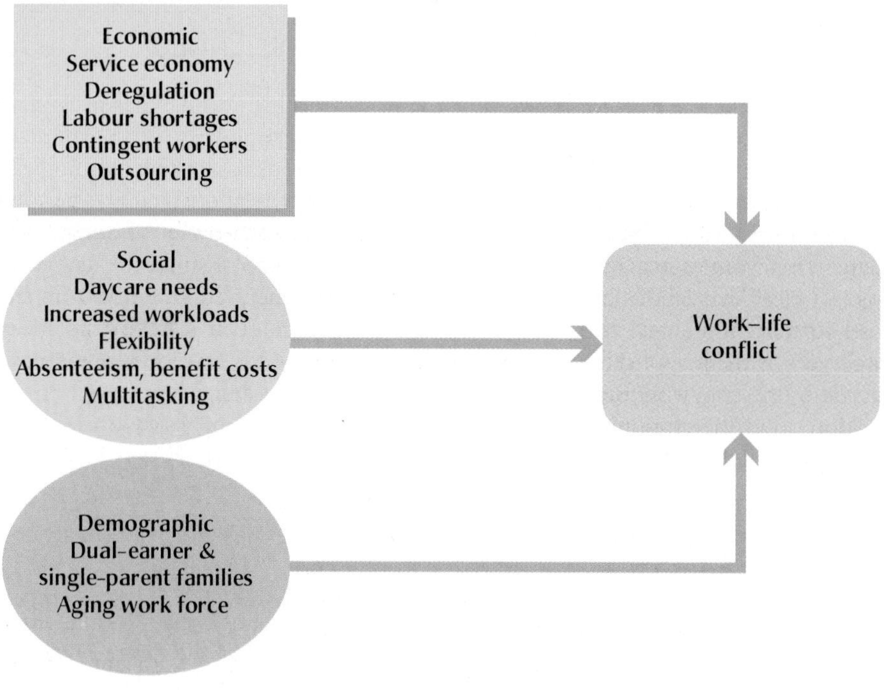

Economic
Service economy
Deregulation
Labour shortages
Contingent workers
Outsourcing

Social
Daycare needs
Increased workloads
Flexibility
Absenteeism, benefit costs
Multitasking

Demographic
Dual-earner &
single-parent families
Aging work force

Work–life conflict

ECONOMIC

As we discussed earlier, the Canadian economy has been undergoing a fundamental restructuring from a manufacturing- to a service-based economy. This is a consequence of free trade and represents a shift that is found in all industrialized countries. Contingent work has grown as part of this restructuring process. A stress point for industrial relations is the pressure on firms for more flexibility. This pressure has, in turn, eliminated plant work rules and reduced economic rewards. Recall that we have discussed above how deregulation, outsourcing, and labour shortages have affected industrial relations.

SOCIAL

Summarizing the previously identified factors, work–life balance will be affected by such issues as daycare needs; increases in workload, including multitasking; job insecurity; and employers' pressure for more flexibility. Firms are concerned about work–life issues because they affect the bottom line through increased absenteeism, benefit costs, and reduced productivity.

DEMOGRAPHIC

Recall the demographic changes of dual-earner and single-parent families, an aging work force, and baby-boomer effects. According to the HRSDC (2005), the most significant labour market changes "include greater labour market participation of women, the increase in dual-wage earner families, the rise in numbers of lone-parent families, the aging of the population, changing immigration patterns, the growth of non-standard work, and new working arrangements."

// THE POLITICAL ENVIRONMENT

In contrast to its American counterpart, the Canadian labour movement has managed to organize new members and avoid the steep decline in union density found in the United States. One of the reasons for this divergence is the more labour-friendly laws in Canada (discussed in Chapter 4). A major factor in the development of Canadian law has been the political support that labour has received from political parties. In Canada, labour has tended to be supported by the New Democratic Party (NDP) in English Canada and the Parti Québécois (PQ) in Quebec.

Two structural elements of the Canadian political system have made it possible for labour parties to translate their pro-labour policies into legislation (Bruce, 1989):

1. *Not all eggs are in one basket.* In the United States, there is only one labour law for the entire private sector. The ability to produce legislative change is lacking in the American system, where only two amendments (Taft-Hartley in 1947 and Landrum-Griffin in 1959) have been made to the *Wagner Act* since its passage in 1935. Since under the Canadian constitution labour is a provincial matter, we have eleven labour laws, including that of the federal jurisdiction (more if we

The RCMP are allowed collective bargaining rights by the Supreme Court of Canada.

include the territories). This fact alone increases the probability of legislative change. The NDP has been in power in four provinces at various times and has held the balance of power in minority governments. This leads to the second enabling element:

2. *The parliamentary system of government.* Unlike the American two-party system, in which it is nearly impossible for parties other than the governing and official opposition parties to have any power and in which minority governments are not possible, the Canadian system favours multiple parties. Moreover, minority governments are possible, meaning that even if no party wins a majority of seats, the party with the largest number may govern with the support of smaller parties. Needless to say, in any minority government, the smaller coalition partners will have a list of demands that must be met for the coalition to exist and the arrangement to survive.

The parliamentary system and constitutional fragmentation mean that labour has been able to use its political association with the NDP, and in Quebec with the PQ, to win significant legislative gains. In Saskatchewan, for example, the NDP labour association produced the first collective bargaining legislation in Canada for public employees (see Sass, 1985). Canada, unlike the United States, has a card system of certification in five out of eleven jurisdictions: federal, Manitoba, Quebec, Prince Edward Island, and New Brunswick. The card system has been associated with success in union-organizing campaigns (Johnson, 2002).

According to Taras (1997), there have been three important social and historical experiences that have caused Canada to reject U.S. opposition to collective bargaining:

- The 1982 *Canadian Charter* protected individual rights but facilitated collective bargaining.

- Even with similar legislation in the United States, American firms in Canada are more restricted in anti-union activities.
- Canada has rejected the U.S. right-to-work approach that prevents unions from forcing nonmembers to join or pay dues despite enjoying the benefits of unionization.

GLOBALIZATION AND POLITICS

The pressure globalization puts on governments to conform to international policy norms means there is less policy space for provincial governments to experiment with reforms. In fact, some theories predict that trade liberalization policies will force a convergence of labour policies. If governments stray too far from international policy norms, they will lose investment (both foreign and domestic), with negative consequences for economic growth.

There is evidence in support of this convergence theory. As more conservative governments took power in such provinces as Saskatchewan, Ontario, and British Columbia, Canadian labour law drifted toward the U.S. model. Saskatchewan, Ontario, and British Columbia, for example, have scrapped the card system of certification in favour of the U.S. *Wagner Act* mandatory voting system.

Whatever the effect of globalization, there is also evidence that the election of an NDP provincial government has not been a guarantee of progressive change in labour legislation. For example, amending labour law proved to be controversial in a case involving the NDP government in Manitoba.

// SUMMARY

This chapter examined the context or environment within which industrial relations take place. We have seen how the economic, social, and political environments affect industrial relations. Also discussed were some of the developments in these environments, brought about by such factors as changing demographics, the forces of globalization and free trade, and labour force composition. There is another important part of the industrial relations context to be studied: the legal environment in Canada. It is to this task that we turn next.

KEY TERMS

deregulation 62
disposable income 75
elasticity of supply (demand) 64
hiring hall 70
macroeconomic policy 62
monopsony 68
North American Free Trade Agreement (NAFTA) 62
privatization 62

WEBLINKS

Campaign 2000's 2009 Report Card on Child and Family Poverty in Canada: 1989–2009:
http://www.campaign2000.ca/reportCards/national/2009EnglishC2000NationalReportCard.pdf

The changing face of Canadian workplaces:
http://www.labour.gc.ca/eng/standards_equity/index.shtml

Research on work–life balance:
http://www.esdc.gc.ca/eng/seniors/reports/cec.shtml

DISCUSSION QUESTIONS

1. Describe two ways in which labour markets have been liberalized in Canada in the past twenty years.
2. What are Marshall's four conditions? How do they affect labour power?
3. What are the barriers to labour supply? Provide examples.
4. Explain how a wage increase affects leisure in terms of the income and substitution effects.
5. What do economists mean by the term *monopsony*? Give two examples of occupations that may be in monopsonistic markets.
6. What positive and negative effects may craft unions have on productivity?
7. According to the Gallup Organization, what evidence has there been of a long-term decline in support for unions? Have union disapproval numbers increased?
8. Does North American polling data show widespread worker dissatisfaction with their jobs?
9. When measured using Gini coefficients, how does Canadian income inequality compare to those of other industrialized countries?
10. What is contingent work? Define five types.
11. What is meant by the term work–life balance? Give two examples of factors that may have upset this balance in the past five years.
12. How have the parliamentary system and constitutional fragmentation helped Canadian unions organize new members compared to their U.S. counterparts?

USING THE INTERNET

1. Using the Internet or another source, find an example of the substitution effect as it affects either the elasticity of demand or the supply of labour.
2. Using the Internet or another source, find an example of a highly labour-intensive organization and an example of a highly capital-intensive organization.

EXERCISES

1. Using Marshall's conditions, analyze the effect on union power of the North American Free Trade Agreement (NAFTA) among Canada, Mexico, and the United States.

2. How does inequality in Canada compare with that of other industrialized countries? How has this changed over time?

3. Describe the factors that account for changes in the balance between work and life in Canada.

CASE	OUTSOURCING AND CANADA—A GOOD PLACE TO OUTSOURCE TO!

"Offshore outsourcing" is the practice of hiring an external organization to perform business functions in another country. This can be contrasted with "offshoring," in which the functions are typically performed by a foreign division or subsidiary of the parent company.

"Nearshore outsourcing" is a form of outsourcing in which functions are relocated to cheaper yet geographically close locations. In the case of the United States, the most obvious nearshore jurisdictions are Canada and Mexico.

CANADA: A UNIQUE OUTSOURCING JURISDICTION

Canada is uniquely situated in the world of offshore outsourcing of Information Technology and Business Process functions. It is a significant importer and exporter of outsourcing activities, is a primary nearshore outsourcing destination for U.S. business, and is emerging as a broker jurisdiction in global outsourcing arrangements.

The statistics are impressive:

- According to the McKinsey Global Institute, in 2002, Canada generated US$3.7 billion in offshore BTO revenue behind only Ireland (US$8.3 billion) and India (US$7.7 billion).[1]

- Canada is the 8th most attractive offshore location overall and places 2nd of all jurisdictions when it comes to quality of people skills and availability of skilled workers (behind India), and quality of business environment (behind Singapore).[2]

- Canada ranks among the top five places in the world for communications providers to offshore call centre and IT operations.[3]

- Canada is a main beneficiary of outsourcing from the United States, which represents approximately 70% of the total global outsourcing market.[4]

- Outsourcing within North America is projected to grow at an average of 10–15% annually.[5]

FOOTNOTES

1. McKinsey Global Institute, "Offshoring: Is it a win-win game?," August 2003. See http://www. mckinsey.com/knowledge/mgi/rp/offshoring/perspective.

2. A. T. Kearney, "Making offshore decisions: 2004 offshore location attractiveness index," 2004. See http://www.atkearney.com/shared_res/pdf/Making_Offshore_S.pdf.

3. Deloitte, "Making the off-shore call: The road map for communication operators," 2004. See http://www.deloitte.com/dtt/cda/doc/content/ca_tmt_offshoreoutlook.pdf.

4. McKinsey Global Institute.

5. PWC, "A fine balance: The impact of offshore IT services on Canada's IT landscape," 2004. See http://www.pwc.com/ca/afinebalance.

Source: Theodore Ling. "Outsourcing to Canada: Legal and tax considerations." Technology Executives Club website. Used with permission of the author. Retrieved from http://www.technologyexecutivesclub .com/Articles/outsourcing/artGlobalOutsourcing.php.

QUESTIONS AND ASSIGNMENTS

1. Using the information provided in this article, ask students to write a short essay on the scope, limitations (if any), and benefits of outsourcing.

2. Using the Internet, find a current example of outsourcing in your province, and ask students to do a cost-benefit analysis of the example.

3. Divide the class into pro- and con-outsourcing. Let each side select a spokesperson (or spokespersons); provide time for preparation, and supervise a debate.

// ENDNOTE

1. For a more in-depth study of the labour market see Drost and Hird (2014).

// REFERENCES

1. Allen, S. G. (1984). Unionized construction workers are more productive. *The Quarterly Journal of Economics, 99*(2), pp. 251–275.

2. Armstrong-Stassen, M. (1998). Alternative work arrangements: Meeting the challenges. *Canadian Psychology, 39*(1/2).

3. Ashenfelter, O. C., Farber, H., & Ransom, M. (2010). Labor market monopsony. *Journal of Labor Economics, 28*(2), pp. 203–210.

4. Audet, M., & Makdissi, P. (2009). Assessing the impact of historical changes in social protection on poverty in Canada. *Applied Economic Letters, 16*, pp. 523–526.

5. Banerjee, R., & Phan, M. (2014). Licensing requirements and occupational mobility among highly skilled new immigrants in Canada. *Relations Industrielles, 69*(2), pp. 290–315.

6. Barling, J., Kelloway, E. K., & Bremermann, E. H. (1991). Preemployment predictors of union attitudes: The role of family socialization and work beliefs. *Journal of Applied Psychology, 76*(5), pp. 725–31.

7. Beach, C. M., Chaykowski, R. P., & Slotsve, G. A. (1997). Inequality and polarization of male earnings in the United States, 1968–1990. *North American Journal of Economics and Finance, 8*(2), pp. 135–l51.

8. Berik, G., & Bilginsoy, C. (2000). Do unions help or hinder women in training? Apprenticeship programs in the United States. *Industrial Relations, 39*(4), pp. 600–625.

9. Bruce, P. G. (1989). Political parties and labour legislation in Canada and the U.S. *Industrial Relations, 28*, pp. 115–141.

10. Byrne, J., Clarke, L., & Van Der Meer, M. (2005). Gender and ethnic minority exclusion from skilled occupations in construction: A Western European comparison. *Construction Management and Economics, 23*(10), pp. 1025–34.

11. Chaykowski, R. P., & Slotsve, G. A. (1996). A distributional analysis of changes in earnings inequality among unionized and nonunionized male workers in the United States: 1982–1990. *The Canadian Journal of Economics, 29*(1), pp. 109–128.

12. Chevan, A., & Stokes, R. (2000). Growth in family income inequality, 1970–1990: Industrial restructuring and demographic change. *Demography, 37*(3), pp. 365–381.

13. Christensen, K. (1990). Here we go into the "high-flex" era. *Across the Board,* July–August, pp. 22–23.

14. Craft, J. A. (1998). The community as a source of union power. *Journal of Labor Research, 11*(2), pp. 145–160.

15. Currie, J., Farsi, M., & Macleod, W. B. (2005). Cut to the bone? Hospital takeovers and nurse employment contracts. *Industrial and Labor Relations Review, 58*(3), pp. 471–493.

16. Devillanova, C., Di Maio, M., & Vertova, P. (2010). Labour mobility and the redistributive effects of trade integration. *Journal of Economics, 100*(2), pp. 95–116.

17. Drost, H., & Hird, R. (2014). *Introduction to the Canadian labour market* (4th Canadian edition). Toronto: Thomson Nelson.

18. Dustmann, C., & Shonberg, U. (2009). Training and union wages. *The Review of Economics and Statistics, 91*(2), pp. 363–376.

19. Duxbury, L., & Haines, G. (1991). Predicting alternative work arrangements from salient attitudes: A study of decision makers in the public sector. *Journal of Business Research, 23* (August), pp. 83–97.

20. Employment and Social Development Canada (ESDC). (2015). Indicators of well-being in Canada: Work–unionization rates. http://www4.hrsdc .gc.ca/.3ndic.1t.4r@-eng.jsp?iid=17

21. Finnie, R. (2004). Who moves? A logit model analysis of inter-provincial migration in Canada. *Applied Economics, 36*(16), pp. 1759–1779.

22. Foot, D. K., & Soffman, D. (1996). *Boom, bust, and echo: How to profit from the coming demographic shift.* Toronto: Macfarlane Walter & Ross.

23. Foot, D. K., & Venne, R. A. (1990). Population, pyramids and promotional prospects. *Canadian Public Policy, 16*(4), pp. 387–399.

24. Government of Canada. (2011). Canada's Economic Action Plan comprises five main elements. Canada's Economic Action Plan website, retrieved 22 April 2011 from http://www.actionplan.gc.ca/eng/feature.asp?pageId=90. Reproduced with the permission of the Minister of Public Works and Government Services Canada, 2011.

25. Gray, M., Hodson, N., & Gordon, G. (1993). *Teleworking explained.* New York: John Wiley & Sons.

26. Gunderson, M., & Riddell, W. C. (1988). *Labour economics* (2nd edition). Toronto: McGraw-Hill, p. 616.

27. Gunderson, M., & Verma, A. (1992). Canadian labour policies and global competition. *The Canadian Business Law Journal, 20*(1), pp. 63–90.

28. Hayden, A. (2003). International work-time trends: The emerging gap in hours. *Just Labour, 2* (Spring), pp. 23–35.

29. Hsing, Y. (2005). Economic growth and income inequality: The case of the U.S. *International Journal of Social Economics, 32*(7), pp. 639–648.

30. Human Resources and Skills Development Canada (HRSDC). (2002). Summary: Adaptive measures accommodating an aging workforce–recommendations. Published in Overview of the Aging Workforce Challenges. http://www.rhdcc-hrsdc.gc.ca/eng/lp/spila/wlb/aw/10overview_recommendations.shtml#5. Human Resources and Skills Development Canada, 2002. Reproduced with the permission of the Minister of Public Works and Government Services Canada, 2011.

31. Human Resources and Skills Development Canada (HRSDC). (2004). The changing face of Canadian work-places. Retrieved 15 January 2011 from http://www.rhdcc-hrsdc.gc.ca/eng/labour/employment_standards/fls/resources/resource01.shtml. Human Resources and Skills Development Canada. Reproduced with the permission of the Minister of Public Works and Government Services Canada, 2011.

32. Human Resources and Skills Development Canada (HRSDC). (2005). Overview of the aging workforce challenges: Recommendations. Retrieved 22 April 2011 from http://www.rhdcc-hrsdc.gc.ca/eng/lp/spila/wlb/aw/10overview_recommendations.shtml#50. Reproduced with the permission of the Minister of Public Works and Government Services Canada, 2011.

33. Institut économique de Montréal (IEDM). (2010, 19 March). Léger Marketing poll on negotiations with public sector unions. Retrieved 22 April 2011 from http://www.iedm.org/3411-legermarketing-poll-on-negotiations-with-public-sector-unions-only-10-of-quebecers-support-theunion-demands

34. Johnson, S. (2002). Mandatory votes or automatic certification: How the choice of union recognition procedure affects certification success. *The Economic Journal, 112*, pp. 334–361.

35. Kim, C. H., & Sakamoto, A. (2010). Assessing the consequences of declining unionization and public-sector employment: A density-function decomposition of rising inequality from 1983–2005. *Work and Occupations, 37*(2), pp. 119–136.

36. Koen, C., Mitchell, M., & Crow, S. (2010). Your workers may be contingent but your liability for them is certain: Part III: Other employment issues. *The Health Care Manager, 29*(3), pp. 213–222.

37. Lero, D., Richardson, J., & Korabik, K. (2009). Cost–benefit review of work–life practices. Report for the Canadian Association of Administrators of Labour Legislation. 115 pp.

38. Lipset, S. M., Meltz, N. M., Gomez, R., & Katchanovski, I. (2004). *The paradox of American unionism: Why Americans like unions more than Canadians do but join much less.* Ithaca, NY: ILR Press.

39. Long, R. J. (1987). *New office information technology: Human and managerial implications.* London: Croom Helm.

40. Luizer, J., & Thornton, R. (1986). Concentration in the labor market for public school teachers. *Industrial and Labor Relations Review, 39*(4), pp. 573–85.

41. MacDonald, B.-J., Andrews, D., & Brown, R. (2010). The Canadian elder standard: Pricing the cost of basic needs for the Canadian elderly. *Canadian Journal on Aging, 29*(1), pp. 39–56.

42. Marshall, A. (1920). *Principles of economics* (8th edition). London: Macmillan and Co., Ltd.

43. Milligan, K. (2008). The evolution of elderly poverty in Canada. *Canadian Public Policy, 34*, Supplement, pp. 79–94.

44. Morganson, V., Major, D., Oburn, K., Verive, J., & Heelan, M. (2010). Comparing telework locations and traditional work arrangements; Differences in work–life balance support, job satisfaction, and inclusion. *Journal of Managerial Psychology, 25*(6), pp. 578–595.

45. Neville, J., & Kriesler, P. (2008). Minimum wages, unions, the economy and society. *The Economic and Labour Relations Review, 19*(1), pp. 25–38.

46. Ontario, Ministry of Finance. 2014. Long-term report on the economy, part II, population and labour force trends and projections, pp. 7–30. Retrieved 21 September 2014 from http://www.fin.gov.on.ca/en/economy/ltr/2014/ch1.html

47. Organisation for Economic Co-operation and Development. (2001). *Employment outlook.* Paris: OECD.

48. Organisation for Economic Co-operation and Development. (2009). Economy: Thoughts on the crisis, tipping back the balance. *OECD Observer, 270/271* (December 2008–January 2009).

49. Organisation for Economic Co-operation and Development. (2014). *OECD employment outlook 2014: How does Canada compare?* http://www.oecd.org/canada/EMO-CAN-EN.pdf

50. Oxfam. (2014, October 29). Even it up: Time to end extreme inequality? Retrieved 1 November 2014 from http://www.oxfam.ca/sites/default/files/file_attachments/even-it-up-end-extreme-inequality-291014-summ-en.pdf

51. Picketty, T. (2014). *Capital in the twenty-first century*. Harvard University Press.

52. Sass, R. (1985). *Union Amendment Act*, 1983: The public battle. *Relations Industrielles, 40*(3), pp. 591–623.

53. Statistics Canada. (1995). *Labour force annual averages 1995*. Ottawa: Statistics Canada.

54. Statistics Canada. (2004). *Perspectives on labour and income*. Ottawa: Statistics Canada.

55. Statistics Canada. (2014a). Catalogue no. 71-001-X Labour Force Information September 14 to 20, 2014.

56. Statistics Canada. (2014b). Highlight. http://www.statcan.gc.ca/pub/91 -215-x/2014000/aftertoc-aprestdm1-eng.htm

57. Taras, D. G. (1997). Collective bargaining regulation in Canada and the United States: Divergent cultures, divergent outcomes. In B. Kaufman (Ed.), *Government regulation of the employment relationship* (pp. 295–341). Madison, WI: Industrial Relations Research Association.

58. Weber, M. (1922; 1978 ed.). *Economy and society: An outline of interpretive sociology*. Berkeley & Los Angeles: UCLA Press.

59. Weeden, K. A. (2002). Why do some occupations pay more than others? Social closure and earnings in the United States. *The American Journal of Sociology, 108*(1), pp. 55–101.

60. Winefield, H., Boyd, C., & Winefield, A. (2014, Nov–Dec). Work–family conflict and well-being in university employees. *Journal of Psychology*, pp. 683–697.

61. Zeytinoglu, I. U., Cooke, G. B., & Mann, S. L. (2009). Flexibility: Whose choice is it anyway? *Relations Industrielles, 64*(4), pp. 555–574.

THE LEGAL ENVIRONMENT

LEARNING OBJECTIVES

BY THE END OF THIS CHAPTER, YOU WILL BE ABLE TO DISCUSS

- the basic elements of the Canadian model of union recognition and collective bargaining;
- collective agreement administration;
- the role of the *Charter* in industrial relations;
- the impact of international law on labour relations policy; and
- the impact of employment law on employee rights and conditions.

A breakthrough collective agreement was reached September 21 between UFCW [United Food and Commercial Workers] Canada and Floralia Growers of Abbotsford, B.C.

The new UFCW Canada Local 1518 contract provides wage improvements, but is particularly noteworthy for the protections it establishes for the rights of seasonal migrant agriculture workers to return to Canada under the federal government's Seasonal Agricultural Workers Program (SAWP).

"We have had a lot interest from migrant farm workers in joining the union," said Ivan Limpright, President of UFCW Canada Local 1518, "and this contract is a huge step forward in providing the kinds of basic protections and recall rights that migrant farm workers in Canada deserve."

"These are among the most vulnerable workers in Canada, because too often when workers would dare complain, let alone join a union, the farm employers would make sure they didn't call those workers back for the next season's work, or just send them straight back to their home country," said Limpright.

"This contract establishes a real measure of justice and dignity for the Floralia workers."

The new contract establishes recall rights for migrant agriculture workers, and the union and employer have agreed to a process for recalling SAWP workers that will enhance workers' opportunities to return year after year.

In addition, when the growing season slows down and a smaller workforce is needed, a process is now established whereby those volunteering to return home would be the first to go, and if necessary, other workers would then return to their home based on seniority.

"Previously, the workers would be 'repatriated', as the employers like to call it, and strictly at the employer's whim," said Limpright. "For example, we have had cases where there was a slowdown in the growing season and a worker volunteered to go home because his wife was pregnant or there was another family emergency, but the employer would refuse and send someone else home instead. Now, under this contract, the workers at least have some control over their own fates, and this is a huge and important breakthrough."

The migrant agriculture workers at Floralia are from Mexico, and make up approximately 90 percent of the Floralia workforce.

In addition to recall rights, the crucial topic of overtime was also addressed in the new contract. It had been apparent that when workers developed an interest in joining UFCW, those workers were punished by having their overtime eliminated or minimized.

The new contract has a process by which overtime will be balanced among all workers, and monitored so that it is not awarded by favouritism nor used as a form of punishment against workers interested in the union…

Source: UFCW Canada. *Historic victory for migrant farm workers.* Reprinted with permission. Retrieved from http://www.ufcw.ca/index.php?option=com_content&view=article&id=661&catid=5&Itemid=99&lang=en.

The preceding vignette highlights why understanding the regulatory framework is so important in industrial relations. Migrant workers have tended to be excluded from Canadian collective bargaining laws. In this chapter, we will uncover the origins of the current industrial relations legislation in Canada; examine the principles upon which the law is based; canvass the current state of employment law in Canada; and identify legislative trends. Since the origin of Canadian labour law can be traced to the American *Wagner Act* of 1935, we will employ a comparative approach to illuminate the key aspects of labour legislation.

// WAGNER ACT HISTORY

Prior to the passage of the *Wagner Act* in the United States, unions were seldom recognized without a violent power struggle between management and labour. In Canada, while

Migrant workers from Mexico achieved a collective agreement after joining the UFCW.

Photos.com/Thinkstock/Getty Images

unions had achieved legal recognition in the *Trade Union Act* of 1872, they encountered the same hostile employers in the Canadian context. Unions in both countries struggled to attain recognition or any degree of democracy in the workplace (Panitch & Swartz, 1993). The state tried to contain labour conflict in the 1907 *Industrial Dispute Investigations Act* (IDIA) in Canada but again failed to provide an orderly mechanism for union recognition. In the second decade of the twentieth century, a number of broader social and economic factors would contribute to the decline of organized craft labour in both countries: the influence of **scientific management** and mass production; the increasing use of company unions as a method of union substitution; and a generally hostile legal environment. It would take a new model of unionism–industrial unionism–for workers in Canada and the United States to achieve industrial democracy.

The Great Depression of the early 1930s gave rise to a new wave of unionism. As the paternalist model of company unions declined and unemployment surged, workers increasingly distrusted companies to provide basic rights and benefits. Industrial unions, who sought to organize all workers in an industry regardless of skill or occupational status, emerged as a more active and socially oriented movement to protect workers. In the United States, the cause of industrial unionism was advanced by the 1932 election of President Franklin D. Roosevelt. A major feature of Roosevelt's New Deal was the 1935 *National Labor Relations (Wagner) Act*, which protected–under federal law–the right to organize unions for the purpose of collective bargaining and the right to strike. While the *Wagner Act* model might have been enacted principally to reduce conflict and aid in the rebuilding of the American economy, it had the effect of legitimizing industrial unionization. As such, union density increased from 12.9 percent in 1930 to 22.5 percent in 1940 (Troy & Sheflin, 1985).

> **scientific management**
> the application of engineering principles to define specific tasks in the production process thereby removing the autonomy of skilled craft workers (associated with Frederick Taylor)

THE *SNIDER* CASE

The case of *Toronto Electric Power Commissioners v. Snider et al.* grew out of a labour dispute between the commission and its employees in 1923. The established protocol of the day provided that a conciliation board would be appointed under the *Industrial Dispute Investigations Act*. This federal statute called for the conciliation board to analyze the circumstances of the dispute and the probable impact on the public before a strike could be taken. However, in this case, Toronto Electric Power refused to acknowledge the conciliation board, arguing that the federal statute did not apply to a labour dispute in Toronto. This line of argument derived from the *British North America (BNA) Act*, the statute that effectively served as Canada's constitution until 1982. In the *BNA Act*, civil and property matters were the responsibility of the provinces. Thus, the underlying issue was whether labour relations legislation would be a provincial or federal responsibility.

The **Snider case** went to the British Privy Council, the highest court in Canada at that time. The Privy Council found that the federal government had exceeded its jurisdiction in applying the 1907 IDIA to a province and that in the absence of a national emergency, the provincial responsibility over civil matters must be respected. As a result of this decision, the distinctive Canadian system of shared jurisdiction was given legal authority. The federal government was given responsibility over such interprovincial industries as communication and transportation, while the provinces were given responsibility for all other areas of commerce. But not every province had labour legislation in 1925. The next twenty years would see each province and the federal government design separate labour policies to govern industrial relations within their jurisdiction.

> **Snider case**
> a landmark court case in 1925 that determined that labour matters fell under the purview of the provinces under the *British North America Act*

CANADA'S P.C. 1003

It would be nine years before Canada passed its own version of the *Wagner Act* model in 1944. The outbreak of World War II in 1939 and employer resistance delayed the introduction of labour legislation. The dissatisfaction of Canadian workers with their employment conditions resulted in increased conflict—especially in the all-important steel industry. It was this unrest that gave rise to a new political movement. When the strength of the Canadian labour movement appeared to threaten the survival of the Liberal Party in 1944, Prime Minister William Lyon Mackenzie King enacted **P.C. 1003**. This legislation was almost a copy of the American *Wagner Act* except that P.C. 1003 was not intended to be a permanent measure. Only with sustained pressure from organized labour was the 1948 *Industrial Relations and Dispute Investigation Act* (IRDIA) introduced to replace P.C. 1003 at the federal level. Soon thereafter, because of the *Snider* case and the provincial jurisdiction over labour policy (discussed next), each province either extended the IRDIA or enacted a comparable act of its own. By 1948, union density had grown to 30 percent in Canada from 16 percent in 1940 (Lipset & Meltz, 2004). Thus, the *Wagner Act* model would prove to be the underlying framework for the postwar system of industrial relations, which saw increasing unionization and economic growth in both Canada and the United States.

According to the *Constitution Act* and its interpretations, the Parliament of Canada has jurisdiction for labour relations in a number of key industries. For the purposes of the *Canada Labour Code*, Part I, these include

- broadcasting (radio and television);
- chartered banks;
- postal service;
- airports and air transportation;
- shipping and navigation (including loading and unloading of vessels);
- interprovincial or international transportation by road, railway, ferry, or pipeline;
- telecommunications; and
- industries declared to be for the general advantage of Canada, such as grain handling and uranium mining and processing.

Thus, each province and territory has its own version of the *Wagner Act* model. These private-sector labour laws can be found by following the links to each provincial and territorial Labour Ministry as provided by the Government of Canada, Labour Program (see www.labour.gc.ca/eng/resources/info/publications/collective_bargaining/collective_bargaining.shtml).

> **P.C. 1003**
> the Canadian government imported the *Wagner Act* model in 1944; under the *War Measures Act*, it was introduced by the Privy Council as P.C. 1003

// UNION RECOGNITION UNDER THE *WAGNER ACT* MODEL

Recall that the *Wagner Act* was passed in a period of intense conflict between labour and management. The conflict, however, was not restricted to labour and management. Because the employees of a given firm could belong to more than one union, interunion conflict over representation rights was not uncommon.

To deal with this conflict, the *Wagner Act* provided the following:

1. Recognition strikes and lockouts were declared illegal.
2. As a substitute for industrial conflict over union recognition, labour boards were established to provide a process where employees could obtain union recognition by a free expression of support.
3. The union that obtained recognition was granted exclusive jurisdiction to represent all employees in a given bargaining unit. This is known as the **exclusivity principle**.

LABOUR BOARDS

Neutral labour relations boards serve a vital function in the North American model of industrial relations. Their purpose is to provide an alternative to the courts that is faster, cheaper, and has greater expertise in matter pertaining to industrial relations. Their structure is **tripartite**, where cases are heard by a panel consisting of union- and management-appointed representatives and a neutral chairperson. Quebec employs a labour court model but the functions of the board are very similar to those in the rest of Canada. In broad terms, the main function of a labour board is to enforce the *Labour Relations Act*. Boards may hear several kinds of cases:

1. certification and decertification;
2. unfair labour practices; and
3. declarations of illegal strikes or lockouts.

Certification is the process of gaining recognition under the appropriate labour act. A key element that defines the Canadian version of the *Wagner Act* model is the possibility of automatic certification—that is, certification based on the number of signed cards without a formal vote. A union can obtain certification without a vote under private-sector law in the federal sector and in those of Manitoba, New Brunswick, Prince Edward Island, and Quebec. In B.C. a vote is required when 45 percent of the bargaining unit have signed cards in the union. However, in Manitoba only 40 percent is required to obtain a vote and certification without a vote (i.e., automatic) occurs if 65 percent or more of the bargaining unit have signed cards in the union. In several provinces, however, the board may certify without a vote if a firm has been found guilty of an unfair labour practice and if the true wishes of the employees would likely not be expressed through a vote.

Two important elements of the recognition process require explanation: the **bargaining unit** and **unfair labour practices**.

BARGAINING UNIT

Unless the parties agree, the labour board will be called upon to make a critical determination of which employees are eligible to be covered by the union. This is an important question, because the percentage of employees needed by the union to win a vote or get an automatic certification is expressed as a proportion of the defined bargaining unit. Labour boards typically apply several criteria to decide which employees are eligible to be included in the bargaining unit.

> **exclusivity principle**
> the idea that a union is granted the sole right to represent all employees in the defined bargaining unit

> **tripartite**
> a tripartite board has three stakeholders: management, labour, and government

> **certification**
> recognition of a union by a labour board after completion of the procedures under the labour act

> **bargaining unit**
> the group of employees in an organization that are eligible to be represented by a union

MANAGEMENT EMPLOYEES Management employees are excluded from union representation. They are defined as those employees who have supervisory responsibility over bargaining-unit employees, including the ability to effectively recommend the hiring, firing, or discipline of employees. Management employees may also be defined as those having confidential information with respect to labour relations.

The rationales for excluding managers are

1. access to confidential labour relations information might compromise management's position in bargaining; and
2. the union would be in a conflict of interest if a union member was disciplined by another union member.

On the other hand, persons are not excluded simply because they have a job title that may indicate management responsibilities or if they have access to confidential information not related to labour relations. The labour board will examine the actual duties of the job in question.

COMMUNITY OF INTERESTS The fundamental criterion to form a bargaining unit is that a community of interests should exist among employees. The board must settle disputes, for example, over the inclusion of part-time employees into a unit of full-timers or to combine office and plant employees. Too many bargaining units in a company may lead to labour instability and threaten labour peace. Also, if bargaining units are too small, they may not be viable entities—that is, they may lack the bargaining power to effectively represent their members.

WISHES OF EMPLOYEES Boards will take into account the desires of employees to be separate from or part of a defined group. For example, stationary engineers have a history of craft unionism and organize on the basis of a single occupational unit. The result has been that in hospital settings, stationary engineers responsible for a steam plant have been allowed by labour boards to have their own bargaining units. The history of the craft or profession also matters in these cases.

EMPLOYER STRUCTURE The labour board must consider the employer's structure in determining appropriate bargaining units for collective bargaining. Suppose, for example, a firm has two plants in a city producing similar products with the same management, pay structure, and array of jobs. A board might determine that the employees of these two plants constitute a single bargaining unit for purposes of collective bargaining. The union would then have to organize both plants if it wished to represent the employees. The selection of a bargaining unit can be a major source of conflict between management and labour.

UNFAIR LABOUR PRACTICES

Unfair labour practices are alleged violations of the *Labour Relations Act* by employers, unions, or employees. To ensure that workers are free to choose a union, companies and unions are prevented from using intimidation or coercion. Other prohibited actions include the calling or counselling of illegal strikes or lockouts and the failure or refusal to bargain collectively (see IR Notebook 4.1). Criticism of the current Canadian system of processing unfair labour practices has recently surfaced in the academic literature.

unfair labour practice
an alleged violation of
the labour relations act

Scholars argue that employer penalties are insufficient (Slinn, 2008) and forced speeches by management (captive-audience meetings) may violate the *Canadian Charter of Rights and Freedoms* (Doorey, 2008).

To redress these violations, labour board remedies include cease-and-desist orders for coercion or intimidation; reinstatements if fired for union activities; and orders to resume bargaining if a party refuses to bargain in good faith.

IR NOTEBOOK   4.1

UNFAIR LABOUR PRACTICES UNDER THE *P.E.I. LABOUR ACT*

Employer Unfair Labour Practices

10. (1) No employer, employers' organization or an agent or any other person acting on behalf of an employer or employers' organization shall

(a) interfere with, restrain or coerce an employee in the exercise of any right conferred by this Act;

(b) participate or interfere with the formation, selection or administration of a trade union or other labour organization or the representation of employees by a trade union or other labour organization; or contribute financial or other support to such trade union or labour organization;

(c) suspend, transfer, refuse to transfer, lay-off, discharge, or change the status of an employee or alter any term or condition of employment, or use coercion, intimidation, threats or undue influence, or otherwise discriminate against any employee in regard to employment or any term or condition of employment, because the employee is a member or officer of a trade union or has applied for membership in a trade union;

(d) refuse to employ any person because such person is a member or officer of a trade union or has applied for membership in a trade union or require as a condition of employment that any person shall abstain from joining or assisting or being active in any trade union or from exercising any right provided by this Part;

(e) fail or refuse to bargain collectively in accordance with this Act;

(f) call, authorize, counsel, procure, support, encourage or engage in a lockout except as permitted by section 41.

Prohibitions re Employees, Trade Unions Etc.

(2) No employee, trade union or person acting on behalf of a trade union shall

(a) interfere with the formation, selection or administration of an employers' organization or the representation of employers by an employers' organization, or by intimidation or any other kind of threat or action, seek to compel an employer to refrain from becoming or to cease to be a member or officer or representative of an employers' organization;

(b) except with the consent of the employer, attempt at the employers' place of employment during working hours to persuade an employee of the employer to join a trade union;

(c) fail or refuse to bargain collectively in accordance with this Act;

(d) call, authorize, counsel, procure, support, encourage or engage in a strike except as permitted by section 41;

(e) use coercion or intimidation of any kind with a view to encouraging or discouraging membership in or activity in of for a trade union or labour organization.

Source: Government of Prince Edward Island. *P.E.I. Labour Act, Unfair Labour Practices*, p. 10. Used with permission. Retrieved from http://www.gov.pe.ca/ law/statutes.

DUTY OF FAIR REPRESENTATION

duty of fair representation
a legal obligation on the union's part to represent all employees equally and in a non-discriminatory manner

Finally, a union has a **duty of fair representation**. Under this duty, a union must not discriminate or act in an arbitrary manner in the representation of all employees. An example of a breach of this duty might be a union that fails to support a grievance by an employee because she is in a faction of the union that is in opposition to the current union leadership. McQuarrie (2010) examined 138 duty-of-fair-representation cases before the British Columbia Labour Relations Board over the period 2000–2006. She found that complaints against the union were upheld in only eight of the cases, or 5.8 percent.

// COLLECTIVE BARGAINING

GOOD FAITH BARGAINING

good faith bargaining
an obligation on union and management to make a serious attempt to reach a settlement

Labour laws in North America all require the parties to bargain in good faith. The idea of **good faith bargaining** is that union and management must make a serious attempt to negotiate a collective agreement. The concept of good faith bargaining is not easy to define, because it has been rarely tested, and boards have displayed a reluctance to interfere in private negotiations between the parties. One of the reasons that good faith bargaining rarely goes before labour boards is that between 75 and 90 percent of all cases are settled by mediation (Davenport, 2003). In general, unless there is a clear demonstration of antiunion bargaining behaviour, labour boards will not interfere. Boards will not hear bad faith bargaining charges based on the reasonableness of offers and counteroffers. An exception might be a first agreement, in which a firm deliberately makes offers that it knows the union will not or cannot accept.

DISPUTE RESOLUTION

voluntarism
the notion that collective bargaining is a private matter between the parties and that government intervention should be kept to a minimum

mediation
a dispute-resolution process in which a neutral third party acts as a facilitator

conciliation
see mediation

Canadian labour laws have always differed from their *Wagner Act* parent in several respects. Generally, the *Wagner Act* is crafted on the principle of **voluntarism**, which involves minimal government intervention in collective bargaining. Under the *Wagner Act*, for example, **mediation** of disputes is used only if either party requests it. Canadian laws generally provide for greater government intervention especially on the question of industrial conflict. Thus, distinguishing features of Canadian labour law include the ban on strikes during the term of a collective agreement (Haiven, 1990) and mandatory government **conciliation**, or mediation, in the collective bargaining process before a legal strike can take place.

The latter feature has been a controversial intrusion in the negotiation process. Described as a cooling-off period before a strike, unions complain that it gives management time to prepare for a strike by stockpiling or building up inventories and simply delays serious bargaining. Policymakers, on the other hand, argue that conciliation gives third parties a chance to avoid costly strikes. They also claim that Canada's greater dependence on the exports of raw materials and the need for stability of supply requires a stronger government role in dispute resolution to avoid strikes. We will return to this topic in Chapter 9.

In several Canadian jurisdictions—federal, Alberta, British Columbia, Manitoba, Quebec, and Saskatchewan—the requirement to complete the conciliation/mediation procedure before a strike has been removed, but the procedure is still required in New Brunswick, Newfoundland and Labrador, Nova Scotia, Quebec, Ontario, and Prince

Edward Island. Despite this move toward *Wagner Act* voluntarism by removing concilia-tion/mediation as a required step before a strike, Canadian governments have gradually expanded the role of government in collective bargaining. Three examples of this trend are the ability of the minister of labour (or in some jurisdictions, the parties) to create an industrial inquiry commission, order a vote on the last offer in bargaining, or settle a dispute over the first collective agreement by **arbitration**.

EXAMPLES OF THE EXPANDED GOVERNMENT ROLE IN COLLECTIVE BARGAINING

INDUSTRIAL INQUIRY COMMISSION

Inquiry commissions are employed, though rarely, by governments to investigate the causes and consequences of industrial actions and strikes. After a long and bitter strike between Vale and the United Steelworkers of America, the Newfoundland Government created an Inquiry Commission in 2010, the terms of reference of which are outlined next.

> *NOW THEREFORE, pursuant to Section 140 of the Labour Relations Act, I hereby appoint an Industrial Inquiry Commission, composed of John F. Roil, Q.C., as Inquiry Chairperson, and V. Randell J. Earle, Q.C., and Brian R. Gatien as Inquiry Members, to inquire into and investigate the following industrial matters at Voisey's Bay, Labrador:*
>
> 1. *the positions of the parties in relation to the outstanding collective bargaining issues;*
> 2. *the factors which have led to the existing labour-management relations climate at the Voisey's Bay project site in Labrador and options to improve these relations;*
> 3. *the identification of local, provincial, national or international matters that maybe contributing factors in this dispute;*
> 4. *a discussion of any impacts this dispute may be having on other labour management relationships;*
> 5. *a discussion of the ramifications of this dispute, and its costs to the Province and the parties involved;*
> 6. *the options to resolve this dispute, including proposed terms of settlement, should the parties fail to conclude a collective agreement before the filing of the Commission's report; and,*
> 7. *other matters the Commission may deem appropriate.*
>
> *The Commission shall report its findings together with such recommendations as it may deem necessary to the Minister by a date not to exceed two months from the date of this appointment unless otherwise extended by the Minister. (Government of Newfoundland and Labrador, 2010)*

LAST-OFFER VOTE

Employers have complained that unions call strikes without putting the last offer to their members. To accommodate these employer concerns, labour laws have been amended to permit forced votes. There are several variants of this process across Canada. In Newfoundland the right is restricted to cases in which the strike or lockout poses a threat

arbitration
a quasi-judicial process whereby a neutral third party makes a final and binding determina-tion on all outstanding issues in dispute

to an industry or region. In Ontario the request by an employer for a last-offer vote must be granted when a strike is in progress (one vote per dispute). Also, the Ontario minister may order a vote if it is deemed in the public interest to do so. In several other jurisdictions, including the federal one, a vote is at the discretion of the minister.

FIRST CONTRACT ARBITRATION

The U.S. *National Labor Relations Act* (*Wagner Act*) has been amended only twice since 1935. The Taft-Hartley amendments in 1947 were designed to strengthen management in bargaining, and the Landrum-Griffin changes in 1959 promoted internal union democracy. In contrast, because of the *Snider* decision and pressure from labour-friendly political parties, Canadian labour laws have changed on a regular basis (Bruce, 1989), generally becoming more supportive of collective bargaining and unions. The law on first contract arbitration is a good illustration of this point.

In the United States, winning a free election does not necessarily guarantee the security of a union. One study, for example, found that unions were able to obtain a collective agreement in the first round of bargaining in fewer than 60 percent of the cases (Department of Labor study, reported in Abraham, 1997). To correct this problem in Canada, eight of eleven jurisdictions have adopted one of three models of first contract arbitration. Only Alberta and New Brunswick have no provision for first contract arbitration.

The three models according to Abraham (1997) are (1) a bad faith bargaining remedy; (2) a complete breakdown in bargaining; and (3) a no-fault approach.

In the federal, British Columbia, and Newfoundland jurisdictions, a union must establish that the employer has been bargaining in bad faith in order to obtain first contract arbitration. According to Abraham (1997), "there has been a trend away from this concept because of the difficulty of defining and establishing 'bad faith bargaining.'" In Ontario and British Columbia, first contract arbitration is available only when the labour board determines that a complete breakdown in negotiations has occurred. Finally, the no-fault approach of Quebec, Prince Edward Island, and Manitoba does not require the union to establish either bargaining in bad faith or a complete breakdown in negotiations.

REPLACEMENT WORKER LAWS

Finally, we canvass the wide variation in policies with respect to replacement employees during a strike or lockout. Quebec and British Columbia have outright bans on strikebreakers during a strike. Ontario, Manitoba, and Alberta prohibit the use of professional strikebreakers. Manitoba, Prince Edward Island, and Saskatchewan prevent replacement workers from permanently replacing employees but only after a strike. The federal *Canada Labour Code* prevents the use of replacement workers but only when their purpose is to undermine the union rather than pursue legitimate collective bargaining objectives. New Brunswick, Newfoundland, and Nova Scotia have no significant policies with respect to the use of replacement workers.

// COLLECTIVE AGREEMENT ADMINISTRATION

The law in Canada dealing with collective agreement administration again differs significantly from its American parent. In all Canadian jurisdictions, strikes are illegal during the term of a collective agreement. The *Wagner Act* contains no such prohibition. In Canada, all laws substitute arbitration for the right to strike during the contract term. However, this restriction on strikes is known as the "labour peace" provision of the law. Not all scholars agree that restricting strikes produces labour peace, since Canada has a relatively high number of illegal strikes during the term of the agreement (Haiven, 1990).

The labour peace provision is also known as the "deemed provision" of the labour law, because the law deems it be included in every collective agreement. The Nova Scotia law provides a typical example of how this provision works (see IR Today 4.1). Note that even if labour and management choose not to include an arbitration provision in the collective agreement, the law puts it in the agreement as if the parties had agreed to it (see 42(2) in IR Today 4.1).

IR TODAY 4.1

EXCERPT FROM NOVA SCOTIA *TRADE UNION ACT*

Final Settlement Provision

42(1) Every collective agreement shall contain a provision for final settlement without stoppage of work, by arbitration or otherwise, of all differences between the parties to or persons bound by the agreement or on whose behalf it was entered into, concerning its meaning or violation. (2) Where a collective agreement does not contain a provision as required by this Section, it shall be deemed to contain the following provision:

> *Where a difference arises between the parties relating to the interpretation, application or administration of this agreement, including any question as to whether a matter is arbitrable, or where an allegation is made that this agreement has been violated, either of the parties may, after exhausting any grievance procedure established by this agreement, notify the other party in writing of its desire to submit the difference or allegation to arbitration. If the parties fail to agree upon an arbitrator, the appointment shall be made by the Minister of labour for Nova*

> *Scotia upon the request of either party The arbitrator shall hear and determine the difference or allegation and shall issue a decision, and the decision is final and binding upon the parties and upon any employee or employer affected by it.*

(3) Every party to and every person bound by the agreement, and every person on whose behalf the agreement was entered into, shall comply with the provision for final settlement contained in the agreement. R.S., c. 475, s. 42; 2010, c. 37, s. 145; 2010, c. 76, s. 1.

Powers and Duty of Arbitrator or Arbitration Board

43B An arbitrator or an arbitration board appointed pursuant to this Act or to a collective agreement . . .

(h) has power to treat as part of the collective agreement the provisions of any statute of the Province governing relations between the parties to the collective agreement.

Source: Nova Scotia House of Assembly. Retrieved from http://nslegislature.ca/legc/statutes/trade%20union.pdf.

Because the law provides "labour peace" by banning strikes during the collective agreement term, there is an implicit role for the arbitrator. Under Canadian law, both the collective agreement and the law give arbitrators the jurisdiction to settle disputes, defining a significant public policy role for arbitration. This public policy role has expanded in the decades since World War II with the passage of employment law governing such matters as human rights, health and safety, employment equity, pensions, and plant closures. Arbitrators across Canada have been increasingly called upon to apply these laws in arbitration decisions.

We have chosen two examples where Canadian laws explicitly mandate arbitrators to interpret employment law. The first is found in section 43 B of the Nova Scotia law (see IR Today 4.1). The Nova Scotia law gives the power to the arbitrator to treat relevant employment laws as part of the collective agreement. In the second case, Ontario, arbitrators are more explicitly given the power to interpret employment law (see excerpt in IR Today 4.2).

IR TODAY 4.2

ONTARIO LABOUR RELATIONS ACT: ARBITRATOR POWERS

(j) to interpret and apply human rights and other employment-related statutes, despite any conflict between those statutes and the terms of the collective agreement. 1995, c. 1, Sched. A, s. 48 (12).

In summary, Canadian laws define an important public policy role for arbitrators in two respects. First, arbitration, as a strike substitute procedure, gives arbitrators a public policy role in settling all disputes during the contract term—hence the term "labour peace." Second, labour legislation and arbitrational jurisprudence have given arbitrators an increasingly important role in interpreting relevant employment law (human rights, employment equity, health and safety, plant closure, pension, termination, etc.).

// ROLE OF THE *CHARTER*

In the process of repatriating the Constitution in 1982, Canada preserved labour as a provincial responsibility and created a *Charter of Rights and Freedoms* (see IR Today 4.3). The important question raised by the *Charter* was its effect on existing Canadian labour laws. Since the Canadian constitution requires that all laws be consistent with the *Charter* (section 52), it was an open question whether the *Charter* would negatively or positively affect existing law. Note that the rights set out in the *Charter* (e.g., freedom of association) are subject to s. 1: "reasonable limits prescribed by law as can be demonstrably justified in a free and democratic society." In addition, governments could invoke the "notwithstanding clause," which provided a legislative override of the freedom or right for five years (s. 33).

REVIEW OF SUPREME COURT *CHARTER* DECISIONS

In this section, we canvass some of the important decisions affecting labour and management.

RIGHT TO STRIKE

The most significant early interpretation of freedom of association was found in three cases that have together become known as the Labour Trilogy: restrictions on the right to strike in Alberta, the federal government wage controls, and back-to-work laws in Saskatchewan and various unions (reference *Public Service Employee Relations Act* (*Alta.*), [1987] 1 S.C.R. 313 ("*Alberta Reference*"); *PSAC v. Canada*, [1987] 1 S.C.R. 424; *RWDSU v. Saskatchewan*, [1987] 1 S.C.R. 460). In these three 1987 cases, the court found that freedom of association did not include a right to strike and bargain collectively (Swinton, 1995). These trilogy outcomes have since been fully reversed by subsequent decisions of the court, as we will discover below.

For organized labour in Canada, the early trilogy losses resulted in some negative views about the *Charter*'s ability to protect workers' right to freedom of association.

In a landmark decision for labour, the Supreme Court finds that freedom of association included a right to strike.

Andrew Balfour/Supreme Court of Canada

More recently, however, several (but not all) cases have produced more positive outcomes and indicated a more labour-friendly direction (Cameron, 2002). We will discuss these cases more fully below.

UNION DUES

The *Lavigne* decision in 1991 was interesting because an earlier case in the United States very similar to this one was heard by the Supreme Court of Canada (SCC). Both the Abood case (*Abood v. Detroit Board of Education*, 431 U.S. 209 1977) and the Lavigne case (*Lavigne v. Ontario Public Service Employees Union*, [1991] 2 S.C.R. 211) involved teachers who objected to their union dues going to political causes that they did not support. These decisions provide an example of a major difference between U.S. and Canadian views of freedom of association and collective bargaining. In the U.S. Supreme Court decision, the court upheld Abood's complaint and ordered the union to rebate that portion of his dues that was for purposes other than collective bargaining. In the *Lavigne* case, on the other hand, the Canadian court justified the restriction on his freedom of association by a view of unionism that includes legitimate social and political goals that go beyond collective bargaining. Whereas the U.S. constitution has emphasized individual rights, the Canadian *Charter* has respected both individual and collective rights (Sack, 2010).

Here is an excerpt from *Lavigne v. OPSEU*:

> *The limitation on appellant's freedom of association is justified under s. 1 of the Charter. The state objectives in compelling the payment of union dues which can be used to assist causes unrelated to collective bargaining are to enable unions to participate in the broader political, economic and social debates in society, and to contribute to democracy in the workplace. . . .*

PICKETING

The SCC has decided that secondary picketing is part of freedom of expression. In the *Pepsi-Cola* case (*R.W.D.S.U., Local 558 v. Pepsi-Cola Canada Beverages (West) Ltd.*, [2002] 1 S.C.R. 156, 2002 SCC 8), the court held that it was legal to picket at locations other than the firm's premises as long as the picketing is peaceful. Here is an excerpt from the decision:

> *The union engaged in a variety of protest and picketing activities during a lawful strike and lockout at one of the appellant's plants. These activities eventually spread to "secondary" locations, where union members and supporters picketed retail outlets to prevent the delivery of the appellant's products and dissuade the store staff from accepting delivery; carried placards in front of a hotel where members of the substitute labour force were staying; and engaged in intimidating conduct outside the homes of appellant's management personnel. An interlocutory injunction was granted which effectively prohibited the union from engaging in picketing activities at secondary*

locations. A majority of the Court of Appeal upheld the order against congregating at the residences of the appellant's employees, as these activities constituted tortious conduct. However, the section restraining the union from picketing at any location other than the appellant's premises was quashed, thus allowing the union to engage in peaceful picketing at secondary locations. (Supreme Court of Canada, 2002)

UNION RECOGNITION

In 1994, during the term of the New Democratic Party (NDP) government, the Ontario legislature enacted the *Agricultural Labour Relations Act*, 1994 (ALRA), which extended trade union and collective bargaining rights to agricultural workers. Prior to the adoption of this legislation, agricultural workers had always been excluded from Ontario's labour relations regime. A year later, under the Harris Conservative government, the legislature repealed the ALRA in its entirety, in effect subjecting agricultural workers to section 3(b) of the *Labour Relations Act*, 1995 (LRA), which excluded them from the labour relations regime set out in the LRA. Section 80 also terminated any certification rights of trade unions, and any collective agreements certified, under the ALRA.

The United Food and Commercial Workers (UFCW), on behalf of Tom Dunmore and other farm workers, brought an application challenging the repeal of the ALRA and the union's exclusion from the LRA, on the basis that it infringed its workers' rights under sections (d) and 15(1) of the *Canadian Charter of Rights and Freedoms (Dunmore v. Ontario (Attorney General)*, [2001] 3 S.C.R. 1016, 2001 SCC 94). While both the Ontario Court (General Division) and the Ontario Court of Appeal upheld the challenged legislation, the Supreme Court struck it down as follows:

Here, the appellants do not claim a constitutional right to general inclusion in the LRA, but simply a constitutional freedom to organize a trade association. This freedom to organize exists independently of any statutory enactment, although its effective exercise may require legislative protection in some cases. The appellants have met the evidentiary burden of showing that they are substantially incapable of exercising their fundamental freedom to organize without the LRA's protective regime. While the mere fact of exclusion from protective legislation is not conclusive evidence of a Charter violation, the evidence indicates that, but for the brief period covered by the ALRA, there has never been an agricultural workers' union in Ontario and agricultural workers have suffered repeated attacks on their efforts to unionize. The inability of agricultural workers to organize can be linked to state action. The exclusion of agricultural workers from the LRA functions not simply to permit private interferences with their fundamental freedoms, but to substantially reinforce such interferences. The inherent difficulties of organizing farm workers, combined with the threat of economic reprisal from employers, form only part of the reason why association is all but impossible in the agricultural sector in Ontario. Equally important is the message sent by the exclusion of agricultural workers from the LRA, which delegitimizes their associational activity and thereby contributes to its ultimate failure. The most palpable effect of the LRESLAA and the LRA is, therefore, to place a chilling effect on non-statutory union activity. (Supreme Court of Canada, 2001)

In an 8–1 vote, the Supreme Court of Canada (SCC) granted the appeal and declared the impugned legislation unconstitutional. The Harris government was given eighteen months to comply with section 2(d) of the *Charter* and to provide a statutory framework that would be consistent with the principles established in the case.

The *Dunmore* decision may be important for several reasons (Adams, 2003; Fudge, 2008). For a more critical view of the court's interpretation of freedom of association, see Langille (2009):

1. Until *Dunmore*, the SCC had tended to defer to elected legislatures.
2. All Canadian workers have the right to organize to advance employment interests without fear of reprisals.
3. Canadian governments have legal responsibility to proactively intervene to ensure freedom of association.
4. The *Charter* extends rights to both individuals and collectivities.
5. Finally, the SCC acknowledged the importance of the core labour standards established through the International Labour Organization (ILO), in which freedom of association is viewed as a fundamental human right:

27. The notion that underinclusion can infringe freedom of association is not only implied by Canadian Charter jurisprudence, but is also consistent with international human rights law. Article 2 of Convention (No. 87) concerning freedom of association and protection of the right to organize, 67 U.N.T.S. 17, provides that "[w]orkers and employers, without distinction whatsoever, shall have the right to establish and . . . to join organisations of their own choosing" (emphasis added), and that only members of the armed forces and the police may be excluded (Article 9). In addition, Article 10 of Convention No. 87 defines an "organisation" as "any organisation of workers or of employers for furthering and defending the interests of workers or of employers" (emphasis added). Canada ratified Convention No. 87 in 1972. The Convention's broadly worded provisions confirm precisely what I have discussed above, which is that discriminatory treatment implicates not only an excluded group's dignity interest, but also its basic freedom of association. (Supreme Court of Canada, 2001)

POLITICAL ACTIVITY

In 1991 the Supreme Court upheld a challenge to restrictions on the political activities of civil servants (*Osborne v. Canada (Treasury Board)*, [1991] 2 S.C.R. 69). Under section 33 of the *Public Service Employment Act*, it was illegal on threat of dismissal to engage in work for or on behalf of a political party or candidate. The court found that the restrictions violated freedom of expression under 2(b). Here is an excerpt from the decision:

Section 33 of the Act, which prohibits partisan political expression and activity by public servants under threat of disciplinary action including dismissal from employment, infringes the right to freedom of expression in s. 2(b) of the Charter. Where opposing values call for a restriction on the freedom of speech, and, apart from exceptional cases, the limits on that freedom are to be dealt with under the balancing test in s. 1, rather than circumscribing the scope of the guarantee at the outset. In this case, by prohibiting public servants from speaking out in favour of a political party or candidate, s. 33 of the Act expressly has for its purpose the restriction of expressive activity and is accordingly inconsistent with s. 2(b) of the Charter. (Supreme Court of Canada, 1991)

A NEW DIRECTION FOR THE SUPREME COURT

It has been argued that the *Pepsi-Cola* and *Dunmore* cases, together with the *Advanced Cutting* decision (*R. v. Advanced Cutting and Coring Ltd.*, [2001] S.C.R. 70), in which collective rights trumped individual rights, have resulted in a new Labour Trilogy being defined by Canada's highest court (Cameron, 2002). Contrary to the earlier trilogy of cases (discussed above), these more recent decisions provide more positive outcomes for labour. While the former trilogy limited labour's ability to strike, the later cases strengthened collective rights, expanded picketing and freedom of expression, and gave new meaning to union recognition and freedom of association.

The case for a new direction was made even stronger by a landmark decision of the Supreme Court of Canada on June 8, 2007. In a dramatic reversal of past decisions, the Court declared collective bargaining a constitutional right under the freedom of association guarantee. Once again, the Court relied on international labour standards as established by the ILO in its reasoning. The preamble and decision excerpt in IR Today 4.4 explain the context of the case. For a more recent Supreme Court of Canada case that represents a follow-up to *Dunmore*, see IR Today 4.5.

IR TODAY 4.4

SUPREME COURT RELIES ON ILO STANDARDS

Preamble

The *Health and Social Services Delivery Improvement Act* was adopted as a response to challenges facing British Columbia's healthcare system. The *Act* was quickly passed and there was no meaningful consultation with unions before it became law. Part 2 of the *Act* introduced changes to transfers and multi-worksite assignment rights (sections 4 and 5), contracting out (section 6), the status of contracted-out employees (s. 6), job security programs (ss. 7 and 8), and layoffs and bumping rights (s. 9). It gave healthcare employers greater flexibility to organize their relations with their employees as they see fit, and in some cases to do so in ways that would not have been permissible under existing collective agreements and without adhering to requirements of consultation and notice that would otherwise obtain. It invalidated important provisions of collective agreements then in force, and effectively precluded meaningful collective bargaining on a number of specific issues. Furthermore, s. 10 voided any part of a collective agreement, past or future, that was inconsistent with Part 2, and any collective agreement purporting to modify these restrictions. The appellants, who are unions and members of the unions representing the nurses, facilities, or community subsectors, challenged the constitutional validity of Part 2 of the Act as violative of the guarantees of freedom of association and equality protected by the *Canadian Charter of Rights and Freedoms*. Both the trial judge and the Court of Appeal found that Part 2 of the Act did not violate ss. 2(d) or 15 of the *Charter*.

Decision Excerpt

Freedom of association guaranteed by s. 2(d) of the Charter includes a procedural right to collective bargaining. The grounds advanced in the earlier decisions of this Court for the exclusion of collective bargaining from the s. 2(d)'s protection do not withstand principled scrutiny and should be rejected. The general purpose of the Charter guarantees and the broad language of s. 2(d) are consistent with a measure of protection for collective bargaining. Further, the right to collective bargaining is neither of recent origin nor merely a creature of statute. The history of collective bargaining in Canada reveals that long before the present statutory labour regimes were put in place, collective bargaining was recognized as a fundamental aspect of Canadian society, emerging as the most significant collective activity through which freedom of association is expressed in the labour context. Association for purposes of collective bargaining has long been recognized as a fundamental Canadian right which predated the Charter. The protection enshrined in s. 2(d) of the Charter may properly be seen as the culmination of a historical movement towards the recognition of a procedural right to collective bargaining. Canada's adherence to international documents recognizing a right to collective bargaining also supports recognition of that right in s. 2(d). The Charter should be presumed to provide at least as great a level of protection as is found in the international human rights documents that Canada has ratified. Lastly, the protection of collective bargaining under s. 2(d) is consistent with and supportive of the values underlying the Charter and the purposes of the Charter as a whole. Recognizing that workers have the right to bargain collectively as part of their freedom to associate reaffirms the values of dignity, personal autonomy, equality and democracy that are inherent in the Charter. (Health Services and Support–Facilities Subsector Bargaining Assn. v. British Columbia, 2007 S.C.C. 27)

IR TODAY   4.5

SUPREME COURT RULES ON COLLECTIVE BARGAINING FOR AGRICULTURAL WORKERS

There is a difference between winning the battle and winning the war. In the April 29, 2011, Supreme Court of Canada decision in *Ontario (Attorney General) v. Fraser*, the UFCW (United Food & Commercial Workers) and Ontario's agricultural workers lost in their argument that the *Agricultural Employees Protection Act* (AEPA) was insufficient to protect their Charter freedom of association. That was the battle.

But what was really at stake in this case was whether the Supreme Court's earlier *B.C. Health Services* decision, which established limited Charter protection for collective bargaining, was going to be overturned or substantially weakened—and it wasn't. That was the real danger for Canadian workers—the war, if you will—and Canadian workers did not lose this war today.

Summary

This case dealt with the question of whether collective representation legislation applying to agricultural workers in Ontario, the AEPA, lacks sufficient protections for collective representation and bargaining such as to violate the workers' section 2(d) *Charter*-protected freedom of association. The Ontario Court of Appeal had held that it was an unjustifiable violation of this freedom, and held that the *B.C. Health Services* decision effectively constitutionalized the Wagner Model of collective bargaining. The Court of Appeal had held that because the AEPA did not include key features of the Wagner Model, it violated these workers' freedom of association, and this breach was not saved under section 1 of the *Charter*. The Ontario government appealed this decision to the Supreme Court of Canada.

A majority of the Supreme Court of Canada held that the AEPA does not violate either section 2(d) or 15 (equality rights) of the *Charter*. However, the majority opinion of five justices, drafted by Chief Justice McLachlin and Justice LeBel, affirmed the *B.C. Health Services* decision, noting that it was "consistent with previous cases on the issue of individual and collective rights" and that the "unworkability of Health Services has not been established. There is no concrete evidence that the principles enunciated in *Dunmore* and *Health Services* are unworkable or have led to intolerable results. It is premature to argue that the holding in *Health Services*, rendered four years ago, is unworkable in practice."

Emphasizing that the *Health Services* decision does not guarantee any particular model of collective bargaining, the majority concluded that because the AEPA does not make association by these workers in pursuit of workplace goals impossible, it does not meet the necessary threshold of substantially impairing the workers' section 2(d) rights. In coming to this conclusion, the majority ruled that, by implication, the collective bargaining provisions of the AEPA must impose a duty on employers to consider employee representations in good faith.

Addressing the UFCW's argument that the AEPA has not been sufficient to permit effective collective bargaining, the majority concluded that this was a premature argument, that "the union has not made a significant attempt to make it work," and that "the process has not been fully explored and tested."

The decision is a disappointment to the UFCW and Ontario's agricultural workers, as it makes clear that the *Charter* and *B.C. Health Services* does not constitutionalize or entrench the Wagner Model—or any particular system—of collective bargaining. However, the decision does offer strong support for the *B.C. Health Services* decision and inclusion of limited protection of the process of collective bargaining in the *Charter*'s freedom of association. It also offers some guidance on the content and extent of this protection of collective bargaining and good-faith negotiations.

Source: Report by Prof. Sara Slinn, Osgoode Hall Law School, York University, and the Centre for Industrial Relations and Human Resources, University of Toronto. Reprinted with permission. See also Adams (2012) and Fudge (2012).

In addition to extending collective bargaining rights to agricultural workers, on January 16, 2015 the Supreme Court also found that members of the RCMP should be allowed to join unions and participate in collective bargaining. Previously the RCMP had consultation rights only, with management having the final say on all conditions of employment (known as the SRRP). The Supreme Court held that:

We have concluded that s. 2(d) protects the right of employees to associate for the purpose of meaningfully pursuing collective workplace goals. The government therefore cannot enact laws or impose a labour relations process that substantially interferes with that right. This raises the question—what are the features essential to a meaningful process of collective bargaining under s. 2(d)? In this section, we conclude that a meaningful process of collective bargaining is a process that provides employees with a degree of choice and independence sufficient to enable them to determine their collective interests and meaningfully pursue them. (para 81)

Collective bargaining constitutes a fundamental aspect of Canadian society which "enhances the human dignity, liberty and autonomy of workers by giving them the opportunity to influence the establishment of workplace rules and thereby gain some control over a major aspect of their lives, namely their work" (Health Services, at para. 82). Put simply, its purpose is to preserve collective employee autonomy against the superior power of management and to maintain equilibrium between the parties. This equilibrium is embodied in the degree of choice and independence afforded to the employees in the labour relations process. (para. 82) (Supreme Court of Canada, 2015)

A RIGHT TO STRIKE

On January 30, 2015, the Supreme Court constitutionalized the right to strike in Canada by concluding in a 5–2 decision that freedom of association includes this right. This completed the reversal of the court's trilogy decision in 1987 discussed above (see IR Today 4.6).

SUPREME COURT "CONSTITUTIONALIZES" A RIGHT TO STRIKE

OTTAWA, ON—The Canadian Union of Public Employees is celebrating today's Supreme Court decision recognizing the constitutional right of public sector workers to go on strike. CUPE, Canada's largest union, is calling the decision a huge victory for all workers across the country.

"The ability of workers to go on strike is a fundamental part of collective bargaining;

a corner stone of our free and democratic society. It is extremely important to have the highest court in our country recognize this as a right of all workers, private and public sector alike," said Paul Moist, national president of CUPE. "No union ever wants a strike, but without the right to strike, employers have an unfair advantage. This decision secures a balance between workers and employers in negotiations."

Source: http://cupe.ca/supreme-court-recognizes-constitutional-right-strike-canadian-workers.

One final case, which is summarized in IR Today 4.7, involved a 5–2 decision of the Supreme Court authored by Mr. Justice Louis LeBel. The court ruled that Walmart violated a section of the Quebec labour code that prevents an employer from changing its workers' conditions of employment, without the union's consent, during the negotiation of a first collective agreement. According to the court, closing the store and cancelling contracts amounted to an illegal change of working conditions.

WALMART IN VIOLATION OF QUEBEC'S LABOUR CODE

The Supreme Court of Canada has ruled that Walmart violated Quebec's labour code when it closed a store in Jonquiere, Quebec after workers tried to unionize it.

A decision that some experts believe could have ramifications for the rest of the country.

"Walmart may be able to close stores again but they will have to pay (we will see by how much) and this may have a positive impact on unionizing," Robert Hebdon told Global News.

Hebdon is a professor in McGill University's Faculty of Management and specializes in organizational behaviour and industrial relations. He said the Supreme Court of Canada's decision could have implications for all of Canada.

"All Canadian labour laws have a provision that provides for a freeze on conditions during a union recognition

drive, thus I think this decision does have implications for the rest of Canada," he said.

"Closure should be intrepreted as a change in conditions and thus contrary to all Canadian labour laws."

In August 2004, the Quebec store was the first Walmart to unionize in North America.

When the collective bargaining dispute was ordered to arbitration, Walmart announced that it would close the store, citing financial reasons.

Quebec employees, represented by United Food and Commercial Workers Union Canada, said that the retailer made the decision after they exercised their right to organize, and demanded to be reinstated.

In 2009, Canada's top court defended the company's right to close the store, and refused an appeal by Walmart employees.

The company now owes compensation to the workers, which has not yet been determined.

However, Hebdon suggested it could be considerable.

"I would not be surprised if was quite large taking into account retroactivity and interest costs."

Source: Amanda Kelly. (27 June 2014). "Supreme Court rules Walmart broke Quebec labour code by closing store." Global News. Retrieved from http://globalnews.ca/news/1420291/supreme-court-rules-walmart-broke-quebec-labour-code-by-closing-store/.

// EMPLOYMENT LAW

Some scholars argue that private-sector union decline has led to the emergence of a new regime defined by individual employment rights (Piore & Safford, 2006). The argument is more compelling in the United States than in Canada, since union decline is much greater south of the border. Nonetheless, employment law has also expanded in Canada. The essence of the argument is that collective bargaining under the *Wagner Act* model has been replaced by a system of rights and obligations that apply to all firms and employees whether unionized or not. This trend has created a tension between individual and collective rights. In this section, we summarize the conditions of employment and the rights that apply to both union and nonunion firms and to all employees.

The Supreme Court of Canada found in favour of Quebec workers who were fired from a Walmart in Jonquière, Que., after it suddenly shut its doors, and says the former employees must be compensated.

EMPLOYMENT CONDITIONS

We make a distinction between employment conditions—commonly known as *employment standards*—and employment rights. However, it should be borne in mind that these two categories cannot be easily separated; in the case of health and safety regulation, for example, we will find both conditions and rights.

Generally, conditions are established in legislation by minimums (e.g., hours of work, overtime, minimum wages, vacation, meal breaks). Unionized employees may typically build on these minimum conditions. Like most employment conditions, there is wide variation across Canada. This section draws on the summary provided by Human Resources and Social Development Canada (HRSDC).

HOURS OF WORK

According to Human Resources and Social Development Canada, there are two models for the regulation of hours of work provisions. In one model, the law provides for a standard workday or workweek and overtime pay if the standard is exceeded; in the other, there are standard hours of work and a legal maximum number of hours per day or per week.

OVERTIME

This excerpt from HRSDC provides a summary of the law with regard to overtime in Canada:

The overtime rate is payable to the employees for each hour or part of an hour they work in excess of the standard hours. Most jurisdictions have established an overtime rate equivalent to one and a half times the employee's regular rate of pay. British Columbia further provides that hours in excess of 12 in a day must be remunerated at twice the regular rate. New Brunswick and Newfoundland and Labrador have established the overtime rate as being one and a half times the minimum wage. In many jurisdictions, subject to certain conditions, an employer and an employee may agree to replace the payment of overtime by paid leave equivalent to one and a half times the overtime hours worked. (HRSDC, 2006)

SCHEDULING OF HOURS

Some employers may be required to give notice to employees in advance of changes in scheduled hours. For example, where there is a change in shift, some employers depending on jurisdiction might need to give twenty-four hours' notice to affected employees. In addition, companies might have to provide a minimum period between shifts (at least eight hours) and a rest day wherever practicable.

COFFEE AND MEAL BREAKS

British Columbia, Manitoba, New Brunswick, Ontario, Prince Edward Island, Quebec, and Saskatchewan provide an employee entitlement to a meal break of at least half an hour after each period of five consecutive hours of work. This meal break is normally unpaid unless an employee is required to remain at their workstation or to be available for work during the meal break. There is no legislation that requires an employer to provide a coffee break. However, if a coffee break is provided in Ontario, Quebec, or Saskatchewan, employers have to consider it time worked.

EXCLUSIONS

The long list of exclusions usually includes students, members of designated professions, ambulance drivers and attendants, domestics, fishermen, farm workers, construction workers, and managerial staff. Additionally, more flexible arrangement of work hours for certain jobs may be permitted by the statutes as explained below:

The modification of the standard work week or the averaging of hours over a period of two or more weeks, for example, can be authorized under the terms of the Canada Labour Code, the Labour Standards Act in Saskatchewan and in all three territories. Similarly, Quebec allows the staggering of hours of work on a basis other than a weekly basis with the authorization of the Labour Standards Commission (Commission des normes du travail). These provisions are especially useful to employers because they provide flexibility while allowing to economize on overtime premiums. (HRSDC, 2006)

EMPLOYEE RIGHTS

Rights have been granted to all employees in the following areas: human rights and discrimination, health and safety, plant closure, pension, maternity, pay equity, employment equity, and dismissal. In this section, we provide examples of how the laws vary across Canada.

HUMAN RIGHTS

Human rights are protected in each of the eleven jurisdictions by means of a human rights commission. There is some variation in the human rights codes with respect to the protected groups, but the administration of the law is quite uniform across Canada. We have chosen the federal jurisdiction as representative. Under the *Canadian Human Rights Act*, it is against the law for any employer or provider of a service that falls within federal jurisdiction to discriminate on the basis of

- race;
- national or ethic origin;
- colour;
- religion;
- age;
- sex (including pregnancy and childbearing);
- sexual orientation;
- marital status;
- family status;
- physical or mental disability (including dependence on alcohol or drugs); or
- pardoned criminal conviction.

Enforcement of human rights is by means of an employee (or group of employees) complaint. Complaints are heard by tribunals of the respective provincial or federal commission that are composed of neutral adjudicators.

The *Human Rights Act* also protects employees against harassment by other employees. According to the Canadian Human Rights Commission, "harassment, whether by a supervisor or co-worker, creates a barrier to equality by demeaning its victims, interfering with their ability to work effectively and, in some instances, even forcing them to resign. Despite the publicity surrounding this issue, studies consistently show that employees continue to face harassment in the workplace."

HEALTH AND SAFETY

In Canada, we have what is known as the internal responsibility model (IRM), which places emphasis on establishing the framework within which the workplace parties mutually address health and safety concerns (Hebdon & Hyatt, 1998). The IRM mandates employee involvement by conferring three basic rights and responsibilities upon workers:

- the right to know about the hazards to which they are exposed;
- the right to participate in mandatory joint worker–management health and safety committees; and
- the right to refuse unsafe work without fear of reprisal.

Research indicates that IRM has a significant effect on reducing lost-time injury rates, especially where labour and management have co-managed health and safety issues through the joint committee (Lewchuk, Robb & Walters, 1996).

PAY AND EMPLOYMENT EQUITY

Pay equity is parity in wages and salaries between men and women. **Employment equity** is a broader term that involves the removal of barriers that have an adverse impact on certain designated groups. The federal employment equity legislation, for example, targets employment levels of visible minorities, women, Aboriginals, and the disabled (Mentzer, 2002).

It is important to make a distinction between direct and systemic discrimination:

- *Direct discrimination* occurs when, for example, an employee discriminates against a fellow employee.
- *Systemic discrimination* occurs when the organizational rules are followed but protected groups are disadvantaged.

Direct discrimination may be dealt with through a complaint under a human rights code or under a union's grievance procedure. Systemic discrimination is much harder to prove and to remedy. It might be built into human resources functions such as recruitment, selection, training, staff development, compensation, performance evaluation, and discipline (Weiner, 1995).

The federal government has the only employment equity legislation in Canada. The coverage of the act was defined in the HRSDC *Employment Equity Act* annual report 2004:

> *Four types of employers are covered by the* Employment Equity Act: *federally regulated private sector employers, the Federal Public Service, Separate Employers, and employers under the Federal Contractors Program (FCP). In 2003, these employers accounted for 13 percent of the Canadian workforce or over 2.2 million employees, compared to 2 million in 2002. (HRSDC, 2004)*

From 2002 to 2003, there were employment gains in the combined totals of all reporting employers as follows:

- Women went from 95.9 to 97.9 percent.
- Aboriginal peoples went from 80.7 to 84.6 percent.
- Persons with disabilities went from 46.9 to 58.5 percent.
- Members of visible minorities went from 77.5 to 90.5 percent (HRSDC, 2004).

Pay equity and employment equity have proven to be difficult goals to achieve despite the apparent success shown in employment equity above. Singh and Peng (2010) argue that Ontario's *Pay Equity Act* is one of the world's most progressive pieces of pay equity legislation. They find that by targeting the discriminatory aspect of women's work evaluations the *Act* has resulted in pay increases for thousands of women, especially in the public sector. For a comprehensive analysis of the Canadian experience, see Jain, Lawler, Bai, and Lee (2010). Appendix A at the end of this chapter provides a comprehensive review of pay equity legislation in Canada. Note that all provinces have a version of pay equity legislation that covers both the public and the private sector.

The reader will note that several conditions and rights are not discussed in this section. There are laws that provide employee rights and conditions, for example, in the areas of pensions, statutory holidays, vacation, plant closures, workers' compensation, and more.

pay equity
women and men being paid relatively equally for work of equal value

employment equity
equity in employment levels and opportunities between targeted community groups (women, visible minorities, Aboriginals, and disabled employees) and major employers

INTERNATIONAL LAW

The globalization of trade and the increased mobility of capital have resulted in new challenges and opportunities for labour. Labour policy is shifting from a state-centred model to one in which international considerations must be taken into account. Globalization is creating some new international rules that apply to the labour market. The International Labour Organization (ILO), a tripartite agency of the United Nations, is playing a key role in this process. Labour rights such as freedom of association and expression are seen as fundamental human rights not subject to the whims of politicians.

We have already seen the references made to ILO standards in the *Dunmore* and *B.C. Health Care* decisions of the Supreme Court. The ILO governing body has established international labour standards. To give effect to these standards, it passed three key conventions that nation states are encouraged to ratify through their political processes. They are

- *Convention 87,* freedom of association and protection of right to organize (1948). Ratified by Canada in 1972.
- *Convention 98,* right to organize and collective bargaining (1949). Not ratified by Canada.
- *Declaration on Fundamental Principles and Rights at Work* (1998). Canada voted for it.
- *Declaration on Social Justice for a Fair Globalization* (2008). Canada voted for it.

The 1998 *Declaration* states:

all Members, even if they have not ratified the Conventions in question, have an obligation arising from the very fact of membership in the Organization to respect, to promote and to realize, in good faith and in accordance with the Constitution, the principles concerning the fundamental rights which are the subject of those Conventions, namely:

> *(a freedom of association and the effective recognition of the right to collective bargaining;*
>
> *(b) the elimination of all forms of forced or compulsory labour;*
>
> *(c) the effective abolition of child labour; and*
>
> *(d) the elimination of discrimination in respect of employment and occupation.*

The 2008 declaration went even further to urge ILO members to implement a decent work agenda. It said:

The Declaration calls upon the ILO to assist its Members in their efforts towards its implementation, according to national needs and circumstances. To that end, it presents a challenge to the International Labour Conference, the Governing Body and the International Labour Office, signalling that "the Organization should review and adapt its institutional practices to enhance governance and capacity building in order to make the best use of its human and financial resources and of the unique advantage of its tripartite structure and standards system". Therefore, the Organization and its Members must mobilize all available means of action, both nationally and internationally, to promote the objectives of the Declaration and implement its commitments in the most effective and efficient way. (ILO, 2008)

// SUMMARY

Earlier we introduced the debate about a shift from an emphasis on collective rights under labour legislation to a greater role for individual rights under various employment laws. We wish to revisit this debate and ask the question "Is there a new individual-rights regime in Canada?"

There is no doubt that Canadian employment laws have significantly expanded both union and nonunion employee rights and conditions, as the chapter illustrates. There are two problems, however, with the argument that a new individual-rights regime has replaced the old one based on collective rights.

1. The argument advanced by Piore and Safford (2006) is more relevant in the U.S. case, because union decline is so much more pervasive there. Moreover, the idea that employment laws are a substitute for unionization has less resonance when placed in international comparative perspective. As the Canadian case shows, stronger employment laws are associated with more powerful labour movements, not vice versa.

2. The Supreme Court of Canada strengthened collective rights in the more recent decisions affecting labour discussed above.

KEY TERMS

arbitration 99
bargaining unit 95
certification 95
conciliation 98
duty of fair representation 98
employment equity 114
exclusivity principle 95
good faith bargaining 98
mediation 98
P.C. 1003 94
pay equity 114
scientific management 93
Snider case 93
tripartite 95
unfair labour practice 95
voluntarism 98

DISCUSSION QUESTIONS

1. Using Appendix A, determine which provinces provide for the strongest pay equity legislation.

2. What has been the impact of the *Snider* decision on the development of Canadian labour legislation?

3. How do labour boards determine which persons should be eligible for inclusion in a bargaining unit? Which employees are not eligible?

4. What are the steps in a typical organizing drive?

5. What is an unfair labour practice? Give examples. What is the duty of fair representation? Give examples.

6. How does public policy play a role in arbitration during the term of a collective agreement?

7. What is evidence of a new pro-labour direction of the Supreme Court?

8. Discuss how any three laws covering conditions of employment vary across Canada.

9. Discuss the proposition that there is a new individual-rights regime in Canada.

USING THE INTERNET

Blogs on labour law:

- Dr. David Doorey's Workplace Law Blog: http://lawofwork.ca/
- Freedom of Association discussion blog: http://foa2010.blogspot.com
- List of labour and employment law blogs: http://www.lawblogs.ca/category/labour-employment

There are several websites containing information about the principles upon which the law is based, the current state of employment law in Canada, and legislative trends. A few of these are listed below.

- Department of Justice Canada: http://www.justice.gc.ca/eng/index.html
- Canadian Human Rights Act: http://laws-lois.justice.gc.ca/eng/acts/H-6/
- Canadian Human Rights Tribunal: *www.chrt-tcdp.gc.ca/NS/index-eng.asp*
- Understanding pay equity: http://www.labour.gc.ca/eng/standards_equity/eq/pay/
- International Labour Organization: http://www.ilo.org/global/lang--en/index.htm#3

For industrial relations journals and cases, have a look in a law library such as one of the following:

- Nahum Gelber Law Library, McGill University: http://www.mcgill.ca/library/branches/law
- Bora Laskin Law Library, University of Toronto Faculty of Law: http://library.law.utoronto.ca/
- Bibliothèque de droit, Université de Montréal: http://www.bib.umontreal.ca/DR

1. Why does each province have its own human rights commission?

2. Use the links here to find a typical human rights commission or tribunal. What are the functions of the tribunal?

3. Find a website that provides links to labour legislation in Canada. Find the *Manitoba Labour Relations Act*. Have you found a current version of the legislation?

See also YouTube videos on labour law, history, legislation, etc.

EXERCISES

1. Do research on the Internet to find the labour relations act of any of the provinces. Summarize the sections of the act that define the jurisdiction of the labour board and its duties.

2. Select any two provinces and obtain the minimum wage law and human rights code.

Collective bargaining under the *Canada Labour Code* begins when a group of employees decides to organize in order to negotiate a collective agreement with their employer. The employees must first form their own trade union or join an existing one. Recognition of the union as their bargaining agent may be acquired by the employer voluntarily agreeing to enter into a collective agreement or by the union applying for certification. When this occurs, the following general framework for collective bargaining, as set out in Part I of the *Canada Labour Code*, applies:

GENERAL PRINCIPLES

Role of the Canada Industrial Relations Board:

- The Canada Industrial Relations Board decides the certification of bargaining agents and determines questions of membership support.
- The board also decides matters such as the appropriateness and structure of the negotiating unit and polling constituency, and questions of employee status or exclusion.
- Management may voluntarily recognize a union, thereby bypassing the formal certification procedures.

Management and union obligations:

- Bargaining agents and employers have a duty to meet and negotiate in good faith and to make every reasonable effort to conclude a collective agreement.
- The Canada Industrial Relations Board adjudicates allegations of failure to bargain in good faith and other unfair labour practices.

How bargaining starts and what may be negotiated:

- Notice to bargain for renewal and revision of an existing collective agreement may be given by either party within three months of the expiry date. The parties are required to notify the Minister of Labour of any dispute that they cannot resolve before they may acquire the right to strike or to lock out.
- The scope of collective bargaining is not limited by the Code; all subjects are potentially negotiable and, subject to the agreement of the parties, may be included in a collective agreement.

How strikes are restricted:

- Conciliation procedures may be imposed at the discretion of the Minister of Labour, and no strike or lockout may legally take place unless the dispute notification and settlement procedures have been completed or dispensed with by authority of the Minister.
- Strikes and lockouts are not permitted during the term of an agreement. The agreement must contain a provision for the settlement by arbitration or otherwise of disputes concerning the interpretation of the agreement that arise during its term, without resort to a work stoppage.

Term of agreements:

- Collective agreements must be for a fixed term of at least one year.

QUESTIONS

1. If union or management fails to bargain in good faith, what recourse does an affected party have under the *Code*?

2. What restrictions are there on the right to strike? Why do you think these restrictions exist?

3. What are the functions of the Canada Industrial Relations Board?

4. What action may I take under the *Code* if I want to become unionized?

CASE 2   AN USWA ORGANIZING DRIVE AT CANADA METALS, WINNIPEG

To help you understand how the law works to provide an orderly process of union recognition, we have constructed a representative case based on the Manitoba law. The steps in a typical organizing campaign between the United Steelworkers of America and Canada Metals are set out below:

1. Employees of Canada Metals contact USWA.

2. An internal committee is established and an organizing drive to sign cards in the union begins.

3. An application is made to the labour board, and signed cards are submitted.

4. (i) If the union has more than 40 percent of the bargaining unit but less than 65 percent of the employees signed up, there will be a vote; if a vote is ordered, the union must win 50 percent plus one of the ballots cast.

   (ii) If the union has more than 65 percent of the cards signed, there is automatic certification without a vote.

5. If the union is certified, the company and union must bargain in good faith and conclude a collective agreement.

QUESTION

1. How would the procedure differ if the province were Ontario, British Columbia, or your province?

// REFERENCES

1. Abraham, S. E. (1997). Relevance of Canadian labour law to US firms operating in Canada. *International Journal of Manpower, 18*(8), pp. 662–674.

2. Adams, R. (2003). The revolutionary potential of Dunmore. *Canadian Labour and Employment Law Journal, 10,* pp. 83–116.

3. Adams, R. (2012). Bewilderment and beyond: A comment on the *Fraser* Case. *Canadian Labour & Employment Law Journal,* pp. 313, 316, 326–28.

4. Bruce, P. G. (1989). Political parties and labour legislation in Canada and the U.S. *Industrial Relations, 28,* pp. 115–141.

5. Cameron, B. J. (2002). The "second labour trilogy": A comment on *R. v. Advance Cutting, Dunmore v. Ontario,* and *R.W.D.S.U. v. Pepsi-Cola. Supreme Court Review, 16*(2d), pp. 67–102.

6. Davenport, G. (2003). Approach to good faith negotiations in Canada: What could be the lesson for us? *New Zealand Journal of Industrial Relations, 28,* pp. 150–156.

7. Doorey, D. (2008). The medium and the "anti-union" message: "Forced listening" and captive audience meetings in Canadian labor law. *Comparative Labor Law and Policy Journal, 29,* pp. 79–118.

8. Fudge, J. (2008). The Supreme Court of Canada and the right to bargain collectively: The implications of the *Health Services and Support* case in Canada and beyond. *Industrial Law Journal, 37*(1), pp. 25–48.

9. Fudge, J. (2012). Introduction: Farm workers, collective bargaining rights, and the meaning of constitutional protection. In Fay Faraday, Judy Fudge, and Eric Tucker, eds, *Constitutional Labour Rights in Canada: Farm Workers and the Fraser Case, 7–8* Toronto: Irwin Law.

10. Government of British Columbia. (6 October 2005). Commission appointed to improve teacher bargaining. News release. Retrieved 11 January 2011 from http://www2.news.gov.bc.ca/news_releases_2005-2009/2005LCS0016-000902 .htm

11. Government of Newfoundland and Labrador. (23 October 2010). *Industrial inquiry: Voisey's Bay–Report of the Industrial Inquiry Commission, Report No. 1.* Retrieved from http://www.gov.nl.ca/LRA/voisey_bay.html

12. Haiven, L. (1990). Industrial conflict and resolution in Canada and Britain. *Employee Relations, 12*(2), pp. 12–19.

13. Hebdon, R., & Hyatt, D. (1998). The impact of industrial relations factors on health and safety conflict. *Industrial and Labor Relations Review, 51*(4)(July), pp. 579–593.

14. Human Resources and Social Development Canada. (2004). Annual report: Employment Equity Act 2004. Retrieved 15 January 2011 from http://www .hrsdc.gc.ca/en/lp/lo/lswe/we/ee_tools/reports/annual/2004/2004Annual Report.pdf

15. Human Resources and Social Development Canada (HRSDC). 2006. Hours of work, overtime, meal and other breaks. Retrieved 31 July 2011 from http://www .hrsdc.gc.ca/eng/lp/spila/clli/eslc/21Hours_Work_Overtime_Meal.shtml Human Resources and Skills Development Canada. Reproduced with the permission of the Minister of Public Works and Government Services Canada, 2011.

16. ILO. (2008). ILO declaration on social justice for a fair globalization. Retrieved from http://www.ilo.org/gender/Informationresources/Publications/ WCMS_100531/lang--en/index.htm

17. Jain, H. C., Lawler, J. J., Bai, B., & Lee, E. K. (2010). Effectiveness of Canada's employment equity legislation for women (1997–2004). *Relations industrielles, 65*(2), pp. 304–329.

18. Langille, B. (2009). The freedom of association mess: How we got into it and how we can get out of it. *McGill Law Journal, 54,* pp. 177–212.

19. Lewchuk, W., Robb, L. A., & Walters, V. (1996). The effectiveness of Bill 70 and joint health and safety committees in reducing injuries in the workplace: The case of Ontario. *Canadian Public Policy, 22*(3), pp. 225–244.

20. Lipset, M., & Meltz, N. M. (2004). *The paradox of American unionism*. Ithaca, NY: ILR Press.

21. McQuarrie, F. (2010). In good faith? An analysis of the features and outcomes of duty of representation cases. *Relations industrielles, 65*(1), pp. 118–133.

22. Mentzer, M. S. (2002). The Canadian experience with employment equity legislation. *International Journal of Value-Based Management, 15*(1), pp. 35–50.

23. Panitch, L., & Swartz, D. (1993). *The assault on trade union freedoms*. Toronto: Garamond Press.

24. Piore, M. J., & Safford, S. (2006). Changing regimes of workplace governance, shifting axes of social mobilization, and the challenge to industrial relations theory. *Industrial Relations, 45*(3), pp. 299–325.

25. Sack, J. (2010). U.S. and Canadian labour law: Significant distinctions. *American Bar Association Journal of Labor and Employment Law* (Chicago), *25*(2), pp. 241–258.

26. Singh, P., & Peng, P. (2010). Canada's bold experiment with pay equity. *Gender in Management: An International Journal, 25*(7), pp. 570–585.

27. Slinn, S. (2008). No right (to organize) without a remedy: Evidence and consequences of the failure to provide compensatory remedies for unfair labour practices in British Columbia. *McGill Law Journal, 53*, pp. 687–737.

28. Supreme Court of Canada. (1991). *Osborne v. Canada (Treasury Board)*, [1991] 2 S.C.R. 69. Judgments of the Supreme Court of Canada. Retrieved from http://scc.lexum.umontreal.ca/en/1991/1991rcs2-69/1991rcs2-69.html

29. Supreme Court of Canada. (2001). *Dunmore v. Ontario (Attorney General)*, [2001] 3 S.C.R. 1016, 2001 SCC 94. Judgments of the Supreme Court of Canada. Retrieved 1 August 2010 from http://csc.lexum.org/en/2001/2001scc94/2001scc94.html

30. Supreme Court of Canada. (2002). *R.W.D.S.U., Local 558 v. Pepsi-Cola Canada Beverages (West) Ltd.*, [2002] 1 S.C.R. 156, 2002 SCC 8. Judgments of the Supreme Court of Canada. Retrieved 15 January 2011 from http://scc.lexum.umontreal.ca/en/2002/2002scc8/2002scc8.html

31. Supreme Court of Canada. (2015). *Mounted Police Association of Ontario v. Canada (Attorney General)*, 2015 SCC 1. Retrieved from https://www.documentcloud.org/documents/1503704-supreme-court-of-canada-rcmp-union-ruling.html

32. Swinton, C. (1995). The *Charter of Rights and Freedoms*. In G. Swimmer & M. Thompson (Eds.), *Public sector collective bargaining in Canada*. Kingston, ON: IRC Press, pp. 53–77.

33. Troy, L., & Sheflin, N. (1985). *Union sourcebook: Membership structure, finance, and directory* (1st edition). West Orange, NJ: Industrial Relations Data Information Services.

34. Weiner, N. (1995). Workplace equity. In G. Swimmer & M. Thompson (Eds.), *Public sector collective bargaining in Canada*. Kingston, ON: IRC Press, pp. 78–10.

APPENDIX A

EQUAL PAY LEGISLATION IN CANADA BY JURISDICTION

Note: To save space, the footnotes have been omitted. They may be found on the HRSDC website.

(Continued)

Jurisdiction	Application	Type of Prohibition	Basis for Measuring Equal Pay	Basis for the Comparison of Work	Factors That Justify a Difference in Pay	Time Limit to File Complaint	Restrictions on Recovery
Federal Jurisdiction (*Canadian Human Rights Act* Equal Wages Guidelines, 1986)	Federal public service and federally regulated undertakings	Male-female pay differential	Wages [*Act*, s. 11(1))	Work of equal value performed in the same establishment, assessed by the composite of the skill, effort and responsibility required and the working conditions under which work is performed. (*Act*, s. 11(1), (2))	Different performance ratings; seniority; a re-evaluation and downgrading of an employee's position; a rehabilitation assignment; a demotion procedure or a procedure of gradually reducing an employee's wages on the same grounds that justify a demotion procedure; a temporary training position; the existence of an internal labour shortage in a particular job classification; a reclassification of a position to a lower level; or regional rates of wages. Gender is not a reasonable factor justifying a difference in pay. [*Act*, ss. 11(4), (5); Guidelines, s. 16)	1 year (an extension of time is possible) (s. 41(1) (e))	No

APPENDIX A Equal Pay Legislation in Canada by Jurisdiction

Jurisdiction	Application	Type of Prohibition	Basis for Measuring Equal Pay	Basis for the Comparison of Work	Factors That Justify a Difference in Pay	Time Limit to File Complaint	Restrictions on Recovery
Alberta (*Human Rights, Citizenship and Multiculturalism Act*)	Private and public sectors	Male-female pay differential	Rate of pay s. 6(1)	The same or substantially the same work for an employer in an establishment. s. 6(1)	The contravention of the Act was reasonable and justifiable in the circumstances. (s. 11)	1 year (s. 20(1)(b))	Recovery is limited to wages, income lost and/ or expenses incurred during the 2 years preceding the complaint. A limit also applies for civil proceedings, (s. 34)
British Columbia (*Human Rights Code*)	Private and public sectors	Male-female pay differential	Rate of pay (s. 12(1))	Similar or substantially similar work. This must be assessed by the concepts of skill, effort and responsibility, subject to factors in respect of pay rates, such as seniority systems, merit systems and systems that measure earnings by the quantity or quality of production. (ss. 12(1), (2))	A factor that would reasonably justify the difference, other than sex. (s. 12(3))	6 months (an extension of time is possible) (s. 22)	No (a limit does apply for civil proceedings)

Jurisdiction	Application	Type of Prohibition	Basis for Measuring Equal Pay	Basis for the Comparison of Work	Factors That Justify a Difference in Pay	Time Limit to File Complaint	Restrictions on Recovery
Manitoba (*Human Rights Code*)	Private and public sectors	Male-female pay differential	Scale of wages (s. 82(1))	The kind or quality of work and the amount of work required of, and done by, the employees, is the same or substantially the same. (s. 82(1))	No provisions	6 months (s. 82(2))	Recovery is limited to wages due and payable in the 6 months before the date the complaint was filed or, if employment was terminated, in the last 6 months of employment. (s. 96(2))
New Brunswick (*Employment Standards Act*)	Private and public sectors	Male-female pay differential	Rate of pay (s. 37.1(1))	Work that is substantially the same in nature, performed under similar working conditions in the same establishment and requiring substantially the same skill, effort and responsibility. (s. 37.1(1))	A seniority system; a merit system; a system that measures earnings by quantity or quality of production; or any other system or practice that is not unlawful. (s. 37.1(1))	12 months (s. 61(1))	No
Newfoundland and Labrador (*Human Rights Code*)	Private and public sectors	Male-female pay differential	Wages, pension rights, insurance benefits and opportunities for training and advancement. (ss. 11(1), (2))	The same or similar work on jobs requiring the same or similar skill, effort and responsibility, performed under the same or similar working conditions in the same establishment. (s. 11(1))	A seniority system or a merit system. (s. 11(1)) These factors apply only in respect of wages (i.e. not for insurance benefits or opportunities for training and advancement).	6 months (s. 20(1))	No

(Continued)

Jurisdiction	Application	Type of Prohibition	Basis for Measuring Equal Pay	Basis for the Comparison of Work	Factors That Justify a Difference in Pay	Time Limit to File Complaint	Restrictions on Recovery
Northwest Territories (*Human Rights Act*)	Private and public sectors	General antidiscrimination	Rate of pay (s. 9(1))	The same or substantially similar work performed by employees in the same establishment. Work is deemed to be similar or substantially similar if it involves the same or substantially similar skill, effort and responsibility and is performed under the same or substantially similar working conditions. (ss. 9(1), (5))	A seniority system; a merit system; a system that measures earnings by quantity or quality of production or performance; a compensation or hiring system that recognizes the existence of a labour shortage in respect of the field of work or of regional differences in the cost of living; a downgrading, reclassification or demotion process or system; the existence of a temporary rehabilitation or training program; or any other system or factor. These cannot be based on a prohibited ground of discrimination. (s. 9(2))	2 years (an extension of time is possible) (ss. 29(2), (3))	No
Nova Scotia (*Labour Standards Code*)	Private and public sectors	Male-female pay differential	Rate of wages (s. 57(1))	Substantially the same work performed in the same establishment, the performance of which requires substantially equal skill, effort and responsibility and that is performed under similar working conditions. (s. 57(1))	A seniority system; a merit system; a system that measures wages by quantity or quality of production; or another differential based on a factor other than sex. (s. 57(2))	6 months (s. 21(3A))	No

Jurisdiction	Application	Type of Prohibition	Basis for Measuring Equal Pay	Basis for the Comparison of Work	Factors That Justify a Difference in Pay	Time Limit to File Complaint	Restrictions on Recovery
Ontario (*Employment Standards Act, 2000*)	Private and public sectors	Male-female pay differential	Rate of pay (s. 42(1))	Substantially the same kind of work performed in the same establishment under similar working conditions and that requires substantially the same skill, effort and responsibility. (s. 42(1))	A seniority system; a merit system; a system that measures earnings by quantity or quality of production; or any factor other than sex. (s. 42(2))	2 years (s. 96(3))	An order to pay unpaid wages made by an employment standards officer cannot exceed $10,000 per employee. (ss. 42(5), 103(4)) Furthermore, an officer cannot make an order to pay unpaid wages if the wages became due more than 6 months before the complaint was filed. (s. 111)
Prince Edward Island (*Human Rights Act*)	Private and public sectors	General antidiscrimination	Rate of pay (s. 7)	Substantially the same work, requiring equal education, skill, experience, effort and responsibility and which is performed under similar working conditions. (s. 7)	A seniority system; a merit system; or a system that measures earnings by quantity or quality of production. The factor cannot be based on discrimination. (s. 7)	1 year (s. 22(1)(b))	No (a limit does apply for civil proceedings)

(Continued)

Jurisdiction	Application	Type of Prohibition	Basis for Measuring Equal Pay	Basis for the Comparison of Work	Factors That Justify a Difference in Pay	Time Limit to File Complaint	Restrictions on Recovery
Quebec (Charter of Human Rights and Freedoms)	Private and public sectors	General antidiscrimination	Salary or wages (s. 19)	Equivalent work performed at the same place. (s. 19)	Experience; seniority; years of service; merit; productivity; or overtime. These criteria must be common to all members of the personnel in order to justify a difference in pay. (s. 19)	Not specified	No
Saskatchewan (Labour Standards Act)	Private and public sectors	Male-female pay differential	Rate of pay (s. 17(1))	Similar work performed in the same establishment under similar working conditions, requiring similar skill, effort and responsibility. (s. 17(1))	A seniority system or a merit system. (s. 17(1))	Not specified	No
Yukon Territory (Employment Standards Act)	Private sector	Male-female pay differential	Rate of pay (s. 44)	Similar work performed in the same establishment under similar working conditions, requiring similar skill, effort and responsibility. (s. 44)	A seniority system; a merit system; a system that measures earnings by quantity or quality of production; or a differential based on any factor other than sex. (s. 44)	6 months (s. 73(3))	No

Jurisdiction	Application	Type of Prohibition	Basis for Measuring Equal Pay	Basis for the Comparison of Work	Factors That Justify a Difference in Pay	Time Limit to File Complaint	Restrictions on Recovery
Yukon Territory *(continued)* *(Human Rights Act)*	Public sector, including municipalities and their corporations, boards and commissions.	Male-female pay differential	Wages (s. 15(1))	Work of equal value, assessed by the criterion of the composite of skill, effort, and responsibility required and the working conditions. (s. 15(1), (3))	No provisions	6 months (s. 20(2))	No

Source: Employment and Social Development Canada, Equal pay legislation in Canada by jurisdiction, Labour Law Analysis, International and Intergovernmental Labour Affairs Labour Program (2006). Reproduced with permission of the Minister of Employment and Social Development Canada, 2015.

CHAPTER
5

THE UNION PERSPECTIVE

LEARNING OBJECTIVES

BY THE END OF THIS CHAPTER, YOU WILL BE ABLE TO DISCUSS

- the function and role of unions in contemporary Canadian society;
- union purposes and philosophies;
- the organization and structure of unions;
- the differences between craft/occupational, industrial, and public-sector unionism;
- the democratic processes of unions;
- why employees join unions;
- changing union membership patterns; and
- labour and the environment.

Unions in the twenty-first century face many challenges emanating from globalization and the liberalization of markets, changes in the nature of work, and shifts in the composition of the labour force. Globalization has allowed capital to move more freely between countries and has no doubt decreased the bargaining power of unions. Many aspects of the changes in markets and work have affected union identity through a shift to a more individualistic employment relationship. Examples of structural changes that affect union identity are the increase in the participation rate of women; the decline in manufacturing and other heavily unionized industrial sectors; the increase in multiple forms of contingent employment; the increase in diversity by groups such as nonwhite and gay and lesbian minorities; the growing need for higher education; and the increasing importance of knowledge work (Lévesque, Murray & Le Queux, 2005). We will return to these themes in Chapter 12.

The purpose of this chapter is to introduce to the reader the function and role of unions in contemporary Canadian society. We will examine unions' purposes and philosophies; organization and structure, including their democratic processes; and changing membership patterns.

// UNION PURPOSES AND PHILOSOPHIES

UNION PURPOSES

Why do unions exist? Three broad approaches are used to justify the existence of unions: economics, politics, and human rights. Two of these, the economic and political approaches, are derived from the early views expressed by the **institutionalists** in industrial relations (Commons, 1921; Perlman, 1928; Webb & Webb, 1902). The human rights rationale is more recent, and grew out of the internationalization of labour rights after World War II and to some extent in Canada by the adoption of the *Charter of Rights and Freedoms* after 1982.

institutionalists
those subscribing to the theory that the operation of labour markets requires a knowledge and understanding of such social organizations as unions, nongovernmental community organizations, and international institutions

ECONOMICS

The institutional economists believed that unions would improve both the efficiency and equity of markets by providing a greater balance of bargaining power between individuals and firms (Kaufman, 2000). This belief was in part a reaction to the unregulated markets of the nineteenth century that led to exploitative wages, excessive workplace injuries and deaths, and the general lack of "opportunities for personal growth and development at work" (Kaufman, 2000, p. 189).

The macroeconomic purpose of wealth redistribution could be achieved by replacing individual bargaining with collective bargaining through unions. Conditions of unfettered markets that produce such negative outcomes as substandard wages would be replaced with union protection. Thus, the institutionalists envisioned win-win outcomes for employers, workers, and the public at large (Kaufman, 2000).

POLITICS

Even more important than enhancing economic outcomes was the institutionalist objective for unions: promoting industrial democracy. Scholars defined industrial democracy in various ways, ranging from simple profit-sharing to government ownership of the means of production (Kaufman, 2000). For the institutionalists, there were four key elements of industrial democracy:

1. *Employee voice in determining work rules*. "Representative democracy in industry is representation of organized interests" and "it is the equilibrium of capital and labor–the class partnership of organized capital and organized labor, in the public interest" (Commons, 1919, p. 40).

2. *A written law of workplace rules*. "Whether carved on stone by an ancient monarch or written in a Magna Carta by a [sic] King John, or embodied in collective agreement between a union and employer, the intent is the same, to subject the ruler to definite laws to which subjects or citizens may hold him when he attempts to exercise arbitrary power" (Leiserson, 1922, p. 75, cited in Kaufman, 2000).

3. *A binding procedure for the enforcement of the written law*. "Like the Constitution of the United States, the agreement has become a 'government of law and not of men.' A man is not deprived of his job without 'due process of law'" (Commons, 1919, p. 108).

4. *A balance of power between management and labour*. "If one party to the employment relationship has a preponderance of power, it is likely that this power will be used in ways that are both arbitrary and onerous" (Kaufman, 2000, p. 197).

HUMAN RIGHTS

International Labour Organization (ILO)
a tripartite (government, management, and labour) agency of the United Nations with the mandate to establish and enforce global labour standards

The **International Labour Organization (ILO)**, a tripartite (management, labour, and government) agency of the United Nations, has established standards on such human rights as freedom from child or forced labour, freedom of association, and the right to collective bargaining. In 1998, the ILO passed the *Declaration on Fundamental Principles and Rights at Work*. In a unanimous vote (but with some abstentions), it declared a core set of labour standards to be fundamental human rights, thereby bringing them under the umbrella of international human rights law (Adams, 2002; Hebdon 2014). In 2008, these fundamental principles were affirmed in the *Declaration on Social Justice for a Fair Globalization* acclaimed by the 182 member states of the ILO including Canada. Freedom of association is also a freedom guaranteed in the *Canadian Charter of Rights and Freedoms* and has been interpreted by the Supreme Court of Canada to include collective bargaining (see Chapter 2 and the *B.C. Health* case, 2007).

The International Labour Organization (ILO) has as a core labour standard the elimination of child labour.

PHILOSOPHIES

Unions have different world-views than managers and corporate leaders. The democratic mandate of union leaders is both a source of strength and a constraint on their behaviour. We start with the definition of a union derived from Canadian labour law. All eleven labour laws in Canada provide such a definition. The *Saskatchewan Trade Union Act*, for example, defines an employee organization as follows:

> 2 (j) *"labour organization" means an organization of employees, not necessarily employees of one employer, that has bargaining collectively among its purposes;*
>
> and
>
> 2 (l) *"trade union" means a labour organization that is not a company dominated organization. (Government of Saskatchewan, 1978)*

Two elements of this legal definition are essential components of unions. First, unions must have, as one of their purposes, collective bargaining with the firm. Second, it is clear from this typical definition that unions must be independent of the employer. Thus, an organization created by the employer, a **company union**, would not qualify as a union under Canadian labour law.

As long as collective bargaining is one of the functions of a union, unions are free to pursue other goals. Non–collective bargaining activities of unions vary considerably according to such factors as

- the union's history (violent struggle or peaceful recognition);
- industry (private or public); and
- the aims of the founding members (economic, political, or religious).

company union
a union that a company helped create

As we saw in Chapter 2, there have been three great waves of unionization in Canada, each with its own defining elements. The three waves were

- craft (late 1890s to 1920s);
- industrial (1930s and 1940s); and
- public-sector (1960s).

Reflecting their historical roots, Canadian unions tend to fall into one of three broad categories of institutions: craft or occupationally based; industrial or multiple-skill based; or public-sector. The reader will note, however, that these categories are not distinct, nor do they define all unions. The International Association of Fire Fighters (IAFF), for example, is both a craft and a public-sector union. The first union of firefighters was affiliated with the American Federation of Labor (the craft union federation) in 1901 in Washington, D.C. (IAFF, 2006).

CRAFT/OCCUPATIONAL UNIONISM

The earliest wave of unionization was marked by the extensive craft-union organizing that took place between the end of the nineteenth century and beginning of the twentieth. To a great extent this **craft or occupational unionism** was defined by the way goods were produced in North America at the time. Production was very much a skill-based activity often involving a variety of artisans working independently of each other. A modern example is production in the residential housing sector, in which various trades are called upon to contribute toward the completion of a house.

craft or occupational unionism
unions that typically allow into membership only trades or occupations that are in the same family of skills

Single occupation unions tend to focus on the non-collective bargaining activities of maintaining the skill, training, and education of the craft or profession. They may also try to control entry into the craft or profession. The singular focus on standards means that these unions are more likely to have a world-view limited to providing for the security and economic well-being of their members. The philosophy of craft unions is often referred to as business unionism that emphasizes economic gains through collective bargaining. Since the primary non-collective bargaining activities are related to promoting the craft or profession, there is often not a strong social agenda.

We are familiar with craft or occupational unionism in the construction trades (e.g., carpenters, electricians, stonemasons, bricklayers, plumbers) and firefighting. In addition, in some provinces, some professional associations such as those for teachers, nurses, and doctors also fall into this category. Professional organizations may not think of themselves as remotely related to craft unions, but if they are judged objectively by the stated aims of their constitutions, a case can be made for more similarities than differences. To illustrate the philosophy of occupational unionism, we have provided three examples from the constitutions of these organizations: the International Brotherhood of Electrical Workers (IBEW), the Ontario Nurses' Association (ONA), and a bricklayer's union. A more rigorous examination of an organization's character would require a detailed analysis of the full range of activities of each organization, which is beyond the scope of this text. Nonetheless, the aims and purposes as defined in their constitutions provide useful indicators of the nature of these organizations.

Our enquiry begins with an excerpt from the constitution of the International Brotherhood of Electrical Workers (see IR Today 5.1). The objects of the union emphasize conditions of employment for workers in the electrical industry. What is most

CRAFT UNION: INTERNATIONAL BROTHERHOOD OF ELECTRICAL WORKERS CONSTITUTION

Objects

The Objects of the International Brotherhood of Electrical Workers are:

- To organize all workers in the entire electrical industry in the United States and Canada, including all those in public utilities and electrical manufacturing, into local unions,
- To promote reasonable methods of work,
- To cultivate feelings of friendship among those of our industry,
- To settle all disputes between employers and employees by arbitration (if possible),

- To assist each other in sickness or distress,
- To secure employment,
- To reduce the hours of daily labor,
- To secure adequate pay for our work,
- To seek a higher and higher standard of living,
- To seek security for the individual,
- And by legal and proper means to elevate the moral, intellectual and social conditions of our members, their families and dependents, in the interest of a higher standard of citizenship.

Source: International Brotherhood of Electrical Workers. 2001 Constitution, p. 4. Reprinted with permission. Retrieved from www.ibew769.com/library/IBEWConstitution.pdf.

noteworthy about the IBEW is the absence of any focus on social issues that might affect all union and nonunion employees.

The next example is a case of a typical professional union where the focus is again on a single occupation and less on the wider social conditions of society. The Ontario Nurses' Association philosophy and vision statement indicate a focus on nursing practice and care (see IR Today 5.2). Like the IBEW, the emphasis is on the social and economic status of the association's members.

CRAFT UNION: ONTARIO NURSES' ASSOCIATION

Philosophy

Members of the Union are committed to a program, which enhances their social and economic status. As well, the organization's goals include the right to be involved in the determination of policies and legislation concerning nursing practice and the quality of care.

To achieve this goal, it is essential that the organization build positive relationships, and create and maintain harmonious environments within the Union, with employers and other groups to stimulate a free exchange of ideas and information.

Objectives

- The advancement of the social, economic and general welfare of nurses.
- The regulation of employee/employer relations and the negotiation of written contracts that implement progressively better conditions of employment.
- The promotion of effective communication with employers.
- The promotion of knowledge of nurses in all areas related to their social and economic welfare through education and research.

A typical construction craft, bricklayers at work.

Digital Vision/Thinkstock/Getty Images

Our final example of a craft or occupational union is the International Union of Bricklayers and Allied Craftworkers; information on the BAC union can be found at http://www.bacweb.org/about_us/who_we_are/pdf/member_booklet-english.pdf. From the union's constitution objectives, we can see that the most important aim is to "improve members' quality of life—both on and off the job—through access to good jobs, fair wages and quality benefits, and by building solidarity and support" among all its members' interests. While raising the standard of the craft is an important goal, the International Union of Bricklayers and Allied Craftworkers also shows a concern for the wider interests of all workers.

Note the distinction here between national or international unions and local unions. Locals are subunits of the parent national or international union, and as such may have aims that diverge somewhat from the parent organization, which in this case is the International Union of Bricklayers and Allied Craftworkers.

INDUSTRIAL OR MULTI-SKILL UNIONISM

The second great wave of union organizing began in the 1930s, after manufacturing enterprises introduced the assembly-line method of production. With this method, the typical production worker became more of a generalist lacking specific training in any particular craft or trade. Craft unions were not interested in organizing these new generalists. Thus, as a competing vision to craft unionism, **industrial unionism** welcomed both skilled and unskilled occupations into membership. Rather than organize a single occupation or craft in a firm, industrial unions sought to represent all of the production or office workers of a firm at a given location or at several locations or plants.

The vision of most industrial unions is more class-based and goes beyond collective bargaining to include societal reform. Members' interests are served by promoting a wide agenda of social issues. Within industrial unionism, there is also considerable

industrial unionism
a type of inclusive unionism that represents a broad range of skills and occupations

variation in the scope of the social agenda and the radical nature of the reforms sought. The unions in this category often use the term *social unionism* to describe their philosophy (see Ross, 2007).

These excerpts from Unifor's constitution provide an illustration of this type:

In our workplaces

- *To promote, conduct and safeguard collective bargaining and to strengthen practices of more broadly based bargaining, including coordinated and pattern bargaining.*

- *To regulate and improve wages, pensions and benefits, hours of work, employment security and working conditions through collective bargaining and political action.*

- *To protect and strengthen our rights at work.*

- *To strive for a safe and healthy work environment.*

- *To ensure fair treatment, dignity and respect at work.*

- *To make workplaces more democratic.*

- *To organize the unorganized.*

- *To strive for a safe workplace free of discrimination and harassment*

In our communities

- *To fight for good jobs in our communities and throughout the economy.*

- *To provide support to those in need.*

- *To build our union's presence in the community and encourage our members to be involved in all aspects of community life.*

- *To work in common cause with other progressives to promote social justice and environmental sustainability at a community level.*

- *To work on labour-based campaigns with other affiliates of Labour Councils.*

- *To encourage unorganized workers to join our union and be open to new members in our communities.*

In broader society

- *To safeguard, protect and extend freedom, civil liberties, democracy and democratic trade unionism.*

- *To be broadly politically active at the municipal, provincial and federal levels and to mount issue-based campaigns.*

- *To fight for social and economic reform by giving priority to good jobs, equality and social justice.*

- *To protect and safeguard the health and safety of the planet by supporting the goal of an environmentally sustainable future.*

- *To build and unify the labour movement and to act in solidarity with other labour organizations in Canada and throughout the world with objectives similar to ours.*

- *To support and work in common cause with progressive organizations in Canada and around the world.*

- *To resist corporate globalization and provide alternatives to job-destroying trade deals and policies.*

- *To work to end war and contribute to world peace. (Unifor, n.d.)*

Unifor's broad social agenda stands in stark contrast to those of the occupational unions. Unifor stands on the left of the Canadian political spectrum, but its support for the NDP and the mainstream left in Canada has waxed and waned over the years. Unifor president Jerry Dias encouraged members to support Liberal candidates in the 2015 federal election in those ridings where the NDP had little or no chance of winning (see Livingston, 2006). This practice intensified existing splits within labour between unions that support the NDP and those that do not—some from the right (e.g., craft unions) and others (e.g., Unifor) from the left (see IR Notebook 5.1).

IR NOTEBOOK 5.1

UNIFOR AIMS TO DEFEAT HARPER TORIES

The NDP's traditionally strong ties to the labour movement won't be enough to secure a blanket endorsement from Canada's largest private sector union in next year's federal election.

Unifor will urge its 300,000-plus members to vote strategically and will pour its resources behind the local candidates — be they NDP or Liberal — best positioned to defeat Stephen Harper's Conservatives.

The union infuriated many New Democrats when it took a similar stance in last spring's Ontario election in a bid to stop Tim Hudak's Progressive Conservatives.

In that case, Conservative support collapsed, allowing Kathleen Wynne's Liberals to cruise to a majority victory.

Unifor national president Jerry Dias says the union has a strong relationship with the federal NDP and will support re-election of all incumbent New Democrat MPs.

But he says the need to defeat the Harper government must trump Unifor's loyalty to the party.

"For us, we know that another four years of Harper will be disastrous for working class people in Canada, period. So, that in itself trumps going out there and putting support in a riding where we know that the New Democrats have no chance," Dias said in an interview.

"If the New Democrats have a legitimate, good shot at winning, absolutely that's where we're going, no question about it. But if there's not a hope in hell, why would I waste resources? It doesn't make a stitch of sense."

For example, in a riding like Manitoba's Brandon-Souris, where the Liberals came within a whisker of defeating the Conservatives in a byelection late last year, Dias said Unifor will throw its support and resources behind the Liberal candidate next year.

"The New Democrat got wiped right out (in the byelection). So for us to even consider supporting the New Democrats in Brandon-Souris, in my opinion, may very well just hand the seat back to the Conservatives."

The decision to pursue strategic voting in the next federal election was taken unanimously at a weekend meeting of Unifor's national council. Ironically, the gathering featured a keynote speech by NDP Leader Tom Mulcair, who announced his plan to reinstate a minimum wage for workers in federally regulated sectors, rising to $15 per hour over four years.

NDP labour critic Alexandre Boulerice conceded Unifor's decision is disappointing.

"Frankly, I would have preferred clear support for the NDP as the real choice for the next election," Boulerice said Thursday.

Still, he said most labour unions are solidly behind the NDP and it's no surprise Unifor is not among them, given its history of strategic voting. Unifor was formed last year from a merger of the Canadian Auto Workers and the Communications, Energy and Paperworkers unions.

The CAW endorsed Paul Martin's Liberals in the 2006 election in a failed bid to prevent Harper from becoming prime minister.

Dias acknowledged the labour movement has no stronger political ally than the NDP. But while Justin Trudeau's Liberals are less supportive of unions than the NDP, he said he doubts they're intent on destroying the movement, as he believes Harper's Conservatives are determined to do.

"So, if my choice is Stephen Harper or Justin Trudeau, then that's a no-brainer."

Dias said anti-union measures are "red meat" that Harper throws out to pacify "right-wing extremists" in the Conservative party.

He pointed to government and Conservative private members' bills which labour advocates complain would impose unfair financial transparency rules on unions, gut public service collective bargaining and make it harder for federally regulated workers to join a union while making it easier to decertify a union.

Unifor's refusal to unequivocally back the New Democrats in the Ontario election prompted more than 600 federal NDP parliamentary staffers, who are members of Unifor, to look for another union to represent them.

Anthony Salloum, president of the Unifor local that represents the staffers, said members will vote early next month to choose a new union home. They have three options: the United Steelworkers, the United Food and Commercial Workers or the International Association of Machinists.

All three "have indicated full support for the NDP," Salloum said.

Source: Joan Bryden. (18 September 2014). "Unifor aims to defeat Harper Tories." The Canadian Press. Used with permission of The Canadian Press. Retrieved from http://www.nationalnewswatch.com/2014/09/18/union-puts-defeat-of-harpers-tories-ahead-of-support-for-ndp/#.VFJd2FfQp1s.

Another example of industrial unionism can be seen in the constitution of the United Food and Commercial Workers (UFCW) (IR Today 5.3). The UFCW constitution also highlights two of the key elements of a social union: namely, a wide social agenda and a desire to have this progress apply to all workers, not just the members of the UFCW.

IR TODAY   5.3

INDUSTRIAL UNION: UNITED FOOD AND COMMERCIAL WORKERS CANADA

Article 2

Objectives and Principles

The object of this International Union shall be the elevation of the position of its members, and further:

- to conduct an International Union of persons engaged in the performance of work within its jurisdictions;
- to encourage members and all workers to register and vote;

- to support research in its industries for the benefit of its members;
- to advance and safeguard the full employment, economic security, and social welfare of its members and of workers generally;
- to protect and extend democratic institutions, civil rights and liberties, and the traditions of social and economic justice of the United States and Canada. . . .

Source: United Food and Commercial Workers Canada Constitution 2013. "Article 2: Objectives and principles." UFCW Canada Constitution. Used with permission. Retrieved from http://www.tuac.ca/templates/ufcwcanada/images/our_union/ufcw_canada_constitution_2014/CONSTITUTION_EN_ALL_email.pdf

public-sector or social justice unionism
unions of public-sector employees at all three levels of government: local, provincial, and federal; typically advocates of a philosophy of social justice

The third phase of unionism was the most recent to develop. Public-sector collective bargaining took off in the 1960s in Canada due to expansion in services, the passage of favourable public-sector collective bargaining laws, and the social activism brought on by the civil rights and antiwar movements (Rose, 1995). Most public-sector unions have embraced some form of **public-sector or social justice unionism**, as the example of the Canadian Union of Public Employees below aptly illustrates (see IR Today 5.4).

IR TODAY   5.4

PUBLIC-SECTOR UNION: CANADIAN UNION OF PUBLIC EMPLOYEES CONSTITUTION

Objectives

2.1 The Union has as its objectives:

(a) The organization of workers generally, and in particular all workers in the public service of Canada.

(b) The advancement of the social, economic and general welfare of active and retired employees.

(c) The defence and extension of the civil rights and liberties of public employees and the preservation of free democratic trade unionism.

(d) The improvement of the wages, working conditions, hours of work, job security and other conditions affecting all employees including retirees' pension benefits.

(e) The promotion of efficiency in public service generally.

(f) The promotion of peace and freedom in the world, and the cooperation with free and democratic labour movements throughout the world.

(g) The utilization of our world's natural and human resources for the good of all the world's people while promoting the respect and conservation of the environment and the creation of sustainable communities and jobs.

(h) The elimination of harassment and discrimination of any sort or on any basis; for the equality of treatment regardless of class, race, colour, nationality, age, sex/gender, language, sexual orientation, place of origin, ancestry, religious beliefs, or mental and physical disability; and the active opposition to discrimination of same wherever it occurs or appears.

(i) The establishment of strong working relationships with the public we serve and the communities in which we work and live.

Source: Canadian Union of Public Employees. "Article II: Objectives." CUPE Constitution 2009. Used with permission. Retrieved from http://cupe.ca/updir/Constitution_2009.pdf.

The CUPE constitution has some elements that warrant closer examination. There is a wide range of objectives, from promoting efficiency in the provision of public services to the elimination of discrimination in the workplace, the conservation of the environment, and the pursuit of world peace.

Almost all unions engage in some form of political activity in the form of lobbying for, endorsing, and supporting candidates, or fully affiliating with a political party. With respect to the latter activity of political-party affiliation, some public-sector unions prefer to be nonpartisan organizations. The last paragraph in the objects of the British

Columbia Government and Service Employees' Union (BCGEU) indicates such: "The Union shall not affiliate to any political party" (BCGEU, 2008).

OTHER UNION CATEGORIES

There are unions that do not fit into the categories of craft or professional, industrial or social, or public-sector. One is CLAC (Christian Labour Association of Canada). IR Today 5.5 provides excerpts from the CLAC website that reveal its policies on political affiliation, strikes, and cooperation. The CLAC world-view illustrates the pluralist nature of unions in Canada.

IR TODAY   5.5

CLAC

What Makes Us Different?

WE THINK DIFFERENTLY THAN OTHER UNIONS

We believe in cooperation, not confrontation. We work to make your workplace a better place—so that you and your co-workers can grow both as a workplace community and as individuals.

It's why we seek to balance individual and collective interests when we negotiate. It's why we only strike as a last resort. It's why we don't tell our members where to work, or our signatory employers who they can hire. It's why we don't force anyone to join us, or fine them when they leave. It's why we use your dues money to represent and support you, not politicians or political parties.

WHY DO WE THINK DIFFERENTLY?

Our view of work and labour relations is based on respect, dignity, and fairness for everyone in the workplace. Every one of us is unique, with different ideas and goals. The best workplace is one in which we work together, treat each other as we would like to be treated, and go out of our way to help others.

We believe that work is more than simply a paycheque and a means to an end. It enriches individual lives and society. It gives us a sense of meaning and fulfilment, and the opportunity to take pride in a job well done—no matter what the job is.

At the same time, there's more to your life than work. You belong to many groups—your family, a sports team, a religious group, a gardening club, a political party, a union, and more. Each one is important and plays a role in your life.

We work to improve your workplace so that you can enjoy your life both at work and outside of work. We bring individuals together to create a strong voice in the workplace, while still respecting their individuality. We believe in working together to make everyone's life better.

Unionizing with CLAC

If and when a collective agreement is in place, you will be required to pay union dues. Our dues policy is set by the union's National Convention at a very competitive rate. CLAC dues are among the lowest in the country. And unlike some unions, your dues stay in Canada and are used to support you and your co-workers—not political parties or candidates. . . .

Source: Used with permission of CLAC. Retrieved from https://www.clac.ca/About-us/What-makes-us-different.

A final union type that reinforces this pluralist portrayal of unions is the independent local union or enterprise union. It is possible to organize a union that is not affiliated with either a national or international union. Since the focus of local unions is typically on enterprise concerns, these organizations tend to have limited political and social objectives. For an example, read about the NHL Players' Association in IR Today 5.6.

Much like a craft union, the focus of the NHLPA is almost exclusively on hockey. Mentions of collective bargaining on the website are limited to bargaining agreement updates and arbitration schedules.

// ORGANIZATION AND STRUCTURE

UNION SIZE

You should by now have a sense of the purpose and objectives of unions and their diversity in Canada. We will now take a look at union democracy and the external links that give unions much of their power to influence Canadian society.

Our starting point is a simple introduction to the largest unions in Canada as measured by membership. The relative size of unions in Canada is a rough measure of their power and influence as organizations. In Table 5.1, we see Canada's 27 largest unions and associations as of 2001 and 2014. It is significant that the two largest unions both represent public-sector employees. With over half a million members, the largest union is the Canadian Union of Public Employees (CUPE). CUPE represents workers mostly at the municipal level of government. The National Union of Public and General Employees (NUPGE) is second-largest, and represents mostly employees at the provincial level of government. CUPE has grown by 25 percent since 2001, while NUPE membership has also increased but by a more modest amount.

The third-largest union, Unifor, was created in 2013 out of a merger of the Canadian Auto Workers (CAW) and the Communication, Energy and Paperworkers (CEP) unions. The CAW has been highly active in terms of mergers and takeovers of existing unions, listing mergers with 34 unions since 1985, adding about 148,000 members. Union mergers have helped to compensate for member losses resulting from the decline in manufacturing in Canada. Another example is the recent merger of the Telecommunication Workers with the United Steelworkers (see IR Today 5.7).

TABLE 5.1

UNIONS WITH LARGEST MEMBERSHIP, 2001 AND 2014

	MEMBERSHIP (000s)		
	2001	2014	% CHANGE
Canadian Union of Public Employees (CLC)	505.0	630.1	0.25
National Union of Public and General Employees (CLC)	325.0	340.0	0.05
Unifor (CLC)	0.0	308.0	0.0
United Food and Commercial Workers Canada (UFCW-Can)	220.0	245.3	0.12
United Steel, Paper and Forestry, Rubber, Manufacturing, Energy, Allied Industrial and Service Workers International Union (USW)	190.0	230.7	0.21
Public Service Alliance of Canada	148.7	187.5	0.26
Fédération de la santé et des services sociaux (CSN)	102.0	129.0	0.26
Service Employees International Union- Canada (AFL-CIO/CLC)	65.0	118.9	0.83
Teamsters Canada (TC)	100.2	93.1	−0.07
Alberta Union of Provincial Employees (AUPE)		80.1	
Laborers' International Union of North America (AFL-CIO/CLC)	85.0	80.0	−0.06
Elementary Teachers Foundation of Ontario (CLC)	50.4	76.2	0.51
Ontario Secondary School Teachers Federation (CLC)	55.0	65.6	0.19
Fédération des employées et employés de services publics inc. (CSN)	32.2	60.7	0.89
Ontario Nurses Association (CLC)	45.0	59.5	0.32
Professional Institute of the Public Service (Ind.)	32.5	58.7	0.81
International Brotherhood of Electrical Workers (AFL-CIO/CLC)	80.1	57.1	−0.29
Canadian Union of Postal Workers (CLC)	44.1	54.5	0.24
United Association of Journeymen and Apprenctices of the Plumbing and Pipe Fitting Industry of the United States and Canada (AFL-CIO/CLC)	36.0	50.4	0.40
United Brotherhood of Carpenters and Joiners of America (AFL-CIO/CLC)	46.0	50.0	0.09
International Association of Machinists and Aerospace Workers (AFL-CIO/CLC)	46.1	50.0	0.08
Ontario English Catholic Teachers Association (CLC)	45.6	48.6	0.07
Alberta Teachers Association (Ind.)	35.0	44.5	0.27
British Columbia Teachers' Federation (Ind.)	39.6	43.6	0.10
International Union of Operating Engineers (AFL-CIO/CLC)	46.8	42.0	-−0.10

TABLE 5.1

UNIONS WITH LARGEST MEMBERSHIP, 2001 AND 2014 (CONTINUED)

	MEMBERSHIP (000s)		
	2001	2014	% CHANGE
Syndicat de la fonction publique du Québec (Ind.)	40.0	35.5	−0.11
Fédération du commerce inc. (CSN)	33.0	32.7	−0.01

Affiliations Legend
AFL-CIO: American Federation of Labor and Congress of Industrial Organizations
CCU: Confederation of Canadian Unions
CLC: Canadian Labour Congress
CSD: Centrale des syndicats démocratiques
CSN: Confédération des syndicats nationaux
CSQ: Centrale des syndicats du Québec
CtW: Change to Win
ITUC: International Trade Union Confederation
NUPGE: National Union of Public and General Employees

Source: Adapted from Employment and Social Development Canada, Labour organizations in Canada. (2014). Reproduced with the permission of the Minister of Employment and Social Development Canada, 2015. http://www.labour.gc.ca/eng/resources/info/tools/labour_organizations_canada/organization.shtml; and Statistics Canada. Union perspectives, 2001.

IR TODAY 5.7

TELECOMMUNICATIONS WORKERS UNION VOTES TO MERGE WITH UNITED STEELWORKERS

The Telecommunications Workers Union is merging with the United Steelworkers. Union leaders issued a statement Friday saying TMU members had voted 73.7 per cent in favour of the merger.

The TWU represents 12,000 members across Canada who work for telecommunications companies including TELUS (TSX:T) and Shaw Communications (TSX:SJR.B), as well as employers in related telecommunications sectors.

"This is a great result for our membership, our families and our communities across Canada," TWU national president Lee Riggs said, adding that the decision to join the much larger union would "help us improve the working lives of our members."

USW National Director Ken Neumann said the merger was an example of a "shared, positive vision for the labour movement."

The merger agreement does not take effect until January 1, but both unions said they planned to begin joint activities immediately.

"With the USW's extensive international network of allies and resources and the TWU's deep expertise in the sector, our newly merged union can become a global leader in the telecommunications sector," Riggs and Neumann said in a joint statement.

The United Steelworkers is a diverse private-sector union with 225,000 members working in every region and sector in Canada.

Source: "Telecommunications Workers Union Votes to Merge with United Steelworkers." (7 November 2014). The Canadian Press. Used with permission of The Canadian Press. Retrieved from http://www.timescolonist.com/telecommunications-workers-union-votes-to-merge-with-united-steelworkers-1.1529790.

The fourth-largest, the United Food and Commercial Workers (UFCW), also experienced modest growth since 2001. This unusual private-sector growth may be explained by the service (non-manufacturing) orientation of the UFCW members.

UNION AFFILIATION

The list in Table 5.1 also identifies whether the union is affiliated. CUPE, for example, is affiliated with the Canadian Labour Congress (CLC), and the British Columbia Teachers' Federation is independent (i.e., unaffiliated). Table 5.2 shows union membership by affiliation. By far, the dominant federation is the Canadian Labour Congress, representing 70.2 percent of the 4.6 million union members in Canada. The Quebec-based federations account for another 9.7 percent. Finally, unaffiliated national and local organizations represent 19 percent of union members in Canada.

TABLE 5.2

UNION MEMBERSHIP BY CONGRESS AFFILIATION, 2004–2014

CONGRESS AFFILIATION	2004 MEMBERSHIP	%	2014 MEMBERSHIP	%
CLC	3,121,010	73.2	3,257,196	70.2
CLC only	1,960,530	46.0	2,131,443	45.9
AFL-CIO/CLC	1,160,480	27.2	668,084	14.4
CtW/CLC			457,669	9.9
CSN	278,170	6.5	323,586	6.9
CSQ	126,060	3.0	126,486	2.7
CSD	63,070	1.5	5,000	.1
CCU	8,940	0.2	7,958	0.2
AFL-CIO only	17,630	0.4	36,040	0.8
Unaffiliated national unions	488,200	11.5	698,931	15.1
Unaffiliated international unions	2,120	0.0	1,992	0.0
Independent local organizations	155,800	3.7	181,723	3.9
Total	**4,261,000**	**100.0**	**4,638,912**	**100.0**

Note: Due to rounding, sums may not always equal totals. Legend:
CLC: Canadian Labour Congress
AFL-CIO: American Federation of Labour—Congress of Industrial Organizations
CtW: Change to Win
CSN: Confederation of National Unions (Quebec) CSQ: Union Central (Quebec social services and education) CSD: Democratic Central of Unions (Quebec—construction)
CCU: Confederation of Canadian Unions

Sources: (2001 data) Employment and Social Development Canada, Table 3: Union Membership by Congress Affiliation, published in Union Membership in Canada 2010; (2014 data) Employment and Social Development Canada, Workplace Information and Research Division, Strategic Policy, Analysis, and Workplace Information Directorate, Labour Program, Employment and Social Development Canada (2013). Retrieved from http://www.labour.gc.ca/eng/resources/info/publications/union_coverage/union_coverage.shtml. Both are reproduced with the permission of the Minister of Employment and Social Development Canada, 2015.

FIGURE 5.1

UNION AFFILIATION IN CANADA

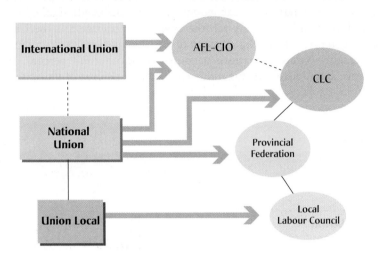

To better understand why unions affiliate with the CLC, study the flow chart of affiliations in Figure 5.1, which outlines the CLC's and components—provincial labour federations and local labour councils. The CLC's mandate is to advance a broad social agenda to improve the lives of all workers—that includes the principles of social justice, economic security, a sustainable environment, and a peaceful world (see IR Today 5.8).

In the next section, we will examine the links that unions sometime forge with national and international organizations to gain strength and exert influence over Canadian governments at all levels—local, provincial, and federal.

IR TODAY   5.8

CANADIAN LABOUR CONGRESS CONSTITUTION

Preamble

- The strength of the labour movement is built on solidarity and respect among workers.
- We commit ourselves to the goals of worker democracy, social justice, equality, and peace.
- We are dedicated to making the lives of workers and their families safe, secure, and healthy.
- We believe that every worker is entitled, without discrimination, to a job with decent wages and working conditions, union representation, free collective bargaining, a safe and healthy workplace, and the right to strike.
- We believe that we, as members of society, are entitled to basic human rights, political freedom, quality public services, good democratic government, a safe and sustainable environment, a just and equitable society, and a peaceful world.

Source: Canadian Labour Congress. (May 2008). Constitution. Used with permission. Retrieved from http://www.canadianlabour.ca/sites/default/files/pdfs/clc-constitution-english.pdf.

The arrows in Figure 5.1 indicate the options that unions have in Canada to affiliate and in which organizations' activities they can participate. International unions will usually be affiliated with the AFL-CIO (the American equivalent of the CLC), and most are also affiliated with the CLC. The thick lines indicate an organic connection between organizational units; thus, Canadian unions that can affiliate with the CLC have the option of also affiliating with provincial federations and local labour councils in the provinces and cities where members are located.

The organizational functions of the CLC and its components are set out in Figure 5.2. The CLC's primary duties are to lobby the federal government on such policy concerns as national social programs (e.g., Medicare, child care, pensions, employment insurance, trade arrangements) and to represent member unions internationally—for example, at meetings of the International Labour Organization).

The provincial federations perform similar tasks but at the provincial level of government. Since labour is a provincial responsibility under Canada's constitution, there is an important emphasis on a range of laws affecting all citizens whether union members or not. To illustrate this point, here is an excerpt from the Newfoundland and Labrador Federation of Labour:

> ... The NLFL is dedicated to advancing the cause of working people and promoting a progressive civil society where no one gets left behind. We advocate for improved workplace rights and stronger laws including occupational, health and safety laws as well as workers' compensation and Employment Insurance programs that are fair and there when people need them.
>
> We fight for better labour laws and strong, accessible public services such as universal health care, education, worker training, elder/home care and child care and early learning.
>
> We stand up for the principles of equality, equity and social justice and we work with our affiliate unions and social partners to build a better world for all citizens. (Newfoundland and Labrador Federation of Labour, 2014)

FIGURE 5.2

ORGANIZATIONAL FUNCTIONS

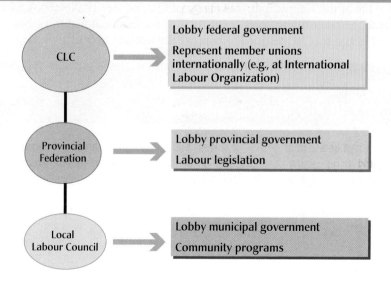

CLC → Lobby federal government
Represent member unions internationally (e.g., at International Labour Organization)

Provincial Federation → Lobby provincial government
Labour legislation

Local Labour Council → Lobby municipal government
Community programs

Canada Post workers ask for support in protecting postal services.

Labour councils are an important and often critical link between unions and the wider community. Some scholars believe that forming labour–community coalitions is critical to the revitalization of the labour movement and the organizing of the service sector (Cornfield, 2005).

As a representative example of a labour council in Canada, we examine the activities of the Toronto and York Region Labour Council. This council works with a number of community and labour organizations to effect change in public policy and in the quality of life in the Toronto and York region of Ontario. See IR Notebook 5.2 to learn more about the range of campaigns from local to international that this labour council is engaged in and that are designed to improve the working lives of all working people.

IR NOTEBOOK   5.2

TORONTO AND YORK REGION LABOUR COUNCIL CAMPAIGNS

SAVE CANADA POST   Canadians were shocked to hear of the plans of Canada Post to begin dismantling residential delivery of mail across Canada, raise prices of mail, and deeply cut its workforce. This decision will have a serious impact on working families and communities across Canada. It will particularly hurt people with disabilities and seniors.

It is clear that this action is part of the ongoing austerity agenda of the Harper Conservatives, which seeks to make workers pay for the 2008 financial melt-down caused by corporate greed and speculation. It continues the pattern of attacks on fundamental labour rights, exploitation of foreign temporary workers, and gutting of social programs such as Employment Insurance.

Armine Yalnizyan's insightful response is a must-read (http://www.theglobeandmail.com/globe-debate/article15981676.ece).

The Toronto & York Region Labour Council will extend our full support to CUPW and its local unions in our region in whatever form of fight-back the union undertakes. We support the union's call for to preserve public postal service and improve Canada Post's financial position by expanding parcel delivery and adding banking and financial services. Send a message to your Member of Parliament—www.cupw.ca.

A JOB SHOULD LIFT YOU OUT OF POVERTY… *"A job should lift you out of poverty, not keep you in it".* Not many years ago, that statement would have seemed unnecessary to most Canadians. But in today's economy, the assertion that people working a full-time job should not be in poverty is not so obvious. The statement is at the core of the challenge facing the Ontario government – does it believe that poverty will be addressed without fundamentally addressing the issue of poverty wages? Labour Council is part of the coalition fighting for a $14 Minimum Wage www.RaiseTheMinimumWage.ca

Joint Statement by Community and Labour Groups Concerning Federal Changes to Employment Insurance

STUDENT + LABOUR UNITY On June 12th over 70 representatives of student unions, campus labour unions and members of the Labour Council met to dialogue about their common interests in tackling austerity. The symposium called "Students and Workers Unite" was hosted by Labour Community Services, the Labour Council and the Canadian Federation of Students - Ontario office.

Workers and students discussed the many challenges faced in the post-secondary arena with added pressures of declining government support and increased privatization on university and college campuses. The common consensus build was that a united front of both students and workers must be presented in order to protect public education. Campus labour unions and student unions committed to building a framework of ongoing communication and mutual solidarity in each of Toronto's three universities.

DEFEND WORKERS RIGHTS Stephen Harper and Tim Hudak are promoting changes to labour law that would drive down wages and harm Canadian society. Ontario Conservative leader Tim Hudak has announced that he will weaken unions by making major changes to labour laws – if he wins the next Ontario election. Prime Minister Harper has already pushed Bill 377 through Parliament. This legislation was designed to disrupt unions by requiring extraordinary financial reporting. Next in line is Bill 525, making it far harder for workers to join unions in a number of sectors. To learn more about the campaign to defend workers against these attacks, go to http://www.labourcouncil.ca/workers-rights.html.

COMMUNITY BENEFITS + TRANSIT Metrolinx is building a Light Rail Transit (LRT) network worth $8.4-billion across Toronto. Labour Council is working with a number of community groups and unions to achieve a Community Benefit Agreement (CBA) to ensure that residents from marginalized and low-income communities have a chance at some of the jobs created between now and 2020. www.community benefits.ca

FIX EI—SCRAP THE CHANGES People in greater Toronto need to start fighting to improve unemployment insurance, and defend what is left of this vital social safety net. Only 1 in 5 unemployed Torontonians received Employment Insurance (EI) benefits at any given time last year and the recent changes by the Conservatives government will only make matters worse. Many workers will now be forced to accept jobs that pay up to 30% less than their previous income or risk being cut off benefits. The role of construction union hiring halls is being severely curtailed.

"This reform will undermine overall wages and will have huge long-term implications on local economies across Canada" said Armine Yalnizyan, a senior economist with the Canadian Centre for Policy Alternatives, as she traced the history of unemployment insurance at a special teach-in on EI changes held in June 2013. Good Jobs for All Coalition is leading the effort to scrap the changes and bring back a system that covers all workers between jobs (www.goodjobsforall.ca).

FIRST VICTORY FOR BANGLADESHI WORKERS Mobilization by global union federations and NGOs may have changed the rules of the game for garment workers in Bangladesh. A number of major companies have signed an accord on worker safety measures, including H&M, Marks & Spencer, Carrefour, Loblaws and Benetton. In agreeing to the binding programme of fire and building safety reforms based on independent inspections, worker-led health and safety committees and union access to factories, signatories commit to underwrite improvements in dangerous factories and properly confront safety problems. But Walmart, the world's largest retailer, has refused to sign on.

CAW member Joachim Victor Gomes and John Cartwright co-authored a letter in May 13, 2013, Toronto Star "What do Bangladeshi workers deserve." (http://www.thestar.com/opinion/letters_to_the_editors/2013/05/13/what_do_bangladeshi_workers_deserve.html)

MONTREAL SOLIDARITY, January 2013 Leaders of the Montreal and Toronto Labour Councils signed a Common Declaration of Solidarity mid-January in Montreal. A group from Toronto including President John Cartwright, Organizer Preethy Sivakumar and Steve Shallhorn of Labour Education went for three days of intense learning about the work of the Montreal Council, and Cartwright addressed their Delegates meeting on January 15th. This builds on an ongoing exchange between the two Councils and the decision by our Labour Council to develop a greater understanding of Quebec labour's unique role in our movement. Go to http://www.labourcouncil.ca/uploads/8/8/6/1/8861416/joint_declaration.docx for The Declaration. To see the video of President John Cartwright go to http://www.youtube.com/watch?v=bJolYGedOcY

RETIREMENT SECURITY FOR EVERYONE Canada is at a crossroads, just like it was forty years ago when it was time to do something about our health care system. Today, we need to do something about retirement income, and we need to do it soon. There's too much risk and not enough security to ensure that, after a lifetime of work, people can retire and live out their last years in dignity. To find out more about the CLC's national campaign for retirement security, go to http://www.canadianlabour.ca/action-center/retirement-security-for-everyone

ONTARIO HEALTH COALITION We are a non-partisan group committed to maintaining and enhancing our publicly-funded, publicly-administered health care system. For further information about Ontario Health Coalition and to find out how you can help please visit the website at www.ontariohealthcoalition.ca

Source: Adapted from the Toronto and York Region Labour Council. Used with permission. Retrieved from http://www.labourcouncil.ca/campaigns.html.

Courtesy Canadian Federation of Students - Ontario.

Students and workers unite to fight for public education.

UNION DEMOCRACY

Institutional scholars have identified the necessity for unions to practise strong internal democratic procedures (Kaufman, 2000). After all, how can unions fulfill the expectations of industrial democracy if they are autocratic themselves?

> *If labor organizations also exercise autocratic powers over their members, then workers may merely be substituting dictatorial rule of union officials for the arbitrary authority of the employer or his managers. (Leiserson, 1959, p. 54)*

Internal union democracy has been shown to be an important factor in winning union elections (Catano, 2010), union renewal (Ashby & Hawking, 2009), and worker perceptions of union power (Peetz & Pocock, 2009). Not only is democracy intrinsically good, but it is also important for unions for the following reasons (Strauss, 2000, p. 211):

1. Unions exist not just to better workers' economic conditions but to give them a voice. Democracy gives them that voice. It is not enough to assume that union officers know what members want, for the officers are often wrong (Gallagher & Strauss, 1991). In any case, democracy to me means government by the people, not just for them.

2. Over the long run, democracy makes unions more effective: it weeds out the corrupt and incompetent. It gives the officers an incentive to perform better.

3. Decisions made by the members (such as a decision to go on strike) are more likely to be implemented by the members. Democracy helps mobilize member support.

4. Having a choice is of great symbolic value and considerably increases the members' identification with their union.

5. Democracy unearths and trains leaders, especially the unpaid, shop-level leaders who would seem to be essential for strong unions. The paid staff can't do it all (see Frost, 2000).

There is no comprehensive theory of union democracy, but scholars have identified several factors that may influence their democratic practices:

- Newly organized groups of workers will be highly active in the union—control by members over leaders is highest at this stage.

- Member control and influence may decline over time as the union establishes itself.

- As product markets grow, local unions amalgamate into larger more centralized entities—unions can become large, bureaucratic, and more remote from the rank and file (Webb & Webb, 1902).

- This bureaucratization leads to a dependence on professionals and nonelected officials—rank and file inevitably lose some control.

- Internal democracy can be diminished in unions by the apathy and ignorance of the members; except in a crisis (e.g., a strike vote), members do not attend meetings.

- Elected leaders tend to stifle opposition, but bargaining requires some discipline and control in order to maintain solidarity; the challenge is to achieve a balance between these competing forces.

The evidence of union democracy is often anecdotal. In Canada, there is little regulation of union democracy (Lynk, 2000). The United States, on the other hand, has more intrusive restrictions on union behaviour, probably as a result of the following case. The most infamous and well-documented story of union corruption was the case of Jimmy Hoffa, president of the International Brotherhood of Teamsters (IBT) (see Belzer & Hurd, 1999). The IBT, a union mostly of truck drivers, was America's largest union in the 1950s and 1960s. Despite the IBT's connections to organized crime, serious misuse of members' pension funds by union officials, and strong pressure against him from the AFL-CIO, Hoffa was reelected in 1957 by an overwhelming majority of IBT members (Sloane, 1991). After a major investigation led by the then attorney general, Bobby Kennedy, Hoffa was finally sent to prison in 1967 on charges of jury tampering and mail fraud (Sloane, 1991). This case highlights one of the dilemmas of union democracy. Despite the corruption, the IBT rank and file repeatedly elected Hoffa because he delivered the goods at the bargaining table.

Some research on U.S. unions shows that, measured by turnover of elected officials, union democracy is improving. The other mixed finding was that corruption among some unions persists but seems to be declining overall (Strauss, 2000).

Information technology has undoubtedly had a positive impact on democracy in unions, enabling members to participate more in the activities of the union in such areas as collective bargaining and union governance (Greer, 2002). Email has made top union officials more accessible, involvement in union politics has increased, and some union dissidents are able to use alternative websites as forums for opposition politics (Greer, 2002).

UNION DEMOCRACY IN PRACTICE

All unions have democratic structures. This means that decisions about collective bargaining, grievances, policies, political affiliation, etc., are made by union members. One of the consequences of this is that the decision-making process is often slower than management's. In collective bargaining, for example, unions must be careful to seek a strong mandate. Changes to the mandate will frequently involve renewing it by holding another membership meeting and voting. Management, on the other hand, is better positioned to make faster decisions as the situation changes. To gain an understanding of what democracy means for the typical union member, we provide an example of how it works in the network of political positions and connections in a national union—Unifor (formerly CAW). (See the OPSEU case discussed at the end of this chapter.) Democracy plays an important function in a union's national structure. To illustrate this, we reproduced an organizational chart of the CAW (see Figure 5.3). CAW members may be elected to bargaining committees, local union executive positions, and local committees (e.g., health and safety, grievance, trustee). The CAW organization goes further to reveal member paths for elected delegates to CAW councils, constitutional conventions, industry councils, and ultimately to the national executive council.

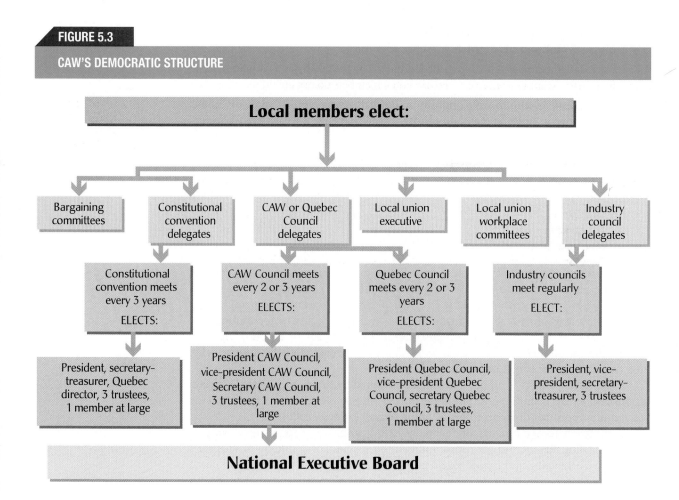

FIGURE 5.3

CAW'S DEMOCRATIC STRUCTURE

// WHY EMPLOYEES JOIN UNIONS

There are three major theories in the industrial relations literature that help us understand why workers join unions: collective voice, utility, and ideology (Wheeler & McClendon, 1991).

COLLECTIVE VOICE

When dissatisfied or frustrated on the job, employees join unions to remedy the sources of dissatisfaction through collective representation. Existing research suggests that non-union employees who are dissatisfied with their jobs and the companies for which they work want union representation more than those employees who are satisfied with their jobs and companies. Employees who perceive that their company is doing better financially or that their industry has more growth potential have a much greater desire to join a union. This desire is perhaps due to a feeling of entitlement to share in the company success. Thus, it is also important to consider a company's performance variables (Friedman, Abraham & Thomas, 2006).

UTILITY

This theory asserts that employees will join unions if the unions are able to satisfy a **utility function** consisting of such economic concerns as wages and benefits or anxiety over job security. Unions have to be seen as able to "deliver the goods."

> utility function
> the sum of individual preferences for such measurable items as wages and benefits

POLITICS OR IDEOLOGY

Under this theory, employees join unions for political or ideological reasons. Employees who have more positive attitudes to unions are more likely to want to join. Reasons for supporting a union may range from purely political to familial (having a family member in a union) to communal (community attitudes are supportive of unions). One study found, for example, that prounion youth workers had a predisposition for "collective solutions to social and economic issues" (Lowe & Rastin, 2000).

Research shows that union support is linked to employee dissatisfaction, but adds attitudes toward work, perceived company performance, and intention to quit as other factors for supporting unions (Friedman, Abraham & Thomas, 2006; Moody, 2014). When determining the desire for unionization among blue-collar workers, economic or extrinsic satisfaction appears to be more important than noneconomic or intrinsic satisfaction. In addition, workers who had more company tenure were more likely to want to join a union. The study also found that women and minorities were significantly more likely to want unionization than men and non-minorities. Immigrants also show a higher than average propensity to unionize (Catron, Rosenfeld, Jake & Kleykamp, 2013). Forrest (2001) argues that women organize around "women's issues" such as pay equity, harassment, child care, and maternity. She also adds that if unions are to be successful in organizing women, they will have to find ways of accommodating their needs. Finally, in the case of professionals, research shows that there are often shared values between joining a union and a profession (Campbell, 2013).

CHAPTER 5 The Union Perspective

// WHY EMPLOYEES LEAVE UNIONS

Unionized employees who work for larger companies are more likely to want to leave their unions. This might be because of the union security clauses of larger companies requiring their employees to join unions even if the employees have no desire to do so (Friedman, Abraham & Thomas, 2006). Unionized employees who are less satisfied with their compensation and benefits also have a greater desire to leave their unions. Research also identified a strong relationship between the employees' level of dissatisfaction with the company and their desire to leave both the company and the union (Friedman, Abraham & Thomas, 2006).

Generally, unionized employees will express discontent with the union if it fails to fulfill its primary function of providing distributive justice for its members. A company's performance appears to significantly influence employees' desire to join and, to a lesser extent, leave an existing union. Employees will generally seek change if they perceive that their current working environment is not in their best interests.

// MEMBERSHIP PATTERNS

We have gained an understanding of the aims and purposes of unions and their structure. In this next section, we examine union membership patterns. To explore the reasons for union decline and to generally measure the strength of the labour movement, researchers express union members as a percentage of the nonagricultural labour force (agricultural workers have traditionally been excluded from labour laws in Canada and most other industrialized countries). This is known as **union density** (see Figure 5.4). Union density statistics answer the question of whether the growth in union membership has kept pace with the natural growth in the labour force.

$$\text{Union density} = \frac{\text{Union members}}{\text{Labour force}} \times 100$$

Industrial relations scholars often use another measure of unionization, called **union coverage**. To explain the difference between union density and union coverage, we need to explain the various forms of union security.

Union security refers to the ability of the union to sign up new members that are hired by the firm into their bargaining unit. Certain aspects of union security may be found in labour legislation or in the collective agreement. As a result of some bitter conflict over union security clauses in the collective agreement, the policy in Canada has been to provide for a minimum form of security in the legislation. The important categories of union security include **closed shop**, **union shop**, and **Rand Formula**.

The closed shop still exists in Canada in sectors such as construction, but it is rare. Hiring is through a union hiring hall. The union shop, more common than the closed shop, requires employees to join the union after a probation period (typically ninety days). The Rand Formula, the most common union security arrangement in Canada, requires that all bargaining unit employees pay dues and is based on the legal requirement that the union must represent all employees whether union members or not.

Thus, we can see that in most bargaining units today, employees do not have to belong to the union. This means that bargaining units have a mix of members and nonmembers—typically about 90 percent of the bargaining unit is union members, and 10 percent is dues-paying nonmembers. Union coverage is then a higher number than union density, because nonmembers are included. Union coverage is particularly important to

union density
a fraction that expresses union members as a percentage of the nonagricultural labour force

union coverage
a broader measure than union density; includes nonmembers covered by the collective agreement

closed shop
a form of union security in which membership in the union is a condition of employment

union shop
a form of union security in which new employees must join the union but only after a probation period

Rand Formula
a union security provision in which employees do not have to join the union but all employees must pay dues

FIGURE 5.4

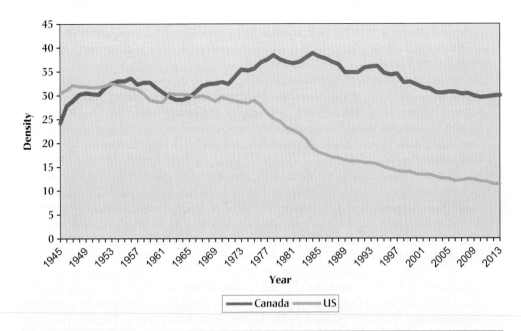

Sources: United States Bureau of Labor Statistics. (2014). "Current population survey" (press release). Retrieved from http://www.bls.gov/news.release/union2.nr0.htm; Workplace Information Division, Strategic Policy, Analysis, and Workplace Information Directorate, Labour Program, Employment and Social Development Canada; and Statistics Canada, the Labour Force Survey, Labour Statistics Division, CANSIM 282-0002 & 282-0011. Retrieved from http://www.labour.gc.ca/eng/resources/info/publications/union_coverage/union_coverage.shtml.

take into account when making comparisons between North American and European industrial relations systems. France provides a good illustration of our point. Union density in France is only about 10 percent, but union coverage is close to 90 percent. This is because, in France, the outcomes of union negotiations are often automatically applied to nonunion firms in the same industry (Bamber, Lansbury & Wailes, 2004).

In Figure 5.4, union density patterns in Canada and the United States are compared from the post–World War II period to 2013. Despite the many economic, social, and legal similarities between our countries, union density patterns dramatically diverged beginning in the 1960s. Both Canadian and U.S. unions had equal densities of 30 percent in the mid-1960s, but the U.S. density fell to just 12.3 percent and in Canada rose to a high of 38 percent in the mid-1980s and fell back more recently to about the 1960 level of 30 percent.

There are many reasons for the Canadian–U.S. divergence in union density. In the first place, about one-third of the difference can be explained by the higher rate of public-service unionization in Canada, over 60 percent, as against the U.S. rate of 37.4 percent (United States Bureau of Labor Statistics, 2010). Rose and Chaison (2001) argue that the difference can be explained by a greater ability of Canadian unions to recruit new members. Unions are better able to recruit in Canada because of more favourable laws; the affiliation between organized labour and the New Democratic Party (NDP); and an ability to resist concession bargaining (Rose & Chaison, 2001).

In Canada, it is easier for unions to organize because labour laws provide for faster certification procedures and card systems that provide for automatic recognition without the requirement of a vote. These more favourable Canadian laws came about, in part, because the labour movement has been able to exert influence on legislation through the NDP. Godard (2003) argues that, in fact, the stronger laws in Canada are the main factor in explaining differences in union density. In addition, because labour in Canada has the strength of numbers, it has been able to resist some of the concessions made by its counterpart unions south of the border.

To attempt to explain U.S.–Canadian differences in union density, Lipset and Meltz (2004) compared various attitudes toward unions and work in Canada and the United States. They predicted that higher union density in Canada would be a result of more favourable attitudes toward unions in Canada: Canadians tend to hold positive collectivist views, while Americans are more individualistic in outlook, leading to less support for unions. (See Table 5.3.)

To their surprise, Lipset and Meltz (2004) found very little difference in public support for unions between the two countries (see Table 5.3). In fact, in the United States a slightly higher proportion of workers (70 percent) approved of unions than in Canada (67 percent). When the nonunion workers were asked the same question about whether they would vote for a union, the lower percentage (33 percent) in Canada, in contrast to 47 percent in the U.S., can be entirely explained by the smaller pool of nonunion employees in Canada. That is, if the "already in a union" category is added to the "would vote for a union" category in each country, the result in both the U.S. and Canada is just over 50 percent. Similarly, other cross-border differences (e.g., union preferences and power) in answers between union and nonunion employees are explained by the higher unionization rates in Canada. Thus, surprisingly, there was very little difference between U.S. and Canadian attitudes toward unions.

The Lipset and Meltz (2004) study provided a breakdown of union voting intentions of nonunion Canadian and American employees by gender and age, believing it was possible, for example, that Canada–U.S. density differences could be explained by union-preference differences for women and younger employees. Table 5.4 reveals that both women and youth (15 to 24 years old) had higher than average union propensities.

TABLE 5.3

EMPLOYEE ATTITUDES TO UNIONS

% OF EMPLOYED WORKERS	CANADA	UNITED STATES
Workers who approve of unions	67	70
Workers who believe that, as a whole, unions are good	52	57
Nonunion employees who, if an election were held tomorrow, would vote for unionization	33	47
Nonunion employees who would personally prefer to belong to a union	21	29
Nonunion employees who think unions do not have enough power	7	20
Nonunion workers who feel that unions have too much power	40	26
Nonunion employees who, when hearing of a labour dispute and before knowing all the details, would side with the union	40	57

Source: Reprinted from *The Paradox of American Unionism: Why Americans Like Unions More Than Canadians Do but Join Much Less*, edited by Seymour Martin Lipset, Noah M. Meltz, Rafael Gomez, and Ivan Katchanovski. Copyright © 2004 by Cornell University. Used by permission of the publisher, Cornell University Press.

It further showed that this was equally true for both countries (recognizing that Canada had higher numbers already in unions).

This result is significant for the future of unionization in both countries, because these are key cohorts for new members. The emerging service sector has a higher proportion of female employees, and the attitudes of our nations' youth are a good indicator of union growth potential. It's still an open question, of course, whether unions will be able to satisfy this apparently strong demand for unionization.

Despite the general support for unions, workers had very positive attitudes toward work and working conditions (see Table 5.5). Again, Canadian and American workers shared similar attitudes. A vast majority of employees in each country were satisfied with their jobs, thought they were paid fairly, and took pride in their work.

We can only conclude from these apparently contradictory results that the majority of Canadian and U.S. workers want unions for reasons other than economics or job dissatisfaction. Employee demand for a collective and independent voice in the workplace in Canada and the United States appears to be strong despite some profound changes over the past three decades in work organization, labour force composition, and the individualization of human resources.

TABLE 5.4

UNION VOTING INTENTIONS OF NONUNION EMPLOYEES BY GENDER AND AGE, 1996 (%)

	UNITED STATES		CANADA	
	VOTE FOR UNION	ACTUAL DENSITY	VOTE FOR UNION	ACTUAL DENSITY
Male	45.6	18.8	37.9	34.4
Female	55.7	14.3	45.7	30
Total	48.2	16	33	36
Youth (15–24)	60.5	6.6	58.5	10.7
Adult (25+)	45.2	19.8	37	35.7
Total	48.2	16	33	36

Source: Reprinted from *The Paradox of American Unionism: Why Americans Like Unions More Than Canadians Do but Join Much Less*, edited by Seymour Martin Lipset, Noah M. Meltz, Rafael Gomez, and Ivan Katchanovski. Copyright © 2004 by Cornell University. Used by permission of the publisher, Cornell University Press.

TABLE 5.5

VIEW OF WORK, 1996 (% OF EMPLOYED WORKERS)

	CANADA	UNITED STATES
Workers who are somewhat or very satisfied with their jobs	86	85
Workers who think they were paid fairly in the past year	73	74
Workers taking some or a great deal of pride in their work	97	99
Workers who agree that they would do their best regardless of pay	77	75

Source: Reprinted from *The Paradox of American Unionism: Why Americans Like Unions More Than Canadians Do but Join Much Less*, edited by Seymour Martin Lipset, Noah M. Meltz, Rafael Gomez, and Ivan Katchanovski. Copyright © 2004 by Cornell University. Used by permission of the publisher, Cornell University Press.

CHAPTER 5 The Union Perspective

// THE CHANGING FACE OF UNIONIZATION

As discussed above, Figure 5.4 shows a small decline in Canadian unionization from the late twentieth century. When gender, age, and region differences are taken into account the decline is far from uniform.

THE GROWING PROPORTION OF WOMEN

Historically, the union density of male employees was higher than that of female employees. In 1997, it stood at 35.2 percent for male employees compared to 32.1 percent for female employees. However, in 2005 the unionization rates for male and female employees were roughly equal (32 percent). By 2012, there has been a significant shift where the union density of 32.8 percent for female employees exceeded that of for male employees of 30.2 percent (see Figure 5.5).

FIGURE 5.5

UNION DENSITY BY GENDER

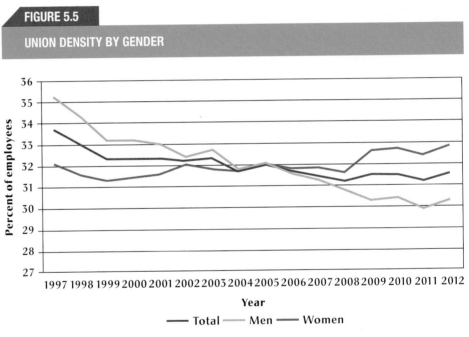

Source: HRSDC calculations based on Statistics Canada. Table 282-0078 - Labour force survey estimates (LFS), employees by union coverage, North American Industry Classification System (NAICS), sex and age group, annual (persons), CANSIM (database). Retrieved from http://www4.hrsdc.gc.ca/.3ndic.1t4r@-eng.jsp?iid=17#M_3. Reproduced with the permission of the Minister of Employment and Social Development Canada, 2015.

DENSITIES BY AGE

Figure 5.6 shows that in 2012, unionization rates ranged from 16.0 percent for employees aged 15 to 24 to 38.1 percent for those employees aged 55 to 64. Thus employees under the age of 25 and over the age of 64 were much less likely to belong to a union or to be covered by a collective agreement than employees between the ages of 25 and 64.

Researchers attribute the youth–adult difference in union density rates to variation in the costs and benefits for younger workers (Bryson, Gomez, Gunderson & Meltz, 2005).

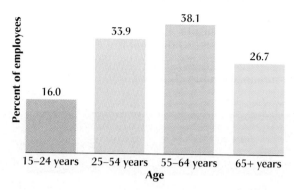

Source: HRSDC calculations based on Statistics Canada. Table 282-0078 - Labour force survey estimates (LFS), employees by union coverage, North American Industry Classification System (NAICS), sex and age group, annual (persons), CANSIM (database). Retrieved from http://www4.hrsdc.gc.ca/.3ndic.1t.4r@-eng.jsp?iid=17#M_3. Reproduced with the permission of the Minister of Employment and Social Development Canada, 2015.

DIFFERENCES BY REGION

Union density varies widely by province (see Figure 5.7). In 2012, 39.9 percent of Quebec employees belonged to a union, followed closely by Newfoundland and Labrador (38.9 percent), Manitoba (36.0 percent), and Saskatchewan (35.4 percent).

Alberta had the lowest unionization rate in 2012 at 23.5 percent, followed by Ontario at 28.2 percent and New Brunswick at 29.8 percent.

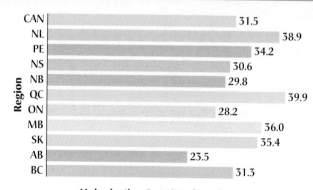

Source: HRSDC calculations based on Statistics Canada. Table 282-0078 - Labour force survey estimates (LFS), employees by union coverage, North American Industry Classification System (NAICS), sex and age group, annual (persons), CANSIM (database). Retrieved from http://www4.hrsdc.gc.ca/.3ndic.1t.4r@-eng.jsp?iid=17#M_3. Reproduced with the permission of the Minister of Employment and Social Development Canada, 2015.

// LABOUR AND THE ENVIRONMENT

Unions have been slow to fully embrace environmental issues out of fear of job losses in such sectors as energy and natural resources. Coalitions between unions and environmentalists often dissolved because unions were forced to choose between job security and occupational or environmental health (Mayer, 2008; Senier, Mayer, Brown & Morello-Frosch, 2007). To respond to this problem the Canadian Labour Congress developed a program that involves allaying job loss fears by transitioning to a green economy and a more sustainable future (Burrows, 2001; see IR Today 5.9).

IR TODAY   5.9

EXCERPT FROM CLC PLAN FOR GREEN JOBS

Canada can create hundreds of thousands of jobs through investment into green job creation. Not only can we build an economy of good jobs, strong enough to lift people out of poverty, but we can invest in climate change solutions.

What Is a "Green Job"?

Green collar jobs will grow our economy in a greener and more sustainable direction. In general a green job is any job that greens our economy.

The solutions are simple yet multifaceted; we need to:

- Increase energy efficiency, building retrofits and green building;
- Invest in rail and mass transit infrastructure;
- Reduce the distance between producer and consumer and encourage production of everything from green vehicles to windmill blades here in Canada; and
- Develop renewable energy sources.

Source: Canadian Labour Congress. "Green Jobs." Used with permission. Retrieved from http://www.canadianlabour.ca/issues/green-jobs.

BLUE–GREEN COALITIONS

Mayer (2008) shows how labour and environmental groups can work together by focusing on the role health-related issues have played in creating a common ground between the two groups. His cases reveal that the same toxins that cause workplace hazards escape into surrounding communities and the environment; thus, workers and environmentalists are able to collaborate for the protection of all. The Good Jobs for All Coalition is an example of a successful coalition in Canada's largest urban centre. The coalition, formed in 2008, is an alliance of community, labour, social justice, youth, and environmental organizations. Here is an excerpt from a Good Jobs for All campaign directed at Toronto Hydro that began in 2010:

> The Good Jobs for All Coalition is calling on Toronto Hydro to:
>
> • Plan for an aggressive expansion of Toronto Hydro's role in renewable energy generation in partnership with other public institutions, such as the city, school boards, colleges, universities and hospitals;
>
> • Make local procurement of green products a priority in all activities;

- *Use Toronto Hydro's buying power to attract green manufacturers to Toronto and/ or assist existing manufacturers to retool; and*

- *Work with local training organizations and Toronto's Social Development Office to ensure equitable access and inclusion of workers of colour and youth from marginalized communities in new job opportunities in the sector. (Good Jobs for All Coalition, 2010)*

In addition to forming coalitions and generally working with environmental organizations, unions are also using the collective bargaining process to promote environmental issues. Below is an example from a collective agreement between DaimlerChrysler and the CAW (now Unifor):

Letter (15.3): Joint National Environmental Committee

During these negotiations the Company demonstrated its concern for the environment by outlining the programs and policies which are in place in the plants and offices.

As well, the CAW has become deeply involved in environmental issues, at both the National and local levels.

Therefore, it is agreed that to demonstrate this joint interest a National Environmental Committee will be established by the parties. The committee will consist of two people from the Union, the National Health & Safety Coordinator and a Representative designated by the President of the National Union for the CAW and two people, from the company, the Manager of Health & Safety and Manager of Environment representing DaimlerChrysler Canada.

The National Committee shall:

- *Meet 4 times annually at mutually agreeable times and place to review and discuss issues involving the environment, recycling and energy conservation which pertain to DaimlerChrysler Canada employees.*

- *Develop and issue a joint statement regarding the environment, recycling and energy conservation pertaining to DaimlerChrysler Canada employees.*

- *Discuss and make recommendations regarding possible future programs for the plants and offices concerning the environment, recycling and energy conservation.*

- *Promote and support ongoing programs in the plants and offices relating to the environment [and] recycling....*

- *Receive and discuss appropriate issues referred to them by the plants and offices.*

- *Develop and issue educational materials to employees and their families concerning the environment, recycling and energy conservation.*

- *Discuss other duties and responsibilities of this Joint Environmental Committee at its regular meetings as jointly agreed on.*

- *Be agreed by the parties that this committee and its functions will not be adversarial and its clear purpose is to promote environmental awareness of all DaimlerChrysler Canada workers.*

- *Be agreed by the parties that environmental issues and statistics pertaining to DaimlerChrysler Canada discussed at this committee are to be held confidential if so requested by any member. (Canadian Auto Workers, 1996)*

// SUMMARY

This chapter has introduced you to the function and role of unions in contemporary Canadian society. We studied the range of union purposes and philosophies found in craft or occupational, industrial, and public-sector unions. The pluralism of unions in Canada was further demonstrated by national and local independent unions. We discovered that public-sector unions are the largest unions and that most unions are affiliated with the Canadian Labour Congress. It was shown how union affiliations with federations at the local, provincial, and national levels give union members a voice in the economic and social affairs of Canada. There was a special focus on the democratic character of unions and the importance of this function to industrial democracy. Changing membership patterns and density decline were examined in an international comparative perspective. We found that women make up a larger proportion of union members, and younger workers a smaller one. Finally, we discovered that the greater decline in union density in the United States was due to public-sector, legal, and organizing differences and not public attitudes.

KEY TERMS

closed shop 154
company union 133
craft or occupational unionism 134
industrial unionism 136
institutionalists 131
International Labour Organization (ILO) 132
public-sector or social justice unionism 140
Rand Formula 154
union coverage 154
union density 154
union shop 154
utility function 153

WEBLINKS

Canadian Legal Information Institute:
http://www.canlii.org/en/index.html

International Brotherhood of Electrical Workers constitution and bylaws:
www.ibew769.com/library/IBEWConstitution.pdf

Ontario Nurses' Association statement of beliefs:
http://www.ona.org/publications_forms/constitution_booklets_guides.html

CAW mergers:
http://53.15.200-74.q9.net/en/3012.htm

Good Jobs for All Coalition:
http://goodjobsforall.ca/endorse-the-good-green-jobs-for-all-at-hydro -campaign/

Videos

Jerry Dias, Unifor President, on strategic voting:
http://news.yahoo.com/video/jerry-dias-interview-232038141.html

DISCUSSION QUESTIONS

1. Give an economic, political, and human rights rationale for the existence of unions.
2. What were the three waves of union organizing? Give examples.
3. Describe the five largest unions in Canada by type. What are the main occupations in each union's membership?
4. What proportion of Canadian workers are not affiliated with a national labour federation?
5. What are the purposes of the Canadian Labour Congress?
6. What do local labour councils do?
7. Name four ways that union democracy makes a positive contribution to unions' well-being.
8. How has information technology positively affected unions?
9. Give three reasons that workers join unions. What three factors may cause workers to leave unions?
10. Compare Canadian and U.S. union membership patterns.
11. Define and compare three types of union security.
12. What does union density measure? Compare Canadian and American union density.
13. Compare Canadian and American public attitudes toward unions. Also compare proportions that would vote for a union. Why is the proportion lower in Canada if support for unions is the same?
14. Highlight provincial differences in union density in Canada.
15. Explain why unions and environmental organizations may have competing interests. How have unions managed to overcome this problem and form successful coalitions with environmentalists?

USING THE INTERNET

1. On the Internet, find a union and its constitution not discussed in this chapter. From the constitution or from other information on its website, describe the union's aims, objectives, and main activities. Determine the union's type: craft/occupational, industrial, or public-sector. (You may use the list of unions found in Table 5.1.)
2. Find a local labour council in any Canadian community. Determine what its main activities on behalf of its members are. Do any of these activities include actions on behalf of nonmembers?
3. Find the Walmart campaign organized by the UFCW through email. What are the goals of the campaign? Has it achieved any of them?

EXERCISES

1. Compare and contrast the aims and purposes of the IBEW and the CAW (now Unifor).
2. By finding the aims and purposes of the United Steelworkers of America, determine what type of union it is. What is the purpose of the USWA development fund? What has it achieved?

CASE	DEMOCRACY AND FINANCES IN AN OPSEU LOCAL

This case is about a typical local of the Ontario Public Service Employees Union. Unions are nongovernmental organizations (NGOs) run by their members. All union officers are elected by the members in their workplace. The OPSEU president, executive board, and council members stand for election every two years. Job stewards are also elected from their work areas. At the heart of every union is the local union. The following information taken from the OPSEU website describes the purpose and functions of union locals.

OPSEU WHERE YOU WORK—YOUR LOCAL

The purpose of establishing Locals of the Union is to encourage participation of all Members in their Union.
—The OPSEU Constitution

Your OPSEU Local is your primary link to the union. It represents you where you work, and you elect its leaders—your stewards, your Local president and other officers, your delegates to Convention and so on. It's your first step to getting involved.

Locals have the autonomy and resources to do what they think is important for their members. You have a vote on those decisions.

WHAT CAN LOCALS DO?

- Participate in negotiating collective agreements
- Process grievances to enforce the collective agreement
- Establish joint labour–management committees to resolve Local or unit issues
- Control their own money
- Join the local Labour Council or other organizations
- Organize social or community activities
- Publish newsletters or websites
- Elect delegates to the OPSEU Convention
- Send members for union education and training
- Monitor workplace health and safety
- Adopt bylaws
- Help craft union policy
- Promote human rights and equity

OPSEU HAS THREE KINDS OF LOCALS:

1. Single unit Locals, where all members work for the same employer in the same location.

2. Multi-unit Locals, where all members work for the same employer but at different locations.

3. Composite Locals, where members work for more than one employer at one or more locations.

HOW DO LOCALS WORK? For starters, democratically.

Local elections normally take place at membership meetings, but in special cases, there may be polling stations.

The front-line voice of the union in the workplace is the shop steward. Your Local (or your unit in a multi-unit or composite Local) decides how many shop stewards it needs, and how they should be distributed. You elect the steward for your work area. It takes a clear majority to win.

From among your shop stewards, you elect your Local Executive Committee (LEC in OPSEU jargon). So every member of the LEC has already been elected as a steward. Your LEC must have a president and at least two other officers (vice-president, secretary, treasurer, secretary-treasurer, chief steward etc.) In single unit Locals, all shop stewards are automatically on the LEC.

Each unit in a multi-unit or composite Local elects one or more unit stewards from among their shop stewards to sit on the LEC, and the officers are elected from these unit stewards.

Locals can define their structure in Local bylaws, which must conform to the union's Constitution. Article 29 of the Constitution governs Locals without their own bylaws.

HOW ARE LOCALS FUNDED?

- Local funds come from your union dues. A portion of your dues comes back to your Local.

- OPSEU Locals get quarterly "rebates" from the union, depending on how many members have signed union cards. In January, April, July and October, each local gets a cheque. Composite Locals get a supplement to reflect their more complex structure.

- Rebate levels are revised annually.

- A typical OPSEU Local with 250 members would receive nearly $15,000 annually in operating funds.

WHAT DO LOCALS SPEND THEIR MONEY ON? A wide variety of things, actually.

In OPSEU, most member expenses are covered by the central union. This includes travel, accommodation, meals and lost wages for members attending Convention, education courses, bargaining sessions, grievance hearings, and the many other meetings and events that the union organizes or participates in.

That leaves Local funds for things like sending extra members as observers to Convention, child care or refreshments at meetings, publishing newsletters or other things the Local decides. Locals can also support the local food bank or a kids' soccer team or make other contributions to their community. Some Locals set up their own strike fund to augment strike pay from the central union. Others send fruit baskets to members in hospital. It's up to the Local to decide.

Source: OPSEU. The Members' Owners' Manual. Used with permission. Retrieved from http://www.opseu .org/information/members-owners-manual.

QUESTION

1. After reading the information provided above and visiting the OPSEU website, describe how democracy works at the local level in OPSEU.

// REFERENCES

1. Adams, R. (2002). Implications of the International Human Rights Consensus for Canadian labour and management. *Canadian Labour and Employment Law Journal, 1,* pp. 119–139.

2. Ashby, S., & Hawking, C. J. (2009). *Staley: The fight for a new American labor movement.* Champlain: University of Illinois Press.

3. Bamber, G. J., Lansbury, R. D., & Wailes, N. (2004). *International and comparative employment relations* (4th edition), chapter 7. London: Sage.

4. Belzer, M., & Hurd, R. (1999). Government oversight, union democracy, and labor racketeering: Lessons from the Teamsters experience. *Journal of Labor Research, 20*(3), pp. 343–365.

5. British Columbia Government and Service Employees' Union. (2008). Article 3: Objects. *Constitution 2005* (p. 7). Retrieved 26 April 2011 from http://www .bcgeu.ca/sites/default/files/BCGEUConstitandbylaws2008_0.pdf

6. Bryson, A., Gomez, R., Gunderson, M., & Meltz, N. (2005). Youth–adult differences in the demand for unionization: Are American, British, and Canadian workers all that different? *Journal of Labor Research, 26*(1), pp. 155–167.

7. Burrows, Mae. (2001). Just transition: Moving to a green economy. *Alternatives Journal, 27*(1), pp. 29–32.

8. Campbell, S. M. R. (2013). The applicability of commitment models in a unionized professional workplace. *International Journal of Organizational Analysis, 21*(4), pp. 488–503.

9. Canadian Auto Workers (CAW). (15 September 1996). Agreement between Chrysler Canada Ltd. and the CAW. Retrieved 10 May 2011 from http://206.191.16.137/eng/agreement/history/0193510a.pdf. Used with permission of CAW-Canada.

10. Canadian Auto Workers (CAW). (2009). Statement of principles: Social unionism. *CAW constitution.* Retrieved 27 April 2011 from http://www.caw.ca/ en/about-the-caw-policies-and-papersstatement-of-principles.htm

11. Catano, V. (2010). Union members' attitudes and perceptions about their union: Winning a representational election following a merger of four hospitals. *Economic and Industrial Democracy, 31*(4), pp. 579–592.

12. Catron, P., Rosenfeld, J., and Kleykamp, M. (2013). Immigrant unionization through the Great Recession. *American Sociological Review, 78*(2), pp. 315–338.

13. Commons, J. (1921). *Industrial government*. New York: Macmillan.

14. Cornfield, D. B. (2005). Tactics and the social context of social movement unionism in the service economy. *Labor History, 46*(3), p. 347.

15. Edmonton Community Foundation. (2011). Retrieved from www.ecfoundation. org. Used with permission of the Edmonton Community Foundation.

16. Forrest, A. (2001). Connecting women with unions: What are the issues? *Relations industrielles, 56*(4), pp. 647–676.

17. Friedman, B. A., Abraham, S. E., & Thomas, R. K. (2006). Factors related to employees' desire to join and leave unions. *Industrial Relations, 45,* pp. 102–110.

18. Frost, A. C. (2000). Union involvement in workplace decision making: Implications for union democracy. *Journal of Labor Research, 21*(2) (Spring), pp. 265–286.

19. Gallagher, D., & Strauss, G. (1991). Union attitudes and participation. In G. Strauss, D. Gallagher & J. Fiorito (Eds.), *The state of the unions*. Madison, WI: Industrial Relations Research Association, pp. 139–174.

20. Godard, J. (2003). Do labor laws matter? The density decline and convergence thesis revisited. *Industrial Relations, 42*(July), pp. 458–492.

21. Good Jobs for All Coalition. (2010). "Support Green Jobs in TO." Used with permission. http://goodjobsforall.ca/endorse-the-good-green-jobs-for-all-at -hydro-campaign/.

22. Good Jobs for All. (2014). http://goodjobsforall.ca/endorse-the-good-green-jobs-for-all-at-hydro-campaign/ (updated 20 November 2014).

23. Government of Saskatchewan. (1978). *Saskatchewan Trade Union Act*, R.S.S. 1978, c. T-17. Retrieved 24 April 2006 from http://www.canlii.org/sk/laws/sta/t-17/20060310/whole.html

24. Greer, C. R. (2002). E-voice: How information technology is shaping life within unions. *Journal of Labour Research, 23*(2), pp. 215–236.

25. Hebdon, R. (2014). Public sector labor policy: a human rights approach. *University of Nevada Law Journal, 14*(2) (Spring), pp. 209–221.

26. International Association of Fire Fighters. (2006). History and mission of the IAFF. Retrieved 18 May 2006 from http://www.iaff2400.org/history.html

27. Kaufman, B. (2000). The early institutionalists on industrial democracy and union democracy. *Journal of Labor Research*, Spring 2000, pp. 189–210.

28. Leger Marketing–Quebec Federation of Labour. (24 March 2001). Public opinion poll.

29. Leiserson, W. (1922). Constitutional government in American industries. *American Economic Review, 12,* pp. 56–79.

30. Leiserson, W. (1959). *American trade union democracy*. New York: Columbia University Press.

31. Lévesque, C., Murray, G., & Le Queux, S. (2005). Union disaffection and social identity: Democracy as a source of union revitalization. *Work and Occupations, 32*(4), pp. 400–422.

32. Lipset, M., & Meltz, N. M. (2004). *The paradox of American unionism*. Ithaca, NY: ILR Press.

33. Livingston, G. (2006). New Democrats unmoved by CAW decision to end traditional support of NDP. *The Brockville Recorder and Times*, April.

34. Lowe, G. S., & Rastin, S. (2000). Organizing the next generation: Influences on young workers' willingness to join unions in Canada. *British Journal of Industrial Relations, 38*(2), pp. 203–222.

35. Lynk, M. (2000). Union democracy and the law in Canada. *Journal of Labor Research, 21*(1) (Winter), pp. 37–63.

36. Mayer, B. (2008). *Blue–green coalitions: Fighting for safe workplaces and healthy communities*. Ithaca, NY: ILR Press, Cornell.

37. Moody, K. (2014). Competition and conflict: Union growth in the US hospital industry. *Economic and Industrial Democracy, 35*(1), pp. 5–25.

38. Newfoundland and Labrador Federation of Labour. (2011). Used with permission. http://www.nlfl.nf.ca/about-us.

39. Newfoundland and Labrador Federation of Labour. (2014). Used with permission. http://www.nlfl.nf.ca/about-us.

40. Peetz, D., & Pocock, B. (2009). An analysis of workplace representatives, union power and democracy in Australia. *British Journal of Industrial Relations, 47*(4), pp. 623–652.

41. Perlman, S. (1928). *The theory of the labor movement*. New York: Macmillan. Public Interest Alberta. (2011). Retrieved from www.pialberta.org. Used with permission of Public Interest Alberta.

42. Rose, J. (1995). The evolution of public sector unionism. In G. Swimmer & M. Thompson (Eds.), *Public sector collective bargaining in Canada*. Kingston, ON: Queen's University IR Press, pp. 20–52.

43. Rose, J., & Chaison, G. (2001). Unionism in Canada and the United States in the 21st century: Prospects for revival. *Relations industrielles, 56*, pp. 34–65.

44. Ross, S. (2007). Varieties of social unionism: Towards a framework for comparison. *Just Labour: A Canadian Journal of Work and Society, 11*, pp. 16–34.

45. Senier, L., Mayer, B., Brown, P., & Morello-Frosch, R. (2007). School custodians and green cleaners: New approaches to labor–environment coalitions. *Organization & Environment, 20*(3), pp. 304–325.

46. Sloane, A. (1991). *Hoffa*. Cambridge, MA: MIT Press, p. 430.

47. Strauss, G. (2000). What's happening inside U.S. unions: Democracy and union politics. *Journal of Labor Research, 21*(2), pp. 211–225.

48. Unifor. (n.d.). Retrieved from http://www.unifor.org/en/search-cross-site ?search_api_views_fulltext=constitution

49. United States Bureau of Labor Statistics. (2010). Current population survey [press release]. Retrieved 20 January 2011 from http://www.bls.gov/news .release/union2.nr0.htm

50. Webb, S., & Webb, B. (1902). *Industrial democracy*. London: Longmans Green.

51. Wheeler, H. N., & McClendon, J. A. (1991). The individual decision to unionize. In G. Strauss, D. Gallagher, & J. Fiorito (Eds.), *The state of the unions* (pp. 201–236). Madison, WI: Industrial Relations Research Association.

CHAPTER 6

THE MANAGEMENT PERSPECTIVE

LEARNING OBJECTIVES

BY THE END OF THIS CHAPTER, YOU WILL BE ABLE TO DISCUSS

- the evolving managerial view;
- the growing role of management in the industrial relations system;
- the relationship between business and industrial relations strategies;
- the various management strategies related to unionization; and
- current managerial perspectives and trends.

CANADIAN HOCKEY LEAGUE: EMPLOYEES OR STUDENT ATHLETES?

Many of the North American professional sports leagues, such as the CFL, NBA, NHL, and NFL, comprise unionized professional athletes. Certainly we have seen large-scale negotiations, strikes, lockouts, and potential work stoppages among these sports bodies. More recently in Canada, we have seen both union drives as well as court challenges related to the Canadian Hockey League (CHL).

The CHL represents the development league for the National Hockey League (NHL). Many NHL players play in this league prior to turning professional. In fact, no other league provides as many players to the NHL. The CHL is the umbrella organization for three leagues and 60 junior hockey teams (52 Canadian and 8 American). The three leagues within the CHL, comprising 1,300 players, are the Ontario Hockey League (OHL), the Quebec Major Junior Hockey League (QMHL), and the Western Hockey League (WHL).

The typical CHL player is between 16 and 20 years old and signs a contract when he agrees to play for a team. The contracts are fairly standard with similar, if not identical, terms. Payment is minimal. Some players earn as little as $35 a week, with the higher end being about $120 a week. In exchange, players devote as much as 65 hours a week for practice, games, travel, etc.

Concerns regarding the low payments received by players relative to their long hours, coupled with the revenues earned by the teams and their owners, have received considerable attention lately. This situation has prompted union drives. In 2012, there was a failed attempt to unionize the junior players by a group then called the Canadian Hockey League Players Association. A union certification application was filed, and subsequently withdrawn, in Nova Scotia. More recently, Canada's largest private-sector union, Unifor, has announced plans to unionize the league, with the QMHL being its first campaign target.

In addition to union drives, the players have filed a class action suit. Specifically, the players were seeking $180 million for unpaid wages, overtime, holidays, vacations, and unpaid employer payroll contributions (e.g., Canada Pension Plan, Employment Insurance). In contrast, the CHL leadership and owners assert that the players are student athletes versus employees. They argue that they contribute heavily to player education. For example, players receive a scholarship equivalent to one year's education (e.g., an amount equal to books and tuition at the university closest to their hometown) per year they play with the CHL. In fact, in 2013 CHL teams spent close to $5 million in tuition for former junior players. However, any athlete who fails to attend college within 18 months of leaving the CHL, or any player who plays with the NHL, forfeits this education payment.

No new union certification applications have been filed, and no decision on the class action lawsuit has occurred. In the event of a successful certification or lawsuit, the league will face significant changes.

Sources: CHL. (14 January 2015). "About the CHL." Retrieved from http://www.chl.ca/aboutthechl; Cribb, R. (20 October 2014). "Class action lawsuit filed against Canadian Hockey League over wages." *Toronto Star.* Retrieved from http://www.thestar.com/news/world/2014/10/20/class_action_lawsuit_filed_against_canadian_hockey_league_over_wages.html; The Canadian Press. (9 July 2014). "Unifor finalizing plans to unionize Canadian Hockey League." CBC News. Retrieved from http://www.cbc.ca/news/canada/windsor/unifor-finalizing-plans-to-unionize-canadian-hockey-league-1.2701355; Westhead, R. & Cribb, R. (7 July 2014). "Major junior hockey gets new push to unionize." *Toronto Star.* Retrieved from http://www.thestar.com/sports/hockey/2014/07/07/major_junior_hockey_gets_new_push_to_unionize_from_familiar_controversial_figure.html.

// THE EVOLVING MANAGERIAL VIEW

To understand the current management perspective, it is helpful to briefly review some of the most significant perspectives that have influenced managerial thinking. These can be labelled as

- the master–servant relationship;
- scientific management;
- human relations; and
- human resources management.

Many professional hockey players are unionized, while attempts are now being made to unionize junior players.

MASTER–SERVANT RELATIONSHIP

As is discussed in Chapter 2, the early employment relationship was marked by a significant power imbalance. The employment relationship was, in essence, a contractual agreement whereby the employee was obligated to perform work and the employer was required to pay wages. However, the power imbalance between parties was such that the worker was often forced into agreeing to employment terms and conditions. For example, it was illegal for employees to quit; it was deemed a conspiracy for employees to bargain collectively or to form a union; and management controlled virtually all aspects of the employment relationship (for more details, please see Labour Law Casebook Group, 2011).

As outlined by Labour Law Casebook Group (2011), under this **master–servant relationship** the third actor of the IR system, namely the government and its legislature, did little for the employee. There was rarely interference by courts, and when there was, it was usually in the employers' favour. In a nutshell, this philosophy marked a time where labour was viewed as a commodity that could be bought and sold at will, with little ramification to the employer, limited consideration of the employee, and marginal court protection of the employee. You might recall that it was the very environment that spurred the onset of organized labour as a way to "balance" the power between management and labour.

master–servant relationship
the essence of the common-law employment relationship pertaining to nonunion workplaces

SCIENTIFIC MANAGEMENT (TAYLORISM)

The Industrial Revolution brought forth a new form of workplace organization. We saw a movement toward large-scale industrial workplaces employing large groups of workers. In these workplaces, much of the focus was on mass production through assembly lines. Workers went from performing a large number of tasks to becoming specialists in a small number of tasks, and in some cases, a single task. Much of the push for task specialization started in the early 1900s with the advent of Frederick Taylor's theory of scientific management (Taylor, 1911). Two key principles of Taylor's theory follow. First, work should be divided into simple tasks, and workers should be trained to perform a small number of these simple tasks. Second, managers should perform all planning and decision-making tasks while workers merely perform simple tasks in accordance with the plans and decisions made by management. Given the role of management in the planning and decision making, and the employees' role of following directions, we see that elements of the master–servant relationship remained in this industrial-based perspective. That is, the master made the rules, and the worker followed with little say in work processes or the workplace as a whole. In many ways, this perspective saw the employee as an extension of the machines they ran; the goal was to reduce costs by making the production line (and those running it) as efficient as possible. This quest for efficiency exists today, as we see in IR Notebook 6.1.

RAY KROC, FREDERICK TAYLOR, AND THE QUEST FOR EFFICIENCY

Management has often focused on issues of efficiency. Taylorism was based on two factors: (1) the search for the best and most efficient way to perform a task and (2) the quest for the best way to divide a large, complex task into small, simple tasks. Many people assume that the principles of scientific management are no longer used in modern organizations. Yet a trip to a local McDonald's would suggest that Ray Kroc, the founder of the chain, followed the principles of Frederick Taylor's scientific management. Next time you are at a McDonald's, take a look at the food packaging. You will notice that the drink container has a line showing how much of the container should contain ice versus soda. McDonald's also provides a complete nutrition breakdown on the "Nutrition Centre" section of its website and in a publication called "Food Facts" where it presents detailed ingredient information. This suggests to us a very high focus on efficiency and consistency across stores.

For more information, please see "Food Facts," McDonald's Canada website, http://www1.mcdonalds.ca/NutritionCalculator/IngredientFactsEN.pdf; "Nutrition Centre," McDonald's Canada website, http://www.mcdonalds.ca/ca/en/food/nutrition_centre.html#/.

HUMAN RELATIONS

Whereas earlier managerial perspectives saw workers as akin to machines, a movement in the 1930s presented a more enlightened approach to management. This new approach, called **human relations**, was largely influenced by Elton Mayo and the Human Relations School that he founded (Reece, 2011).

Human relations was grounded in the belief that while managers and workers have conflicting views and values, these differences could be resolved using effective policies and procedures. Accordingly, this paradigm focused heavily on the role of effective leadership (i.e., improved communication, humanistic workplace designs, and participative decision-making processes) as a way to improve the workplace (Godard & Delaney, 2000).

The human relations school and Mayo are probably best known for the Hawthorne studies, conducted in the Hawthorne plant of Western Electric in the 1930s (Mayo, 1933). These studies focused on the effects of lighting, breaks, and other factors on plant workers' productivity. The results revealed that productivity increased when lighting was either increased or decreased, leading to the conclusion that management needed to pay attention to the work environment, and the social needs and satisfaction of workers, if they wished productivity to increase.

While this perspective put more emphasis on employees than the managerial views of master–servant and scientific management, it was heavily criticized by the labour movement as anti-union. This anti-union view of human relations may well have been spawned by the funding of the human relations school. Many of the early founders of this school were CEOs of enterprises, including John Rockefeller, who sought ways to improve the relationship between workers and management without reducing managerial control (Bruce & Nyland, 2011; Hassard, 2012). However, not all scholars agree that the human relations school was anti-union, and some unionists even embraced the human relations concepts (Kaufman, 2001).

> **human relations**
> a managerial view that believes that effective management practices can minimize the conflict between managers and employees

HUMAN RESOURCES MANAGEMENT (HRM)

Many of the concepts of the HRM perspective grew out of the human relations school and the closely associated field of organizational behaviour (Godard, 2014; Van Buren, Greenwood & Sheehan, 2011). At the core of this view is the relationship between individual employees and their employers, often represented by management. As such, as you can see by examining any HRM textbook, most HRM practitioners and scholars focus on issues associated with the selection, performance appraisal, training, and compensation of individual employees. In this role, the HRM professional seeks to balance the need for fairness in workplace procedures with the organization's need to remain efficient and productive. It can be argued that the HRM perspective minimizes the elements of industrial democracy, or democratic processes in the workplace (since it is not focused on collective representation), as well as the inherent conflict between management and worker as they attempt to achieve their competing needs (Godard, 2014; Godard & Delaney, 2000).

While some argue that this perspective, like human relations, is a nonunion view, others disagree. For example, Barbash's (1987) seminal equity-efficiency theory has long been advocated as a theoretical link between the HRM and traditional IR perspectives (Meltz, 1997). In essence, Barbash (1987) defined *efficiency* in terms of the organizational outputs such as profits, revenues, and productivity. Therefore, *efficiency* focuses on the needs of the organization. In contrast, Barbash described *equity* in terms of fair, or ethical, treatment of employees by employers. In particular, Barbash (1987) highlighted five elements of equity:

1. Employees need to have a say in the work they perform (also known as voice).
2. Employees require due process in the handling of complaints.
3. Employees are entitled to fair treatment at work.
4. Employees are entitled to meaningful work.
5. Employees need fair compensation and secure employment.

In the pluralist view of IR, unions are seen as focusing their efforts on these five elements of equity while management is seen as focusing its efforts on elements of efficiency. The result is that collective agreement terms protect employees from exploitation, inconsistent management practices, and potentially unsafe work practices while still ensuring that the operation remains financially viable (Barbash, 1987).

Although the equity–efficiency theory had been discussed extensively in IR circles, Barbash (1987) argued that management itself could introduce equity through HRM practices. Thus, we should not be surprised that the essence of Barbash's concept of equity is very similar to the organizational justice theory that entered mainstream HRM literature in the 1980s. For a detailed overview of **organizational justice** theory and research, we refer the reader to *The Handbook of Organizational Justice* (Greenberg & Colquitt, 2013). A brief summary of organizational justice follows.

In its broadest meaning, organizational justice can be thought of as one's perception of fairness in the workplace. There are three elements of organizational justice (Crawshaw, Cropanzano, Bell & Nadisic, 2013):

- **Distributive justice,** or perceptions of the fairness of workplace outcomes or decisions;
- **Procedural justice,** or perceptions of the fairness of the procedures used to decide workplace outcomes; and

organizational justice employees' perception of fair treatment at work

distributive justice employees' perception of fairness in workplace outcomes and decisions

procedural justice employees' perception of fairness in workplace procedures

- **Interactional justice**, or perceptions of the fairness of interpersonal interactions and exchanges. This can include elements of respect and dignity as well as whether one receives explanations for workplace outcomes and decisions.

interactional justice
employees' perceptions
of the fairness of inter-
personal interactions
and exchanges

In many ways the elements procedural justice and distributive justice mirror Dunlop's concepts of procedural rules (i.e., rules concerning processes and procedures) and substantive rules (i.e., rules concerning the outcomes) that we discussed in Chapter 1. Given the similarities between these theories that ground the IR and HRM disciplines, we argue that the HRM perspective is not inherently anti-union, as both see the importance of equity and fairness.

// THE GROWING ROLE OF MANAGEMENT

As is discussed in Chapter 1, IR system models have been the cornerstone of IR teaching and research in Canada. In these pluralist IR systems, the concept of shared ideology was key. It meant that each of the three actors (management, labour, and government) saw a legitimate role for the other two actors. Yet these systems, and most textbooks, tend to minimize the role of management in IR. As we will now see, management has taken a strong role in the IR system.

THE STRATEGIC CHOICE FRAMEWORK

In the 1980s, a seminal work by Kochan, Katz, and McKersie (1986) focused largely on the role of management, claiming that management was a driving force in transforming the IR system. In their review of the changing IR climate in the United States from the 1960s through the 1980s, they noted a number of trends in the U.S.:

- a rapid decline in the number of unionized workers (see Chapter 5);
- a large number of employers opening new locations in largely nonunion areas or states;
- a large number of plant and business closures in the more heavily unionized states;
- decreased capital expenditures in nonunionized versus unionized plants;
- a shift of products from union to nonunion plants; and
- a movement toward "union-free" workplaces—for example, there was a push toward progressive HRM strategies that some saw as ways to avoid unionization (i.e., employees would not see the value in unionizing since their employer could provide the benefits as a union).

During the 1980s, the United States also saw several anti-union trends in the National Labor Relations Board and the government:

- the appointment of "employer-friendly" and "anti-union" members to the National Labor Relations Board, and
- a pro-management/anti-union approach to labour relations by political leaders and governments of the time—for example, in what was considered a milestone event of the 1980s, former president Ronald Reagan fired striking air-traffic controllers in what some members of the labour movement saw as a "union-busting" approach.

Taken together, these trends called into question Dunlop's (1958) concept of shared ideology. The clear trend was that the actors of management and government were questioning, if not reducing, the role of labour. Thus, it should not be surprising that Kochan, Katz, and McKersie (1986) titled their book *The Transformation of American Industrial Relations* and highlighted the role of strategic decisions (or choices) made by management. The **strategic choice framework** highlighted three elements:

First, IR decisions are made at three levels: the business level (i.e., long-term strategic level); the collective bargaining level; and the day-to-day workplace level. The business (or strategic) level would represent the senior management of the organization where long-term strategies are developed and implemented. The collective bargaining level would represent the level of the firm where collective agreements are negotiated and implemented. The workplace level focuses on the front-line management group that deals with day-to-day workplace issues within the organization.

Second, effective strategies require these three levels (i.e., strategic, collective bargaining, and workplace) to work in one direction in order to achieve major goals. Thus, these strategic choices must be designed to achieve a significant goal, planned and executed from the highest level, and must have a long-term focus.

Third, strategic choices can have a longer-term impact on all actors of the industrial relations system. The key here is that the strategic choice of one actor can impact the other actors and indeed the IR system.

Let's consider a hypothetical example. If a manufacturing company had a number of unionized plants in Ontario and wanted to establish a new, nonunion plant in Alberta, the following scenario could occur. At the strategic level of the firm, there would be a plan to build and invest in a plant in Alberta and a conscious decision that it be union-free. This might involve an assessment of which areas of the province are least at risk for a union drive and which areas have low union-density rates. At the collective bargaining level, the negotiators would ensure that the collective agreements in Ontario did not provide any access to jobs, or union member rights, for the new Alberta location. At the workplace level, the company would ensure that managers of the new plant worked in such a way that employees did not see any reason to unionize. This could be done using any of the managerial union avoidance tactics discussed later in this chapter.

It is important to note that while strategic choice often focuses on management choice, unions and governments also have similar choices, as shown in Table 6.1.

> **strategic choice framework**
> a view that emphasizes the role of management and strategies in the industrial relations system

TABLE 6.1

STRATEGIC CHOICES: THREE-LEVEL, THREE-ACTOR SUMMARY

	LONG-TERM STRATEGIC LEVEL	COLLECTIVE BARGAINING LEVEL	WORKPLACE LEVEL
MANAGEMENT	Business and investment strategies	Human resources policies and negotiation priorities	Front-line supervisor style, contract administration, employee involvement, job design
LABOUR	Political, representation, and organizing strategies	Negotiation priorities	Shop steward style, contract administration, employee involvement, job design
GOVERNMENT	Overall economic and social mandate/ policies	Labour and employment law administration	Individual worker rights and protection

Source: Reprinted from *The Transformation of American Industrial Relations*, Second Edition, edited by Thomas A Kochan, Harry C. Katz, and Robert B. McKersie. Copyright © 1994 by Cornell University Press. Used by permission of the publisher, Cornell University Press. P. 17,

For example, as we covered in Chapter 5, unions face choices concerning which industrial sectors to unionize, how to balance the current members' needs and new union drives, etc. For any of the union's strategic, long-term plans, they would also need to ensure that all levels of the union operated in concert to achieve major goals.

STRATEGIC CHOICE AND CANADA

A logical question is: "To what extent does the strategic choice framework, and the associated transformation of IR, hold true in Canada?" Not surprisingly, arguments concerning the potential for "nonunion" industrial relations system in Canada arose shortly after the release of Kochan et al.'s (1986) book (e.g., Chaykowski & Verma, 1992; Verma & Chaykowski, 1999).

Several arguments, from the previous sources and our interactions with industry stakeholders, might support the idea that we will see movement toward a nonunion IR system in Canada:

- Canada has historically followed the industrial relations trends of the United States;
- the number of multinational corporations that are headquartered in the United States and operate in Canada will encourage a similar transition here in Canada;
- there is a low level of union density in the private sector;
- increased global competition will encourage employers to avoid the increased wage and benefit costs associated with unionization;
- progressive HRM techniques may result in employees no longer seeing significant advantages to unionization, making such workers difficult to organize;
- there has been a rise in largely nonunionized industries (e.g., retail, business services); and
- governments are taking actions that may be seen as "pro-management." For example, we have seen governments include the traditionally negotiated issues of wages and benefits in back-to-work legislation, or threaten to use such legislation to end a strike (Rose, 2008; Thompson & Slinn, 2012).

On the other hand, other factors support the argument that Canada will not see a huge shift away from unionization. For example, while the union density rate in Canada has decreased slightly, it still remains in the 30 percent range with limited evidence of a radical drop (see Chapter 5). The highly unionized public sector shows little likelihood of becoming union-free. Also, we have seen unions make inroads into new sectors of the economy. For example, some of Atlantic Canada's offshore oil fields are unionized. In addition, unions are making headway with youth as evidenced in unionization of small retail workplaces, such as the Just Us! Coffee Roasters Co-op in Nova Scotia (Kimber, 2014) discussed later in this chapter, and union drives such as the CHL union drive discussed in the opening vignette.

Finally, there is the argument that we may see a movement to a nonunion system in some sectors of the economy but not others. Chaykowski and Verma (1992) suggest that in heavily unionized industries (e.g., automotive) and in the public sector, we are unlikely to see the movement to a union-free model. However, in the private sector and in largely nonunion industries (e.g., the financial sector), we may see trends toward union-free workplaces as these workplaces face more pressure from the external environment (e.g., increased competition, global trade).

Overall, our view of the evidence suggests that Canada is not going down the union-free road. Thirty years after Kochan et al. (1986) published their influential book, unionization rates in Canada remain near 30 percent, the public sector remains heavily unionized, there is limited evidence of a pro-management government agenda, and unions have made inroads into new industries. Nevertheless, it is clear that we are seeing changes in the union–management relationship and that management is becoming a more dominant actor in the IR system. Morever, as suggested by the trends noted in Chapter 5, there may be some evidence to support the argument that different sectors of the economy may experience a transformation in the IR system.

// INDUSTRIAL RELATIONS AND BUSINESS STRATEGIES

Given the importance of the strategic choice framework in current IR teaching and research, it is essential to understand the key elements of an overall business or organizational strategy. There is general agreement that a business/organizational strategy process includes four phases: an assessment of the external and internal environments, strategy formation, strategy implementation, and strategy evaluation (Wheelen, Hunger, Hoffman & Bamford, 2015).

1. *Assessment of the external and internal environments.* This assessment often includes a SWOT-like analysis, in which the firm will determine its own strengths (S) and weaknesses (W), and assess the opportunities (O) and threats (T) in the external environment.

2. *Strategy formation.* Three actions are key in this phase. First, on the basis of the SWOT analysis, the organization will develop a mission statement that maps out its overall purpose. Second, the organization will then break the mission into specific performance goals to determine a more targeted direction. A wealth of evidence shows that specific and challenging goals are very effective in bringing about high levels of performance (Brown & McCracken, 2010; Locke & Latham, 2013), so management will want to ensure that the set goals are SMART: *specific, measurable, attainable* (i.e., difficult but attainable), *relevant to the vision and recorded*, and *time-based* (Brown & Latham, 2000). Third, the firm will develop strategies to achieve these performance goals. More specifically, these plans should mark the path to achieve the goals developed previously.

3. *Strategy implementation.* During this step, the organization puts the strategy it formulated in step two into action.

4. *Strategy evaluation.* During this step, the organization examines the effectiveness of its strategy implementation—namely, whether it achieved its goals. Key players might also examine what factors impacted the success (or lack of success) of the industrial relations strategy. Post-evaluation, the organization will often determine next steps, resulting in a refinement of the strategy and a restart of the previous steps.

Within this organizational strategy framework, an organization has to examine the fit of its strategy with its overall people-management strategy. In other words, the goals of and plans for the broader organizational strategy should include elements related to employee and people management. Thus strategic HRM can be defined in terms of managing HRM philosophies, policies, and practices in a manner that supports the achievement of the organizational strategy (Belcourt & McBey, 2015):

- *Overall human resources philosophy*. In essence, this defines the values of the organization as it relates to employees and human resources issues.
- *Specific policies*. These include formal (and usually written) policies and guidelines that can outline, and even constrain, specific human resources strategies. For example, an employer may have a formal diversity or employment equity policy.
- *Specific practices*. For example, those related to various typical human resources functions (i.e., selection, promotion, layoff, performance management, compensation, training, etc.). For example, a formal diversity or employment equity program could influence an organization's selection (or hiring) practices.

MANAGEMENT STRATEGIES RELATED TO UNIONS

Strategic HRM traditionally includes a discussion of how human resources functions of staffing (i.e., recruitment and selection), training and development, performance appraisal, and compensation need to be aligned to the organizational direction (Belcourt & McBey, 2015). However, the effectiveness of human resources management also includes an analysis of industrial relations (Huselid, Jackson & Schuler, 1997) as well as the organization's strategy vis-à-vis labour relations and unionization (Greer, 2001). Canadian scholar Thompson (1995) long ago identified four specific management strategies related to unions. Today, we continue to look at these four strategies in IR circles:

- union acceptance;
- union resistance;
- union removal; and
- union substitution.

UNION ACCEPTANCE

A strategy of **union acceptance** is grounded in the belief that unionization is somewhat inevitable. Management accepts the fact that unionization is a democratic right and part, if not all, of the company's operations will be unionized. However, this does not mean that management will relinquish control of the operation to the union. Rather, the goal is for management to obtain the best deal that it can to meet its operational needs. A good example of this would be global retailer H&M; UFCW's Shimmin has described the company's response as follows: "In my 10 years of organizing, this was unique. The employer was not nearly as intimidating as they usually are," he said. According to H&M spokesperson Emily Scarlett the Swedish retailer has had a long history of working with unions in Europe, including the Union Network International, a global trade union. "For us, we believe in people. It's one of our fundamental values that we work with our employees. We value their decision," Scarlett said, adding several U.S. outlets are already represented by UFCW in New York. "We encourage our employees to make a decision for themselves and to look at the information" (Lu, 2011).

> **union acceptance**
> management's seeing unionization as a democratic right, and accepting that part, if not all, of its operations will be unionized

Some companies, like H&M, present a union acceptance model.

UNION RESISTANCE

A **union resistance** strategy in essence contains two somewhat contrasting elements. On one hand, management accepts the right of employees to organize and may follow a union-acceptance strategy in the parts of the organization that are currently unionized. In such unionized workplaces, management will seek to get the best deal that it can and will negotiate in good faith without any attempt to remove the union. On the other hand, management will oppose any further unionization of its workforce. This attempt to stop union inroads may include active opposition to union drives and challenging certification procedures. Examples of union avoidance behaviours include illegally firing union organizers or supporters, restricting union access to the workplace, hiring consultants to assist in an anti-union campaign, training managers to oppose the drive, and threatening to close the operation if it becomes unionized (Bentham, 2002; Jacobs, 2010; Thomason & Pozzebon, 1998).

One example of this could be the Just Us! Coffee Roasters Co-op in Atlantic Canada. That firm faced an unfair labour practice complaint from the Nova Scotia Labour Relations Board as it had allegedly fired two employees who had been organizing co-workers to join the Service Employees International Union (SEIU) (Kimber, 2014).

> **union resistance**
> a management policy seeking to limit the spread of unions in the firm

UNION REMOVAL

Simply put, managers using **union removal** seek to remove the union wherever it exists in the workforce. This is also sometimes called "union busting." Again, it essentially has two elements. In unionized workplaces, management endeavours to ensure that unionized employees' working conditions, wages, and benefits are not superior to those of nonunion employees. In so doing, they attempt to send a message to union members that the union is not getting them a better employment package than they would receive if they were not union members. In nonunionized workplaces, management will try to discourage union activity by sending the message that there is little to gain from unionization and will openly resist any union certification drives. For an example, see the YouTube posting from a former union buster listed in the Weblinks section at the end of this chapter. Another example is the type of training presented in IR Today 6.1.

Another example could be the recent Walmart decision by the Supreme Court of Canada (CBC News, 2014). As discussed in Chapter 4, the Supreme Court ruled that Walmart violated Quebec's labour laws when it closed the Jonquière, Quebec store, the very first Walmart store to unionize in North America. The same retailer also closed the tire centre in its Gatineau, Quebec, location a few months after the tire employees negotiated the very first collective agreement in the store's history (CBC News, 2014).

> **union removal**
> a management strategy designed to remove the union from the workplace

ONLINE COMPLIANCE PANEL
Comprehensive GRC Solutions

Toll Free: 510-857-5896

Live Webinar on

Register Now and Grab 5% discount
using the coupon code **ZX5YW**
on Early bird registration valid till September 05, 2014

Register Now

Union Avoidance Policies

Instructor: Cynde Jackson Clarke
Date: Tuesday, September 23, 2014
Time: 10:00 AM PDT | 01:00 PM EDT
Duration: 60 Minutes
Price: $143.00 Live Session for one participant
Super combo offer Live + Training CD at $479.00

Webinar Description:
Join this webinar to learn about whether your organization is a potential high conflict "hot spot" and steps you can take to create the type of work environment where employees and the business flourish without the labor union involvement. Section 7 of the National Labor Relations Act (NLRA) gives employees the right to form labor union giving them the ability to unionize or not to unionize.

- Bargain collectively through representatives of employee's own choosing
- Engage in other concerted activities for the purpose of collective bargaining or other mutual aid or protection.

Why Should you Attend:
Employees today are concerned about job security, off shoring and outsourcing, the hiring of temporary employees to replace permanent workers, reductions in benefits and a variety of social issues. These are the concerns that move a workforce toward unionization.
Employers should be aware of their companies' susceptibility to union organization and the impact a labor union would have on their business. More importantly, they should know what it takes to create a work environment where employees are engaged and content so that forming the labor union is the last thing they think about.

Objectives of the Presentation:
This webinar will help the attendee:

- Understand what drives a workforce to consider forming a labor union
- Identify labor's organizing tactics and the implications
- Learn about positive employee relations, including lawful ways to respond to union tactics

Who can Benefit:
Human resource professionals should be aware of labor's organizing tactics and their implications in order to educate managers and supervisors on positive employee relations as well as lawful ways to respond to unionizing activities.

Instructor Profile:

Cynde Jackson Clarke
Consultant-Talent Acquisition,
Cynde Jackson Clarke, SPHR is a veteran human resources consultant and educator, whose expertise includes recruitment, onboarding, organization assessment &design, training and, coaching. Her training facilitation experience includes behavioral interviewing skills; applicant tracking systems; and coaching/delivering meaningful feedback. More...

About Us | Email | Webinars

For more offers please contact customer support.

Customer Support :
Email: customersupport@onlinecompliancepanel.com.
Call us at this Toll Free number: 510-857-5896
Fax: 510-509-9659

If you do not wish to receive this training alerts from OnlineCompliancePanel Click Unsubscribe

www.onlinecompliancepanel.com

Source: Courtesy of OnlineCompliancePanel.

UNION SUBSTITUTION

union substitution
a management strategy
designed to give
nonunion employees
all the advantages of
unionization

The strategy of union substitution applies to nonunion operations and workplaces. In essence, taken to its fullest, **union substitution** is designed to give nonunion employees all of the due process elements (e.g., appeal procedures, clear policies applied consistently), representation (e.g., teams), and compensation advantages of unionization. Take for example the fact that many nonunion employers have employee handbooks that contain policies concerning discipline, discrimination, hours of work, wages, benefits, appeal processes, and performance expectations (Smith & Harris, 2014). In essence, these handbooks are very similar to a collective agreement with the exception that each individual employee signs the book as there is no collective agreement negotiated by a union. Therefore, it can be argued that management, through its HRM policies and practices, attempts to provide a substitute to unionization that makes employees see unionization as unnecessary (Donaghey, Cullinane, Dundon & Dobbins, 2012). Some would argue that the nonunion employee representation plans we discuss later in the chapter are good examples of this strategy (see review in Campolieti, Gomez & Gunderson, 2013). Note that this strategy is also called a union avoidance strategy in that one avoids unionization through a substitution strategy.

MANAGEMENT STRATEGIES TOWARD UNIONS: EVIDENCE TO DATE

As discussed previously, the evidence from Kochan et al. (1986) suggests that union substitution, removal, and resistance strategies are widely used in the United States. But what about Canada? The evidence to date suggests that these strategies are not as prevalent in Canada. One study (Thompson, 1995) of industrial relations executives suggests that over 70 percent of Canadian organizations have a union acceptance strategy (i.e., they seek to negotiate the best deal), while just over 9 percent have a union resistance strategy (i.e., they seek to limit spread of unions), and none have a union removal strategy. The remaining 20 percent or so used a combination of strategies. However, that same study found that in new plants, approximately 37 percent of the executives preferred to be nonunion (i.e., they accept employees' right to unionize and, thus, remain neutral) while another 34 percent actively oppose unionization.

A second Canadian study by Godard (1997) found similar results. In that study, approximately 56 percent of managers surveyed used union acceptance (i.e., tougher negotiation) policies toward unions, 17 percent used a union avoidance policy, and 9 percent used a union reduction or elimination strategy.

However, one study of certification applications in eight Canadian jurisdictions suggests that Canadian employers are increasingly adopting a union resistance strategy. That study (Bentham, 2002) found that 80 percent of employers stated that they had taken specific actions that opposed a union certification drive. Moreover, 12 percent of the survey respondents openly admitted to taking actions that are considered unfair labour practices (e.g., promised pay/benefit increases, threatened to fire or layoff employees, transferred employees).

Taken together, these three studies suggest that we have not seen a radical shift toward union removal policies in Canada. However, the trend toward a nonunion approach in newer operations suggests there is a movement toward union resistance–employers may well accept the legitimacy of a union in their currently unionized workplaces, but many in nonunion environments are attempting to block union inroads into them.

Interestingly, since the last of these studies in 2002 we have seen few studies that compare the prevalence of these strategies. However, we as will discuss later in this chapter, we have seen the movement toward many strategies that may be seen as methods of union substitution (e.g., nonunion representation) as well as studies outlining the union substitution, resistance, and removal strategies present in some sectors (Coulter, 2013).

// CURRENT MANAGERIAL PERSPECTIVES AND TRENDS

Given the strategies toward unionization, it is logical to question what the current trends are as they relate to the management perspective. Over the past years, we have seen a number of trends toward managerial practices that include elements of voice, due process, or alternative forms of collective relationships with the employer. In particular, the following trends will be discussed:

- high-performance workplaces and work practices;
- nonunion representation; and
- nonstandard work arrangements.

HIGH-PERFORMANCE WORKPLACES AND WORK PRACTICES (HPWPs)

High-performance work practices (HPWPs) have become important to management and are a topic of significant interest in the IR field. For a thorough review of the topic from a Canadian perspective, we encourage you to see the recent book edited by Murray, Belanger, Giles, and Lapointe (2013). A summary of HPWPs now follows.

Huselid (1995), an early scholar in the field, defined HPWPs to include comprehensive staffing (i.e., recruitment and selection), incentive compensation, performance management, training and development, and employee involvement systems designed to: (1) improve the knowledge, skills, and abilities of employees, (2) motivate high levels of employee performance, (3) minimize employee turnover, (4) reduce work avoidance and poor work quality, and (5) encourage nonperformers to leave the organization. In the years since this seminal work, these elements of HPWPs, and their impact on organizational performance, have continued to be examined. The general consensus is that HPWP have a positive relationship on organizational performance (Gill, 2009; Kehoe & Wright, 2013; Liu, Guthrie, Flood & MacCurtain, 2009).

However, while the evidence of a positive relationship exists, researchers have struggled to prove causation, namely that these HPWPs cause organizational performance improvements (Guest, 2011). Nevertheless, the data showing a positive relationship between HPWPs and firm performance are such that the area has become of significant interest to the management actor of the IR system. After all, a key focus for management is efficiency.

HPWPs can be categorized into three clusters (Kehoe & Wright, 2013), defined as follows (Delaney & Huselid, 1996; Huselid, 1995; Kehoe & Wright, 2013):

- *Ability enhancing practices.* These practices are designed to ensure that employees have the needed skills, knowledge, and abilities to enhance organizational performance. Thus, HR practices related to the selection and training of employees are critical here.
- *Motivation-enhancing practices.* Motivational HR practices can include individual and group pay incentives, performance appraisals, promotion based on

> **high-performance work practices (HPWPs)** comprehensive human resources practices designed to improve organizational performance

High-performance workplaces and work practices (HPWPs) include having employees involved in decision making.

merit/performance, and due process mechanisms (e.g., grievance and appeal processes) designed to ensure fair treatment in the workplace.

- *Opportunity-enhancing practices.* Here we see the importance of practices related to voice and employee involvement. Thus, HR practices related to information sharing, autonomy, teams, and participation fall into this cluster.

Given the prevalence of HPWPs today, scholars have examined the adoption of HPWPs in unionized workplaces. For example, we see arguments that HPWPs can have both beneficial and detrimental effects for workers and their unions (see Gill, 2009; Godard, 2004; Pohler & Luchak, 2014). For example, HPWPs can be a way for unions to move away from their traditional adversarial role toward a partnership role that extends beyond the typical labour issues associated with negotiations and contract administration. In addition, they provide for employee benefits related to better pay, fairer treatment of workers, improved work environments, and greater voice. However, reviews of the literature also suggest that these high-performance practices can negatively impact employees and their unions in terms of increased stress, fatigue, and workload (Godard & Delaney, 2000; Pohler & Luchak, 2014).

Scholars have also examined whether the presence of a union facilitates or impedes the implementation of HPWPs. Overall the results are inconclusive, with some researchers finding a positive relationship between unions and HPWPs and others finding a negative relationship (see Gill, 2009; Gill & Meyer, 2013; Liu et al., 2009; Pohler & Luchak, 2014). A review of these studies suggests the following reasons for why one could expect a positive relationship between HPWP adoption and unionization: (1) unions can facilitate the employee trust and job security needed for the long-term adoption of HPWPs, (2) unions can advocate for the longer-term investments needed to successfully implement HPWPs, (3) many of the HPWP elements related to promotion from within, training, and fair selection processes are consistent with union interests; (4) unionized workplaces have lower turnover and higher retention rates, reducing the costs of HPWPs related to training and selection, (5) unions have a communication infrastructure that can be used to facilitate the implementation of HPWPs, and (6) unions enable an independent, collective voice (complementary to, but separate from, the management-sponsored individual voice contained in HPWPs) that can improve the level of employee commitment needed for successful implementation of HPWPs.

A review of these studies also provides arguments for why unionized workplaces may be less likely to adopt HPWPs. Firstly, the traditional adversarial role of unions and management is such that unions may be less likely to support what can be seen as pro-management HPWPs. Second, unions may resist HPWPs, perceiving that these practices are a threat to job security. Third, unions have often fought for, and negotiated, clear rules that limit management's flexibility and discretion in hiring, training, pay, etc. HPWPs may be seen as a way for management to regain such flexibility and discretion at the expense of employees. Finally, HPWPs (given their focus on voice, good pay, increased training, etc.) may be seen as a form of union substitution. As pointed out by Gill and Meyer (2013, p. 508), we see "… evidence that managers regard unions as hindrances to workplace performance … resulting in union avoidance, suppression and substitution" via HPWPs.

These preceding arguments reveal that, like many things in IR, we cannot simply conclude that there is a consistently positive or negative relationship between unionization and the presence of HPWPs. However, like many of the union effects we will discuss in Chapter 11, we can conclude that the relationship between the union and management plays an important role in the successful adoption of HPWPs. As Gill (2009) concluded following her comprehensive review of the HPWPs literature, unions that have a cooperative relationship with management can overcome many barriers to HPWP adoption. In her words (p. 45), it is the "quality of Industrial Relations, or the relationship between unions and management" that determines whether or not unionization results in successful or unsuccessful implementation of HPWPs. In fact, her follow-up study confirmed that "good employee relations" both facilitated the implementation of HPWPs in unionized Australian workplaces and had positive impacts on organizational competitiveness (Gill & Meyer, 2013). In particular, unionized workplaces with good employment relations were more likely to introduced HPWPs related to employee voice and empowerment than both nonunion workplaces and union workplaces with poor employment relations.

Similarly, an Irish study found that when job security was low, the presence of a union was associated with reduced usage of HPWPs (Liu et al., 2009). In contrast, very high job security was associated with greater presence of HPWPs in unionized firms. This finding makes sense to us. When there is low job security, unions may use their collective voice and bargaining power to resist HPWPs out of concern that such practices will reduce in job loss. However, where job loss is not perceived to be an issue, and the risk to employees is lower, unions may be more likely to support HPWPs.

Turning now to Canadian evidence, Pohler and Luchak (2013) found that unionization and an employee-focused business strategy (i.e., a strategy containing HPWPs related to enhancing workers' skills, increasing employee involvement/participation, and improving labour–management cooperation) was associated with increased profitability, workplace climate, employment growth, and dispute resolution. The authors suggest that: "when management signals … that it intends to invest in and co-operate with employees, the negative effects of unions are attenuated, and the positive effects are enhanced" (Pohler & Luchak, 2013, p. 25).

These same Canadian authors (Pohler & Luchak, 2014) examined the effects of HPWPs that focused on employee involvement (e.g., participation in teams or joint labour–management committees, information sharing concerning workplace events/changes; employee suggestion plans, use of self-directed teams). Overall, they found that increased use of HPWPs was associated with increased usage of sick days, unpaid over-time, and disputes/grievances. These findings could be seen to support the argument that HPWPs can have a negative effect on workers. However, when they teased out the union effects, interesting patterns emerged. Specifically, they discovered that the presence of a union negated the aforementioned positive relationships between HPWPs and sick-day usage, unpaid overtime, and disputes/grievances. Moreover, the job satisfaction HPWP was most positive for unionized employees.

Taking all of the evidence together, we conclude that HPWPs can be successfully implemented by management in a unionized workplace and that such practices are not inherently anti-union. However, it is also clear that a positive union–management climate, job security, and an employee-focused business strategy can facilitate the successful implementation of HPWPs in unionized workplaces.

NONUNION EMPLOYEE REPRESENTATION

Nonunion employee representation (NER) can be defined as groups of employees who meet with management on matters related to the terms and conditions of their workplace, often using a committee structure (Taras, 2006). The basic philosophy of NER has been described as *quid pro quo*, or "this for that" (Taras & Kaufman, 2006). Managers hope to achieve cooperative and consultative workplace interactions with workers that minimize worker–management conflict, whereas workers seek a voice mechanism that allows them to influence managerial decision making and facilitate a respectful work environment. As such, the primary goals of such plans are said to include:

- to improve communication between workers and management;
- to increase access to workplace dispute resolution and justice mechanisms; and
- to negotiate better terms and conditions of employment. (Taras & Kaufman, 2006)

While statistics concerning NER are not as easily available as those concerning union representation, reviews suggest that about 15 to 20 percent of Canadian employees have access to some form of nonunion representation (see reviews in Campolieti, Gomez & Gunderson, 2013; Taras, 2002; Taras & Kaufman, 2006). Similar rates have been reported in the United States (Campolieti et al., 2013).

It is interesting to note that despite the similarities between Canadian and American NER rates and labour laws, NER is often considered illegal in the United States. This is because such forms of representation have often been considered akin to company unions, which are prohibited under the *National Labor Relations Act* (NLRA) (Tara & Kaufman, 2006). While legislation that would have allowed NER in the States, namely the *Teamwork for Employees and Management Act* (TEAM), was proposed, it was vetoed by former president Bill Clinton in 1996 (Chansler & Schraeder, 2003). In Canada, there has been a history of NER dating back to the 1910s, and these mechanisms are deemed lawful unless specifically designed to prevent union organizing (Taras, 1999). Arguably, it was Mackenzie King's past experience promoting nonunion representation that ensured that NER was not deemed illegal by the labour law legislation passed in the 1940s when he was Prime Minister (Taras & Kaufman, 2006).

While there is a tendency to group all NER plans into a single category, scholars agree that there are indeed four types of nonunion representation (Campolieti et al., 2013; Taras & Kaufman, 2006). These are described below.

> nonunion employee representation (NER) occurs when a group of nonunion employees meets with management regarding employment terms and conditions

EVOLUTIONARY This form of representation enables a gradual improvement in workers' economic position and voice. However, this venue lacks the presence of an independent union that can advocate for the employees. Thus, the basic premise here is that this is a temporary state. As workers experience the importance of voice, but grow frustrated with their limited ability to create change given that all decision-making power still resides with management, this form of representation can often become the springboard to union. A potential current example of this form of nonunion representation would be the Royal Canadian Mounted Police (RCMP). Past studies have shown that the RCMP has a form of nonunion representation (Taras, 1999; Taras & Copping, 1998). Arguably issues related to the sovereignty of the nation, and the special role of the RCMP, precluded their unionization. However, a recent Supreme Court of Canada ruling declared that RCMP officers should be able to bargain collectively. Specifically, the court ruled that the:

> ... *in-house labour relations scheme that was imposed on RCMP rank and file members in 1967 by management and leaves all final decisions up to the commissioner breaches the Charter guarantee of freedom of association. It denies their right to form an independent labour association and hold "meaningful" collective bargaining talks with their employer. (MacCharles, 2014)*

While the ruling fell short of legislating their right to unionize, we argue that this is an example of evolutionary NER. Frustration with the balance of power remaining in management's hand pushed the court challenge that can now facilitate a union-like, independent, employee advocate within the RCMP.

UNITY OF INTEREST Managers generally oppose unionization, believing that it leads to adversarial (or win-lose) relationships. In this form of NER, the focus is on a "win-win" scenario. Specifically, this NER, usually initiated by management, seeks to foster a harmonious organization. It involves the alignment of employees to the organization's goals, increased cooperation, and improved communication/information sharing. In exchange, employees receive better working conditions and voice. In many ways, this type of NER is seen to include many of the employee voice and involvement HPWPs we just reviewed. Good examples of this form of NER would include the joint council of Imperial Oil dating back to the 1910s, or Dofasco's NER model dating back over half a century (Taras & Kaufman, 2006).

UNION AVOIDANCE The primary purpose of this form of NER is to avoid unions and use NER as a substitute. Given a great hostility toward unions, employers using this form of NER deliberately design the plan to reduce the likelihood of unionization. Here employers will "buy off" employees by providing them more than the union can in terms of higher wages, improved working conditions, and some access to dispute resolution and voice (Taras & Kaufman, 2006). However, this type of NER is often accompanied with scare tactics, punishment, and even unfair labour practices as ways to minimize the likelihood of unionization. As noted by Campolieti et al. (2013, pp. 380–381), among some IR scholars "there is a commonly held belief that NER is always and everywhere a union avoidance strategy."

COMPLEMENTARY VOICE (DUAL CHANNEL) Whereas the previous two NER categories saw NER as a substitute to unionization, the complementary voice sees NER and unions as two different yet complementary employee representation models. Thus, it is also called the dual channel model. One channel represents the internal NER voice mechanisms, while the second channel represents the collective voice of a union. In so doing, this model provides advantages to firms in terms of standardization of pay, benefits, and working conditions (via union voice) combined with non-confrontational NER governance models. For the employee, there is the advantage of union protection and bargaining power combined with access to individual voice via NER. For the union, they retain their role of employee advocate and negotiator, but face the challenge of having to prove their value relative to a nonunion NER model.

A recent study examined these four types of NER and unionization in both Canada and the United States (Campolieti et al., 2013). Specifically, they examined the extent that NER was complementary to unionization (a combination of evoluntionary and complementary NERs) or a substitute to unionization (a combination of avoidance and unity of interest NER types). That study found that NER was negatively associated with unionization in Canada and the United States. Moreover, Canadians with an NER showed less desire to unionize. In fact, they were 12 percent less likely to prefer being a union member relative to Canadians without an NER. Given these findings, the authors conclude that NERs had a stronger substitution than complementary effect in Canada and that NER may indeed be harmful to unions.

Regardless of the NER form used, research (Kaufman & Taras, 2000) suggests that the long-term success of these plans requires two managerial practices: (1) pay and benefits must meet (or exceed) what unionized workers of that industry (or comparable industries) receive, and (2) there must be considerable effort and commitment to make the plan work. One might also argue a third factor is needed: the ability to have voice and make significant changes in the workplace. While these plans may start as nonunion, they create the collective mechanisms akin to unionization as pointed out in the evolution form of NER (see Timur, Taras & Ponak, 2012). For example, as will be discussed in Chapter 12, while association-consultation was a nonunion employee representation plan in many public-sector workplaces, employees quickly opted for the union option when it was provided to them. A potential explanation for this rapid movement to unionize in the public sector was that these associations had limited power, given that management still had final say on all matters. Clearly, issues of NER will continue to be closely examined over the next decade.

PROFESSIONAL ORGANIZATIONS—A SPECIAL FORM OF NER

An NER by definition represents a representation plan for employees. Yet Canadian union certification procedures often exclude professionals such as lawyers, physicians, engineers, and architects. A potential explanation for this exclusion may be that such professionals are often self-employed or employed under contract. Thus, they would not meet the definition of "employee" in most Canadian laws. However, many of these professionals are members of professional associations. These associations often set minimum standards for licensing (e.g., lawyers must pass a bar exam in each province in which they provide services); provide mechanisms for group access to (and discounts for) health benefits and retirement investment planning; and set provincial standards for fees. Therefore, we see professional associations that are "quasi-union" in status as they act as a closed shop, limiting employer ability to hire outside of the "union."

In some cases, we are seeing employers also moving to a "quasi-union" model—negotiating collectively with elected members of these associations, using joint committees, and even agreeing to arbitration processes to settle disputes. A good example of such an approach involves the Newfoundland and Labrador Medical Association (see IR Notebook 6.2).

IS THE NLMA A PROFESSIONAL ASSOCIATION OR A UNION?

The *Medical Act* of Newfoundland and Labrador requires that all physicians register with the Newfoundland and Labrador Medical Association (NLMA) in order to practise in the province. Physicians who fail to join render their medical licence "null and void"; they also face financial penalties and/or late-payment fees. Currently, the association represents 1,200 practising physicians. Medical students enrolled in the province's only med school can also join the association. Working members are either "fee for service" (they bill the provincial government for patient visits/services) or "salaried" (they are employed by a healthcare facility and paid a salary).

In many ways, the NLMA functions similarly to a nonunion employee representation plan. For example, NLMA positions itself as "the voice of organized medicine" in the province, and representatives of the NLMA (who are elected by the NLMA membership) and representatives of the government meet at least once per month to discuss issues of mutual concern. Joint committees came to an arrangement concerning vacation and job descriptions for salaried physicians. Other committees have been tasked with examining ways of recovering the current deficit in the fee-for-service budget.

The association provides its members with a number of services, including access to group insurance plans (mental, dental, accidental death and dismemberment), professional assistance plans (referral and counselling services for a variety of personal issues), and group RRSPs (for salaried members only), to name a few. In addition to offering these services, the NLMA is the voice of physicians with the government, which acts as the employer either directly (for salaried physicians) or indirectly (most fee-for-service physicians gain the bulk of their earnings from billing the provincial health plan). In this role, the NLMA negotiates with the provincial government on issues related to salaries, provincial budget allocations for fee-for-service providers, on-call rates, retention bonuses, etc.

Since 2000, the parties found it difficult to reach an agreement. In 2003, the result was a service withdrawal, in which both fee-for-service and salaried physicians withdrew all nonessential services. Arguably, this was akin to a strike or work-to-rule initiative. Approximately sixteen days later no agreement had yet been reached, so the parties agreed to have a third party determine the remaining issues. The third party process used was very similar to interest arbitration. In fact, upon agreement of the parties, the government enacted legislation stating an arbitration process mirroring that used in labour relations issues would be used.

In the fall of 2010, the parties were again deeply divided. A small group of physicians who were salaried employees of a health board resigned in protest. While the majority of these physicians rescinded their resignation when the parties settled, it was noteworthy that the 2010 settlement contained an "agreement in principle" that any future disputes between the parties would be resolved by a third party, an arbitration process similar to what we would see for unionized firefighters and police officers in the public sector.

As these facts show, this professional association has many of the elements associated with unionization: membership fees (akin to union dues), elective officials (akin to elected union representatives), collective bargaining, third party dispute resolutions (akin to arbitration), etc. As such, one could argue that the NLMA is akin to a union.

Sources: "About the NLMA." Retrieved from http://www.nlma.nl.ca/About/About-NLMA/; "Arbitration award between Newfoundland and Labrador Medical Association and Government of Newfoundland and Labrador." (15 April 2003). Retrieved from http://www.gov.nl.ca/publicat/2003/NLMAArbitration.pdf; NLMA 2005: *Book of Reports for the Annual General Meeting.* (4 June 2005). St. John's: Health Sciences Centre. Retrieved from http://www.nlma.nf.ca/documents/annual_reports/annual_ report_3.pdf; NLMA website, http://www.nlma.nf.ca; "NLMA board recommending acceptance of new offer from government." (16 December 2010). *The Telegram.* Retrieved from http://www.thetelegram.com/News/Local/1969-12-31/artide-2048073/NLMA-board-recommending-acceptance-of-new-offer-from-government/1; Memorandum of Agreement between Newfoundland and Labrador Medical Association and Government of Newfoundland and Labrador. (15 May 2003 to 30 September 2005). Retrieved from http://www.nlma.nl.ca/documents/agreements_negotiations/agreement_ negotiation_1.pdf.

NONSTANDARD WORK ARRANGEMENTS

While the trends of high-performance work practices, participative management, and nonunion representation have presented workplaces with ways that management can increase voice and/or due process, **nonstandard work arrangements** arguably were not designed to enhance such mechanisms. Rather, such arrangements are often implemented as a way to lower labour costs, more readily adjust labour levels to match business production/service needs, and generally improve business performance (Grant, 2014). However, employers have argued that nontraditional work arrangements can offer the advantages of flexibility, work–life balance, improved ability to recruit and retain employees, lower turnover rates, less employee stress and anxiety, less commuting time, and lower childcare costs (Burton, 2011; Manitoba Civil Service Commission, 2015).

> **nonstandard work arrangements**
> work arrangements that differ from the norm in terms of employment term, location, schedule, hours of work, or pay

In Canada, considerable research on this topic has been conducted by Isik Zeytinoglu and Gordon Cooke. As argued by these scholars, there is also a body of literature that discusses how nonstandard work arrangements, particularly those designed to provide flexibility in work schedules and hours, are driven by employees' desire to maximize work–life balance—though these scholars did conclude that business drivers, rather than employee drivers, were the main reason for such arrangements (Zeytinoglu, Cooke & Mann, 2010).

Broadly speaking, nonstandard work arrangements are employment agreements that differ from those of typical full-time jobs in terms of (1) term of employment (e.g., nonpermanent), (2) location (e.g., telecommuting), (3) work schedule and hours of work, and (4) pay (Cooke, 2005). Regardless of how we define these practices, they are increasingly prevalent in the Canadian economy. Evidence suggests that more than about 40 percent of Canadians are employed in some form of nonstandard work arrangement (Connelly, Gallagher, & Wilkin, 2014). In fact, looking at one type of nonstandard work, 57 percent of Canadians have some form of flexibility in work schedules or hours (Zeytinoglu et al., 2010). Moreover, the majority of new jobs are now considered nonstandard (Grant, 2014; Zeytinoglu & Cooke, 2006), suggesting that this work arrangement may be more common for new entrants into the labour force (immigrants, university graduates, high school graduates, etc.).

Interestingly, despite the increased use of nonstandard work, it is clear that not all employees have the same exposure to this trend. For example, Zeytinoglu et al. (2010) found that (1) part-time workers had more access to flextime, variable work weeks, and schedules than did full-time employees, and (2) unionized workers generally had less access to a variable work week length or schedule. There are two potential arguments for the latter union finding. First, details concerning work hours and schedules for unionized workers are usually contained in a collective agreement that would potentially restrict flexibility in that area. Second, building on equity-efficiency theory, these initiatives are usually linked to the firm's desire for efficiency, versus the union's focus on equity, thereby potentially reducing union acceptance of such practices.

Building on the equity argument, the evidence to date suggests that employees in nonstandard work arrangements have fewer benefits, lower wages, and less job security relative to workers in "standard" jobs (Grant, 2014; Zeytinoglu & Cooke, 2006; Zeytinoglu, Denton, Plenderleith & Chowhan, 2015).

Given these potentially negative impacts on workers—and the fact that unions have traditionally tried to standardize work relationships and improve job security, working conditions, and wages, as well as limit managerial discretion (see Chapter 5)—it is not surprising that labour often frowns upon these work arrangements, calling them "precarious," as shown on the Unifor website (for the link, see the list of Weblinks at the end of this chapter).

// SUMMARY

As we discovered in this chapter, management has faced new challenges over the past two decades, due largely to increased global competition. Although many textbooks underestimate the role of the management actor in the industrial relations system, we have shown that management plays an important role in the current system, as it continues to respond to a more competitive product and service environment.

This chapter highlights the evolution of management perspectives from thinking of workers as akin to slaves and machines to their being a strategic resource. We have also discovered the extent to which an organization's industrial relations strategy and human resources practices must be consistent with its overall business strategy. In so doing, we have seen how the importance of managerial strategy, in particular as it relates to unions, plays a key role in current management thinking.

Moving forward, we see a number of strategic trends emerging, particularly HPWPs, NER, and nonstandard work practices. Some argue that these plans will reduce the influence of labour, intentionally or unintentionally, given that many of these practices produce mechanisms of due process and voice. Others argue that such trends will have a negative impact on workers and their unions. Alternatively, one can argue that if employees feel that these substitutes fail to provide the equivalent benefits of unionization, they may drive employees toward unions. Only time will tell whether these new trends will have a negative or positive impact on employees and their unions. However, the current evidence suggests that management is moving toward a union resistance strategy.

KEY TERMS

distributive justice 174
high-performance work practices (HPWP) 183
human relations 173
interactional justice 175
master–servant relationship 172
nonstandard work arrangements 190
nonunion employee representation (NER) 186
organizational justice 174
procedural justice 174
strategic choice framework 176
union acceptance 179
union removal 180
union resistance 180
union substitution 182

WEBLINKS

McDonald's Food Facts and Nutrition Information:
http://www.mcdonalds.ca/ca/en/food/nutrition_centre.html
http://www1.mcdonalds.ca/NutritionCalculator/NutritionFactsEN.pdf

Firing of the U.S. air traffic controllers in 1981:
https://www.youtube.com/watch?v=4HId3EaWTq4

Newfoundland and Labrador Medical Association:
http://www.nlma.nl.ca/About/About-NLMA/

Management strategies to unions:

• Southwest Airlines:
http://www.youtube.com/watch?v=GiiOHgE8ADg
• WestJet:
https://www.youtube.com/watch?v=cWJWDI1MPgw

Union busting:
http://www.youtube.com/watch?v=2qajBfEdzoE http://www.youtube.com/watch?v=vGl3HQL-gxo&feature=related

Unifor's web page on an educational program concerning precarious work:
http://www.unifor.org/en/member-services/education/precarious-work

DISCUSSION QUESTIONS

1. Some argue that high-performance work practices, nonunion employee representation, and nonstandard work practices are designed to be forms of union substitution and/or union avoidance. Do you feel this is true? Why or why not?

2. Many students using this textbook have yet to start a full-time career path. These students will enter the full-time labour force at a time of massive retirements due to the aging baby boomers. Do you feel that the movement toward high-performance work practices, nonunion representation, and nonstandard work practices will continue during these students' careers? Justify your answer.

3. Assume you are a labour leader and you are trying to organize a nonunion firm that has high-performance work practices and nonunion employee representation practices in place. What would you tell employees are the advantages of unionization even with these progressive HRM practices?

4. Given the number of multinational companies and companies that operate in both Canada and the United States, do you believe that Canada will see an increased usage of the union removal and substitution strategies that are more common in the U.S.? Why or why not?

5. In your opinion, can employers expect highly engaged employees who seek to improve the performance of the firm if they continue to use nonstandard work arrangements? Justify your answer.

USING THE INTERNET

Many colleges and universities use part-time instructors, faculty, and teachers in addition to full-time staff. As examples, look at the websites for the Association of Part-Time Professors at the University of Ottawa (http://www.aptpuo.ca) and the Concordia University Part-Time Faculty Association (http://www.cupfa.org). Also examine an article on the Canadian Association of University Teachers, or CAUT, website written by

Diane Huberman-Arnold that outlines the challenges of part-time faculty (http://www.cautbulletin.ca/en_article.asp?articleid=2185).

On the basis of what you have learned from this chapter, and of insights gleaned from these websites, why do you think university administrations (i.e., management) use part-timers and would prefer that they remain nonunion?

EXERCISES

You will find on many universities' and colleges' websites advertisements for faculty positions, information concerning university-wide strategic plans, and collective agreements. Alternatively, you may this information in other places easily accessible by students.

1. Have a look at the faculty collective agreement (or handbook if your faculty is not unionized) for your college or university. Does it contain language concerning any of the current managerial trends in terms of high-performance work practices, nonunion employee representation, and nonstandard work practices? Look for keywords such as *committees, work schedules, alternative work arrangements, contractual, part-time appointments, quality, teams, TQM, etc.*

2. Look at recent job postings for your academic institution. How many of the postings are for nonstandard work versus permanent full-time work? How many are for unionized versus nonunionized positions?

3. In looking at the job postings and/or the collective agreement, would you say your university or college has a traditional (i.e., hourly or salaried human resources) model or a high-performance model? Justify your answer.

4. Of the forms of management strategies toward unions, which do you feel exists on your campus? Why?

| CASE | PROVINCIAL WINE CORPORATION (PWC) |

Provincial Wine Corporation (PWC) launched on April 1, 2012. Prior to its incorporation, customers could purchase wines from three organizations in the metro area: (1) Provincial Liquor Corporation (PLC), a provincial Crown corporation which sold wines, spirits, and beers; (2) Vintage Wines Inc. (Vintage), a private company that sold higher-end, specialty wine products not available at PLC; or (3) small agency outlets that were not government-run and had a small inventory of Canadian wines. The newly formed PWC is a merger of PLC and Vintage. The current merger has resulted in 20 PWC stores in the metro area. On average, each store has one manager, two assistant managers, and 14 full-time and 30 part-time employees. Full-time employees work 37.5 hours a week while part-time employees are guaranteed a minimum of 25 hours a week. As permanent employees, they receive pay and a full benefit package (e.g., pension, medical, etc.). In addition, there are approximately 60 casual workers who can be called in as needed and can work at any of the metro stores. These casual employees are not guaranteed a minimum number of work hours a week. They are paid the same hourly rate as permanent employees but have no access to the organization's benefit plan. All non-managerial employees, whether full-time, part-time, permanent or casual, are unionized.

Luke Davis (CEO), Kate Hong (Vice-President Retail Sales & Operations), and Jason Williams (Vice-President HRM) are discussing the strategic plan for PWC for the next five years. Luke feels strongly that the key business strengths relate to the product knowledge of the staff, the extensive variety of wines available in each store, and customer service. As he stresses, the province still allows the existing agency stores to offer some wine products. If PWC stores do not provide great service, products, and product knowledge, there is a huge threat—customers can simply go to one of the numerous agency outlets that still exist throughout the metro area. This threat is even more significant as the provincial government has recently hinted that agency outlets may soon be able to sell non-Canadian wines, allowing these nonunion outlets to compete more directly with product offerings of PWC. As Luke stresses, the agency stores also have an operational advantage of lower labour costs as none of the agency outlets are unionized.

Kate adds that from an operational perspective, employees need to be encouraged to maximize sales while ensuring social responsibility (i.e., not selling to underaged people, not selling to those under the influence, etc.). Kate also stresses that information sharing between staff and teamwork are key to business success, as employees often have to assist others, cover for each other, etc. However, she feels that this area needs improvement. She proposes that PWC increase training and move toward having employees work in teams to facilitate knowledge sharing.

Jason then starts to focus on the HRM implications. The organization is in transition. About 80 percent of the full-time employees came from the former PLC, and were formerly covered by the provincial government's collective agreement. A new collective agreement was signed when PWC was formed, with the understanding that the new operation had to generate sufficient revenues to cover its own operating cost and maintain its current level of contributions to the provincial government in terms of taxes on alcohol. Failure to meet these financial goals would result in PWC being shut down. In fact, at the time of formation, there was pressure from some members of the legislature that PWC should be a standalone, non-government-based, private company like Vintage. However, the social responsibility associated with alcohol sales resulted in the organization remaining within the public sector.

Given the environment at the time of formation, the union and management realized that they needed to reach a settlement that would help ensure the long-term viability of the newly formed PWC. The union encouraged the workers to accept the 2012 deal, even though wage increases were lower than what other provincial employees received. The union argued that this was needed in order to firmly establish the organization and enhance job security. The resulting collective agreement provided a $1,000 signing bonus in year one, and a one percent increase over the next three years. The resulting contract also allowed PWC enhanced staffing flexibility with the ability to hire more part-time and casual workers. Such hiring provisions did not exist in the former PLC. However, the contract required that any employee who worked a minimum of 1,800 hours in a two-year period would be converted to permanent part-time status.

Three years after the initial collective agreement was signed, the restructuring has taken place, and the operation has seen many changes. While the organization lost money in year 1, it has now achieved its financial goals of covering costs and contributing tax dollars to the province; new products and new in-store wine-tasting equipment have been introduced; and there has been an increased use of casual staff for peak periods (weekends and the holiday season). However, as they map out the strategy for the upcoming five years, they realize that their largest cost is labour but also that the success of any future quality and product improvements will require employee engagement. Therefore, the human resources strategy of Jason's department must mesh with the overall business strategy.

As they prepare to map out the plan, they have been hit with unexpected financial news. Over the past six weeks, oil prices have plummeted, causing both a stall in the overall Canadian economy and a drop in the Canadian dollar. The rapid drop in the loonie over the past two months means that all wines purchased from the U.S. are now 13 percent more expensive, while European wines have increased by 8 percent. This is due solely to exchange rate effects. Locally, a number of large firms have laid off staff, and a few higher-end restaurants (which purchase their speciality wines from the organization) have shut their doors. While no one had expected this financial slump, estimates are that oil prices, a leading cause of the economic slow down, will remain low for at least a year.

With this as the backdrop, they start to form a plan that will continue to ensure financial stability, product quality, and a stable, committed workforce.

QUESTIONS

1. What type of union strategy is PWC using?
2. Do you see evidence of the managerial trends of high-performance work practices, nonunion employee representation, and nonstandard work practices present in the case?
3. Has there been a strong linkage between the industrial relations and business strategies of the organization? To what extent?
4. Given the case at hand, what would you suggest the firm do in terms of making changes to its current strategies?

// REFERENCES

1. Barbash, J. (1987). Like nature, industrial relations abhors a vacuum. *Relations industrielles, 42,* pp. 168–179.
2. Belcourt, M., & McBey, K. J. (2015). *Strategic human resources planning* (5th edition). Toronto: Nelson.
3. Bentham, K. J. (2002). Employer resistance to union certification: A study of eight Canadian jurisdictions. *Industrial Relations, 57*(1), pp. 159–187.
4. Brown, T. C., & Latham, G. P. (2000). The effects of goal setting and self-instruction training on the performance of union employees. *Relations industrielles, 55,* pp. 80–94.
5. Brown, T., & McCracken, M. (2010). Which goals should participants set for effective management development? *Journal of General Management, 35,* pp. 27–44.

6. Bruce, K., & Nyland, C. (2011). Elton Mayo and the deification of human relations. *Organization Studies, 32*, pp. 383–405.

7. Burton, B. (2011). Non-standard work: an Employer perspective. *New Zealand Journal of Employment Relations, 36*(3), pp. 37–43.

8. Campolieti, M., Gomez, R., & Gunderson, M. (2013). Does non union employee representation act as a complement or substitute to union voice? Evidence from Canada and the United States. *Industrial Relations: A Journal of Economy and Society, 52*, pp. 378–396.

9. CBC News. (27 June 2014). Quebec unionized Wal-Mart workers win Supreme Court victory. Retrieved 19 January 2015 from http://www.cbc.ca/news/canada/montreal/quebec-unionized-wal-mart-workers-win-supreme-court-victory-1.2689646

10. Chaykowski, R., & Verma, A. (1992). Canadian industrial relations in transition. In R. P. Chaykowski & A. Verma (Eds.), *Industrial relations in Canadian industry* (pp. 448–475). Toronto: Dryden.

11. Chansler, P., & Schraeder, M. (2003). Will the TEAM work for employees and managers: A closer look at the TEAM Act. *Journal for Quality and Participation, 26*, pp. 31–37.

12. Connelly, C. E., Gallagher, D. G., & Wilkin, C. L. (2014). The potential "spill-over" of temporary agency work. In B. A. S. Koene, N. Galais, & C. Garsten (Eds.), *Management and Organization of Temporary Agency Work*. New York: Routledge, pp. 103–117.

13. Cooke, G. (2005). The nature and incidence of non-standard work arrangements. Ph.D. dissertation. McMaster University. Unpublished.

14. Coulter, K. (2013). Raising retail: Organizing retail workers in Canada and the United States. *Labor Studies Journal, 38*(1), pp. 47–65.

15. Craig, A. W. J. (1967). A model for the analysis of industrial relations systems. Paper presented to the annual meeting of the Canadian Political Science Association.

16. Crawshaw, J. R., Cropanzano, R., Bell, C. M., & Nadisic, T. (2013). Organizational justice: New insights from behavioural ethics. *Human relations* (early view). doi: 10.1177/0018726713485609

17. Delaney, J. T., & Huselid, M. A. (1996). The impact of human resource practices on perceptions of organizational performance. *Academy of Management Journal, 38*, pp. 949–968.

18. Donaghey, J., Cullinane, N., Dundon, T., & Dobbins, T. (2012). *Non-union employee representation, union avoidance and the managerial agenda. Economic and Industrial Democracy, 33*(2), pp. 163–183.

19. Duffy, T. (2 July 2001). Alternative work arrangements. Retrieved 18 July 2011 from http://www.itworld.com/NWW010702work

20. Dunlop, J. T. (1958). *Industrial relations systems.* New York: Henry Holt and Company.

21. Gill, C. (2009). Union impact on the effective adoption of high performance work practices. *Human Resource Management Review, 19*, pp. 39–50.

22. Gill, C., & Meyer, D. (2013). Union presence, employee relations and high performance work practices. *Personnel Review, 42*, pp. 508–528.

23. Godard, J. (1997). Whither strategic choice: Do managerial IR ideologies matter? *Industrial Relations, 36*, pp. 206–228.

24. Godard, J. (2004). A critical assessment of the high-performance paradigm. *British Journal of Industrial Relations, 42*, pp. 349–378.

25. Godard, J. (2007). Unions, work practices, and wages under different institutional environments: The case of Canada and England. *Industrial & Labor Relations Review, 60*(4), pp. 457–476.

26. Godard, J. (2014). The psychologisation of employment relations? *Human Resource Management Journal, 24*, pp. 1–18.

27. Godard, J., & Delaney, J. (2000). Reflections on the "high performance" paradigm's implications for industrial relations as a field. *Industrial and Labor Relations Review, 53*, pp. 482–502.

28. Grant, T. (4 October 2014). The 15-hour workweek: Canada's part-time problem. *The Globe and Mail.* Retrieved 4 February 2015 from http://www.theglobeandmail.com/report-on-business/the-15-hour-workweek-canadas-part-time-problem/article20926986/

29. Greenberg, J., & Colquitt, J. A. (Eds.). (2013). *Handbook of organizational justice.* London: Psychology Press.

30. Greer, C. R. (2001). *Strategic human resource management.* Upper Saddle River, NJ: Prentice Hall.

31. Guest, D. E. (2011). Human resource management and performance: Still searching for some answers. *Human Resource Management Journal, 21*, pp. 3–13.

32. H&M. (2015). Employee relations. Retrieved 19 January 2015 from http://career.hm.com/content/hmcareer/en_ca/workingathm/get-to-know-us/EmployeeRelations.html

33. Hassard, J. S. (2012). Rethinking the Hawthorne studies: The Western Electric research in its social, political and historical context. *Human Relations, 65*, pp. 1431–1461.

34. Huselid, M. (1995). The impact of human resource management practices on turnover, productivity, and corporate financial performance. *Academy of Management Journal, 38*, pp. 635–672.

35. Huselid, M. A., Jackson, S. E., & Schuler, R. S. (1997). Technical and strategic human resource management effectiveness as determinants of firm performance. *The Academy of Management Journal, 40*(1), pp. 171–188.

36. Jacobs, K. (3 November 2010). Delta flight attendants reject union. Retrieved 7 February 2011 from http://www.reuters.com/article/2010/11/03/us-delta-idUSTRE6A27M620101103

37. Kaufman, B. E. (2001). The theory and practice of strategic HRM and participative management: Antecedents in early industrial relations. *Human Resource Management Review, 11*, pp. 505–533.

38. Kaufman, B. E., & Taras, D. G. (2000). (Eds.) *Nonunion employee representation: History, contemporary practice and policy.* Armonk, NY: ME Sharpe.

39. Kaufman, B. E., & Taras, D. G. (2010). Participation through non-union forms of representation. In A. Wilinson, P. Goll, M. Marchington, & D. Lewin (Eds.), *The Oxford Handbook of Participation in Organizations.* Oxford: Oxford University Press, pp. 258–285.

40. Kehoe, R. R., & Wright, P. M. (2013). The impact of high-performance human resource practices on employees' attitudes and behaviors. *Journal of Management, 39,* pp. 366–391.

41. Kimber, S. (15 December 2014). Brewhaha. *Atlantic Business (Jan/Feb).* Retrieved 15 January 2015 from http://www.atlanticbusinessmagazine.net/article/brewhaha/

42. Kochan, T., Katz, H., & McKersie, R. (1986). *The transformation of American industrial relations.* New York: Basic Books.

43. Labour Law Casebook Group. (2011). *Labour and employment law: Cases, material and commentary* (8th edition). Toronto: Irwin Law.

44. Liu, W., Guthrie, J. P., Flood, P. C., & MacCurtain, S. (2009). Unions and the adoption of high performance work systems: Does employment security play a role? *Industrial & Labor Relations Review, 63,* pp. 109–127.

45. Locke, E. A., & Latham, G. P. (Eds.). (2013). *New developments in goal setting and task performance.* New York, NY: Routledge.

46. Lu, V. (31 October 2011). Retail workers organize H&M outlet. *Toronto Star.* Reprinted with permission–Torstar Syndication Services. http://www.thestar.com/business/2011/10/31/retail_workers_organize_hm_outlet.html

47. MacCharles, T. (16 January 2014). Supreme Court strikes down rule that bans RCMP from forming union. *Toronto Star.* Retrieved 25 January 2015 from http://www.thestar.com/news/canada/2015/01/16/supreme-court-strikes-down-rule-that-bans-rcmp-union.html

48. Manitoba Civil Service Commission. (2015). *Job sharing and/or part-time work arrangements guidelines.* Retrieved 4 February 2015 from http://www.manitoba.ca/csc/pdf/jobshare.pdf

49. Marchington, M., & Suter, J. (2013). Where informality really matters: Patterns of employee involvement and participation (EIP) in a non union firm. *Industrial Relations: A Journal of Economy and Society, 52,* pp. 284–313.

50. Mayo, E. (1933). *The human problems of an industrial civilization.* New York: Macmillan.

51. Meltz, N. M. (1997). Introduction to employment relations. Paper presented to the Conference on Teaching in Human Resources and Industrial Relations. Atlanta.

52. Murray, G., Belanger, J., Giles, A., & Lapointe, P. A. (Eds.). (2013). *Work and employment in the high performance workplace.* New York: Routledge.

53. Pohler, D., & Luchak, A. (2013). Are unions good or bad for organizations? The moderating role of management's response. *British Journal of Industrial Relations* (early view).

54. Pohler, D. & Luchak, A. (2014). Balancing efficiency, equity, and voice: The impact of unions and high-involvement work practices on work outcomes. *ILR Review,* 0019793914546295 (early view).

55. Reece, B. (2011). Human relations: principles and practices. Cengage Learning.

56. Rose, J. (2008). Regulating and resolving public sector disputes in Canada. *Journal of Industrial Relations, 50,* pp. 545–59.

57. Smith, K. J., & Harris, L. M. (2014). Drafting an effective employee handbook. *Employment Relations Today, 41*(1), pp. 71–79.

58. Taras, D. G. (1999). Evolution of nonunion employee representation in Canada. *Journal of Labor Research, 20,* pp. 31–51.

59. Taras, D. G. (2002). Alternative forms of employee representation and labour policy. *Canadian Public Policy, 28,* pp. 105–116.

60. Taras, D. G. (10 March 2006). Non-union representation and employer intent: How Canadian courts and labour boards determine legal status of non-union plants. *Socio-Economic Review, 4,* pp. 321–336.

61. Taras, D. G., & Copping, J. (1998). The transition from formal nonunion representation to unionization: A contemporary case. *Industrial and Labor Relations Review, 52*(1), pp. 22–44.

62. Taras, D. G., & Kaufman, B. E. (2006). Nonunion representation in North America: Diversity, controversy and uncertain future. Working paper. Jason Young School of Policy Studies. Atlanta, GA: Georgia State University.

63. Taylor, F. W. (1911). *The principles of scientific management.* New York: Harper.

64. Thomason, T., & Pozzebon, S. (1998). Managerial opposition to union certification in Quebec and Ontario. *Industrial Relations, 53*(4), pp. 750–771.

65. Thompson, M., & Slinn, S. (2012). Public sector industrial relations in Canada: Does it threaten or sustain democracy? *Comparative Labor Law & Policy Journal, 34,* pp. 393–414.

66. Thompson, M. (1995). The management of industrial relations. In M. Gunderson & A. Ponak (Eds.), *Union–management relations in Canada* (3rd edition) (pp. 105–130). Toronto: Addison-Wesley.

67. Timur, A. T., Taras, D., & Ponak, A. (2012). "Shopping for Voice": Do pre-existing non-union representation plans matter when employees unionize? *British Journal of Industrial Relations,* 50, pp. 214–238.

68. Van Buren III, H. J., Greenwood, M., & Sheehan, C. (2011). Strategic human resource management and the decline of employee focus. *Human Resource Management Review, 21,* pp. 209–219.

69. Verma, A., & Chaykowski, R. P. (1999). Business strategies and employment relations. In A. Verma & R. P. Chaykowski (Eds.), *Contract & commitment: Employment relations in the new economy* (pp. 338–354). Kingston, ON: Industrial Relations Centre.

70. Wheelen, T. L., Hunger, J. D., Hoffman, A. N., & Bamford, C. E. (2015). *Strategic management and business policy: Globalization, innovation and sustainability.* Global Edition. Toronto: Pearson Higher Ed.

71. Zeytinoglu, I. U., & Cooke, G. B. (2006). Who is working on weekends? Determinants of regular weekend work in Canada. In J. Boulin, M. Lallement, J. C. Messenger, & F. Michon (Eds.), *Decent Working Time, New Trends, New Issues.* Geneva: ILO Publications, pp. 395–417.

72. Zeytinoglu, I. U., Cooke, G. B., & Mann, S. L. (2010). Flexibility: Whose choice is it anyways? *Relations industrielles/Industrial Relations, 64,* pp. 555–574.

73. Zeytinoglu, I. U., Denton, M., Plenderleith, J., & Chowhan, J. (2015). Associations between workers' health and non-standard hours and insecurity: The case of home care workers in Ontario, Canada. *The International Journal of Human Resource Management* (ahead-of-print), pp. 1–20.

NEGOTIATIONS

LEARNING OBJECTIVES

BY THE END OF THIS CHAPTER, YOU WILL BE ABLE TO DISCUSS

- the differences between individual negotiations and collective bargaining;
- the four subprocesses of collective bargaining;
- examples of distributive and integrative bargaining issues;
- a collective bargaining model;
- the pressures on all of the parties to collective bargaining;
- bargaining step by step;
- the dos and don'ts of bargaining;
- the principles of adversarial negotiations;
- the principles of integrative, or win-win, negotiations;
- the elements of interest-based negotiations;
- obstacles to achieving the best bargaining outcome for management and labour; and
- when to use adversarial and win-win negotiations.

June 7, 2013—After weeks of sporadic and limited work actions, Canadian diplomats have started worldwide strikes after negotiations fell apart with their employer, the Canadian government.

"After nearly two years of negotiations and a four-month hiatus in talks, the Government returned to the table with the same position they presented back in the fall of 2011," says Tim Edwards, President of the Professional Association of Foreign Service Officers (PAFSO), in a press release Thursday (June 6, 2013).

"The Government's unwillingness to compromise is an affront to the principles of free and fair bargaining, and to the tremendous value and dedication Foreign Service Officers offer to Canadians and their elected representatives," said Edwards.

The association started with work-to-rule tactics, no overtime, not answering e-mails after 5PM, leaving cell phones at work. That followed with information pickets in Ottawa, then Washington.

The association wants parity with public servants in Canada who do similar work to theirs. It says the diplomats make thousands of dollars less than others in the public service. This even though, postings abroad bring all kinds of extra financial challenges that public servants in Ottawa do not have to face.

A PAFSO spokesperson confirmed late Friday that all Foreign Service Officers in London, Ireland and Paris (not OECD) have withdrawn services. Canada's Prime Minister Stephen Harper arrives in London on Tuesday and goes to Paris and Dublin before a G8 summit in Ireland.

The withdrawal of services affects Canadian immigration departments in Beijing, Shanghai, Delhi, and Chandigarh.

All Foreign Service officers have withdrawn services from Tokyo, Tel Aviv, Ramallah, Washington and the EU in Brussels.

Source: Wojtek Gwiazda. (7 June 2013). "Strike by Canadian diplomats worldwide ends." Radio Canada. Used with permission of CBC Licensing. Retrieved from http://www.rcinet.ca/en/2013/06/07/strike-by-canadian-diplomats-spreads-worldwide/.

Collective bargaining is a complex, multilateral process involving the bargaining teams at the table and those in management and labour that are directly affected by the outcome. It is made difficult by the range of issues that are typically negotiated at the same time. Some issues, such as employee safety and pensions, may be best resolved using a cooperative approach. On the other hand, adversarial negotiations remain the fundamental process for most labour–management problems. A central question to be answered, therefore, is how to get the best outcome for both parties when there is a mix of issue types.

Canadian foreign service employees protest the Government of Canada's unwillingness to engage meaningfully at the negotiating table.

// CONFLICT-OF-INTEREST ASSUMPTION

An important assumption of the employment relationship is the existence of a conflict of interests between managers and those whom they manage. The assumption holds equally in public- and private-sector enterprises. While some conflict is inevitable, it is not all-pervasive. In fact the labour–management relationship is defined by cooperation most of the time. Cooperation may apply to little things such as agreeing to the timing and location of meetings or major issues like jointly lobbying governments over industry trade policies. A complicating factor is that cooperation and its opposite—adversarial or competitive negotiations—often take place during the same set of negotiations and sometimes between the same parties. In any successful union–management relationship, there must be a synergy between cooperation and competitiveness. This may be true because the conflict of interest does not extend to all situations, and the relationship in any union–management setting is long-term. A goal is to understand those circumstances where cooperation and competitiveness are likely to work and where they may not.

// HOW COLLECTIVE BARGAINING DIFFERS FROM INDIVIDUAL NEGOTIATIONS

Individual negotiations are very different from bargaining over the terms of a collective agreement.[1] When two people bargain over the price of a car, there is a defined process. The seller inflates the price and exaggerates the positive qualities of the car. The potential buyer offers less than the seller's price and deflates the car's attributes. The seller and buyer then haggle over a price somewhere between the seller's asking price and the buyer's offer. If a deal is struck, the buyer and seller sign the necessary papers. The buyer gets the car, and the seller obtains the best acceptable price he or she can get. Typically, neither party gets everything they want out of the deal. And they go their separate ways.

THE CANADIAN PRESS/Michelle Siu

Even adversarial bargaining has its lighter moments.

In collective bargaining, the process is more complex for several reasons that we will examine. First, there are multiple parties involved, often with different interests and pressures. Second, the issues are not all the same type. Some issues have the potential for a win-win or mutual gains outcome, where both sides come out ahead. Others may be more like the adversarial bargaining described earlier over the price of a car. A third set of issues may result in a combination of elements of win-win and adversarial bargaining. Finally, unlike individual bargaining, collective bargaining involves a continuing relationship between the parties. As we will discover, a sound relationship is critical to effective union–management outcomes.

In summary, here are the main differences between individual and collective negotiations:

- Individual negotiations are bilateral in nature: there are only two parties involved in their outcome. Collective bargaining, on the other hand, is multilateral, involving employees, unions, supervisors, and higher-level managers. Each party may have distinct interests and pressures.

- Issues may be inherently adversarial, may have some potential for mutual gain, or may be a combination of both. Collective bargaining is more complex because all three types of issues are often negotiated at the same time.

- In collective bargaining, the relationship between the parties is ongoing. In individual bargaining, the parties will most likely never see each other again.

// THE FOUR SUBPROCESSES OF COLLECTIVE BARGAINING

Scholars have broken collective bargaining down into four subprocesses (Walton & McKersie, 1965):

- distributive bargaining;
- integrative bargaining;
- intra-team or intra-organizational bargaining; and
- building trust or attitudinal structuring.

DISTRIBUTIVE BARGAINING

Distributive bargaining is a category of negotiations usually characterized by an adversarial or competitive style. Note that even though the outcome is distributive, the style is a matter of choice. In our car negotiations, for example, one or both of the parties may choose to bargain cooperatively by trying to avoid haggling. It is unlikely, however, that one party will be able to bargain cooperatively if the other party chooses to haggle. To be legitimate, distributive bargaining assumes some degree of conflict between the parties—labour and management. Thus, distributive bargaining is consistent with an industrial relations system that assumes an inherent conflict of interest between management and labour. It is distributive in the sense that the conflict is over some fixed economic reward for the work performed on the job. Conflict can also occur over the control management exerts over such issues as the pace of work, downtime, and disciplinary standards and procedures.

Distributive not only defines a process but can also be used to describe certain collective bargaining issues. For example, issues such as wages and job security are often described as inherently distributive in nature because the parties have competing interests. Economists describe distributive bargaining as a zero-sum game in which one side's gain is the other's loss. Under this characterization, for example, wage increases directly reduce profits.

> **distributive bargaining**
> a form of negotiations in which two parties compete over the distribution of some fixed resource

INTEGRATIVE BARGAINING

In contrast with distributive bargaining, where the pie may be fixed, **integrative bargaining** is founded on the assumption that bargaining outcomes can expand the pie to enable both sides to win. It is assumed that the parties have shared interests in any settlement. Like the word *distributive*, *integrative* may be used to refer not just to a process but also to the bargaining issues themselves. The issue of health and safety, for example, clearly has aspects of mutual interests, but providing a safe and healthy workplace also involves costs.

A subprocess of collective bargaining is integrative bargaining, whereby labour and management adopt a problem-solving approach.

LuckyImages/Shutterstock

> **integrative bargaining**
> a form of bargaining in which there is potential for a solution that produces a mutual gain; also called win-win bargaining, principled negotiations, and interest-based bargaining

INTRA-TEAM BARGAINING

intra-team (or intra-
organizational)
bargaining
bargaining within
union and manage-
ment teams during the
collective bargaining
process; individual
union team members,
for example, may
represent a group with
particular interests,
such as shift workers

attitudinal structuring
the difficult process
of building the mutual
respect and trust nec-
essary for an enduring
and positive collective
bargaining relationship

Bargaining that takes place within each side's team is known as **intra-team (or intra-organizational) bargaining**. Union bargaining teams may be elected to represent an array of internal groups and their interests—shift workers, women, older workers, married employees, etc. The team consists of union members with a common interest or solidarity. But each will also have his or her own agenda with competing priorities. The reality is that in collective bargaining, often more time is spent negotiating within teams or organizations than is spent between management and labour. This usually comes as a shock to the uninitiated bargaining team member.

ATTITUDINAL STRUCTURING

Attitudinal structuring is the stage in which trust is built between the parties. Typically, this is a long-term process and may not be limited to activities directly associated with collective bargaining itself. For example, many unions and managements have established a permanent joint committee that meets at regular intervals during the term of a collective agreement to discuss problems of mutual interest.

Distributive issues generally lack the potential of a win-win mutual gains outcome. Wages or, more generally, labour cost items tend to directly affect the organization's bottom line. Profits or surpluses are proportionately reduced by a wage increase. This applies to employee benefits, overtime rates, vacations, holidays, leaves of absence, etc.

Perhaps the best example of an integrative issue with mutual gains potential is occupational health and safety. Management has a direct interest in providing safe and healthy working conditions. Workers have a similar interest in reducing occupational health and safety hazards in the workplace.

Hybrid issues combine distributive and integrative elements. Pensions, for example, are a direct cost to the employer. To the extent that providing a pension plan enhances career opportunities and reduces turnover costs, it may also produce a mutual gain for an organization and its employees.

In summary, collective bargaining may involve all three types of issues described above: distributive, integrative, and hybrid (see Table 7.1). Given this reality, a problem in achieving the optimal collective bargaining outcome is that the strategies and tactics of negotiations are quite different for each issue type. We examine these strategies and tactics next.

TABLE 7.1

EXAMPLES OF DISTRIBUTIVE, INTEGRATIVE, AND HYBRID ISSUES

DISTRIBUTIVE	INTEGRATIVE	HYBRID
Wages	Health And Safety	Pensions
Benefits	Rest breaks	Plant closure/severance
Overtime rates		Technological change
Vacations		
Holidays		

// STRATEGIES AND TACTICS OF THE BARGAINING SUBPROCESSES

Each of the four subprocesses has a distinct set of strategies and tactics. As we will see, the tactics of distributive and integrative bargaining are almost mirror opposites. Since in any round of collective bargaining there are likely to be distributive, integrative, and hybrid issues on the table simultaneously, employing the appropriate tactic at the right time poses a challenge to even the most experienced negotiator. This problem will become more apparent as we examine the strategies and tactics of each process.

DISTRIBUTIVE BARGAINING TACTICS

As in our car sale example at the beginning of the chapter, the parties will typically inflate their positions so they have issues that can be traded off later. The notion is that to get what you want, you have to ask for more than your **bottom line**. A party will often keep secret its true position, but to withhold this information requires some control over the communication at the bargaining table. As a rule, in distributive bargaining, the parties each have one spokesperson, which helps them avoid revealing unnecessary or even damaging information. It is important for negotiators to disguise their own bottom line while trying to discover that of the other party. Your outcome may well be affected by how well you implement these tactics.

Distributive bargaining has been criticized for unduly raising expectations since the parties will seek support from their constituencies for their inflated positions. In fact, strikes have occurred because the union executive or bargaining team has raised expectations about goals that are not possible to achieve in collective bargaining or a management team has oversold a package of concessions to their principals. Third-party intervention can help avoid these situations but fortunately they appear to be very infrequent events. As long as collective bargaining exists there will be strikes that might have been avoided by a more responsible union or management team. But collective bargaining is a manifestation of a fundamental human right—freedom of association; thus occasional excesses must be weighed against the inviolability of these rights.

> **bottom line**
> the minimum position necessary in negotiations to avoid a strike or lockout; it represents for the union the best possible outcome short of strike

INTEGRATIVE BARGAINING TACTICS

During integrative bargaining, the parties are less likely to inflate the issues. For example, unions will probably focus more on real cases and clearly defined remedies in discussions about the health and safety of their members. A necessary component of cooperation is the sharing of information. In fact, information sharing can often be a test of commitment to a joint problem-solving approach to conflict resolution.

The form that integrative bargaining takes is different from distributive bargaining, with issues often resolved through a joint-committee structure. Unions and management typically set up joint committees on such matters as health and safety (may be required by law), pensions, and plant closures. The parties will relax the strict distributive bargaining requirement of a single spokesperson, instead involving many voices and an array of solutions rather than a single bottom line.

INTRA-TEAM TACTICS

Union and management bargaining teams represent a diversity of interests. For example, on the management team there might be line managers concerned about more flexibility, financial executives focusing on costs, human resources managers concerned about recruitment, and a chief spokesperson whose job is to produce a settlement that satisfies all of these interests. On the union team, for example, there might be a member whose priority is the pension plan, another who is stressing wages, a member who wants improvements in the maternity leave contract provisions, and one who wants better job security.

The teams within union and management groups might use the team caucus to resolve differences over which issues to drop off the table and which to keep. Negotiators must take into account the mandates that their teams have been given. In the union's caucus, the spokesperson will probably attempt to resolve by consensus but ultimately will rely on a democratic majority to decide on priorities. Special interests that lack strong constituent support will probably not make it into the final settlement package. The union spokesperson will have to represent the union on the issues that affect only the administration of the union's affairs (e.g., dues deduction).

BUILDING TRUST TACTICS

Trust in the labour–management relationship cannot be achieved overnight. But clearly, parties who trust each other's word will have a higher chance of positive outcomes in collective bargaining. Unfortunately, there is no easy formula for creating trust. If there are meetings between high-level management and labour officials during the term of the agreement and if they are used creatively to bring forward issues of common concern, using a problem-solving approach, then these away-from-the-table meetings can help to build trust.

Examples of meeting discussion topics might include the following:

- management plans to introduce new technology;
- union concerns about delays in the grievance process;
- surpluses or deficits in group benefits plans; and
- firm policies on such issues as hiring and retention.

A COLLECTIVE BARGAINING MODEL

The Katz, Kochan, and Hicks (KKH) collective bargaining model provides an economic explanation of collective bargaining outcomes (Katz & Kochan, 2000). It is limited, therefore, to conflict that is derived from wages, benefits, and other monetary issues in collective bargaining. In reality, however, disputes arise over a range of nonmonetary issues, including union recognition, union security (union dues and membership requirements), outsourcing, and union roles in promotions, transfers, and layoffs. On the other hand, in the vast majority of strikes, economic issues are important issues in dispute.

In Scenario 1 below, we will assume that the parties have the same expectations about the outcome of a strike. We will also assume that all monetary issues can be aggregated into a wage-dollar-per-hour amount. In our example, both parties have the same expectations: that a strike would increase the total monetary value of the union contract to a $10 per hour wage (see Figure 7.1). At W(Es), the expected strike wage, the union expected wage outcome of W(Esu) is equal to the management expected wage of W(Esm).

FIGURE 7.1

Wage Line

$W(Es) \rightarrow$ $10.00

$W(Es)$ = expected strike wage {$W(Esu)$ = $W(Esm)$}

In Scenario 1, employees estimate the cost of a strike per worker at $0.50 per hour (Wu). This is calculated by aggregating the total losses in pay less the costs of strike pay and other income earned during the strike and converting that to an hourly rate. Management makes a similar forecast based on losses from a strike (lost production, length of strike, etc.) converted to a wage of $0.40 per hour (Wm).

For management the estimated costs of a strike are added to the expected strike wage to produce a bottom line of $10.40 (see Figure 7.2). This is the highest-cost package that management will offer to avoid a strike. For ease of presentation all costs (wages, benefits, vacation, etc.) are expressed in wage units (i.e., dollars per hour). Similarly, the union deducts its costs of striking from the expected wage to produce a bottom-line cost package of $9.50 per hour. The range between the parties' bottom lines creates a **contract zone**.

In Scenario 2, the parties have widely different expectations of what a strike outcome might be (see Figure 7.3). The union predicts that a strike would produce a package costing $10.50 per hour. Management, on the other hand, forecasts a package worth $9 per hour. Now, if union and management factor in the same costs of striking as in Scenario 1, there is a gap between the parties' bottom lines. The union will not go lower than $10 per hour and management will offer no more than $9.40 per hour to avoid a strike.

> **contract zone**
> exists if each side's bottom line overlaps; in other words, to avoid a strike or lockout, management will offer more and the union will accept less than the point where their negotiating positions intersect

FIGURE 7.2

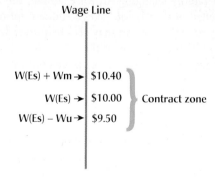

Wage Line

$W(Es) + Wm \rightarrow$ $10.40
$W(Es) \rightarrow$ $10.00   } Contract zone
$W(Es) - Wu \rightarrow$ $9.50

$W(Es)$ = expected strike wage {$W(Esu)$ = $W(Esm)$}

FIGURE 7.3

SCENARIO 2: PARTIES HAVE DIVERGENT EXPECTATIONS

The fact that the parties are able to freely negotiate a settlement about 95 percent of the time when they have a right to strike or lock out supports the existence of a contract zone most of the time. It is instructive, however, to examine the conditions that may give rise to divergent expectations as described in Scenario 2.

NEW RELATIONSHIP OR NEGOTIATORS

If the parties are negotiating a first contract or are new to the bargaining relationship, they are more likely to have unrealistic expectations about what a strike may produce. To reduce the probability of conflict in these cases, the parties may benefit from third-party intervention. Mediators and conciliators may assist by reducing the parties' expectations (see also Chapter 10). It may be that distributive bargaining would be less successful in avoiding strikes where expectations diverge. We will also learn below that more cooperative forms of negotiations such as interest-based bargaining are more common during first agreement negotiations. Finally, it is noteworthy that most jurisdictions in Canada have legislated arbitration in the special circumstances of first contract negotiations.

CHANGING ECONOMIC CONDITIONS

Divergent expectations can occur because economic conditions for the organization or the economy are rapidly changing. If, for example, the organization has a number of large orders cancelled or if inflation takes a sudden upturn, the parties' expectations may diverge. Third-party intervention may also help to reduce unrealistic expectations. In extreme cases, such as the oil crisis in the 1970s that produced rapid inflation and a severe recession, incomes policies (wage and price controls) were instituted.

THE TRIANGLE OF PRESSURES

In any negotiations, a deadline may be necessary to pressure the parties into a settlement. In collective bargaining, there is always a deadline imposed on the parties by provincial or federal legislation. By serving notice to bargain and completing the conciliation or mediation steps, the union (or management) can place itself in a legal strike (or lockout) position. Just the potential of this happening creates pressure on the parties. Even when no strike mandate has been obtained or no discussion of a lockout has taken place, the parties are always aware of the potential of a strike or lockout. Their behaviour in collective bargaining will be affected by this reality. Thus, there are pressures on the parties throughout the bargaining process that affect their desire to settle. To be a more effective negotiator, it is important that the negotiator appreciate the pressures on the other party and understand the strengths and weaknesses of both parties.

We have grouped the pressures of bargaining into three broad categories of relationships that form a triangle: union–employer, employer–employee, and union–employee (see Figure 7.4). The union–employer relationship depicted in Figure 7.4 is simply the traditional collective bargaining process. Employer–employee relations are referred to today as human resources management. Finally, the relationship between the union, its members, and all employees in the bargaining unit is called the "intra-union dynamics" of collective bargaining. The next section hones in on these three categories of pressures, starting with the traditional labour–management relationship.

UNION–EMPLOYER PRESSURES

PRESSURES ON THE FIRM

In the traditional union–management collective bargaining relationship, the potential of a strike may put pressure on the firm because of the potential loss of sales, revenue, profits, and market share; decreased stock prices; bad publicity; etc.

The firm may relieve some of this pressure by *stockpiling*, or building up inventory. To the extent possible, it will have a plan to shift production to alternative sites. All this depends on the level of competition in the market for the firm's goods or services (discussed in Chapter 3). In the public sector, governments may ensure that collective agreements expire in non-election years, although governments are not above exploiting collective bargaining with their own employees as an election issue.

FIGURE 7.4

TRIANGLE OF PRESSURES

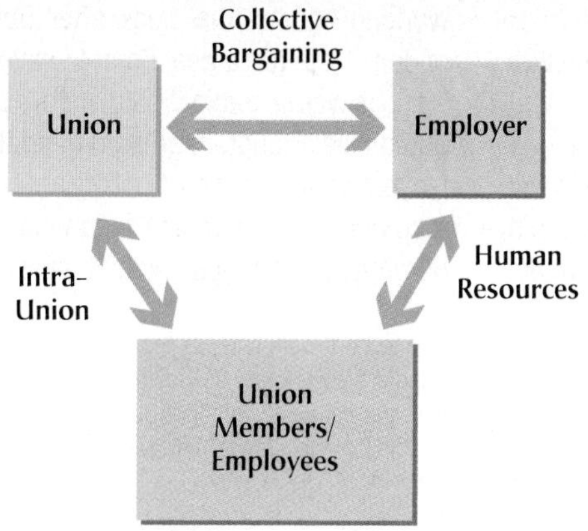

Collective Bargaining

Union ⟷ Employer

Intra-Union

Human Resources

Union Members/ Employees

A firm's ability to withstand a strike may also depend on its debt load. The lower the fixed costs of operating the plant, the less pressure there will be on it during a strike. The likelihood of losing some market share also raises the spectre of uncertainty. A strike is a venture into the unknown, especially if there is no prior history. Every strike has an element of unpredictability to it. How will the bottom line be affected? How long will the strike last? What will it take to get a settlement? Buyers like stability of supply, and uncertainty is their enemy (see IR Today 7.1 for news of a 10-year settlement).

IR TODAY 7.1

NHL LOCKOUT OVER AFTER 16-HOUR NEGOTIATING SESSION

Someone said, well, you might as well put your tie on, Shane, so Shane Doan took the blue diamond-checked tie out of his pocket and affixed it around his neck. He did it because the National Hockey League lockout of 2012–13 was over at 5 a.m. Eastern time, after a vast 16-hour bargaining session, and the cameras were coming in. He was the only player in the ballroom wearing a suit. Might as well look his best.

That is what the NHL and its players will have to do now, after 113 days spent battling and bickering and burning games. They will have to put the best face on a sport that was marred by a lockout that didn't need to go this long, and didn't need to be this ugly. The NHL needs to make amends, because the damage could be deep.

After six long months of negotiations, it took one extremely long night to get the NHL out of the boardroom and back on the ice.

A tentative deal to end the 113-day NHL lockout was reached early Sunday morning following a marathon 16-hour negotiating session.

"We have reached an agreement on the framework of a new collective bargaining agreement, the details of which need to be put to paper," NHL commissioner Gary Bettman told a news conference. "We've got to dot a lot of i's and cross a lot of t's. There's still a lot of work to be done but the basic framework of the deal has been agreed upon."

Before the new CBA officially comes into effect, it must be ratified by a majority of both the league's 30 owners and the union's membership of approximately 740 players.

"Hopefully we're at a place where all those things will proceed fairly rapidly and with some dispatch," said Donald Fehr, executive director of the NHL Players' Association.

"We'll get back to business as usual just as fast as we can."

Neither side has announced details of the deal—which came together with the help of U.S. federal mediator Scot Beckenbaugh—but according to a source, it's a 10-year agreement with an opt-out option after eight years.

It also includes defined benefit pensions for the players as well as a $64.3-million salary cap in 2013–14.

Other highlights, according to a source, include a seven-year contract term limit for free agents and eight years for players re-signing with the same team. The deal also includes a 35% yearly variance in salary and no more than 50% difference between any two seasons.

"Everyone is obviously relieved that it's over and done with, for all intents and purposes, and we're able to kind of move on to what we kind of enjoy doing a lot more than this," said Phoenix Coyotes captain Shane Doan, who was involved in the negotiations.

It's not clear when the season will start or how many games will be played, though Winnipeg Jets defenceman Ron Hainsey—also a key figure in the negotiations—said he expects it to be 48 or 50 games.

The league was on the verge of cancelling a second season due to a work stoppage. The two sides were working against the clock after Bettman set a deadline of Jan. 11 to get a deal done to save a shortened season.

"It was a battle," said Hainsey. "Gary said a month ago it was a tough negotiation and that's what it was. The players obviously would rather not have been here but our focus now is to give the fans whatever it is—48 games, 50 games—the most exciting season we can."

Sources: Bruce Arthur. (6 January 2013). "NHL lockout ends and now begins the long, hard work to repair the damage," *National Post*. Material reprinted with the express permission of: National Post, a division of Postmedia Network Inc. Retrieved from http://sports.nationalpost.com/2013/01/06/nhl-lockout-ends-and-now-begins-the-long-hard-work-to-repair-the-damage/; and Chris Johnston. (6 January 2013). "NHL lockout is over after 16-hour negotiating session,: *National Post*. Used with permission of The Canadian Press. Retrieved from http://sports.nationalpost.com/2013/01/06/nhl-lockout-is-over-after-16-hour-negotiating-session/.

Management bargaining teams might be under pressure from both local managers and central or corporate management. For example, line managers will have their own agendas that they will want addressed at the table. They might want previous grievance losses reversed through collective bargaining. Corporate management, on the other hand, might choose from a range of cooperative to more aggressive strategies according to the demands of the business. In the paper industry, for example, some firms have tried a strategy of cooperating with unions, while others have taken hard-line bargaining approaches, often taking long strikes by using replacement workers (Dachis & Hebdon, 2010; Duffy & Johnson, 2009; Eaton & Kriesky, 1998). Local management teams may negotiate under rigid constraints on costs imposed from some central or corporate authority. In the public sector, financial controls over lower levels of government are typical (e.g., provinces over municipalities and school boards).

Public-sector employers will be under different kinds of pressures. The pressures on bargaining teams from line managers and central authorities will likely parallel those of private-sector firms. But since public services are very labour-intensive, payrolls will be a high proportion of total costs. Thus, public employers are likely to save money during a strike. The pressures they face will be more political than financial.

NHL players are locked out by the NHL.

PRESSURES ON THE UNION

Since unions exist to benefit their members, a strike can put this fundamental purpose on the line. There are potentially seriously damaging consequences for the union as an institution. A long strike with little or no gains may have a major impact on the strike fund, future organizing, and even the continued existence of the union.

Particularly when there are changes in economic conditions (e.g., increases in inflation), unions must deal with changing member expectations in bargaining. Unions are democracies and must listen to their members. Moreover, if a strike is to be avoided, the contract must be ratified by these same members. How should unions assist in adjusting member expectations? Critics might answer that they shouldn't—the union's role is not to dampen expectations. We believe that nearly all unions support a collective bargaining model based on realistic achievements at the table, not conflict for its own sake. Thus, there are times when union leaders and bargaining teams must explain the art of the possible to the rank and file or, alternatively, when the union members have to remind the leadership of their priorities. The tension between union leaders and members often plays out in the union negotiating team caucus meetings.

Before making its last offer, management will usually insist that the union's bargaining team unanimously recommend it to its membership. If there are dissenters, there is a higher probability that the last offer would be rejected. A rejected offer may increase the likelihood of strike and undermine the union's authority to negotiate a settlement at the bargaining table. Ideally, if expectations have to be lowered, the union leadership will try to do this at the time of setting proposals. Mediators can also play a useful role in explaining reality to a union team that has inflated expectations about what is possible when there is a disconnect between the union's leadership and its membership.

Unions also face pressures from settlements achieved by rival unions. Ross (1948) coined the phrase "orbits of coercive comparison" to describe the relative standard used by competing unions in collective bargaining. The final pressure here is derived from the active tactics and strategies of management. The inventory buildup discussed above may put pressure directly on employees (speedups, overtime, more shifts, schedule changes, etc.) and indirectly on the union by sending a signal that the firm can sustain a long strike.

PRESSURES ON UNION MEMBERS

The pressures on individual employees and union members[2] to avoid a strike are many. Union members know that strike pay usually comes after a waiting period of one or two weeks. When it finally arrives, it will normally pay only for subsistence items. The loss of income during a strike can adversely affect an employee's debt situation. Employees may have mortgage or rent payments, loan payments for cars, appliances, or schooling, and upcoming expenses for a scheduled vacation. There may be pressures from the union and other members for strike solidarity, and family pressures against striking. However, studies show that communities with a strong union presence often rally behind striking employees. Employees about to take a strike vote will be feeling psychological stress from the fear of the unknown and the insecurity a strike presents: How long will the strike last? Will the family survive financially? Will I have a job when the strike is over?

EMPLOYER–UNION MEMBER/EMPLOYEE PRESSURES

Planning for a possible strike poses a significant challenge to the management team. Those responsible for production will do everything possible to maintain production and sales during a strike. This may include a plan to use managers and supervisors to sustain production and to hire temporary replacement employees. In British Columbia and Quebec there are laws limiting the use of replacement workers in the event of a strike or lockout.

In the pre-strike period management may attempt to stockpile inventory to keep up sales during a strike. During this buildup period, managers may face increasing discontent and resistance from employees. Employee dissatisfaction is often manifested as grievances, slowdowns, or other individual or collective actions designed to disrupt production. For an example, see the opening vignette.

UNION–UNION MEMBER PRESSURES

Before and during a strike there are often powerful tensions between the union leadership and its members. If the leaders (national or international office, local executive, and bargaining team) can see a settlement coming, they will apply pressure on members to prepare for this eventuality. They might hold information meetings to explain the issues, use third-party procedures, or work at lowering expectations—actions all designed to prepare the way for settlement and avoid a strike. Union leaders must lead, but they also have to get reelected if they wish to remain in office, so they have to be sensitive to the condition and mood of their members.

If, on the other hand, a strike is likely, a very different strategy will be adopted. The union leaders will prepare for this probability by building support in the membership for their bargaining position. They will prepare a contingency strike plan that includes a strike policy covering everything from the production of picket signs to the allocation of additional strike pay to cases of family hardship.

// BARGAINING STEP BY STEP

1. Management and the union prepare for bargaining
   - Obtain a mandate from the constituents.
     a. Management is given its mandate from the corporate or strategic level
     b. Union holds membership meeting to establish bargaining proposals and elect negotiating team.
   - Management solicits input from line managers—this includes a grievance analysis.
   - Both union and management examine comparators—for example, industry settlement patterns.
2. The union or management serves notice to bargain.
   - The parties prepare their proposals to amend the current collective agreement based on constituent input and research.
   - Before the current collective agreement expires, the management or union may give written notice to start negotiations for renewal agreement—the notice period is usually required by legislation.
3. The parties meet.
   - The parties agree to meet at a mutually acceptable location and time.
   - The purpose of this first meeting is to establish the ground rules for bargaining, including a timetable for future meetings; to introduce the teams to each other; to explain the proposed changes to the agreement; and to provide a rationale.
4. Each party communicates its priorities.
   - Each side provides a written list of its priority issues together with a rationale. Sometimes the priorities are indicated by the order of the list. Other guides to the importance attached to each issue are the amount of time spent on the rationale and potency of language each party uses.
   - This is the art of negotiations—skilled negotiators are able to indicate priorities with a single sentence. If, for example, the management negotiator responds to a union proposal with "We cannot do what you want; our hands are tied," this will likely be a major obstacle to a settlement.
   - On the other hand, if the management response is "We will take a look at it," the negotiator will likely test his or her committee to see if there are objections to the union proposal.
5. Momentum builds for a settlement.
   - The parties will often combine issues into packages. These are small groups of easily resolved issues that involve dropping union or management proposals for some modest gains.

- A technique that is used at this stage and throughout negotiations is the caucus meeting—both management and union teams will frequently break away from the bargaining table to meet as an individual team to assess moves and countermoves.

6. The contract zone is reached.
   - If a settlement is possible in direct talks, then there must be an overlap in bottom lines; this is defined as a contract zone.
   - At this stage, each negotiator should have an idea of the other side's bottom line.

7. Settlement or impasse?
   - If there is a contract zone and the parties have good negotiating skills, a settlement is reached in direct talks.
   - If there is no contract zone or the parties lack the necessary negotiating skills, negotiations may reach an impasse.
   - If there is an impasse, the parties may seek the services of a conciliator or mediator to assist them in bridging the remaining gaps.

8. Ratification.
   - When a settlement occurs before or after an impasse, an agreement will have to undergo **ratification** by both sides. This unratified agreement between the two bargaining teams is referred to as a *tentative settlement*, because the parties must each approve it for it to take effect.

ratification
the process by which each party approves the settlement reached at the bargaining tables by the management and union teams

// THE DOS AND DON'TS OF BARGAINING

Our first question is: What issues should be discussed first at the table and why? Students often answer this question by asserting that it would be logical that the parties start with the tough issues first. After all, if the hard ones can be successfully tackled, then the rest of the issues will fall into place. Then, assuming that economic issues are high on each party's list, it might be logical to start with the economic issues and end with the noneconomic ones.

There are at least two major problems with starting with the tough issues. The first problem is tactical. If the parties cannot generate any movement on the tough issues, talks could simply collapse, producing a premature impasse caused by the failure of the parties to fully understand each other's positions and to psychologically prepare for compromise. Starting with lesser issues can produce positive momentum, getting negotiations headed in the right direction as progress is made on the minor issues.

The second problem is more strategic. Both sides may have important nonmonetary issues that they want dealt with. The union might want improvement in job security; management, for example, might want more flexibility in scheduling weekend work via a reduction in the minimum notice period. If wages and benefits are resolved, the parties are likely to encounter difficulties in generating support for any noneconomic issues. To put it simply, neither side will want to lock out or strike over issues of lesser importance.

To illustrate the folly of settling the highest priority issues first, we present an example from a class bargaining simulation. A student bargaining team drew a line in the sand over the issue of cleaning the washrooms. It is highly unlikely that a union would get membership support for a strike over this type of issue if all other issues have been settled—especially all economic ones. A better strategy, given the minor cost nature of this issue, might be to include it in an appropriate package that includes some economic issues. Timing may be everything. By linking its resolution to more important economic issues, the union may use its leverage on wages to achieve this relatively minor issue of health and hygiene.

For a typical example of a round of negotiations in which the most important priorities were presented as the last issues, see IR Today 7.2.

When union leader Buzz Hargrove sauntered out of a tough bargaining session at Ford the other day, he heard a familiar voice behind him.

"Put two women in charge and they'll get it done," one of his top negotiators, Peggy Nash, said to chief Ford negotiator Stacey Allerton Firth as they walked down a Sheraton Centre hallway.

The women chuckled, and Hargrove, head of the Canadian Auto Workers, smiled. "Yes, they're right," he said later.

The two women had just found a way around a nagging money issue at the negotiating table to put another piece of the puzzle in place for a new contract.

They had also broken new ground in high-octane auto negotiations, a male bastion replete with decades of screaming, fist pounding and even the occasional scrap punctuated by a knuckle sandwich.

For the first time in Canada, two women were in the front seat of Big Three auto bargaining. They played a significant role in negotiating the tentative contract at Ford that set a pattern for the other auto giants, General Motors and DaimlerChrysler.

Both have participated in major auto bargaining before, but never with this much influence and so much at stake.

The atmosphere in this year's bargaining was noticeably different than a generation ago, according to officials familiar with talks.

On one side of the table was Nash, a former passenger agent at Air Canada who quickly took an interest in unions and women's rights, eventually rising to the CAW's inner circle. On the other side was Allerton Firth, a Ford labour relations veteran who became the first woman vice-president of human resources at Ford of Canada in 2003. The appointment meant she would automatically become the company's lead negotiator in contract talks this year.

And there they were—two married women juggling family life sitting across from each other at a bargaining table in a downtown hotel dealing with issues affecting millions of dollars and thousands of workers.

"I didn't really see gender as an issue," Nash said. "It's a different era. People now just want to see if you can do the job. That's the bottom line."

Allerton Firth added in a separate interview she also didn't give gender much thought in negotiations because both sides had to focus on resolving major issues including how to deal with pending job losses. Ford is losing money and needed to cut production because of sliding sales.

Insiders said one or two local bargaining committees still experienced heated arguments, but a lot of the macho nature of past bargaining on both sides had disappeared.

Hargrove, who has bargained contracts for more than 30 years, said he remembers occasions when chauvinism ran rampant. Some previous negotiators felt women had no place at the bargaining table or an auto plant, he said.

Although Hargrove didn't recall any CAW and Big Three negotiators resorting to fisticuffs, he remembers members of union committees trying to settle disputes physically among themselves after knock-down, drag-'em-out debates.

Nash said there are still some situations where people stereotype women as not tough or confrontational enough for contract bargaining.

"It's a Victorian notion of women as delicate flowers," added Nash, who has fought for more programs for women in the workplace.

She remembers a time when negotiators would ask her, "What's a woman doing in a job like this? … Don't your kids miss you? … How does your husband feel about you being away so much?"

It left her with the impression they felt she was abandoning her responsibilities as a mother.

Nash said bargaining was more of "a boys' club" a generation ago.

"I don't mean to be disrespectful but it was a different time and the bargaining style was different."

Nash said although there is still some occasional yelling as nerves become frayed and frustration sets in during all-night bargaining sessions, "the decibel level has gone down."

Allerton Firth added her approach in bargaining was sharing a lot of information and "active listening."

"If you're yelling at someone, they're not listening but thinking about defending themselves," she said.

"We were facing serious issues and had to concentrate on finding solutions."

Allerton Firth noted that as a working mother, organization is essential because she is usually "juggling several balls in the air" and that skill helps in bargaining.

Allerton Firth and Nash stressed their senior positions show young women choosing a career can break through barriers to holding non-traditional jobs.

The two negotiators received high praise for their work from colleagues because of strong communication skills, respect and trust between each other.

Hargrove said the women played a strong role in resolving impasses in local negotiations affecting Ford parts plants in Windsor that could have held up a settlement.

The deal must still be ratified by union members in a vote this weekend.

Whitey MacDonald, chairman of the union's master bargaining committee at Ford, said Allerton Firth listened intently, had a good understanding of the issues and made decisions quickly. "She put her best foot forward for the people affected by Ford's restructuring. Quite frankly, I had a better relationship with her than other people in that position in the past."

Source: Tony Van Alphen. (16 September 2005). "At auto talks, women grabbed the front seat. For the first time Canadian Big Three bargaining that females led talks," *Toronto Star*. Retrieved from, Reprinted with permission of Torstar Syndication Services.

// INTEREST-BASED BARGAINING (IBB)

WHAT IS IT?

> **interest-based bargaining (IBB)**
> a cooperative form of bargaining in which the parties focus more on the interests of the parties and not the exaggerated positions; also called *principled, integrative, cooperative, positive-sum,* or *collaborative negotiations*

Interest-based or cooperative bargaining is just one of the many labels given to integrative bargaining. In this section, we define **interest-based bargaining (IBB)**, discuss its usage by management and labour, and examine the conditions under which it might be most appropriate to use it in collective bargaining.

Economists describe distributive or competitive bargaining as a zero-sum game. One party's gain is the other party's loss. In theory, IBB is a positive-sum game, where the size of the pie may be increased. Hence IBB is often called *win-win* or *mutual gains negotiations*. Other labels for IBB include *principled, integrative, cooperative, positive-sum,* or *collaborative negotiations*. An early form of IBB, called "relations by objectives" (RBO), was developed by the U.S. Federal Mediation and Conciliation Service in 1977 (Cutcher-Gershenfeld, Kochan & Wells, 2001). Designed as a special form of preventive mediation during the term of a collective agreement to improve the union–management relationship, RBO was used in high-conflict relationships, such as those involving a strike aftermath or an unusually high rate of grievances.

Modern-day IBB is often based on four assumptions (Corry, 2000):

- both labour and management can win;
- each can assist the other to win;

- open discussions expand area of mutual interests; and
- decision making is based more on standards for evaluating options than on power.

Its main elements include (Fisher & Ury, 1981):

- a focus on issues, not personalities;
- a problem-solving approach;
- a free exchange of information;
- an emphasis on interests, not positions;
- the creation of options to satisfy mutual and separate interests; and
- an evaluation of options with objective standards.

To illustrate how IBB causes a shift in focus from positions to interests, we present the following example. Suppose the union proposes a no-contracting-out clause in the collective agreement. The intent of the proposal would be to prevent management from contracting out existing bargaining unit jobs during the life of the agreement. The position advanced by the union is apparently absolute and inflexible. Management's counterposition, on the other hand, is that it will under no circumstances give up its right to contract out work. To survive in a highly competitive environment, management needs the flexibility to outsource. The parties appear to be on a collision course on this issue alone.

Under an IBB process, the parties would be asked to shift their focus away from their extreme and seemingly intractable positions. They would be asked to reveal their real interests. What is the real interest of the union and its members? What is management's real interest on this issue? In a more open process in which both sides are willing to explore solutions, the union reveals that its real priority is job security and the protection of its members' jobs. Management reveals that its real interest is flexibility. It has no direct plans to outsource jobs, but to remain competitive in the future, it cannot rule out this possibility.

A matrix of options that shows the positions, interests, and creative solutions that are revealed using an IBB problem-solving approach is set out in Table 7.2. A simple clause that prevents layoffs but not contracting out would appear to satisfy the interests of both management and labour. Compensation may also be included. Another option is to limit the outsourcing to work not currently preformed by current union members.

TABLE 7.2

CONTRACTING OUT MATRIX OF SOLUTIONS

POSITION/INTEREST	UNION	MANAGEMENT
Hard-line position	No contracting out	Contracting out is a management right
Interest	Protection of members' jobs	Flexibility
IBB solutions	There will be no layoffs as a result of contracting out. Employees affected by contracting out will be compensated. Contracting out will apply to new work only.	

IBB STEPS

1. Identify the problem.
   - Convene frequent sessions by mutual agreement.
   - Develop agenda items that have joint problem-solving potential.
   - Formulate negotiation subjects as specific problems rather than general concerns.
2. Search for alternative solutions.
   - Give adequate notice of negotiation times.
   - Engage in informal exploratory discussion before making formal proposals.
   - Tackle easy-to-resolve issues first.
3. Systematically compare alternatives.
   - Accurately report preferences.
   - Arrange (e.g., combine) proposals to make patterns of agreement more visible.
   - Consider remedial actions that improve the relationship to be part of the general solution.

A criticism of Fisher and Ury's (1981) application of win-win negotiations in collective bargaining is that it narrowly assumes a dichotomy between integrative and distributive processes. It is our view that this is a false dichotomy and that cooperation and competition must coexist in every labour–management relationship. In fact, some scholars argue that cooperation and competition are part of the same dynamic (Kolb & Bartunek, 1992). Moreover, as we discussed above, collective bargaining often involves integrative, distributive, and hybrid issues at the same time. IBB may be inappropriate, therefore, where issues are inherently distributive. We will explore this further below.

To summarize, for integrative bargaining to be successful, there should be a free exchange of information, a problem-solving approach, an understanding of each other's needs and objectives, and a sufficient level of trust.

WHY IS IBB SO DIFFICULT TO ACHIEVE?

MIXED-ISSUE BARGAINING

Any round of collective bargaining will have a mix of inherently distributive and integrative issues. As discussed, wages are distributive while the issue of employee health and safety has integrative potential. Hybrid issues such as technological change and pensions have both distributive and integrative components. Given the complex nature of collective bargaining issues, it is sometimes difficult in the heat of battle to fully exploit integrative potential. Negotiators who prefer a highly adversarial style are most likely to ignore the integrative potential in integrative or hybrid issues. But to achieve optimal outcomes, negotiators need to adapt their tactics to meet the needs dictated by the mix of issues. This may be easier said than done.

BARGAINING HISTORY

The parties may have had a long history of adversarial negotiations characterized by conflict and a lack of trust. In this climate, it is common for bargaining positions to harden. Additionally, there are unions that, for ideological reasons, oppose all forms of cooperation. For these unions, to collaborate is to be co-opted by management.

THEORY

Another difficulty in achieving integrative bargaining follows from theory. Unless there is complete certainty that the other side will bargain in a cooperative manner throughout the negotiations, the risk of adopting such a strategy may be too great. This is because the party that switches to distributive bargaining during negotiations will likely obtain a much greater outcome at the expense of the other party. The cooperative style of multiple spokespersons, information sharing, etc., will not work against a disciplined hard-line approach. Thus, unless there is ironclad agreement to the negotiating rules, there is a strong incentive for a party to switch from an integrative to a distributive style.

DOES IBB WORK?

Studies show that it works in specific sectors. It works in union–management negotiations in such diverse industries as libraries, airlines, and railways (Hargrove, 2010; Miller, Farmer & Peters, 2010). On a national basis, two scholars and a U.S. Federal Conciliation Mediation Services official conducted a national survey of union and management negotiators to determine the usage of IBB (Cutcher-Gershenfeld, Kochan & Wells, 2001). At the heart of this important research is the notion that process matters; that is, the way negotiations are conducted affects outcomes. The authors frame their research in terms of the following provocative questions:

- Is IBB an important innovation to allowing collective bargaining to keep pace with other organizational innovations (e.g., team-based work systems)?
- Alternatively, is IBB a new label for an old process called "integrative bargaining" and a well-crafted ploy to undercut the bargaining power of unions?

They argue that this important debate is fuelled by anecdotal evidence. The key element in the controversy is whether IBB can produce "mutual gains" outcomes across the full range of issues of interest to the parties. They assume that a mutual-gains outcome must be viewed as a gain by both management and labour; otherwise, it is a product of the relative power of the parties. Hence, in the study, management and union negotiators are asked a series of questions about the same bargaining outcomes on a range of issues.

Some of the salient questions posed to both manager and union negotiators about IBB are shown together with some survey results in Figure 7.5.

Interestingly, there were significant differences between female and male negotiators and large and small bargaining units. Female negotiators were more likely to prefer IBB, and the management–labour gap in attitude to IBB was wider in large bargaining units. Also, negotiators in first contract situations were more likely to prefer IBB.

The authors compared contract outcomes for labour and management who prefer IBB with those who do not. Labour and management who both prefer IBB were more likely to negotiate a mutual gains outcome for only one issue—increased worker input in decision making. On all other issues, the pattern reflected a power outcome rather than a mutual gains approach. For example, work-rule flexibility and benefit reductions were more likely outcomes among union negotiators who prefer IBB. The authors conclude, "Thus, adopting a more problem-solving approach by unions will make them more vulnerable to concessions or management power tactics" (Cutcher-Gershenfeld et al., 2001).

IBB SURVEY RESULTS: U.S., 1996

Are you familiar with IBB or win-win or mutual gains bargaining?
62.6% of management and 77.2% of union said yes

Have you employed IBB?
35.4% of management and 48.9% of union said yes

Do you prefer it?
79.8% of management and 59.6% of union said yes

As the authors indicate, these attitudes can be interpreted two ways. On the one hand, these are relatively high acceptance rates, but a significant number of negotiators did not like IBB (about 20% of managers and 40% of union). If the groups that were not aware of IBB are included, 26.2% of management and 24.8% of union negotiators prefer IBB overall.

Source: Cutcher-Gershenfeld, Kochan & Wells, 2001.

Here is a summary of the key results:

- Highly distributive issues do not work in a mutual gains approach.
- A high degree of lead negotiators are familiar with IBB and have used it.
- Union negotiators rate it lower than managers do.
- On average, female and newer negotiators give IBB a higher rating.
- IBB is a relatively new innovation that is still at an experimental stage and is not fully accepted by either labour or management.

IBB appears to have taken a permanent place in the arsenal of labour–management negotiations. However, its apparent failure to produce results that are seen by both parties as mutual gains suggests that adversarial bargaining has not been replaced, nor is it likely to be in the near future. Today's negotiator needs to know both integrative and distributive negotiating styles.

UNDER WHAT CONDITIONS DOES IBB WORK OR NOT?

To help determine under which conditions IBB works and which it doesn't, let us look at two Canadian articles, one that examined the impact of IBB (Paquet, Gaétan & Bergeron, 2000) and another that evaluated twenty-four relations by objectives (RBO) programs (Hebdon & Mazerolle, 1995). Two of the authors of the first article are academics who perform training in IBB for Quebec private- and public-sector firms and unions. In their paper, they revisit several of their own cases to evaluate the outcome of negotiations after the training was given. Results are compared with matched samples of negotiations that did not use IBB. According to the research, IBB produced a broader range of changes to the collective agreement and was more innovative than adversarial negotiations. This is consistent with a problem-solving approach. However, there were more union concessions and fewer union gains with IBB. The latter finding reinforces the results of the U.S. national survey discussed above. Today's negotiator needs to know both cooperative and adversarial negotiating styles.

RBO is a form of preventive mediation first developed by the U.S. Federal Mediation and Conciliation Service in 1977. It is referred to in the Cutcher-Gershenfeld et al. (2001) article as an earlier form of IBB. The problem-solving techniques used in IBB and RBO are very similar. Research on twenty-four RBO cases in school board and teacher negotiations in Ontario in the 1990s also produced mixed results. As the authors conclude,

> RBO seemed to exhibit a "half-life" effect. For example, over a period of more than three contracts, the RBO boards returned to levels of conflict above the norm for the education sector, lending support to the view that economic (or other) differences ultimately determine the relationship. However, this conclusion does not rule out RBO as a useful tool for the reduction of conflict since even a "short-run" effect can be beneficial. In addition, our definition of the short run is three rounds of bargaining; that is, a minimum of three years and a probable average of four to six years—a substantial period of time.

The authors also noted that a return to previous high levels of conflict after RBO was due to the difficulty of institutionalizing change in the collective agreement. Like RBO, IBB involves a considerable investment in the training of both union and management bargaining teams. An obvious problem is that with the normal turnover in these teams, the full effect of IBB may be diluted over time if no automatic process is in place to provide training for new and inexperienced negotiators.

In summary, some of the conditions where IBB may be the most beneficial to the parties include the following:

- In a crisis. Cooperative bargaining works under crisis conditions (we are in this together). A private-sector example is the UAW and Chrysler negotiations in the 1980s, where the survival of the company was at stake. In the public sector, cooperative bargaining occurred at the local level during Ontario's economic crisis in the early 1990s (Hebdon & Warrian, 1999).

- In an exceptionally bad relationship. The positive effects of IBB may be difficult to sustain in the long run unless they are institutionalized in the relationship with collective agreement language and processes. IBB can be particularly effective where a bad relationship is due to a clash of personalities. It also appears to work for grievances as long as the issues in dispute are not distributive in nature.

- Where monetary conflicts of interest do not exist. Research shows that interest-based bargaining has a half-life effect when the issues are economic in nature and that distributive issues seldom produced a mutual gains outcome.

Thus, in collective bargaining there is a mix of what Walton and McKersie (1965) call distributive and integrative issues. Recall that distributive issues are those where win-win outcomes are almost impossible (e.g., economic issues, job security); integrative issues, in contrast, have mutual gains possibilities (e.g., health and safety, pensions). The challenge to negotiators is to realize the full potential on both types of issue. We argue that in order to do this, it is best to separate distributive from integrative issues and to isolate the integrative components of those issues that appear to be a mix of both types.

// SUMMARY

Students should understand the difference between distributive and integrative collective bargaining processes and issues. The other bargaining processes are intra-team and building trust. Intra-team occurs because of the diversity of interests on each team, and building trust is the most difficult process because of the inherent obstacles to establishing trust in labour–management relations.

To appreciate the other side's bargaining positions, it is important for negotiators to understand the pressures that they are under. These are presented in our triangle of pressures, which shows the union–management, union–employee, and management–employee relationships. In this chapter, we also examined the bargaining steps in a typical set of negotiations, including a look at the dos and don'ts.

To facilitate an understanding of the difficulties in achieving the best outcomes of collective bargaining, we examined the principles of the two contrasting bargaining styles of adversarial and win-win negotiations. The origins and elements of interest-based bargaining were studied, including the necessary conditions that ought to apply for it to be effective.

KEY TERMS

attitudinal structuring 204
bottom line 205
contract zone 207
distributive bargaining 203
integrative bargaining 203
interest-based bargaining (IBB) 216
intra-team (or intra-organizational) bargaining 204
ratification 214

WEBLINKS

Collective bargaining and workplace information (see below for details):
http://www.labour.gc.ca/eng/resources/info/index.shtml

- Collective bargaining:
  - Agreements and settlements
  - Directory of labour organizations
  - Collective agreement provisions
  - Information on Canadian legislation and client services
  - Federal mediation and conciliation service
  - Preventive mediation
- Workplace information:
  - Wage adjustments
  - Current and upcoming key negotiations

- Current settlements
- Negotech access to settlement summaries and full-text collective agreements
- Collective agreement expiries and reopeners
- Working conditions and benefits
- Work stoppages
- Directory of labour organizations
- Union membership
- Innovative workplace practices

Collective agreements in Canada:
http://cirhr.library.utoronto.ca/research/best-ir-hr-websites/collective-agreements

DISCUSSION QUESTIONS

1. What are the key differences between individual and collective bargaining?
2. What are the differences among the four subprocesses of bargaining? Why is building trust so difficult?
3. Can strikes occur when a contract zone exists? What are the weaknesses of the KKH model?
4. Why would you begin with bargaining minor issues and save the priority ones until the end of negotiations?
5. How do adversarial tactics differ from integrative ones?
6. Give examples of distributive, integrative, and hybrid issues.
7. What is interest-based bargaining? When does it work best?

USING THE INTERNET

The full texts of collective agreements are increasingly available on the Internet. The Centre for Industrial Relations and Human Resources, for example, provides links to full texts: http://cirhr.library.utoronto.ca/research/best-ir-hr-websites/collective -agreements. Find collective bargaining wage settlement trends as reported by any provincial labour department. Compare settlements this year and last year.

1. Find a current settlement of a strike or lockout in Canada. What were the issues that caused the strike?

EXERCISES

1. Find the full text of a collective agreement and analyze it by separating issues by type: distributive, integrative, and hybrid.
2. Take any unionized industry in Canada and analyze the pressures on the three parties to collective bargaining: management, union, and employees.

INTRODUCTION

This strike was without doubt the most important strike in Canada in past several years. It was a confrontation between Vale, a mammoth multinational corporation based in Brazil, and the strong Sudbury local of one of Canada's largest and most powerful private-sector unions—the United Steelworkers. The strike lasted almost a year from July 13, 2009, to July 7, 2010.

HISTORY

Since 1966 there have been seven strikes at this same mine when it was owned by INCO and the same USW local 6500. But the 2009 strike was very different from past ones in the manner described next.

Vale continued to run and upgrade its operations both during a shutdown prior to the strike and over the subsequent twelve months. Following the precedent set by the former Canadian mining giant Falconbridge a decade earlier, Vale used its 1,200 contract staff to do maintenance, upgrading, mining, and metal processing. It then had many of its contractors hire more workers in order to ramp up production in early 2010. After upgrading and maintenance work was completed in the plant, estimates from workers inside the operation and out estimated that the mines and facilities were functioning at near 30 per cent of capacity over the course of the year-long strike. (Peters 2010)

GLOBALIZATION OF THE MINING INDUSTRY

- The mining industry accounts for 19 percent of exports and 55 percent of all Canadian port traffic in 2007.
- The rapid expansion of ore extraction and processed ore and metal in nickel, aluminum, and iron figured in much of this growth, with exports more than doubling in value from $20 billion in 2000 to over $50 billion in 2008.

CANADA: A LOW-COST COUNTRY

- With internationally "competitive" tax and finance regimes and royalty levels that are among the lowest in the world, Canada ranks with the friendliest government regimes for mining companies. This seriously limits union political effectiveness and influence on the major political parties, as well as curtails trade union opportunities to improve wages and working conditions in the sector.

THE DEMAND FOR MINERALS

- Three billion tonnes of ore were mined in 1980. In 2002, 5.9 billion tonnes were extracted. By 2020, the UN predicts the annual volume of ores to exceed 11.2 billion tonnes. In recent years, such rapid extraction and consumption of structural metals (iron ore, bauxite, copper, and nickel) has risen three times faster than global GDP.

- China and India's rapid industrialization has been a chief factor in this boom.

- For mining companies, economies of scale and increasing rates of extraction are now key, as a hedge against good times turning bad, or to strengthen their hand in specific metals for economic booms in contexts of resource scarcity.

THE FINANCIAL CRISIS, 2008

- The credit crunch that began in late 2008 led to prices plunging as the world economy slumped and China's red-hot growth cooled off. As prices fell, steelmakers cut production, dramatically reducing demand for iron ore.

- Mining companies suffered a rapid decline in prices and returns.

- Estimates of the top companies' earnings before tax and depreciation fell by a third, though net profit margins remained above 15 percent over the course of 2008–2009.

THE PARTIES—MANAGEMENT & UNION

VALE

- By 2010, mining had been completely transformed. Inco and Falconbridge, along with hundreds of other small and medium sized mining operations, had completely disappeared.

- Vale expanded more than twentyfold, and climbed the ladder of globally diversified mining giants.

- It was in this context of rapid global growth and ever-expanding profits that Vale entered Canada in 2007, buying Inco Ltd. for $20 billion and establishing an independent but integrated corporate subsidiary, initially called "Vale-Inco" before it was shortened to "Vale."

- Vale adopted a more complex corporate strategy than a number of the other diversified mining giants. It set up operations around the world through direct ownership, joint ventures, and independent subsidiaries. Involved in everything from mining to railways, shipping to steelmaking, pulp and paper to reforestation and road building, the Brazilian corporation's goal was not only mining diversification but corporate diversification.

VALE REACTION TO FINANCIAL CRISIS

- Measures mining multinationals took to remain profitable during the recession were to cut capital expenditures, temporarily shut down operations, eliminate jobs, and in Vale's case, demand concessions from its workers.
- Vale-Inco reacted to the decline in nickel prices by
  - cutting 900 jobs at its global nickel operations including 423 in Canada and 261 in Sudbury;
  - announcing plans to shut down the Sudbury operations in June and July in an effort to reduce supply; and
  - letting go former executives and upper managers prior to launching a much wider restructuring initiative

THE UNITED STEELWORKERS

- The USW is the largest private-sector union in both Canada and North America, with more than 225,000 members in Canada and more than 800,000 members continent-wide.
- Members work in nearly every industry and in every job imaginable, in all regions of the country—call centres and credit unions, mines and manufacturing plants, offices and oil refineries, restaurants and rubber plants, sawmills and steel mills, and security companies as well as in nursing homes, legal clinics, social agencies, and universities.
- The USW goes global. Workers Uniting, representing three million members, is the international union created by Unite, the biggest union in the United Kingdom and Republic of Ireland, and the United Steelworkers, North America's largest private-sector union (http://www.usw.ca/union/uniting).

UNION STRATEGY

- The USW believed that by adopting a traditional strategy of coordinating three of its Canadian collective agreements with Vale to expire in the summer of 2009, with a fourth ending in January 2010, the union would have more than enough leverage for a "wait it out" strategy against Vale.
- This would leave the union ample opportunity to bargain a common agreement for all three workplaces that would have few concessions.
- The USW believed that such a withdrawal of labour power from Vale's facilities across Canada would be more than enough to pressure the company to step back from its concessionary demands.
- Relied on public support and member mobilization.
- Traditional financial support from other unions, and community rallies and events would raise the visibility of the strike and put pressure on the company to settle.

BARGAINING PROCESS ISSUES

A lack of trust and respect:

- The Vale strike was notable for the degree of acrimony involved.
  - The company routinely launched lawsuits and court cases proliferated.
  - Vale hired private security forces and burdened the municipality with millions of dollars in police protection and bylaw hearings.
  - Vale commonly neglected to set any dates to meet with the locals or make any promises to negotiate, let alone compromise.
- Vale demands initially included
  - a freeze in wages (though a cost-of-living clause was continued);
  - a sharp reduction in the miner nickel bonus to 15 percent of the employee's base pay; and
  - a switch in the company's pension plan from defined benefit to defined contribution.
- For workers, these concessions amounted to tens of thousands of dollars in lost income, a far less secure and far smaller pension, and the loss of jobs. The capping of the bonus was among the most contentious issues. Under the previous collective agreement, the miner's nickel bonus had no maximum limit and kicked in once nickel prices rose above $2.50 per pound.
  - As nickel prices were regularly low in the 1980s and 1990s, the bonus was often small, costing the company little.
  - But at the start of this decade, with the dramatic rise in the price of nickel from $3 to over $25 per pound, miners began to earn nearly as much in bonus as their regular pay, in some cases in excess of $60,000 per year.
  - By capping the bonus at a fixed rate of salary, the company's goal was to reduce the bonus to a fixed maximum of $15,000.
- Following wider corporate trends, Vale sought to replace its existing plan with a private defined-contribution one, in which workers carry most of the risk. Vale's third set of demands was driven by a desire to promote the retirement of older, high-paid workers and increase the flexibility of the workforce that remained.

TACTICS

- To win such concessions from the Steelworkers, Vale launched a wide public relations campaign prior to the strike deadline that let them and the community know that the company would not engage in any negotiations without the union first agreeing to its basic "pre-conditions":
  - changing to a defined contribution pension plan for new employees, a seriously reduced nickel bonus plan, and amendments to the collective agreement which the company said were necessary for competitiveness.

- Vale then maintained an active public relations profile throughout the strike, regularly commenting in the media on "new international realities" and the need for "efficiencies," placing full-page ads about the strike in local newspapers.
- Following tactics well developed in the United States, Vale launched a comprehensive campaign to ensure its success in bargaining. Over the course of the year, Vale instructed its lawyers to use every legal option to tie up union resources in the courts and at the labour board.
  - It fired nine strikers and sued them for damages ranging from $75,000 to $120,000 because of alleged incidents on picket lines. Twice it levied lawsuits of $25 million against the union for not following picket line protocol.
  - It launched further lawsuits against the union and individuals for information posted on the USW website, and for a blockade staged by community and individual union members in May 2010.

MEDIATION

- Labour talks between Vale and the USW collapsed for a third time over a disagreement about eight workers who were fired during the prolonged strike at the company's Sudbury nickel operations in Ontario.
- There was common ground after ten days of mediation for all other issues, including pensions, the nickel price bonus, and transfer rights.
- The parties were deadlocked over a single issue: the legal process to determine whether Vale will rehire eight of the nine employees who were fired for alleged blockading, harassment, and intimidation on the picket line, according to Ontario provincial mediator Kevin Burkett. (Excerpts from "Vale and USW fail to reach deal", *Metal Bulletin Weekly*, London: 5 July 2010, 9. Used with permission of Metal Bulletin).

OUTCOMES

- The Union was forced to accept major concessions on bonuses, layoffs, and pension plans, but got marginal improvements for current retirees and early retirement incentives for those with 27 years or more of experience.
- The losses to the local community over the course of the year were equally significant. Local estimates put the direct loss of wages and income due to the strike at $20 million a month and more than $250 million over the year.
- The company tactics were largely successful.
  - In the final contract offer, the bonus was capped at 25 percent of straight-time hours, effectively limiting the nickel bonus to $15,000 a year.

- The defined contribution plan was implemented for all new hires.
- Approximately 500 workers retired over the course of unionized workforce.
- Vale also gained new controls over the number of jobs, transfer rights, and the new grievance procedure, while having no restrictions placed on its use of contract workers throughout operations.
- The strike undoubtedly cut into Vale's profits.

MORE UNION VIEWS

http://www.usw.ca/workplace/campaigns/campaigns/vale

VIDEOS ON THE STRIKE

MANAGEMENT:
http://www.youtube.com/watch?v=O0JgNtH-RLE

UNION:
http://www.youtube.com/watch?v=4f59bCnkJqI&feature=related
https://www.youtube.com/watch?v=ev0FdY6bpyA

NEWS:
http://www.youtube.com/watch?v=DPRqqVqDM48&feature=related
http://www.youtube.com/watch?v=zjA2YCMRDJ0&NR=1
http://www.youtube.com/watch?v=9m2mjZInoxA&feature=related

USEFUL LINKS

IMPORTANT STRIKE DOCUMENTS

THE SUDBURY STAR:
http://www.thesudburystar.com/ArticleDisplayGenContent.aspx?e=15737

UNITED STEEL WORKERS:
http://www.usw.org/

UNITE THE UNION:
http://www.unitetheunion.org/

WORKERS UNITING:
http://www.workersuniting.org/connect/news/workers-uniting-questions-vales-cancellation-of-investor-events

OPEN LETTER TO THE SUDBURY COMMUNITY:
http://www.usw.ca/legacy_assets/UserFiles/File/radio_ads/sudbury_star_ad.pdf

Source: This case is drawn from multiple sources but relies primarily on John Peters. (Fall 2010). "Down in the Vale: Corporate globalization, unions on the defensive, and the Local 6500 strike in Sudbury, 2009–10," *Labour, 66*, pp. 73–105.

QUESTIONS

1. Outline the legal, social, and economic context of the bargaining between Vale and the United Steelworkers.
2. Analyze the pressures on the parties before and during the strike.
3. What were the strike issues? Why did the strike last so long?
4. What were the gains and losses of Vale and the union?

// ENDNOTES

1. For a popular work on getting the most out of individual bargaining, see *Getting to Yes* by Roger Fisher and William Ury (1981).
2. In most bargaining units, unless there exists a "union or closed shop," not all employees are union members. In Canada, nonmembers are typically required to pay dues.

// REFERENCES

1. Corry, D. J. (2000). *Negotiation: The art of mutual gains bargaining.* Aurora, ON: Canada Law Book.
2. Cutcher-Gershenfeld, J., Kochan, T., & Wells, J. C. (2001). In whose interest? A first look at national survey data on interest-based bargaining in labor relations. *Industrial Relations, 40*(1), pp. 1–21.
3. Dachis, B., & Hebdon, R. (2010). *The laws of unintended consequences: The effect of labour legislation on wages and strikes.* Toronto: C. D. Howe Institute.
4. Duffy, P., & Johnson, S. (2009). The impact of anti-temporary replacement legislation on work stoppages: Empirical evidence from Canada. *Canadian Public Policy, 35*(1), pp. 99–120.
5. Eaton, A. E., & Kriesky, J. (1998). Decentralization of bargaining structure: Four cases from the U.S. paper industry. *Relations industrielles, 53*(3), pp. 486–517.
6. Fisher, R., & Ury, W. (1981). *Getting to yes: Negotiating an agreement without giving in.* New York: Random House Business Books.
7. Hargrove, S. (2010). Achieving improved relationships through collaboration. *Library Management, 31*(4/5), pp. 229–240.

8. Hebdon, R., & Mazerolle, M. (1995). Mending fences, building bridges: The effect of RBO on conflict. *Relations industrielles, 50*(1), pp. 164–183.

9. Hebdon, R., & Warrian, P. (1999). Coercive bargaining: Public sector restructuring under the Ontario Social Contract 1993–96. *Industrial and Labor Relations Review, 52*(2), pp. 196–212.

10. Katz, H., & Kochan, T. (2000). *An introduction to collective bargaining and industrial relations* (2nd edition). New York: McGraw Hill.

11. Kolb, D., & Bartunek, J. (1992). *Hidden conflict in organizations: Uncovering behind-the-scenes disputes.* Newbury Park, CA: Sage Publications.

12. Miller, J. K., Farmer, K. P., & Peters, L. M. (2010). Panacea or snake oil? Interest-based bargaining in the U.S. airline and rail industries. *Negotiation Journal, 26*(2), pp. 177–201.

13. Paquet, R., Gaétan, I., & Bergeron, J.-G. (2000). Does interest-based bargaining really make a difference in collective bargaining outcomes? *Negotiation Journal,* July, pp. 281–296.

14. Peters, J. (2010). Down in the Vale: Corporate globalization, unions on the defensive, and the Local 6500 strike in Sudbury, 2009–10, *Labour, 66* (Fall), pp. 73–105.

15. Ross, A. (1948). *Trade union wage policy.* Berkeley: University of California Press, p. 133.

16. Walton, R. E., & McKersie, R. B. (1965). *A behavioral theory of labor negotiation.* New York: McGraw-Hill.

CHAPTER
8

COLLECTIVE AGREEMENT ADMINISTRATION

LEARNING OBJECTIVES

BY THE END OF THIS CHAPTER, YOU WILL BE ABLE TO DISCUSS

- the role of the collective agreement in unionized workplaces;
- the common layout of a collective agreement;
- the types of clauses typically found in collective agreements;
- why management and labour may prefer certain wording in collective agreements; and
- the importance and meaning of collective agreement language.

Jim Power, the nursing manager for Unit 4B, was meeting with employment relations manager Marc Picard. They were very carefully reading the collective agreement language concerning job sharing, vacation entitlement, and calculation of seniority. Both had represented management in the last round of collective bargaining, where the union and management agreed on new language concerning job sharing. This new language allowed two nurses to "share" a single nursing position providing that: (1) the two employees agreed on a schedule that covered off the normal work schedule for a single, full-time nursing position; (2) both nurses were qualified to perform the job that they wished to share; (3) the proposed job share schedule ensured that each nurse worked a minimum of two 8-hour shifts a week; and (4) the nursing manager of the unit in question approved the job sharing arrangement proposed by the employees. This was the first time the agreement contained such language. Both union and management teams believed that job sharing would facilitate work–life balance among staff, as well as help recruit and retain nurses. Both parties considered it a win–win solution.

"Marc, the language concerning calculation of seniority and vacation entitlement is very clear to me," Jim said. "Article 20.2 states that annual vacation will be scheduled by order of seniority such that the most senior nurse in the unit gets first choice of vacation, then the second most senior gets to choose his/her vacation, and so on. The table in Article 20.8 then presents the number of days of vacation an employee receives based on his or her years of service."

"Right," replied Marc. "But the employee in question is Maria Santos, who is job-sharing with Heather Scott. So we also need to look at Clause 43 concerning job sharing. Clause 43.4.2 states that all leaves, including vacation, will be provided to employees who job share on a prorated basis."

Jim replied, "That makes total sense. It basically means that as Maria's normal work schedule is three shifts a week, or 60 percent of a normal work week, her vacation entitlement is 60 percent of her 'normal' entitlement. In looking at Article 20.8, her 14 years of service would normally entitle her to 20 days of vacation. However, given her 60 percent job share, she is entitled to only 12 vacation days."

"That's how I read it as well," said Marc. "Now, what we need to figure out is seniority for the purposes of when Maria gets to pick her vacation. Remember, Maria and Heather in essence share one job. Maria has 14 years of seniority; Heather has two years of seniority. Looking at the seniority list of nurses in Unit 4B, it means that Maria gets to pick fifth, as the fifth most senior nurse on the unit. To me, absent any other language, it means that Maria gets to schedule her vacation well before Heather, who is twentieth on the seniority list, even though they share a single job that Maria used to work full-time."

"Ah, Jim, the joys of trying to interpret new language in a collective agreement. This is one area we never fully discussed when we negotiated the new agreement in December. I'm going to call Sharon Andrews, the president of the union local. Given that Sharon negotiated the language with us, let's see if she interprets the language as we do."

// ROLE AND LAYOUT OF A COLLECTIVE AGREEMENT

As you may recall, the collective agreement is the agreement between the union—representing all workers included in the bargaining unit (i.e., union members and nonmembers)—and the employer. The role of the agreement is to establish clear rules and procedures governing both workplace practices and the relationship between the parties. While it is probably safe to say that no two collective agreements are identical, most have similar features. For example, most are printed in pocket-sized format, so workers and supervisors can carry them during the workday and refer to them as needed. Moreover, many workplaces now put their collective agreements online. Union leaders have also posted YouTube videos concerning collective agreements.

In order to provide concrete examples of typical elements found in collective agreements, please examine the example in IR Notebook 8.1. More specifically, it, like most agreements, includes:

- *A cover page.* The cover usually states the name of the union (including local number), the employer, and the start and end dates of the collective agreement.
- *A table of contents.* The table of contents, usually found at the front of the agreement, and sometimes called an index, enables the reader to quickly identify where certain terms of the agreement can be found. See IR Notebook 8.1 for an example.
- *Articles.* Collective agreements are divided into a number of **articles**, each covering a certain workplace issue. Generally, each article is numbered and has a heading. For example, Article 4 of the University of Toronto agreement in IR Notebook 8.1 concerns management rights, Article 7 covers union representation, and Article 9 focuses on grievances.
- *Sections.* Within an article, there might be a number of sub-areas, called **clauses or sections**, also usually numbered. For example, in Article 12 (Staffing Related Issues) of the University of Toronto agreement, section 12.2 states how seniority, a key factor in staffing decisions, is calculated, section 12.4 describes job posting procedures, and section 12.6 focuses on issues related to layoffs.
- *Appendixes/schedules.* In some collective agreements, you will find schedules or appendixes that provide specific information. These, which are located toward the end of the contract, often relate to wages and benefits, or to items usually updated during each round of collective bargaining. In the University of Toronto example, Appendix A is the salary schedule.
- *Letters of understanding.* A **letter of understanding** usually describes a specific practice the parties have agreed to follow. In some cases, these are a result of a grievance or arbitration settlement. They too are usually put at the end of an agreement. An example from the University of Toronto agreement would be the letter of understanding concerning seniority listed at the end of the table of contents.

article
a larger section of a collective agreement

clause (or section)
a specific section of an article

letter of understanding
letter between the parties, usually placed at the end of an agreement and describing a specific practice they have agreed to follow

---

IR NOTEBOOK   8.1

SAMPLE TABLE OF CONTENTS: UNIVERSITY OF TORONTO

Union leaders, managers, and employees regularly refer to collective agreements for guidance concerning workplace rules and practices. Thus collective agreements have typically included a Table of Contents enabling the parties to quickly find relevant information. The following represents an abbreviated version of a typical table of contents that can help users of the collective agreement locate the information they seek.

Table of Contents

Source: Adapted from University of Toronto Schools and the United Steelworkers. *Collective Agreement.* Used with permission. Retrieved from http://www.usw1998.ca/2008-2011_UTS-USW%20Collective%20Agreement.pdf.

TYPES OF CLAUSES

Not only is the layout of an agreement fairly consistent, but so are the types of clauses found in them. For several decades, the federal government tracked collective agreements and clustered collective agreement language into several groupings (Human Resources and Social Development Canada, 2008). The following is adapted from HRSDC's list:

- *The rights of parties.* The rights of the union (e.g., union security clauses, restrictions on contracting out), employers, and employees.
- *The organization of work.* This includes provisions concerning how work is organized and distributed (e.g., technological change, job sharing, teams, etc.).
- *Labour relations processes.* These clauses concern the grievance procedure, arbitration, and any language about joint committees. Collective agreement language concerning joint committees will often examine issues related to

working conditions/environment, contracting out, and technological changes. We also include health and safety issues in this category given that legislation requires joint health and safety committees.

- *Education, training, and development.* Language in this grouping can include issues concerning training leave, required/provided training, financial assistance for training, and apprenticeship programs.
- *Working conditions.* This is perhaps the broadest grouping of clauses, including issues related to hours of work/work schedules, overtime, pay and benefits, job security, termination, corrective action/progressive discipline, and part-time work.

In the following sections we provide sample contract language for each of these groupings.[2] These examples come from Negotech (2014), a federal government database that allows you to access and search through collective agreement language. Negotech, and the following sample clauses, may be particularly helpful if your instructor assigns a collective bargaining simulation (such as that found in Appendix B).

RIGHTS OF PARTIES

RECOGNITION OF UNION SECURITY

Unions often seek collective agreement language that provides some form of union security (e.g., dues check-off, union shop, closed shop, Rand Formula). There might also be language regarding leave for union business and restrictions on management's ability to contract out as a way to ensure union member security. Examples follow from the collective agreement between Ivaco Rolling Mills and the United Steelworkers (2012). The first excerpt, from Article 1 (Union Recognition), discusses the role of the union as the exclusive bargaining agent as well as the parameters concerning contracting out. The second excerpt, from Article 5, covers union security, including dues check-off.

Article 1—Union Recognition

1.01—The Company recognises the Union as the sole collective bargaining agent for all employees of the Company at the plant in L'Orignal, Ontario, save and except Foremen, persons above the rank of Foreman, office and clerical staff, sales staff, security guards.

1.06 a) While it is not the intent of the Company to utilize outside contractors in lieu of its own employees to perform normal production and maintenance work required to operate and maintain the Company's equipment, the Company reserves the right to continue to use outside contractors. However, when employees are laid off to the street who have the skills to perform the required work, the Company will have such work performed by employees within the bargaining unit…

Article 5—Union Security

5.01—Employees who are members of the Union must remain members of the Union.

5.02—The Company shall deduct union dues including, where applicable, initiation fees, on a weekly basis, from the wages of each employee covered by this agreement. The amount of dues shall be calculated in accordance with the Union's Constitution.

MANAGEMENT RIGHTS

Under the principle of **residual rights**, management retains all rights and privileges it held before unionization, with the exception of rights restricted by the agreement (and, of course, any that are now illegal under changes in legislation). Thus, not all agreements have these clauses, as some employers feel that they are unnecessary. Other employers will seek to negotiate such clauses to emphasize their rights. The following is an example of a management rights clause (Article 6) from the Greater Vancouver Hotel Employers Association (2010).

In rare cases, employees can be asked to partake in drug and alcohol testing. Collective agreements often have language concerning how and when such testing can occur.

6.01 Management Rights

(a) The entire management of the operation including discipline of the employees is vested exclusively in the Employer at his place of business.

(b) In the exercise of management rights, the Employer will not treat any employee in an unfair or discriminatory manner and will observe the provisions of this Agreement at his place of business.

In addition, we have recently seen a number of employers seeking to include language concerning drug/alcohol testing, selection tests (e.g., medical, aptitude, and intelligence), or performance tests (i.e., electronic monitoring of performance). See the sample from the Saskatchewan Liquor and Gaming Authority (2013) that discusses drug testing of employees.

1.7 Drug and Alcohol Testing

Management may do drug testing of employees only with the prior approval of the Union

EMPLOYEE RIGHTS/SECURITY

These clauses include language concerning antidiscrimination (employment equity, harassment, disabled workers, etc.), substance abuse, recreational and health services, and childcare/eldercare programs. In general, there are two types of equity clauses found in agreements: the first, which we call **legislative reference**, refers to legislation, and the second, which we call **explicit reference**, explicitly states

residual rights
a principle whereby management retains all rights it held before unionization except those changed by the agreement

legislative reference
equity clause in collective agreements that references legislation

explicit reference
equity clause in collective agreements that specifies which groups are covered

As Canadian families become more diverse, collective agreements have broadened access to benefits for same-sex couples, common-law couples, etc.

inappropriate grounds for discrimination. The following are examples of each:

Legislative reference—*"The Company shall not discriminate against an employee on grounds prohibited by the Ontario Human Rights Code. An allegation that this clause has been violated shall be a fit matter for redress under the grievance and arbitration procedure." (From Article 6.03 [No Discrimination], Ontario Power Generation, 2012)*

Explicit reference—*"Subject to Section 10 of the Yukon Human Rights Act, the parties agree that there shall be no discrimination, interference, coercion, harassment, intimidation or disciplinary action exercised or practised by employees, the Union or the Employer with respect to an employee by reason of age, race, creed, colour, national origin, religious affiliation, sex, sexual orientation, family status, mental or physical disability, or membership or activity in the Union. For clarity, the parties agree that "sex" includes transgender identity or expression." (From Clause 5.01 [Discrimination] from the Yukon Government collective agreement, 2013)*

One might wonder why the parties would choose to use a legislative reference rather than the more detailed, explicit reference clause. Our conversations with union and management leaders provide some insights. Some argue that the legislative reference is preferred as it ensures that the agreement is current with the law. Others argue that the explicit reference is better because (1) most managers, union leaders, and employees look to their collective agreement for guidance on these issues, and the lack of specifics would not meet this need; (2) explicitly referencing specific groups ensures that these groups remain protected if the law changes; and (3) the parties may feel that they wish to include a group not covered by legislation.

DESIRED RELATIONSHIP

In some agreements, the parties will also set out expectations concerning the desired, positive relationship between the parties. A good example of such language is found in IR Today 8.1.

IR TODAY   8.1

TONE OF THE UNION–MANAGEMENT RELATIONSHIP

When you hear people refer to collective agreements, they may often sigh, voice discontent, discuss conflict, etc. However, some parties now include preambles designed to establish the desired, positive relationship between the parties. Let's look at the preamble from the University of Alberta collective agreement and see how it sets the desired relationship between the parties.

"Preamble

The University of Alberta (the Employer) and the Support Staff of the University share a common interest in achieving the University's goal of excellence in teaching, research and service to the community. The University and the Non-Academic Staff Association (NASA) are committed to working together for common goals, recognizing that NASA's role is

---

to represent the interests of its members and the Employer's role is to manage in the best interests of the University.

This Collective Agreement provides a foundation for achieving our common goals of:

- building positive working relationships at all levels of the organization, and
- creating safe, healthy, effective, innovative work environments in support of teaching, research and service excellence.

Support employees make a vital contribution to the University's success. We are committed to creating a work environment that contributes to the overall well-being of staff and enables them to be the "best they can be". We will strive to ensure that all members of the University community achieve their full potential, contribute to the University's success, and are valued and recognized for their contributions. We will help build a sense of pride and community at the University by actively fostering the behaviours, principles and accountabilities that guide our relationship must be based on a high level of trust between the Employer, NASA and Support Staff. In working to build and sustain trust, each party commits to and is entitled to expect frankness and honesty. We also recognize that:

- Mutual efforts at problem solving on issues that affect employee interests can build trust when based on recognition of each party's legitimate role.
- Actions that disappoint reasonable expectations or place the other party in an untenable or embarrassing position can undermine trust and should be avoided.

A trusting, effective working relationship depends on the manner in which we share information and consult with each other on issues that significantly affect our interests. We recognize that:

- It is to our mutual advantage to notify each other in a timely way of issues that may have a significant impact on our respective responsibilities as employer or bargaining agent.
- It is important that University decision makers consider the interests of employees when deciding upon a course of action.

- There is value in consultation on matters that directly affect the interests of NASA and its members.
- Consultation, when engaged in, needs to be timely, meaningful and efficient.
- Some matters may, of necessity, need to be handled with discretion—we need to be clear with each other when the exercise of discretion is necessary.
- Breaches of confidence in a breach of trust.
- Our interests may differ in particular circumstances, but failure to agree on an issue should not undermine our relationship or the integrity of the process used to discuss an issue.

We recognize that our working relationship relies on respectful behaviour, including:

- Behaving with honesty, consistency and integrity
- Listening to what others have to say, without interruption
- Being open-minded to other's feedback, ideas and suggestion
- Managing emotions
- Identifying and addressing differences quickly, encouraging people in conflict to try to resolve disagreements themselves through constructive, face-to-face dialogue before involving others
- Intervening when personal differences (or tests of will) are impairing ability to solve issues, taking steps to resolve such differences and to re-focus energies on problem solving
- Preventing personal attacks and behaviours that intentionally discredit or undermine others
- Following through on commitments
- Supporting people who work together and processes that promote cooperation, and working to correct disrespectful behaviour
- Making effective use of existing processes to resolve disagreements and overcome impasse

We will work to ensure that all members of the University community understand the importance and value of this Agreement and live up to their Collective Agreement responsibilities."

Source: University of Alberta and University of Alberta Non-Academic Staff Association. (2012). *Collective agreement.* Used with permission. Retrieved from http://negotech.labour.gc.ca/eng/agreements/12/1260507a.pdf.

ORGANIZATION OF WORK

TECHNOLOGICAL CHANGE

Since the Industrial Revolution we have seen ongoing change in the technologies used in workplaces. So it should not be surprising that, as is discussed in Chapter 1, Dunlop included technology in his IR system, nor that many parties negotiate technological change (often referred to as *tech-change*) language in their agreement. Usually, the union desires such language as a way to protect workers from the potentially negative impacts of the new technology. Hence, collective agreement language here may include elements such as the union being notified of the change, any restrictions concerning layoffs, any employer requirements concerning employee training for new jobs/equipment, and any wage protection for employees (often called **red-circling**) who might be demoted and/or moved to a lower-paying position as a direct result of tech change. The following excerpt from Article 17 (Technological Change) of the Bombardier (2011) agreement is one example of tech-change language.

red-circling
protecting employees' pay at a level higher than the normal rate of their current job

> *17.1 In order to provide maximum opportunities for continuing employment, the Union and the Company agree to cooperate in the introduction or operation of new equipment or changes in operating methods.*
>
> *If as a result of such change, a classification will be discontinued, and/or members of the Bargaining Unit will be displaced, the Company will inform the Union Bargaining Committee in advance of such changes and will discuss with the Union Bargaining Committee prior to the inception of such changes, means by which existing employees of the Bargaining Unit may qualify for positions created by such changes.*
>
> *17.2 In the event of the installation of new equipment that may affect the job status of employee(s) in the Bargaining Unit, the Company will, as far in advance as possible, before the installation of such equipment, meet with the Union Bargaining Committee, provide them with information regarding the new equipment and advise them of the number and classification of employees likely to be affected by such installation. The parties will discuss the feasibility of providing training on such new equipment to employees affected by such changes with the intent that the Company will give first consideration to present employees for such newly created positions.*
>
> *If training is required, such training shall be extended first to affected employees with the greatest seniority.*
>
> *17.3 In the event that a job stream is eliminated by new equipment or other changes in operating methods, the Company will provide training to affected employees in order to upgrade their skills to meet current technical and operational requirements if such training is required for said upgrade. The Union and the Company shall meet to discuss and arrive at a fair and equitable training plan.*

DISTRIBUTION OF WORK

Distribution of work clauses examine issues concerning job rotation, job sharing, teams/workgroups, and flexibility in work assignment. As is discussed in Chapter 6, many employers seek increased flexibility in work assignment and the organization of work in their workplaces. The following is from a letter of understanding (Flexible Work Practices) between Canfor Pulp Limited Partnership and Pulp, Paper and Woodworkers of Canada (2012). Notice how the first section of the excerpt focuses on the relationship between flexible work practices and operational efficiency and how the latter sections focus on employee safety and training for employees. As such, you can see how the needs of management and the union are presented.

1. *The introduction of flexible work practices is designed to improve productivity, improve product quality, reduce downtime and lower costs while ensuring that the work is completed in a safe manner. The efficiencies that result from flexible work practices are also intended to assist in fulfilling the intention of Article XXIII of the Labour Agreement.*

2. *The parties agree that this letter on flexible work practices recognizes that the primary responsibility for the operation of the mill will remain with operators and the primary responsibility for maintaining the mill will remain with trades persons and steam plant maintenance employees.*

3. *It is understood that the intent of this letter will supersede local practices, and verbal and written agreements, which would impair the implementation of flexible work practices.*

4. *All work will be performed in a manner consistent with safety articles of the Labour Agreement as well as the company's safety rules and the regulations issued by the Workers' Compensation Board of B.C. It is recognized that some tasks can only be performed by employees who possess certain government certifications and in that instance, the work will only be performed by employees who possess the required government certificate.*

5. *The intent of this agreement is to provide that all employees will safely utilize all of their existing skills and maximize their productivity and learn and use new skills to enhance their effectiveness.*

6. *The Company and the Union will meet to discuss a module-based training program that will enhance the existing skills of employees. They will also discuss the option of using trainers from the bargaining unit to assist in the design and delivery of the training modules. The Company will design and introduce new training programs to facilitate the implementation of an evolution of flexible work practices.*

Similarly, the following section from a letter of understanding from the City of Winnipeg Police collective agreement (2010) examines job sharing. Note how the letter seeks to balance the employees' need for flexibility with the police force's need to ensure qualified, available officers are available to work:

The City of Winnipeg and the Winnipeg Police Association encourage employees to retain their employment with the City of Winnipeg, particularly during child bearing/child rearing years. One way of doing this is through a formal job sharing agreement.

Job sharing restructures full-time work to meet the particular needs of employees who might otherwise be forced to resign from their jobs.

1. Ending this Agreement

This Job Sharing Program may be ended at any time by either the Police Service or the Association, after thirty (30) working days' written notice.

2. Application for Job Sharing

1. *Any two (2) members may submit a request to share a job to the Chief of Police;*

2. *Both the applicants must be employed in positions of the same rank at the time the request is submitted (the rank of Constable will be considered a single rank level);*

3. *One (1) of the applicants must currently hold the job to be shared, and*

4. *Positions which become vacant due to a job sharing arrangement will be filled, temporally, through the normal promotion/recruitment/acting process.*

5. *The Police Service will reasonably exercise discretion in approving a job sharing arrangement.*

3. Eligibility for Job Sharing

Applicants must have:

1. *at least four (4) years' Police experience; and*

2. *satisfactory performance in their current position.*

4. Division of Duties

Members sharing a job must work:

1. *full days/shifts only, and*

2. *at least two (2) days/shifts per week.*

LABOUR RELATIONS

Labour relations clauses in collective agreements specifically deal with issues concerning the relationship between the parties. Typical clauses examine grievance/arbitration procedures, participatory mechanisms (e.g., joint committees), and preferred bargaining methods.

GRIEVANCE AND ARBITRATION

You may recall that the right to a grievance procedure is not a requirement under common law. Thus, most agreements have specific language related to grievances and arbitration. Some, like the Nuna Contracting contract (2010), even define grievances (see Article 22.02):

22.02 "Grievance" will mean a complaint or claim concerning improper discipline or discharge, or a dispute with reference to the interpretation, application, administration or alleged violation of this Agreement.

A "Group Grievance" is defined as a single grievance, signed by a Steward or EI Union Representative on behalf of a group of employees who have the same complaint. Such grievance must be dealt with at successive stages of the Grievance procedure commencing with Step 1. The grievors will be listed on the grievance form.

A "Policy Grievance" is defined as one which involves a question relating to the interpretation, application or administration of this Agreement. A Policy Grievance will be signed by a Steward or a Union Representative, or in the case of an Employer's Policy Grievance, by the Employer or their representative.

The following excerpt from an agreement of the University of Lethbridge agreement with the Alberta Union of Provincial Employees (Article 12, 2011) outlines a typical grievance procedure. As will be discussed in more detail in Chapter 9, notice how the language highlights the representatives involved and the time frames.

Step I

If the difference is not resolved in the informal discussion, it becomes a grievance provided that it is reduced to writing specifying the complete and full statement of the difference pursuant to a declared, specific sub-clause of 12.01 and the particular relief requested on behalf of the grievor. The grievance must be signed by the Employee and submitted to the Human Resources Department and the Senior Supervisor within ten (10) work days from the date of the informal discussion. The decision of the Senior Supervisor shall be issued to the Employee, in writing, within ten (10) work days of receipt of the written grievance. At the request of either party, a meeting shall be held at this step.

Step II

If no settlement is reached in Step I, the grievance may be referred to Step II within ten (10) work days of the receipt of the written decision from Step I. The President, or a mutually agreeable designate, shall hear from representatives of the Board and the Union, at a hearing to be convened within fifteen (15) work days of receipt of the grievance. He shall issue his decision in writing within ten (10) work days of hearing the grievance. If it is a grievance as defined in 12.01 (i), (ii), (iii) or (iv) the decision of the Step II Officer shall be final and binding upon the Board, the Employee and the Union.

Step III

If it is a grievance as defined in 12.01 (v), (vi) or (vii) and no settlement is reached in Step II, and the employee has the approval of the Grievance Committee, the grievance may be referred to arbitration as provided in the Act. Where either party requests that a grievance be submitted to arbitration, the request shall be submitted to the other party in writing within fifteen (15) work days of the receipt of the written decision from Step II.

As you can imagine, the grievance language is very important to all parties but can also be very complicated to follow. As shown in the excerpt from the Iron Ore Company of Canada collective agreement (Table 8.1), some places use visuals to summarize key elements.

TABLE 8.1

GRIEVANCE PROCEDURE

ORIGINATE AT STEP	TIME LIMITS TO ORIGINATE GRIEVANCE	TIME LIMITS TO HEAR/AND ANSWER	HEARD BY	MAXIMUM UNION REP. (PAID REGULAR WAGES OR 1 HR. ON OWN TIME)	COMPANY REP	TIME LIMITS FOR ANSWER
Step I- Individual or Group*	5 days	5 days	Superintendent	1 Grievance Representative Union Co Chair (if requested)	1 Company Representatives Additional Company Representative if requested by Superintendent	Included in 5 days to hear
Step II- Individual or Group* or Policy	5 days	10 days to hear plus additional 5 days to answer	Manager or designate HR Representative HR Manager (Policy) Supervisor (if involved)	3 Grievance Representatives	3 Company Representatives	Included in 10 days to hear plus additional 5 days to answer
Arbitrator	Union has 30 days to refer to Arbitration		Rotational list of arbitrators			Arbitrator has 30 Days to answer grievance

* For group grievances - 1 grievor will represent the group and can be accompanied by no more than 3 grievance representatives

Source: Iron Ore Company of Canada and the United Steel, Paper and Forestry, Rubber, Manufacturing, Energy, Allied Industrial and Service Workers. (2012). P. 26 of the *Collective Agreement*. Retrieved from http://negotech.labour.gc.ca/eng/agreements/00/0013909a.pdf.

PARTICIPATORY MECHANISMS AND BARGAINING METHODS

Sometimes parties include language to enable ongoing negotiations to address specific issues rather than wait for the next round of collective bargaining. The following example is from the Hydro One agreement (2013), which defines membership on the committee and sets the expectation that the employer (Hydro One) and the union (The Society of Energy Professionals) will negotiate in good faith to resolve issues quickly.

92 *Problem Solving Committee*

92.1 A Problem Solving Committee shall be established and constituted by Hydro One Senior Management representatives and the Society Local VP and Unit Directors. The Problem Solving Committee shall meet upon request of either party and when mutually agreed.

92.2 The Problem Solving Committee Oversight Committee shall consist of the President and CEO of Hydro One and the President of the Society and shall meet upon request of either party and when mutually agreed.

92.3 Negotiations between Hydro One and the Society shall take place through a body to which each party will appoint an equal number of representatives. Negotiations shall be conducted in good faith and both parties shall make every reasonable effort to reach agreement on matters of mutual interest as expeditiously as possible.

HEALTH AND SAFETY COMMITTEES

Building on the previous theme of participatory mechanisms, joint health and safety committees are required by law. Many collective agreements include language on the role of such committees. This language may discuss committee membership, roles, record keeping, and pay. As one example, see the following language from the Montreal Gazette (2012) collective agreement:

20.04 One (1) employee of the Mailroom department will sit on the Health & Safety Committee comprised of representatives of the other GCIU bargaining units at the plant, and shall meet once every two months. It is agreed that the discussion shall be limited to matters of safety and health.

Minutes will be taken by the Company and both parties shall receive a copy of these minutes after verification. It is understood that Union representatives to the Committee shall attend meetings without loss of wages or shall be compensated at their regular rate of pay for the duration of the meetings when such meetings are held outside regular working hours.

It is agreed that representatives of either party may request the assistance at meetings of Company resource persons.

It is understood that this committee shall have all rights and obligations generally recognized to such committees and that their members' and the person responsible for the Human Resources department's unanimous recommendations shall be implemented by the Company.

CerebroCreative/iStock/Thinkstock/Getty Images

In many workplaces, safety clothing is required including hard hats, safety eyewear, safety vests, etc. Collective agreements often have language pertaining to the employer provision of these items.

EDUCATION, TRAINING, AND EMPLOYEE DEVELOPMENT

As we will discuss in more detail in Chapter 11, unionized workers often have increased access to workplace training. Thus, many collective agreements contain specific language about leaves for education, repayment of educational expenses (e.g., tuition, books), access to training, the employer's ability to provide **multi-skill training**, contributions to a training fund, and apprenticeship training programs. A few examples of such clauses follow.

> **multi-skill training**
> training to provide employees with a variety of skills, some of which may not normally be part of their job

REPAYMENT OF EDUCATIONAL EXPENSES

The following is from Article 12.13 (Education Leave) of the Greater Moncton International Airport Authority (2011) agreement. Notice how the language discusses issues related to paid versus unpaid leave, access to time off, and job-relatedness of the training/education.

12.13 Education Leave

(a) *The Employer shall grant education leave with pay during an employee's normally scheduled hours for the purpose of taking any courses, seminars or training required by the Employer. The Employer will provide time off with pay for the purposes of writing required examinations and will pay course registration fees and tuition.*

(b) *The Employer recognizes that generally there is a mutual benefit to be derived from employees who seek to improve their educational qualifications. The Employer agrees to reimburse employees the cost of tuition fees for those employees who successfully complete a course of study pre-approved by the Employer and provided by a recognized educational institution outside their normal hours of work. The Employer further agrees to provide the employee time off with pay to write exams during their normal working hours.*

(c) *An employee may be granted education leave without pay for varying periods of up to one (1) year, which may be renewed by mutual agreement. The career development leave shall be for attendance at a recognized institution for studies in some field of education which the Employer agrees will enhance the employee's present role or provide a required service in the future.*

APPRENTICESHIPS

Collective agreements that include skilled tradespersons usually have provisions for apprenticeships. This language will distinguish apprentices from journeypersons (or fully qualified tradespeople who have successfully completed an apprenticeship and passed any required examinations). Such language may cover off pay rates and progression, number of apprentices, legislative training requirements, hiring upon completion of the apprenticeship, etc. The following excerpts from the Iqaluit Housing Authority's 2011 collective agreement (Article 43–Apprentices) are examples of such language:

43.01 *The following are agreed upon terms and conditions of employment for employees engaged as apprentices.*

(a) The Apprenticeship, Trades and Occupational Certification Act *and pursuant regulations shall apply to all apprentices. A copy of the applicable regulations shall be supplied to the apprentice upon appointment.*

(b) *Apprenticeship Training programs shall be those designated under the* Apprenticeship, Trade and Occupations Certification Act.

(c) *Pay increases shall not be automatic but will be based upon levels of certification issued by the Apprentices Branch and shall be effective from the date of certification.*

And

(g) *Upon successful completion of the Apprenticeship program, the Employer will make every reasonable effort to provide the apprentice with a permanent full time position in the area of their trade. All time spent as an apprentice shall count towards continuous employment.*

CONDITIONS OF WORK

North American unionism has often been described as "bread and butter" in nature given its focus on improving the wages, job security, and working conditions of its members. Thus, one could argue that conditions of work is the most referenced section of a collective agreement, because it includes issues related to work schedules, overtime, pay, health and welfare benefits (vacation, retirement, health plans, etc.), and layoff/termination of employment (including progressive discipline, probationary periods, and violations of company rules that can lead to termination). We now present several examples of collective agreement language related to such work conditions.

HOURS OF WORK

Most collective agreements provide an overview of a typical workday (e.g., number of work hours). In workplaces with shift work, information concerning shift schedules may also be discussed. The following excerpt is from Article 6 (Hours of Work) of the Jazz Aviation (2012) collective agreement where both the work week and shifts are defined.

6.02 *The working week will average forty (40) hours which will be accomplished by various schedules, as follows… [NOTE: Collective agreement then presents, in detail, numerous shift schedules for the airline employees]*

6.03 Shift Definitions:

Day Shift—*will be any shift which starts on or after 0600 hours but before 1200 hours.*

Afternoon Shift—*will be any shift which starts on or after 1200 hours but before 1900 hours. On the 5x2, 4x3, 5x4 and 3x3 shifts in accordance with Article 6.02 Table 1, the afternoon shift will not run for four (4) or more consecutive hours between midnight and 5AM.*

Night Shift—*will be any shift which starts on or after 1900 hours but before 0600 hours.*

OVERTIME

Provincial labour/employment standards legislation includes provisions for overtime payment. However, most collective agreements have language concerning overtime that usually goes beyond the minimum legislative requirements. Such language often includes how overtime, which can be financially lucrative to workers, is to be assigned. The following example from Rolls-Royce (5.05 Overtime, 2013) shows how overtime is defined, paid, and allocated:

> Overtime for all work schedules will be paid at time and three-fourths (1 ¾) for all hours worked in excess of the normal work week of forty (40) hours for employees working on day or evening shifts, thirty four (34) hours for employees working on night shift and thirty (30) hours for employees working on the weekend shift and for all hours worked on a statutory holiday. Annual vacation, statutory holidays, union leaves, full days off taken as per article 5.18.2, exit passes up to a maximum of three (3) or a total of five (5) hours per four week period (AP), bereavement leaves, personal days and preparatory retirement course will be considered hours worked.

> Except for overtime worked directly before and after the shift, priority for overtime will go to employees on their day off (unscheduled day) from the department on the shift where the overtime occurs, who have accumulated the least overtime hours and are able to perform the work required.

Firms often seek to minimize what might be called *compounding*, or **pyramiding**, of payments. For example, many agreements would not allow a person to get 1.5 times their base pay and 1.5 times their shift premium when calculating overtime. Take a look at how Gray Line (2010), in Article G15 (Overtime), included language to avoid pyramiding:

pyramiding
compounding of premiums or benefits

> G15.04 There shall be no compounding of overtime payments or any other premium payments.

HOLIDAYS

As is the case with overtime, minimum requirements for paid holidays are provided in employment/labour standards legislation, and unionized workplaces often exceed these minimums. You will often find that language in this area will present the days considered to be holidays (often called "plant holidays" in manufacturing) as well as how employees who work these holidays will be paid. Let's look at a section of Section 14 (Statutory and Designated Holidays) of the Toronto Transit Commission (TTC) 2011 collective agreement. Given that some workers will have to work on certain holidays to keep the buses and subways operating, note how the end of this excerpt discusses how some holidays will be observed if they fall on Sunday.

> Statutory and designated holidays for employees covered by this Agreement shall be the day of each eligible employee's birthday, one floater holiday, and the days on which the following holidays are observed by the Commission: New Year's Day, Family Day, Good Friday, Victoria Day, Canada Day, Simcoe Day, Labour Day, Thanksgiving Day, Christmas Day, Boxing Day, and any other special holiday observed by the Commission. Student employees are not eligible for the Birthday/ Floater Holidays.

> If the appropriate governmental authority provides an additional paid statutory holiday during the term of this Agreement for the employees covered by this Agreement and the legislation compels the observance of this holiday over and

above the agreed number of statutory and designated holidays, the Statutory and Designated Holidays Section of Article 1 will be amended to provide such holiday.

For uniformed employees and Divisional Clerks, when Christmas Day falls on a Sunday and is observed on Monday, December 26th, Boxing Day will be observed on Tuesday, December 27th. In such cases, uniformed employees and Divisional Clerks, who are assigned to work on Sunday, December 25th, shall be paid one and one-half times the basic rate for each hour actually worked and they shall be given first consideration, for the following Christmas Day, when determining eligibility with respect to being released from work for the Statutory holiday.

When Boxing Day falls on a Sunday, the Commission will observe the holiday on Monday, December 27th. When Christmas Day falls on a Sunday and is observed on Monday, December 26th, Boxing Day will be observed on Tuesday, December 27th.

VACATION LEAVE

Collective agreement language concerning vacations often states how vacation is calculated, the amount of vacation time an employee receives, and when an employee is eligible for vacation. Such language may even state the order in which employees get to choose vacation and how it will be paid. Let's look at a section of Article 32 (Vacation) of the General Motors (2013) collective agreement. Note again how a table is included in the collective agreement for ease of interpretation:

A team member's entitlement to vacation with pay in any vacation year will be dependent upon the team member's seniority as of July 1 of that year and the number of hours which have been paid to each team member in the preceding vacation year.

For team members who have worked one thousand (1,000) hours or more in the preceding vacation year, earned hours of vacation will be in accordance with the following schedule:

SENIORITY AS OF JULY 1	TOTAL VACATION ENTITLEMENT	MAX. HOURS OF VACATION HOLD BACK
One (1) but less than two (2) years	80	24
Two (2) but less than three (3) years	88	24
Three (3) but less than five (5) years	140	24
Five (5) years but less than ten (10) years	160	24
Ten (10) years but less than fifteen (15) years	180	24
Fifteen (15) years but less than twenty (20) years	200	24
Twenty (20) or more years	240	24

For each fifty (50) hours or part thereof by which a team member fails to work the specified qualifying hours, hours of vacation with pay entitlement will be reduced by five (5%) per cent. Vacation with pay will be the team member's applicable base rate and COLA.

TERMINATION, LAYOFF, AND DISCIPLINE

One of the biggest differences between employment under common law and collective bargaining law is management's restricted ability to terminate employees. Thus, collective agreements will often contain language concerning probationary employees, just cause–based discipline and termination, layoff provisions (including recall), and progressive discipline steps, which normally take place prior to discharge. Examples of each follow.

PROBATIONARY EMPLOYEES Language in this area usually highlights the length of the probationary period as well as the fact that the employee can be terminated (without just cause) during the probationary period. This language is important to both the union and management as at the end of the probationary period, an employee can only be terminated with just cause. As one would imagine, employers often seek longer probationary periods while the union would desire shorter ones. While there is no consistent probationary period across all collective agreements, six months' probation is not unusual. The following example is from the Sunwing Airlines collective agreement (Article 19.1: Cabin Crew Probation, 2012):

19.1.1 A Cabin Crew Member will be required to serve a Company probationary period of one hundred and eighty (180) cumulative days of active service which will commence on his first scheduled flight after his line indoctrination flight.

19.1.2 The Company reserves the sole right to dismiss a Cabin Crew Member during this probationary period for any reason satisfactory to the Company.

19.1.3 A Cabin Crew Member dismissed during his probationary period, other than dismissal for cause, shall only be entitled to the minimum notice as required under the Canada Labour Code.

JUST CAUSE Many collective agreements include clauses which state that employers cannot discipline or discharge an employee without just cause. For example, the College of New Caledonia (2010) agreement (Article 15–Dismissal, Suspension and Discipline) states:

15.01 No employee shall be disciplined, suspended or dismissed except for just cause. Demonstration of just cause is the responsibility of the College.

LAYOFF Layoff language (sometimes called workforce adjustment language) often discusses issues such as the process to be used for a layoff and the notice period provided to the employees and the union. Such language often makes reference to seniority, as seniority is a key factor in collective agreements. Generally speaking, unions will seek to protect senior workers from layoff, while management will seek to ensure they can efficiently run the organization with qualified staff. This usually means that employers seek language stating that any employees remaining after the layoff must have the skills needed to effectively perform their jobs. Take a look at the role of seniority versus efficiency in the layoff language from sections of the Ontario Hospital Association's (2014) agreement with the Ontario Nurses' Association.

10.09 Layoff–Process and Options

(a) *In the event of a layoff, nurses shall be laid off in the reverse order of seniority provided that the nurses who are entitled to remain on the basis of seniority are qualified to perform the available work. Subject to the foregoing, probationary nurses shall be first laid off.*

[....]

(b) *iii. A nurse who has been notified of a long-term layoff may*

(A) *accept the layoff; or*

(B) *opt to retire if eligible under the terms of the Hospital's pension plan as outlined in Article 17.04; or*

(C) *elect to transfer to a vacant position provided that she or he is qualified to perform the available work; or*

(D) *displace another nurse in any classification who has lesser bargaining unit seniority and who is the least senior nurse on a unit or area whose work the nurse subject to layoff is qualified to perform.*

DISCIPLINE Most collective agreements present discipline language related to the concept of **corrective action**. These clauses often present forms of discipline, grounds for discipline, the progression of discipline (e.g., verbal warning to discharge), how discipline is to be administered, what records will be kept, where these records will be kept, and how long they will be kept, as well as who will be involved in the discipline process (i.e., level of union and managerial representation). Given that the union is the advocate for the employee, the norm is for such language to state that any employee being disciplined is entitled to union representation. The following sections from Article 8 (Progressive Discipline, Suspension and Dismissal) of the agreement for Thompson Rivers University faculty (2012) present an example of discipline language.

> **corrective action**
> a warning process designed to improve employee performance or behaviour

8.1 Right to Have Steward Present

An employee shall have the right to have his/her steward present at any discussion with supervisory personnel that the employee believes might be the basis of disciplinary action. Where a supervisor intends to interview an employee for disciplinary purposes, the supervisor shall notify the employee and the Union of the purpose of the interview in order that the employee may contact his/ her steward, providing that this does not result in an undue delay of the appropriate action being taken. This clause shall not apply to those discussions that are of an operational nature and do not involve disciplinary action.

8.2   Progressive Discipline

8.2.1 Progressive discipline steps shall be initiated for inappropriate conduct as warranted. Such discipline would normally begin with verbal warning(s), then progress to a written warning, then progress to suspension (if applicable) and finally to dismissal, as the situation may warrant.

In addition, collective agreements may have special language for discipline for specified infractions. Given the health and safety issues associated with operating a vehicle and cell phones, some agreements have language concerning cell phone usage. As one example, take a look at IR Today 8.2.

IR TODAY 8.2

COLLECTIVE AGREEMENT LANGUAGE CONCERNING CELL PHONES

Smartphones are such a normal part of our lives that we rarely leave home without them. Yet, as we know from public awareness campaigns and legislation, these devices can distract people—especially when operating motorized vehicles or machinery. Increasingly, we are seeing collective agreement language that outlines the restrictions on cell phone usage as well as disciplinary action that may result from improper usage of these devices. As one example, see the following Article from the collective agreement for the Association of Commercial and Industrial Contractors of Prince Edward Island (2011).

ARTICLE 11—CELL PHONE

11.01 Uses of cell phones/blackberries/smart-phones/i-pods/walkmans/etc, shall not be permitted by employees on site during working hours, except as explicitly authorized by the employer. Violations of this article shall be subject to the following disciplinary action.

(1) Warn the employee in writing of the offence, copy of letter mailed to the Union office.

(2) Any further offence calls for a possible suspension, the length of the suspension to be at management's discretion, but not to exceed three (3) days.

(3) Repetition of offence after suspension, employee is to be dismissed.

This article shall not apply to stewards or foremen using cell phones in the course of their duties.

// SPECIAL ISSUES IN COLLECTIVE AGREEMENTS

In addition to the types of clauses shown above, there are a few special types of clauses and language that can found in collective agreements concerning bumping, super seniority, and the importance of language.

BUMPING

> **bumping**
> a process whereby senior employees pass on their layoff to more junior employees

Given the importance of seniority in collective agreements, there are often clauses that protect senior employees from being let go in a downsizing; this is known as **bumping**. Bumping is a process whereby a union member with greater seniority who is about to be laid off is allowed to use his or her seniority rights to remove (or bump) a more junior union member (who otherwise would not have been affected by the layoff) from a job (Stringer & Brown, 2008). In essence, he or she "bumps" his or her layoff notice to the more junior employee. Unions prefer such a bumping clause as it provides additional protection to more senior employees. These clauses can be very complicated as they set out to define the conditions under which bumping can occur. One example of bumping language from Xstrata Nickel (2013) follows. As you can see, a single layoff can result in numerous employees being affected through a bumping process as the layoff notice is bumped from employee to employee.

17.02 LAYOFF IN EXCESS OF 14 DAYS

In all cases of reduction in the workforce of duration in excess of 14 days, including those of an emergency nature, other than as provided in section 17.05 (Vacation Shutdown) employees affected will have the opportunity to be relocated in the order of their seniority ranking in accordance with the following placement and bumping sequence:

a) Production Occupations

I. Placement into Vacancy within his Occupation in his Department

II. Placement into Vacancy within his Occupation in his Business Unit

III. Bump within his Occupation in his Department

IV. Bump within his Occupation in his Business Unit

V. Placement into Vacancy within his job class in his Department

VI. Placement into Vacancy within his job class in his Business Unit

VII. Bump within his job class in his Department

VIII. Bump within his job class in his Business Unit

IX. Placement into Vacancy in the next lower job class in his Department

X. Placement into Vacancy in the next lower job class in his Business Unit

XI. Bump in the next lower job class in his Department

XII. Bump in the next lower job class in his Business Unit

Where the surplus employee in the highest Job Class with the most seniority is to bump the junior employee, where possible, in his Department or in his Business Unit in the next lower Job Class in an occupation which has been redesigned by the company, such senior employee will be allowed to exercise his seniority provided he can perform the duties of one of the former occupations which now comprise the redesigned job. If the Business Unit requires such senior employee to perform the duties of more than one of the former occupations in the redesigned job, the Business Unit shall provide the senior employee with such reasonable training as will enable the employee to meet the requirements of operations.

SUPER SENIORITY

Union leaders are often given special protection from layoffs. Possible reasons for this are: (1) an unscrupulous manager might declare a layoff to get rid of a challenging, but junior union rep; (2) union reps are needed to be present to represent employees' rights until the very end in the event of a massive layoff or business closing; or (3) to encourage people to take on union leadership roles.

The following clause from Article 8.08 (Layoff) from the Coca-Cola (2011) collective agreement is an example of a **super seniority** clause:

> (f) *Notwithstanding their seniority, the Union's Stewards, President and Financial Secretary, all of whom must be regular full-time employees shall, when layoffs occur, retain their shift status if possible, or otherwise retain a job that they are willing and qualified to perform. At any rate, no more than one (1) regular Steward shall be retrained per shift due to such super seniority.*

> **super seniority**
> the status of union representatives who, while in office, have highest seniority in the bargaining unit

THE SUBTLETIES OF LANGUAGE

As you read through this chapter, you will have noticed that collective agreement language can often be very cumbersome to read. However, in negotiations, both parties make serious efforts to ensure that the language is specific and clear, and that it meets their needs. They may even consult past arbitration rulings in works such as Brown and Beatty (2006) to help them decide on the language they use. In particular, pay special attention to words such as *will*, *shall*, and *must*, all of which provide no flexibility to either party–they are bound to follow the language. Words such as *will usually*, *will normally*, and *may*, on the other hand, imply a level of flexibility or discretion. You will also see parties add phrases or sentences to qualify previous statements. Some agreements even explicitly highlight the differences of these terms. For example, in clause 3.01(p), the Yukon College (2013) collective agreement clearly defines and differentiates the words *may*, *shall*, *will*, and *should* by stating:

> (p) *"May" shall be regarded as permissive, "Shall" and "Will" as imperative, and "Should" as informative only;*

IR NOTEBOOK   8.2

COMPLEXITY OF COLLECTIVE AGREEMENT LANGUAGE

Employees, managers, and union representatives regularly refer to collective agreements for guidance concerning workplace rules and practices; however, the language in them is often very complex. In fact, one study of thirty collective agreements suggests that many collective agreement clauses had the same reading difficulty as legal journals such as *Osgoode Hall Law Review* and the *Ottawa Law Journal* (Elliott, 1990, rev. 1998). The following represents suggestions by Elliott for ways to improve clarity in collective agreements:

- Break long text sections into short sentences.
- Divide long sections of text into paragraphs.

- Use clear headings.
- Minimize wording by using a single word (e.g., *if*) rather than a phrase (e.g., *in the unlikely event that*).
- Remove cumbersome language such as *aforementioned*, *hereinbefore*, *aforesaid*, etc.

Table 8.2 provides some of Elliott's examples to show how clauses can be rewritten to improve clarity. Notice how much easier it is to understand the clauses on the right.

Source: Elliot, D. (1990, revised 1998). Writing Collective Agreements in Plain Language. Paper was first presented to the 8th Annual Labour Arbitration Conference in 1990. Used with permission. Retrieved from http://www.davidelliott.ca/papers/5b3.htm.

TABLE 8.2

WRITING FOR CLARITY

THE ORIGINAL	THE REVISED VERSION
The time limits expressed in the foregoing shall be exclusive of Saturdays, Sundays and statutory holidays, and normal time off.	Saturdays, Sundays, statutory holidays, and normal time off are not counted when calculating time limits in this article.
All settlements arrived at shall be final and binding upon the Company and the Union and the employee or group of employees concerned.	Settlements are final and binding on the Company, the Union, and employees concerned.

Source: Elliot, D. (1990, revised 1998). Writing Collective Agreements in Plain Language. Paper was first presented to the 8th Annual Labour Arbitration Conference in 1990. Used with permission. Retrieved from http://www.davidelliott.ca/papers/5b3.htm.

// SUMMARY

A key difference between unionized and nonunionized workplaces is the presence of a collective agreement that governs much of the employment relationship. After reading this chapter, you should understand the role of the collective agreement in unionized workplaces, know the typical layout of a collective agreement, be familiar with the common types of clauses that are found in collective agreements, and understand the importance and meaning of special collective agreement language and terms.

As shown in this chapter, the role of the collective agreement is largely to define workplace practices and procedures as they relate to the parties of the employment relationship; namely, employees, their union, and management. Thus, we saw that collective agreements often contain language related to five groupings: (1) the rights of parties; (2) the organization of work; (3) labour relations processes; (4) education, training, and development; and (5) working conditions. While the types of clauses, and in some cases even the language used, may be similar, we must remember that every collective agreement is unique to the relationship at hand and that the specific clauses found in each were crafted to meet the needs of the two actors involved (management and labour).

The text examples also highlight the importance of language. Parties can negotiate language that provides flexibility or language that is "airtight." Regardless of the specific language chosen, it is fair to say that agreements have become increasingly legal in nature. While the original intent of collective agreements may have been to provide the actors of the IR system with plain, simple language to aid them in their daily work, the reverse is now true. The language is often very complex. Only time will tell if we will see a movement away from legalist language and back toward "everyday" wording.

KEY TERMS

article 234
bumping 252
clause 234
corrective action 251
explicit reference 237
legislative reference 237
letter of understanding 234
multi-skill training 246
pyramiding 248
red-circling 240
residual rights 237
super seniority 254

WEBLINKS

YouTube postings from unions:

Concordia Part-Time Faculty Association:
http://www.youtube.com/watch?v=jYXDA37yrKY

IATSE for Visual Effects Artists (VFX):
http://www.youtube.com/watch?v=rPq2rcJa1yw

Negotech:
http://negotech.labour.gc.ca/

DISCUSSION QUESTIONS

1. Seniority is a key issue for unions; thus, seniority is a key factor in many articles of a collective agreement. At the same time, unions are trying to increase their youth membership. How do you suggest that unions balance these competing needs in terms of their collective agreement language?

2. As shown in this chapter, collective agreements are often complex written documents. As a result, they are often difficult for employees to understand and/or navigate when seeking answers to their workplace questions. What would you suggest that the parties can do to improve the user-friendliness of agreements?

3. We have often heard two sayings in IR circles: (1) once language has been placed in a collective agreement it is almost impossible to remove it; and (2) you can place a manager's name next to each clause of a collective agreement (e.g., that manager's actions resulted in the need for the clause). To what extent do you feel these sayings are true?

4. The demographics of the Canadian labour force are changing. For example, we see increased ethnic and visible diversity; increased focus on attracting youth given the aging workforce; and the ability of employees to remain at work beyond the typical retirement age of 65. Given these demographic changes, do you feel we will see changes in the types of clauses contained in collective agreements or even in their format? Explain.

5. Collective agreements are often produced in paper format. Do you feel that we will see a movement toward electronic versions of such agreements? Why or why not?

USING THE INTERNET

Many of the collective agreement clauses used as examples in this text were gathered using Negotech (see http://negotech.labour.gc.ca or just google the word "Negotech"). This database is an excellent way for labour and business leaders to examine the contract language of other workplaces when they are setting out to negotiate their own collective agreements. Go to the Negotech site and conduct searches on any of the following keyword sets; feel free to restrict the sample to your province or a particular industry:

- overtime assignment
- job sharing (*or* flexible work patterns)
- job posting
- layoff (*or* workforce adjustment)
- promotion

1. Examine the specific language in five or so different collective agreements. In particular, pay attention to the extent to which they provide flexibility to management or provide protection to employees.
2. Of the clauses you found, which would you prefer if you were a union representative? Why?
3. Which of the clauses would you prefer as a management representative? Why?

EXERCISES

1. As you might imagine, employers often seek to maximize their flexibility and discretion, whereas unions often try to minimize it fearing that it could lead to management favouritism. The following two clauses are from two different police collective agreements. Read both and pay particular attention to the role of seniority in layoffs.

CLAUSE 1: VICTORIA POLICE

14.02 Layoff Order

(i) Regular employees shall be laid off on the basis of classification and department designated for the layoff by the Employer, with the senior employee(s) being retained in that classification and section, provided always that they have the required qualifications, experience, skill and ability to perform the work in question.

All determinations of qualifications, experience, skill and ability shall be made by the Employer in a fair and equitable fashion. (From the Victoria Police Board collective agreement, Article 14 [Layoffs, Recall and Bumping], 2011)

CLAUSE 2: YORK POLICE

31.1 Where the Board has made a decision to reduce the complement of the York Regional Police and such reduction in personnel cannot be accommodated through attrition and where such action is not in contravention of the Police Services Act, layoffs of members shall be in reverse order of seniority with the York Regional Police, and recall of members shall be in order of seniority with the York Regional Police. Members shall retain seniority rights for recall purposes for a period of eighteen (18) months.

Prior to a full-time member being laid off, all part-time, temporary members or summer students shall be laid off, provided that the full-time member who will replace them has the requisite skill and ability to perform the job in question. (From Article 31.1 [Lay-Off Protection] of the Regional Municipality of York Police Services Board collective agreement, 2010)

(a) Does the York or Victoria language give the most flexibility to management in the event of layoff?

(b) Which, in your opinion, gives the most protection to senior employees?

(c) As a management negotiator, would you prefer the York or the Victoria language? Why?

(d) As a union negotiator, would you prefer the York or the Victoria language? Why?

2. Collective agreements are often readily available in university libraries and on websites. Such agreements can also be easily found in most unionized workplaces. Find a collective agreement or two and answer the following questions:

(a) Some people say that you can sense the tone of the relationship between the parties on the basis of the first few articles of a collective agreement. Is this the case with your agreement? If so, what is the tone?

(b) Look at the wording of issues such as layoffs and promotions. Does it provide much flexibility to the parties? Is the language about these issues clear? Can you apply elements of IR Notebook 8.2 to improve the language?

3. The media often discuss issues of labour unrest and contract negotiations. Find one or two examples from a news media outlet (newspaper, TV, website, etc.).

(a) What are the main issues at hand?

(b) What type of language do you think management would aim to craft in the agreement?

(c) What type of language do you think the union seeks?

4. One could argue that a university calendar is like a collective agreement in that it governs the student's relationship with the university. Take a look at the section concerning your degree program.

(a) Is the language flexible in nature or very specific?

(b) Is the language easy to understand?

(c) Can you apply any of the suggestions from IR Notebook 8.2 to improve the clarity of the language?

5. Many employees do not understand the cost of shutting down a workplace for a day. As such, some employers, like the TTC example in this chapter, are moving to floating holidays (or one's birthday) rather than a single holiday day that all

employees take at one time. Let's look at one fictitious example. In collective bargaining, the union seeks an additional plantwide holiday. Thus, all 500 manufacturing employees would be off on the same day. Now let's assume that the company seeks to run the production line on that newly proposed holiday, meaning that 250 employees will need to work an 8-hour shift on that day. The average rate of pay is $20 per hour; employees receive double time if they work a plant holiday. Management counters with the proposal that each employee will get one additional holiday, to be taken on his/her birthday.

(a) What is the cost of having the 250 employees work the newly proposed holiday?

(b) What are the operational implications of management's proposal versus that of the union?

(c) Why will the union seek the fixed holiday available to all employees while management will seek the birthday holiday?

6. There has been a recent trend toward the use of signing bonuses in multi-year agreements. These signing bonuses are one-time payments that are not added to an employee's base salary. As one example, the recent collective agreement for the transit drivers in Halifax consisted of a $1,500 signing bonus in year 1 and 2.25 percent a year for the next four years (Jeffrey, 2012). Let's assume that 800 employees are covered by this agreement, the average annual salary is $65,000 per employee, and the current total payroll is $52 million (800 employees at $65,000 per year).

(a) Calculate the transit service's annual total payroll cost at the end of the newly negotiated, five-year collective agreement.

(b) Assume that the agreement was a $1,500 addition to base pay in year 1, and then 2.25 percent for the next four years. Calculate the transit service's annual total payroll cost at the end of the five-year agreement.

(c) Given the results of your calculations, which option would the union prefer? Why?

(d) Given the results of your calculations, which option would management prefer? Why?

CASE   MINE RESTRUCTURING

Operations at Wabush Mines are ceasing immediately, parent company Cliffs Resources said Tuesday.

The news came during meetings with union officials in the afternoon, and was followed up with formal letters to all workers employed at the Scully mine.

An estimated 400 people work at the mine and concentrator in Wabush. A small number of staff and supervisors will stay on until mid-February to oversee the safety and technical side of slowing and eventually stopping operations at the mine.

Cliffs said the mine will be "idled," which refers to the process of not entirely turning off all power, should they or another company wish to restart operations in the future.

The decision is a major blow for the western Labrador region, and follows a similar move in March 2013 when Cliffs idled its Pointe Noire iron ore pellet plant in Sept-Iles, Que. The company blamed that decision on high production costs and lower pellet premium pricing "which is expected to persist in certain markets during the year."

At the time, Cliffs said it would move to producing iron ore concentrate only from its Wabush Scully mine.

But in a statement released later Tuesday, the company said costs at Wabush had become "unsustainably high."

"It is not economically viable to continue running this operation," said Cliffs president and chief operating officer Gary Halverson.

"Over the past three years we have seen pricing drop and Wabush Mine's costs escalate, all while we have made significant capital investments into the operation.

"This is a regrettable but necessary decision. We simply cannot continue operating a high-cost mine while pricing and freight markets are so volatile. We do value the hard work of all our employees and are committed to easing the transition for the people and communities, including providing severance and other support services as a result of this decision."

Cliffs said it expects to spend about $100 million idling the Scully mine, considered the third largest iron ore mine in Canada.

Source: "Wabush Mines shutting down: Almost 400 workers affected by closure/idling of Scully Mine." (11 February 2014). CBC News. Used with permission of CBC Licensing. Retrieved from http://www.cbc.ca/news/canada/newfoundland-labrador/wabush-mines-shutting-down-1.2532744.

QUESTIONS

1. Assume that you are either the union representative or the human resources/labour relations manager for Wabush Mines. What areas of the collective agreement would be relevant for you to review as the plant becomes idle? (*Hint:* Look at IR Notebook 8.1 or the various clauses in the text of this chapter.)

2. Assume that you are the human resources/labour relations manager for a northern iron ore mine not affected by the recent announcement and that you are about to enter negotiations. What would be your priorities for collective agreement language changes?

3. Assume that you are the union representative of a northern iron ore mine not affected by the recent announcement and that you are about to enter negotiations. What would be your priorities for collective agreement language changes?

// ENDNOTES

1. The opening vignette is fictional and was created by the authors. It is not based on a real company or situation.

2. Note that all clauses were retrieved from the Negotech website rather than from hard copies. Consequently, their appearance may differ from that of the hard copy. Also note that, in some places formatting such as spacing, bullets, capitalization, etc., were adjusted to improve the readability of the clauses. In no case was the actual wording altered.

// REFERENCES

1. Association of Commercial and Industrial Contractors of Prince Edward Island, Construction and General Labourers & General Workers in Construction, Industrial and Commercial. (2011). *Collective Agreement*. Retrieved 29 July 2014 from http://negotech.labour.gc.ca/eng/agreements/02/0249911a.pdf

2. Bombardier Transportation & Canadian Office and Professional Employees Union. (2011). *Collective Agreement*. Retrieved 23 July 2014 from http://negotech.labour.gc.ca/eng/agreements/02/0203310a.pdf

3. Brown, D., & Beatty, D. (2006). *Canadian labour arbitration* (4th edition). Aurora, ON: Canada Law Book.

4. Canfor Pulp Limited Partnership & Pulp, Paper and Woodworkers of Canada. (2012). *Collective Agreement*. Retrieved 27 July 2014 from http://negotech.labour.gc.ca/eng/agreements/01/0116410a.pdf

5. City of Winnipeg & Winnipeg Police Association. (2010). *Collective Agreement*. Retrieved 27 July 2014 from http://negotech.labour.gc.ca/eng/agreements/07/0721913a.pdf

6. Coca-Cola Refreshments Canada Company & National Automobile, Aerospace, Transportation and General Workers Union of Canada (CAW Canada). Local 126. (2011). *Collective Agreement*. Retrieved 30 July 2014 from http://negotech.labour.gc.ca/eng/agreements/14/1417801a.pdf

7. College of New Caledonia & Canadian Union of Public Employees, Local 4951. (2010). *Collective Agreement*. Retrieved 30 July 2014 from http://negotech.labour.gc.ca/eng/agreements/11/1173406a.pdf

8. Elliott, D. (1990, rev. 1998). Writing collective agreements in plain language. Paper presented to the 8th Annual Labour Arbitration Conference in 1990. Retrieved 11 October 2006 from http://www.davidelliott.ca/papers/5b3.htm

9. General Motors of Canada Limited–Cami Assembly & Unifor, Local 88. (2013). Retrieved 29 July 2014 from http://negotech.labour.gc.ca/eng/agreements/08/0850109a.pdf

10. Gray Line of Victoria Ltd. & National Automobile, Aerospace Transportation and General Workers Union of Canada (2010). *Collective Agreement*. Retrieved 29 July 2014 from http://negotech.labour.gc.ca/eng/agreements/03/0373211a.pdf

11. Greater Moncton International Airport Authority & Public Service Alliance of Canada. (2011). *Collective Agreement*. http://negotech.labour.gc.ca/eng/agreements/12/1263104a.pdf

12. Greater Vancouver Hotel Employers' Association & Unite Here. (2010). *Collective Agreement*. Retrieved 23 July 2014 from http://negotech.labour.gc.ca/eng/agreements/06/0647109a.pdf

13. Human Resources and Social Development Canada. (18 March 2008). *Negotiated benefits and working conditions*. Retrieved 25 January 2011 from http://www.hrsdc.gc.ca/eng/lp/wid/07Provisions.shtml

14. Hydro One Inc. & The Society of Energy Professionals (2013). *Collective Agreement*. Retrieved 28 July 2014 from http://negotech.labour.gc.ca/eng/agreements/06/0647109a.pdf

15. Iqaluit Housing Authority & Nunavut Employees Union. (2011). *Collective Agreement*. Retrieved 29 July 2014 from http://negotech.labour.gc.ca/eng/agreements/08/0897309a.pdf

16. Ivaco Rolling Mills & United Steelworkers. (2012). *Collective Agreement*. Retrieved 23 July 2014 from http://negotheque.travail.gc.ca/fra/ententes/01/0175309c.pdf

17. Jazz Aviation LP & National Automobile, Aerospace, Transportation and General Workers Union of Canada. (2012). *Collective Agreement*. Retrieved 29 July 2014 from http://negotech.labour.gc.ca/eng/agreements/12/1272006a.pdf

18. Jeffrey, D. (11 March 2012). Transit union, city reach deal. *Herald News*. Retrieved 7 July 2014 from http://thechronicleherald.ca/metro/72299-transit-union-city-reach-deal

19. Nuna Contracting Ltd. & Construction Workers Union, Local 63. (2010). *Collective Agreement*. Retrieved 27 July 2014 from http://negotech.labour.gc.ca/eng/agreements/13/1378202a.pdf

20. Ontario Hospital Association & Ontario Nurses' Association. (2014). *Draft Collective Agreement*. Retrieved 30 July 2014 from http://negotech.labour.gc.ca/eng/agreements/09/0913310a.pdf

21. Ontario Power Generation & Power Workers' Union. (2012). *Collective Agreement*. Retrieved 23 July 2014 from http://negotech.labour.gc.ca/eng/agreements/14/1411502a.pdf

22. Regional Municipality of York Police Services Board & York Regional Police Senior Officers Association. (2010). *Collective Agreement*. Retrieved 30 July 2014 from http://negotech.labour.gc.ca/eng/agreements/08/0874211a.pdf

23. Rolls-Royce Canada & International Association of Machinists and Aerospace Workers. (2013). *Collective Agreement*. Retrieved 29 July 2014 from http://negotech.labour.gc.ca/eng/agreements/01/0189713a.pdf

24. Saskatchewan Liquor and Gaming Authority & Saskatchewan Government and General Employees' Union. (2013). *Collective Agreement*. Retrieved 23 July 2014 from http://negotech.labour.gc.ca/eng/agreements/04/0450011a.pdf

25. Stringer, K. G., & Brown, T. C. (2008). A special kind of downsizing: An assessment of union member reaction to bumping. *Relations industrielles Industrial Relations, 63*, pp. 648–670.

26. Sunwing Airlines Inc. & CUPE Airline Division, Local 4055. (2012). Retrieved 30 July 2014 from http://negotech.labour.gc.ca/eng/agreements/14/1435301a.pdf

27. The Montreal Gazette Group & Teamsters/Graphic Communications Conference. (2012). *Collective Agreement*. Retrieved 29 July 2014 from http://negotech.labour.gc.ca/eng/agreements/08/0847807a.pdf

28. The Victoria Police Board & Canadian Union of Public Employees, Local No. 50. (2011). *Collective Agreement*. Retrieved 30 July 2014 from http://negotech.labour.gc.ca/eng/agreements/13/1383902a.pdf

29. Thompson Rivers University & Thompson Rivers University Faculty Association. (2012). *Collective Agreement*. Retrieved 30 July 2014 from http://negotech.labour.gc.ca/eng/agreements/11/1169606a.pdf

30. Toronto Transit Commission & Amalgamated Transit Union, Local 113. (2011). *Collective Agreement*. Retrieved 29 July 2014 from http://negotech.labour.gc.ca/eng/agreements/03/0377011a.pdf

31. University of Alberta & University of Alberta Non-Academic Staff Association. (2012). *Collective Agreement*. Retrieved 23 July 2014 from http://negotech.labour.gc.ca/eng/agreements/12/1260507a.pdf

32. University of Lethbridge & Alberta Union of Provincial Employees (2011). Yukon Government and The Public Service Alliance of Canada. (2013). *Collective Agreement*. Retrieved 28 July 2014 from http://negotech.labour.gc.ca/eng/agreements/05/0533713a.pdf

33. Xstrata Nickel Subury Operations & Sudbury Mine, Mill and Smelter Workers Union Local 598 (CAW). (2013). *Collective Agreement*. Retrieved 30 July 2014 from http://negotech.labour.gc.ca/eng/agreements/00/0017810a.pdf

34. Yukon College & The Public Service Alliance of Canada. (2013). *Collective Agreement*. Retrieved 30 July 2014 from http://negotech.labour.gc.ca/eng/agreements/10/1007509a.pdf

35. Yukon Government & The Public Service Alliance of Canada. (2013). *Collective Agreement*. Retrieved 23 July 2014 from http://negotech.labour.gc.ca/eng/agreements/06/0675711a.pdf

CHAPTER

9

CONFLICT RESOLUTION: GRIEVANCES AND STRIKES

LEARNING OBJECTIVES

BY THE END OF THIS CHAPTER, YOU WILL BE ABLE TO DISCUSS

- the different types of industrial disputes;
- the steps that must be taken prior to a strike;
- the various statistics used to measure strikes;
- the theories, causes, and impacts of strikes;
- typical grievance procedure in unionized workplaces; and
- common types of nonunion grievance procedures and why they are used.

B.C. TEACHERS' STRIKE

On May 28, the British Columbia Teachers' Federation (BCTF) confirmed that rotating strikes would continue for at least one more week. All 41,000 teachers in every school in all 16 BC school districts would continue miss at least one day of teaching time next week.

This is all part of an ongoing labour dispute between BCTF and the BC government. The main areas of disagreement include wages and working conditions related to numbers of specialized teachers, class composition, and class size. The current government offer is a 7.25 percent wage increase over six years plus a signing bonus; the union is seeking a four-year deal and a 15.9 percent wage improvement.

The rotating strikes are just one phase in the dispute. In early March, almost 90 percent of teachers voted in favour of the union taking strike action. At that time, the union commented that they sought to negotiate a settlement and that any initial job action would not impact students. The union stated that job action would likely start with limiting communication between teachers and management, then move to rotating strikes, and finally conclude with a full strike.

In late April, the initial job action began. Specifically, teachers left students unsupervised during recess and lunch times. The next phase occurred in May, when the employer partially locked out all teachers. The negotiators for the BC government then cut pay for teachers who participated in any job action and locked out teachers. In essence, the lockout restricted teachers' work hours and duties. Teachers could not arrive (or leave) more than 45 minutes before (or beyond) instruction times; teachers could not work recess and lunch breaks.

The current events build on a conflict-ridden relationship. In the past ten years, the parties have managed to negotiate only a single collective agreement, with the other settlements often requiring back-to-work legislation. While closed-door negotiations between the parties will continue, the parties remain far apart at the moment. Not surprisingly, the media has speculated that back-to-work legislation could again be brought in to end the strike. However, Peter Fassbender (BC Education Minister) has stated that the earliest they could legislate an agreement would be the end of the BC Legislature's spring session. Until then, over 500,000 students across the province can expect to be missing some class time and parents will struggle to manage the schedule and childcare implications of rotating strikes.

Sources: Laanela, M., & Sheppard, M. (28 May 2014). "B.C. teachers' strike to continue next week: B.C. Teachers' Federation confirms 4 more days of strikes." CBC News. Retrieved from http://www.cbc.ca/news/canada/british-columbia/b-c-teachers-strike-to-continue-next-week-1.2656893; Sherlock, T., & Shaw, R. (26 May 2014). "B.C. braces for four days of rotating teacher strikes, and maybe more to come: If no progress is made in negotiations following this round of strikes, another could follow next Monday." *Vancouver Sun.* Retrieved from http://www.vancouversun.com/business/braces+four+days+rotating+teacher+strikes+maybe+more+come/9876170/story.html; Tahirali, J. (25 May 2014). "Dispute between B.C. teachers, province leads to rotating strikes." CTVNews. Retrieved from http://www.ctvnews.ca/canada/dispute-between-b-c-teachers-province-leads-to-rotating-strikes-1.1837923#ixzz337H3FGIL; Talmazanm, Y. (8 March 2014). "UPDATE: B.C. teachers vote in favour of strike action, bring offer to negotiation table." Global News. Retrieved from http://globalnews.ca/news/1191102/results-of-b-c-teachers-strike-vote-released-today/.

As we have seen in several instances in this text, strikes are one mechanism that parties can use to resolve conflict and achieve their bargaining goals. Thus, they are a conversion mechanism in the IR system. In this chapter, we will focus primarily on two of the conversion mechanisms that can be used by the management and labour actors of the IR system to resolve conflict: namely, strikes and grievances. Third-party dispute resolution procedures such as arbitrations and alternative dispute resolution will be presented in detail in Chapter 10.

Over the past few years, many students have witnessed faculty strikes, or near strikes, at their campuses—a few examples are Mount Allison (CTV News, 2014); UNB (CBC News, 2014); the University of Manitoba (Bender, 2013); and the University of Windsor (Wildeman, 2014). Strikes often cause student reactions, including YouTube postings. Given the importance of strikes in the IR system, let's start this chapter with a review of strikes.

// STRIKES

As we have seen throughout this textbook, strikes and lockouts receive considerable media attention. In this section, we will define industrial disputes (one of which is strikes), review statistics concerning strike prevalence, and discuss some of the causes of strikes.

DEFINING INDUSTRIAL DISPUTES

In its simplest form, we can think of an industrial dispute as a disagreement between employers and employees. However, in industrial relations, **industrial dispute** has a more precise meaning. The *Canada Labour Code* (section 3(1), 1985) defines it as "a dispute arising in connection with the entering into, renewing, or revising of a collective agreement." Should the parties not be able to come to agreement (using any or all of the dispute resolution techniques we cover in this textbook), they may end up in a strike or lockout position.

In essence, the difference between a strike and a lockout depends on whether management or labour initiated the action.

industrial dispute
a disagreement arising from entering into, renewing, or revising a collective agreement

STRIKE

A **strike** occurs when a number of workers refuse to continue working or they stop working (*Canada Labour Code*, 1985). For example, in the opening vignette, the teachers had a rotating strike as they "walked off the job."

Note that the *Canada Labour Code* (section 3(1), 1985) also includes work slowdowns as a form of a strike when it states that a "strike includes a cessation of work or a refusal to work or to continue to work by employees … and a slowdown of work or other concerted activity … that is designed to restrict or limit output." This would mean that worker efforts to reduce productivity would also be considered a strike. These concerted slowdowns are often referred to as **work to rule**. In the opening vignette, the BCTF's decision to no longer supervise recess or lunch could be seen as an example of work to rule. There are also **wildcat strikes**, which occur when employees who are not in a legal strike position walk off the job. When these happen, employers will often go to court to seek a formal injunction that requires employees to return to work on the threat of legal penalties. Some strikes are restricted, meaning that there are a limited number (or type) of employees who can go on strike. These are often called **essential services agreements**. For example, there are often restrictions on the number of nurses who can go on strike at one time as hospitals must continue to operate for the public good. These essential services agreements will be discussed in more detail in Chapter 12 on public-sector industrial relations.

Naturally, students may wonder why a union would use work to rule or wildcat strikes versus just going on a traditional strike. As we discuss later in this chapter, certain steps must be followed before a legal strike and a legal strike can occur only when a collective agreement expires. Hence, if the union wishes to withdraw labour in response to an employer's actions during the term of the collective agreement, or when back-to-work legislation is used, their only recourse may be a wildcat strike or work to rule. As one example, Air Canada's ground workers took part in a 13-hour wildcat strike in March of 2012 (National Post Staff, 2012). The workers were subject to back-to-work legislation tabled by then Federal Minister of Labour Lisa Raitt. When Ms. Raitt arrived at Toronto's Pearson Airport, she was heckled by three ground workers. Air Canada disciplined the three workers. Tensions mounted, and 150 Toronto workers walked off the job in protest resulting in a wildcat strike. The strike then spread to other airports, including Montreal

strike
a work stoppage invoked by a union

work to rule
the strategy of employees who perform only to the minimum standard required

wildcat strike
an illegal strike during the term of the collective agreement

essential services agreement
used when some workers must remain on the job during a strike to provide key services

Air Canada employees, in uniform, protest in Calgary Airport.

Ted Rhodes, Calgary Herald

and Quebec. Over 100 flights were cancelled or delayed, thirty-seven employees were fired, and Ms. Raitt announced that fines of $1,000 per day per worker and $100,000 a day for the union could result if the strike continued. At the end of the wildcat strike, Air Canada agreed that no employees would be disciplined and that the thirty-seven fired employees would get their jobs back.

Work to rule can be used by the union as a way to strengthen their bargaining position and, technically, not be on strike. Rather, employees do arrive to their workplace to perform their jobs but tend to work to the exact duties of their job description. Again, a union may choose this strategy when they are not in a legal strike position, or when back-to-work legislation or essential service agreements make a traditional strike unlikely. Take, for example, the Newfoundland and Labrador Nurses' Union (NLNU) overtime strike (CBC News, 2009). Unlike a traditional strike, nurses reported to work for their normal shifts. However, they would not accept any overtime. Given that one health board paid 18,000 hours of overtime in a single month, this was a very powerful bargaining chip for the union. While the essential services agreement would require that about half of the 5,000 nurses remain at work during a traditional strike, there was no such provision for an overtime strike. The fact that parties settled about seven days after the overtime strike began suggests that the overtime strike may have been a very powerful intervention (Executive Council, 2009).

As both the Air Canada and NLNU examples show, work to rule and wildcat strikes may result due to restrictions on strikes. One could even speculate that we may see more of such actions as governments continue to place restrictions on strikes. Given the increased restrictions on strikes in the public sector we will pick up on this theme later in the text.

LOCKOUT

A **lockout** represents a work stoppage initiated by the employer. As shown by the *Canada Labour Code* (section 3(1), 1985), the definition of a lockout is broad and can include:

the closing of a place of employment, a suspension of work by an employer or a refusal by an employer to continue to employ a number of their employees, done to compel their employees, or to aid another employer to compel that other employer's employees, to agree to terms or conditions of employment.

In the opening vignette we see that the employer partially locked out teachers, restricting their access to the workplace. Sports fans have seen several lockouts. For example, there was a 136-day lockout in the National Football League (NFL) in 2011 (CNN, 2013). And avid hockey fans will recall the 113-day NHL lockout that occurred in the 2012–2013 season, the second following a similar lockout in 2004–2005 (Johnston, 2013).

We have also seen issues related to lockouts at universities. Over the summer of 2014, there were intense negotiations between the University of Windsor and the Windsor University Faculty Association (WUFA). In an open letter to WUFA members dated July 3, 2014, the president of the university stated the university was in a position where it could lock out faculty, and that if a deal were not reached by July 7 they would no longer honour many elements of the now-expired collective agreement (Wildeman, 2014). For example, the university would no longer pay some health insurance premiums, contribute to parts of the pension plan, deduct union dues, or engage in grievance and arbitration procedures. As the union acknowledged, Ontario law allows the employer to alter employment terms and conditions when they are in a legal lockout position; however, they often do not take such actions as doing so can have negative, long-term consequences on union–management relations (Forrest, 2014).

Faculty members picketing at the University of Windsor.

NICK BRANCACCIO/The Windsor Star

STRIKE STEPS

Before we discuss strike statistics, we need to discuss the mechanisms that have to occur for a legal strike in Canada. As we discussed in Chapter 4, provinces each have their own legislation so slight variations may exist from province to province. However, in essence, the following steps have to occur prior to a legal strike in Canada:

- A certified union must be in place—recall that only certified unions can legally go on strike in Canada.
- The current collective agreement must have expired—remember that strikes and lockouts cannot occur when a collective agreement is in place.
- The parties must fail to reach an agreement—note that Canadian legislation requires that the parties bargain in good faith and seek to negotiate a collective agreement.
- The union must have a **strike mandate**, which is normally gained by a positive **strike vote** (usually a secret ballot vote) from the membership. In

essence, the union will have members vote to support (or not support) strike action. If the majority of the membership supports the strike action, it is said that the union has a strike mandate. For example, in the opening vignette 90 percent of BC Teachers supported the union, giving the BCTF a strong mandate.

- Conciliation and other third-party dispute resolution procedures are needed. Canadian legislation requires conciliation prior to a strike. Then once the union has a strike mandate, it will still need to undergo conciliation and wait a period of time specified by legislation.
- The union must give notice of the strike.
- Only after all these steps can the union legally strike.

Note that the steps required for management to call a lockout are very similar. For an example of the steps for the province of Alberta, please see IR Today 9.1.

IR TODAY   9.1

REQUIREMENTS FOR A LEGAL STRIKE

According to the Alberta Labour Relations Board (2014a), the requirements for a union to go on strike include:

1. Any collective agreement between the union and the employer must be expired.
2. The parties must enter into collective bargaining.
3. The parties must work with a government-appointed mediator.
4. A 14-day cooling-off period must elapse following mediation.

5. A Labour Board-supervised strike vote (unions) or lockout poll (employers) must be taken and a majority of those voting must agree to the strike or lockout.
6. One party must serve the other (as well as the mediator) with 72 hours of notice before the strike or lockout commences.

Source: Alberta Labour Relations Board. (2014a). FAQ—strikes and lockouts. Retrieved from http://www.alrb.gov.ab.ca/faq_strikes.html.

STRIKE STATISTICS

Now that we understand what constitutes a strike, it is time to examine the statistics in this area. In particular, we will look at how strikes are tracked, as well as at regional and industry differences in tracking. As we examine this area, it is important to note that the statistics reported in this chapter include strikes and lockouts. Statistical agencies do not differentiate according to who initiated the work stoppage.

In Canada, Human Resources and Social Development Canada (HRSDC) compiles statistics on strikes and makes these data publicly available. In this chapter, we will largely focus on data from the last 30 years or so. Tables 9.1 to 9.3 and Figure 9.1 present data taken from the HRSDC site that show strike trends, for strikes involving 500 or more workers. Table 9.1 presents national data (Figure 9.1 shows these data as a graph); Table 9.2 presents data by industry; Table 9.3 presents strike statistics by region.[1,2,3,4]

TABLE 9.1

CANADIAN STRIKE STATISTICS FOR ALL INDUSTRIES, 1980–2014

YEAR	TOTAL STRIKES	WORKERS INVOLVED	PERSON-DAYS NOT WORKED	% OF ESTIMATED WORKING TIME
2014	2	1,130	10,130	NA
2013	15	193,064	884,730	0.02
2012	43	113,988	468,565	0.01
2011	14	80,243	996,527	0.03
2010	21	44,625	598,301	0.02
2009	19	55,178	1,402,520	0.04
2008	13	26,704	269,840	0.01
2007	27	49,172	1,243,190	0.03
2006	11	27,583	260,230	0.01
2005	41	179,482	3,645,060	0.10
2004	37	236,843	2,396,220	0.07
2003	26	56,730	1,076,560	0.03
2002	31	142,089	2,273,000	0.07
2001	44	189,240	1,296,960	0.04
2000	44	112,468	779,410	0.02
1999	55	126,822	1,408,430	0.04
1998	63	214,847	1,631,460	0.05
1997	32	237,246	2,855,740	0.09
1996	32	250,406	2,484,250	0.08
1995	39	125,531	993,430	0.03
1994	29	55,283	736,470	0.03
1993	25	73,757	498,680	0.02
1992	44	121,831	1,145,810	0.04
1991	36	218,377	1,452,400	0.05
1990	66	226,665	3,520,150	0.12
1989	67	394,351	2,177,040	0.08
1988	54	158,888	3,393,880	0.12
1987	63	530,720	2,406,350	0.09

TABLE 9.1

CANADIAN STRIKE STATISTICS FOR ALL INDUSTRIES, 1980–2014 (CONTINUED)

YEAR	TOTAL STRIKES	WORKERS INVOLVED	PERSON-DAYS NOT WORKED	% OF ESTIMATED WORKING TIME
1986	89	431,986	5,673,310	0.21
1985	56	100,107	1,348,850	0.05
1984	67	130,852	2,331,350	0.09
1983	61	279,818	2,881,950	0.12
1982	70	410,559	3,859,810	0.16
1981	99	240,452	6,169,150	0.24
1980	137	363,470	6,901,450	0.28

Source: Workplace Information and Research Division, Labour Program, Employment and Social Development Canada. (2014). *Work Stoppages in Canada involving 500 or more workers, 1987 to 2013* [Data File].

FIGURE 9.1

ESTIMATED LOST TIME DUE TO WORK DISPUTES FOR CANADA, 1980–2014

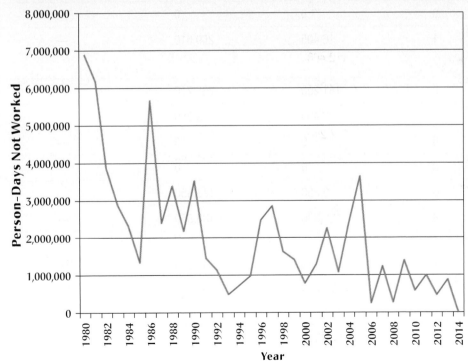

Source: Workplace Information and Research Division, Labour Program, Employment and Social Development Canada. (2014). *Work Stoppages in Canada involving 500 or more workers, 1987 to 2013* [Data File].

TABLE 9.2

CANADIAN STRIKE STATISTICS BY SELECTED INDUSTRIES, SELECTED YEARS 1990–2013

PERIOD	TOTAL NUMBER	WORKERS INVOLVED	PERSON-DAYS NOT WORKED	% OF ESTIMATED WORKING TIME[1]
PRIMARY INDUSTRIES				
2013	0	0	0	—
2010*	0	0	0	—
2005	4	3,273	140,260	—
2000	4	4,150	148,960	—
1995	1	985	6,890	—
1990	5	7,757	305,030	—
UTILITIES				
2013	0	0	0	—
2010*	0	0	0	—
2005	1	850	60,260	—
2000	0	0	0	—
1995	0	0	0	—
1990	1	16,405	259,610	—
CONSTRUCTION				
2013	9	181,200	768,710	—
2010*	2	1,450	9,380	—
2005	0	0	0	—
2000	0	0	0	—
1995	6	9,550	173,350	—
1990	8	122,300	1,136,950	—
MANUFACTURING				
2013	2	1,459	86,870	—
2010*	4	5,317	467,530	—
2005	4	4,550	154,230	—
2000	8	20,228	138,270	—
1995	13	14,327	366,470	—
1990	22	42,654	1,407,280	—

TABLE 9.2

CANADIAN STRIKE STATISTICS BY SELECTED INDUSTRIES, SELECTED YEARS 1990–2013 (CONTINUED)

PERIOD	TOTAL NUMBER	WORKERS INVOLVED	PERSON-DAYS NOT WORKED	% OF ESTIMATED WORKING TIME[1]
WHOLESALE AND RETAIL TRADE				
2013	1	8,744	26,230	—
2010*	0	0	0	—
2005	2	4,830	147,640	—
2000	2	7,815	16,080	—
1995	0	0	0	—
1990	1	609	30,380	—
INFORMATION AND CULTURE				
2013	0	0	0	—
2010*	0	0	0	—
2005	3	20,600	1,533,960	—
2000	3	3,330	36,740	—
1995	0	0	0	—
1990	0	0	0	—
FINANCE, REAL ESTATE, AND MANAGEMENT SERVICES				
2013	0	0	0	—
2010*	0	0	0	—
2005	1	1,100	41,640	—
2000	2	1,143	26,370	—
1995	1	580	1,740	—
1990	0	0	0	—
EDUCATION, HEALTH, AND SOCIAL SERVICES				
2014	2	1,130	10,130	—
2013	0	0	0	—
2010*	11	29,905	108,979	—
2005	19	101,427	934,040	—
2000	15	36,035	190,190	—
1995	7	36,265	87,810	—
1990	24	29,240	314,960	——

TABLE 9.2

PERIOD	TOTAL NUMBER	WORKERS INVOLVED	PERSON-DAYS NOT WORKED	% OF ESTIMATED WORKING TIME[1]
CANADIAN STRIKE STATISTICS BY SELECTED INDUSTRIES, SELECTED YEARS 1990–2013 (CONTINUED)				
ENTERTAINMENT AND HOSPITALITY				
2013	1	627	1,880	—
2010*	1	500	4,150	—
2005	1	1,071	15,000	—
2000	2	3,740	34,240	—
1995	2	2,919	70,090	—
1990	0	0	0	—
PUBLIC ADMINISTRATION				
2013	2	1,034	1,040	—
2010*	2	6,623	4,112	—
2005	5	40,831	605,500	—
2000	7	34,950	184,250	—
1995	3	25,900	65,500	—
1990	3	4,400	36,030	—

*Person-days not worked as a percentage of estimated working time is only available for "All Industries" and "Canada Total."

Source: Workplace Information and Research Division, Labour Program, Employment and Social Development Canada. (2014). *Work Stoppages in Canada involving 500 or more workers, 1987 to 2013* [Data File].

As these tables suggest, strike statistics can be calculated in a number of ways. You will note that HRSDC provides several measures of strikes:

- total number, or frequency, of strikes;
- number of workers involved in the strike;
  - person-days not worked (or the estimated number of days lost due to the strike calculated as number of workers multiplied by number of days on strike); and
- percentage of working time lost due to strike.

It is important to remember that a single statistic can be misleading. For example, as shown in Table 9.1, there were about the same number of strikes in 2008 (13 strikes) and 2011 (14 strikes), suggesting that strikes were relatively equivalent those years. However, the statistics in that table show that, relative to 2008, 2011 had more than double the number of workers involved, almost four times the person-days lost, and three times the working time lost. Thus, we would conclude that 2011 was a bigger year for strikes. As this comparison reveals, it is important to be aware of which statistic you are examining. For us, person-days not worked is the better of the statistics to use for

TABLE 9.3

STRIKE STATISTICS, SELECTED YEARS 1985–2013

YEAR	PERSON-DAYS NOT WORKED						
	1985	1990	1995	2000	2005	2010	2013
Newfoundland	35,320	100,020	0	13,950	9,960	0	0
P.E.I.	0	0	2,000	0	0	0	0
Nova Scotia	730	49,350	3,900	0	21,000	0	0
New Brunswick	3,600	211,200	0	13,920	105,600	0	0
Quebec	482,960	517,890	267,990	19,560	1,284,050	113,034	668,760
Ontario	561,280	2,374,390	270,500	345,350	182,180	440,907	187,320
Manitoba	0	0	19,820	2,090	0	7,500	0
Saskatchewan	25,090	15,510	0	0	31,370	0	0
Alberta	12,150	71,020	0	17,000	73,130	0	26,230
B.C.	24,740	120,970	213,770	287,350	498,840	0	2,420
Territories	0	0	0	0	0	0	0
Total federal	202,980	59,800	215,460	80,190	1,438,930	4,150	0

Source: Workplace Information and Research Division, Labour Program, Employment and Social Development Canada. (2014). *Work stoppages covering 500 or more workers by jurisdiction, Year, and Sector* [Data File].

comparison purposes. The overall economic impact of lost work days can be significant in terms of workers' losing take-home pay and firms' losing profits. "These two effects might reduce the productivity of both labour and capital, the two main components of economic productivity" (Dachis & Hebdon, 2010, p. 5).

NATIONAL STATISTICAL TRENDS

A review of Tables 9.1 through 9.3 and Figure 9.1 reveals a number of trends in terms of strikes over time, by industry, and by region. You will note that, historically, the general trend has been a reduction in lost time since 1980, with a sharp decrease after 1990. You will also note that certain industries (e.g., manufacturing, public administration) seem more strike-prone, particularly when we look at the number of workers involved and the person-days not worked relative to other industries (e.g., finance, real estate, management services). Similarly, we see that some regions of the country have low levels of strikes (e.g., Prince Edward Island, the territories) compared to others (e.g., Quebec, Ontario, and British Columbia). However, we need to be careful in interpreting these trends. For example, we would expect a large province such as Ontario and Quebec, which have high concentrations of manufacturing and public-sector jobs (heavily unionized industries that Table 9.2 shows are prone to strikes) to have higher strike rates than a relatively small province such as Prince Edward Island, which is known for its hospitality/tourism industry (an industry that Table 9.2 shows has fewer strikes).

INTERNATIONAL TRENDS

Given the increased focus on global markets and international competition, it is also important to examine Canada's strike rates relative to those of other countries. A report by Hale (2008) presents the strike statistics for the Organisation for Economic Co-operation and Development (OECD) countries. The report examines the number of working days lost per 1,000 employees in all sectors and services of the economy. That report suggests that Canada's average number of working days not worked (or lost) due to strike (per 1,000 employees) dropped by 6 percent between the two five-year periods of 1997–2001 and 2002–2006. However, with an average of 186 working days lost per 1,000 workers over 1997–2006, only Iceland had more lost time due to strikes, at 486 days. Moreover, Canada's strike rate was almost six times that of our largest trading partner, the United States (34 days).

As was the case with our review of the Canadian strike trends, we must be careful to ensure that we "compare apples to apples" when examining international strike data. In particular, the technical notes from Hale (2008) discuss the subtleties of how strikes are measured and tracked in one country versus another. Take a look at differences in the minimum criteria used by some countries for inclusion in strike statistics:

- Belgium has no size restrictions but excludes public-sector disputes.
- Denmark requires 100 workdays not worked.
- Finland statistics include all strikes of greater than one hour's duration.
- United States statistics include strikes of one day (or one shift) involving at least 1,000 employees.
- United Kingdom statistics include strikes of ten or more workers for a minimum of one day's duration, unless 1,000 workers were involved.

Table 9.4 and Figure 9.2 provide summary data on strikes from several countries. Consistent with the previous trend, you will note that Canada has a higher level of strikes relative to many of its comparators.

TABLE 9.4

STRIKE DATA FROM SELECTED COUNTRIES, SELECTED YEARS: DAYS NOT WORKED

COUNTRY	1990	1995	2000	2005	2012
Canada	8,599,340	2,576,500	2,436,200	4,147,580	904,027
Chile	245,192	350,124	114,306	99,931	1,871
Denmark	195,200	394,600	124,800	51,100	10,200
France	528,000	1,567,765	1,389,114	1,997,000	
Germany		247,460	10,776	18,633	86,051
Israel	1,071,300	515,596	2,011,263	244,236	462,960
Japan	144,511	76,971	35,050	5,629	3,839

TABLE 9.4

STRIKE DATA FROM SELECTED COUNTRIES, SELECTED YEARS: DAYS NOT WORKED (CONTINUED)

COUNTRY	1990	1995	2000	2005	2012
Korea, Republic of	4,487,200	785,162	1,893,563	847,697	933,267
Mexico	3,197,500	1,454,123	895,968	260,124	99,029
New Zealand	661,846	106,704	11,495	30,028	78,589
Norway	139,047	101,338	496,568	10,998	360,643
Poland	159,000	56,300	74,266	413	12,853
Spain	2,612,900	1,457,100	3,616,907	951,495	1,290,114
Sweden	770,356	627,291	272	568	37,072
Turkey	3,466,550	4,838,241	736,950	176,824	36,073
United Kingdom	1,903,000	415,000	498,800	223,801	249
United States	5,925,500	5,771,200	20,419,500	1,348,000	1,130,800

Source: ILOSTAT, International Labour Organization. (2014). Days not worked due to strikes and lockouts by economic activity [Data File]. Used with permission of International Labour Organization. Retrieved from http://www.ilo.org/ilostat.

FIGURE 9.2

INTERNATIONAL COMPARISON DAYS NOT WORKED, 2012

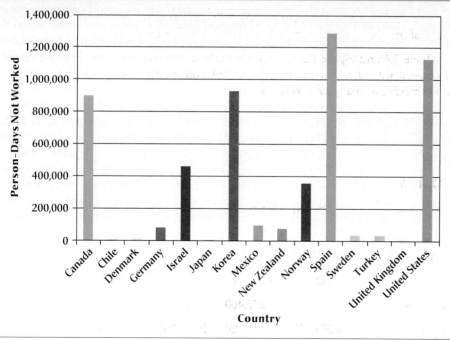

Source: ILOSTAT, International Labour Organization. (2014). Days not worked due to strikes and lockouts by economic activity [Data File]. Used with permission of International Labour Organization. Retrieved from http://www.ilo.org/ilostat.

// THEORIES, CAUSES, AND IMPACTS OF STRIKES

Having defined the various types of industrial disputes and examined the statistics and trends of strikes, it is time to turn to the theories, causes, and impacts of strikes.

STRIKE THEORIES

Kramer and Hyclak (2002) outline the three common theories of strikes, namely, the accident theory (i.e., the Hicks theory), total joint costs, and asymmetric information. While these researchers focused on unions striking, we assert that managers can also lock out employees for these same theoretical reasons.

ACCIDENT (OR HICKS) THEORY

The accident theory, often referred to as the Hicks theory, is grounded in the premise that strikes represent accidents. The assumption is that "rational" negotiators would seek to avoid strikes and lockouts in order to avoid their high costs (lost wages, lost productivity, etc.). Thus, the theory states that strikes should be unexpected and that when they do occur, they are the result of errors made at the bargaining table, misunderstandings of bargaining goals, or mismatches between the expectations of the bargaining team and the group they represent.

THE TOTAL JOINT COSTS THEORY

As stated previously, both the management team and the union membership face potential costs associated with a strike. In its simplest form, this theory argues that strikes are more likely when the cost of the strike is relatively low for both parties. Note that we must look at the total and joint costs to both the union and management groups to fully understand the model. If the cost of a strike is low to one party but high to another, a strike may not be likely given the clear power imbalance. In essence, the difference in the cost of the strike to one party, relative to the other, results in a difference in bargaining power (Maki, 1986). For example, the cost of snowplow operators going on strike in July may be high to the workers (e.g., lost wages) but low to the city, as there is little need for snow clearing in July. The power dynamic is such that the workers may settle because of the high cost to them. The city, however, may readily accept a strike since citizens would not be in need of snow-clearing services at that time. Not surprisingly, then, snowplow operators often choose winter months for strike action when they have the most power and a city would not want to take a strike. For example, in Ontario's Grey County the parties settled in late November, with one reporter stating (Fell, 2013), "With winter fully underway, Grey County has avoided a possible strike by operators of their snowplows."

In contrast, if a company created a great deal of inventory anticipating a strike, and workers were paid overtime to create the inventory, the costs of the strike would be relatively low to both parties. The firm could continue to receive revenue in selling the product in inventory, and workers could use savings from their overtime pay to compensate for the loss in earnings. In essence, the total joint costs theory predicts that parties go on strike only when the cost of the strike is low or, in contrast, when the cost of settling is high in comparison to the cost of striking.

ASYMMETRIC INFORMATION THEORY

Remember that during collective bargaining, parties may not candidly share goals and priorities. In fact, they might use deceptive tactics to shade the truth about their true priorities. The asymmetric information theory is grounded in the assumption that parties may strike or lockout as a way to see if the other side is bluffing. In so doing, the parties gather more information about the claims of the other party—information that would not be easily accessible in other ways. As a concrete example, we can look at strikes in professional sports. One analysis of pro sport strikes in hockey, basketball, baseball, and football found that many disputes were long and centred on issues concerning player salaries (Fisher, 2007). In many of these cases, the employer argued that players' salaries would negatively impact the long-term viability of the teams and the sport. We might surmise that the unions representing these players went on strike in an effort to see whether management was bluffing about the effect of the union's desired pay levels on team viability. The longer the employer accepted the strike, the more likely it was being honest about the potential impact. On the other hand, a quick settlement at (or near) the desired pay level might signal that the management groups were bluffing. Interestingly, Fisher (2007) concluded that management often gained concessions when the sports unions settled, suggesting they were not bluffing.

STRIKE CAUSES

While these previous theories provide us with the tools to understand potential causes of strikes, they tend to assume that strikes are rational and that their causes can be easily explained. However, there are other possible causes of strikes. In this section, we present several, many of which have been argued to have sparked strikes for over forty years.

CATALYSTS

Over forty years ago, the idea that one event or action could act as a catalyst for a strike was examined in a study of the New Zealand meat industry (Geare, 1972). That study

Locked-out Teamsters members picketing their employer (IKEA).

argued that strikes may have been sparked by a single trigger event. For example, in the 1960s GM suspended seventeen union members, which resulted in the plant chairperson calling for a wildcat strike; this snowballed into 240,000 workers from twenty-two of GM's twenty-three assembly plants going on strike (Zetka, 1995). Clearly, the suspensions were a catalyst in that strike. Similarly, the previously mentioned Air Canada wildcat strike in 2012 that started in Toronto and spread to other locations appears to have been triggered by two potential catalysts: (1) the presence of the Minister of Labour who tabled back-to-work legislation for Air Canada workers preparing to board an Air Canada flight in Toronto; and (2) the suspension of three workers who heckled the minister.

ISOLATED AND HOMOGENEOUS GROUPS

Researchers have argued that intact groups of similar workers—particularly if they are in unpleasant jobs—may be more prone to strikes. For example, Geare's (1972) study discusses how factors such as monotonous jobs, unpleasant conditions, and geographic isolation from others (i.e., company hostels/camps) may explain some strike experiences. Similarly, "the solidarity work group thesis" (Zetka, 1995) argues that collective action, including strikes, is more likely to occur when workers form strong bonds between them (which can happen, for example, when working together to try to beat a production quota). These bonds place workers in a collective struggle that can then be mobilized for strike action (Zetka, 1995).

MANAGEMENT INDIFFERENCE OR UNRESOLVED GRIEVANCES

You may recall that one of the potential outcomes of the industrial relations system is employee satisfaction and commitment. Thus, it should not be surprising that management (particularly lower-level management) indifference to worker complaints has been identified as a potential catalyst for strikes (Geare, 1972). Likewise, grievances that are allowed to fester or left unresolved may become a catalyst for strike action.

FRUSTRATION-AGGRESSION

Some scholars have presented a frustration-aggression hypothesis. This hypothesis argues that workers with feelings of work-related frustration, alienation, or dissatisfaction will naturally seek to improve the situation through their involvement in union activities and strikes (see review in Blackwood, Lafferty, Duck & Terry, 2003).

ECONOMIC FACTORS

Workers and management do not exist in isolation from the external labour market. Thus, research dating back to at least the 1960s has examined the relationship between the unemployment rate and the overall state of the business cycle (see reviews in Ashenfelter & Johnson, 1969; Maki, 1986). The general trend shows that strikes are more common when the economy is doing well and unemployment is low. This may be because in "good times" business is better and employers are able to pay better wages— workers may strike in an effort to make economic gains from employers. Alternatively, it may be because when the market is in an upswing, striking workers have other sources of income to turn to (i.e., a part-time job).

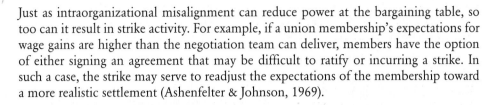

INTRAORGANIZATIONAL FACTORS

Just as intraorganizational misalignment can reduce power at the bargaining table, so too can it result in strike activity. For example, if a union membership's expectations for wage gains are higher than the negotiation team can deliver, members have the option of either signing an agreement that may be difficult to ratify or incurring a strike. In such a case, the strike may serve to readjust the expectations of the membership toward a more realistic settlement (Ashenfelter & Johnson, 1969).

STRIKE IMPACTS

ECONOMIC

Research into the impacts of strikes has often focused on economic factors such as the relationship between strikes and market value of the affected firm (Hanrahan, Kushner, Martinello & Masse, 1997), decreased production that can result in decreased revenues and market share in the longer term (Barton & Weernink, 2003), and the fact that any negotiated wage and benefit increases can represent substantial increases in organizational expenditures (Burns, 2000). Striking workers themselves face economic impacts as they are not receiving a pay cheque and have only limited access to funds via strike pay. Thus, it is not surprising that long strikes can result in significant (and negative) financial impacts on striking employees, their families, and even the communities in which they live.

WORKER WELL-BEING

However, the consequences of a strike on affected workers stretch beyond economics. A strike can have an impact on workers in terms of their employment experience and psychological well-being. For example, Giesbrecht, Markle, and Macdonald (1982) have examined the impact of a long strike on alcohol consumption. From a workplace perspective, Nicholson and Kelly (1980) suggest that a strike can result in several organizational changes that may significantly affect the employment relationship and impact the rapport between employer and employees once workers return to their jobs. As has been pointed out in a practitioners' journal, actions taken by employers or employees during the strike (e.g., verbal abuse or other regrettable actions) can result in the employment relationship never being fully restored (Herald, 2002).

To date there has been limited examination of worker perception outputs of the industrial system (employee satisfaction, commitment, union satisfaction, union commitment, etc.). One study measured several of these variables following a three-week strike (Barling, Wade & Fullagar, 1990). Its goal was to assess the relationships between strikes and predictors of organizational and union commitment; it did not, however, assess the extent that the strike affected these variables. Similarly, Barling, Fullagar, McElvie, and Kelloway (1992) examined the relationship between organizational commitment, union loyalty, and how likely it would be for union members to strike. However, we know of only one Canadian study that examined the impact of strikes on employee perception variables of organizational commitment, job satisfaction, work environment, management satisfaction, and union commitment (Chaulk & Brown, 2008). It found that strikes had a significantly negative impact across all of these measures.

UNEXPECTED RESULTS: THE RELATIONSHIP BETWEEN STRIKES AND LEGISLATION

Canada has perhaps more restrictions on strikes than any other country. However, as outlined in a recent report from Dachis and Hebdon (2011), the use of legislation to restrict strikes has resulted in some unexpected outcomes.

- Essential service requirements have no impact on the likelihood of a strike but may increase the length of strikes by as much as 60 percent.
- Banning the employer's use of **replacement workers** during a strike increased strike rates by approximately 15 percent and increased strike duration by 60 percent.

- **Reinstatement rights** increase strike length by 50 percent.
- Over the term of a collective agreement, back-to-work legislation results in a 2.9 percent decrease in wages compared to settled agreements.
- Likelihood of a back-to-work legislation being used to settle the next agreement is almost 3.5 times higher if back-to-work legislation was used to settle the present agreement.
- **Mandatory strike vote** may increase the number of strikes but reduces the length of a strike by 28 percent.

Source: Dachis, B., & Hebdon, R. (2010). *The laws of unintended consequences: The effect of labour legislation on wages and strikes.* Toronto: C. D. Howe Institute.

---

replacement workers employees hired to replace striking workers

reinstatement rights employees are guaranteed their old jobs after the strike

mandatory strike vote a majority of the workers must vote in favour of a strike; the union leaders cannot call a strike on their own

As we conclude our discussion of strikes, the trend of fewer strikes has caused at least one scholar to question "What has happened to strikes?" (Godard, 2011, p. 282). By their very nature, strikes represent a way for the parties to express and resolve conflict. Godard (2011) suggested several avenues for where the conflict formerly managed through strikes may have gone:

- Routed to alternative conflict resolution mechanisms. For example, the use of mechanisms from individual employment law to express and/or resolve conflict.
- Resolved through the restructuring of the economy. Collective strike action is less prevalent in the growing service versus declining industrial sectors (e.g., mining, manufacturing, etc.) that were often associated with poor work environments.
- Internalized. Perhaps the conflict has been driven internally into the employee resulting in "cynicism and escapism, general malaise and depression, alcohol and drug abuse, widespread normlessness and resentment, low levels of civic and political engagement" (p. 294).
- Cyclical. As shown in the history chapter, strike occurrences have not been consistent. Perhaps this is merely a trend that will revert as it has in the past.

// GRIEVANCES IN UNIONIZED WORKPLACES

Having discussed the conversion mechanism of strikes, we turn our attention to another internal conflict resolution process, namely, grievances. A formal grievance procedure is a requirement of Canadian labour relations legislation. Arguably, the grievance procedures given by lawmakers were in exchange for Canada's "no strike" requirement. Remember, Canadian unionized workers cannot legally strike when a collective agreement is in place. Instead, unionized workers have the right to have their complaints resolved through another mechanism, namely the grievance procedure. Accordingly, grievance procedures are one of the employment practices that formally differentiate employment under common law versus employment under collective bargaining law. Only unionized Canadian workers have the legal right to file a formal grievance and have management formally respond to it. However, it is also clear that many nonunion employers are choosing to provide nonunion employees with a grievance or appeal process (Walker & Hamilton, 2011). As noted by Walker and Hamilton's (2011, p. 42) international review of grievance procedures, "(e)xit, voice and loyalty has been a dominant theoretical approach in research on how employees respond to a grievance, and grievance outcomes." Consistent with exit voice theory, unionized employees also have the ability to "voice" their complaints using the grievance procedure as an alternative to exiting the organization. This view was supported by Rees's (1991) study of schoolteachers. He found that teachers with the strongest grievance procedures had a lower probability of quitting than those with weaker grievance procedures.

In this section, we will define grievances, present a typical grievance procedure, and discuss research findings concerning the determinants of grievance initiation.

GRIEVANCES DEFINED

In its simplest form, a grievance may be considered a complaint. However, the meaning is more precise in the field of industrial relations. In industrial relations, a **grievance** is a formal complaint that a specific (and identified) clause contained in the collective agreement was not properly followed (Bemmels & Foley, 1996). A copy of an actual grievance is presented in Figure 9.3. (Note that the names of the people involved, the company, and the union have been blacked out.)

In addition, there are three key types of grievances in work environments: individual, group, and union. An example of each follows.

> **grievance**
> a formal complaint that a specific clause in the collective agreement has been violated

INDIVIDUAL GRIEVANCE

Perhaps the most common grievance filed at the workplace is the individual grievance. Examples of this type of grievance include an employee who grieves that she was not paid overtime in accordance with the collective agreement or a worker who grieves that he was inappropriately denied his vacation request.

GROUP GRIEVANCE

Here, a group of employees grieve that the collective agreement has been violated. We could see, for example, a group of workers alleging that vacation is not being allocated per the process outlined in the collective agreement or a group of employees grieving that protective clothing is not being provided in accordance with the collective agreement.

UNION OR POLICY GRIEVANCE

With a union or policy grievance, the union leadership, rather than members, initiates the complaint. For example, the union might grieve that a new attendance policy developed by management violates the collective agreement, or that work has been inappropriately contracted out in violation of the collective agreement.

THE GRIEVANCE PROCEDURE

A review of the literature suggests that there are several key parties and steps to the grievance procedure (see Bemmels, 1994; Bemmels & Foley, 1996; Bemmels, Reshef & Stratton-Devine, 1991; Brown & Beatty, 2006; Peterson & Lewin, 2000), which we outline below.

FIGURE 9.3

GRIEVANCE

GRIEVANCE FORM AND RECORD OF PROCEEDINGS

Employee ▮▮▮▮▮▮▮▮▮▮▮▮▮▮▮ Date grievance occurred _June 12, 2006_
If space in any step is inadequate
attach separate sheets.

The aggrieved employee(s) should follow carefully each step of the grievance procedure, answer all questions and pay close attention to the specified time limits.

STEP 1

Have you attempted to resolve your grievance with your immediate supervisor?   YES ✔ NO ____

Have you had disciplinary action taken against you?   YES ✔ NO ____

Have you consulted with your shop steward?   YES ✔ NO ____

Describe your grievance, pointing out the article(s) of the agreement which is alleged to have been violated and the corrective action you request. This must be presented to your area superintendent/plant manager within 15 days of the occurrence of the grievance. ____

Article 6 – Managment Rights, Article 9.05 – discrimination
Article 37 – Subjugation, when grievor was wrongfully disciplined.
Settlement Requested: letter of written reprimand be removed
from personnel file, and replaced with written apology.

Signed ▮▮▮▮▮▮▮▮▮▮▮   Signed ▮▮▮▮▮▮▮▮▮▮▮
        Aggrieved employee   Steward

PARTIES

The three key parties in the grievance process are

- the employee, who often is the initial initiator of the grievance;
- the union, who is usually first represented by the shop steward; and
- management, who at the start of the process is usually represented by the immediate supervisor.

Many unions, such as PSAC, provide training to shop stewards concerning the grievance process.

However, we should note that if the grievance is not settled through the "normal" grievance process, external third parties may become involved (grievance mediators, arbitrators, etc.). We will discuss these third-party procedures in more detail in the next chapter.

PROCESS

We can think of the grievance process in terms of a formal (i.e., usually a paper-based process outlined in the collective agreement) as well as an informal (what some call pre-grievance) process. Given that these steps are specified in collective agreements, they differ between employment relationships. Nevertheless, while there is no standard process, most agreements have an informal stage followed by three or four formal stages. An example of an internal grievance procedure (up to but not including arbitration) can be found in Table 9.5. A typical process follows:

1. *Informal stage.* While not a requirement, and often not outlined in the collective agreement, an employee (with or without the assistance of the shop steward) may bring a complaint to his or her immediate supervisor in an attempt to settle the issue (Bemmels, Reshef & Stratton-Devine, 1991). If the complaint is resolved (either because the supervisor changes the employee's mind or because the employee is satisfied with the supervisor's answer), the process stops here. If not, the employee can take it through the formal grievance process.

2. *Formal step 1.* In a formal grievance, the employee will, usually with a union shop steward, present a written grievance to the immediate supervisor. The supervisor will have a specified period of time (as dictated by the collective agreement) to investigate the situation and respond. If the grievance is resolved, either because the supervisor changes the employee's mind or because the employee or union is satisfied with the answer, the process stops here. If not, it moves to step 2.

3. *Formal step 2.* The grievance is reviewed by the next level of management and sometimes the next level of the union hierarchy (i.e., the department manager and a member of the union grievance committee). As in step 1, management will have a set period of time to respond to the grievance. If the grievance is not resolved to the satisfaction of the grievor or union, the process can proceed to the next step.

4. *Formal step 3.* This repeats the previous step but with an even higher level of management and union hierarchy present (i.e., the plant manager or HR manager and a senior member of the union, such as an executive member or union local president). Note that it is not uncommon for several members of both management and the union to be present at this stage. If the grievance is resolved, either because the supervisor changes the employee's mind because or the employee or union is satisfied with the answer, the process stops here. If not, it moves to third-party intervention (e.g., arbitration).

If the grievance has not been settled at the end of the internal, formal procedure, the parties turn to third-party interventions such as arbitration. We will discuss these mechanisms in Chapter 10.

There are a few key points to remember about the grievance process. First, management has a specific time frame to investigate the grievance, and the union has a specific time frame to file a grievance or move it to the next step. These time frames are usually strictly enforced. Arbitrators will often refuse to hear grievances if the union filed after the time limit specified in the collective agreement, and unions can move to the next step when management fails to respond within the time frame permitted in the agreement (Brown & Beatty, 2006).

Second, note that at each stage of the grievance, the parties can agree to settle. Very few grievances go all the way to arbitration.

Third, at each stage of the process, higher levels of both the union and management hierarchy are often involved. These higher levels will usually consult with the lower levels to understand the issues at hand. In fact, as is shown in Table 9.5, it is not uncommon for several levels of union and management to be present during the latter steps of the procedure.

Fourth, the union is said to formally carry the grievance for the employee in question. Thus, you will note that the titles of labour arbitration cases refer to the union and organization involved—the grievor will be named in the text of the case but not the case title. However, as is also shown in the table, the employee is often present at all levels of the process.

Fifth, while the industrial relations department (whether called *human resources*, *labour relations*, *employment relations*, or *industrial relations*) may not be formally named in the collective agreement until the later steps of the process, it is often involved earlier. This is because (1) most members of the management team will consult with their industrial relations representative for guidance on how to handle the grievance; (2) given the importance of consistent interpretation of the agreement, IR staff members often have access to information concerning how the collective agreement language in question has been interpreted in the past; and (3) IR staff members have specialized training and expertise in the industrial relations field that may not exist in the rest of the organization.

GRIEVANCE INITIATION

A theme across the literature is that few of the actual work contract violations actually result in grievances, with some suggesting that for every one written grievance there are ten more unwritten ones (Walker & Hamilton, 2011). Naturally the question becomes what factors cause an individual to initiate a grievance. Considerable research has examined factors that can be linked to grievance initiation (Bamberger, Kohn &

TABLE 9.5

AN INTERNAL GRIEVANCE PROCEDURE

STEP	UNION REPRESENTATIVE	MANAGEMENT REPRESENTATIVE	TIME FOR MANAGEMENT TO RESPOND
1	Employee and his/ her shop steward	Shift supervisor	Meeting within 7 days of filing. Oral decision within 4 days of meeting.
2	Employee and, his/ her shop steward	Supervisor and the Distribution Manager (or designate)	Meeting within 7 days of referral to step 2. Written decision within 5 days of meeting.
3	Employee, his/ her shop steward, and representative of local union	Supervisor and the Distribution Director (or designate)	Meeting within 20 days of referral to step 3. Written decision within 7 days

Source: National Grocers Ltd. and Teamsters, Local 91. *Collective Agreement*. Retrieved from http://negotech.labour.gc.ca/eng/agreements/04/0418907a.pdf.

Nahum-Shani, 2008; Bemmels, 1994; Bemmels & Foley, 1996; Bemmels, Reshef & Stratton-Devine, 1991; Peterson & Lewin, 2000; Walker & Hamilton, 2011). A summary of some of the key findings from various fields (economics, industrial relations, and psychology) follows.

GRIEVOR CHARACTERISTICS

From a demographic perspective, past research found that grievors (as against non-grievors) were more likely to be young, male, well educated, and highly skilled (Peterson & Lewin, 2000). Interestingly, a newer study by Bamberger, Kohn, and Nahum-Shani (2008) suggests that there is no difference between the filing rate of men versus women and ethnic minorities versus whites per se; however, their findings did suggest that women and minorities may be less likely than their male and white colleagues to file grievances in positive environments (non-abusive supervisors, few workplace hazards, etc.). Overall, these findings lead us to conclude that demographics alone probably play a very small role in whether a person files a grievance. In addition to demographics, grievors, relative to non-grievors, are also found to be less satisfied with their jobs, have stronger views that employees should participate in workplace decisions, feel less commitment to their employers, and have less positive views of management (Bemmels & Foley, 1996).

MANAGEMENT CHARACTERISTICS

A general trend is that the stricter the management practices in terms of enforcement of performance and disciplinary standards (what some call a structure focus), the higher the level of grievances. In contrast, supervisors having a good knowledge of the collective agreement, as well as supervisors who are considerate of employees and have friendly relations with them, experience lower levels of grievances (Bemmels & Foley, 1996; Peterson & Lewin, 2000).

UNION CHARACTERISTICS

Unions encouraging employees to file grievances, union leadership advocating "putting complaints in writing" (i.e., making formalized complaints), and shop stewards receiving a large number of complaints from employees result in more grievances, but unions that have stewards who attempt to informally resolve grievances see fewer grievances (Bemmels, 1994; Bemmels & Foley, 1996; Bemmels, Reshef & Stratton-Devine, 1991). In addition, when stewards have completed union steward training and received years of formal education, there tends to be an increased use of informal grievance resolution (Bemmels, Reshef & Stratton-Devine, 1991).

Regardless of factors that may be associated with the initiation of grievances, a review by Peterson and Lewin (2000) concluded that the presence of a grievance procedure is associated with increased productivity, lower turnover, and longer job tenure. Regression analyses found that the current status of a grievance had the greatest impact on employees' perceptions of the process. However, use of the procedure is associated with lower company performance. As such, this review presented several recommendations for human resources and labour relations executives (Peterson & Lewin, 2000):

- View the grievance system as a high-performance human resources practice, given its positive relationship with organizational performance. In fact, research has shown that perceptions of fairness in a unionized grievance system are positively correlated with organizational commitment (Mandville & Brown, 2009). Similarly, Fiorito, Bozeman, Young, and Meurs (2007), in a study of a HRM practices in union and nonunion firms, found that organizational commitment was positively related to grievance processes, defined by them as any formal procedure for resolving disputes.

- Understand the relationship between the presence of and usage of grievance procedures. The presence of the procedure is an important method to instill voice and fairness in the workplace; however, overly high usage rates may suggest that there is an ineffective use of informal conflict resolution. High usage of the formal process can result in employees (i.e., those filing grievances and their union representatives) and the management team directing their time away from work and toward the administration of grievance activities, thus reducing organizational performance.

- Assess the extent to which supervisors are treating workers democratically (i.e., with consideration) as opposed to focusing on issues of performance and productivity (i.e., structure), and whether any "rebalancing" between the two is needed, given that consideration reduces grievance filing.

- Ensure that front-line supervisors have a good knowledge of the collective agreement, as lack of such knowledge increases grievance rates.

In a similar vein, Nurse and Devonish's (2007) work provides guidance to practitioners. They suggest that effective grievance management systems should give workers (1) a well-defined process that is easily understood and ensures their issue is addressed in a timely manner; (2) the opportunity to be heard, without fear of management repercussions; (3) the right to union representation; and (4) the ability to shape workplace decisions that affect them.

GRIEVANCE EFFECTIVENESS AND OUTCOMES

EFFECTIVENESS

Given the importance of grievance processes in industrial relations, a key question would be how do we access the effectiveness of these processes? Two key effective criteria have been used in the grievance literature: speed and satisfaction (Walker & Hamilton, 2011). Speed, or the length of time to settle the grievance, is important to all parties. As the old saying goes, "justice delayed is justice denied." The second effectiveness criterion is satisfaction, or the extent that the parties (in particular employees) perceive the process as being fair. Overall, Walker and Hamilton's (2011) review concluded that satisfaction was more important than speed for employees.

OUTCOMES

Walker and Hamilton's (2011) review also provided interesting insights as it relates to outcomes of grievance processes. Overall, the outcome of grievance processes is more likely to support the employee (e.g., the "winner" is usually the employee). While exit-voice theory would predict that employees would improve performance and reduce turnover (exit) post-grievance settlement, this may not always be the case. In fact, Walker and Hamilton concluded that among union and nonunion grievors, voluntary turnover increased while performance ratings and promotion rates decreased relative to their counterparts who did not file grievances. Interestingly, supervisors who had grievances filed against them by employees also experienced similar effects of higher voluntary turnover rates, and lower performance ratings and promotion rates.

IR NOTEBOOK   9.1

GRIEVANCES AS A UNION ADVANTAGE

As we review grievance procedures, it is important to note that a formal grievance procedure is a key differentiator of union versus nonunion employment models. Historically, access to such procedures has been a benefit solely for union members, making such procedures a key advantage for unionization. As shown below, unions have often promoted grievance procedures as a reason to join unions. As one example, let's look at an excerpt from the Alberta Federation of Labour's webpage entitled "Why Join a Union."

"Grievance Procedure

In a nonunion workplace, workers are at the mercy of the boss. If an employee has a complaint related to the workplace, he or she can attempt to talk to a manager about it, but the manager doesn't have to do anything. The manager might act on the complaint, ignore it or even punish the employee for raising the issue—it all depends on the nature of the complaint, the company's labour–management philosophy or even the manager's mood on that particular day.

In a unionized workplace, on the other hand, grievances and complaints are handled in an entirely different manner. Unlike the nonunion environment where the workers are basically subject to the whims of management, workers in unionized firms have a clear set of rights which are outlined in detail in their collective agreements. If the employer breaches provisions of the collective agreement—for example, if he or she fires a worker without just cause or if an employee is being harassed in some way on the job—then the worker can take defensive action through the established grievance procedure.

Union members don't have to face the boss or make their way through the red tape of labour law alone. Union shop stewards and representatives are there to support individual workers who have been treated unfairly."

Source: Alberta Federation of Labour. (2014b). Why Join a Union? Used with permission. Retrieved from http://www.afl.org/index.php/Unions/why-join-a-union.html.

// NONUNION GRIEVANCES

While nonunion grievance procedures have become increasingly common in recent years, the concept is not new. We know that such procedures date back to before the Second World War (Patmore, 2013). In fact, by 2003, 35 percent of employees in a Statistics Canada survey of over 10 million workers stated that they had access to a grievance procedure (Akyeampong, 2003). As such, we will now discuss the common types of nonunion grievances and why nonunion employers would opt to use such procedures.

TYPES OF NONUNION GRIEVANCES

As noted by Colvin (2014), there is considerable variation in the types of nonunion procedures used in nonunion workplaces. These procedures can range from the simple open-door policy to peer review panels and formal, almost jury-like procedures. We will now briefly outline three common forms found in Colvin's review.

OPEN-DOOR POLICY

By far the most common procedure, this type of grievance consists of a policy stating that employees should feel comfortable bringing areas of concern to a member of the management team. Such policies may state that the complaint can be brought to one's supervisor, the human resources department or a senior manager and may state that the employee cannot be retaliated against for voicing concerns. There is considerable range in the formality of such policies from very informal procedures to ones that have a formal investigation stage. Unfortunately, "...many open door policies involve little more than aspirational statement by the organization with very little to back them up..." (Colvin, 2014, p. 170).

FORMAL GRIEVANCE OR APPEAL

In this type of nonunion procedure, the policy specifies how the grievance is to be made and to whom. A common approach is to follow a chain of command model, meaning that employees would first voice their concern with their immediate supervisor. If that was unsuccessful, they would appeal to the next level of the management hierarchy. As such, it mirrors the step process of the unionized grievance model with the notable absence of a union advocate for the employee.

INDEPENDENT REVIEW

Though less common, some nonunion grievance procedure provides for an independent review outside of the immediate management team. Again, the range of options in nonunion processes is large. Some procedures include only members of management. For example, an independent review by a manager outside of the chain of command related to the employee who filed the grievance.

Other independent reviews include non-management personnel. These can include panels comprising peers of the employee and managers (the majority of the panel will be peers). A small number of firms have policies that include formal arbitration where a labour relations arbitrator will make final decision.

WHY WOULD MANAGEMENT OPT FOR A NONUNION GRIEVANCE PROCEDURE?

A natural question would be why management would opt to include nonunion grievance procedures. Arguably, such procedures might limit management flexibility and decision making. Colvin (2014) presents several reasons for their usage in nonunion firms. First, they can be a way to minimize the risk of unionization. More specifically, if employees are provided with grievance procedures akin to those provided by a union, some employers believe that their employees will be less likely to seek unionization. Second, just like the arguments concerning exit-voice for unionized workers, grievances represent voice and may reduce employee exit (or turnover). Third, the increasing usage and costs associated with litigation and lawsuits make grievance procedures attractive. More specifically, the provision of internal conflict resolution procedures via grievance procedures may help resolve issues before they lead to legal battles. Fourth, such procedures may enhance employee perception of justice, or fairness, in their workplace as workers have the ability to challenge workplace decision. As we discussed in Chapter 6, perceptions of organizational justice are becoming increasingly important in workplaces. Similarly, as we also discussed in Chapter 6, such procedures are part of a high-performance human resources strategy.

// SUMMARY

As is shown in this chapter, strikes and grievances are two conflict resolution–based conversion mechanisms contained in the IR system.

In terms of strikes, we examined three theories—the Hicks or accident theory, asymmetrical information, and total joint costs—as well as several factors known to potentially cause strikes (e.g., management indifference, unresolved grievances). We also discovered that Canada has one of the higher strike rates globally but that our strike rates are generally declining over time. Yet, we explored how the increased use of strike restrictions through back-to-work legislation and essential service agreements may result in wildcat strikes and work to rule behaviour.

Given the decrease in strikes, some scholars have concluded that "(t)he focus of industrial conflict has shifted from collective confrontation (or strikes) to grievances between employee and employer (Walker & Hamilton, 2011, p. 40). Our review of grievances in unionized workplaces shows the extent to which they provide employees with a formal process to voice concerns with the support of their union. We further noted that formal grievance procedures, once the exclusive domain of unionized workplaces, are becoming increasingly common in nonunion firms. As time unfolds it will be most interesting to see the extent to which these mechanisms become embedded in nonunion firms.

KEY TERMS

essential services agreement 266
grievance 283
industrial dispute 266
lockout 268
mandatory strike vote 282
reinstatement rights 282
replacement workers 282
strike 266
strike mandate 268
strike vote 268
wildcat strike 266
work to rule 266

WEBLINKS

HRSDC requirements for a legal strike in different Canadian jurisdictions:
http://www.hrsdc.gc.ca/en/lp/spila/clli/irlc/votes(e).pdf

For a full overview of the Halifax Transit strikes, see
http://thechronicleherald.ca/tags/transit-strike?page=1

YouTube posting of Mount Allison faculty and librarians thanking students:
https://www.youtube.com/watch?v=8qiWmI2XfPM

DISCUSSION QUESTIONS

1. Think of a current strike/lockout that is receiving media coverage in your community. Can you apply the strike theories to explain why this strike/lockout occurred? What do you feel was the primary cause of this strike/lockout?

2. Canadian legislation has perhaps the greatest restrictions on strikes. Yet we have one of the highest strike incidents on a global basis. Why do you think this is so?

3. It has been argued that restrictions on strikes, back-to-work legislation, and essential services are making legal strikes all but obsolete. As a result, we are more likely to see work to rule, wildcat strikes, etc. What do you think?

4. With more nonunion firms providing dispute resolutions that are akin to those of the labour movement, will unions become obsolete in the future?

5. Some scholars argue that grievances rather than strikes will be the focus of union moving forward. What do you think?

USING THE INTERNET

1. Go to a local or national news website and look for information concerning a strike or lockout. Can you apply the strike theories to explain why this strike/lockout occurred? What do you feel was the primary cause of this strike/lockout?

2. Many organizations place collective agreements online. Have a look at one or more of these collective agreements. To what extent

   a. is the grievance procedure similar to that presented in the text?

   b. does it contain (or refer to) strikes?

3. Go to an Internet search engine and search for a recent media story concerning strikes. To what extent do you feel the causes of strikes presented in this chapter apply to this strike?

4. Go to a website that compares the values of Generation Y to those of Baby Boomers. As we see more Generation Y enter the full-time labour force, we can expect to see their impact on workplaces and IR systems. As more Generation Y enter the workplace, what do you think will be the impact on strikes and workplace dispute resolution procedures?

5. Search the Internet to determine the growing sectors of the economy in the province where you attend this course. Based on the industry makeup of the economic growth sectors, will strike rates increase, decrease, or remain stable in the next 10 years? Justify.

EXERCISES

1. Reread the opening vignette. To what extent are the theories and causes of strikes represented?

2. Look at any recent media stories about strikes and choose one such strike. To what extent can the three theories of strikes be used to explain the strike in question?

3. Godard (2011) suggests several avenues for where the conflict formerly managed through strikes may have gone. These include: (1) routed to alternative conflict resolution mechanisms; (2) resolved through the restructuring of the economy; (3) internalized into the employee; and (4) cyclical. The instructor may break you into four groups and have you argue one of these positions.

4. In the chapter we discuss nonunion grievance procedures. Most colleges and universities have a calendar that discusses appeal processes. These are often available online. How similar is the process to the grievance process we presented in this chapter? (see pp. 285–286)

5. Find a collective agreement from your workplace, the workplace of a friend or family member, or online. Have a look at the grievance procedure contained in one collective agreement from your institution.

   a. Is there an informal (pre-grievance) step mentioned?

   b. How many steps are in the formal process?

   c. Which levels of management and the union are present at each step?

6. Interview a parent, sibling, friend, or someone else who has been on strike. Ask what he or she feels was the cause of the strike as well as what impact it had on the workplace, workers, and management. To what extent does his or her personal experience mirror the findings discussed in this chapter?

On February 2, for the first time in almost 15 years, the Halifax transit system faced a strike. The largest transit system in Atlantic Canada was shut down with all 300 buses and three ferries at a standstill. The 750 employees represented by the Amalgamated Transit Union (ATU), Local 508, walked off the job after the parties failed to reach a settlement. Almost 100,000 commuters would now need to find alternative transportation in the midst of winter.

The most contentious issue at the time of the strike was the management-proposed shift scheduling system called rostering. Previous collective agreements had a scheduling system based on seniority and workers could pick different shifts during a week. This system had been in place for decades. In the newly proposed rostering system, workers would be assigned to weekly schedules. The union felt that this weekly schedule reduced worker flexibility as members tried to maintain work–life balance. Management believed that the rostering system was needed to reduce costs, including the high overtime costs of their current scheduling system.

Immediately prior to the strike, the Halifax Regional Municipality bargaining team presented two offers. The first included a wage increase of 6 percent and rostering; the second included a 3.5 percent wage increase but no rostering. Neither offer was accepted by the union, and a strike occurred. Within a few hours of the strike, media stories were quoting citizens concerned about the impact of the strike on commuters, calling for transit to be declared an essential service (thereby reducing or eliminating strikes), and even speculating on the likelihood of back-to-work legislation.

On February 14, with little headway being made, the union members voted unanimously in favour of binding arbitration to end the strike. The City rejected that offer, opting instead to seek the assistance of a conciliator appointed by the provincial government.

About three weeks into the strike, the City made what it called its final offer. The offer included 14 million in wages ($1,500 signing bonus, 2.25 percent a year for four years) but would save the City $8 million in efficiencies (largely due to the inclusion of rostering). The union members voted to reject the offer and the strike continued on in the midst of a cold winter. Commuters during this time moved to ridesharing, walking, and in some cases working from home or not going to work or classes as they attempted to cope with the strike.

After a 41-day strike, almost 90 percent of union members voted in favour of a deal negotiated by the parties with the aid of a conciliator. City councillors too voted 19 to 2 in support of the deal. The final agreement included a wage package for workers worth $14.5 million over five years and efficiencies for the City in the range of $8.9 million. In terms of the specifics of the agreement, employees would receive a lump-sum payment of $4,000 in year one, and 2 percent increases in years two through five. However, new hires would now take five years to reach the top of the salary scale versus the 18 months it took in the old contract. The City accomplished its goal of the rostering schedule system; however, it agreed that the union would have at least two opportunities to provide feedback on the rostering system before it become operational in November.

While the majority of both sides were satisfied with the deal, not all were. Some union members felt that junior employees had lost the most in the strike and that little had been gained following a 40-day strike. At least one City councillor felt that scheduling should have remained solely a management decision and that the union should have had the opportunity to comment on the new system during the development phase.

As the transit system became operational, both sides realized that public opinion had been damaged. Estimates were that 5 percent of commuters will not return to the transit system after the strike. As a result, a public relations campaign was being launched and the City was offering free transit services during the month of March at an estimated cost of $1.5 million in lost revenue.

Sources: CBC, 2012; CTV Atlantic, 2012; CTV News, 2012; Fraser, 2012; Halifax, 2012; Jeffrey, 2012; Logan, 2012.

QUESTIONS

1. Media reports tend to call all work stoppages "strikes." Please justify if this case represents a strike or a lockout.

2. Please discuss the extent to which the three theories of strikes can be used to analyze this work stoppage.

3. On the basis of the list of potential causes of strikes presented in this chapter, what do you feel caused this strike?

4. It is arguably society's more vulnerable members (low-income earners, students, seniors, etc.) who are most impacted by labour disputes involving public transportation. The case makes reference to back-to-work legislation and essential service provisions. Do you feel that transit workers should be able to strike or do you feel that other dispute resolution procedures should be used as strike replacements?

5. Do you feel the proposed PR campaign and free transit during the month of March will minimize the loss of transit users post-strike?

// ENDNOTES

1. These data report work stoppages involving more than 500 workers. However, the HRSDC website also allows you to restrict the strike statistics to include smaller strikes.

2. Data for 2014 reflect only part of the year and should be interpreted cautiously.

3. Note that percent of estimated working time lost is only by industry and province.

4. All data reported were downloaded in the period June 2 to July 9, 2014.

// REFERENCES

1. Akyeampong, E. B. (2003). Unionization and the grievance system. *Perspectives on Labour and Income: The Online Edition, 4*(8). Retrieved 8 July 2014 from http://www.statcan.gc.ca/pub/75-001-x/00803/6606-eng.html

2. Alberta Labour Relations Board. (2014a). FAQ–strikes and lockouts. Retrieved 7 July 2014 from http://www.alrb.gov.ab.ca/faq_strikes.html

3. Alberta Federation of Labour. (2014b). Why join a union? Retrieved 8 July 2014 from http://www.afl.org/index.php/Unions/why-join-a-union.html

4. Ashenfelter, O., & Johnson, G. E. (1969). Bargaining theory, trade unions, and industrial activity. *The American Economic Review, 59*(1), pp. 35–49.

5. Bamberger, P., Kohn, E., & Nahum-Shani, I. (2008). Aversive workplace conditions and employee grievance filing: The moderating effects of gender and ethnicity. *Industrial Relations: A Journal of Economy and Society, 47*(2), pp. 229–259.

6. Barling, J., Fullagar, C., McElvie, L., & Kelloway, E. K. (1992). Union loyalty and strike propensity. *Journal of Social Psychology, 132*(5), pp. 581–590.

7. Barling, J., Wade, W. C., & Fullagar, C. (1990). Predicting employee commitment to company and union: Divergent models. *Journal of Occupational Psychology, 63*, pp. 49–61.

8. Barton, G., & Weernink, W. O. (30 June 2003). Strikes interrupt German output. *Automotive News, 8*(13), p. 3.

9. Bemmels, B. (1994). Determinants of grievance initiation. *Industrial and Labor Relations Review, 47*(2), pp. 285–301.

10. Bemmels, B., & Foley, J. R. (1996). Grievance procedure research: A review and theoretical recommendations. *Journal of Management, 22*(3), pp. 359–384.

11. Bemmels, B., Reshef, Y., & Stratton-Devine, K. (1991). The roles of supervisors, employees, and stewards in grievance initiation. *Industrial and Labor Relations Review, 45*(1), pp. 15–30.

12. Bender, J. (21 October 2013). Strike averted at University of Manitoba. *Winnipeg Sun*. Retrieved 29 May 2014 from http://www.winnipegsun.com/2013/10/21/university-of-manitoba-nears-midnight-strike-deadline.

13. Blackwood, L., Lafferty, G., Duck, J., & Terry, D. (2003). Putting the group back into unions: A social psychological contribution to understanding union support. *The Journal of Industrial Relations, 45*(4), pp. 485–504.

14. Brown, D. J. M., & Beatty, D. M. (2006). *Canadian labour arbitration* (4th edition). Aurora, ON: Canada Law Book Inc.

15. Burns, M. (2000). Nurses strike prompts increased health spending. *Europe, 393*(February), pp. 45–47.

16. *Canada Labour Code*. R.S., 1985, c. L-2.

17. CBC News. (27 April 2014). UNB and striking faculty ordered back to bargaining table. Retrieved 27 April 2014 from http://www.cbc.ca/news/canada/new-brunswick/unb-and-striking-faculty-ordered-back-to-bargaining-table-1.2512666

18. CBC News. (15 May 2009). Expect picket lines next Wednesday, N.L. nurses say. Government insists it is not locking out nurses. Retrieved 7 July 2014 from http://www.cbc.ca/news/canada/newfoundland-labrador/expect-picket-lines-next-wednesday-n-l-nurses-say-1.785846

19. CBC News. (2 February 2012). Transit strike hits Halifax. Retrieved 7 July 2014 from http://www.cbc.ca/news/canada/nova-scotia/transit-strike-hits-halifax-1.1225921

20. Chaulk, K., & Brown, T. C. (2008). An assessment of worker reaction to their union and employer post-strike: A Canadian experience. *Relations industrielles/ Industrial Relations, 63*(2), pp. 223–245.

21. Colvin, A. J. S. (2014). Grievance procedures in non-union firms. In W. K. Roche, P. Teague, & A. J. S. Colvin (Eds.), *The Oxford Handbook of Conflict Management in Organizations* (pp. 168-189). Oxford, UK: Oxford University Press.

22. CTV Atlantic. (15 February 2012). Halifax transit workers ask for binding arbitration. CTV News. Retrieved 7 July 2014 from http://atlantic.ctvnews.ca/ halifax-transit-workers-ask-for-binding-arbitration-1.768505

23. CTV News. (10 February 2014). New Brunswick names mediator in bid to end Mount Allison University strike. Retrieved 23 April 2014 from http://www .ctvnews.ca/canada/new-brunswick-names-mediator-in-bid-to-end-mount-allison-university-strike-1.1679521

24. CNN Library. (3 September 2013). Pro sports lockouts and strikes fast facts. CNN. Retrieved 29 May 2014 from http://www.cnn.com/2013/09/03/us/ pro-sports-lockouts-and-strikes-fast-facts/

25. Dachis, B., & Hebdon, R. (2010). *The laws of unintended consequences: The effect of labour legislation on wages and strikes*. Toronto: C. D. Howe Institute.

26. Executive Council. (20 May 2009). Tentative agreement reached; Nurses' strike avoided. Retrieved 7 July 2014 from http://www.releases.gov.nl.ca/ releases/2009/exec/0520n01.htm

27. Fell, C. (28 November 2013). County averts strike by snowplow operators. *Meaford Express*. Retrieved 10 June 2014 from http://www.simcoe.com/ news-story/4243451-county-averts-strike-by-snowplow-operators/

28. Fiorito, J., Bozeman, D. P., Young, A., & Meurs, J. A. (2007). Organizational commitment, human resource practices and organizational characteristics. *Journal of Managerial Issues, 6*(2), pp. 186–207.

29. Fisher, G. H. (2007). Can strikes pay for management? Pro sports' major turn-arounds. *Relations industrielles/Industrial Relations, 62*(1), pp. 3–30.

30. Forrest, A. (2014). A message from Anne Forrest, WUFA President. Retrieved 7 July 2014 from http://www.wufa.ca/

31. Fraser, L. (13 March 2012). Halifax transit strike over. *Herald News*. Retrieved 7 July 2014 from http://thechronicleherald.ca/metro/73157 -halifax-transit-strike-over

32. Geare, A. J. (1972). The problem of industrial unrest: Theories into the causes of local strikes in a New Zealand meat freezing works. *Journal of Industrial Relations, 14*(1), pp. 13–22.

33. Giesbrecht, N., Markle, G., & Macdonald, S. (1982). The 1978–79 INCO workers' strike in the Sudbury basin and its impact on alcohol consumption and drinking patterns. *Journal of Public Health Policy, 3*(1), pp. 22–38.

34. Godard, J. (2011). What has happened to strikes? *British Journal of Industrial Relations, 49*(2), pp. 282–305.

35. Hale, D. (2008). International comparisons of labour disputes in 2006. *Economic & Labour Market Review, 2*(4), pp. 32–39.

36. Halifax. (24 February 2012). News release: ATU Local 508 rejects HRM's five-year offer. Retrieved 7 July 2014 from http://halifax.ca/mediaroom/pressrelease/pr2012/untitled.php

37. Hanrahan, R., Kushner, J., Martinello, F., & Masse, I. (1997). The effect of work stoppages on the value of firms in Canada. *Review of Financial Economics, 6*(2), pp. 151–167.

38. Herald, D. (2002). Back to work doesn't mean back to normal. *Canadian HR Reporter.* Retrieved 13 July 2007 from http://www.fgiworld.com/eng/articles/back_to_work.pdf

39. Human Resources and Social Development Canada. (2011). Chronological perspective on work stoppages. Retrieved 16 January 2011 from http://srv131.services.gc.ca/dimt-wid/pcat-cpws/recherche-search.aspx?lang=eng&ind=1&jurs=1

40. Jeffrey, D. (11 March 2012). Transit union, city reach deal. *Herald News.* Retrieved 7 July 2014 from http://thechronicleherald.ca/metro/72299-transit-union-city-reach-deal

41. Johnston, C. (6 January 2013). NHL lockout is over after 16-hour negotiating session. *National Post.* Retrieved 7 July 2014 from http://sports.nationalpost.com/2013/01/06/nhl-lockout-is-over-after-16-hour-negotiating-session/

42. Kramer, J., & Hyclak, T. (2002). Why strikes occur: Evidence from their capital markets. *Industrial Relations, 41,* pp. 80–93.

43. Laanela, M., & Sheppard, M. (28 May 2014). B.C. teachers' strike to continue next week: B.C. Teachers' Federation confirms 4 more days of strikes. *CBC News.* Retrieved 29 May 2014 from http://www.cbc.ca/news/canada/british-columbia/b-c-teachers-strike-to-continue-next-week-1.2656893

44. Logan, N. (2 February 2012). Halifax Metro Transit workers on strike for first time in 14 years. Global News. Retrieved 7 July 2014 from http://globalnews.ca/news/206664/halifax-metro-transit-workers-on-strike-for-first-time-in-14-years/

45. Maki, D. (1986). The effect of the cost of strikes on the volume of strike activity. *Industrial and Labour Relations Review, 39*(4), pp. 552–563.

46. Mandville, S., & Brown, T. C. (2009). How do employees view their grievance system? A survey of unionized healthcare workers. Paper presented at the Annual Meeting of the Administrative Sciences Association of Canada. Niagara Falls, ON.

47. National Post Staff. (23 March 2012). Air Canada ground crew sent back to work after wildcat strike causes flight chaos. *National Post.* Retrieved 7 July from http://news.nationalpost.com/2012/03/23/air-canada-ground-crew-return-to-work-after-wildcat-strike-causes-flight-chaos/

48. Nicholson, N., & Kelly, J. (1980). The psychology of strikes. *Journal of Occupational Behaviour, 1*(4), pp. 275–284.

49. Nurse, L., & Devonish, D. (2007). Grievance management and its links to workplace justice. *Employee Relations, 29*(1), pp. 89–109.

50. Patmore, G. (2013). Unionism and non-union employee representation: The interwar experience in Canada, Germany, the US and the UK. *Journal of Industrial Relations, 55*(4), pp. 527–545.

51. Peterson, R. B., & Lewin, D. (2000). Research on unionized grievance procedures: Management issues and recommendations. *Human Resource Management, 39*(4), pp. 395–406.

52. Rees, D. (1991). Grievance procedure strength and teacher quits. *Industrial and Labor Relations Review, 45*(1), pp. 31–43.

53. Sherlock, T., & Shaw, R. (26 May 2014). B.C. braces for four days of rotating teacher strikes, and maybe more to come: If no progress is made in negotiations following this round of strikes, another could follow next Monday. *Vancouver Sun*. Retrieved 29 May 2014 from http://www.vancouversun .com/business/braces+four+days+rotating+teacher+strikes+maybe+more +come/9876170/story.html

54. Tahirali, J. (25 May 204). Dispute between B.C. teachers, province leads to rotating strikes. CTV News. Retrieved 29 May 2014 from http://www .ctvnews.ca/canada/dispute-between-b-c-teachers-province-leads-to-rotating -strikes-1.1837923#ixzz337H3FGIL

55. Talmazanm, Y. (8 March 2014). UPDATE: B.C. teachers vote in favour of strike action, bring offer to negotiation table. Global News. Retrieved 29 May 2014 from http://globalnews.ca/news/1191102/results-of-b-c -teachers-strike-vote-released-today/

56. Walker, B., & Hamilton, R. T. (2011). Employee–employer grievances: A review. *International Journal of Management Reviews 13*(1), pp. 40-58.

57. Wildeman, A. (3 July 2014). Letter to Windsor University Faculty Association. Retrieved 7 July 2014 from http://www.wufa.ca/sites/default/ files/July%203%20Letter%20to%20WUFA%20members.pdf

58. Zetka, J. R. (1995). Union homogenization and the organizational foundations of plant-wide militancy in the US automobile industry, 1957–1975. *Social Forces, 73*(3), pp. 789–810.

CHAPTER 1

THIRD-PARTY DISPUTE RESOLUTION PROCEDURES

LEARNING OBJECTIVES

BY THE END OF THIS CHAPTER, YOU WILL BE ABLE TO DISCUSS

- the process of grievance arbitration
- types of grievance arbitration
- interest arbitration
- mediation and conciliation procedures
- alternative dispute resolution procedures (ADR)

Black Friday is best known as the day when big-box retailers rake in money, but it has also become a time for some of their employees to demand a share of the proceeds. At Walmart, this year's Black Friday protests will be the widest-reaching ever, organizers say, with pickets and strikes planned at 1600 stores to remind shoppers that the people serving them often can't afford to feed themselves.

"I have to depend on the government mostly," says Fatmata Jabbie, a 21-year-old single mother of two who earns $8.40 an hour working at a Walmart in Virginia. "Walmart should pay us $15 an hour and let us work full-time hours," she says. "That would change our lives. That would change our whole path. I wouldn't be dependent on government too much. I could buy clothes for my kids to wear."

The nation's largest employer, Walmart employs 1.4 million people, or 10 percent of all retail workers, and pulls in $16 billion in annual profits. Its largest stockholders—Christy, Jim, Alice, and S. Robson Walton—are the wealthiest family in the United States, collectively worth $145 billion. Yet the company is notorious for paying poverty wages and using part-time schedules to avoid offering workers benefits.

The group behind the Black Friday protests, the union-backed Organization for Respect at Walmart (OUR Walmart) was founded in 2011 to pursue a new approach to improving labor conditions at the retail giant. Rather than try to overcome Walmart's union-busting tactics, OUR Walmart has focused on publicly shaming the company through a relentless PR campaign and mass demonstrations. Organizers say the approach is working: Since 2012, Walmart has instituted a new pregnancy policy and a scheduling policy that helps workers get more shifts.

Like the holiday retail season, this year's Walmart protests actually started before Black Friday. On Wednesday, Jabbie walked off her shift along with other workers who are demanding a $15 wage and full-time hours. Other Walmart workers walked off the job throughout the U.S. "It felt great," Jabbie told me. "I feel like doing it over and over again until they get the message."

Source: Adapted from http://www.motherjones.com/politics/2014/11/walmart-protests-black-friday.

Strikes and grievances are the most common forms of conflict found in labour–management relations. In this chapter we will examine the various procedures that labour, management, and governments have developed to resolve these conflicts. Note that there are some new developments in the nonunion sector that are worth looking at. See, for example, the Walmart strike outlined in the opening vignette. This is not a traditional industrial work stoppage. It occurred in a nonunion company and doesn't appear to have included a majority of employees. Thus the chapter will go beyond the usual labour–management dispute resolution procedures to include disputes in nonunion workplaces. We begin with grievance arbitration.

// GRIEVANCE ARBITRATION

Recall that the three key parties in the grievance process are

- the employee, who often is the initial initiator of the grievance;
- the union, who is usually first represented by the shop steward; and
- management, who at the start of the process is usually represented by the immediate supervisor.

Walmart employees strike on Black Friday.

However, we should note that if the grievance is not settled through the "normal" grievance process, external third parties may become involved (grievance mediators, arbitrators, etc.).

As we discovered in Chapter 4, grievances in Canadian unionized workplaces must by law be resolved by third-party binding arbitration. The arbitration procedures provided by lawmakers were in exchange for Canada's "no strike" requirement during the term of collective agreements. Remember, Canadian unionized workers cannot legally strike when a collective agreement is in place.

As discussed above, the parties can turn to arbitration when they are unable to resolve a grievance themselves. At times, because of the union's duty of fair representation, a union member may want to take an issue to arbitration even if the union does not agree that it is warranted. Regardless of how the parties get there, arbitration is a final and binding process where a third party resolves the dispute. Remember, there are two forms of arbitration processes: rights and interest.

RIGHTS ARBITRATION

As discussed in Chapter 9, rights (or grievance) arbitration addresses alleged violations of the collective agreement. When the parties cannot resolve a grievance through the internal grievance process, it can be taken to arbitration. It is for this reason that this type of arbitration is also referred to as grievance arbitration. While we present this as the next logical step in the grievance process, we should be clear that very few grievances go as far as arbitration. Remember that the industrial systems framework that grounds this textbook includes the concept of a feedback loop. Before any arbitration, and during various steps of the grievance procedure, both union and management representatives will seek guidance from past grievance resolutions. For example, both union and management representatives may look internally to see how similar issues in the past were handled. This is because consistent application and interpretation of the collective agreement is critical. The parties may also look to external resources. One often used external resource is commonly referred to as *Brown and Beatty*. This source presents trends in arbitration and references specific arbitration rulings (known as labour arbitration cases, or LACs) by topic, so that parties can see how other parties have interpreted similar issues and collective agreement language.

THE PROCESS

The rights arbitration process has many of the same characteristics of a legal proceeding in that witnesses are sworn in, give evidence, and can be cross-examined, and evidence is formally presented and reviewed. However, it differs from a legal court proceeding in several ways: there is never a jury present; there is no true judge as the arbitrator may not be a lawyer or judge; and the proceeding does not take place in a courthouse.

The process also differs on some of the key legal principles grounding the process. For example, take the issue of proof. In a criminal proceeding, the judge must be convinced beyond a reasonable doubt that the charged person committed the crime. In arbitrations, the decision is based on probable cause (i.e., is it most probable that the grievor did what management alleges?). It also differs in that arbitrators are not bound to follow

A typical labour arbitration proceeding often takes place in hotel meeting rooms.

Westend61/Getty Images

jurisprudence
past decisions (usually in a legal context)

jurisprudence, the past decisions of other arbitrators, and that arbitration decisions are considered final and binding. Only under very rare and exceptional circumstances will a court examine an arbitration ruling. However, we should stress that most arbitrators (even if not formally required to) will consult and follow past decisions. Remember, an arbitrator is deemed to be a neutral third party; it can be tough to be seen as a neutral third party if one creates rulings that contradict current arbitration trends.

Given this backdrop, let's walk through a typical arbitration process. Since a number of arbitration cases involve discipline and discharge, we will examine a typical discharge arbitration using guidance from Brown and Beatty (2006). A summary of the key events for a discharge case on the grounds of excessive absenteeism follows, and a summary of key arbitration issues is presented in Table 10.1.

prima facie case
union establishes, at arbitration, that the collective agreement was in place and that that the grievor was employed, covered by that agreement, and disciplined

First, the union will need to establish a **prima facie case**. In other words, they must show that (1) the collective agreement was in place, (2) the grievor in question was covered by that agreement, (3) the grievor was employed, and (4) the grievor was disciplined. In essence, it will establish that the employee has a right to have his or her grievance heard. Note also that in disciplinary cases only, management has the primary burden of proof. That is, management must prove on a balance of probabilities that the grievor committed the alleged acts.

Second, the management group will need to present evidence to answer the following questions in order to show that there was just cause for its disciplinary actions:

- *Did the alleged events take place?* Management would need to present evidence of excessive absenteeism (e.g., attendance records, payroll records).

- *Was it reasonable for the employer to provide some form of discipline?* Management would most likely present evidence on the basis of its interpretation of the discipline clause (and perhaps other language) of the collective agreement to justify its disciplinary actions. Similarly, it would likely present evidence (using LACs likely found in Brown and Beatty) to show how arbitrators have ruled that similar employee conduct has warranted some level of discipline.

TABLE 10.1

KEY ARBITRATION ISSUES

Three Elements of Culpable Behaviour
1. The grievor was aware of what was required of him or her.
2. The grievor was capable of performing what was required of him or her.
3. The grievor chose to do otherwise.

Three Questions Examined for Discharge Cases
1. Did management have reasonable grounds to impose some form of discipline?
2. Was the level of discipline imposed reasonable given the circumstances?
3. If the level of discipline imposed was excessive, what level of discipline (if any) is appropriate?

Common Mitigating Factors	
The grievor's work record	Isolation
Inconsistent application of rules	Grievor's length of service
Premeditation	Economic hardship
Remorse/likelihood to repeat	Seriousness of the offence
Provocation	Lack of understanding

Management will need to prove that the grievor is **culpable**—that he or she is blame-worthy for his or her actions—and that the conduct warrants discipline. For the grievor's conduct to be considered the management representative will need to show that

1. the grievor was aware of what was required of him or her;

2. the grievor was capable of performing what was required of him or her; and

3. the grievor chose to do otherwise.

If management cannot demonstrate all three elements of culpability, the employee is considered nonculpable.

Let's consider two examples. Let's say that a grievor was aware of the attendance policy stating that he was to call in sick if he could not report to work; that he was able to follow the policy (i.e., nothing impeded his ability to phone in sick); and that he failed to call in sick. In this case, the grievor would be culpable, and some form of discipline would be appropriate. Now let's say that a second grievor who was also absent was aware of the attendance policy but that she was unable to phone in because the phone lines were down due to an ice storm. In that case, her conduct would not make her culpable. It is also important to stress that if management cannot provide evidence to support all three culpability elements, then the employee is nonculpable. That is, the burden of proof is on management.

- *Was the level of discipline imposed by management reasonable?* In discipline cases, management has several sanctions available. These include a verbal warning, a written warning, a suspension, and a discharge. In the hearing, management would again argue (using data from collective agreement language) that the level choice of the discipline imposed (e.g., discharge) was appropriate. Remember that discharge is the most serious sanction available—it is akin to capital punishment in a criminal trial. To have the grievance denied (i.e., a ruling in favour of management), management will have to provide considerable evidence to support its decision to discharge. Given the long-standing doctrine of progressive discipline discussed in Chapter 8, you would expect management to present evidence either that it followed the concept of progressive discipline or that the alleged conduct was such that immediate discharge was warranted. Note that as discussed in Chapter 6, nonunion workplaces often use the doctrine of progressive discipline. See the example in IR Today 10.1.

Third, remember that the union representative will have an opportunity to question the management witness and provide counterevidence. Often, the union will present what is known as **mitigation factors** during arbitration (particularly with regard to the issue of whether the level of discipline imposed was appropriate). These factors are used as a way to reduce or remove the sanction (in our example, discharge) imposed by management. A review of Brown and Beatty (2006; see section 7:440) shows several mitigation factors that the union may argue:

- *The grievor's work record.* If the grievor has had few or no warnings, a good level of performance, etc., the union will often ask that this be used to lessen the sanction.

- *The grievor's length of service.* Similar to the previous factor, a long record of service (particularly if it is unblemished) may be used by the union as a reason to reduce the sanction.

- *Isolated event.* As with the previous two factors, an isolated event can be used as a mitigating factor. For example, the union could argue that a single failure to call in sick was an isolated incident unworthy of discipline (or of the level of discipline imposed).

culpable
at fault, guilty

mitigation factors
factors argued by the union for a reduction in a sanction

- *Inconsistent application of rules or treatment.* If the union can find examples in which other employees conducted themselves in a similar manner and a less severe sanction or no sanction was imposed, it will argue that the management group acted inconsistently. For example, if in our case the union could find evidence that other employees with similar records of absenteeism received written warnings, not discharges, this mitigating factor might be used to argue for a reduction in the sanction imposed.

- *Premeditation.* If there is evidence that the grievor's actions were "spur of the moment" and not premeditated (i.e., planned in advance), the union may use this to argue for a reduction in sanction.

- *Remorse/likelihood to repeat.* When grievors are remorseful for their actions, their unions will often assert that there is little likelihood that the same conduct will occur again. Thus, they will argue that this factor should be used to give the grievor another chance (i.e., reduce the sanction).

- *Economic hardship.* A union can argue that the sanction imposed presents severe economic hardship, and thus should be reduced. For example, if the employee in our attendance example was one year away from qualifying for his pension, the union might argue that discharge poses extreme hardship.

- *Provocation.* If the grievor's actions were provoked by a management action, the union will often request reduction or removal of the sanction. For example, if the employee is being disciplined for swearing at his supervisor and it turns out that the supervisor swore at him first, the union might argue provocation.

- *Seriousness of the offence.* For example, the impact of an employee who stole a blank USB drive would be minimal for the organization relative to an employee who downloaded the entire customer list and sold it to a competitor.

- *Lack of understanding.* A union can argue that an employee did not truly disobey a work order as she did not fully understand it.

IR TODAY 10.1

CYGNUS GYMNASTICS

The concept of progressive discipline (or corrective action) is a cornerstone of unionized workplaces and is becoming increasingly common among nonunion firms. In essence, it is grounded in the beliefs that the punishment should fit the crime, that employees should be given the chance to improve their conduct, and that workers should be aware that failure to improve can result in discharge (Brown & Beatty, 2006). Thus, employees will normally receive lower levels of sanctions (i.e., verbal and written warnings) prior to more serious sanctions (i.e., a suspension or discharge). For example, the first time an employee failed to follow the company's dress code, he or she might receive a verbal warning. If he or she continued to ignore the dress code, a more severe sanction (i.e., a written warning) might be issued. This would continue until the behaviour improved or the employee was discharged.

The following is a (verbatim) example of a corrective action policy from a nonunionized, nonprofit gymnastics club.

Corrective Action Policy for Cygnus Gymnastics

1. Cygnus believes in the concept of progressive discipline for all of its employees. In situations where discipline is required, such actions should, wherever possible, be

corrective rather than punitive in nature. The normal progression of corrective action will be as follows:

Step 1: Verbal counseling

Step 2: Written warning

Step 3: Suspension without pay (equivalent to 20% of normal workweek)

Step 4: Suspension without pay (equivalent to 100% of normal workweek)

Step 5: Termination

2. It is understood that certain offences are sufficiently serious to warrant immediate termination and/or a faster progression through the process outlined in section 1 of this policy. While not inclusive, the following are examples of grounds for immediate termination.

   a. Using or being under the influence of alcohol and/or narcotics and/or illicit prescription drugs in the workplace or during work time.

   b. Failure to comply with a direct order from a person of authority, unless compliance would be in violation of a law or statute.

   c. Endangering the safety or well-being of athletes, staff, or parents.

   d. Fighting or committing assault in the workplace or during work time.

   e. Theft or misappropriation of Cygnus funds, equipment, materials, or property, or of the property of others that is positioned on Cygnus-owned or -operated premises or equipment.

   f. illegal activities conducted at the workplace or during work time.

3. Wherever possible, all corrective action must be approved by the Director of Human Resources (or delegate) prior to implementation.

4. Wherever possible (a) the Director of Human Resources (or delegate) will be present when any form of discipline is presented to an employee, and (b) all forms of corrective action will be presented and discussed in a meeting between the employee, his/her immediate supervisor, and the Director of Human Resources (or delegate).

5. The primary purpose of a verbal counseling is to make the employee aware of the issue at hand; discuss expectations going forward; and (c) inform the employee that repeated performance/behavioural issues can result in further correction action. Given the counselling nature of this form of corrective action, the only documentation placed in the employee's human resources file will relate to the date of the counselling and the issue at hand.

6. With the exception of verbal counselling, all corrective action must be documented with a hard copy placed in the employee's human resources file and a copy provided to the employee. The Director of Human Resources (or delegate) and the employee in question will be asked to sign both copies. Provided that no subsequent corrective action steps have occurred, documentation referring to corrective action will be removed from the employee's human resources file after twenty-four (24) calendar months.

Source: Courtesy of Cygnus Gymnastics Training Centre.

While we have presented mitigation factors in terms of how the union might argue them, management can argue the reverse (poor work record, consistent application of rules, etc.). Also note that while we have presented them as separate factors, either party might use multiple mitigating factors in its argument (e.g., twenty-year employee, clean work record with no performance issues, isolated event provoked by management).

Fourth, after hearing all of the evidence, a decision will be written. In the case of discharge, the arbitrator will examine three key questions:

1. Did management have reasonable grounds to impose some form of discipline?

2. Was the level of discipline imposed reasonable given the circumstances?

3. If the level of discipline imposed was excessive, what level of discipline (if any) is appropriate?

Thus, the ruling will be either "Grievance denied," meaning that management's position is supported and no changes are awarded, or "Grievance upheld," meaning that management's decision was not supported. In some cases, the ruling grievance is "partially upheld," meaning that part, but not all, of the union's argument is accepted. In many cases, when the grievance is upheld or partially upheld, the ruling will include a substitution of the sanction. For example, the discharged employee may be reinstated and the discharge replaced by a lesser penalty (e.g., suspension). Key elements in any sanction substitution or reinstatement will be seniority provisions and pay. Remember that it can be months (or even years) from the time an employee is discharged to the time he or she is reinstated. The ruling will also need to determine whether the reinstated employee accumulates seniority for any portion of the period between discharge and reinstatement and whether he or she is paid for any of that period.

Students have often asked us, "What does it take for management to win an arbitration concerning discharge?" A review of Brown and Beatty (2006) provides guidance here. Generally speaking, management's actions are most likely to be supported when management shows that (1) progressive discipline was used; (2) its treatment of the grievor was consistent with that of other employees in similar situations; (3) there is little likelihood of the grievor's conduct being reformed given his or her current employment record; and (4) past corrective action steps have failed. Of course, when management cannot prove such issues, the union is likely to win the arbitration. Thus, we see that documentation of events and progressive action steps are key. For this reason, one of the authors of this text has often reminded managers of the need to watch their *ABCDs* in discipline steps: "Always Be Consistent and Document."

THE FORMS OF ARBITRATION

As we discussed in Chapter 4, Canadian labour relations laws are largely similar in content but have subtle differences between them. When it comes to grievance arbitration, the forms of arbitration differ slightly from jurisdiction to jurisdiction. Some of the following may not be available in your province.

CONVENTIONAL TRIPARTITE ARBITRATION

This three-person arbitration panel is a common method used for rights arbitration. Both management and the union each choose a representative and mutually agree to a third chairperson, who is registered with the appropriate labour relations board. The chair is sometimes called the *neutral chair* as the person must be mutually agreed upon by union and management; thus, it is unlikely that the chair is seen as being either pro-management or pro-union. While it is not a requirement, common wisdom states that each side's representative be present to ensure that its side's view is heard, so the union nominee will argue for the union's position and the management nominee will argue for the management's position. Therefore, split decisions (2–1) are not uncommon in tripartite arbitration rulings.

This model is particularly useful in complex cases where the side persons can be used in a sounding board capacity for the parties by the neutral chair.

SOLE ARBITRATION

The primary difference between this form of arbitration and the previous is that there is just a neutral chair. No nominees (i.e., people on the side of management or the union) are present to represent the union or management. This form is often used in conjunction with expedited arbitration. In jurisdictions such as Ontario, this model is by far the most common. It tends to be faster and cheaper for the parties.

EXPEDITED ARBITRATION

Given the long time frame that parties can wait before an arbitration hearing, some jurisdictions allow expedited arbitration. Under this form of arbitration, the labour relations board guarantees a hearing within a specified time frame, but the parties have no choice on the selection of the arbitrator.

// THE PROBLEMS WITH CURRENT GRIEVANCE ARBITRATION PROCESSES

Our conversations with labour leaders and industrial relations practitioners suggest there are several problems with the current system. First is the long delay between the actions that prompted the grievance and the arbitration ruling. As outlined by Williams and Taras (2000), even if the employee is reinstated, the extended time delay can make reintegration into the workplace difficult for all parties involved. In fact, it can result in some employees who are reinstated opting to financially settle with the employer and not return to work. As rightly pointed out by Zerbe (2009), there is an emotional element to arbitration processes, and we can imagine that significant time delays would enhance any emotional responses.

Second, arbitrations are costly. A typical arbitration requires each side to pay for its respective nominees and share the cost of the chair, the room where the hearings take place, etc. Moreover, many unions and management teams will hire lawyers to represent them, adding to the cost. Finally, there are the hidden costs of the staff time spent preparing for the arbitration.

Third, there is what can be called the "outsider" factor. Remember that the collective agreement represents a mutual understanding of the terms and conditions of the work negotiated by representatives of the union and management groups. As such, these parties have first-hand knowledge of the workplace and the implications of any language they create. On the other hand, the arbitrators who will make the final decision often lack such first-hand experience with the workplace and work relationship in question. This lack of personal understanding of the relationship can be problematic considering that the final arbitration decision is final and binding.

Fourth, the process is becoming increasingly legalistic, as is the case with collective agreement language in general. Many unions and employers hire lawyers to represent them in arbitration, while others hire legal counsel as full-time employees. Thus, it is rare that management would send a manager or the union would send a front-line representative to argue the merits of the grievance. Yet, we must remember that the grievance process was conceived as a simple process to resolve workplace issues.

For these reasons, we are seeing a number of alternative dispute resolution techniques being used as potential precursors (or substitutes) to arbitration. These will be discussed in more detail later this chapter.

INTEREST ARBITRATION

Designed to resolve a disagreement during collective agreement negotiations, **interest arbitration** is used as an alternative to strikes when parties are not permitted to strike or lockout. When they fail to reach a collective agreement on their own, they must turn to arbitration. While private-sector parties can mutually agree to such forms of arbitration, interest arbitration is most commonly used in public-sector employment relationships. Interestingly, recent evidence suggests that in places where legislation requires interest arbitration to settle public-sector disputes, wage settlements are higher than where there is no legislation (i.e., a right to strike exists). (Campolieti, Hebdon & Dachis, 2014). In Canada, there are two common forms of interest arbitration: conventional and final-offer selection (Hebdon & Stern, 2003).

CONVENTIONAL INTEREST ARBITRATION

In **conventional interest arbitration**, the parties submit separate potential solutions to the outstanding issues. The arbitrator can then choose among the options or craft his or her own to settle the outstanding issues.

FINAL-OFFER ARBITRATION

In **final-offer arbitration**, the parties submit a final offer to the arbitrator. The arbitrator must then choose the full final offer (i.e., without making any changes) of either management or the union. The rationale for the final-offer method is that the parties would be likely to submit reasonable alternatives given that the arbitrator would have to choose *all* of one of the two packages placed before him or her.

FIRST AGREEMENT ARBITRATION

Some jurisdictions require that when the parties cannot come to a mutually agreeable collective agreement during the very first round of negotiations, they must submit to interest arbitration. This is known as **first agreement (or first contract) arbitration**. Interestingly, recent evidence suggests that this form of arbitration is effective, reducing first agreement work stoppages by at least 50 percent (Johnson, 2010; Riddell, 2013).

THE PROS AND CONS OF INTEREST ARBITRATION

The principal strength of interest arbitration is its ability to reduce the incidences of strikes, especially for employees performing essential tasks (Campolieti, Hebdon & Dachis, 2014; Currie & McConnell, 1991; Ichniowski, 1982; Olson, 1986; Rose, 1994). While interest arbitration laws may reduce the number of formal strikes, there is evidence that they have the unintended effect of increasing grievance arbitrations, unfair labour practices, absenteeism, and job actions (Hebdon, 2005; Hebdon & Stern, 1998, 2003). A job action could be any collective action designed to disrupt or slow down work (e.g., booking off sick, working to rule) or simply a button-wearing action to inform the public of union grievances.

The weaknesses of interest arbitration have been widely canvassed. Many (but not all) studies show that interest arbitration has a negative impact on the parties' ability to freely negotiate settlements.

// OTHER CONVERSION MECHANISMS

CONCILIATION AND MEDIATION

In addition to grievances and arbitrations, conciliation and mediation represent important conversion mechanisms in the Canadian industrial relations system. Since each province has its own legal system of dispute resolution (see Chapter 4), for our purposes mediation and conciliation will be treated as identical processes. For example, in six Canadian jurisdictions—federal, Alberta, British Columbia, Manitoba, Quebec, and Saskatchewan—there is no requirement to complete the conciliation/mediation procedure before a strike has been removed, but the procedure is required in New Brunswick, Newfoundland, Nova Scotia, Quebec, Ontario, and Prince Edward Island.

We defined mediation/conciliation in Chapter 4 as a process that involves a third party as facilitator. The facilitator has no power to impose a settlement but uses his/her abilities to bring the parties together. There are no real theories of mediation but the process can be broken into three stages as follows:

- Passive stage 1—the mediator/conciliator selects a neutral location to meet with the parties to introduce each other and determine the issues in dispute
- Probing stage 2—having identified the issues the mediator attempts to find areas of compromise on selected issues
- Active stage 3—if he/she is successful in stage 2 then the final stage involves a push to settlement with both labour and management making concessions to avoid a strike or lockout

alternative dispute resolution (ADR) resolving disputes without going to court

grievance mediation a voluntary nonbinding process whereby a neutral third party examines the grievance

ALTERNATIVE DISPUTE RESOLUTION (ADR) OPTIONS

Practitioners' journals discuss **alternative dispute resolution (ADR)**, a term commonly used in Canada. A keyword Internet search of this phrase will result in numerous hits about the previously discussed conversion processes of arbitration, mediation, and conciliation—mechanisms akin to ADRs (Carver & Vondra, 1994). The Canadian Human Rights Commission (2015) provides a good definition of ADR: "resolving disputes in ways other than going to court, including arbitration, mediation, negotiation, conciliation, etc."

In addition to the conversion mechanisms already discussed, some jurisdictions provide grievance mediation services as a form of ADR. **Grievance mediation** is a voluntary process whereby the parties can have a neutral third

UCCO-SACC-CSN, Pacific Region

The mediator brings labour and management together in a face-to-face meeting.

party examine the grievance. The mediator works with the parties to attempt to have them broker the resolution; yet it still leaves open the option for a formal arbitration hearing. IR Notebook 10.1 provides more details on this form of ADR.

ALTERNATIVE DISPUTE RESOLUTION IN NONUNION FIRMS

While ADR is core to the unionized employment relationship, it also exists in nonunion workplaces. For example, mediation and conciliation interventions are available to all workers who bring forward complaints to the Canadian Human Rights Commission (Canadian Human Rights Commission, 2015).

In addition, as is discussed in Chapter 6, many nonunion firms have due process and voice mechanisms such as grievance/complaint processes and third-party review of grievances/complaints (i.e., akin to arbitration). As Colvin (2003) points out, there are three possible reasons for the adoption of ADR in nonunion firms. First, ADR can be seen as part of a high-performance work system; that is, it is seen as a way to emphasize fair treatment of employees in an effort to increase employee commitment, retention, and performance. Second, under common law, litigation was the only way employees could attempt to resolve disputes with employers; ADR provides an alternative to litigation. Third, the implementation of ADR is a form of union substitution. By having access to dispute resolution mechanisms that mirror those of the union movement, employees may be less likely to seek unionization.

Regardless of the reason, the trend is clear. Many nonunion workplaces, as well as agencies such as the Canadian Human Rights Commission, are moving to forms of ADR in an effort to provide alternatives to legal action.

IR NOTEBOOK   10.1

GRIEVANCE MEDIATION: AN ALTERNATIVE TO COSTLY ARBITRATION

Given the high cost and the long time frame of dealing with grievances, many jurisdictions offer grievance mediation services. Here is an example from Saskatchewan.

After exhausting any grievance procedure established by the collective agreement, the parties can agree to request the Director of Labour Relations and Mediation to appoint a labour relations officer to assist the parties in resolving a dispute arising from an unresolved grievance.

Grievance mediation is a less formal process than arbitration. The outcome is decided by the two parties directly affected by the dispute, unlike arbitration, where a decision is handed down by a third party.

Grievance mediation is a mutually agreed to process by which the parties to a collective agreement, with the assistance of a mediator, work toward the resolution of a grievance arising from the interpretation, application, administration or alleged contravention of a collective agreement.

Instead of the formality of an arbitration hearing, a mediator meets with representatives of both parties in an informal setting, in joint and/or separate sessions. The mediator provides a neutral viewpoint on the relative merits of the parties' positions on the grievance and may provide suggestions for its resolution. The mediator is a third party who works constructively with the parties, in a flexible and creative manner, to assist the parties in resolving their dispute(s).

Here's How It Works:

- The program is voluntary; both parties must agree to participate.

- The mediation is informal in nature and the mediator will not produce any formal report. If an agreement is reached, the terms of settlement will be recorded.

- Arbitration remains an option if the grievance is unresolved after grievance mediation.

- Issues in industrial relations can be both unique and complex. Our mediators have extensive experience in dispute resolution in labour relations.
- All grievance mediation proceedings are without prejudice and are confidential between the parties, unless otherwise agreed.

Why Consider Grievance Mediation?

There are several reasons why employers and unions may want to consider grievance mediation:

- Attitudes—grievance mediation is designed to alleviate the build-up of negative attitudes which can develop when conflict goes unresolved.
- Control—grievance mediation allows the parties to shape a settlement. If the grievance goes to arbitration, a settlement will be imposed.
- Cost—arbitration can be an expensive process. A grievance mediator is assigned without cost for their services.
- Time—grievance mediation is designed for resolving disputes as quickly as possible. Time delays can lead to serious morale and personnel problems.

Source: Ministry of Labour Relations. Government of Saskatchewan. (2015). Conciliation and Mediation Services. Used with permission. Retrieved from http://www.saskatchewan.ca/work/collective-bargaining-and-mediation/conciliation-and-mediation#grievance-mediation.

// SUMMARY

As is shown in this chapter, there are a variety of conversion mechanisms in the current industrial relations system in addition to strikes and grievances, such as mediation, conciliation, arbitration, and alternative dispute resolution (ADR).

Given the potential high cost of grievances and strikes to employers, employees, and the Canadian economy as a whole, various alternative mechanisms designed to address workplace conflict and disagreements have been widely instituted. In terms of resolving impasses at collective bargaining, we reviewed first contract arbitration, conciliation, mediation, and interest arbitration.

We also looked at various mechanisms that can be used to address conflicts during the term of the collective agreement, and often regarding the interpretation of the collective agreement. Here, we studied the important mechanisms of grievances and rights arbitration—two mechanisms that are legally required only under collective bargaining law. However, we saw that given the movement toward more progressive human resources management policies in nonunion firms, these mechanisms are becoming increasingly more common in all workplaces—unionized and nonunionized.

In our discussion of rights arbitration, we examined how legalistic it has become in terms of language and process. The process is not without its problems, however, causing many jurisdictions to provide alternative dispute resolution mechanisms.

Overall, this chapter has shown the diversity and indeed sometimes the complexity of dispute resolution procedures. As time unfolds it will be most interesting to see the extent to which these mechanisms become embedded in nonunion firms as well as the extent to which these processes become increasingly—or decreasingly—legalistic.

KEY TERMS

alternative dispute resolution (ADR) 311
conventional interest arbitration 310
culpable 305
final-offer arbitration 310
first agreement (or first contract) arbitration 310
grievance mediation 311
interest arbitration 310
jurisprudence 304
mitigation factors 305
prima facie case 304

WEBLINKS

Resources for Grievance Arbitration:
http://guides.library.utoronto.ca/employmentandlabourlaw

Canadian Human Rights Commission and ADR:
http://www.chrc-ccdp.ca/eng/content/how-develop-internal-dispute-resolution-process

Saskatchewan Federation of Labour grievance mediation process:
**http://www.saskatchewan.ca/work/collective-bargaining-and-mediation/conciliation
-and-mediation#grievance-mediation**

DISCUSSION QUESTIONS

1. With more nonunion firms providing dispute resolutions that are akin to those of the labour movement, will unions become obsolete in the future?

2. Given the limitations of traditional rights arbitration, do you believe that we will see an increase in alternative dispute resolution processes?

3. Some unions require that all discharge cases can be taken to arbitration; others look at the issue of arbitration on a case-by-case basis. What do you see as the pros and cons of each of these options?

4. What are the three stages of mediation? In your opinion what type of person would make the best mediator?

5. Identify the issues that might be raised by labour and management in a dismissal arbitration case.

USING THE INTERNET

1. Many provincial labour relations boards provide third-party dispute resolution procedures in addition to arbitration. Go to your province's website.

   a. What forms of third-party assistance are offered to help parties resolve grievances?

b. What forms of third-party assistance are offered to help parties conclude a collective agreement?

c. Which of these third-party mechanisms are compulsory versus voluntary?

2. Go to an Internet search engine and search using keywords such as *grievance*, *dispute*, and *alternative dispute resolution*. What do you find? Are there union and nonunion examples? If so, what are some key differences between these union and nonunion examples?

3. In this chapter, we discussed that management training can reduce the number of grievances filed. Conduct a search for industrial relations or labour relations training for managers/supervisors. Do you believe that the training you have found can better inform managers and thus reduce grievances?

4. Unions often provide training for shop stewards. Search the websites of three to five large unions in your area. To what extent do you see training programs for union leaders? Is there evidence that they are trained on matters related to grievances, arbitrations, and other forms of dispute resolution?

EXERCISES

1. Reread the opening vignette. How does the strike described differ from traditional ones?

2. Many students work while they attend school. As a group or class project, check for a progressive discipline policy in your organization. If it has one, bring a copy into class.

a. Does the policy you found contain the elements discussed in IR Notebook 10.1?

b. Are there significant differences between the policies of unionized and nonunionized workplaces? If so, what are these differences?

3. Many university and college libraries have access to LACs and Brown and Beatty either electronically or in hard copy. Using Brown and Beatty, find an LAC that deals with discipline and discharge.

a. Was the employee culpable or not? Why?

b. What mitigating factors, if any, did the union raise?

c. To what extent did these mitigating factors impact the final decision?

d. What is the time frame between the date of the disciplinary action in question and the final decision?

4. Most universities are unionized and have collective agreements readily available in hard copy or on their websites. Have a look at the grievance procedure contained in one collective agreement from your university.

a. Is there an informal (pre-grievance) step mentioned?

b. How many steps are in the formal process?

c. Which levels of management and the union are present at each step?

On January 29, Island Air Flight 101 departed from Vancouver Island Airport en route to Montreal. Upon landing in Montreal, Flight 101 skidded off the runway and crashed. No passengers or crew were injured. There was light snow and a temperature of –4 degrees Celsius. A safety board conducted an investigation. The case facts are as follows: (1) The pilot, James Brown, was forty years old, had fifteen years of service, and had no prior incidents or warnings on his employment record; (2) Captain Brown was later discharged by Island Air; (3) as a unionized Canadian employee, he filed a grievance that went to arbitration; and (4) at the arbitration, the facts were not in dispute.

QUESTIONS

1. What questions must the arbitrator examine to determine whether the employer had just cause for discharging the pilot?

2. Assume that the safety board investigation determined that the plane crashed for two reasons: (a) due to a mechanical failure, the engines were not producing maximum power; and (b) the ground crew did not de-ice the plane. As a result, once the plane was airborne, ice formed on the wings and this extra weight contributed to the crash. Hence, the crash was not caused by pilot error. Given these facts, walk through the questions raised in question 1 above and discuss how you would rule if you were the arbitrator. Justify your ruling.

3. Now, assume that the safety board determined the following: (a) The plane was landing at a speed of 600 kilometres per hour, above the recommended landing speed of 400 kilometres per hour; (b) the pilot was aware of the recommended speed; (c) the pilot had landed the plane on many occasions at the recommended speed of 400 kilometres per hour; and (d) there was no evidence that the excessive speed was justified or caused by a mechanical failure (i.e., the safety board found that the crash was caused by pilot error). Again walk through the questions you presented in question 1 above and present how you would rule if you were the arbitrator. Justify your ruling.

// ENDNOTE

1. This case is not based on any real person, company, or event.

// REFERENCES

1. Brown, D. J. M., & Beatty, D. M. (2006). *Canadian labour arbitration* (4th edition). Aurora, ON: Canada Law Book Inc.

2. Campolieti, Michael, Robert Hebdon, and Benjamin Dachis. 2014. "Collective Bargaining in the Canadian Public Sector, 1978-2008: The Consequences of Restraint and Structural Change", *British Journal of Industrial Relations*, published on-line June 23 DOI: 10.1111/bjir.12082.

3. Canadian Human Rights Commission. (2015). Alternative dispute resolution. Retrieved 4 February 2015 from http://www.chrc-ccdp.ca/eng/content/how-develop-internal-dispute-resolution-process

4. Carver, T. B., & Vondra, A. A. (1994). Alternative dispute resolution: Why it doesn't work and why it does. *Harvard Business Review*, May–June, pp. 120–130.

5. Colvin, A. J. S. (2003). Institutional pressures, human resource strategies, and the rise of nonunion dispute resolution procedures. *Industrial and Labor Relations Review, 56*, pp. 375–392.

6. Currie, J., & McConnell, S. (1991). Collective bargaining in the public sector: The effect of legal structure on dispute costs and wages. *American Economic Review, 81*(4), pp. 693–718.

7. Government of Saskatchewan. (2015). Grievance mediation: An alternative to costly arbitration. Retrieved 5 February 2015 from http://www.saskatchewan.ca/work/collective-bargaining-and-mediation/conciliation-and-mediation#grievance-mediation

8. Hebdon, R. (2005). Toward a theory of workplace conflict: The case of U.S. municipal collective bargaining. *Advances in Industrial and Labor Relations, 14*, pp. 35–67.

9. Hebdon, R., & Stern, R. (1998). Tradeoffs among expressions of industrial conflict: Public sector strike bans and grievance arbitrations. *Industrial and Labor Relations Review, 51*(2), pp. 204–221.

10. Hebdon, R., & Stern, R. (2003). Do public-sector strike bans really prevent conflict? *Industrial Relations, 42*, pp. 493–512.

11. Ichniowski, C. (1982). Arbitration and police bargaining: Prescriptions for the blue flu. *Industrial Relations, 21*(2), pp. 149–166.

12. Johnson, S. J. T. (2010). First contract arbitration: Effects on bargaining on work stoppages. *Industrial & Labour Relations Review, 63*, pp. 585–605.

13. Olson, C. (1986). Strikes, strike penalties, and arbitration in six states. *Industrial and Labor Relations Review, 39*(4), pp. 539–551.

14. Riddell, C. (2013). Labor law and reaching a first collective agreement: Evidence from a quasi-experimental set of reforms in Ontario. *Industrial Relations, 52*(3), 702. Retrieved from http://search.proquest.com/docview/1370368458?accountid=12339

15. Rose, J. B. (1994). The complaining game: How effective is compulsory interest arbitration? *Journal of Collective Negotiations in the Public Sector, 23*(3), pp. 187–202.

16. Williams, K., & Taras, D. (2000). Reinstatement in arbitration: The grievors' perspective. *Relations industrielles, 55*, pp. 227–249.

17. Zerbe, W. (2009). Chapter 6: Emotional deviance and organizational discipline: A study of emotions in grievance arbitration. In Neal M. Ashkanasy, Wilfred J. Zerbe & Charmine E. J. Härtel (Eds.), *Emotions in groups, organizations and cultures* (*Research on emotion in organizations*, Volume 5) (pp. 123–149). Bingley, UK: Emerald Group Publishing Limited.

CHAPTER
11

IMPACTS OF UNIONIZATION

LEARNING OBJECTIVES

BY THE END OF THIS CHAPTER, YOU WILL BE ABLE TO DISCUSS

- the impacts of unions on management practices, in particular those related to human resources management (HRM) practices;
- the relationship between unions and firm measures; and
- the impact of unionization on employee measures.

Nick Williams and Emily Hong decide to grab a bite to eat between classes. Nick notices a newspaper left on the table with a headline concerning a recent public-sector pension agreement and asks, "Have you seen the news stories today about the public-sector pension plan?" Emily replies, "I have only heard that the unions and the government reached a deal. Though Mom did say this morning that it has no impact on her as she retires in four years. What do you know about it?"

"Let's see." Nick picks up the paper and starts to read. "It says here that the current pension plan was not sustainable. Wow!! Sixty-four cents of every dollar of provincial debt was due to the unfunded public-sector pension liability with a total unfunded pension liability of $5 billion. No wonder they say it was not sustainable."

"Anything else of interest?" asks Emily. "Sure is," Nick continues. "It will take about 30 years for the pension to become self-funding—can you believe that? It will be self-funded by the time we retire. What else. . . . The unions and the government agreed that the premiums paid by employees will increase, the age needed to take early pension will increase by a few years, and the pension payment a retiree receives will be based on their best six years of earnings, up from their best five years of earnings. In exchange, the new pension plan will be jointly managed by the union and the government. And you are right, anyone who retires in the next five years will see no changes—so your Mom is not affected by the new deal. So, all in all, it looks like employees will have to pay a bit more but continue to have a defined pension. It seems that both the government and the various unions are happy with the deal—both are highlighting the fact that employees retain a defined benefit pension. What's the big deal about a defined pension?"

Emily replies, "It's a big deal because defined benefit means that employees are guaranteed a specific pension payment when they retire. In the other type of pension, defined contribution, employees know what they contributed to the pension plan but the payment they receive when they retire is not guaranteed—instead, it will depend on how the pension fund performs."

"That makes perfect sense," says Nick with a smile. "I'd much prefer the security of a defined benefit plan. Now the next story makes sense as well. It says the city and the union are potentially at an impasse in their current round of collective bargaining. The city is proposing that existing employees will retain their current defined benefit pension but that all new hires will move to a defined contribution pension plan."

Emily looks at the time on her phone. "We have to run. We've got an industrial relations class in ten minutes. How funny, the topic today is the impact of unionization. I wonder if we will discuss these pension issues!"

Sources: Antle, R. (2 September 2014). "Pension reform deal targets 'sustainable' future for plan: Premiums and retirement ages to rise, but defined benefits will remain in place." CBC News. Retrieved from http://www.cbc.ca/news/canada/newfoundland -labrador/pension-reform-deal-targets-sustainable-future-for -plan-1.2753102; Benefits Canada Staff. (20 September 2014). "Pension reforms won't affect N.L. public sector." Retrieved from http://www.benefitscanada.com/pensions/governance-law/ pension-reforms-won%E2%80%99t-affect-n-l-public-sector -retirees-44172; Executive Council Finance. (2 September 2014). "Sustainable solutions to pension reform." Retrieved from http://www.releases.gov.nl.ca/releases/2014/exec/0902n05 .aspx; "City of St. John's workers ratify contract." (19 September 2014). The Telegram. Retrieved from http://www .thetelegram.com/News/Local/2014-09-19/article-3875901/ City-of-St.-Johns-workers-ratify-contract/1.

// IMPACT OF UNIONS ON MANAGEMENT PRACTICES

As you may recall from previous chapters, nonunion workplaces operate under the master–servant relationship. The employer is free to determine workplace policies and practices, and employees are dutifully required to follow their employer's requests. About the only restrictions on employers in common law are statutory legislation covering minimum wage, overtime, grounds of discrimination, etc. However, in a unionized workplace, the numerous conversion mechanisms we discussed in Chapters 9 and 10 mean that the employer cannot have unilateral ability to determine all terms and conditions of employment. In many unionized workplaces, the collective agreement will spell out both processes and requirements related to such issues.

In this section, we focus on how unions impact management practices, in particular those related to human resources management (HRM). Traditional HRM functions include staffing, training and development, performance appraisal, job evaluation, and compensation. For decades, scholars have proposed several reasons for why such HRM practices would differ between union and nonunion firms (see Brown & Warren, 2010; Freeman & Medoff, 1984; Hirschmen, 1970; Ng & Maki, 1994; Slichter, Healy & Livernash, 1960, Verma, 2005; Wagar, 1997). A summary of these reasons follows:

1. The **shock effect**, which states that the increased protection and costs associated with unionization shock management into adopting both stricter HRM practices and methods of improving production/service efficiency.

2. Differing preferences of union versus nonunion workers. Because unionized employees are often older, and remain with a firm for a longer period of time because of the advantages associated with seniority, their preferences for HRM practices may differ from those of nonunion employees.

3. Exit–voice theory states that dissatisfied employees have two choices: leave the firm (i.e., exit) or voice their dissatisfaction. Unions represent a **collective voice**, enabling workers to express their discontent. As a collective, they have greater power to convince employers to adopt HRM practices that reflect worker preferences relative to a single employee under common law.

We will now briefly examine several specific HRM functions in more detail to see the key differences between union and nonunion firms. As argued by Jacobson, Rubin, and Donahue (2008), while studies examining the relationship between unions and compensation are common, fewer studies have examined the impact of unionization on specific HR practices. Unfortunately, it means that some of the literature on noncompensation practices is becoming dated.

STAFFING

Recruitment, selection, and deselection represent key staffing functions. We will now look at how each function can be impacted by unionization.

RECRUITMENT

Recruitment techniques are used to make potential employees aware of job openings. The literature shows that unionized employers use often use fewer **recruitment** techniques (e.g., newspaper ads, private and government agencies, employee referrals, direct applicants; see Koch & Hundley, 1997). However, union firms often use more formal job posting methods (i.e., internal recruitment; see Ng & Maki, 1994). Potential reasons for these trends are that unionized jobs, with the higher security and voice provisions, may reduce the need for extensive, and expensive, recruitment techniques (Koch & Hundley, 1997). A second explanation may be the use of recruitment processes outlined in the collective agreement, such as closed-shop clauses, job posting procedures, etc. Such clauses, for all intents and purposes, limit the employer's ability to recruit externally while reinforcing internal recruitment practices.

shock effect
occurs when increased costs and protection shock management into stricter management practices

collective voice
the ability of a group or union to express concerns

recruitment
techniques designed to make potential employees aware of job openings

SELECTION

Selection techniques are used to decide which employee should fill a job opening. Recall that union security clauses can play a role in selection. For example, in a closed shop, where new hires must be members of the union before an employer can hire them, management plays a small role in hiring; the union itself may even decide which employees are hired. Canadian evidence historically suggests that unionized firms are more likely to hire from within versus externally; have **probationary periods**; institute formal promotion criteria; and promote workers on the basis of seniority (Ng & Maki, 1994). Interestingly, a more recent Canadian study (Haines, Jalette & Larose, 2010) did not find a significant relationship between unionization and the usage of internal labour markets (hiring from within the workplace or from another workplace within the same employer).

Help wanted ads or signs are typical recruitment techniques used by many organizations.

DESELECTION/TERMINATION

Deselection in essence represents the removal of an employee from a job. As discussed previously, collective agreements often contain detailed layoff and bumping procedures. Remember that the concept of *layoff*, whereby an employee can be released from work and **recalled** (rehired later), applies only to unionized workplaces. In nonunionized workplaces, termination for any reason, including downsizing, does not imply the right of recall; rather, it signals the end of the employment relationship.

> **probationary period**
> a short period of time after an employee is hired in which he or she is not fully protected by a union
>
> **recall**
> the process by which a laid-off employee gets rehired

STAFFING AND JOB DESIGN FLEXIBILITY

As we discussed in Chapter 6, many employers have introduced alternative work schedules and have increased their use of temporary and casual employees. One review of the literature (Verma, 2005) clearly shows that unionized firms are much less likely to have numerical flexibility (the ability to contract out work, to use temporary and part-time workers, etc.) and are often prohibited from assigning a worker job tasks that fall into another worker's job description. Hence, you will often hear managers of unionized firms discussing that employees (and their union) will grieve if they assign work outside an employee's job description.

In terms of job design flexibility, it is often argued that unions will seek to minimize the management flexibility in this regard. Not surprisingly, then, recent Canadian evidence found a negative relationship between unionization and flexible job design elements of "job rotation, job enrichment/redesign (broadened job definitions), and job enrichment (increased skill variety or autonomy of work)" (Haines et al., 2010, p. 236).

TRAINING AND DEVELOPMENT

Globally, the research supports the notion that unionized workers receive more training than nonunion workers. Data from Canada, the UK, Germany, and Australia all show that unionized workers have increased access to training relative to nonunion employees

(Boheim & Booth, 2004; Booth, Francesconi & Zoega, 2003; Dustmann & Schönberg, 2009; Livingstone & Raykov, 2005, 2008; Waddoups, 2012). The most recent of these studies reported that the probability of unionized workers having access to training was approximately five probability points higher for men and ten percent higher for women (Waddoups, 2012).

PERFORMANCE APPRAISAL

Performance appraisal has two purposes. First, it has a developmental purpose—namely, to develop and motivate staff. Second, it has an administrative function—namely, to determine pay, promotion, termination, and disciplinary decisions (Brown & Warren, 2010). Given that the collective agreement would contain language concerning much of the administrative functions of appraisal, it should not be surprising that research from Britain (Brown & Heywood, 2005) and Canada (Ng & Maki, 1994) has found that unionized firms were much less likely to have a formal appraisal system compared to nonunion firms.

Interestingly, Canadian studies by Brown and colleagues involving newly introduced performance appraisal processes in unionized mining (Krats & Brown, 2013) and telecommunications companies (Brown & Latham, 2000) suggest that unions appear supportive of performance appraisals when they focus on developmental purposes versus administrative purpose. These studies further suggest that union involvement in the design of the system is beneficial to effective implementation.

Perhaps Brown & Waren (2011) best summarized the literature when they concluded that in unionized workplaces: (1) performance appraisals are less common; (2) in cases where such processes exist, the union appears to have no preference regarding the format of the instrument but does prefer that the process be developmentally focused; (3) unions are more supportive of performance appraisal processes in which they have been involved in the process design and in which the primary goals are not geared toward discipline and/or individual pay; and (4) goal setting has been used to introduce, or improve upon, performance appraisal systems. We believe that two factors support these conclusions. First, as unions represent a voice process, it seems natural that they would seek involvement in these issues. Second, the bulk of the administrative functions of performance appraisal in unionized firms (e.g., pay, promotion, layoff, etc.) are covered by the specific language and procedures found in collective agreements. Thus, unions would most likely prefer that these administrative functions not be the primary goal of performance appraisal processes.

JOB EVALUATION AND JOB ANALYSIS

job evaluation
a process whereby the firm determines the value of a job

job analysis
a process whereby the key competencies for a job are identified

A key element in HRM is to ensure that HRM practices (e.g., selection, promotion, pay, performance appraisal) reflect the skills needed to effectively perform the job at hand (Long, 2014). In fact, as is discussed in Chapter 4, it is a legal requirement that such decisions be based on the worker's ability to perform the key functions of a job. If firms do otherwise, they risk discrimination charges. Thus, most organizations use some form of **job evaluation** or **job analysis** to gather such data. Evidence suggests that unionized firms are as likely as nonunion firms to use what can be seen as objective methods (e.g., point-factor methods, in which key job duties are assessed and given points according to a classification system, or classification methods, in which jobs are placed into groups or grades with each group representing jobs requiring certain skills or knowledge, and each job description then being compared to the group description). However, unionized firms are much less likely to use a subjective ranking of jobs in which jobs are ranked in terms of overall worth to the organization (Ng & Maki, 1994; Verma, 2005). While job evaluation is often seen as a managerial function, it is interesting to note that some workplaces use joint union–management job evaluation committees (Long, 2014).

COMPENSATION

Of all the possible impacts of unionization on human resources practices, the area of compensation has received the most focus. As we point out in IR Notebook 10.1, the union often has to balance the desire to increase wages with the potential of few jobs for members. For at least 30 years scholars have argued that unions place two significant impacts on compensation: the monopoly effect and the voice effect (Freeman & Medoff, 1984). The **monopoly effect** is shown by unions raising wages above the rate of nonunion employees. In so doing, unions are argued to reduce employment levels as employers choose to hire fewer employees given the high wage rate. The second union effect on wages is known as the collective voice impact. While much of the research has focused on wages and wage rates, it is important to remember that an organization's **total compensation mix** contains three elements: base pay, performance pay, and indirect pay (also known as *benefits*) (Long, 2014):

- **Base pay** represents the portion of a worker's pay that is based on time worked and not based on performance or output. For example, many students work in jobs in which their base pay is an hourly rate (e.g., $14 per hour).

- **Performance pay** represents the portion of an employee's pay provided only if certain specific performance targets are achieved. These can be both individual and group targets. For example, salespeople often make a commission based on their sales.

- **Indirect pay** includes anything that the employer pays for that is not part of an employee's base or performance pay. This often includes various forms of benefits such as paid leaves of absence (e.g., vacation), retirement/pension plans, and health and life insurance plans. Accordingly, we will refer to indirect pay as benefits throughout this chapter.

> **monopoly effect**
> the union's ability to raise wages above nonunion rates
>
> **total compensation mix**
> the total base pay, performance pay, and indirect pay that an employee receives

> **base pay**
> the part of pay that is solely based on time worked
>
> **performance pay**
> the part of pay that is based on output or performance
>
> **indirect pay (or benefits)**
> anything that an employer pays for, to the benefit of the employee, that is not part of base or performance pay

IR NOTEBOOK 11.1

THE UNION DILEMMA: PAY OR JOBS?

As the evidence in this chapter shows, union members have significantly higher pay than their nonunion counterparts. A natural question is whether this pay premium results in lower employment levels. Some claim that evidence "(t)hat unions suppress employment growth among their employers has been such a ubiquitous finding that it has been dubbed 'the one constant' in industrial relations research" (Walsworth & Long, 2012, p. 654). Yet the Canadian evidence suggests that the effect is not universal. One study suggests that private unionized firms reduce employment by the small amount of about 2 percent a year (Walsworth, 2010a), while a second study found that unionization may even increase employment in small service firms (Walsworth & Long, 2012).

Given the potential of lower employment caused by higher wages, unions have often been faced with a tough decision. Do they focus on getting wage and benefit gains for members—which, remember, is a key reason why employees join unions—or do they focus on increasing/maintaining employment? The following newspaper article highlights the tightrope unions must walk as they balance wages and jobs.

The Conservative government, which has cut nearly 26,000 jobs in Canada's public service over the past three years, is poised to shed another 8,900 jobs by 2017.

Treasury Board's latest employment numbers show 257,138 people working in the core public service at the end of March, compared to 2010–11 when the federal payroll peaked at 282,980.

But the plans and priorities reports done by federal departments indicate they are braced to eliminate another 8,900 jobs over the next three years, said Mostafa Askari, the assistant Parliamentary Budget Officer.

"Those 8,900 reductions are presumably beyond what has already been done," he said. That would bring total cuts to about 35,000.

That's a far cry from the 19,200 jobs the Conservative government pledged to cut in its major austerity budget of 2012, which launched a downsizing that trimmed $5.2 billion in spending over three years. Most of those cuts were managed by attrition and done in the first year.

The additional reductions are the result of all the other spending cuts—particularly the operating freezes imposed on departments in 2010 and another one this year—that are still working their way through the system.

The latest two-year operating freeze, which affects all departments and separate agencies, came into effect this year and is expected to generate $1.7 billion is savings over two years.

It comes on top of the billions of dollars' worth of spending reductions that departments have been swallowing since 2010. The impact, once the latest operating freeze is factored in, will leave departments managing yearly ongoing savings of $13.7 billion by 2017–18.

With that kind of cumulative impact, federal managers have little room to manoeuvre in managing this operating freeze, which probably means no hiring and more layoffs.

It also puts unions in a tough position at the bargaining table because any wage increase they win for public servants would have to be absorbed by departments—which could further increase job losses.

The government and union are in the early days of what is expected to be a very tough round of collective bargaining over the Conservatives' plans to replace public servants' existing regime of accumulated sick leave with a short-term disability plan.

As part of those contract talks, the government tabled a proposed wage increase of 0.5 per cent a year over three years. During a freeze, departments must absorb any wage increases and can't rely on Treasury Board for funds to compensate for the extra costs of the wage settlements.

That puts unions in the unenviable position of a negotiating a deal that could result in more job losses. The 17 unions have already lost bargaining clout under the new ground rules for collective bargaining that the government has implemented.

Sources: May, K. (27 August 2014). "Federal government on track to cut 35,000 public service jobs." *Ottawa Citizen*. Material reprinted with the express permission of: Ottawa Citizen, a division of Postmedia Network Inc. Retrieved from http://ottawacitizen.com/news/national/federal-government-on-track-to-cut-35000-public-service-jobs.

BASE PAY

Data from multiple countries have consistently shown that unionized workers earn more than nonunion workers. Decades of research, largely based on U.S. data, has shown that unionized employees earn about 15 percent more than their nonunion counterparts (Blanchflower & Bryson, 2004; Freeman & Medoff, 1984; Lewis, 1986). More recent American and UK data suggest that the union premium may even be over 20 percent (Bahrami, Bitzan & Leitch, 2009; Blanchflower & Bryson, 2010; Eren, 2007).

Turning to Canadian data, we see similar trends. Union members, on average, have had a 10 to 15 percent range premium since the 1970s [i.e., a 13 to 16 percent differential in the early 1970s (Grant, Swidinsky & Vanderkamp, 1987); 10.4 percent in the late 1980s (Renaud, 1998); between 8 to 15 percent in the 1990s (Kuhn, 1998; (Verma & Fang, 2002), and in the 9 to 13 percent range in the first decade of 2000 (Godard, 2007)]. While much of the data have examined traditional industries (manufacturing, construction, private sector, public sector), the same 10 to 15 percent premium has been found in low-wage service jobs, such as those of child-care workers (Cleveland, Gunderson & Hyatt, 2003). Thus, the evidence concerning a Canadian union premium in the 10 to 15 percent range appears to be very robust.

However, this does not mean that every unionized worker receives a 10 to 15 percent premium. For example, public versus private sector can play a role. Evidence from the United States suggests that the union premium in the private sector is almost 23 percent, as against 11 percent for public sector (Bahrami, Bitzan & Leitch 2009), while UK data show that the union premium is higher for lower skilled jobs in the private sector (Blanchflower & Bryson, 2010). Immigration status too can play a role, with evidence from Ireland showing that the hourly union wage premium is approximately 8 percent for immigrants (Turner, Cross & O'Sullivan, 2014). Finally, Canadian evidence suggests that industry plays a significant role, with a union premium of 11 percent in the service sector compared to approximately 1 percent in manufacturing (Walsworth & Long, 2012). Perhaps the low-union effect in Canadian manufacturing is due to the highly unionized nature of that industry as study of Ontario professors (Martinello, 2009), also a highly unionized sector, concluded that unionization did not impact wages.

A natural question is whether the 10 to 15 percent wage increase for unions results in a wage decrease in the nonunion sector. Two arguments are key here (Kuhn, 1998):

1. The **spillover effect** argument states that the increased wages in the union sector cause a decrease in demand for labour in that sector, which would in turn increase supply for labour in the nonunion sector and thus reduce wages in the nonunion sector.

2. The **threat effect** argument states that nonunion employers will increase non-union wages in an attempt to make unionization of their workplace less likely.

It is interesting to note that unions impact both wage rates and wage structures. A consistent finding in the literature is that the **wage differential** between the highest- and lowest-paid workers is smaller in unionized workplaces than in nonunionized workplaces (Card, Lemieux & Riddell, 2004; Hayter & Weinberg, 2011). As this evidence concerning wages and wage structures shows, unions generally have what can be called an inequity-reducing effect as they often reduce wage inequality. As we discuss in more detail in IR Today 11.1, some attribute the global increase in wage inequality to the reduction in unionization.

spillover effect
a belief that increases in union wages result in decreases in nonunion wages

threat effect
a belief that nonunion employers increase wages to avoid unionization

wage differential
the difference in wages earned by two groups of workers

Courtesy of Unifor.

Unions often promote their benefits to encourage nonunion members to unionize.

IR TODAY 11.1

IMPACT OF UNIONIZATION ON THE BROADER ECONOMY AND SOCIETY

Markey and Patmore (2011) assert that the three criteria for assessing union effectiveness are the extent that unions: (1) organize new members; (2) provide positive outcomes from collective bargaining; and (3) impact the larger society. Over the past few decades, we have seen a general decline in unionization. In some places, such as the United States, New Zealand, and France, union density has dropped by as much as 60 percent. Naturally, then, a question to answer is whether we have seen broader societal impacts associated with decreased unionization. While there is no quick answer to this question, some interesting trends can be seen.

An analysis of data from 22 OECD countries by Pontusson (2013) suggests a negative pattern between rates of unionization and wage inequity (or the spread between the highest- and lowest-paid members of society). Figure 11.1 examines wage inequity using a measure called the 90–10 ratio. This is the ratio of a person in the 90th percentile of earnings relative to a person in the 10th percentile of earnings. The figure clearly shows that countries with higher unionization (measured here as union density), have more equal wage distribution (i.e., lower wage inequality). Notice how the United States (coded as US), with one of the most drastic drops in unionization, has the highest level of wage inequality in contrast to Sweden (SE), with a high level of unionization and a low level of wage inequality.

Interestingly, Pontusson goes on to examine the average rate of voter turnout for political elections and union density (Figure 11.2). Note that as shown below, the trend is very similar. High union density countries like Sweden have high voter turnout; low union density countries like the United States how low voter turnout.

While this study does not allow us to conclude that higher unionization rates cause wage equality and voter turnout, the relationships are certainly interesting. They further suggest that unionization can impact the broader economy and society.

Source: Pontusson, J. (2013). Unionization, inequality and redistribution. *British Journal of Industrial Relations, 51*, pp. 797–825. doi: 10.1111/bjir.12045.

FIGURE 11.1

EARNING INEQUALITY (FULL-TIME EMPLOYEES) AND UNION DENSITY, 2008

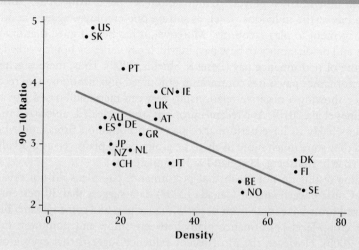

Note: Australia (AU), Austria (AT), Belgium (BE), Canada (CN), Denmark (DK), Finland (FI), France (FR) , Germany (DE), Greece (GR) , Ireland (IE) ,Italy (IT) 1976, Japan (JP), New Zealand (NZ)), Norway (NO), Portugal (PT), South Korea (SK), Spain (ES), Sweden (SE), Switzerland (CH), The Netherlands (NL), United Kingdom (UK), United States (US)

Sources: Pontusson, J. (2013). Unionization, inequality and redistribution. *British Journal of Industrial Relations, 51*, p. 805. Reproduced with permission of John Wiley & Sons Ltd.

FIGURE 11.2

AVERAGE VOTER TURNOUT IN 2000–09 AND UNION DENSITY IN 2005

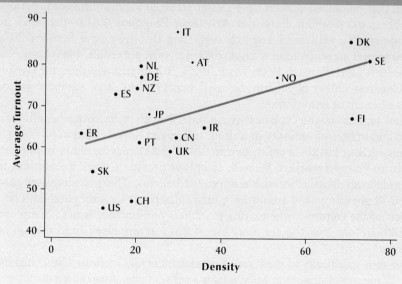

Note: Australia (AU), Austria (AT), Belgium (BE), Canada (CN), Denmark (DK), Finland (FI), France (FR) , Germany (DE), Greece (GR) , Ireland (IE) ,Italy (IT) 1976, Japan (JP), New Zealand (NZ)), Norway (NO), Portugal (PT), South Korea (SK), Spain (ES), Sweden (SE), Switzerland (CH), The Netherlands (NL), United Kingdom (UK), United States (US)

Source: Pontusson, J. (2013). Unionization, inequality and redistribution. *British Journal of Industrial Relations, 51*, p. 809. Reproduced with permission of John Wiley & Sons Ltd.

PERFORMANCE PAY

As is shown in our discussion of wage structures, unions have tried to minimize pay differences between individual employees. Unions often see performance pay, particularly performance pay at the individual level, as pitting one employee against another and allowing management to play favourites. Moreover, it has been argued that unions prefer the security and predictability of base pay, in which pay varies by hours worked, to the uncertain nature of performance pay (Long & Shields, 2009). Thus, there is general consensus that performance pay is less common in unionized organizations, with recent Canadian evidence showing a negative relationship between merit/skill-based pay and unionization (Haines et al., 2010). As a recent European study revealed, unionized firms were 21 percent less likely to have performance pay than nonunion firms, and where such plans existed they were much more likely to be group-based plans versus individual performance pay (Barth, Bratsberg, Hægeland & Raaum, 2012).

These preceding results do not mean that performance pay plans do not exist in unionized firms. Conference Board of Canada (2002) data suggest that 30 percent of Canadian unionized firms have some form of performance pay, and some research finds no differences in group-level performance plans between union and nonunion firms (Long & Shields, 2009). However, the most recent evidence suggests that even group-level performance plans such as **gain sharing** and **profit sharing** are less common in unionized workplaces (Haines et al., 2010; Long & Fang, 2013).

> **gain sharing**
> a group performance pay that is based on firm productivity gains
>
> **profit sharing**
> a group performance pay that is based on firm profits

INDIRECT PAY/BENEFITS

Given that benefits account for as much as 30 percent of the total payroll of many organizations (Long, 2014), and that benefit costs are increasing, indirect pay structures have come under increasing scrutiny over the past few years. Decades of research has concluded that unionized workers have greater access to various forms of benefits—for example pensions, vacations, **Employee Assistance Programs (EAPs)**—than their nonunion counterparts, with some research suggesting that they have between 20 and 45 percent greater access (Altonji & Usui, 2007; Freeman & Medoff, 1984; Long, 2006; Long & Shields, 2009; Renaud, 1998; Wagar, 1997). Not surprisingly, then, the Canadian Labour Congress (2011) highlights increased benefit plans (e.g., vacation, pension, health) as a benefit of unionization.

> **Employee Assistance Program (EAP)**
> a counselling service available to employees

Several reasons might explain why unionized firms have better benefits. First, given the importance of seniority in unions, unionized workers tend to be older, and thus issues such as health benefits, pensions, and EAPs may be more important to them than to younger workers. Second, as unions provide a voice mechanism, they may provide a mechanism to enable improved benefits. Third, as discussed during our review of grievances and arbitrations, many arbitrators look for good-faith efforts on the part of the employer when trying to address performance issues of employees. We would therefore expect to see more use of EAPs in unionized firms than in nonunion firms.

As we turn specifically to the issue of pensions, the CLC website (2011) highlights that only 27 percent of nonunion workers have a pension plan versus about 80 percent of unionized workers. Luchak and Gunderson (2000) provide several reasons why unionized organizations would be more likely to have pension plans, particularly those that are of the **defined benefit** type, in which employees are essentially guaranteed a certain pension value upon retirement. For example, the median union member may be older, with less mobility (meaning that employers may be hesitant to hire an older worker), and thus may

> **defined benefit**
> a type of pension plan that guarantees a specific payout

have more to gain from a pension plan. In addition, the union can provide employee voice. Thus, union members may be more comfortable relying on the union to (1) protect them from a "bad" plan, (2) maintain knowledge concerning the complex technical issues concerning pension investments, and (3) ensure that their retirement needs are protected.

EQUALITY, PARTICIPATION, AND SAFETY

In addition to influencing traditional human resources functions, unions can also affect other factors that come under the umbrella of HRM in many organizations, namely workplace equality, voice, and health and safety. As summarized by Bacon and Hoque (2012, p. 239):

> It is generally acknowledged that trade unions have had a significant impact recently in terms of promoting fair treatment at work and advancing the interests of disadvantaged workers. Studies have shown, for example, that equal opportunities (EO) practices are more likely to have been adopted in unionized than non-union workplaces, and outcomes such as pay rates have been found to be more equitable in unionized workplaces than elsewhere

Over the past 30 years, Canadian labour has made great strides in the equality arena (Brown, 2003; Hart, 2002b; Hunt & Rayside, 2000; Parker & Foley, 2010). Thus, as is shown in Chapter 8, many collective agreements now contain specific clauses on employment equity, equal pay, disability, and sexual harassment, as well as special committees dedicated to such issues. In addition, we see that CLC and union websites often contain sections dedicated to equity issues, where issues of relevance to visible minorities and women are presented (e.g., CLC 2014a; CUPE, 2014).

Encouraging health and safety has become an important role of unions. Historically, Canadian unions have sought to bring in safer working conditions for their members and have lobbied the government for increased legislation to protect workers (Hart, 2010). This theme still holds a special place in the labour movement. As the CLC (2014b) highlights, on average four Canadians a day die on the job—over 1,000 a year. Given these factors, it should not be surprising that labour organizations often devote considerable space on their websites to issues concerning workplace health and safety as well as cite the improved safety records of unionized workplaces as a key benefit of joining a union (e.g., CLC, 2014b; Unifor, 2014).

While all workplaces are subject to the same equality and safety legislation, unions, with collective voice, have more power than an individual employee. In recent years, equality and safety issues have been closely examined in IR literature. This literature suggests that unions play an important role in the successful implementation of such programs (Hart, 2002a, 2002b, 2010), and that unions, in particular strong ones, are effective in both addressing longer-term health hazards and improving safety outcomes (Bornstein & Hart, 2010). Moreover, several studies have highlighted the effectiveness of unions in improving workplace safety practices, through training programs offered by labour organizations as well as the use of joint committees (Hart, 2002a, 2010; Hilyer, Leviton, Overman & Mukherjee, 2000; Nick & Walters, 2002; Walters, 2004). In particular, one Australian historical analysis (covering a 70-year period) found that the effectiveness of these committees depended upon the relationship with unions, the degree of management commitment, and the overall industrial relations climate (Markey & Patmore, 2011). As we will see later in the chapter, **IR climate**, or attitudes concerning IR and the union–management relationship (Snape & Redman, 2012), play an important role in the IR system.

IR climate
attitudes concerning IR and the union–management relationship

Unions often promote workplace equality and diversity.

HR PRACTICES IN UNIONS

As we close out this section, it is important to remember that unions are also employers and manage employees. While research on the HRM practices of unions has been limited, some have concluded that "unions have been slow to embrace a strategic outlook on human resources and adopt HR practices that could improve union effectiveness and rejuvenate the union movement"; when greater than 50 percent of union expenses relate to the hiring and retention of employees (Rau, 2012, p. 27). However, Clark and Gray (2008) find that unions are increasingly moving toward formalized HRM practices similar to those found in private-sector, governmental, and nonprofit organizations. They found that over 60 percent of unions had an HRM director or department; more than 50 percent had formalized, written policies concerning affirmative action, discipline/discharge, and performance appraisal for their headquarters and professional staff; and over 45 percent had similar policies for training and hiring.

OVERALL IMPACT

After reviewing the impact of unions on human resources practices (see Table 11.1), several conclusions can be drawn. First, there is no question that unionized organizations

TABLE 11.1

OVERALL UNION IMPACT ON HRM PRACTICES

HRM PRACTICE	UNION IMPACT
Recruitment	Some evidence that unionized firms use fewer recruitment techniques; more likely to use internal job postings.
Selection	Union firms more likely to hire from within, have formal promotion criteria, and have probationary periods.
Deselection/ termination	Unionized workplaces usually have more formal rules, bumping processes, recall rights, and just-cause termination requirements.
Staffing and job design flexibility	Unionized workplaces have more restrictions concerning job design, contracting out, task assignment, and use of part-time or casual workers.
Training and development	More training and development opportunities in unionized firms.
Performance appraisal	Unionized firms are less likely to have formal performance appraisal systems. When they do exist, they usually focus on developmental as oppose to administrative purposes. Union involvement is likely to bolster plan acceptance.
Job evaluation/ job analysis	Unionized firms are as likely as nonunion firms to use objective(e.g., point factor) job evaluation methods versus subjective ranking of jobs.
Base pay	On average, union pay in Canada is 10-15% higher than nonunion; wage differentials are lower in unionized firms.
Performance pay	Less use of individual and group performance pay in union firms
Indirect pay (benefits)	Unionized workers have greater access to benefits in the range of 20–45% and have more elements included in their benefit plans.

differ significantly in the types of HRM practices put in place. Second, unionized workplaces are less likely to have HRM practices that focus on individual rewards and recognition (e.g., performance pay and performance appraisal). Third, unionized firms often have more HRM practices that limit managerial flexibility and/or management's ability to make unilateral decisions. Fourth, in unionized firms, the element of seniority plays an important role in many HRM practices. Fifth, the increased formality in processes may explain why unionized firms are more likely than nonunionized firms to have dedicated HRM departments and staff. Sixth, unions (as employers) are moving to more formalized HRM practices in their workplaces.

// UNIONS AND FIRM MEASURES

It has historically been argued that the primary concern of the employer in the IR system is efficiency (e.g., productivity, profitability) (Barbash, 1987). In their landmark book, Freeman and Medoff (1984) concluded that unions increase firm efficiency due to the shock effect. Since the publication of that book, there has been considerable research (and debate) concerning the relationship between unionization and firm effectiveness. In this section, we will examine the research evidence concerning the impact of unionization on productivity, profitability, and innovation, as well as investment/return on investment (ROI).

PRODUCTIVITY

The relationship between a company's productivity and unionization is a controversial one. There are two opposing arguments on the topic (Doucouliagos, Laroche & Stanley, 2005; Morikawa, 2010):

1. *Economic theory.* According to theory, we would expect that collective agreement language would reduce management flexibility, foster an adversarial employee–management climate, create the potential for lost labour due to strikes, and increase wages. All of which would likely decrease productivity. Moreover, one often hears the argument that unions "protect the lazy and the incompetent," given that it is much more difficult to terminate employees in unionized workplaces (Kuhn, 1998, p. 1047).

2. *Collective voice.* Voice may increase productivity by improving communication between employees and managers, enabling methods of voicing discontent (and thus reducing quit rates and absenteeism), providing formal grievance procedures to address workplace conflicts, and shocking management into improved people- and production-management practices.

From their analyses, Freeman and Medoff (1984) concluded that the voice argument held and that the productivity of unionized firms was higher than that of their nonunion counterparts. As the authors readily admit, their conclusion that unions are associated with increased productivity is "the most controversial and least widely accepted" finding of their research study (Freeman & Medoff, 1984, p. 180).

Evidence since that time has been mixed. One review states that studies reveal "that most estimates are positive, with the negative effects largely confined to industries and periods known for conflictual union-management relations and the public sector"

(Kuhn, 1988, p. 1048). A **meta-analysis** (Doucouliagos & Laroche, 2003) found both positive and negative results. Specifically, they found that in their sample of 73 studies, 45 studies reported a positive relationship between unions and productivity while 28 reported a negative relationship. They also found that the total productivity gain of unionized firms over nonunionized firms was 4 percent (unweighted) and 1 percent when sample size was considered. Overall, they concluded that there is a slightly negative relationship between unionization and productivity in the United Kingdom and a slightly positive one in the United States—in particular, in American manufacturing.

Perhaps Morikawa (2010, p. 1031) best summarizes the current trends, stating: "(a)lthough empirical studies in the U.S. and in European countries have produced widely varying results, including coefficients with opposite signs, unions have, at most, a small positive effect on productivity, at least in the U.S."

Overall, the evidence (see Table 11.2) to date produces several conclusions. First, the impact of unions on productivity appears to be small, and positive. Second, the relationship is not always positive and can vary by context (e.g., industry, country). Third, as with most measures in this section, we have to watch for the "which came first—the chicken or the egg" debate. We cannot conclude that unions cause increased productivity. Rather, the evidence states that unionization is *associated with* a small increase in productivity. The causes for such productivity increases could be a number of factors, such as increased health and safety focus, management being shocked into improved practices, less turnover, and so on.

PROFITABILITY AND INNOVATION

A consistent finding in the literature is that profits are lower in unionized versus non-unionized firms (Doucouliagos & Laroche, 2009; Laroche & Wechtler, 2011), with a typical estimate of the impact being in the 10 to 20 percent range (Hirsch, 2004). A meta-analytic study using data from 45 union-profit studies found a country effect: in the United States, union decreased profits by about 23 percent, whereas the impact in non-U.S. countries was relatively insignificant, at 1 percent (Doucouliagos & Laroche, 2009).

TABLE 11.2

UNION IMPACT ON ORGANIZATIONAL MEASURES

ORGANIZATIONAL MEASURE	UNION IMPACT
Productivity	Varied results. Trend is a small, positive association between unionization and productivity (< 5%).
Profitability	While results suggest profits drop by 10–20%, there is a country effect, with U.S. seeing a 20% drop as against 1% for other countries.
Innovation	Limited data and inconsistent results. Most recent and most comprehensive data suggests a negative union effect in the range of 7%.
Investment and ROI	Tend to be lower in union firms – particularly in North America

Interestingly, recent Canadian research suggests that the union-profit relationship is not always negative. Analysis of data from approximately 5,000 Canadian workplaces found a positive relationship between union density and profit when employee-focused business strategy (e.g., employee involvement, positive union–management cooperation, skills development focus) was high.

In addition, the issue of innovation has become an important area to the Canadian economy. As is pointed out by Walsworth (2010b), the few studies that have examined the impact of unions on innovation found a negative impact in the United States. In Canada, one study did not find any significant relationships between unions and innovation (Verma & Fang, 2003), while Walsworth (2010b) found a positive relationship. Specifically, he found that the presence of a union increased a firm's propensity to innovate, over the seven years examined, by almost 4 percent, and that workplaces in which the majority of employees were unionized were about 7 percent more likely to innovate.

However, in perhaps the most comprehensive study of the relationship between unions and innovation, Doucouliagos and Laroche (2013) find less favourable results. In their meta-analysis of 25 studies, they concluded that "(a)ll the available evidence indicates that unions are associated with depressed levels of innovation" (p. 487). In fact, they found that unionization was associated with an innovation decrease of about 7 percent. However, these effects were not universal, as the union-innovation relationship was more negative in North America than Europe. On the basis of this more comprehensive study, we conclude that the relationship between unions and innovation is most likely negative.

INVESTMENT AND RETURN ON INVESTMENT

It would stand to conventional wisdom that firms with lower profits would have less money to invest in equipment, technology, etc. A review of the literature supports the notion that unionized firms see less investment than nonunion firms (Hirsch, 2004). However, it is clear that these effects are not universal. For example, an interesting trend is that countries like Germany and Finland (with high unionization and very centralized wage bargaining at the industry and national level) have high levels of investment in R&D in Europe, whereas for countries with lower unionization and decentralized collective bargaining (on a firm by firm basis), such as Canada and the United States, we find "consistently strong and negative impacts of unions on R&D" investments (Manasakis & Petrakis, 2009, p. 666).

Looking specifically at investment, the trend also appears to be negative. A recent American study examining almost 40 years of data found that unionization resulted in a 10 percent reduction in equity value of a firm (Lee & Mas, 2009), suggesting lower returns on investment.

In conclusion, it is clear that unionization has impacts on many organizational measures, many of which could be seen as "negative" by the employer (e.g., reduced profits, investments, innovation). However, we must be cautious in interpreting the data as it can be difficult to tease out the unique effect of unionization versus other variables. Interestingly, despite the association of unionization with negative profit, innovation, and investments, there is no evidence to conclude that unionization results in higher rates of business failure.

// THE IMPACT OF UNIONIZATION ON EMPLOYEE MEASURES

Thus far in this chapter, we have focused on the impact of unionization on the employer, in terms of both management practices and efficiency outcomes. Now we turn to the impact of unionization on employee measures, many of which are attitudinal measures (see Table 11.3).

Given the increasing focus on employee measures, we now review several that are influencing today's workplace. Interestingly, the IR literature has largely focused on economic versus employee measures, particularly those that are attitudinal in nature. A potential explanation for the lack of attitudinal research in IR was provided over 25 years ago by Craig (1988), who argued that concepts from organizational psychology/behaviour, an area in which employee attitudinal measures are often researched, have largely been overlooked in IR. That same year, Barling (1988), a prominent researcher in organizational psychology/behaviour, concurred, stating that his field had largely ignored issues relevant to IR. Since that time, we have seen works that integrate these fields. For example, studies have looked at employee reactions to strikes (Chaulk & Brown, 2008) and bumping (Stringer & Brown, 2008). Building on such works, we will now examine the employee measures of job satisfaction, intention to quit, organizational commitment, union satisfaction, union commitment, work climate, and desire to leave a union.

VOLUNTARY TURNOVER (QUIT RATES)

Arguably the ultimate employee measure is voluntary turnover, or quitting. Employee turnover is very expensive, with some estimating that the cost of replacing a single employee equates to 100 to 150 percent of that employee's annual salary. Second, there is growing evidence that turnover is negatively associated with customer service, profitability, as well as operational performance (Mohr, Young, & Burgess, 2012).

TABLE 11.3

UNION IMPACT ON TRADITIONAL HRM EMPLOYEE MEASURES

EMPLOYEE MEASURE	UNION IMPACT
Voluntary Turnover (Quit Rates)	Significantly lower in unionized firms, potentially by as much as 30%
Satisfaction	Bulk of evidence shows a negative union relationship
Intention to quit	Results vary but generally lower in unionized workplaces. Few studies to date.
Organizational commitment	Commitment to the employing organization may facilitate union commitment, particularly if the work climate is positive.

The evidence is clear that unionized works are much less likely to quit their job relative to their nonunion peers. For example, evidence suggests that voluntary quit rates are between 5 and 34 percent lower in unionized firms (see review in Pfeifer, 2011). Not surprisingly, a recent analysis of data from almost 4,200 Canadian workplaces found a negative relationship between voluntary turnover and unionization (Haines et al., 2010). In fact, Pohler and Luchak (2013) found that this negative union-turnover effect was even stronger when a high-employee-focus business strategy was used whereby management focused on skills development, employee involvement, and union–management cooperation.

Given the total compensation, due process, seniority-based rights, and voice advantages of unionization, these results should not be surprising. Simply put, the real benefits of unionization for workers make the cost of quitting high, and thus reduce the likelihood of voluntary turnover.

JOB SATISFACTION AND INTENTION TO QUIT

Job satisfaction has historically been defined as an employee's assessment of his or her job experience (Locke, 1976), and is frequently studied in the fields of human resources and organizational behaviour. **Intention to quit**, which is closely related, has historically been assessed in terms of the likelihood of an employee leaving the organization (Freeman & Medoff, 1984). Both concepts are linked to the previously discussed measure of voluntary turnover. As summarized by Chen et al. (2011, p. 159) "... central to most turnover theories is the notion that job satisfaction directly and negatively relates to employees' intentions to quit their jobs (i.e., turnover intentions), which in turn positively relate to actual turnover." Thus, research has often examined issues related to both job satisfaction and intention to quit (sometimes called intention to leave).

> **job satisfaction**
> an employee's assessment of his or her job experience
>
> **intention to quit**
> a survey measure assessing the likelihood that an employee will quit

Almost 50 years of research concludes that several factors—namely, compensation, promotional opportunities, supervisor, job responsibilities, and coworker relationships—contribute to an employee's job satisfaction (Rogelberg et al., 2010; Smith, Kendall & Hulin, 1969). Not surprisingly, then, low pay and low job satisfaction among unionized workers have been linked to high turnover intentions (Singh & Loncar, 2010), while the lower pay levels often associated with outsourced call centres (which were largely nonunion) were associated with higher quit rates, increased absenteeism, and lower employee performance (van Jaarsveld & Yanadori, 2011).

Since collective agreements and unionization can impact many of these factors, it would be reasonable to assume that job satisfaction might differ between union and nonunion workers. In fact, in a milestone study conducted some 30 years ago, Freeman and Medoff (1984) suggested that unionized employees have lower levels of job satisfaction than nonunionized employees. Specifically, they found that unionized workers were more satisfied with their level of total compensation (wages plus benefits) and less satisfied with (1) their supervisors, (2) their relationships with their supervisors, (3) physical conditions of work, and (4) job safety level. Yet their intention to quit and actual quit rates were lower than those of nonunion employees. This seems contradictory, as one would expect that if the unionized workers were truly dissatisfied, they would be more likely to seek jobs elsewhere—but the reverse is true. A potential explanation to this contradiction that they offered was the voice mechanism of the union. They argue that true dissatisfaction would result in turnover or intention to quit, while "voiced" dissatisfaction results from negative attitudes toward the workplace and a willingness to complain about problems. We can well imagine that the increased protection of just-cause termination and grievance procedures would increase the willingness of unionized employees to voice their dissatisfaction relative to nonunion employees, who have little or no protection.

Since that time researchers have continued to examine, and speculate, as to the union–job satisfaction relationship. The general consensus in the field has been that unionized workers have lower job satisfaction (see review in Donegani & McKay, 2012). Scholars offer several possible explanations for lower levels of satisfaction among unionized workers (Artz, 2012; Donegani & McKay, 2012; Hammer & Avgar, 2005). First, unions may choose to organize workers with poor working conditions, low pay, and/ or unsafe tasks in order to increase the likelihood of a successful certification vote. Second, unions may create unrealistic expectations, thus raising worker dissatisfaction when these expectations are not met. Third, unionized and nonunionized workers may have different job outcome preferences. For example, unions may socialize members to value the areas that the union can improve (pay, benefits, safety, etc.) rather than job content. Fourth, unions and collective agreements may restrict job tasks and narrowly define jobs, resulting in workers not being able to fully use all of their skills and abilities. This can result in lower autonomy, challenge, and sense of achievement—all of which are associated with higher job satisfaction. Fifth, the working conditions may be worse in unionized workplaces. If these poor working conditions are not taken into account, the lower satisfaction can be attributed to unionization.

We stress, however, that a growing body of evidence suggests that the union–nonunion difference in satisfaction levels may be more complex than it first appears. For example, one study of almost 30,000 survey respondents across 18 European studies found that the satisfaction levels differed by country. Interestingly, that study found a positive union–job satisfaction relationship in all but five of the 18 countries. Renaud's (2002) study of over 3,000 Canadians found that unionized workers were less satisfied with their jobs than nonunionized workers. However, when he factored out the work environment (e.g., opportunities for promotion, physical surroundings, freedom at work, and routine) there was no longer a significant difference between union and nonunion employee job satisfaction. Finally, Artz (2010) examined over 20 years of data and argued that results can be misleading if one examines only union status. He argued that one must also consider union experience, as many nonunion workers have worked previously in union jobs and vice versa. Taking these factors into account, he found that job satisfaction (1) increases for people who are in the union for the first time; (2) decreases the longer a person is a union member; (3) increases with tenure when tenure is known to be higher for unionized workers; and (4) increases for formerly unionized workers the longer they have been in their new nonunion jobs. Artz offers several explanations for these findings. First, first-time union members may experience an increase in satisfaction due to the benefits of unionization, but the voice mechanism experienced through their union experience subsequently causes a reduction in satisfaction. Second, the longer an employee works in a unionized firm, the more they can find workplace dissatisfiers that can be used as leverage during subsequent collective bargaining. Third, unions enable a workplace culture of discontent that stays with the employees even after they leave a unionized firm.

ORGANIZATIONAL COMMITMENT

organizational
commitment
an employee's
commitment to the
organization

Organizational commitment can be defined in terms of an employee's acceptance of the organization's goals and values, exertion of a substantial amount of effort on behalf of the organization, and aspiration to remain a member of the organization (Mowday, Steers & Porter, 1979; Vakola & Nikolaou, 2005). There is a long history of research concerning organizational commitment in organizational psychology/behaviour literature. In fact, a meta-analysis by Cooper-Hakim and Viswesvaran (2005) cited almost 1,000 studies on the issue. That study found a positive relationship between organizational commitment and both job satisfaction and performance, and a negative relationship between organizational commitment and turnover. Overall, these results suggest that organizations in which employees have high levels of organizational commitment will see positive employee reactions and performance.

Given that commitment is argued to increase with communication and participation (Brown, McHardy, McNabb & Taylor, 2011), we could speculate that the voice mechanisms of unionization would increase employee commitment in unionized firms. Unfortunately, few studies have examined the relationship between union status and organizational commitment (Hammer & Avgar, 2005). One study found that being a unionized worker reduced the probability that a worker would be in the top commitment category by a modest 1 percent (Brown et al., 2011). Other studies have often examined union-member commitment to both employer (i.e., organizational commitment) and union (i.e., union commitment). For example, Snape, Redman, and Chan (2000) concluded from their review of the studies that commitment to the employing organization facilitates union commitment. Stringer and Brown (2008) also found a positive relationship between these variables, even in an environment of downsizing. A meta-analysis concluded that organizational commitment was an antecedent to union commitment (Bamberger, Kluger & Suchard, 1999). On the other hand, another study that examined employees' reactions toward their employer and union following a strike (Chaulk & Brown, 2008) found a negative relationship between organizational commitment and both union commitment and job satisfaction. To us, this reinforces the need for a positive work environment to facilitate joint commitment.

UNION SATISFACTION AND COMMITMENT

Scholars have argued that **union satisfaction** is akin to job satisfaction, while **union commitment** is akin to organizational commitment (Kuruvilla, Gallagher & Wetzel, 1993). Kuruvilla, Gallagher, and Wetzel (1993) suggest that union satisfaction is a reflection of, and reaction to, the immediate actions taken by the union, whereas union commitment is less specific and focuses less on the performance and actions of the union. The authors indicate that the primary distinction between these measures is that union commitment is developed over a longer period of time and is more stable than union satisfaction.

Kuruvilla, Gallagher, and Wetzel's (1993) survey study of Canadian and Swedish employees indicates that contact with the union is a key determinant of union commitment. Their study concluded that members who read union newsletters and who actively take part in union activities demonstrate more union commitment than those members who do not. They also found that friends of union members influence commitment toward unions. For example, when friends of union members have positive attitudes toward unions, the members will also develop positive attitudes and therefore will become committed to the union.

As we discussed previously, researchers (Kuruvilla, Gallagher & Wetzel, 1993; Snape, Redman & Chan, 2000) often associate union commitment with organizational commitment. These researchers indicate several antecedents to union commitment by using the "parallels model," which suggests that commitment to the union can be studied and

> union satisfaction
> an employee's assessment of his or her union experience
>
> union commitment
> an employee's commitment to his or her union

based on previous organizational commitment research. The model highlights personal characteristics, job characteristics, work experience, and industrial relations climate as antecedents to union commitment. Thus, scholars have concluded that commitment to the employing organization also facilitates positive union commitment (Snape, Redman & Chan, 2000), and research has found a positive relationship between these measures (Stringer & Brown, 2008). Moreover, when the industrial relations climate is perceived to be positive, commitment to the union and the employer are both positive.

However, the relationship between IR climate and union commitment is not always positive. While US studies have generally found a positive relationship, recent UK data found a negative relationship potentially as in positive climates employees feel less of a need for the protection of their union (Snape & Redman, 2012).

What can be concluded from these results is that employers and unions do not essentially compete for commitment and that a favourable work climate may have positive implications for both of these actors of the industrial relations system. Interestingly, though, it appears that IR events, such as strikes, may impact this relationship, as following a lengthy strike union commitment was seen to drop and the relationship between union and organization commitment, when controlling for work environment, was also negative (Chaulk & Brown, 2008).

WORK CLIMATE

Patterson et al. (2005), reflecting upon a study conducted by Brown and Leigh (1996), concluded that a positive work environment had a positive impact on employee performance. As we have seen throughout this chapter, a positive union–management relationship is often positively associated with organizational and employee outcomes.

EMPLOYEES' DESIRE TO LEAVE A UNION

union renewal
quantity and quality of
union membership

Given the global decrease in union membership, we are seeing an increased focus on **union renewal**, or increasing the quantity and quality of union membership (Gall & Fiorito, 2012). The reverse of this concept would relate to desire to leave a union. Recall that low job satisfaction and perceptions of poor work environments can encourage unionization. As was the case with the organizational measure of intention to quit, studies have also examined the concept of desire to leave a union. Remember that, as we discussed in Chapter 4, unions can face decertification, in which union members ask the labour relations board to rescind the certification order. Thus, unions too are concerned with issues of "quitting." In a U.S. study involving over 3,000 workers, Friedman, Abraham, and Thomas (2006) found that desire to leave a union increased with firm size, possibly due to larger firms having collective agreement clauses requiring that employees be union members as a condition of employment. They also found that employees less satisfied with their compensation and benefits were more likely to desire leaving the union. Given the "bread and butter" focus of unions in North America, this finding should not be surprising. If a union cannot "deliver the goods" in terms of economic gains, members are more likely to want out. Interestingly, that study, along with a second of Polish workers (Zientara & Kuczynsk, 2009), found a positive relationship between one's intention to leave a firm and one's desire to leave the union. Zientara and Kuczynsk (2009) argue that this relationship is likely explained by the fact that employees who plan to leave a firm likely have no interest in remaining with the union associated with it.

// SUMMARY

As we have seen throughout this chapter, unionization has several impacts on the employment relationship and the outcomes of the IR system. In particular, we see that unionization impacts management practices (especially those of HRM), firm measures, and employee measures.

Generally speaking, unionization results in more formalized HRM practices, less managerial discretion, fewer individualized practices, less differential between employees, and HRM practices heavily influenced by seniority. We also see increased total compensation levels and increased focus on equality and health and safety in unionized firms. This difference can be explained in three ways. First, the addition of the union greatly restricts management flexibility and unilateral decision making relative to nonunion employers operating under common law. Second, the collective voice of the union allows employees to express their needs and serves as an alternative to quitting. Third, unionized workers have increased wages and benefits—probably due to the fact that North Americans often seek economic returns from unionization.

Turning to efficiency measures, the research suggests that unions are associated with at most a modestly positive impact on productivity and largely negative impacts on profitability, innovation, as well as return on investment and investment. Clearly, the increased total compensation package of unionized workers is not offset by improved productivity. However, there is no evidence that this reduced profitability results in more unionized firms going out of business.

But what about the worker him- or herself? The evidence suggests that unionized workers are often less satisfied with their jobs than their nonunion counterparts. However, this reduced job satisfaction does not lead to increased intention to quit or actual quitting of jobs. In fact, unionized workers are much less likely to quit. Other studies concerning organizational commitment and union commitment suggest these employers and unions do not "fight" for employee affect—rather, union commitment and organizational commitment tend to go hand in hand.

Perhaps the most significant lesson from this chapter is the importance of an effective labour–management relationship and a positive work climate. Considering both productivity and commitment, a positive climate plays an important role in unionization having a positive impact.

Perhaps Freeman and Medoff (1984, p. 190) best summarized the impact of unions some 30 years ago when they stated:

> *Beneficial to organized workers, almost always; beneficial to the economy, in many ways; but harmful to the bottom line of company balance sheets; this is the paradox of American trade unionism, which underlies some of the ambivalences of our national policies toward the institution.*

KEY TERMS

base pay 323
collective voice 320
defined benefit 328

WEBLINKS

YouTube postings concerning the union impact in the construction industry:

Michigan Associated Builders and Contractors:
http://www.youtube.com/watch?v=k3vBA3Hm5Mk

Association of Union Constructors:
http://www.youtube.com/watch?v=tw610qHGyM8

Canadian Labour Congress discussion of unions improved compensation:
http://www.canadianlabour.ca/about-clc/union-advantage-2014

Canadian Labour Congress's Day of Mourning:
http://www.canadianlabour.ca/issues/day-mourning

Alberta Federation of Labour health and safety activities of unions:
http://www.afl.org/index.php/Unions/why-join-a-union.html

Health and safety section of UFCW's website:
**http://www.ufcw.ca/index.php?option=com_content&view=article&id=32
&Itemid=112&lang=en**

Canadian Federation of Labour on equality activities of unions:
http://www.canadianlabour.ca/human-rights-equality

DISCUSSION QUESTIONS

1. The evidence in this chapter shows that unions can have positive effects on the firm. Why then are employers generally not supportive of unionization?

2. Many students work while in school, and typically they work in nonunion jobs. If you move to a unionized workplace upon graduation, what do you expect will be the biggest challenges you will see in terms of HRM practices?

3. Union organizers are often tasked with encouraging workers to seek union representation. Let's assume you were a union organizer trying to unionize a retail workplace in your community. Based on the evidence presented in this chapter, what would you tell employees are the greatest advantages of becoming unionized?

4. On the basis of the data in this chapter, what do you feel are the biggest impacts of a union for the management team of a firm?

5. As is mentioned in the chapter, we are seeing an increase in the earnings gap between the rich and the poor. At the same time, union density is dropping in many countries. Do you believe the two are related? Why?

6. The evidence presented in this chapter suggests that the "union advantage" concerning wages and benefits may be decreasing over time. What do you feel is causing this trend?

USING THE INTERNET

The health and safety of workers has always been a key concern of unions. Have a look at what information you find related to health and safety on several union web pages. (*Hint*: Look for health and safety committees.)

1. What is the role of the union concerning health and safety?

2. Do these activities have an impact on the employer? How so?

3. If there is a health and safety committee, what is its role and structure?

4. Does the union use improved health and safety as a "recruiting" method to attract new union members?

EXERCISES

1. Take a look at recent media stories related to industrial relations. To what extent do you see issues related to unions' impact on any of the firm or employee measures discussed in this chapter?

2. Your instructor may divide you into groups where you will debate the relative merits of unionization versus nonunionization for young workers (under the age of 25). Based on the evidence in this chapter, prepare arguments to either: (1) support unionization for youth; or (2) not support unionization for youth.

3. In most universities, employees are unionized, many placing their collective agreements online. Take a look at a collective agreement from your university (or any other workplace you choose) and examine the following human resources functions:
   - staffing (look for language on job postings, selection, promotions, and layoffs);
   - training and development; and
   - compensation.

Then answer the following questions:

a. To what extent does seniority play a role in these practices?

b. To what extent is management flexibility restricted?

c. Do you feel that any of these clauses impact employer measures such as productivity, profitability, innovation, investment, and return on investment (ROI)?

CASE   **WHAT IF THE CANADIAN HOCKEY LEAGUE UNIONIZES?**

The world of professional sports is highly unionized. Professional players in basketball, baseball, football, and hockey all have union representation. The Canadian media have recently reported several stories related to the Canadian Hockey League (CHL). The CHL comprises about 60 teams that play in the Ontario Hockey League, Quebec Major Junior Hockey League, and Western Hockey League. The goal for many of the league's 1,300 junior players, aged 16–20, is to play professionally in the National Hockey League.

In particular, recent media stories have also highlighted union drives for junior hockey players. A previous unionization attempt in Halifax by what was then known as the Canadian Hockey League Players' Association failed. That union then sought the assistance of the largest private-sector union in Canada–Unifor. Unifor is now creating a leadership team and legal entity so it can start a more formal certification drive. According to Unifor, the union seeks to improve pay, reduce the restrictions currently in place on scholarships, and enhance health insurance. Union organizers argue that players can, in essence, earn less than one dollar an hour while owners make profits from ticket, food/beverage, and clothing sales. Leadership of the league assert that fewer than one-third of teams are profitable, that they spent $5 million a year in tuition for former players, and that they have always looked for ways to better meet the needs of players (both as athletes and as young people). In short, they feel the introduction of a third party (a union) will likely not do any better.

On top of the union drive, the CHL has been hit with a class-action lawsuit of $180 million. The lawsuit alleges that the players (who are often paid between $35 and $50 a week for hours of practice, training, games, and travel) are owed millions of dollars as the league has failed to pay minimum wage, holiday, overtime, and vacation pay. The lawsuit further alleges that these players were, in essence, forced to sign contracts that violated minimum wage legislation. The CHL leadership argue that these laws do not apply as the players are in essence amateur student athletes (eligible for scholarships) and independent contractors.

Sources: "Canada's junior hockey teams violate minimum wage laws: lawsuit: Player contracts include weekly pay of between $35 and $50." (20 October 2014). CBC News. Retrieved from http://www.cbc.ca/news/canada/toronto/canada-s-junior-hockey-teams-violate-minimum-wage-laws-lawsuit-1.2806008; Cribb, R. (20 October 2014). "Class action lawsuit filed against Canadian Hockey League over wages. Suit alleges junior hockey league breaches minimum wage laws. President of league says it 'will vigorously defend the way our teams operate.'" *Toronto Star*. Retrieved from http://www.thestar.com/news/world/2014/10/20/class_action_lawsuit_filed_against _canadian_hockey_league_over_wages.html; Russell, S. (7 October 2014). "Major junior hockey gets new push to unionize." *Toronto Star*. Retrieved from http://www.thestar.com/sports/hockey/

QUESTIONS

1. Let's assume that the CHL becomes unionized. You need to brief the management team on the changes they will face as a result of unionization.

   (a) What would you inform them are the key changes they can expect to see in terms of management and HRM practices?

   (b) The managers will likely be concerned about efficiency. How would you advise that they best ensure that profitability and productivity remains the same or improves?

2. Employees, some of whom supported the union and some of whom did not, may have many questions. Let's assume that you and a Unifor representative hold a joint meeting with the players. What three or four changes would you highlight as they move to a collective employment relationship?

// REFERENCES

1. Altonji, J. G., & Usui, E. (2007). Work hours, wages, and vacation leave. *Industrial & Labor Relations Review, 60*(3), pp. 408–428.

2. Artz, B. (2010). The impact of union experience on job satisfaction. *Industrial Relations, 49*, pp. 387–405.

3. Artz, B. (2012). Does the impact of union experience on job satisfaction differ by gender? *Indus. & Lab. Rel. Rev., 65*, p. 225.

4. Bacon, N., & Hoque, K. (2012). The role and impact of trade union equality representatives in Britain. *British Journal of Industrial Relations, 50*, pp. 239–262. doi: 10.1111/j.1467-8543.2011.00865.x

5. Bahrami, B., Bitzan, J., & Leitch, J. (2009). Union worker wage effect in the public sector. *Journal of Labor Research, 30*(1), pp. 35–51.

6. Bamberger, P. A., Kluger, A. N., & Suchard, R. (1999). The antecedents and consequences of union commitment: A meta-analysis. *Academy of Management Journal, 42*, pp. 304–18.

7. Barbash, J. (1987). Like nature, industrial relations abhors a vacuum. *Relations industrielles, 42*, pp. 168–179.

8. Barling, J. (1988). Industrial relations: A blind spot in the teaching, research and practice of I/O psychology. *Canadian Psychology, 29*, pp. 103–108.

9. Barth, E., Bratsberg, B., Hægeland, T., & Raaum, O. (2012). Performance pay, union bargaining and within-firm wage inequality. *Oxford Bulletin of Economics and Statistics, 74*, pp. 327-362. doi: 10.1111/j.1468-0084.2011.00656.x

10. Blanchflower, D. G., & Bryson, A. (2004). What effect do unions have on wages now and would Freeman and Medoff be surprised? *Journal of Labor Research, 25,* pp. 383–414.

11. Blanchflower, D. G., & Bryson, A. (2010). The wage impact of trade unions in the UK public and private sectors. *Economica, 77*(305), pp. 92–109.

12. Boheim, R., & Booth, A. L. (2004). Trade union presence and employer-provided training in Great Britain. *Industrial Relations, 43,* pp. 520–545.

13. Booth, A. L., Francesconi, M., & Zoega, G. (2003). Unions, work-related training, and wages: Evidence for British men. *Industrial and Labor Relations Review, 57,* pp. 68–91.

14. Bornstein, S., & Hart, S. (2010). Evaluating occupational health and safety management systems: A collaborative approach. *Policy and Practice in Health and Safety, 8*(1), pp. 61–76.

15. Brown, M., & Heywood, J. S. (2005). Performance appraisal systems: Determinants and change. *British Journal of Industrial Relations, 43,* pp. 659–679.

16. Brown, S., McHardy, J., McNabb, R., & Taylor, K. (2011). Workplace performance, worker commitment, and loyalty. *Journal of Economics & Management Strategy, 20,* pp. 925–955.

17. Brown, S. P., & Leigh, T. W. (1996). A new look at psychological climate and its relationship to job involvement, effort, and performance. *Journal of Applied Psychology, 81,* pp. 358–368.

18. Brown, T. C. (2003). Sexual orientation provisions in Canadian collective agreements. *Relations Industrielles/Industrial Relations, 58,* pp. 644–666.

19. Brown, T. C., & Latham, G. P. (2000). The effects of goal setting and self-instruction training on the performance of union employees. *Industrial Relations, 55,* pp. 80–94.

20. Brown, T. C., & Warren, A. M. (2011). Performance management in unionized settings. *Human Resource Management Review, 21*(2), pp. 96–106.

21. Canadian Labour Congress (CLC). (2011). *The union advantage.* Retrieved 11 January 2011 from http://www.canadianlabour.ca/about-clc/union-advantage

22. Card, D., Lemieux, T., & Riddell, W. C. (2004). Unions and wage inequality. *Journal of Labor Research, 25,* pp. 519–562.

23. Chaulk, K., & Brown, T. C. (2008). An assessment of worker reaction to their union and employer post-strike. *Relations Industrielles/Industrial Relations, 63*(2), pp. 223–245.

24. Chen, G., Ployhart, R. E., Thomas, H. C., Anderson, N., & Bliese, P. D. (2011). The power of momentum: A new model of dynamic relationships between job satisfaction change and turnover intentions. *Academy of Management Journal, 54*(1), pp. 159–181.

25. CLC. (2014a). Human rights and equality. Retrieved 2 November 2014 from http://www.canadianlabour.ca/human-rights-equality

26. CLC. (2014b). Day of mourning. Retrieved 2 November 2014 from http://www.canadianlabour.ca/issues/day-mourning

27. Clark, P. F., & Gray, L. S. (2008). Administrative practices in American unions: A longitudinal study. *Journal of Labour Research, 29,* pp. 42–55.

28. Cleveland, G., Gunderson, M., & Hyatt, D. (2003). Union effects in low-wage services: Evidence from Canadian childcare. *Industrial and Labor Relations Review, 56*, pp. 295–305.

29. Conference Board of Canada. (12 September 2002). *News release 02-30: Variable pay offers a bonus for unionized workplaces.* Retrieved 26 July 2006 from http://www.conferenceboard.ca/press/2002/variable_pay.asp

30. Cooper-Hakim, A., & Viswesvaran, C. (2005). The construct of work commitment: Testing an integrative framework. *Psychological Bulletin, 131,* pp. 241–259.

31. Craig, A. W. J. (1988). Mainstream industrial relations in Canada. In G. Hebert, C. J. Jain & N. Meltz (Eds.), *The state of the art in industrial relations* (pp. 9–43). Kingston, ON: Industrial Relations Centre, Queen's University, and Centre for Industrial Relations, University of Toronto.

32. CUPE. (2014). Pay equity. Retrieved 2 November 2014 from http://cupe.ca/pay-equity.

33. Donegani, C. P., & McKay, S. (2012). Is there a paradox of lower job satisfaction among trade union members? European evidence. *Transfer: European Review of Labour and Research, 18*(4), pp. 471–489.

34. Doucouliagos, C., & Laroche, P. (2003). What do unions do to productivity? A meta-analysis. *Industrial Relations, 42,* pp. 650–691.

35. Doucouliagos, C., & Laroche, P. (2009). Unions and profits: A meta-regression analysis. *Industrial Relations, 48,* pp. 146–184.

36. Doucouliagos, C., & Laroche, P. (2013). Unions and innovation: New insights from the cross-country evidence. *Industrial Relations, 52,* pp. 467–491.

37. Doucouliagos, C., Laroche, P., & Stanley, T. (2005). Publication bias in union–productivity research? *Industrial Relations, 60,* pp. 320–346.

38. Dustmann, C., & Schönberg, U. (2009). Training and union wages. *Review of Economics & Statistics, 91*(2), pp. 363–376.

39. Eren, O. (2007). Measuring the union–nonunion wage gap using propensity score matching. *Industrial Relations, 46*(4), pp. 766–780.

40. Freeman, R. B., & Medoff, J. L. (1984). *What do unions do?* New York: Basic Books.

41. Friedman, B. A., Abraham, S. E., & Thomas, R. K. (2006). Factors related to employees' desire to join and leave unions. *Industrial Relations: A Journal of Economy and Society, 45,* pp. 102–110.

42. Gall, G., & Fiorito, J. (2012). Union commitment and activism in Britain and the United States: Searching for synthesis and synergy for renewal. *British Journal of Industrial Relations, 50,* pp. 189–213 doi: 10.1111/j.1467-8543.2011.00855.x

43. Godard, J. (2007). Unions, work practices, and wages under different institutional environments: The case of Canada and England. *Industrial & Labor Relations Review, 60*(4), pp. 457–476.

44. Grant, E. K., Swidinsky, R., & Vanderkamp, J. (1987). Canadian union–nonunion wage differentials. *Industrial and Labor Relations Review, 41,* pp. 93–107.

45. Haines, III, V. Y., Jalette, P., & Larose, K. (2010). The influence of human resource management practices on employee voluntary turnover rates in the

Canadian nongovernmental sector. *Industrial and Labor Relations Review, 63,* pp. 228–246.

46. Hammer, T. H., & Avgar, A. (2005). The impact of unions on job satisfaction, organizational commitment, and turnover. *Journal of Labor Research, 26,* pp. 241–266.

47. Hart, S. M. (2002a). Norwegian workforce involvement in safety offshore: Regulatory framework and participants' perspectives. *Employee Relations, 24,* pp. 486–499.

48. Hart, S. M. (2002b). Unions and pay equity bargaining. *Relations industrielles, 57,* pp. 609–628.

49. Hart, S. (2010). Self-regulation, corporate social responsibility, and the business case: Do they work in achieving workplace equality and safety? *Journal of Business Ethics, 92*(4), pp. 585–600.

50. Hayter, S., & Weinberg, B. (2011). Mind the gap: Collective bargaining and wage inequality. *The Role of Collective Bargaining in the Global Economy: Negotiating for Social Justice,* pp. 136–186.

51. Hilyer, B., Leviton, L., Overman, L., & Mukherjee, S. (2000). Union-initiated safety training program leads to improved workplace safety. *Labor Studies Journal, 24*(4), pp. 53–66.

52. Hirsch, B. T. (2004). What do unions do for economic performance? *Journal of Labor Research, 25,* pp. 415–455.

53. Hirschmen, A. O. (1970). *Exit, voice and loyalty.* Cambridge, MA: Harvard University Press.

54. Hunt, G., & Rayside, D. (2000). Labor's response to diversity in Canada and the United States. *Industrial Relations, 39,* pp. 401–444.

55. Jacobson, W. S., Rubin, E. V., & Donahue, A. K. (2008). Integrating labor relations and human resource management: Impacts on state workforces. *International Review of Public Administration, 13*(2), pp. 13–31.

56. Koch, M. J., & Hundley, G. (1997). The effects of unionism on recruitment and selection methods. *Industrial Relations, 36,* pp. 349–370.

57. Krats, P., & Brown, T. C. (2013). Unionised employees' reactions to the introduction of a goal based performance appraisal system. *Human Resource Management Journal, 23*(4), pp. 396–412.

58. Kuhn, P. (1998). Unions and the economy: What we know; what we should know. *Canadian Journal of Economics, 31,* pp. 1033–1056.

59. Kuruvilla, S., Gallagher, D. G., & Wetzel, K. (1993). The development of members' attitudes toward their unions: Sweden and Canada. *Industrial and Labor Relations Review, 46,* pp. 499–514.

60. Laroche, P., & Wechtler, H. (2011). The effects of labor unions on workplace performance: New evidence from France. *Journal of Labor Research, 32*(2), pp. 157–180. doi:10.1007/s12122-011-9106-9

61. Lee, D., & Mas, A. (2009). *Long-run impacts of unions on firms: New evidence from financial markets, 1961–1999 (No. w14709).* National Bureau of Economic Research. Retrieved 21 October 2014 from http://www.nber.org/papers/w14709.pdf

62. Lewis, H. G. (1986). *Union relative wage effects: A survey.* Chicago: University of Chicago Press.

63. Livingstone, D. W., & Raykov, M. (2005). Union influence on worker education and training in Canada in tough times. *Just Labour, 5*, pp. 50–64.

64. Livingstone, D. W., & Raykov, M. (2008). Workers' power and intentional learning among nonmanagerial workers: A 2004 benchmark survey. *Relations Industrielles/Industrial Relations, 63*(1), pp. 30–56.

65. Locke, E. A. (1976). The nature and causes of job satisfaction. In M. D. Dunnette (Ed.), *Handbook of industrial and organizational psychology.* Chicago: Rand McNally pp. 1319–1328.

66. Long, R. J. (2006). *Compensation in Canada: Strategy, practice, and issues* (3rd edition). Toronto: ITP Nelson Publishers.

67. Long, R. J. (2014). *Compensation in Canada: Strategy, practice, and issues* (5th edition). Toronto, ON: Nelson.

68. Long, R. J., & Fang, T. (2013). Profit sharing and workplace productivity: Does teamwork play a role? (No. 7869). IZA Discussion Paper.

69. Long, R. J., & Shields, J. L. (2009). Do unions affect pay methods of Canadian firms? A longitudinal study. *Relations Industrielles/Industrial Relations, 64*(3), pp. 442–465.

70. Luchak, A. A., & Gunderson, M. (2000). What do employees know about their pension plan? *Industrial Relations, 39*, pp. 646–670.

71. Manasakis, C., & Petrakis, E. (2009). Union structure and firms' incentives for cooperative R&D investments. *Canadian Journal of Economics/Revue canadienne d'économique, 42*, pp. 665–693.

72. Markey, R., & Patmore, G. (2011). Employee participation in health and safety in the Australian steel industry, 1935–2006. *British Journal of Industrial Relations, 49*(1), pp. 144–167. doi:10.1111/j.1467-8543.2009.00756.x

73. Martinello, F. (2009). Faculty salaries in Ontario: Compression, inversion, and the effects of alternative forms of representation. *Industrial & Labor Relations Review, 63*(1), pp. 128–145.

74. Mohr, D. C., Young, G. J., & Burgess, J. F. (2012). Employee turnover and operational performance: The moderating effect of group-oriented organisational culture. *Human Resource Management Journal, 22*, pp. 216–233. doi: 10.1111/j.1748-8583.2010.00159.x

75. Morikawa, M. (2010). Labor unions and productivity: An empirical analysis using Japanese firm-level data. *Labour Economics, 17*, pp. 1030–1037

76. Mowday, R. T., Steers, R. M., & Porter, L. W. (1979). The measurement of organizational commitment. *Journal of Vocational Behavior, 14*, pp. 224–247.

77. Ng, I., & Maki, D. (1994). Trade union influence on human resource management practices. *Industrial Relations, 33*, pp. 121–135.

78. Nick, P., & Walters, D. (2002). Worker representation in health and safety: Options for regulatory reform. *Industrial Relations, 33*, pp. 141–156.

79. Parker, J., & Foley, J. (2010). Progress on women's equality within UK and Canadian trade unions: Do women's structures make a difference? *Relations Industrielles/Industrial Relations, 65*(2), pp. 281–303.

80. Patterson, M. G., West, M. A., Shackleton, V. J., Dawson, J. F., Lawthom, R., Maitlis, S., Robinson, D. L., & Wallace, A. M. (2005). Validating the

organizational climate measure: Links to managerial practices, productivity and innovation. *Journal of Organizational Behavior, 26,* pp. 379–408.

81. Pfeifer, C. (2011). Works councils, union bargaining and quits in German firms. *Economic and Industrial Democracy, 32,* pp. 243–260.

82. Pohler, D., & Luchak, A. (2013). Are unions good or bad for organizations? The moderating role of management's response. *British Journal of Industrial Relations.* Online version. Retrieved 2 November 2014 from http://onlinelibrary.wiley.com/doi/10.1111/bjir.12042/full

83. Rau, B.L. (2012). The diffusion of HR practices in unions. *Human Resource Management Review, 22,* pp. 27–42

84. Renaud, S. (1998). Unions, wages and total compensation in Canada: An empirical study. *Industrial Relations, 53,* pp. 710–729.

85. Renaud, S. (2002). Rethinking the union membership/job satisfaction relationship: Some empirical evidence in Canada. *International Journal of Manpower, 23,* pp. 137–150.

86. Rogelberg, S. G., Allen, J. A., Shanock, L., Scott, C., & Shuffler, M. (2010). Employee satisfaction with meetings: A contemporary facet of job satisfaction. *Human Resource Management, 49*(2), pp. 149–172.

87. Singh, P., & Loncar, N. (2010). Pay satisfaction, job satisfaction and turnover intent. *Relations Industrielles/Industrial Relations, 65,* pp. 470–490.

88. Slichter, S., Healy, J., & Livernash, E. R. (1960). *The impact of collective bargaining on management.* Washington, DC: Brookings Institution.

89. Smith, P. C., Kendall, L. M., & Hulin, C. L. (1969). *The measurement of satisfaction in work and retirement.* Chicago: Rand-McNally.

90. Snape, E., & Redman, T. (2012). Industrial relations climate and union commitment: An evaluation of workplace-level effects. *Industrial Relations, 51,* pp. 11–28.

91. Snape, E., Redman, T., & Chan, A. W. (2000). Commitment to the union: A survey of research and the implications for industrial relations and trade unions. *International Journal of Management Reviews, 2,* pp. 205–230.

92. Stringer, K., & Brown, T. C. (2008). A special kind of downsizing: An assessment of union member reaction to bumping. *Relations Industrielles/Industrial Relations, 63*(4), pp. 648–670.

93. Turner, T., Cross, C., & O'Sullivan, M. (2014). Does union membership benefit immigrant workers in 'hard times'? *Journal of Industrial Relations,* 0022185613515462.

94. UFCW. (2011). *Health & safety.* Retrieved 2 February 2011 from http://www.ufcw.ca/index.php?option=com_content&view=article&id=32&Itemid=112&lang=en

95. Unifor. (2014). *Health & safety.* Retrieved 2 November 2014 from http://www.unifor.org/en/why-unifor/know-your-rights/health-safety

96. Vakola, M., & Nikolaou, I. (2005). Attitudes towards organizational change: What is the role of employees' stress and commitment? *Employee Relations, 27,* pp. 160–174.

97. van Jaarsveld, D. D., & Yanadori, Y. (2011). Compensation management in outsourced service organizations and its implications for quit

rates, absenteeism and workforce performance: Evidence from Canadian call centres. *British Journal of Industrial Relations, 49*, pp. s1–s26. doi: 10.1111/j.1467-8543.2010.00816.x

98. Verma, A. (2005). What do unions do to the workplace? Union effects on management and HRM policies. *Journal of Labor Research, 26*, pp. 415–449.

99. Verma, A., & Fang, T. (2002). Union wage premium. *Perspectives on Labor and Income 14*(4): 17–23.

100. Verma, A., & Fang, T. (2003). Workplace innovation and union status: synergy or strife? *Proceedings of 55th Annual Meeting, Industrial Relations Research Association,* January 2–5, 2003, Washington, DC (pp. 189–198). Retrieved 11 April 2011 from http://www.press.uillinois.edu/journals/irra/proceedings2003/verma.html

101. Waddoups, C. (2008). Unions and wages in Australia: Does employer size matter? *Industrial Relations, 47*(1), 136–144.

102. Waddoups, C. J. (2012). Employer sponsored training and longer tenured workers: Evidence from Australia. *Industrial Relations: A Journal of Economy and Society, 51*(4), pp. 966–986.

103. Wagar, T. H. (1997). Factors differentiating union and non-union organizations: Some evidence from Canada. *Labor Studies Journal, 22*(1), pp. 20–37.

104. Walsworth, S. (2010a). Unions and employment growth: The Canadian experience. *Industrial Relations, 49*(1), pp. 142–156.

105. Walsworth, S. (2010b). What do unions do to innovation? An empirical examination of the Canadian private sector. *Relations Industrielles/Industrial Relations, 65*, pp. 543–561.

106. Walsworth, S., & Long, R. J. (2012). Is the union employment suppression effect diminishing? Further evidence from Canada. *Relations Industrielles/Industrial Relations, 67*(4), pp. 654–680.

107. Walters, D. (2004). Worker representation and health and safety in small enterprises in Europe. *Industrial Relations, 35*, pp. 169–186.

108. Zientara, P., & Kuczynsk, G. (2009). Employees' desire to join or leave a union: Evidence from Poland, *Industrial Relations, 48*, pp. 185–192.

CHAPTER 12

PUBLIC-SECTOR ISSUES

LEARNING OBJECTIVES

BY THE END OF THIS CHAPTER, YOU WILL BE ABLE TO DISCUSS

- why the public sector is a special industry;
- the factors accounting for public-sector union growth;
- theoretical differences between private and public sectors;
- bargaining power;
- essential services and special dispute resolution procedures; and
- management issues such as restructuring, privatization, and HR practice differences.

Montreal firefighters blocked entry to the Port of Montreal, part of a one-day strike across Quebec by unionized municipal workers who oppose Bill 3—the province's pension reform plan.

"Nothing is going to make it into the Port of Montreal," union leader Ronald Martin told Radio-Canada.

The Coalition syndicale pour la libre négociation (The Union Coalition for Open Negotiation) is calling the movement "Le Grand Dérangement," or The Great Disturbance.

"We are one week from having this piece of legislation adopted, so we wanted to show we won't stop the battle," said coalition spokesman Marc Ranger.

"Today's the start of a new kind of mobilization for our membership. We're sending the message that yes, the government has the power to put forth this legislation. But we have a power."

"Not Looking for Conflict"

"In 47 years of existence as a union, this is our first day of any kind of work stoppage," said city employee Pierre Laporte. "We're not people looking for conflict. We're looking for a solution, a negotiated solution."

Police officers also gathered for a rally at their union headquarters.

"They think that once the [bill to reform pensions] becomes law, everything will be OK and will be back to the way it was before," said union president Yves Francoeur. "Do you think we're going to be motivated? Do you think we're going to want to give our time to this police department and to this city administration? No."

About 5,500 municipal workers across Quebec will be on strike, and protest actions are expected to take place all day. Demonstrations were expected to take place outside the city hall buildings in municipalities across Quebec.

Ranger said he would not unveil any action plans organized by the coalition so as to maintain an element of surprise. He also refused to say whether the protests would affect traffic, public transit or other services.

Some transit users in Montreal rode the bus and subway for free as city buses had sticker pasted over cash boxes and gates at certain subway stations were left wide open.

Municipal workers are against the government's proposed bill to modify their pension plans.

Bill 3, introduced in June, would bring employer and employee contributions to a 50/50 split. It could make city employees pay more, and some retirees might also be on the hook for pension shortfalls in order to make up for a province wide pension plan deficit of $4 billion.

Source: Adapted from "Quebec municipal workers in 1-day strike to protest pension reform plan." (November 26, 2014). CBC News. Used with permission of CBC Licensing. Retrieved from http://www.cbc.ca/news/canada/montreal/quebec-municipal-workers-in-1-day-strike-to-protest-pension-reform-plan-1.2850168.

// WHY STUDY PUBLIC-SECTOR LABOUR–MANAGEMENT RELATIONS?

A SIGNIFICANT INDUSTRY

The public sector is an important component in Canada's labour force, representing 24 percent (3,663.9/15,288.4) of total employment in Canada (see Table 12.1).

HIGHLY UNIONIZED

Public-sector employees are more than four times likelier to be unionized than private-sector ones (74.1 percent union coverage as against 16.9 percent in the private sector). (See Table 12.1.)

IMPORTANT PART OF THE LABOUR MOVEMENT IN CANADA

From their growth in the 1960s, public-sector unions have emerged as the largest unions in Canada. Representing primarily employees at the municipal, provincial, and federal

GRAHAM HUGHES

Montreal police can't strike but can protest during wage bargaining.

TABLE 12.1

PUBLIC- AND PRIVATE-SECTOR UNION COVERAGE IN CANADA, 2009–2014

	2009		2010		2011		2012		2013		2014 (OCT.)	
	#	%	#	%	#	%	#	%	#	%	#	%
Total Labour Force (000)	14124.4		14371.2		14635.8		14841.1		15024.5		15288.4	
Public sector labour force	3415	24.2	3511.1	24.4	3563	24.3	3600.8	24.3	3621.9	24.1	3663.9	24.0
Private sector labour force	10709.4	75.8	10860.2	75.6	11072.7	75.7	11240.3	75.7	11402.6	75.9	11624.5	76.0
Union Coverage (total labour force)	4444.4	31.5	4532.6	31.5	4562.2	31.2	4676.8	31.5	4694.6	31.2	4682.7	30.6
Public sector coverage	2541.4	74.4	2629.9	74.9	2638.6	74.1	2684.2	74.5	2702.7	74.6	2715	74.1
Private sector coverage	1903	17.8	1902.7	17.5	1923.6	17.4	1992.6	17.7	1991.9	17.5	1967.7	16.9

Coverage is defined as employees who are members of a union and employees who are not union members but who are covered by a collective agreement or a union contract.
Source: Statistics Canada. Table 282-0077, Labour force survey estimates (LFS), employees by union coverage, North American Industry Classification System (NAICS), sex and age group, unadjusted for seasonality, monthly (persons). Accessed 26 November 2014.

levels, the Canadian Union of Public Employees (CUPE), the National Union of Public and General Employees (NUPGE), and the Public Service Alliance of Canada (PSAC) rank first, second, and fifth in size in Canada, respectively (refer to Table 5.1). Public-sector unions are a vibrant part of the labour movement and are still showing some capacity for growth.

DIFFERENT LEGISLATIVE FRAMEWORK

Special laws govern labour–management relations in the public sector. For example, police officers and firefighters are deemed too essential to have the right to strike. The largest category of provincial and federal civil servants, however, is nonessential employees in clerical and administrative classifications.

ROLE OF GOVERNMENT

An important difference between the sectors is the dual role of government. In public-sector bargaining, the government is both impartial umpire and employer. As employer, the government is a party to collective bargaining; as umpire, it is required to be a neutral to the bargaining process. In general, the government role has been changing in Canada from that of neutral third party to that of a party of direct interest (Swimmer & Thompson, 1995). Some argue that state intervention in collective bargaining (e.g., wage freezes and suspensions of collective bargaining) has resulted in a permanent dismantling of collective bargaining for public employees (Panitch & Swartz, 1993). Gunderson (2005) points out that

> From 1991 to 1997, the federal government suspended collective bargaining for federal employees. Seven other provinces followed with wage freezes and mid-contract pay rollbacks for public sector employees. Numerous provincial governments imposed "social contracts" that mandated employees take a number of days off without pay. Larger proportions of public sector bargaining units were designated as "essential employees" who were denied the right to strike. Ad hoc back-to-work legislation has been increasingly imposed on public sector strikes.

Human Resources and Social Development Canada (2006) keeps a record of governmental orders suspending the right to strike or lock out for public employee unions. Alberta has exercised the suspension nine times; New Brunswick, five times; Newfoundland, once; Quebec, three times; and Saskatchewan, four times. Dachis and Hebdon (2010) show a sharp decline in back-to-work legislation from 1979 to 2009. Their research indicates that the probability of a freely negotiated settlement declines by two-thirds in the round of bargaining immediately after a back-to-work order or law. If the two sides of the agreement know the province will make the hard decisions for them, they have no reason to do so themselves. Back-to-work legislation may be appealing as a way to resume public services, but its long-term consequences for the collective bargaining process could be negative.

IMPERFECT LABOUR MARKET

Public services are often offered in noncompetitive markets. Services provided by teachers, nurses, firefighters, and police officers, for example, may be near monopolies; accordingly, these occupations may have monopoly powers. On the other hand, public employers may possess the power of a monopsony. Characteristics of monopsonistic markets include low wages and chronic labour shortages. Ashenfelter, Farber, and Ransom (2010) found evidence of monopsony in the labour market for teachers and nurses in the United States.

A justification for the monopolistic provision of some services is that they are **public goods**. Public goods might be inefficiently provided in a competitive market either because of abnormally high capital costs (e.g., a space program) or because individuals cannot be charged for the product (e.g., law enforcement). In the case of law enforcement, it would not be efficient or fair to charge only citizens who require police services.

One implication of the monopolistic provision of services of governments is that they are often essential to the health and safety of the public. This is the rationale used for denying these workers the right to strike. The International Labour Organization (ILO) rules allow governments to prevent strikes where services are essential as long as a reasonable substitute (such as arbitration) is made available (see Hebdon, 2014).

> **public good**
> an item whose consumption does not reduce the amount available for others

POLITICS AND PUBLIC OPINION

Politics plays a much greater role in public-sector collective bargaining than in the private sector. Some scholars argue that political power is a substitute for economic power (Swimmer & Thompson, 1995). Since governments actually gain revenue during a strike or lockout, the pressure is generated from the loss of services and the public perception of who is to blame for the job action. Increasingly, the battle for public opinion is important in determining collective bargaining outcomes (see IR Today 12.1).

IR TODAY   12.1

GO BUS RIDERS WARNED TO MAKE ALTERNATE ARRANGEMENTS AS POSSIBLE STRIKE LOOMS

Commuters who rely on GO Transit buses to get to and from work are being warned to make alternate arrangements for Monday's commute in anticipation of a possible strike.

Members of ATU Local 1587 could walk off the job late Sunday night, leaving GO buses idle and disrupting weekend train service to Niagara and Barrie.

Regular GO train service would continue, but trains could be crowded with people who normally take the bus.

"People need to have alternative arrangements ready because we know there will be 53,000 people that are going to be looking to get on a train and while we do have capacity, at some times during the day at peak hours trains are (already) full," Metrolinx spokesperson Anne Marie Aikins told CP24 Friday afternoon. "Use other local services, work from home or if your employer will allow you change your hours to 11 p.m. to 6 p.m. or something like that in order to be able to get on a train that has room."

ATU Local 1587 represents about 1,850 bus drivers, ticket and GO station attendants, maintenance workers, transit safety officers and office staff.

In the event of a strike, Aikins said non-unionized staff will step in to keep stations open and ticket sales going.

Aikins, however, added that the preference is to avoid a work stoppage altogether.

Three years ago Metrolinx and ATU Local 1587 came to an eleventh-hour deal to stave off a work stoppage.

"We are very optimistic that we can avoid one again and we are prepared to work around the clock to do that," Aikins said.

Source: Chris Fox. (30 May 2014). "GO bus riders warned to make alternate arrangements as possible strike looms." CP24.com. Used with permission of CTV News Stox, a division of Bell Media Inc. Retrieved from http://www.cp24.com/news/go-bus-riders-warned-to-make-alternate-arrangements-as-possible-strike-looms-1.1845871.

When politics and public opinion are involved, the parties will settle collective agreement outcomes that are less visible and more long-term (e.g., group benefits and pensions). Public opinion may also play a role in reducing strikes and lockouts.

The final issue involving politics is the line between policymaking in a democracy and the collective bargaining agenda of terms and conditions of employment. Generally, public employees cannot bargain over policy matters including such issues as staffing levels. Public-sector bargaining laws tend to restrict the scope of bargaining to conditions of employment.

// HISTORY OF PUBLIC-SECTOR BARGAINING

After the craft and industrial waves, public-sector unions formed the third wave of unionization in the 1960s. Public-sector membership in Canada grew from only 40,000 in 1946 to 1.5 million by 1981 (Rose, 1995). Today there are about 3.7 million public-sector union members[1] in Canada (see Table 12.1).

UNION GROWTH FACTORS

Several factors account for the rapid rise of public-sector unions in the 1960s.

SOCIAL UPHEAVAL

The civil rights and antiwar movements of the 1960s provided a social context for the rise of public-sector unionism. A 1968 strike of black sanitation workers in Memphis, for example, attracted support from the civil rights movement, including from its leader, Dr. Martin Luther King, Jr. (IR Today 12.2). The main issues in this dispute were union recognition, unsafe working conditions, and the extremely low wages of the sanitation workers, most of whom qualified for social assistance despite working forty hours per week.

THE GROWTH IN PUBLIC SERVICES

Public services grew rapidly in the 1960s and 1970s. The system of community colleges in Canada, for example, was established in this period in most provinces. As healthcare and education services grew, existing unions gained new members without the expense of organizing campaigns.

MEMPHIS SANITATION STRIKE, 1968

Memphis, Spring 1968, marked the dramatic climax of the Civil Rights movement. . . . In the 1960s, Memphis's 1,300 sanitation workers formed the lowest caste of a deeply racist society, earning so little they qualified for welfare. In the film [*At the River 1 Stand*], retired workers recall their fear about taking on the entire white power structure when they struck for higher wages and union recognition.

But local civil rights leaders and the Black community soon realized the strike was part of the struggle for economic justice for all African Americans. The community mobilized behind the strikers, organizing mass demonstrations and an Easter boycott of downtown businesses. The national leadership of AFSCME put the international union's full resources behind the strike. One day, a placard appeared on the picket lines that in its radical simplicity summed up the meaning of the strike: "I am a man."

In March, Martin Luther King, Jr. came to Memphis as part of his Poor People's Campaign to expand the civil rights agenda to the economy . . . . [Dr. King led a rally and gave a speech, and] the next day, April 4, 1968, he was assassinated. Four days later, thousands from Memphis and around the country rallied to [pull off King's] nonviolent march. The city council crumbled and granted most of the strikers' demands. Those 1,300 sanitation workers had shown they could successfully challenge the entrenched economic structure of the South.

Source: "At the River I Stand: About the film," California Newsreel website. Reprinted with permission. Retrieved from http://www.newsreel.org/nav/title.asp?tc=CN0007&s=at%20 the%20river%20i%20stand.

DISSATISFACTION WITH EXISTING EMPLOYEE VOICE MECHANISMS

Many public-sector workers belonged to staff associations in the 1950s and 1960s. These were civil service associations that were unaffiliated with organized labour and that generally shunned militant action. As public employees' demands for decent wages and working conditions increased, many of these weaker organizations were transformed or merged into unions. The motivation for change came from the rising expectations of public servants in the 1960s and 1970s and the inability of these associations to satisfy employee demands. In response to member pressure for full bargaining rights, for example, the Civil Service Association of Ontario gradually transformed itself into a full union, culminating with a name change to the Ontario Public Service Employees Union (OPSEU) in 1975 (Rapaport, 1999; Roberts, 1994). Today, OPSEU is the largest component of the National Union of Public and General Employees (NUPGE), Canada's second-largest union.

UNION MERGERS

Union mergers also played an important role in union growth in the 1960s and 1970s. CUPE, now Canada's largest union, was created out of a merger of two large municipal unions in the 1960s. The merger reduced interunion competition and increased resources for organizing new members. Similarly, NUPGE was created in the 1970s as a national federation of provincial government unions and associations across Canada.

RELATIVE ABSENCE OF EMPLOYER OPPOSITION

Governments at all levels—municipal, provincial, and federal—are reluctant to publicly oppose unions. U.S. research has shown that unions win representation election votes in over 70 percent of the certification applications in the public sector and less than 50 percent in the private sector (Bronfenbrenner & Juravich, 1995). Private-sector employees were also six times more likely to be fired for union organizing than their public-sector counterparts.

REMOVAL OF LEGAL BARRIERS

The passage of collective bargaining laws by the Canadian provinces and federal government in the 1960s and 1970s played an important role in facilitating future union organizing. These laws undoubtedly account for a significant component of union growth. Research shows that the passage of teacher bargaining laws in the United States was the most important factor in the growth of teacher unions (Saltzman, 1985).

// AN ECONOMIC ANALYSIS OF UNION POWER

In this section, we will analyze union power in the context of public-sector bargaining. That public-sector employees might have too much bargaining power was an early rationale used by those arguing against public-sector bargaining rights. According to some, collective bargaining would institutionalize the power of public employee unions so as to leave competing groups at a permanent and substantial disadvantage (Wellington & Winter, 1971). This greater union power, according to this argument, exists for three reasons:

- some services, if disrupted, present a danger to the health and safety of the public;
- demand is relatively inelastic; and
- public-sector strikes affect the public, who have the power to punish only one of the parties.

A theoretical examination of union power can be conducted using Marshall's conditions (1920), which we set out in Chapter 3. To review the four conditions that determine the inelasticity of demand for labour and the wage–employment tradeoff, unions are more powerful when

1. demand for the product or service is inelastic;
2. labour is not easily substituted;
3. supply of substitutes is inelastic (i.e., price of substitutes rises as more are demanded); and
4. labour is a small proportion of total costs.

Applying these factors to the public sector provides the following theoretical analysis. The first condition clearly gives more power to public-sector unions. Many public services have inelastic demand curves, because they are essential and would be demanded at almost any cost.

Similarly, for many services, it is difficult to substitute for labour. Public-safety jobs, for example, are highly skilled and cannot be easily outsourced or replaced with technology. In the case of some services, the public does have other options. For example, citizens can send information today through the post office or by fax, email, or courier. Other jobs can be contracted out to the private sector or replaced by cheaper part-time employees. As we will learn below, private-for-profit is a significant mode of service delivery in Canada.

Both factors 1 and 2 would appear to give public-sector unions more power.

Factor 3 is probably not important in explaining public–private differences in elasticities. The rising prices of substitutes will not likely be a major deterrent to replacing labour in either the public or private sectors.

Factor 4 serves to reduce union power in the public sector. Most public services are highly labour-intensive. In public safety, for example, labour costs can be as high as 70 to 80 percent of total costs.

In the end, we are left with an indeterminate outcome. Two factors (1 and 2) seem to increase union power; the third factor is neutral; and the last reduces union power. The inelasticity of demand for public-sector labour is therefore an empirical question. U.S. research shows that public-sector wages became more elastic over time and were roughly the same as private-sector ones by the 1980s (Lewin, Feuille, Kochan & Delaney, 1988). The wage elasticity of demand for public services undoubtedly increased in the 1970s and 1980s due to the surge in privatization of sanitation and other services in the 1970s.

Thus, the early forecasts that unions would have too much power in the public sector would appear to be unwarranted (Wellington & Winter, 1971).

// DISPUTE RESOLUTION IN THE PUBLIC SECTOR

Public-sector dispute resolution mechanisms were designed in the 1960s and 1970s to avoid strikes. It was believed that essential public employees could not be allowed to walk off their jobs because of the irreparable harm that might be done to the public and because union bargaining power would result in excessive wage gains in negotiations (Hebdon, 1996). These fears provided the rationale for extensive intrusions into the collective bargaining process in the public sector, in contrast to the voluntarism of private-sector dispute resolution.[2] In Canada, each jurisdiction has had to fashion a policy with respect to the right to strike for various categories of public employees. Policies range from a ban on all strikes and lockouts to a private-sector model where all strikes are permitted. In the latter cases, there is almost always a requirement that essential services be provided. In Ontario, for example, public servants can strike, but only after the parties conclude an agreement that provides for essential services. Disputes over what is an essential service in Ontario are decided by the Ontario Labour Relations Board (Adell, Ponak & Grant, 2001). Where strikes are banned, Canadian collective bargaining laws provide for compulsory interest arbitration.

The result of the various strike policies is a legislative patchwork of conditional right to strike, interest arbitration, and in a few cases laws that give the union a choice of striking or arbitration.

Because there is such inconsistency across jurisdictions and occupations, it is difficult to identify patterns of dispute resolution in Canada. Nonetheless, police and firefighters tend to be restricted by laws that ban strikes and substitute interest arbitration. Nova Scotia is an exception; firefighters can legally strike there.

The difficult policy question involves the determination of what constitutes an essential service. Scholars have examined this question and noted the inconsistencies across Canada (Swan, 1985; Swimmer, 1989). In order to assess essential services policies across Canada, Adams (1981) ranks occupational sectors according to the degree of essentiality from the most critical (police and fire) to the least (teachers):

As a general matter, however, there are at least seven principal sectors which are usually considered to have inordinate public interest because the interruption of service threatens one or more of life or limb; peace, order, and good government; or the basic sinews of the economy. These critical areas might be ranked in the following order:

1. Police and firefighters;

2. Hospitals and medical care;

3. Utilities;

4. Transportation;

5. Municipal services;

6. Civil servants;

7. Teachers and educational authorities. (pp. 139–140)

About Ontario's policy, Adams (1981) concludes:

And like other jurisdictions, the uneven application of the process is as much a reflection of different interest group pressures as it is a discriminating concern for the public's welfare and the theoretical dictates of labour-management relations. (p. 140)

The inconsistency is clearest in the variation of teacher dispute resolution across Canada. If we assume that the banning of strikes and lockouts is an indicator of the essentiality of services, then teachers are essential services in British Columbia,[3] Manitoba, and Prince Edward Island but not in the rest of Canada. The inconsistency of application of essentiality is also revealed *within* a province. Alberta, for example, provides a strike/lockout procedure for elementary and secondary teachers, binding arbitration for college teachers, and an arrangement for university faculty whereby they can set up their own procedures.

MORE RECENT DEVELOPMENTS IN DISPUTE RESOLUTION

Adell, Ponak, and Grant (2001) examine three models of dispute resolution in the public sector in Canada: the unfettered strike, the designation system, and interest arbitration.

UNFETTERED-STRIKE MODEL

The unfettered-strike model has been in effect for blue-collar workers at the local level of government in all provinces since World War II. It seems to work best when the services are not essential. When services are essential, unions may have too much bargaining power because they alone determine what services are to be provided in the event of a strike or lockout (Adell, Ponak & Grant, 2001). This model has the advantage of producing the most freely negotiated settlements. It is a positive attribute that is more important during a period of restructuring services, when the parties must resolve complex issues at the bargaining table. A negative attribute, however, is one without any procedure to determine essential services. The strike model invites back-to-work legislation.

DESIGNATION MODEL

In the designation model, the determining of what essential services are is negotiated by the parties either before bargaining starts (Ontario and British Columbia) or at the point of impasse (Quebec). Neutral tribunals are available to adjudicate disputes that arise from these negotiations.

The Quebec model began in 1982 with the establishment of the Essential Services Council, whose function is to determine essential services once impasse is reached. Adell, Ponak, and Grant (2001) conclude:

> As time has passed, both parties have become familiar with the policies and practices of the Quebec Essential Services Council in administering the designation system. This has permitted them to plan in advance for the conduct of strikes, and it has reduced the amount of bargaining and litigation needed with respect to essential services. These developments have given the Quebec public a sense of security which was lacking before the designation model was adopted.

The designation model is most common in Canada for nurses. It is found in Newfoundland, New Brunswick, Quebec, Manitoba, British Columbia, and the federal jurisdiction, and for psychiatric hospital nurses in Ontario (Adell, Ponak & Grant, 2001). The Quebec model for healthcare employees including nurses, however, has such high levels of "essential" designation (80 percent) in the legislation that it effectively removes the right to strike. As such, it is not really a designation model, where essential services determinations are made by independent tribunals.

NO-STRIKE (OR INTEREST ARBITRATION) MODEL

In this model, discussed more fully in Chapter 10, the right to strike is substituted with interest arbitration. It would appear that this category is declining in popularity in Canada. The Adell, Ponak, and Grant (2001) survey of practitioners concluded:

> Among our interviewees, the no-strike model, which substitutes compulsory interest arbitration for the right to strike, had few admirers outside Ontario health care. Almost no one who was operating under either the unfettered-strike model or the designation model advocated moving to the no-strike model.

CHILLING EFFECT

chilling effect
the lack of bargaining flexibility caused by the parties' fear that a concession made in negotiations will reduce the arbitration outcome

Since arbitrators tend to split the difference between the last offers of management and labour at arbitration, the parties are reluctant to move closer to a settlement position in direct talks. This reluctance to negotiate is called the **chilling effect** of interest arbitration (Hebdon, 1996; Hebdon & Mazerolle, 2003; Olson, 1994).

If, for example, management offers 1 percent and the union demands 5 percent at arbitration, there is a good chance that an arbitrator would award a settlement somewhere between these extremes (possibly close to the midpoint of 3 percent). Therefore, if either management or the union were to modify its offer before arbitration, it would run the risk of adversely affecting its arbitration outcome.

NARCOTIC OR DEPENDENCY EFFECT

As its name implies, the **narcotic or dependency effect** is a dependency that occurs because of high rates of arbitration usage. Over time, the parties may no longer be able to negotiate without third-party assistance (Olson, 1994).

A study of collective bargaining settlements in Ontario from 1984 to 1993 revealed a chilling and narcotic effect of interest arbitration:

> *A central finding is that bargaining units covered by legislation requiring compulsory interest arbitration arrive at impasse 8.7 to 21.7 percent more often than bargaining units in the right to strike sectors. Even after controlling for legislative jurisdiction, union, bargaining unit size, occupation, agreement length, time trend, and part-time status, strong evidence was found that compulsory arbitration has a chilling effect on the bargaining process. . . . It was also significant that this effect was greater the more the union operates in the arbitration sector as a proportion of total bargaining activity. This finding is supportive of a dependency effect whereby a union's high usage of arbitration fosters an inability to freely negotiate settlements. (Hebdon & Mazerolle, 2003)*

On the other hand, teachers and school boards who respectively have the right to strike and lock out were able to freely negotiate settlements 97.4 percent of the time.

Final-offer arbitration, explained in Chapter 10, is a modification to interest arbitration designed to reduce these effects. If the problem is the split-the-difference arbitrator behaviour, this is prevented by constraining the arbitrator to select either the union's or management's last offer. Research shows that final-offer arbitration does produce more freely negotiated settlements in some jurisdictions in the United States (Hebdon, 1996). The procedure is not offered as a mandatory procedure in any Canadian jurisdiction.

narcotic or dependency effect
a result of frequent use of arbitration that may cause parties to lose the ability to freely negotiate settlements without third-party assistance

---

IR NOTEBOOK   12.1

B.C. TEACHERS' STRIKE 2014: UNION VOTING ON FULL-SCALE JOB ACTION

As British Columbia's unionized teachers began voting Monday on whether to amplify their job action, the province's education minister pointed to their support staff counterparts as proof bargaining can achieve labour peace.

More than 40,000 members of the B.C. Teachers' Federation were being asked to support a strong mandate for a full strike as a pressure tactic to get a new collective agreement.

The unions representing 34,000 education support staff came to a tentative deal with the province over the weekend after just five days of bargaining.

Education Minister Peter Fassbender said it was another example of a union taking what the government is willing to offer.

"My hope is that this could send a signal to the BCTF," Fassbender told reporters. "This financial agreement is in line with the other public sector unions."

The earliest date that all schools could be shut down is June 16 after the employer gets the required three days' notice of a full walkout.

The vote comes at a time when the union's strike pay account is so depleted it can't pay each teacher $50 a day to walk the picket line and the B.C. government is asking the provincial labour board to declare tests for senior grades to be made essential.

Local union chapters were organizing the ballot, with the union planning to announce results Tuesday night.

"The higher the turnout and the higher the Yes vote, the more pressure it puts on the government to bring resources to the table," said a BCTF memo available online to members last week.

The memo said the economic benefits of a "good settlement" will have a positive long-term effect for members, in spite of salary losses due to job action. Even a one per cent increase for a new teacher will amount to a $15,000 salary boost over a 30-year career, it said.

Teachers have been without a contract since June 2013. Wages and classroom conditions are the major issues.

For every day teachers are on the picket line, the government saves $12 million and another $4.5 million for support staff, according to the Education Ministry.

The union wants a wage hike in the range of 12 per cent over four years, while the government contends that spikes to more than 19 per cent when compounded, and including benefits.

The employer has offered 7.3 per cent over six years plus a $1,200 signing bonus if a deal is reached by the end of the school year.

Vancouver teacher Aeryn Williams said she supports her union.

"I feel like we should be playing hardball because the government isn't putting students first," said the Grades 2 and 3 teacher.

But as teachers consider a full walkout, their co-workers under CUPE and other unions agreed to a 5.5 per cent wage increase over the five-year contract.

The agreement reached on Saturday by the Canadian union of Public Employees and eight other unions representing support staff still needs to be ratified and covers workers including school secretaries, caretakers and bus drivers.

The fact that CUPE has reached a deal as the BCTF remains deadlocked hasn't changed the unions' commitment to support teachers, said B.C. chapter president Mark Hancock.

"Just as the teachers have been at our side as our members have fought for public education, we continue to stand with them," he said in a statement.

Fassbender said there's a difference between the two unions' negotiation strategy: "A willingness to sit in the room and bargain realistically on all the elements."

Support staff will not be punished for refusing to cross BCTF picket lines and they will be compensated for lost wages, the minister said.

Teachers started limited job action on April 23, pulling back some limited duties.

On May 26, a second stage meant rotating strikes closed each school one day per week. A third week of similar strikes begins Tuesday, with districts shutting down schools until Friday.

The employer locked out teachers in conjunction with the rotating strikes and the B.C. Labour Relations Board subsequently ruled it was within its rights to chop teachers' pay by 10 per cent.

The employer has also asked the tribunal to designate the marking of exams for Grades 10 to 12 as essential, although a hearing hasn't yet been set.

Negotiators are scheduled to continue bargaining through to Thursday.

Source: Tamsyn Burgmann. (9 June 2014). "B.C. Teachers Strike 2014: Union Voting on Full-Scale Job Action." The Canadian Press. Used with permission of The Canadian Press. Retrieved from http://www.huffingtonpost.ca/2014/06/09/bc-teachers-2014-vote-job-action_n_5471508.html.

IMPACT ON WAGE OUTCOMES

There is evidence that interest arbitration wage outcomes are higher than in jurisdictions where unions have the right to strike. Dachis and Hebdon (2010), for example, examined wage outcomes in the Canadian public sector from 1979 to 2007. They found that negotiated wage rates are about 1.2 percent higher under interest arbitration than where there is a right to strike. This confirmed an earlier result of Currie and McConnell (1991), who attributed higher settlements under arbitration to arbitrators' attaching greater weight to three factors: wage settlements previously agreed to by bargaining units in the same occupation (i.e., comparability); "catch-up" defined as compensation for prior real wage loss; and less attention to employer ability to pay.

B.C. teachers on strike in 2014 for better wages and classroom conditions.

LOSS OF CONTROL

Finally, Adell, Ponak, and Grant (2001) found opposition to interest arbitration due to the loss of control over outcomes:

> *For employers this means loss of budgetary control—the main reason for the Quebec government's rejection of interest arbitration. Union interviewees, for their part, expressed concern about the growing risk of government manipulation of the appointment of arbitrators and the criteria on which they base their awards.*

In the context of the restructuring of the delivery of services, this loss of control takes on heightened importance. It is crucial that the parties take responsibility for their own solutions to complex problems rather than throwing them into the hands of a third-party arbitrator.

INNOVATIONS IN DISPUTE RESOLUTION

The fiscal pressures of the past two decades have created strains on existing collective bargaining processes. Paradoxically, the pressures have created a unique opportunity for labour and management to experiment with cooperative approaches to dispute resolution. For example, experiments with interest-based bargaining are plentiful at all levels of government in Canada (see Chapter 7).

Despite problems with arbitration, several jurisdictions have instituted a form that involves using the mediator as an arbitrator—called *mediation-arbitration* or simply *med-arb*. Med-arb has been used successfully to resolve grievances before the Grievance Settlement Board in Ontario (Telford, 2000). Also, several public-sector agencies across Canada have institutionalized new forms of mediation to resolve unfair labour practices and grievances.

// THE FOUR GENERATIONS OF PUBLIC-SECTOR BARGAINING

Public-sector collective bargaining may be divided into distinct periods or generations. The first generation represented the growth phase of employment and unions of the 1960s; the second was characterized by the retrenchment and citizen resistance of the 1970s; the third generation, in the 1980s, put a greater emphasis on the performance and productivity of public services (Lewin et al., 1988). In what may be described as a second period of hostility and retrenchment toward public-sector collective bargaining, the period from 1990 to current represents the fourth generation of public-sector collective bargaining. In this current fourth generation, public employees are increasingly under attack on the related fronts of collective bargaining and restructuring of services. Public-sector dispute resolution procedures are at the centre of the pressures on public-sector bargaining. The recent decisions of the Supreme Court of Canada that constitutionalized collective bargaining and the right to strike will make it more difficult for governments to implement retrenchment policies by curbing union rights (discussed in Chapter 4).

// MANAGEMENT ISSUES

As we indicated in the previous section, the current generation of collective bargaining has been marked by the restructuring of public services. In this section, we will examine the challenges facing management in this restraint period and the consequences for public-sector unions and employees. We begin by looking at the international context of public-sector restructuring.

RESTRUCTURING: AN INTERNATIONAL PHENOMENON

There is little doubt that public management has undergone profound changes over the past twenty years. Some claim that a new global paradigm has emerged. It puts greater emphasis on job performance and efficiency in the provision of public services (Osborne & Gaebler, 1992). A **new public management** (NPM) created in the developed world puts much greater emphasis on both private-sector practices and service provision (Hebdon & Kirkpatrick, 2005). But some question the extent to which NPM represents a coherent program of reform (Lynn, 1998). One problem is the appropriateness of exporting private-sector management values and practices into the public domain (Stewart & Walsh, 1992).

> **new public management (NPM)**
> a new approach to public administration in which public organizations are to become more decentralized, market-driven, and concerned with financial control, and managers more empowered and performance-oriented

Of the twenty-five countries in the OECD, twenty-three had a major human resources (HRM) initiative from 1989 to 1992. Of these twenty-three initiatives, nine had a policy to limit government and ten had a major privatization initiative (Swimmer, 2001). The twenty-three governments that implemented these NPM policies spanned the political spectrum from conservative to social democratic.

Evidence of the scope of restructuring can be seen in Table 12.2, with 75 percent of OECD countries planning to decrease the size of their public-sector workforce. Ireland, the Netherlands, Poland, and the United Kingdom all have downsizing initiatives in 2010. Estonia, Japan, and Slovenia all have ongoing workforce reduction programs in place. Finally, Canada, Denmark, and Finland have productivity programs that include such schemes as recruitment freezes and reduction of administrative employees.

Downsizing policies were pursued by strengthening the hands of provincial and federal finance ministries to impose spending limits, reducing transfer payments to lower levels of government, and cutting services and transferring responsibility to individuals and families (Ferrera & Hemerijck, 2003; Hebdon & Kirkpatrick, 2005). Although they were adopted in most OECD countries, these policies were taken furthest in liberal regimes such as the United States, New Zealand, and the United Kingdom.

TABLE 12.2

RESTRUCTURING THE WORKFORCE: SOME INITIATIVES

RECENT DOWNSIZING INITIATIVES	ONGOING REDUCTION PROGRAMMES	PRODUCTIVITY PROGRAMMES
Ireland: 12% of civil service in the next 4 years	Estonia: 15.5% decrease between 2007 and 2010	Canada: Recruitment freeze and review of services
Netherlands: 15% in the next 4 years	Japan: Net reduction by 5% since 2005	Denmark: Reduction of administrative employees in favour of employees in people care
Poland: 10%	Slovenia: 1% reductions per year since 2004	Finland: Productivity programme
United Kingdom: 490,000 jobs as part of the spending reviews	France: General review of public policies (reduction of 100,000 staff since 2007)	

Note: Numbers and percentages about staff adjustment usually exclude some sectors, and apply to parts of the public service that differ across countries.

Source: OECD. (9 December 2010). Getting it Right: Restructuring the government workforce. Public Employment and Management Working Party—annual meeting, Paris. Retrieved from http://www.oecd.org/dataoecd/2/39/46898720.pdf.

CANADIAN CONTEXT

Driven by credit-rating downgrading in some provinces and increases in deficits and debt, public-sector managers struggled to cut costs. From 1988 to 1995, average provincial debt increased from 24 percent to 37 percent of gross domestic product (GDP) and federal debt increased from 50 percent to 70 percent of GDP (Swimmer, 2001). Associated with this process of cost cutting were attempts to reshape the management and organization of public services. One aspect of this was a movement across developed countries to privatize public services. The term *privatization* covers a range of actions that involve the private-for-profit sector. It may mean giving up responsibility for the service entirely by selling it to the private sector, or retaining control by hiring a private company to manage the service. The most common form of privatization in Canada is contracting out, whereby private firms run the service but the public sector retains ultimate responsibility through a contract for a specific term.

In examining the scope of contracting out, we cite a study of Canadian municipal managers in 2004 that summarizes how services are provided (public, private for profit, private not for profit, etc.) for sixty-seven defined services (Hebdon & Jalette, 2008). Since this study replicated an earlier one conducted in the United States in 2002–2003, we can compare Canadian and U.S. privatization rates.

Contrary to expectations, researchers found that the rate of private-for-profit services was significantly higher in Canadian cities and towns than in U.S. ones. In addition, almost 64 percent of Canadian and 58 percent of U.S. municipalities considered privatizing at least one service in the past five years. Privatization is very much on the agenda of both Canadian and American city managers.

TABLE 12.3

COMPARISON OF SERVICE PROVISION AND PRIVATIZATION BY SERVICE CATEGORY:*

AMERICAN (2002-2003) AND CANADIAN (2004) CITIES AND TOWNS (NUMBER OF SERVICES IN PARENTHESES—TOTAL 67)

	UNITED STATES		CANADA	
	% PROVIDED	% PRIVATE FOR PROFIT	% PROVIDED	% PRIVATE FOR PROFIT
Public works/ transportation (20)	49.1	20.9	63.1	33.6
Public utilities (4)	31.4	22.4	22.7	31.6
Public safety (7)	65.3	15.5	58.8	16.8
Parks and recreation (3)	60.6	13	71.1	19.3
Health and human (15)	29.1	11.2	23.4	16.3
Culture and arts (3)	37.1	19.2	57.1	2.8
Support functions (15)	72	18.9	80.7	33.5
Weighted average	**50.3**	**17.4**	**55.4**	**25.8**

*The number of services for each municipal unit was totalled for the categories of "public employees only" and "private for profit." The totals were then divided by total services provided for each city to produce a rate expressed as a percentage of total services.
Source: Hebdon, R., and P. Jalette. (2008). "The Restructuring of Municipal Services: A Canada-United States Comparison." *Environment and Planning C: Government and Policy, 26,* pp. 144–156.

To examine the breadth of cross-border service provision and privatization differences, Table 12.3 provides a breakdown by the seven service categories of public works/transportation; public utilities; public safety; parks and recreation; health and human; culture and arts; and support functions. It presents the mean number of cities providing each of the seven service categories.

On average there were 5.1 percent more cities offering these services in Canada than in the United States. Canadian municipalities provide more services in the categories of public works/transportation, parks and recreation, culture and arts, and support functions. U.S. cities and towns, on the other hand, provide more services in the categories of public utilities, public safety, and health and human or social services.

// IMPLICATIONS OF RESTRUCTURING FOR UNION–MANAGEMENT RELATIONS IN CANADA

GOVERNMENT POLICIES

Swimmer (2001) provides a summary of the restraint policy options available to Canadian governments given the high levels of unionization. These restraint policies applied not only to direct employees of the government but to services like schools, hospitals, and lower levels of government that depend on funding from higher levels. Policies varied according to the managerial or unionization status of the employees.

MANAGEMENT EMPLOYEES

1. At the risk of lowering morale and losing experienced employees, governments were free to downsize and downgrade the conditions of managers.
2. Some governments offered special early retirement to managers.

UNIONIZED EMPLOYEES

1. Some governments demanded concessions from unionized employees using adversarial bargaining.
2. Others adopted a more cooperative approach by opening the books to reveal the bleak financial picture and working toward joint solutions.
3. Governments reduced compensation through legislation or through collective bargaining by threatening legislation if concessions were not made in negotiations (see IR Today 12.3).

IR TODAY   12.3

UNIONS PLAN PUBLIC FIGHT OVER FEDERAL LABOUR REFORMS

In a sign they have all but given up on talks with the Treasury Board over labour reforms proposed in the federal government's budget bill, union leaders say they are taking matters into their own hands.

The Canadian Labour Congress quietly met with more than 100 representatives from unions across the country this week to plot a long-term strategy to engage both the public and union members in pressuring the government to reverse its proposed labour law changes. The CLC represents more than 3 million workers across the country.

The CLC has already wrapped up a series of television ads that ran over the past six weeks. Its next step is to reach out to each of its own members in a campaign that will detail how reforms in the budget bill will affect their bargaining rights.

And then, according to CLC secretary-treasurer Hassan Yussuff, union members must appeal directly to their MPs.

"They need to, of course, take direct responsibility to how they're going to start speaking out on behalf of their union, on behalf of themselves," said Yussuff. "And more importantly, in terms of the gains they have made to ensure this government doesn't take that away."

"Government Had Declared War on Us"

Yussuff said this offensive strategy will become the "new normal" unless policy changes are reversed.

"I think the government had declared war on us," he said. "We didn't start any of these measures—the government itself has done so. I think it's fair for us to respond to their actions."

If passed, Bill C-4 would make sweeping changes to a number of labour laws, including the Canada Labour Code and Public Service Labour Relations Act.

Among other things, it would streamline collective bargaining by allowing the government to determine which services are essential and make it illegal for those workers to strike. In situations where 80 per cent or more of workers in a bargaining unit are designated essential, the only dispute resolution method is arbitration.

In a statement sent to CBC News, Treasury Board president Tony Clement said the Public Service Labour Relations Act is being amended to ensure that the public service is modern and affordable.

"The proposed amendments will bring savings, streamline practices and bring them in line with other jurisdictions. Our government will sit at a bargaining table on behalf of the taxpayer where the rules are fair and balanced."

Unions were not consulted in the drafting of the reforms. Labour leaders have since tried to meet with Clement to present counter-proposals, with little success.

Robyn Benson of the Public Service Alliance of Canada recently had a meeting with Clement during which she proposed he withdraw changes from the budget bill to allow for more consultation.

She wrote on her blog afterwards, "He stated bluntly that he had no intention of consulting with us, and that he wanted all his changes in place for the next round of collective bargaining—in fact, by Christmas."

In response, Clement tweeted, "That's also the meeting where you claimed co-governance with Parliament. Takes 'union boss' to a whole new level."

Source: Trinh Theresa Do. (21 November 2013). CBC News. Retrieved from http://www.cbc.ca/news/politics/unions-plan-public-fight-over-federal-labour-reforms-1.2433850.

The most common strategy for unionized employees was the third one—to reduce compensation either through legislation or the threat thereof (Hebdon & Warrian, 1999). Swimmer's research (2001) revealed that four jurisdictions in Canada relied exclusively on legislation (option 3) and another seven combined legislation with adversarial bargaining. Only four jurisdictions relied exclusively on bargaining (options 1 or 2).

The factors determining the option follow:

- political ideology—left-of-centre governments generally avoided legislation; Liberal and Conservative governments chose legislation in ten out of eleven cases;
- it was more difficult to take the adversarial bargaining option if interest arbitration was the dispute settlement mechanism—in four out of five cases, legislation was used where arbitration existed; and
- when the fiscal problem was more severe, legislation was more likely.

MANAGEMENT ISSUES

INNOVATION

socio-technical systems design systems of new technology in which workers are complements to, not simply extensions of, technology; in which participation, communication, and collaboration are encouraged through an accommodative organizational structure; and in which individual workers achieve control through shared responsibility and minimal supervision

Innovative work practices (e.g., teamwork, job rotation, **socio-technical systems design**) may be more difficult in the public sector than in the private sector, for several reasons (Hebdon & Hyatt, 1996):

- *Higher unionization.* Unions may make the introduction of innovative programs more difficult but, once in, play a positive role in integrating them into the workplace (Meltz & Verma, 1995).
- *Crisis atmosphere.* Enhanced workplace participation and teamwork are less likely under threats of layoffs, privatization, and cost-cutting.
- *Civil service rules.* The civil service bureaucracy may act as a serious deterrent to implementing innovative employee involvement programs. For example,

workplace reorganization that requires the elimination of several layers of supervisors may collide with civil service classification systems that thrive on a multiplicity of levels (Hebdon & Hyatt, 1996).

The conclusion of a case in the Ontario government involving the introduction of new technology combined with a location transfer of the work from Toronto to Thunder Bay is set out below (Hebdon & Hyatt, 1996):

Treasury Board President Tony Clement announces changes to the Public Service Labour Relations Act.

> *The case study revealed some insights into the potential benefits of worker involvement/socio-technical projects for management-labour relations. In the first place we found no evidence of a reduced role for the union after the reorganization. On the contrary, regular meetings between management and labour now take place at the local level. The Thunder Bay union local has been very active in pursuing its agenda of local issues.*

> *The effect of this STS [social technical system] is to enable workers to share in the benefits of the introduction of the new technology. This is manifest in two ways: higher productivity and more pay; and more meaningful jobs, although more research is needed to verify the latter effect. In a traditional collective bargaining sense, the result of the STS initiative can be characterized as "distributive," since it is reasonable to imagine that minimum conditions for agreement to STS would be higher pay, better jobs and a say in workplace design for union members and higher productivity and lower unit costs for the employer.*

There is recent evidence that the human resources practices of public-sector managers are moving closer to those of their private-sector counterparts. Harel and Tzafrir (2002) examined public–private human resources practices in Israel. They looked at several key dimensions of a high-performance workplace and found that

> *public sector management emphasizes HRM domains that deal with employee selection (probably because of the stricter Employment Equity regulations in governmental organizations) and grievance procedures because of the higher level of unionization. On the other hand, private sector management emphasizes employee growth and pay for performance. However, the authors also found evidence that the public sector is "moving" closer and closer to the private sector model by adopting "high performance work practices" in order to overcome the turbulent environment and public demand.*

UNION ISSUES

Because privatization shifts jobs from the public to the private sector, we might expect a decline in public union membership to have resulted from the restructuring of the past decades. But the data in Table 12.1 do not support such a decline; in fact, membership has been increasing.

It is generally assumed in the academic literature that unions will oppose privatization because of the threat to jobs and compensation. Some recent research casts doubt on this assumption. A survey of union reactions to privatization at the municipal level of government in Canada in 2004 revealed that unions may have a range of responses (Jalette & Hebdon, 2012). In the survey, the respondents were asked to indicate whether

TABLE 12.4

UNION REACTION TO PRIVATIZATION CONSIDERATION

CHOICE	VARIABLE	FREQUENCY
Acquiescence	No reaction to the proposal	33
	supported the proposal	3
Traditional collective	strike, work slowdown, etc.	48
bargaining	Court challenge, arbitration	45
Proactive	Offered some alternatives to the proposal sought to	37
	reduce adverse effects through negotiations	52

"some private delivery was considered that affected jobs." Six possible union reactions to the private service delivery consideration were solicited. These reactions were not mutually exclusive categories; unions, for example, might strike and reduce adverse effects through negotiations. The range of reactions is set out in Table 12.4.

The summary shown in Table 12.4 divides the union responses into three categories: acquiescence, traditional collective bargaining, and proactive. The study's authors conclude that unions do make strategic choices in reacting to privatization proposals that affect their members.

ACQUIESCENCE Acquiescence was the least popular category; nonetheless, the choices of support or no reaction were significant (36 cases).

TRADITIONAL COLLECTIVE BARGAINING The most prevalent choices were the traditional collective bargaining ones of collective action (strikes, job actions, etc.) and legal opposition through the courts or arbitration (93 cases); see IR Notebook 12.1.

PROACTIVE The most popular single choice was to try to reduce the worst effects of privatization through negotiations (52 cases). When combined with suggesting alternatives, this category was the second-largest (89 cases).

Research revealed that unionized cities attracted a greater number of new privatization proposals but that unions were successful in having them rejected. The most successful rejection strategy associated with these proposals was suggesting alternatives, while strikes and other industrial action, on the other hand, were not effective. Cities where multiple union strategies were employed had a lower long-term privatization rate. City managers also acted strategically by implementing adjustment policies that facilitated privatization. These results support a pragmatic view of union–management relations in which privatization was modified or mutually acceptable alternatives were found. Where, for example, the municipality created a strong set of adjustment policies (such as minimizing the effects on displaced employees, implementing privatization on a trial basis, or limiting the application of privatization to new or growing services), there were fewer industrial action responses (Jalette & Hebdon, 2008).

// SUMMARY

We have examined why public-sector labour–management relations play an important role in Canadian society today. You should understand the factors that gave rise to the growth of public-sector unionism and the theoretical differences between private and public sectors. You have applied economic analysis to union bargaining power and discovered that there is no a priori case for greater union power in the public sector.

The essential nature of many public services was discussed together with the special dispute resolution procedures developed to accommodate collective bargaining. In particular, the strengths and weaknesses of interest arbitration as a strike substitute were canvassed. We also studied the management problems of restructuring of public services, especially privatization, and some human resources differences between public and private sectors. Finally, we examined some recent evidence on the implications of restructuring for government, management, and labour.

KEY TERMS

chilling effect 360
narcotic or dependency effect 361
public good 354
new public management (NPM) 364
socio-technical systems design 368

WEBLINKS

Employment and Labour Legislation:
http://cirhr.library.utoronto.ca/employment-&-labour-legislation

Public Services International (International Public Sector Union):
http://www.world-psi.org

Research on suspension of the right to strike and lock out in Canada:
http://guides.library.utoronto.ca/content.php?pid=295266&sid=2441811

International Public Management Association for Human Resources:
http://www.ipma-hr.org

International Public Management Association–Canada:
http://ipma-aigp.com/

DISCUSSION QUESTIONS

1. Why study the public sector as a special topic?
2. What factors account for the growth of public-sector unions? What role has the passage of labour laws played?
3. Explain labour market imperfections for some public services.

4. Do public-sector unions have more power than their private-sector counterparts?

5. Are all public services essential? Based on your answer, what would be the most appropriate dispute resolution procedure for people in the following occupations: police, firefighting, hospital, maintenance, transit services, clerical and administrative, and teaching?

6. What are the pros and cons of interest arbitration?

7. What are the restraint policy options available to Canadian governments?

8. Define privatization and describe the range of union reactions to it.

9. How do HR practices differ between public and private sectors?

USING THE INTERNET

1. Using the Internet links provided, find the law that covers firefighters in your province. Fully describe the firefighter dispute settlement procedures in the law.

2. Find two examples in Canada of a provincial order suspending the right to strike for public employees.

3. What are the aims and purposes of the International Public Management Association of Canada and Public Services International?

4. Find an example of a back-to-work order by a government in Canada after 2010. What were its effects on labour, management, and the public?

EXERCISES

1. Find a province that allows teachers to strike and one that bans teacher strikes. Outline the bargaining and dispute resolution procedures in the bargaining law. Why do you think these laws vary from province to province?

2. What has been the impact of public-sector restructuring on governments, management, and labour?

CASE	THE CASE OF THE ONTARIO OFFICE OF THE REGISTRAR GENERAL

The Office of the Registrar General (ORG) is located within the Ontario Ministry of Consumer and Commercial Relations. Its mandate is to record, certify, and provide information (certified copies of registrations) on the province's vital statistics—live and still births, adoptions, marriages, changes of name, divorces, and deaths. In a typical year, the ORG handles about 360,000 registrations and 530,000 proofs of registration. Such revenue-generating services as the issuance of birth and death certificates and provision of certified copies of registration documents may be readily quantified. Unlike most public service, therefore, useful estimates of productivity are possible in this case.

INCITING A CRISIS

Early in 1987, the provincial government in Ontario announced its intention to relocate some government functions to communities in northern Ontario. This initiative intended to promote both economic development and the establishment of a greater presence of the provincial government outside of the provincial capital, Toronto. The Northern Ontario Relocation Program included moving the Office of the Registrar General to Thunder Bay, a community of about 100,000 people located on the northwestern shore of Lake Superior, some 1,375 kilometres from Toronto. The Thunder Bay office was to be operational by April 1991.

The relocation to Thunder Bay was not popular with the Toronto staff, which numbered approximately 150 full-time equivalent (FTE), largely clerical, workers. Most of the Toronto staff members were women who had strong ties to Toronto. In fact, as it would turn out, only six of the Toronto staff would ultimately relocate to Thunder Bay.

The other managerial and clerical staff members chose to use the time between February 1987 and April 1991 to find employment in other areas of the provincial government or in the private sector in order to remain in Toronto. During this four-year period, 95 percent of the staff left the ORG and were replaced by contract staff until the move to Thunder Bay. The average experience level declined from fifteen years before the relocation announcement to less than one year just before the move to Thunder Bay.

REPERCUSSIONS

The result of this staff turnover was predictable. Beginning in the first quarter of 1990, productivity levels began to decline and service delivery suffered enormously. Customers who sent requests for various records through the mail—7,000 per week, accounting for about 75 percent of requests (the other 25 percent of requests came through the walk-up counter service in Toronto)—waited, on average, one week for their requests to be processed in the 1988/89 fiscal year. By April 1990, the average turnaround time for mail requests had increased to slightly over three weeks and by August 1990, the wait was six weeks.

Other indicators provided evidence of the productivity problems facing the ORG. Many of the documents the ORG issues certified copies of are essential for proving status in order to obtain a passport, receive a health card (thus permitting access to medical services), registering in school and organized sporting activities, and settling legal claims. For many of these, time is of the essence to customers, and the slow turnaround time of the mail service incited customers to find ways of "jumping the queue." One was to use the walk-up counter in Toronto, which pro-vided same-day service. The number of people using this service increased steadily from about 60,000 per year to 110,000 within the first year following relocation. The demand on this service began to stretch its limits, resulting in customers waiting at least three days for service. In addition, tens of thousands of Ontario citizens were requesting emergency assistance from their local members of provincial parliament (MPPs) to assist them with their requests. The ORG's response was to set up a special group to deal with these emergency requests. MPPs and their office staff readily determined that this was a more efficient process and began to ask for preferential services for nonemergency requests as well.

The growing demands for the walk-up counter and special MPP emergency service drained resources from the mail-in service. This, combined with lower productivity due to the high staff turnover, contributed to a growing backlog of document requests and vital statistics registrations.

CRISIS? WHAT CRISIS?

Management's response to the growing backlog of requests was to hire more workers. By March 1991, the month prior to the move to Thunder Bay, the number of FTE staff had increased to 170, up from 137 four years earlier, and 25 FTEs more than the ORG's approved staff level. The small amount of training these workers received was applied to an antiquated technological infrastructure. Paper records of over 20 million documents contained in 40,000 volumes were stored in a 929-square-metre warehouse. Document retrieval required considerable expenditures of both time and physical effort.

The organizational structure of the ORG was also not conducive to the maintenance of productivity levels, let alone improvement. There were six layers of management between the director of the branch and the front-line staff. Twelve operational units, twenty-three job classifications, and forty-one separate job descriptions distinguished the 150 FTE staff. The result was that mail requests passed through six functional units before being issued, and communication between the units and management, and the units themselves, followed bureaucratic chains of command.

Between April 1987 and March 1990, productivity levels remained relatively constant—each FTE worker, on average, processed about 6,000 registration and proof of registration requests per year, at a cost of $4.40 per request. In the 1990/91 fiscal year, output per worker had fallen by 20 percent to 5,000 requests per FTE per year, at an average cost of $5.42 per request.

Superimposed over the declining productivity scenario, which was induced by the relocation notice and antiquated technology, was a looming economic recession and pressure for public-sector cost restraint through attrition and increased productivity. For the ORG, this meant a reduction in its approved staff complement of 147 FTEs in 1987 to 135 in 1989.

A WINDOW OF OPPORTUNITY

Although the immediate cause of the productivity woes experienced by ORG was the relocation announcement, the technological and organizational weaknesses were structural barriers to longer-term improvements in staff morale, service delivery, and productivity. The move to Thunder Bay was seen as an opportunity not only to resolve the move-induced productivity problems, but also to address the more fundamental structural problems.

The innovations envisioned for the new workplace were in the areas of

- employment equity;
- customer service;
- technology;

- organizational structure, participation, and flexibility; and
- forging new partnerships with the union, community, and the municipal and federal governments.

The exact policies for these innovations would follow the principles of socio-technical systems design (STS): workers are complements to, not simply extensions of, technology; job content is broad in scope and includes the attainment of new skills, which promote flexibility; participation, communication, and collaboration are encouraged through an accommodative organizational structure; and individual workers achieve control through shared responsibility and minimal supervision.

THE FORMULA FOR REDESIGN

This section reviews the execution of the innovations and how the innovations were achieved.

A. EMPLOYMENT EQUITY

The Ontario government has established for itself employment equity goals. Women, racial minorities, Aboriginal peoples, the physically challenged, and francophones have been designated as groups that are underrepresented in provincial administration.

A concern raised by the Northern Ontario Relocation Program has been its potentially deleterious impact on meeting employment equity objectives. Reid, Foot, and Omar (1992) indicated that for the program as a whole (twelve groups consisting of 1,700 employees), only 12.9 percent of "designated group" employees relocated, compared to 30.9 percent of white, anglophone, able-bodied people. In addition, designated groups accounted for only 59.6 percent of new hires at the new location, compared to 62.6 percent in Toronto.

In order to address the employment equity objectives, the ORG organized a committee of designated group members to assist in recruitment. In addition, a management development program was established to train Native Canadian managers, and the workplace was designed with physical accessibility as a fundamental consideration.

The employment equity program was also expanded to include social assistance recipients and single parents. In conjunction with the federal government, the provincial government designed training programs to help in the development of life and job skills.

B. CUSTOMER SERVICE

New technology provided opportunities to improve customer service. It is now possible for copies of birth, death, marriage, and other certificates to be produced immediately for those who go in person to the Toronto and Thunder Bay offices. The relevant scanned documents are called up onto a computer screen, verified, and printed within minutes. This has significantly reduced the inconvenience of what used to be a process of sorting through archived paper documents, which required a three-day waiting period and two visits to the office.

Other customer service improvements that were part of the broader initiative included extended hours of operation facilitated by the compressed-workweek policy; a more "customer-friendly" office design; better information and instruction on the application process, such as better signs and instruction sheets with examples of how to complete any necessary forms, making it easier for customers to get what they want; and customer service training for all staff.

C. TECHNOLOGY

Existing information storage and processing technology in place at the ORG before the move to Thunder Bay was capturing only about 5 percent of the information gathered by the branch. As a result, 10,000 square feet of space was required in downtown Toronto to store the paper records. In addition to the expense of the storage, there was the threat of time, fire, flood, or security problems that would jeopardize the physical existence of the documents and the pledge that these records would remain confidential.

The decision was made that the move to Thunder Bay would be accompanied by the purchase of an important technological innovation, namely auto imaging technology (AIT). AIT permits paper documents to be optically imaged and the data stored on optical platters. At the time the technology was purchased, it was believed that more than 50 percent of the branch's business information could be imaged and stored on platters. As will be discussed, the introduction of this technology led to better customer service. In addition, the technology resulted in better protection of the integrity of the records and a significant reduction in storage costs, and reduced the amount of labour necessary to manage the records by twenty-two non-bargaining-unit person-years.

The use of an STS approach required the integration of workers and their representatives with the new technology. To this end, it was necessary to establish the continuous involvement and support of OPSEU and the central human resources management agency concerning such administrative arrangements as flexible work time and sustaining community input on equity recruitment and training.

D. ORGANIZATIONAL STRUCTURE, PARTICIPATION, AND FLEXIBILITY

Human resources policies at the Thunder Bay office are based on the assumptions that employees are responsible, individuals are capable of making decisions, and groups can work effectively together with minimal supervision. These philosophies were implemented through organizational delayering, team management, generic job descriptions, pay-for-knowledge, alternative working hours, and workplace childcare.

Before the redesign, there were twelve functional units, each with a seven-level hierarchy between the level of registrar general and clerk. At the clerk level, there were eight more levels of positions. As mentioned earlier, this expansive breadth and depth of bureaucracy is reflected in the fact that in an organization of 150 staff members, there were forty-one different job descriptions and twenty-three different job classifications.

The twelve functional units were integrated into one multifunctional unit consisting of seven teams. The unit is directed by the deputy registrar general. Each team includes twelve team representatives and one team manager. Members of the team are capable of performing all of the necessary job functions.

The net result is a reduction in the hierarchy of seven levels to three, including the removal of two levels of managerial (reporting) hierarchy. In addition, the eight layers within the clerical hierarchy have been replaced by one generic clerical position.

This innovation achieved three fundamental purposes: a flatter organizational structure that permits greater flexibility and encourages more independent lower-level decision making; fewer reporting, communication, and other protocol "seams"; and job enrichment as the forty-one job descriptions were replaced by three generic job descriptions—deputy registrar general, team manager, and team representative.

To encourage team representatives to acquire the skills necessary to perform all of the team's functions, a pay-for-knowledge plan was established. Beginning at an "introductory" or "entry" skill level, at which the worker has no direct experience and little knowledge of the work, workers progress through five knowledge levels for each job function in the team.

In order to better accommodate the widely divergent needs and work–family pressures of its employees, the ORG instituted work scheduling alternatives and a workplace childcare program. The work scheduling options include a compressed work week, a regular part-time night shift, regular part-time jobs for workers with disabilities, and flexible hours for single parents.

E. FORGING NEW PARTNERSHIPS

One of the most notable features of the ORG move to Thunder Bay was the emphasis placed on recasting and enriching old relationships and on establishing new partnerships within the Thunder Bay community.

COMMUNITY PARTNERSHIPS As mentioned, the ORG established an Interagency Placement Committee, intended to encourage the recruitment of staff from the targeted employment equity community. The committee received over 450 referrals from race relations, Aboriginal, and disabled persons' organizations.

As a result of the assistance of this committee, 60 percent of the Thunder Bay ORG is staffed by members of groups that are generally underrepresented in the Ontario public service. The mosaic of the ORG includes 10 percent Aboriginal, 14 percent physically challenged, 5 percent francophone, and 6.3 percent visible minorities. Eighty-one percent of the workforce is female.

Another interesting example of a broad community relationship nurtured as a result of the move was the public/private/nonprofit partnership formed between ORG, Arthur Anderson Consulting, and Goodwill Industries. Together, these organizations worked to scan 10 million paper documents for conversion to optical images. This was achieved by a staff that included eighty-six individuals drawn from the ranks of social assistance recipients, none of whom had any previous computer training. Goodwill Industries provided the training; Arthur Anderson provided technological support; and the ORG provided project management services. According to ORG officials, the project was completed ahead of schedule, and at a savings of $750,000 to the welfare system.

INTERGOVERNMENTAL PARTNERSHIPS Some important intergovernmental partnerships were established through the ORG initiatives. The federal Canadian

Employment and Immigration Commission assisted with funding a strategy that trained some eighty workers from employment-equity-designated groups for employment in the Thunder Bay office of ORG.

A partnership was also formed between the provincial government and the municipal government of Thunder Bay. The Thunder Bay social services department assisted with recruiting and training of sole-support social assistance recipients.

UNION–MANAGEMENT PARTNERSHIPS Last, but most certainly not least, the consultative relationship between the ORG and OPSEU was given an opportunity to be expanded. The ORG and OPSEU agreed to a number of initiatives to assist the overwhelming majority of workers not relocating to Thunder Bay to find employment within the Ontario public service or elsewhere. These measures included restricted job competitions for ORG staff, skills upgrading programs, job interview skills training, and psychological counselling.

An agreement between OPSEU and the ministry provided the framework for the implementation of the project. The pay of the clerical workers increased by as much as two pay grades; the number of workers has actually grown (partly due to an unexpected increase in demand for services); and there is little evidence of deskilling. There was reduced conflict over classification and promotion issues. The collapsing of job classes combined with job rotation has eliminated much interjob conflict through the formal grievance procedure. In addition, the open communications have resulted in workers becoming more active in workplace issues and, rather than threatening the worker–union relationship, enhancing the relationship.

Source: R. Hebdon and D. Hyatt. (1996). "Workplace innovation in the public sector: The case of the office of the Ontario Registrar General." *Journal of Collective Negotiations in the Public Sector*, *25*(1), pp. 63–81.

QUESTION

1. Write a two- or three-page paper evaluating the labour–management relations effects of this innovation case at the Office of the Registrar General. Include in your essay a discussion of the strengths and weaknesses of the management and union actions and policies.

// ENDNOTES

1. The 2.16 million is calculated by multiplying public-sector employment of 3.229 million by union density of 71.4.
2. Recall that in the private sector, third-party intervention was nearly always at the request of one or both parties.
3. The Government of British Columbia changed its teacher bargaining law in 2005 to ban all strikes.

// REFERENCES

1. Adams, G. (1981). The Ontario experience with interest arbitration. In J. Weiler (Ed.), *Interest arbitration.* Toronto: Carswell.

2. Adell, B., Ponak, A., & Grant, M. (2001). *Strikes in essential services.* Kingston, ON: Industrial Relations Centre Press, Queen's University.

3. Ashenfelter, O., Farber, H., & Ransom, M. (2010). Labor market monopsony. *Journal of Labor Economics, 28*(2), pp. 203–210.

4. Bronfenbrenner, K., & Juravich, T. (1995). The impact of employer opposition on union certification win rates: A private/public sector comparison. Working paper no. 113. Washington, DC: Economic Policy Institute.

5. Currie, J., & McConnell, S. (1991). Collective bargaining in the public sector: The effect of legal structure on dispute costs and wages. *American Economic Review 81*(4), pp. 693–718.

6. Dachis, B., & Hebdon, R. (2010). *The laws of unintended consequences: The effect of labour legislation on wages and strikes.* C. D. Howe Institute.

7. Ferrera, M., & Hemerijck, A. (2003). Recalibrating Europe's welfare regimes. In J. Zeltin & D. M. Trubek (Eds.), *Governing work and welfare in a new economy.* Oxford: Oxford University Press, pp. 88–128.

8. Gunderson, M. (2005). Two faces of union voice in the public sector. *Labor Research Journal, 26*(3), pp. 393–413.

9. Harel, G., & Tzafrir, S. (2002). HRM practices in the public and private sectors: Differences and similarities. *Public Administration Quarterly, 25,* pp. 316–355.

10. Hebdon, R. (1996). Public sector dispute resolution in transition. In D. Belman, M. Gunderson & D. Hyatt (Eds.), *Public sector employment in a time of transition* (pp. 85–125). Madison, WI: Industrial Relations Research Association.

11. Hebdon, R., & Hyatt, D. (1996). Workplace innovation in the public sector: The case of the office of the Ontario Registrar General, *Journal of Collective Negotiations in the Public Sector, 25*(1), pp. 63–81.

12. Hebdon, R., & Jalette, P. (2008). The restructuring of municipal services: A Canada–United States comparison. *Journal of Environment and Planning, C–Local Government and Policy, 26,* pp. 144–58.

13. Hebdon, R., & Kirkpatrick, I. (2005). Changes in the organisation of public services and their effects on employment relations. In S. Ackroyd, R. Batt, P. Thompson & P. Tolbert (Eds.), *Oxford handbook of work and organization.* Oxford: University Press, pp. 531–553.

14. Hebdon, R., & Mazerolle, M. (2003). Regulating conflict in public sector labour relations: The Ontario experience (1984–1993). *Relations industrielles, 58*(4), pp. 667–686.

15. Hebdon, R., & Warrian, P. (1999). Coercive bargaining: Public sector restructuring under the Ontario Social Contract 1993–96. *Industrial and Labor Relations Review, 52*(2), (January), pp. 196–212.

16. Hebdon, R. (2014). Public sector labor policy: A human rights approach. *University of Nevada Law Journal, 14*(2) (Spring), pp. 209–221.

17. Human Resources and Social Development Canada. (2006). Orders suspending right to strike or lock out. Retrieved 15 April 2011 from http://www.hrsdc.gc.ca/eng/lp/spila/clli/irlc/10orders_suspending_right_to_strike_or_lock_out.shtml

18. Jalette, P., & Hebdon, R. (2012). Unions and privatization: Opening the "black box." *Industrial and Labor Relations Review, 65*(1), pp. 17–35.

19. Lewin, D., Feuille, P., Kochan, T. A., & Delaney, J. T. (1988). *Public sector labor relations: Analysis and readings* (3rd edition). Lexington, MA: D. C. Heath.

20. Lynn, L. (1998). The new public management as an international phenomenon: A sceptical viewpoint. In L. Jones & K. Schedler (Eds.), *International perspectives on the new public management*. Greenwich, CT: JAI Press, pp. 105–122

21. Marshall, A. (1920). *Principles of economics* (8th edition). London: Macmillan and Co., Ltd.

22. Meltz, N. M., & Verma, A. (1995). Developments in industrial relations and human resource practices in Canada: An update from the 1980s. In T. A. Kochan, R. P. Locke & M. J. Piore (Eds.), *Employment relations in a changing world economy* (pp. 91–130). Cambridge, MA: MIT Press.

23. Olson, C. (1994). Final offer versus conventional arbitration revisited: Preliminary results from the lab. Paper presented at the 4th Bargaining Group Conference. Toronto: Centre for Industrial Relations.

24. Osborne, D., & Gaebler, T. (1992). *Reinventing government: How the entrepreneurial spirit is transforming the public sector*. Reading, MA: Addison Wesley.

25. Panitch, L., & Swartz, D. (1993). *The assault on trade union freedoms*. Toronto: Garamond Press.

26. Rapaport, D. (1999). *No justice, no peace: The 1996 OPSEU strike against the Harris government in Ontario*. Kingston, ON: McGill–Queen's University Press.

27. Reid, F., Foot, D., & Omar, A. (1992). Decentralization of provincial government activities: Implications for employment equity. In T. Kuttner (Ed.), *The industrial relations system*. Proceedings of the Canadian Industrial Relations Association Annual Conference (pp. 345–354). Charlottetown, PE: CIRA.

28. Roberts, W. (1994). *Don't call me servant: Government work and unions in Ontario 1911–1984*. Toronto: Ontario Public Service Employees Union.

29. Rose, J. B. (1995). The evolution of public sector unionism. In G. Swimmer & M. Thompson (Eds.), *Public sector collective bargaining in Canada* (pp. 2–52). Kingston, ON: IRC Press.

30. Saltzman, G. M. (1985). Bargaining laws as a cause and consequence of the growth of teacher unionism. *Industrial and Labor Relations Review, 38*(3), pp. 335–352.

31. Stewart, J., & Walsh, K. (1992). Change in the management of public services. *Public Administration, 70*, pp. 499–518.

32. Swan, K. P. (1985). Differences among provinces in public sector dispute resolution. In D. W. Conklin, T. J. Courchene & W. A. Jones (Eds.), *Public sector compensation*. Toronto: Ontario Economic Council.

33. Swimmer, G. (1989). Critical issues in public sector industrial relations. In A. S. Sethi (Ed.), *Collective bargaining in Canada*. Scarborough, ON: Nelson.

34. Swimmer, G. (2001). *Public sector labour relations in an era of restraint and restructuring*. Don Mills, ON: Oxford University Press.

35. Swimmer, G., & Thompson, M. (1995). *Public sector collective bargaining in Canada*. Kingston, ON: IRC Press.

36. Telford, M. (2000). *Med-Arb: A viable dispute resolution alternative*. Kingston, ON: Queen's University, IRC Press.

37. Wellington, H., & Winter, R. K. (1971). *The unions and the cities*. Washington, DC: Brookings Institution.

APPENDIX A

COLLECTIVE BARGAINING SIMULATION: MARINE METALS LTD. (MML)[1]

INSTRUCTIONS

Below you will find all of the information you need to conduct a collective bargaining simulation, including

- the background of the organization (MML);
- the current collective agreement;
- a comparison of MML's employment package with those of its competitors; and
- a memorandum of agreement to record your final settlement.

Your instructor will assign you to either the management or union team. Before beginning the collective bargaining exercise, each team should do the following:

1. Read the case materials.
2. Develop your bargaining goals and strategies.
3. Prepare the initial set of proposals that you will share with the other team. (Remember, this may not be your final bargaining goals–these are your opening positions.)

Your instructor will provide you with information about

- the length of the bargaining simulation;
- whether interest arbitration is available if you cannot reach a settlement in the time provided; and
- any report/assignment requirement. He or she may choose to use the assignment that follows at the end of this Appendix.

Remember, just as in the real world, your provincial labour relations act requires that you bargain in good faith and make every effort to negotiate a collective agreement.

// MARINE METALS LTD. (MML) CASE[2]

Marine Metals Ltd. (MML) has been in operation for more than 40 years and unionized since it was founded in 1968. It has always operated out of a facility on Water Street in St. John's, Newfoundland, because of that location's access to the harbourfront. Access to the harbourfront is critical for MML, which has traditionally manufactured steel and metal parts for fishing boats and associated cargo vessels. To capitalize on the traditional fishing and trading routes, MML acquired a second (nonunion) plant in 1990, which is located in Gloucester, Massachusetts.

The relationship between the management group of MML and the United Metal Workers of Canada (UMW) has generally been strong. Wages, benefits, and working conditions have usually been on par or better than those of the competition. In particular, the firm has tried to pay slightly above the going market rate. To date, there has been only one strike. It took place in 1990 and was largely centred on the issue of job security given the poor economic conditions of that period and the concern that the acquisition of the Massachusetts plant would result in job losses in Canada. At that time, the fishery was in a crisis due to the collapse of the cod fishery. Given the dramatic decrease in demand for its marine-related metal products, and the need for capital to purchase the new plant, the company laid off about a third of its staff and froze all wages for two years.

Fortunately, the development of several offshore oil fields in the area created a new market for MML. No longer focused on the fishing industry, MML now gets approximately 60 percent of its yearly revenues from the fabrication of metal products for the offshore oil companies and their suppliers. This new market has resulted in the firm hiring about 190 new employees over the past five years. As the parties prepare to enter a new round of bargaining, several key events are taking place.

For the union, the last contract (signed four years ago) was ratified by only 53 percent of the membership. Given the 1990 job cuts and wage freezes, many members felt that the new offshore contracts should have resulted in greater gains at the bargaining table. In fact, the membership voted in a whole new slate of union leaders to form this year's collective bargaining team. Word in the plant is that the membership wanted a more militant negotiations team that would take a firm stand on issues related to job security, increased wages, and improved vacations and pensions. It is also clear the union faces a challenge meeting the needs of a diverse membership. The average union member's age is 43 years old, with about 16 years of service. However, given the downsizing in 1990, and the influx of offshore work, the plant almost has two different age groups. There are close to 200 employees (most who are in their 20s) with fewer than 5 years of service, yet there are about 300 employees (most who are over 40) with more than 15 years of service. The current negotiations team will need to balance the needs of its newer members as well as those of the "old guard."

Management has just received notice that it is at risk of losing its contract with MegaOil. MegaOil is MML's largest offshore oil contract, and represents 30 percent of MML's total revenue stream. The reasons for the potential non-renewal of the MegaOil contract are twofold. First, MML is having problems meeting the offshore production quotas specified in the contract. This has largely been due to reliability issues with MML's now aging production equipment. Second, MML's labour costs are higher than some competitors that could be used to supply the MegaOil contract. Given the recent decreases in global oil prices, MegaOil's management team is under increased pressure to minimize expenses in all areas, including supplier contracts, to retain profitability. There is a rumour that a new firm may get the contract (Plant 2 in the attached comparison). This firm has the advantage of brand-new equipment and a lower labour cost. It currently runs 24 hours a day, 7 days a week. Hence, it is in a better position to meet the needs of the offshore oil industry.

MML management is currently examining the possibility of a substantial reorganization to better meet the needs of the offshore industry. This could include raising production quotas and replacing present equipment with new, up-to-date labour-saving machines in the St. John's plant (cost = $2.1 million). Assuming the current two-shift cycle remains, the new machinery would result in layoffs of about one-third of the staff and the contracting-out to cheaper labour sources in times of high product demand. Two alternative strategies have been openly discussed. First, purchase the new equipment (cost = $2.1 million) and move to a three 8-hour-shift (i.e., 24 hours per day, seven days per week) operation. This option could occur without hiring any new employees or laying off any current staff; however, the firm's total labour costs could not increase to make this a feasible option. Second, close the St. John's plant and move all production to the sister plant contract (Plant 4 in the attached comparison) located in Gloucester,

Massachusetts, a cheaper location. This location would still permit shipping of the products to the offshore oil fields. The management negotiations team has been given a clear message that the collective agreement must facilitate the renewal of the key offshore contract and that total labour costs cannot increase.

OTHER INFORMATION

As is shown in Table 1, MML provides a competitive compensation and benefits package. The average wage in MML is $18.00 per hour. This compares to an average current wage of $17.67 for the other metal manufacturers.

The benefits are co-paid (75 percent company, 25 percent employee). The benefits include dental plan, vision plan, life insurance coverage of two times base salary, medical insurance for hospitalization and prescription drugs, and a sick benefit plan (coverage up to 70 percent of earnings for any absence due to illness, maximum 52 weeks). Current cost of the benefit plan to the employee is $500 per year; the company share is $1,500 per employee per year.

In addition, MML contributes an amount equivalent to 5 percent of each employee's earnings into a retirement fund that can be used by the employee in retirement.

COSTING INFORMATION FOR ANY PROPOSED CHANGES

- *Overtime.* Each employee currently works an average of five hours of overtime per week. Overtime cost is time and a half. At present, employees have to volunteer for overtime. Currently 80% of overtime is worked after midnight to address production issues.
- *Wages.* Present average is $18.00
- *Vacation.* The current entitlement to vacation is as set out below. Any changes to the vacation plan would be costed using the following formula: Average hourly wage × 40 hours a week × Number of employees impacted.

Years of Service	Weeks	No. of Employees
Less than 1	1 day/month of service to a maximum of 2 weeks	50
More than 1 but less than 3	2	60
More than 3 but less than 5	2	80
More than 5 but less than 10	3	20
More than 10 but less than 15	4	40
More than 15 but less than 20	4	90
More than 20 but less than 25	5	120
More than 25 but less than 30	5	80
More than 30	5	10
		Total 550

- *Shift premiums.* Most employees (i.e., 60 percent) work day shift (8 a.m. to 4 p.m.). Forty percent of employees are permanently assigned to evening (i.e., second) shift (4 p.m. to midnight). The shift premium is currently $1.25 per hour. There is no night (i.e., third) shift (midnight to 8 a.m.). If production is needed after midnight, it is voluntary and paid at overtime rates.
- *Retirement fund.* Currently 5 percent of regular wages are placed by MML into a retirement fund for the employee. Any changes should be calculated as follows: Average hourly wage × 40 hours per week × 52 weeks × % invested by the company.

COLLECTIVE BARGAINING AGREEMENT BETWEEN MARINE METALS LTD. (HEREINAFTER REFERRED TO AS THE COMPANY) AND THE UNITED METALWORKERS OF CANADA (HEREINAFTER REFERRED TO AS THE UNION)

ARTICLE 1. RECOGNITION

Section 1.1 The Company recognizes the Union as the sole and exclusive bargaining agent for all employees at the plant located at 1968 Water Street West, St. John's, save and except office employees, human resources management staff, security guards, and production supervisors.

ARTICLE II. MANAGEMENT RIGHTS

Section 2.1 The Union recognizes that the Company has the exclusive right to manage the business and to exercise such right without restriction, save and except such prerogatives of management as may be specifically modified by the terms and conditions of this Agreement.

Section 2.2 The Union recognizes that the Company has the right to discipline and discharge employees for just cause.

ARTICLE III. HOURS OF WORK

Section 3.1 The normal work hours for all employees shall be eight (8) hours per day and forty (40) hours per week, Monday to Friday.

Section 3.2 All time worked by an employee in excess of eight (8) hours per day or forty (40) hours per week, and all time worked on weekends, shall be paid for at an overtime rate of one and one-half times the normal hourly rate. All overtime is voluntary.

Section 3.3 Employees who work the second shift will receive a shift premium of $1.25 per hour worked.

ARTICLE IV. SENIORITY, LAYOFFS, ETC.

Section 4.1 An employee's seniority rights shall be measured on a plant-wide basis, starting from the first day or hour worked.

Section 4.2 In the event of a layoff, employees with the least plant-wide seniority will be laid off first, and employees with the most seniority will be retained, subject to their ability to perform the available work without being trained.

Section 4.3 In the event of layoff, the Company will provide a severance payment equal to four (4) weeks' base pay plus an additional one (1) week's pay per year of service.

ARTICLE V. VACANCIES, NEW JOBS, PROMOTIONS, ETC.

Section 5.1 The Company shall post vacancies or new job openings on designated bulletin boards. Such postings shall include a statement of the required job qualifications, wage rate, and any other pertinent information. Interested applicants shall submit written bids to the Company's Human Resources Department. The job shall be awarded to the senior applicant provided that he or she meets the qualifications on the job posting.

ARTICLE VI. COMMITTEES

Section 6.1 The parties agree to the establishment of a Joint Labour/Management Committee composed of an equal number of representatives of the Company and the Union. The purpose of this Committee will be to provide a means of communication over any matter affecting the interests of either party to this Agreement. The Company may follow the recommendations of the Joint Committee. However, the final decision rests with management.

Section 6.2. The parties agree to the establishment of an Occupational Health and Safety Committee consistent with the requirements of provincial legislation.

ARTICLE VII. WAGES

Section 7.1 The following rates of pay will be operative for the duration of this agreement:

Job Grade	Job Titles	Hourly Rate Range
Grade 10	Janitor, Tool Keeper	$14.50–$15.50
Grade 20	Shipper, Receiver, Forklift Operator	$15.50–$16.50
Grade 30	Materials Handler, Order Processor	$16.50–$17.50
Grade 40	Machine Operator, Tin Cutter, Drill Press Operator	$17.50–$18.50
Grade 50	Quality Inspector, Smelter Operator	$19.50–$20.50
Grade 60	Trades (e.g., Welder, Electrician)	$23.50–$25.50

Section 7.2 All employees shall receive pay increases of $0.25 per hour six months after employment in their job grade, and every six months thereafter, until they reach the maximum rate of pay for their job grade.

ARTICLE VIII. HEALTH AND WELFARE PLAN

Section 8.1 The parties agree to the creation of a Health and Welfare Plan covering absence due to illness, dental care, eye care, life insurance, and supplementary healthcare needs (i.e., hospitalization and prescription drugs).

Section 8.2 The Company agrees to reimburse employees seventy-five percent (75%) of all costs incurred in respect of Section 8.1 above.

ARTICLE IX. RETIREMENT FUND

Section 9.1 The Company agrees to place five percent of each employee's base annual salary, excluding any overtime or shift premiums, into a retirement fund for that employee. This cost is incurred solely by the Company. In addition, the employee can opt to match this contribution by investing up to five percent of his/her base annual salary in the fund.

Section 9.2 When the employee retires, (s)he will receive the entire amount invested per Section 9.1 on his/her behalf.

ARTICLE X. VACATION

Section 10.1 Each employee who has been with the Company for a full year will receive paid vacation as follows:

Years of Service	Weeks of Vacation
More than 1 but less than 5	2 weeks
More than 5 but less than 10	3 weeks
More than 10 but less than 20	4 weeks
Greater than 20	5 weeks

Section 10.2 Employees with less than one (1) year of service will receive one (1) day of vacation per month of service, to a maximum of ten (10) days.

ARTICLE XI. GRIEVANCE

Section 11.1 It is understood that employees (with or without the assistance of the shop steward) may bring a complaint to their immediate supervisor in an attempt to settle the issue at any time without filing a formal grievance.

Section 11.2 The formal grievance process will be as follows:
  Step 1: The employee will (with his/her shop steward) present a written grievance to his/her supervisor. The supervisor will have ten (10) workdays to investigate the situation and respond. If the grievance is not satisfactorily resolved, it moves to Step 2.

TABLE 1

COMPARISON OF WORKING TERMS AND CONDITIONS OF SIMILAR FIRMS

	PLANT 1	PLANT 2	PLANT 3	PLANT 4	PLANT 5	PLANT 6	AVERAGE
No. of employees	500	600	700	525	675	400	566
Unionized?	Yes	No	Yes	No	Yes	Yes	—
Contract duration	3 years	N/A	4 years	N/A	4 years	3 years	3.50
Average wage	$18.25	$17.50	$18.50	$16.50	$17.75	$17.50	$17.67
Year 1 wage increase	Signing bonus $1000	1%	Signing bonus $750	0%	0%	Signing bonus $900	.33% or $883.33 signing bonus
Year 2 wage increase	1.00%	2.00%	1.50%	1.50%	2.00%	1.00%	1.50%
Year 3 wage increase	2.00%	2.00%	2.00%	1.50%	2.00%	1.00%	1.75%
OVERTIME							
Overtime voluntary?	Yes	Yes. But will assign in reverse order of seniority if insufficient volunteers.	No. Management can assign.	Yes	Yes. But will assign in reverse order of seniority if insufficient volunteers.	No	
Overtime rate	1.5	1.5	2	1.5	2	2	1.75
VACATION							
2 weeks at __ years	1	1	1	1	1	1	1.0
3 weeks at __ years	5	3	3	5	3	4	3.83
4 weeks at __ years	10	10	10	15	5	9	9.83
5 weeks at __ years	20	15	15	20	10	15	15.83
6 weeks at __ years		25	20		15	15	20.00

SHIFT							
Regular 2nd shift	Yes	Yes	Yes	Yes	Yes	Yes	Yes
Regular 3rd shift	No	Yes	Yes	No	No	Yes	Yes
SHIFT PREMIUM							
Regular 2nd shift	$1.50	$1.50	$1.25	$1.00	$1.00	$1.25	$1.25
Regular 3rd shift		$1.50	$1.50			$1.75	$1.58
Retirement/pension as % of wage rate	7.50%	7.50%	6.00%	N/A	5.00%	4.00%	6.00%
Contracting out	No language	Only if no one on layoff can perform the work.	Only if no one on layoff can perform the work.	No restrictions	Yes. But only for jobs of < 6 months.	No restrictions	
Layoff/severance pay	4 weeks plus 1 week per year of service, maximum 30 weeks	2 weeks per year of service	2 weeks plus 1 week per year of service	< 5 years' service = 8 weeks > 5 years' service = 15 weeks	2 weeks plus 2 weeks per year of service; maximum of 30 weeks	2 weeks per year of service; maximum of 26 weeks	

Step 2: The grievance is presented to the department manager by the chief shop steward. The department manager will have ten (10) workdays to respond to the grievance. If the grievance is not satisfactorily resolved, it moves to Step 3.

Step 3: The grievance is presented to the plant manager and Union local president. The plant manager will have ten (10) workdays to respond to the grievance. If the grievance is not satisfactorily resolved, it moves to Step 4.

Step 4: The grievance is presented to the Vice-President of Employment Relations by the President of the National Union (or delegate). The Vice-President will have ten (10) workdays to respond to the grievance. If the grievance is not satisfactorily resolved, it moves to arbitration and follows the current process outlined by the provincial labour relations act.

ARTICLE XII. PROGRESSIVE DISCIPLINE

Section 12.1 The Company and the Union believe in the practice of progressive discipline. Prior to formal progressive disciplinary action taking place, the employee may receive a verbal counselling from his/her supervisor. The employee has the right to union representation during this counselling. The only documentation of this meeting will be the time, date, and nature of the discussion. This will be placed in the supervisor's file and will be moved to the employee's human resources file only if progressive discipline steps are taken within twenty-four (24) months of this counselling.

Section 12.2 The normal progression of progressive discipline shall be as follows:

Step 1: Written Warning

Step 2: Suspension

Step 3: Discharge

Section 12.3 It is understood that certain offences will result in a faster progression through the progressive discipline process outlined in Section 12.2.

Section 12.4 Copies of all written warnings, suspensions, and discharges must be given to the employee (in the presence of a union representative). Copies will also be placed in the employee's human resources file. All documentation concerning progressive discipline must be removed from the employee's file after a period of twenty four (24) months if no other disciplinary action occurs.

ARTICLE XIII. DURATION

Section 13.1 This agreement shall be effective November 25, 2011, and will remain in force until November 25, 2015; thereafter, it shall be automatically renewed from time to time for further periods of one year unless either party, at least sixty (60) days prior to November 25, 2015, or any subsequent expiration date, serves on the other party written notice of its desire to terminate or amend the Agreement.

IN WITNESS THEREOF, the parties have caused this Agreement to be executed by their duly authorized representatives on this 25 day of November, 2011.

For the Company
John Smith _____
Samantha Chen _____
Jeff O'Kane _____

For the Union
Rajeev Singh _____
Rita McCracken _____
Glen Brown _____

MEMORANDUM OF SETTLEMENT

Between Marine Metals Ltd. and the United Metalworkers of Canada

The parties agree as follows (use additional pages if necessary):
ARTICLE I. Recognition
ARTICLE II. Management Rights
ARTICLE III. Hours of Work
ARTICLE IV. Seniority, Layoffs, Etc.
ARTICLE V. Vacancies, New Jobs, Promotions, Etc.
ARTICLE VI. Committees
ARTICLE VII. Wages
ARTICLE VIII. Health and Welfare Plan
ARTICLE IX. Retirement
ARTICLE X. Vacation
ARTICLE XI. Grievance
ARTICLE XII. Progressive Discipline
ARTICLE XIII. Duration
Signatures:

COMPANY   UNION

_____   _____
_____   _____
_____   _____
_____   _____

NEGOTIATION ASSIGNMENT

The negotiation assignment and simulation exercise requires each union and management team to participate in a negotiation simulation and to submit an assignment that critically examines the process and outcomes of this experience.

Using information provided in class, your textbook, and the case assigned by your instructor, please answer the following two questions. The first question focuses largely on issues related to bargaining strategy; the second focuses on the collective agreement that resulted from your collective bargaining simulation. Note that the final assignment must not exceed ten pages of double-spaced text.

1. *Bargaining strategy.* Please answer the following:

    a. What bargaining strategy did your team plan to use in the present round of negotiations? Justify this choice.

b. What bargaining strategy did you expect the other team to initially adopt? Why?

c. What bargaining strategy did your team actually use in bargaining? Justify this answer and provide examples of tactics used during bargaining that are consistent with your answer. Explain why your team was, or was not, successful in implementing the strategy you had intended to use (see your answer to part (a) above).

d. What effect, if any, did the bargaining strategies used by both teams have on your team's satisfaction with

i. the outcomes of the negotiation process, and

ii. the quality of the relationship developed with the other team?

e. Do you think the other team was more, less, or equally satisfied with the outcomes and the quality of the relationship developed during negotiations? Justify your answer.

f. Based on your experience from this round of bargaining, what bargaining strategy do you think your team and the other team would adopt if you entered a second round of negotiations? Why?

2. *Collective agreement outcomes*. Please answer the following:

a. What were your team's priorities (maximum of 5 priorities)? Please rank these hoped-for changes in order of importance to your team (1 = most important, 5 = least important). Justify your ranking.

b. Discuss how your five priorities would affect the underlying interests of <u>both</u> your team and the other team.

c. Were any of these priorities strike or lockout issues for your team? Please justify.

d. Was your team successful in negotiating these priorities into the new collective agreement? Why or why not?

e. What effect, if any, did the relative power of the parties have on the outcomes of this round of bargaining? Why? How could power affect the next round? Why?

// ENDNOTES

1. The collective agreement and the assignment used in this case were both adapted from a version created by Andrew Luchak. Used with permission.

2. This case was created solely for educational purposes by the second author. It is not based on any true company, union, or event.

APPENDIX B

COLLECTIVE BARGAINING SIMULATION: WALLY'S JANITORIAL SERVICES[1]

// SIMULATION INSTRUCTIONS AND BACKGROUND INFORMATION

INTRODUCTION

In this simulation, you will play a member either of the management bargaining team representing Wally's Janitorial Services Incorporated (WJS) or of the union bargaining team representing the employees of WJS. You will deal with a complex mix of bargaining issues, and you will be subjected to a variety of pressures during negotiations.

ADVANCE PREPARATION

Before the bargaining session, you should read two sets of information:

1. The "Background Information," presented in this document under that heading. This is information that both management and union teams have access to.
2. The private team information. This information is not to be shared with your bargaining opponents. It will be provided by your instructor once he/she assigns you to a management or union team.

SPECIFIC BARGAINING INSTRUCTIONS

- *Confidentiality of negotiations*. It is *not* necessary to conduct the negotiations in confidence. You are free to discuss your negotiations with other students in the class; however, negotiating may only be conducted during the allotted class time.
- *Bargaining issues*. Teams may only propose changes with respect to the issues provided in the case instructions. As members of bargaining teams, students may not manipulate any costs other than janitor salary costs. In addition, students cannot manipulate the level of firm revenue. They may only negotiate the four issues specified in the case.
- *Legal environment*. The legal framework for this simulation will be the *Employment* (or *Labour*) *Standards Act* and the *Labour Relations Act* of your province. Citing legislation is not appropriate for this simulation.

- *Role profiles.* Students may adopt specific roles as indicated in the text, but no detailed role profiles will be given.
- *Duration of agreement.* The agreement shall be effective for one full year (i.e., the teams are negotiating a one-year contract). Teams may not negotiate an agreement longer than one year.
- *Bargaining in good faith.* Teams are expected to bargain in good faith. In particular, they are required to meet and to bargain with the intention of reaching an agreement. Furthermore, once an item has been agreed upon by both teams, it is not appropriate to reopen negotiation of that item except by mutual agreement of the teams.

BACKGROUND INFORMATION

Wally's Janitorial Services Incorporated (WJS) was founded in 1980 by three competitors who had been working separately as independent janitors in large office settings. As independent providers of janitorial services, these three men would bid on jobs to clean office or retail space for large companies who owned their own facilities or for landlords who included maintenance as part of their rental fee. Compared to an in-house janitorial department, the independent contractors could provide a lower cost option (because they were always bidding against each other) and superior quality (because they were held accountable for their services because their contracts could be terminated).

As a result of this fierce competition, the three independent janitors found they could only make a profit by staying in one location per shift. Generally, an office/retail space was cleaned twice a week. This meant that ideally a contractor would have only three clients at one time (each client is cleaned twice a week for six days of work per week). For an independent contractor to keep himself and his small crew busy for an entire shift (8 p.m. to 4 a.m.), he would require very large clients. Having a number of smaller clients meant additional costs in terms of vehicles and time to transport equipment and labour from one client's site to another. At the time there were only a few large office/retail spaces in Saskatoon, so the independent contractors would fight over these few profitable clients and then fill the remainder of their work week with non-profitable smaller clients as a means of keeping their labour employed. One particularly bleak February evening, the most junior of these men, Wally Wentworth, approached his two main competitors and pitched his idea to consolidate their efforts and form a new firm. The other two agreed to accept minority ownership and employment as executives in the new firm.

Since its inception in 1980, Wally's Janitorial Services Incorporated (WJS) has been growing along with the city of Saskatoon. It has retained market domination and continues to focus on large clients. WJS presently employs 95 people. Of this total 15 are nonunionized employees and work as clerical staff, managers, or executives. The remaining 80 employees are all unionized and are classified into 11 categories of janitors based on seniority. In Table 1 the total number of janitors in each classification and their yearly income is presented. Notice that after 10 years of service an employee is in the 10th classification and earns $50,000 a year. For these employees there is no further classification advancement or pay increase in subsequent years.

TABLE 1

WALLY'S JANITORIAL SERVICES, SALARY SCHEDULE FOR JANITORS

SALARY SCALE	ANNUAL INCOME IN $	2009 NUMBER OF JANITORS	2009 JANITOR SALARY COST IN $	CURRENT NUMBER OF JANITORS	ESTIMATED* 2010 COST IN $
0	24,000	4	96,000	4	96,000
1	25,000	6	150,000	4	100,000
2	26,000	4	104,000	6	156,000
3	28,000	8	224,000	3	84,000
4	30,000	0	0	7	210,000
5	32,000	6	192,000	0	0
6	36,500	5	182,500	6	219,000
7	40,000	3	120,000	5	200,000
8	44,000	4	176,000	3	132,000
9	50,000	5	250,000	4	200,000
10	56,000	35	1,960,000	38	2,128,000
Totals		**80**	**3,454,500**	**80**	**3,525,000**

*The estimated 2010 cost multiplies the 2009 incomes by the current number of janitors.

WALLY'S JANITORIAL SERVICES BUDGET INFORMATION

CURRENT YEAR (NOVEMBER 2010–NOVEMBER 2011) PROJECTED BUDGET

Total Revenue (net of taxes)	$21,222,320
EXPENDITURES	
Administration:	
Professional salaries	$1,137,500
Clerical/secretarial salaries	$ 281,250
Other	$ 250,000
Subtotal	$1,668,750
Capital and Other Business Functions:	
Equipment and vehicles	$ 6,558,100
Marketing and sales	$ 1,420,000

Continued

WALLY'S JANITORIAL SERVICES BUDGET INFORMATION

CURRENT YEAR (NOVEMBER 2010–NOVEMBER 2011) PROJECTED BUDGET		
Aides	$ 1,187,600	
Materials/supplies	$ 943,750	
Subtotal		$10,109,450
Janitorial staff:		
Salaries	$3,525,000	
Training and certification	$ 975,000	
Insurance and safety	$ 258,750	
Subtotal		$4,278,750
Fixed charges:		
Retirement	$ 1,176,450	
Other	$ 425,700	
Subtotal		$1,602,150
Debt servicing		$1,026,000
Transportation:		
Salaries	$ 400,000	
Other	$ 395,000	
Subtotal		$795,000
Total expenditures		$19,960,100
Budget surplus (shortfall)		$1,262,220

WALLY'S JANITORIAL SERVICES BUDGET INFORMATION

PREVIOUS YEAR (NOVEMBER 2009–NOVEMBER 2010)		
Total Revenue (net of taxes)		$22,099,897
EXPENDITURES		
Administration:		
Professional salaries	$ 1,137,248	

Continued

WALLY'S JANITORIAL SERVICES BUDGET INFORMATION

PREVIOUS YEAR (NOVEMBER 2009–NOVEMBER 2010)

Clerical/secretarial salaries	$ 281,067	
Other	$ 261,129	
Subtotal		$1,679,444
Capital and Other Business Functions:		
Equipment and vehicles	$7,748,000	
Marketing and sales	$ 1,394,643	
Aides	$ 1,183,275	
Materials/supplies	$ 842,633	
Subtotal		$11,168,551
Janitorial Staff:		
Salaries	$3,454,500	
Training and certification	$ 812,268	
Insurance and safety	$ 225,198	
Subtotal		$4,011,966
Fixed charges:		
Retirement	$ 1,120,428	
Other	$ 324, 774	
Subtotal		$1,445,201
Debt servicing		$900,260
Transportation:		
Salaries	$ 399,698	
Other	$ 301,527	
Subtotal		$701,225
Total expenditures		$20,386,647
Budget surplus (shortfall)		$1,713,250

The ownership and management team is particularly proud of the work culture at WJS, which is considered a key to the firm's success. Most of the people who work for WJS have had trouble fitting into traditional jobs. Some of them have criminal records, while others are recovering alcoholics and/or drug addicts. Partly because of the difficulty in recruiting night workers who perform routine and sometimes distasteful work, the hiring philosophy at WJS has been much more inclusive than at other firms. An applicant's past is considered less important than an honest handshake and a promise from applicants to do their best and conduct themselves with integrity. This approach has worked very well. With few exceptions the employees are grateful for the opportunity and work very hard. The City of Saskatoon and the Saskatoon Police Services have recognized WJS efforts to successfully reintegrate felons into society with several Corporate Citizenship Awards.

In the late 1990s the city of Saskatoon suffered from an economic downturn. Several of WJS's clients went out of business or left the city. The downturn also created a second problem for WJS. A surplus of office/retail space caused rent levels to fall dramatically. With falling rent prices, the landlords who include janitorial services as part of their rental fee turned to WJS to renegotiate cheaper or reduced services (and sometimes both). The WJS leadership reacted by increasing the pace of work, freezing wages, and replacing any workers who were not willing to accept the "new economic reality." This led to widespread discontent among the janitors and the successful certification of a trade union. In January of 1999, the janitors of WJS formed Local 45 of the Canadian Union of Service Employees (CUSE). After negotiations a first collective agreement was constructed that provided some basic protections for workers. Since then the collective agreement has been successfully renegotiated several times without a strike or lockout.

It is now November 16, 2010. The contract between WJS and CUSE expired on June 30, 2010. Since then the WJS bargaining team and the CUSE bargaining team have met on several occasions in an attempt to finalize the contract, but these attempts have not been successful. There are several remaining bargaining issues, and while both sides are adamant that they wish to avert a work stoppage, they are facing tremendous pressure.

Despite the strong Saskatchewan economy, profits have fallen below acceptable levels. Out-of-province competitors from eastern Canada, fleeing contracting economies, have established a foothold in Saskatoon. Increased competition has forced WJS to lower their fees and reduced revenue. The WJS bargaining team believes that without concessions that allow management to reduce costs and improve productivity, the company is not likely to avoid massive layoffs.

For the members of CUSE, the strong Saskatchewan economy has meant the cost of living has dramatically increased. The workers feel they are entitled to a cost-of-living adjustment to reflect rising costs of housing, food, transportation, etc., in the city of Saskatoon. They also believe management should stick to their original instincts to trust the employees to do their best. They are resentful of policies that either monitor their work or speed it up.

Since the expiration of the collective agreement, there has been more and more talk among the membership of CUSE about the possibility of calling a strike if the contract is not finalized by the end of the fall. However, the executive of the union agreed that, in the interest of demonstrating their willingness to work with the WJS bargaining team, their members would continue with their normal duties, without a contract, on a day-to-day basis.

The union and the leadership team at WJS wish to reach a settlement and avert a strike; however, the union is adamantly committed to improving the conditions of its membership, and the management is just as committed to keeping its costs as low as possible so that it can reposition itself in the new, more competitive market. Nevertheless, each side feels it has room to negotiate on certain issues.

Final Settlement Form for the Four Outstanding Issues between Wally's Janitorial Services and CUSE Local 45 (Hand in one form once negotiations are complete.)

1. Reduction in Staff

_____
_____
_____
_____
_____

2. Salary

_____
_____
_____
_____
_____

3. Benefits

_____
_____
_____
_____
_____

4. Performance Evaluation

_____
_____
_____
_____

_____   _____
Management Names   Union Names
and Signatures   and Signatures

// ENDNOTE

1. The authors gratefully acknowledge and thank Scott Walsworth (creator of this case) for allowing us to use it in the textbook.

APPENDIX C

ARBITRATION: THE CASE OF EMMA WILLIAMS

// INSTRUCTIONS

Your instructor will assign the case to groups or individuals. Once it has been assigned, you will take on the role of management or union (as per your instructor's direction). You will then write an argument appropriate for your assigned role. You may also be required to present your arguments in class on a date designated by your instructor. A key part of this assignment will be the application of arbitral principles of "just cause" for discipline and discharge. This assignment is based on (1) independent research of arbitration jurisprudence; (2) lecture material; (3) the assigned text; and (4) the attached case.

To understand the principles involved in the case, it will be necessary to review relevant arbitral jurisprudence. The texts *Canadian Labour Arbitration* by Brown and Beatty and *Collective Agreement Arbitration in Canada* by Palmer and Palmer offer excellent summaries. Both are probably available at your library. It will also be helpful to review cases reported in the series Labour Arbitration Cases (LACs), which should also be available at the library.

The completed assignment should require a *maximum* of seven typewritten, double-spaced pages (excluding references and cover sheet). To do well on this assignment, you will need to

1. demonstrate a sound knowledge of the elements of just cause;

2. clearly present arguments appropriate for your assigned role of management or union;

3. cite relevant jurisprudence (LACs) to support your argument;

4. present your ideas in a clear manner (correct grammar, punctuation, style, etc.); and

5. ensure that your reasoning is *concise and logically consistent*.

// THE CASE OF EMMA WILLIAMS (VERSION 1)[1]

THE FACTS

The facts of the case are not in dispute. Emma Williams was a registered nurse employed in the oncology (cancer) unit of University General Hospital. Williams is now 46 years old and was hired by University General on March 1, 1996. The hospital has a three-point performance rating system: (1) does not meet expectations; (2) meets expectations; and (3) exceeds expectations. Over the years Williams's performance ratings were "meets expectations" for most years and "exceeds expectations" for her last three years.

In her role as a cancer nurse, Williams was responsible for monitoring patient care, administering potentially lethal drugs (e.g., narcotics), monitoring patient regimes, and counselling patients and their families concerning care options. Accordingly, nurses on this unit were required to maintain certification as "cancer specialists." Williams received this certification in 1995 and had maintained it ever since. Williams was verbally counselled and received two written warnings for absenteeism on January 27, 2013, July 23, 2013, and October 15, 2013, respectively. A union representative was present for all warnings. She was terminated on December 3, 2013, following a three-day leave of absence without permission. The letter of discharge states that she was terminated for failing to call in sick as well as for excessive absenteeism (19 percent as against a hospital average of 7 percent). A union representative was present during each of the meetings where warnings were presented to Williams. Also, on October 15, 2013, Ms. Chang (her manager) reminded Williams about the hospital's confidential Employee Assistance Program (EAP). Chang advised Williams that she could call the EAP about anything, including drug and alcohol addiction or the recent death of her son, that might be affecting her attendance.

Before her discharge, Williams sought treatment for a drug (a painkiller known as oxycodone) and alcohol addiction. She has been in and out of counselling since March 2014. Between the initial treatment in March 2014 and the time of the arbitration hearing (February 25, 2015), she had three major relapses in which she stopped attending her counselling sessions (dates April 20, 2014, July 21, 2014, and October 25, 2014). She has been drug- and alcohol-free since November 11, 2014. At the time of dismissal, management was unaware that she was being treated for her addiction.

Williams's addiction counsellor, Dr. Anderson, believes that she has an 80 percent chance of remaining chemical-free over the next few years. In Dr. Anderson's opinion, it was the unexpected death of Williams's 16-year-old son, who in December 2012 died in the ER of the hospital where she worked, that caused the subsequent addiction. Specifically, Williams lost control of her car when it hit black ice. An accident followed where she was injured and her son subsequently died. Williams was prescribed oxycodone as a painkiller for her accident-related injuries. There is no evidence that Williams ever stole oxycodone from the hospital; however, that medication is readily available on the cancer unit where she works. Now that her patient has recovered from this tragic event shock, Dr. Anderson believes that Williams can maintain an acceptable attendance and performance record as a cancer nurse in the future.

Regarding other employees, Ms. Chang states that only one other cancer nurse, out of a staff of 30, had an absenteeism rate greater than 10 percent (15 percent). That nurse was never given a warning of any kind.

KEY DATES

March 1, 1996: Williams hired
January 27, 2013: Verbal counselling
July 23, 2013: Written warning
October 15, 2013: Second written warning
December 3, 2013: Termination
March 2014: Williams first seeks treatment
February 25, 2015: Arbitration

ARTICLE 15—CORRECTIVE ACTION AND DISCIPLINE

15.1. Employees can be disciplined only for just cause. Such discipline must be reasonable and commensurate with the seriousness of the violation.

15.2. Both the union and the hospital believe in the concept of progressive discipline. Accordingly, they agree that a verbal counselling should normally take place prior to any disciplinary action. Should an employee's conduct or performance not improve after this counselling, the normal progression of discipline will be as follows:

- Step 1: Written warning
- Step 2: Second written warning
- Step 3: Suspension without pay
- Step 4: Termination

15.3 Notwithstanding clause 15.2, it is understood that certain offences are sufficiently serious to warrant immediate discharge and/or a faster progression through the process outlined in 15.2.

15.4 Employees have the right to have a union representative present during any of the steps outlined in clause 15.2.

// THE CASE OF EMMA WILLIAMS (VERSION 2)[2]

THE FACTS

The facts of the case are not in dispute. Emma Williams was a registered nurse employed in the cancer unit of University General Hospital. Williams is now 46 years old and was hired by University General Hospital on March 1, 1996. Her performance was commendable. The hospital has a three-point performance rating system: (1) does not meet expectations; (2) meets expectations; and (3) exceeds expectations. Each year between (and including) 1996 and 2012, Williams received the highest rating of "exceeds expectations."

In her role as a cancer nurse, Williams was responsible for monitoring patient care, administering potentially lethal drugs (e.g., narcotics), monitoring patient regimes, and counselling patients and their families concerning cancer care options. Accordingly, nurses on this unit were required to maintain certification as "cancer specialists." Williams received this certification prior to being hired and had maintained it ever since.

Williams was verbally counselled and received two written warnings for absenteeism on January 27, 2013, July 23, 2013, and October 15, 2013, respectively. She was terminated on December 3, 2013, following a three-day leave of absence without permission. The letter of discharge states that she was terminated for failing to call in sick as well as for excessive absenteeism (19 percent as against a hospital average of 7 percent). A union representative was present during each of the meetings where warnings were presented to Williams. At no point during these meetings was Williams reminded of the hospital's confidential Employee Assistance Program (EAP).

Subsequent to the discharge, Williams sought treatment for a drug and alcohol addiction. She has been in and out of counselling since March 2014. Between the initial treatment in March 2014 and the time of the arbitration hearing (February 25, 2015), she had two major relapses in which she stopped attending her counselling sessions (dates April 20, 2014, and October 25, 2014). She has been drug- and alcohol-free since November 11, 2014.

Williams's addiction counsellor, Dr. Anderson, believes that she has a 65 percent chance of remaining chemical-free over the next few years. In Dr. Anderson's opinion, it was the unexpected death of Williams's 16-year-old son, who in December 2012 died in the ER of the hospital where she worked, that caused the subsequent addiction. Specifically, Williams lost control of her car when it hit black ice. An accident followed where she was injured and her son subsequently died. Williams was prescribed oxycodone as a painkiller for her accident-related injuries. There is no evidence that Williams ever stole oxycodone from the hospital; however, that medication is readily available on the cancer unit where she works. Now that her patient has recovered from this tragic event shock, Dr. Anderson believes that Williams can maintain an acceptable attendance and performance record as a cancer nurse in the future.

Regarding other employees, Ms. Chang (her manager) states that only one other cancer nurse, out of a staff of 30, had an absenteeism rate greater than 10 percent (13 percent). That nurse was given a written warning. Since this warning, her attendance has been improved. Hence, further discipline was not necessary in that case.

KEY DATES

March 1, 1996: Williams hired
January 27, 2013: Verbal counselling
July 23, 2013: Written warning
October 15, 2013: Second written warning
December 3, 2013: Termination
March 2014: Williams first seeks treatment
February 25, 2015: Arbitration

RELEVANT COLLECTIVE AGREEMENT CLAUSE

ARTICLE 15—CORRECTIVE ACTION AND DISCIPLINE

15.1 Employees can be disciplined only for just cause. Such discipline must be reasonable and commensurate with the seriousness of the violation.

15.2 Both the union and the hospital believe in the concept of progressive discipline. Accordingly, they agree that a verbal counselling should normally take place prior to any disciplinary action. Should an employee's conduct or performance not improve after this counselling, the normal progression of discipline will be as follows:

- Step 1: Written warning
- Step 2: Second written warning
- Step 3: Suspension without pay
- Step 4: Termination

15.3 Notwithstanding clause 15.2, it is understood that certain offences are sufficiently serious to warrant immediate discharge and/or a faster progression through the process outlined in 15.2.

Employees have the right to have a union representative present during any of the steps outlined in clause 15.2.

// THE CASE OF EMMA WILLIAMS (VERSION 3)[3]

THE FACTS

The facts of the case are not in dispute. Emma Williams was a registered nurse employed in the cancer unit of University General Hospital. Williams is now 46 years old and was hired by University General Hospital on March 1, 1996. The hospital has a three-point performance rating system: (1) does not meet expectations; (2) meets expectations; and (3) exceeds expectations. Each year between (and including) 1996 and 2012, Williams received a performance rating of "meets expectations."

In her role as cancer nurse, Williams was responsible for monitoring patient care, administering potentially lethal drugs (e.g., narcotics), monitoring patient regimes, and counselling patients and their families concerning cancer care options. Accordingly, nurses on this unit were required to maintain certification as "cancer specialists." Williams received this certification in 1995 and had maintained it ever since.

Williams was verbally counselled and received two written warnings for absenteeism on January 27, 2013, July 23, 2013, and October 15, 2013, respectively. She was terminated on December 3, 2013, following a three-day leave of absence without permission. A union representative was present for the last warning; Williams declined union representation for the first two warnings. At no point was Williams reminded about the Employee Assistance Program (EAP) in place at the hospital. On November 26, 2013, management found oxycodone in her locker. Only Williams had the combination needed to open that locker. The amount of oxycodone found was the exact amount that Williams had signed as being "contaminated and destroyed" on November 24, 2013. The letter of discharge states that she was terminated for failing to call in sick, excessive absenteeism (14 percent as against a hospital average of 7 percent), and theft of medication from the hospital.

Subsequent to the discharge, Williams sought treatment for a drug and alcohol addiction. She has been in and out of counselling since March 2014. Between the initial treatment of March 2014 and the time of the arbitration hearing (February 25, 2015), she had four major relapses in which she stopped attending her counselling sessions (dates April 20, 2014, May 30, 2014, July 2, 2014, and October 25, 2014). She has been drug- and alcohol-free since November 11, 2014.

Williams's addiction counsellor, Dr. Anderson, believes that she has a 75 percent chance of remaining chemical-free over the next few years. In Dr. Anderson's opinion, it was the unexpected death of Williams's 16-year-old son, who in December 2012 died in the ER of the hospital where she worked, that caused the subsequent addiction. Specifically, Williams lost control of her car when it hit black ice. An accident followed where she was injured and her son subsequently died. Williams was prescribed oxycodone as a pain killer for her accident-related injuries. Now that her patient has recovered from this tragic event shock, Dr. Anderson believes that Williams can maintain an acceptable attendance and performance record as a cancer nurse in the future.

In terms of other employees, Ms. Chang (her manager) states that only one other cancer nurse, out of a staff of 30, had an absenteeism rate greater than 10 percent (14 percent). That nurse was given a written warning. Since that warning, her attendance has been meets expectations. Hence, further discipline was not necessary for that nurse.

KEY DATES

March 1, 1996: Williams hired
January 27, 2013: Verbal counselling
July 23, 2013: Written warning
October 15, 2013: Second written warning
November 26, 2013: Oxycodone found in Williams's locker
December 3, 2013: Termination
March 2014: Williams first seeks treatment
February 25, 2015: Arbitration

RELEVANT COLLECTIVE AGREEMENT CLAUSE

ARTICLE 15—CORRECTIVE ACTION AND DISCIPLINE

15.1 Employees can be disciplined only for just cause. Such discipline must be reasonable and commensurate with the seriousness of the violation.

15.2 Both the union and the hospital believe in the concept of progressive discipline. Accordingly, they agree that a verbal counselling should take place prior to any disciplinary action. Should an employee's conduct or performance not improve after this counselling, the normal progression of discipline will be as follows:

- Step 1: Written warning
- Step 2: Second written warning
- Step 3: Suspension without pay
- Step 4: Termination

15.3 Notwithstanding clause 15.2, it is understood that certain offences are sufficiently serious to warrant immediate discharge and/or a faster progression through the process outlined in 15.2.

15.4 Employees have the right to have a union representative present during any of the steps outlined in clause 15.2.

// ENDNOTES

1. This case is pure fiction and is not an actual arbitration. It was created for educational purposes by the second author.

2. This case is pure fiction and is not an actual arbitration. It was created for educational purposes by the second author.

3. This case is pure fiction and is not an actual arbitration. It was created for educational purposes by the second author.

GLOSSARY

A

Alternative dispute resolution (ADR)
Resolving disputes without going to court (p. 311)

Apprenticeship
A process in which trainees learn a trade under the supervision of a senior tradesperson (p. 29)

Arbitration
A quasi-judicial process whereby a neutral third party makes a final and binding determination on all outstanding issues in dispute (p. 99)

Article
A larger section of a collective agreement (p. 234)

Attitudinal structuring
The difficult process of building the mutual respect and trust necessary for an enduring and positive collective bargaining relationship (p. 204)

B

Back-to-work legislation
Legislation requiring that strike action cease and employees return to work (p. 46)

Bargaining unit
The group of employees in an organization that are eligible to be represented by a union (p. 95)

Base pay
The part of pay that is solely based on time worked (p. 323)

Bottom line
The minimum position necessary in negotiations to avoid a strike or lockout; it represents for the union the best possible outcome short of strike (p. 205)

Bumping
A process whereby senior employees pass on their layoff to more junior employees (p. 252)

Business unionism (or pure-and-simple unionism)
Unionism that focuses on improving wages and the working conditions of its members (p. 32)

C

Certification
Recognition of a union by a labour board after completion of the procedures under the labour act (p. 95)

Chilling effect
The lack of bargaining flexibility caused by the parties' fear that a concession made in negotiations will reduce the arbitration outcome (p. 360)

Clause
A specific section of an article (p. 234)

Closed shop
A form of union security in which membership in the union is a condition of employment (p. 154)

Collective agreement
A written document outlining the terms and conditions of employment in a unionized workplace (p. 3)

Collective bargaining
The process by which management and labour negotiate the terms and conditions of employment in a unionized workplace (p. 3)

Collective voice
The ability of a group or union to express concerns (p. 320)

Common law
The legal regime for nonunion employment (p. 28)

Company union
A union that a company helped create (p. 133)

Conciliation
See *mediation* (p. 98)

Contract zone
Exists if each side's bottom line overlaps; in other words, to avoid a strike or lockout, management will offer more and the union will accept less than the point where their negotiating positions intersect (p. 207)

Conventional interest arbitration
Interest arbitration where the arbitrator can choose among the proposals or fashion one of his or her own (p. 310)

Conversion mechanisms
The processes used to convert inputs into outputs of the industrial relations system (p. 14)

Corrective action
A warning process designed to improve employee performance or behaviour (p. 251)

Craft or occupational unionism
Unions that typically allow into membership only trades or occupations that are in the same family of skills (p. 134)

Crown corporations
Corporations owned by the government (p. 45)

Culpable
At fault, guilty (p. 305)

D

Defined benefit
A type of pension plan that guarantees a specific payout (p. 328)

Deregulation
A policy designed to create more competition in an industry by allowing prices to be determined by market forces (p. 62)

Disposable income
Income after taxes and benefits from social programs (e.g., unemployment insurance payments) (p. 75)

Distributive bargaining
A form of negotiations in which two parties compete over the distribution of some fixed resource (p. 203)

Distributive justice
Employees' perception of fairness in workplace outcomes and decisions (p. 174)

Dues check-off
A process whereby union dues are deducted automatically from pay (p. 39)

Duty of fair representation
A legal obligation on the union's part to represent all employees equally and in a nondiscriminatory manner (p. 98)

E

Elasticity of supply (demand)
The labour responsiveness of supply (demand) caused by a change in the wage rate; for example, if a small increase in wages causes a large increase in the supply of labour, the supply curve is said to be *elastic* (p. 64)

Employee Assistance Program (EAP)
A counselling service available to employees (p. 328)

Employee relations
The study of the employment relationship between employers and individual employees, usually in nonunion settings (p. 4)

Employment equity
Equity in employment levels and opportunities between targeted community groups (women, visible minorities, Aboriginals, and disabled employees) and major employers (p. 114)

Employment relations
The study of employment relationships and issues in union and nonunion workplaces (p. 5)

Essential services agreements
Used when some workers must remain on the job during a strike to provide key services (p. 266)

Exchange rate
The value of one country's currency relative to another country's currency (p. 12)

Exclusive jurisdiction
What exists when a single union represents all workers of a trade or occupational grouping (p. 32)

Exclusivity principle
The idea that a union is granted the sole right to represent all employees in the defined bargaining unit (p. 95)

Explicit reference
Equity clause in collective agreements that specifies which groups are covered (p. 237)

F

Feedback loop
The mechanism by which outputs of the industrial relations system flow back to the external environment (p. 8)

Final-offer arbitration
Interest arbitration in which the arbitrator must choose one of the parties' proposals (p. 310)

First agreement (or first contract) arbitration
Arbitration that determines the first collective agreement (p. 310)

G

Gain sharing
A group performance pay that is based on firm productivity gains (p. 328)

Goal
That which a person seeks to obtain or achieve (p. 14)

Good faith bargaining
An obligation on union and management to make a serious attempt to reach a settlement (p. 98)

Great Depression
A period of significant economic downturn resulting from the stock market crash of 1929 (p. 37)

Grievance
A formal complaint that a specific clause in the collective agreement has been violated (p. 283)

Grievance mediation
A voluntary nonbinding process whereby a neutral third party examines the grievance (p. 311)

H

High-performance work practices
Comprehensive human resources strategies designed to improve organizational performance (p. 183)

Hiring hall
A union-run centre that refers union labour to job sites as requested by firms (p. 70)

Human relations
A managerial view that believes that effective management practices can minimize the conflict between managers and employees (p. 173)

Human resources
The study of the employment relationship between employers and individual employees (p. 4)

I

Indirect pay (or benefits)
Anything that an employer pays for, to the benefit of the employee, that is not part of base or performance pay (p. 323)

Industrial dispute
A disagreement arising from entering into, renewing, or revising a collective agreement (p. 266)

Industrial relations
The study of employment relationships and issues, often in unionized workplaces (p. 3)

Industrial unionism
A type of inclusive unionism that represents a broad range of skills and occupations (p. 136)

Industrial unions
Unions that organize all workers of an industry/workplace regardless of trade (p. 38)

Inflation
The increase in prices over time (p. 12)

Institutionalists
Those subscribing to the theory that the operation of labour markets requires a knowledge and understanding of such social organizations as unions, nongovernmental community organizations, and international institutions (p. 131)

Integrative bargaining
A form of bargaining in which there is potential for a solution that produces a mutual gain; also called win-win bargaining, principled negotiations, and interest-based bargaining (p. 203)

Intention to quit
A survey measure assessessing the likelihood that an employee will quit (p. 335)

Interactional justice
Employees' perceptions of the fairness of interpersonal interactions and exchanges (p. 175)

Interest arbitration
An arbitration that determines terms and conditions of the collective agreement while it's being negotiated (p. 310)

Interest-based bargaining (IBB)
A cooperative form of bargaining in which the parties focus more on the interests of the parties and not the exaggerated positions; also called *principled, integrative, cooperative, positive-sum,* or *collaborative negotiations* (p. 216)

Interest rate
The rate a bank charges for borrowing money (p. 12)

International Labour Organization (ILO)
A tripartite (government, management, and labour) agency of the United Nations with the mandate to establish and enforce global labour standards (p. 132)

Intra-team (or intra-organizational) bargaining
Bargaining within union and management teams during the collective bargaining process; individual union team members, for example, may represent a group with particular interests, such as shift workers (p. 204)

IR climate
Attitudes concerning IR and the union-management relationship (p. 329)

J

Job analysis
A process whereby the key competencies for a job are identified (p. 322)

Job evaluation
A process whereby the firm determines the value of a job (p. 322)

Job satisfaction
An employee's assessment of his or her job experience (p. 335)

Jurisprudence
Past decisions (usually in a legal context) (p. 304)

L

Labour relations
The study of employment relationships and issues between groups of employees (usually in unions) and management; also known as union–management relations (p. 4)

Legislative reference
Equity clause in collective agreements that references legislation (p. 237)

Letter of understanding
Letter between the parties, usually placed at the end of an agreement and describing a specific practice they have agreed to follow (p. 234)

Lockout
A work stoppage invoked by management (p. 268)

M

Macroeconomic policy
A policy that applies to economy-wide goals, such as inflation, unemployment, and growth (p. 62)

Mandatory retirement
A requirement that employees retire at age 65 (p. 13)

Mandatory strike vote
A majority of the workers must vote in favour of a strike; the union leaders cannot call a strike on their own (p. 282)

Master–servant relationship
The essence of the common-law employment relationship pertaining to nonunion workplaces; employment relationships in which employees have few rights (p. 172)

Mediation
A dispute-resolution process in which a neutral third party acts as a facilitator (p. 98)

Meta-analysis
A statistical technique that looks for trends across many studies (p. 332)

Mitigation factors
Factors argued by the union for a reduction in a sanction (p. 305)

Monopoly effect
The union's ability to raise wages above nonunion rates (p. 323)

Monopsony
Occurs when a firm is the sole market buyer of a good, service, or labour (p. 68)

Multi-skill training
Training to provide employees with a variety of skills, some of which may not normally be part of their job (p. 246)

N

Narcotic or dependency effect
A result of frequent use of arbitration that may cause parties to lose the ability to freely negotiate settlements without third-party assistance (p. 361)

Neoclassical economics view
A view of industrial relations grounded in economics that sees unions as an artificial barrier to the free market (p. 17)

New model unionism
The movement to trade (or craft) unions (p. 29)

New public management (NPM)
A new approach to public administration in which public organizations are to become more decentralized, market-driven, and concerned with financial control, and managers more empowered and performance-oriented (p. 364)

Nonstandard work arrangements
Work arrangements that differ from the norm in terms of employment term, location, schedule, hours of work, or pay (p. 190)

Nonunion employee representation (NER)
occurs when a group of nonunion employees meets with management regarding employment terms and conditions (p. 186)

North American Free Trade Agreement (NAFTA)
A free trade agreement among Canada, the United States, and Mexico that was signed in 1994 and included a labour side agreement, the North American Agreement on Labor Cooperation (p. 62)

O

Organizational commitment
An employee's commitment to the organization (p. 336)

Organizational justice
Employees' perception of fair treatment at work (p. 174)

P

Pay equity
Women and men being paid relatively equally for work of equal value (p. 114)

P.C. 1003
The Canadian government imported the *Wagner Act* model in 1944; under the *War Measures Act,* it was introduced by the Privy Council as P.C. 1003 (p. 94)

Performance pay
The part of pay that is based on output or performance (p. 323)

Pluralist and institutional view
A view of industrial relations stressing the importance of institutions and multiple actors (including labour) in the employment relationship (p. 17)

Political economy
A view of industrial relations grounded in socialism and Marxism that stresses the role of inherent conflict between labour and management (p. 18)

Political nonpartisanship
A belief that unions should not be aligned with any political party (p. 32)

Power
The ability to make someone agree to your terms (p. 14)

Prima facie case
Union establishes, at arbitration, that the collective agreement was in place and that the grievor was employed, covered by that agreement, and disciplined (p. 304)

Privatization
The transfer or contracting out of services to the private sector (p. 62)

Probationary period
A short period of time after an employee is hired in which he or she is not fully protected by a union (p. 321)

Procedural justice
Employees' perception of fairness in workplace procedures (p. 174)

Profit sharing
A group performance pay that is based on firm profits (p. 328)

Public good
An item whose consumption does not reduce the amount available for others (p. 354)

Public-sector or social justice unionism
Unions of public-sector employees at all three levels of government: local, provincial, and federal; typically advocates of a philosophy of social justice (p. 140)

Pyramiding
Compounding of premiums or benefits (p. 248)

R

Rand Formula
A union security provision in which employees do not have to join the union but all employees must pay dues (p. 154)

Ratification
The process by which each party approves the settlement reached at the bargaining tables by the management and union teams (p. 214)

Recall
The process by which a laid-off employee gets rehired (p. 321)

Recruitment
Techniques designed to make potential employees aware of job openings (p. 320)

Red-circling
Protecting employees' pay at a level higher than the normal rate of their current job (p. 240)

Reinstatement rights
Employees are guaranteed their old jobs after the strike (p. 282)

Replacement workers
Employees hired to replace striking workers (p. 282)

Residual rights
A principle whereby management retains all rights it held before unionization except those changed by the agreement (p. 237)

S

Scientific management
The application of engineering principles to define specific tasks in the production process thereby removing the autonomy of skilled craft workers (associated with Frederick Taylor) (p. 93)

Seniority
The length of time a person has been a member of the union (p. 16)

Shock effect
Occurs when increased costs and protection shock management into stricter management practices (p. 320)

Snider case
A landmark court case in 1925 that determined that labour matters fell under the purview of the provinces under the *British North America Act* (p. 93)

Socialist unionism
Unionism that challenges capitalism and seeks equity for union and nonunion members (p. 32)

Socio-technical systems design
Systems of new technology in which workers are complements to, not simply extensions of, technology; in which participation, communication, and collaboration are encouraged through an accommodative organizational structure; and in which individual workers achieve control through shared responsibility and minimal supervision (p. 368)

Spillover effect
A belief that increases in union wages result in decreases in nonunion wages (p. 325)

Strategic choice framework
A view that emphasizes the role of management and strategies in the industrial relations system (p. 176)

Strategies
Processes developed and implemented to achieve goals (p. 14)

Strike
An action by workers in which they cease to perform work duties and do not report to work (p. 2); a work stoppage invoked by a union (p. 266)

Strike mandate
The majority of the union members support strike action (p. 268)

Strike vote
The union conducts a vote assessing members' support of strike action (p. 268)

Super seniority
The status of union representatives who, while in office, have highest seniority in the bargaining unit (p. 254)

T

Threat effect
A belief that nonunion employers increase wages to avoid unionization (p. 325)

Total compensation mix
The total base pay, performance pay, and indirect pay that an employee receives (p. 323)

Trade union
Unions that organize all workers of a trade regardless of their industry or workplace (p. 29)

Tripartite
A tripartite board has three stakeholders: management, labour, and government (p. 95)

U

Unfair labour practice
An alleged violation of the labour relations act (p. 95)

Union
A group of workers recognized by law who collectively bargain terms and conditions of employment with their employer (p. 3)

Union acceptance
Management's seeing unionization as a democratic right, and accepting that part, if not all, of its operations will be unionized (p. 179)

Union commitment
An employee's commitment to his or her union (p. 337)

Union coverage
A broader measure than union density; includes nonmembers covered by the collective agreement (p. 154)

Union density
A fraction that expresses union members as a percentage of the nonagricultural labour force (p. 154)

Union removal
A management strategy designed to remove the union from the workplace (p. 180)

Union resistance
A management policy seeking to limit the spread of unions in the firm (p. 180)

Union satisfaction
An employee's assessment of his or her union experience (p. 337)

Union security
The method by which unions are able to maintain membership and dues collection in a bargaining unit (p. 154)

Union shop
A form of union security in which new employees must join the union but only after a probation period (p. 154)

Union substitution
A management strategy designed to give nonunion employees all the advantages of unionization (p. 182)

Union renewal
Quantity and quality of union membership (p. 338)

Utility function
The sum of individual preferences for such measurable items as wages and benefits (p. 153)

V

Values
A set of standards or principles (p. 13)

Voluntarism
The notion that collective bargaining is a private matter between the parties and that government intervention should be kept to a minimum (p. 98)

W

Wage differential
The difference in wages earned by two groups of workers (p. 325)

Wagner Act
Named after the bill's sponsor, Senator Robert F. Wagner of New York, and more formally known as the *National Labor Relations Act* of the United States (p. 38)

Wildcat strike
An illegal strike during the term of the collective agreement (p. 266)

Work to rule
The strategy of employees who perform only to the minimum standard required (p. 266)

INDEX

Page references with *f* and *t* notations refer to a figure and table on that page respectively

B

baby boom, 70
BAC, 136
back-to-work legislation, 46, 282, 353
Bacon, N., 329
bad faith bargaining, 100
Bamberger, P., 287
Bangladeshi workers, 149–150
Bank of Canada report, 45
Barbash, J., 174
bargaining methods clause, 244–245
bargaining unit
    community of interests, 96
    defined, 95
    employer structure, 96
    management employees, 96
    union security, 154
    wishes of employees, 96
Barling, J., 281, 334
base pay, 323, 325–326, 330*t*
BCGEU, 140–141
B.C. Health Services decision, 107–109
BCTF, 143*t*, 145, 265, 361–362
Beckenbaugh, Scot, 210
Belcourt, M., 179
Belgium
    income inequality, 76*t*
    strike statistics, 276
    union density impacts, 327*f*
benefits, 323, 328–329, 330*t*
Benson, Robyn, 368
Berlin Convention (1902), 35
Bernard, A., 44
Bettman, Gary, 210
Bill 3, Quebec, 351
Bill C-4, 367
birth rates, 66
Black Friday protests, 301, 302
BNA Act, 93
Bombardier collective agreement, 240
bottom line, 205
Boulerice, Alexandre, 138
Bozeman, D. P., 288
breaks, 112
bricklayer's union, 136

Britain. *See* United Kingdom
British Columbia
    automatic certification, 95
    coffee and meal breaks, 112
    committees, 15
    conciliation/mediation, 98, 311
    designation model, 360
    duty of fair representation, 98
    ecological subsystem, 13
    equal pay legislation, 124
    essential services, 359
    fact-finding, 14
    first contract arbitration, 100
    forestry industry, 41
    Health Services decision, 107–109
    job loss in fishery industry, 44
    overtime, 112
    person-days not worked, 275*t*
    political environment, 83
    public attitudes towards unions, 71
    replacement worker laws, 100, 212
    teachers' strike, 46, 265, 361–362
    temporary foreign workers, 11
    union density, 159*f*
British Columbia Government and Service
    Employees' Union (BCGEU), 140–141
British Columbia Labour Relations Board, 362
British Columbia Teachers' Federation
    (BCTF), 143*t*, 145, 265, 361–362
British North America (*BNA*) *Act*, 93
Brown and Beatty, 303, 304, 308
Brown, James, 316
Brown, T. C., 322, 337
budgetary constraints, in Dunlop's model,
    6–7
bumping, 252–253
Business Affairs department, NHLPA, 142
business/organizational strategies, 178–183
    phases, 178
    related to unions, 179–183
    strategic HRM, 178–179
business unionism, 32, 33*t*, 48

C

California, monopsony in, 68
Campolieti, M., 187

Canada
    AFL in, 32–33
    alternative work arrangements, 79
    base pay, 325
    child poverty in, 73–74
    collective agreement administration,
        100–102
    decentralized legal framework, 9
    designation model, 360
    economic restructuring, 43–45
    employee attitudes to unions, 156
    employee relations, 4
    employee rights, 113–114
    employment law, 111
    equality/participation/safety, 329
    equal pay legislation, 123–129
    events of 1930s and 1940s, 37, 39
    events of 1970s and 1980s, 41
    first contract arbitration, 100, 208
    government policies, 366–368
    government restructuring, 45
    grievance arbitration, 302
    grievance procedure legislation,
        282–283
    high-performance work practices,
        185–186
    immigration, 66–67
    income gap, 61
    income inequality, 75, 76*t*
    interest arbitration, 310
    interest-based bargaining, 220–221
    international strike trends, 276, 277*f*
    IWW membership, 37
    Knights of Labor, 35
    labour boards, 95–97
    labour mobility, 68
    macroeconomic policy, 62
    mediation-arbitration, 363
    money market, 12
    NAFTA, 41–42
    nine-hour movement, 30–32
    nonstandard work arrangements, 190
    nonunion employee representation,
        188
    outsourcing to, 85–86
    performance appraisal, 322
    performance pay, 328